Bottom Line's Household Magic

2,022 Money-Saving, Time-Saving, Make-It-Last Solutions and Surprising New Uses for Everyday Products!

By Joan Wilen and Lydia Wilen

Bottom Line Books

www.BottomLineSecrets.com

Bottom Line's Household Magic
2,022 Money-Saving, Time-Saving, Make-It-Last Solutions and
Surprising New Uses for Everyday Products!
By Joan Wilen and Lydia Wilen

Copyright © 2010 by Boardroom® Inc.

10   9   8   7   6   5   4   3   2   1

ISBN 0-88723-596-4

Bottom Line Books® publishes the advice of expert authorities in many fields.
The use of this material is no substitute for health, legal, accounting or other professional
services. Consult competent professionals for answers to your specific questions.

Offers, prices, rates, addresses, telephone numbers and Web sites
listed in this book are accurate at the time of publication,
but they are subject to frequent change.

Bottom Line Books® is a registered trademark of
Boardroom® Inc.
281 Tresser Boulevard, Stamford, CT 06901

www.BottomLineSecrets.com

Bottom Line Books® is an imprint of Boardroom® Inc., publisher of print periodicals,
e-letters and books. We are dedicated to bringing you the best information from the most
knowledgeable sources in the world. Our goal is to help you gain greater wealth,
better health, more wisdom, extra time and increased happiness.

Printed in the United States of America

Table of Contents

Chapter 7 • Better Bath Basics

Legend

© FYI

$ MONEY SAVER

✍ NOTE

✱ HELPFUL HINT

☛ WARNING

✸ FROM THE CUPBOARD

⚡ CAUTION

🕐 TIME SAVER

★ TIP

Foreword

Smarter. Cheaper. Better. Safer. There's no question that this is how you want to run your life and household. The question is…how?

How can you save time and money on those everyday chores—cleaning, cooking, repairing, maintaining, storing, shopping, grooming, entertaining…living? How can you easily ensure a healthier and nontoxic environment for yourself, your family and your pets—using common household products instead of costly or dangerous commercial products? What are the simple shortcuts and penny-pinching procedures that make quick work of all the necessary jobs around the house…so that you can get more from your rare moments of leisure time?

That's what our readers want to know, so the editors at Bottom Line Books turned to Joan Wilen and Lydia Wilen to research those questions—and countless others. The Wilen Sisters have a knack for finding solutions, consulting the best experts and presenting information in a personal and engaging style.

In their books, the Wilen Sisters offer smart solutions, tips and techniques that use everyday items to make housework hassles disappear—from stubborn stains to annoying insects. You'll get tricks-of-the-trade tips for sleight-of-hand efficiency in the kitchen, laundry room and workshop. You'll discover the wizardry of potent potions made from inexpensive and readily available products that will improve and maintain your furniture, your possessions and even your person.

Each chapter brims with sage advice and uncommon wisdom—and the Wilen Sisters' breezy wit. Whether it's cleaning the carpet or maintaining your car…repairing furniture or growing a garden…preventing disease or preparing dinner…the Wilens suggest a better way—in fact, they offer more than 2,000 of them—to help you cut time, costs and aggravation in virtually everything you need to do around the house.

But rest assured, these remedies are not hocus-pocus. The techniques suggested by the Wilen Sisters have been approved by leading experts who recognized their ingenuity and impact. These helpful hints have worked for them, and we know they will work for you!

The Editors of Bottom Line Books ■

Introduction

When people learn that we're sisters AND writing partners, they often wonder, "How can you possibly work together?" Our answer is that it's a blessing to have a sister (or brother), and we feel that it's a double blessing to be able to work with a sibling. Siblings are together for life, they share memories and a point of view…and they trust each other completely.

After the how-can-you-work-with-your-sibling question, people then ask where we find the information that we share with our readers. It would be fun to say that, like our folk remedies, our household hints have been passed down through many generations of our family. Fun, yes—but true, no. Because of the amazing advances in technology and the invention of time-saving appliances, many of the helpful suggestions that our grandmothers—and even our mother—had to share no longer apply in this day and age.

The true answer is that our information comes from *research*. We've been investigating folk remedies, household hints and environmentally safe cleaning alternatives as well as grooming, cooking, entertaining and space-saving tips for more than two decades. We gather these ideas from the people we meet, from people who contact us, from the Internet and from other published sources.

But make no mistake—gathering information is just the beginning of the process. We know that all of the great things we discover need to be tested and evaluated. So, in addition to ourselves, we ask our family, friends (and our friends' families) as well as our neighbors to be our testers. We also talk to medical doctors, naturopaths, herbalists, chefs, chemists, cleaning experts—you name a specialty, and we've found an expert. We rely on these people to confirm or deny our research, so that we can share the best (and most accurate) information with our readers.

We also make the recipes, mix the formulas and buy LOTS of baking soda and distilled white vinegar, two products that we think are miraculous and endlessly useful. Sometimes our experiments fail…popular or odd-sounding hints may not work as well as some of the more sensible, simple solutions. We're equally happy to help you avoid the remedies that *don't* work as we are to bring you the best. So, we won't suggest that you polish your furniture with SPAM anytime soon!

You may (and we hope you will) find a few surprising suggestions in our books. Be assured that whenever you see something that seems unusual, we feel that it's also wonderful...and useful. We investigate and track down the sources of information whenever we can. For example—a reputable Internet site stated that a very famous daytime soap opera star uses sardines to lighten the dark circles under her eyes. We contacted the star's manager, and when she stopped laughing, she told us that the information was positively untrue. This star has her own cosmetics line—and it has never included sardines!

We prefer to stay away from harsh chemicals like bleach and ammonia, and instead opt for other harmless, lung-friendly, ecologically sound household helpers. Of course, you can always take comedian Joan Rivers' playful advice and just not clean...she said that when you have guests, just put out drop cloths and say you are having the place painted.

Many chapters contain some product ideas from reputable companies. We want you to know that there was absolutely NO advertising or payment for those items to be included in our book. The folks at Bottom Line Books would never permit that! We chose these products simply because we felt they would make your life easier, healthier or just more fun.

We won't be insulted if you don't read our books from cover to cover. In fact, they are designed to be used as reference guides to help you with specific needs and projects. But we do hope that you will enjoy reading them and will discover new ways to use familiar products to manage your everyday tasks.

We're happy to be able to share all of this good stuff with you, hoping it will work like magic. If you have your very own helpful shortcuts and efficient ways of doing chores in and around the house, we'd love to hear from you.

—Joan Wilen & Lydia Wilen ■

About the Authors

The Wilen Sisters—Joan and Lydia—are energetic and enthusiastic health investigators. In a career that's spanned two decades, they have uncovered thousands of amazing "cures from the cupboard," which they share through their best-selling books, dozens of magazine articles and with appearances on numerous national television programs, including NBC's *Today Show* and *CBS This Morning*.

While their passion and search for natural folk remedies continues, they have now broadened their expertise to include household hints. Their wonderful, wide-ranging collection of ways to make your home cleaner, neater and nicer would make their mama proud. ■

A Word from the Authors

We'd like to extend a BIG THANKS to our family and friends for sharing their helpful hints...giving their loving support...and for tasting and testing many of our special remedies.

Our most grateful thanks to Marty Edelston, the master magician who turned an idea into Boardroom Inc.—the publishing empire that includes Bottom Line Books and other publications.

How lucky we are to be Bottom Line authors, working with people like publisher Marjory Abrams, marketing maven Brian Kurtz, chief editor Karen Daly (who waved her magic wand to start this project) and editor Carolyn Gangi (who cast her magic spell on every page).

And to the entire talented, creative and caring Boardroom team—we sincerely thank you for making us proud of our book. ■

CHAPTER 1

Floor-to-Ceiling Magic

Let's start with the basics. Every room in every house —no matter how grand or how humble—will have a floor, a ceiling and walls that need your care and attention.

Take a look around the room you're in now. There are 3 givens…floor, walls and a ceiling. The ceiling is generally out of reach and requires the least amount of care. The walls are an excellent showcase for your inner interior decorator as well as for various do-it-yourself painting or wallpapering projects. (Lots more on that later in this chapter.)

The floor you walk on, however, needs attention on a regular basis. *So let's start with caring for everything underfoot…*

FLOORS

Floors. We all have them. Some common types are vinyl or linoleum in the kitchen… tile in the bathroom or entryway…and hardwood floors in the rest of the rooms. It may surprise you to know that *hardwood* does not refer to the hardness of the wood. It's a classification of broad-leaved flowering trees including oak, maple, ash and elm. Aspen is a hardwood tree whose wood is soft. Needle-leaved trees—pine, fir or evergreen—are softwood trees. Mahogany is from a softwood evergreen. Go figure! Well, don't be floored. *Consider these suggestions…*

Caring for Hardwood Floors

◆ To revive your finished hardwood's shine, mix equal parts of distilled white vinegar and vegetable oil, and put the mixture in a spray bottle. Work small sections of the floor at a time. Start by spritzing the mixture and rubbing it in with a clean cotton cloth. With another clean cotton cloth, buff that section until it's as shiny as can be. Then start on the next section of floor. And so on and so on and so on.

FYI: Are You Protected?
Most newly installed floors have a urethane finish. You can tell simply by looking at the floor. If it looks glossy and as if it has a layer of clear plastic on top of the wood, chances are it is a urethane finish. This kind of finish is a shield, protecting the wood from scratches, water damage and other boo-boos.

◆ To remove any scuff marks, get out an old, clean toothbrush, apply some non-gel toothpaste and scrub off the scuff mark. Then wipe the area clean with a damp cloth or sponge.

◆ Depending on the size of the scuff mark, put a little petroleum jelly or baby oil on a cloth and work it into the floor to remove the mark. Once it's gone, go over the area with dry paper towels, making sure there's not a trace of the slippery jelly or oil.

◆ If a clump of grease dripped on the floor, cover it with 1 or 2 ice cubes. As soon as the grease hardens, carefully scrape it off with the dull side of a knife, an expired credit card or a spatula.

★ Brew Up Beautiful Floors

Boil 1 quart of water, then throw in 2 bags of black tea (such as Pekoe). Let it steep for about 20 minutes, then dampen a cloth or mop with the tea and wash your wood floor with it. The tea's tannic acid should cut through grease and grime. Then buff the wood with a clean, soft cloth—or not. If your floor looks fine, forget the buffing (unless you want the exercise).

Cleaning a Waxed Hardwood Floor

Waxing a hardwood floor is not a popular idea, due to the amount of upkeep necessary. If you insist on it, wax should be applied in light, even coats. Stop when the floor has the sheen and protection level you desire.

◆ If you want the dirt to come off, but the wax to stay on your floor, use a sponge mop that's been dipped in a mixture of ¼ cup of distilled white vinegar and 1 gallon of water. Wring out the mop so that it's damp (not sopping wet) before it touches the floor.

◆ Between waxings, put a piece of waxed paper—waxy side down, of course—over the mop head and give the floor the once over.

⚡ CAUTION: Never wax a urethane floor. Wax and urethane are not compatible.

Sweeping a Hardwood Floor

◆ Try a Japanese cleaning method—sprinkle damp tea leaves on the floor. Don't think of it as adding to the dirt…the tea helps to weigh down the dust, making it easier to sweep up.

◆ If there's a little mound of dirt that can't be swept into the dustpan, wet a paper towel and blot it all up.

$ Make Your Own Dustpan

If you don't have a dustpan and don't want to buy one, cut a paper or plastic plate in half. POOF! A dustpan.

Covering Up a Hardwood Scratch

Hardware stores have wax crayons that match most shades of hardwood. Or look in that old box of crayons for a color that matches your floor. This works best for very long and/or deep scratches—take the paper off the crayon, then put it in a small glass container and melt it in your microwave. Start by setting it for 10 seconds. (You may end up needing to give it another 10 seconds to melt, depending on the power of your microwave.)

Carefully pour the melted wax into the scratch. Before it completely hardens, use a piece of plastic—such as an expired credit card or a section of a yogurt container lid—and glide it over the treated area, removing the extra wax, making the filled-in scratch level with the rest of the floor. (Take care not to scratch the floor again with the plastic.)

⭐ Microwave Alternative

If you don't want to zap a crayon in your microwave, grate the crayon carefully with a knife or your cheese grater (wash it thoroughly afterward). Then line a section of a muffin tin with aluminum foil, and put the grated crayon in it. Put the muffin tin in a preheated 350°F oven. It should take about 2 or 3 minutes for the crayon to melt. And the foil prevents a messy cleanup.

If you don't want to work with the melted crayon, grate a piece of crayon and press the little pieces into the scratch. Next, use a blow-dryer set on *low* to help harden the wax, then level it off with a piece of plastic.

When the melted crayon cools and completely hardens, buff the area with a soft, clean cloth. (If you're into waxing the floor, this would be the time to do it.)

⭐ Put a Sock on It!

◆ *Temporary solution:* If you are rearranging furniture or moving furniture to clean, put old socks—the heavier the better—on the furniture legs. Or rip off pieces from a cardboard box, or cut off the bottom half from a milk or juice carton. Once the carton is washed and dried, it makes a great coaster for furniture legs. You can also use plastic containers that are completely flat on the bottom.

Socks, cartons and containers will protect the floor from scratches, and they make the furniture a lot easier to move around.

◆ *Permanent solution:* Stick clear adhesive tape or strips of weather-stripping on the bottom of furniture legs so that the wood floor will not be scratched when the furniture is moved.

You can also glue pieces of felt or carpet—pile side down—to the bottom of furniture legs. Self-stick bunion pads and moleskin patches will also serve the same purpose.

Managing Creaky/Squeaky Floors

Start by sweeping cornstarch or talcum powder between the noisy floorboards. Once the spaces are completely filled in with the powder, the creaking should be gone.

If the creaking continues, the nails in the floorboard may be loose and need to be hammered back into place. In that case, lay a piece of thin wood or thick cardboard over the part of the floor that seems to creak. This will protect the bare floor or the floor covering (linoleum or carpet) when you pound-pound-pound it with the hammer. But once you hammer down the nails that were loose, there should be no more creaking.

Caring for Vinyl and/or Linoleum Floors

◆ If you want to clean and shine your floor between waxings, mix ½ cup of liquid fabric softener in 1 gallon of water, then mop the floor with the solution. Your floor will get clean and keep its shine.

◆ If your floor has any wax buildup, take club soda and pour it on a small section of the vinyl flooring. Scrub it in with a brush, and give it a few minutes as you start the process on the next small section, then go back to the first section and wipe it off.

◆ If you don't want to wax your floor, but it needs to be mopped clean, you can mix 1 cup of distilled white vinegar into 1 gallon of water and rinse the floor. The linoleum will become clean and shiny. Why bother waxing?

◆ To remove old grease stains from your floor, pour cola on the stain and let it stay there for 1 hour. Then wipe it off—both the soda and the stain. (Legend has it that Coca-Cola works best due to its acidic content, so you might want to try it first.)

Removing Scuff Marks (And Crayon)

- Try scrubbing the mark with non-gel toothpaste on a toothbrush or on a dry cloth. Then wipe it clean with a damp sponge or cloth.

- Pour a little bit of baking soda on a damp cloth and rub the scuff mark, then wipe it with a clean cloth.

- Take a gum or pencil eraser and use it to erase the heel mark.

- When a skid mark is not responding to the toothpaste, baking soda or eraser, rub the mark with nail polish remover. Dab and rub, then quickly wipe it clean with a damp cloth.

> **CAUTION:** Before you use nail polish remover to take off a scuff mark, test a small area of the floor to make sure that it's safe to use. If it is, and you do use the remover to clean the skid mark, wipe it clean with a damp cloth afterward.

> **FYI: Preventing Picasso**
> These solutions should also clean off masterpieces made by young budding artists whose medium is "Crayon on Household Floor and/or Wall."

> **★ High-Heel Horrors**
> Do not wear high, thin heels on linoleum and some wood floors. The heels will make dents in the flooring.

Caring for Tile Floors

- A simple cleaning formula is to mix ½ cup of distilled white vinegar in 1 gallon of water. Dampen a mop or—if you're a down-on-your-knees kind of cleaner—dampen a sponge and clean the tile floor. Depending on the ventilation in the tile-floored room, the vinegar smell will disappear in a short amount of time.

- If the floor hasn't been cleaned in awhile… and you can see the grime…and you suspect that the floor needs to be disinfected, it's probably time to mix up some heavy-duty tile tonic.

  In a large spray bottle, combine 1 cup of distilled white vinegar, 1 cup of rubbing alcohol, 1 cup of water and 3 drops of liquid dish detergent. Spray, mop and rinse the tile with plain water.

CARPETS & RUGS

Carpets and rugs often add warmth to a room. To keep your floor coverings looking their best, you have to take care of them. Do not let your carpet bathe in prolonged periods of direct sunlight—not unless you want it to fade or discolor. Protect it by covering your windows with drapes, blinds or shades.

We hate to have to tell you this, but experts agree that carpets and rugs should be vacuumed at least once a week to stay in good shape, and to keep dirt from getting embedded in the fibers.

To prevent dirt from being tracked into the house, place walk-off mats at each entrance. The mats will absorb and help trap dirt, sand and grit from outside.

Do not forget to clean these mats regularly—either hose them down or vacuum them —so that they don't become the *cause* of the dirt that's being tracked into the house.

Here are more suggestions to help you care for your fibrous floor coverings…

Cleaning Carpets

- Dry-clean your carpet by sprinkling it liberally with baking soda. Use a flour sifter to help distribute it evenly. If you can leave the baking soda on your carpet overnight, do it. If not, let it stay for at least 1 hour.

Meanwhile, sprinkle 1 tablespoon of your favorite fragrant herb—such as lavender, cinnamon or potpourri*—on the floor. After a few minutes, vacuum up the baking soda and whichever herb you used. The unpleasant carpet odors—cigarette smoke, mustiness, wet dog, cat urine—should be gone, and the fragrant aroma of the herb should be in the air.

◆ In a spray bottle, mix 1 part liquid fabric softener (any scent you prefer) to 6 parts water. Spray the carpet with the solution, then vacuum. The carpet should be more dust-resistant, generate less static electricity and smell fresh, too.

*Optional

Cleaning Fringe

Fringe on area rugs looks nice but collects dust and dirt and is difficult to vacuum. Save yourself the trouble by whisking out the dirt instead. With a dry scrub brush, use down-and-away strokes. Then brush the dirt away from the fringe and vacuum it up off the floor.

★ **Keep Your Carpet Clippings!**
When you get new carpeting, be sure to keep several swatches of it. They will come in handy when you're decorating and want to coordinate or match draperies or upholstery fabric or paint. You may also want to use the swatches to test cleaners and stain removers, or if your carpet needs fiber replacements.

Cleaning Stains

You may want to consider treating your carpet with a commercial stain guard, especially if you have children and/or pets or if you do a lot of entertaining.

But if you haven't stain-guarded your floor covering, stock your pantry with a case of distilled white vinegar and club soda, then read on.

⚡ **CAUTION:** Be sure to test any solution you use as a stain remover on a carpet swatch or on a small, inconspicuous spot of your carpet or rug. Not all colors or fabrics will react the same way.

If something is dropped on your carpet and there are pieces involved (for example, a bowl of chili, cornflakes and milk, or chicken noodle soup), pick up all the pieces of food first. Then get paper towels and blot up as much of the liquid mess as possible, as quickly as possible. You may want to step on the towels to help the blotting process.

Once you're finished picking and blotting, you're ready to use 1 of the following stain solutions…

✳ **Be Stain Savvy**
Try not to rub the stain. Rubbing can spread it, embed it deeper and cause damage to the carpet fibers.

◆ Put club soda or seltzer water on a fresh stain and let the carbonation loosen it. After a couple of minutes, blot it up with paper towels, a clean cloth or a sponge.

◆ Work a heaping tablespoon of foam shaving cream into the stain. Wait for it to dry, then rinse with cold water. (The glycerin in shaving cream is the compound that helps dissolve stains.)

◆ Put some vodka on a washcloth and work it into the stain. Wait a minute, then blot it with a paper towel.

◆ If you're sure your carpet or rug is colorfast, work some 3% hydrogen peroxide into the stain, then blot it with a paper towel.

◆ Use a fresh baby wipe to lift the stain off the carpet or rug.

Removing an Existing Stain

If you're wondering how old a stain is—a week, a month, a year or more—we can't tell you. What we do know is that this remedy is worth trying. It should work, but even if it doesn't, it will not make the stain worse.

Combine 1 tablespoon of liquid laundry detergent, 1½ tablespoons of distilled white vinegar and 2 cups of water. Gently work the mixture into the stain, then blot it dry.

Removing Candle Wax

◆ Place a few ice cubes in a plastic bag and put it against the wax that dripped on the carpet. The ice will make the wax brittle, and you will be able to break off or carefully pull off the drippings.

◆ Cut off a section of a plain brown paper bag, and place it on top of the melted wax. With a medium-hot iron, press the paper for several seconds—long enough to soften the wax and have it transfer from the carpet to the paper. If you have to repeat the process a few times, always use a new piece of brown paper.

Removing Pet Urine

◆ Test carpet swatches or a tiny, inconspicuous patch of each carpet and rug in your home with distilled white vinegar. If the color of any of the test patches change, make note *not* to use the vinegar solution on that carpet or rug, if and when your pet has an accident on it. Be on the lookout for such accidents, because you'll want to deal with them immediately.

First, blot up as much of the urine as possible, and rinse the area with warm water. Blot again. Then, for a vinegar-safe rug, mix ½ cup of distilled white vinegar with ½ cup of water, and sponge it into the fibers. After a few minutes, blot it off and repeat the procedure. Then pour equal amounts of table salt and baking soda on the wet area. Wait until it dries—it may take a few hours—then vacuum.

◆ For a fresh accident, blot the spot, then cover it with a thick layer of table salt. More is better, since you want the salt to absorb all of the liquid. Wait until the salt has hardened—overnight if possible—then vacuum over the area.

See "Cleaning Carpets" on pages 4–5 for tips on removing a urine smell.

> **CAUTION:** There is ammonia in urine. Therefore, NEVER use ammonia or a spot remover that contains ammonia to clean urine. It will mislead your pet into believing that this is his/her marked territory. He will return to it on a regular basis, rewetting and restaining the spot.

✳ Dealing with Pet Hair
Give the vacuum a helping hand by sweeping the rug with a damp broom. That will loosen and/or pick up the pet hair. Then finish the job by vacuuming the rug.

Removing Chewing Gum

◆ Start by blow-drying the gum on the *warm* (not *hot*) setting on your hair dryer. You want the gum to melt, not the carpet's fibers. As soon as the gum seems real gooey, put a small plastic bag around it and gently pull off the bag, bringing the gum with it.

Repeat the process until all of the gum is out of the carpet, or there's just a stubborn little bit left. For that little bit, work in a dab of petroleum jelly, rolling the gum into it. Then wash the spot with a gentle laundry detergent formulated to fight grease, rinse with water and blot dry.

Petroleum jelly may stain carpet, so be sure to do a spot-test first.

◆ See the ice-cubes-in-a-plastic-bag remedy for candle wax removal on page 6.

Removing Coffee or Tea

Gulp! You might as well have spilled hair dye. Blot up as much of the spill as possible, as quickly as possible. *Then, depending on what is available to you at the time, use 1 of the following remedies…*

◆ Pour on club soda and blot. Then more club soda and more blotting. If the stain isn't fading fast, pour on a bit of 3% hydrogen peroxide and let it stay on for about 15 minutes. Then blot and rinse with either more club soda or some cold water.

◆ Combine 2 tablespoons of baking soda and 1 tablespoon of borax powder (available at supermarkets and drugstores) in 1 pint of water. Sponge the stain with this solution, then blot dry.

◆ Using a clean, dry washcloth, work a beaten egg yolk into the stain, and then rinse with warm water.

◆ Work a heaping tablespoon of foam shaving cream into the stain, then rinse with club soda or cold water.

Removing Crayon Marks

Put a strip of transparent tape on each crayon mark, then gently remove the tape. Hopefully some of the crayon will come off but none of the fibers.

Removing Fresh Fruit

Try to pick up all of the pieces of fruit and blot up the juice. Then combine 1 tablespoon of liquid laundry detergent, 1½ tablespoons of distilled white vinegar and 2 cups of water. Gently work the mixture into the fruit stain, and then blot dry.

Removing Grease/Oil

◆ Use a paper towel to blot up as much of the grease or oil as possible. Then pour cornmeal or cornstarch on the stain. Let it stay that way overnight and vacuum the carpet in the morning.

◆ Work a heaping tablespoon of foam shaving cream into the stained carpet fibers. Let it dry thoroughly, then vacuum the spot spotless.

Removing Latex Paint

Take action immediately! Make a solution with 1½ teaspoons of distilled white vinegar and 1½ teaspoons of laundry detergent mixed in 2 cups of warm water.

> **NOTE:** You should definitely test this solution on a carpet swatch or on an inconspicuous portion of the carpet *before* using it. If the carpet color is not affected by the mixture, then proceed.

Dip a clean sponge into the solution and use it to wipe away the latex paint. Once the stain is gone, rinse with cold water and blot dry.

If the carpet color on the test patch changed after you applied the vinegar solution, then just use the laundry detergent in warm water. You'll have to work harder to get the paint out, and it may not be as effective.

✳ The Color Cure
Next time, consider using paint that's the exact same color as your carpet so that nobody will ever notice if you spill some.

Removing Mud

Let the mud dry, then use an expired credit card or a dull knife to scrape off as much of it as possible. If the rug is still a little muddy, mix 2 teaspoons of laundry detergent with 1 cup of water, and sponge it on the carpet. Blot with paper towels, rinse with a wet sponge and blot dry with more paper towels.

Removing Red Wine

◆ Open another bottle—seriously! Quickly blot off the red wine with a paper towel, then neutralize it with white wine. Next, wipe it clean with a cold, damp cloth.

◆ If you don't have any white wine, work some table salt or baking soda into the stain, and dab it off with club soda.

Getting Rid of Insects

◆ Moth larvae may be found in carpet fibers. Get rid of them by pouring a thick layer of table salt (a lot of salt!) on the carpet, wait 1 hour, then vacuum up the salt. The salt destroys the moth larvae and also brightens the carpet.

◆ This is a bit of an ordeal, but if you have an insect infestation (especially fleas or ticks) in your carpet, take the time to get rid of the little buggers. Buy boxes of table salt, enough to layer the entire carpet with it.

As you pour the salt into the carpet, use a broom or brush to work the salt down deep where the bugs nest.

Once the salt is in place, let it stay there for 2 to 3 days, giving it time to (somehow) dehydrate and destroy the insects. Then vacuum as usual. To prevent future infestations, it's a good idea to vacuum at least once a week.

✳ Bug Off!
Printer's ink repels moths and silverfish. Put a layer of plain (non-colored) newspaper between the pad and the rug, and be bug-free.

Raising a Matted Nap

If you're into rearranging furniture on a carpeted floor, you'll want to know how to raise matted-down nap or *pile* (the cut or uncut loops of yarn that form the carpet's surface). There's the cold way and the hot way. *So take your pick…*

◆ *Cold:* Put an ice cube on each matted area—most likely where 4 furniture feet rested. Let the ice cubes melt on the dents overnight (just be sure nobody will be walking around the house). In the morning, fluff up the nap with your fingers or an old toothbrush.

◆ *Hot:* Hold a steam iron a few inches above the matted carpet area until the nap is mildly moist. *Do not touch the carpet with the iron.* Then scrape up the nap with an old toothbrush or the edge of a spoon's handle.

Removing Loose Threads

Never pull out threads, unless you want the carpet to unravel. Instead, use scissors to cut each loose thread, making it level with the pile (the surface of the carpet).

Dealing with Static Electricity

If you're tired of getting shocks each time you walk on your carpet, particularly in the winter months, try this solution…

Mix 3 tablespoons of liquid fabric softener with 1 cup of water in a spray bottle. Give the carpet a modest misting. If you wet the carpet too much, dirt will stick to the carpet. Allow it to dry thoroughly before taking a shockless stroll across it.

DID YOU KNOW?

If you get shocks even when you're not walking on carpeting, it's because the humidity levels are low or because you're wearing shoes. The soles of your shoes (especially rubber soles) do not allow you to release the electric charge. Prevent shocks by walking barefoot and discharging the static electricity through your feet. This isn't too practical, though, especially during the cold winter months.

You usually know when you're going to get a shock—when you touch a metal doorknob, the television set, a light switch or a faucet. You can discharge most of the static electricity in your body by touching whatever you want to touch with a wooden pencil *before* touching it with your fingers. You may get a little shock, but nothing like the jolt you would have gotten without the pencil.

✳ Moving Heavy Furniture

On those rare occasions when you have to move a piano or another piece of heavy furniture on wheels, place a protective barrier—such as a piece of heavy cardboard or a plywood plank—between the wheels and the carpet to prevent damage to the carpet.

Anchoring Throw Rugs

If you don't want a throw rug slipping out from under you, make sure it stays put by sewing nonslip rubber rings from mason jars (available at hardware stores) on the underside.

Use strong cotton thread (doubled), and attach each rubber ring by tacking it in 3 or 4 places. Use your discretion as to how many rings to sew on each rug. If you have a rectangular throw rug, consider putting a rubber ring under each corner.

Bathtub decals are also a good idea, as is double-sided "carpet" tape.

Velcro adhesive strips (available at hardware, crafts and sewing-supply stores) are also an option. Velcro strips come in pairs…an upper strip and a lower strip. On the outside of both strips is adhesive…on the inside of both strips are the Velcro fibers that interlock with each other. Stick 1 side on the floor under where the rug is going to stay. Line the rug up and stick the other portion of the Velcro on the underside of the rug. Then lay the 2 pieces of Velcro (the 1 on the floor and the 1 on the underside of the rug) on top of each other.

This is sounding so complicated…if it's not making sense, but the thought of using Velcro appeals to you, go to a store that sells it and just look at it. You will be able to figure it out once you see it. And if you don't want to deal with that…just buy a nonskid rug.

⭐ Can't Beat It

Do you still beat your rugs to get them clean? Save yourself the trouble and toss the throw rug in a dryer on a "no-heat" setting. Let it run for its usual cycle. The rug should come out clean and lookin' good.

Vacuuming

Aside from the contents of accidental spills, have you ever wondered what exactly you're vacuuming up? Brace yourself for a surprise. Household "dirt" is about 75% to 80% sloughed-off human skin cells. Who would have thought that most of the vacuum cleaner dirt comes directly from the people who own the vacuum cleaner? The other 25% to 30% is hair, animal dander, dust mites and just a small amount of actual dirt—sand, earth and pollen—that has been blown in or tracked in from outside. *Now that you know **what** you're vacuuming, here are some ideas on how to get the best results…*

When vacuuming a carpet or a rug, use long, slow strokes. That gives the vacuum time to loosen the dirt and then let it be sucked up. For a lightly soiled area, try to make 3 passes with the vacuum…for a heavily soiled area, go over it at least 5 to 7 times.

 Best Time to Vacuum

When it's raining or humid outside, open the windows and vacuum. The moisture in the air helps prevent dust from flying up and landing on the carpet again.

Extend Your Reach

Figure out which outlet is most central in terms of the areas you vacuum. Next, measure the farthest distance the vacuum needs to go from that outlet. Then buy a lightweight extension cord that will accommodate that measurement, even if it has to be 50 feet long. Using the extension cord will save you the time and effort of going from one outlet to another.

Sweet Smells

Vacuum up a tablespoon of your favorite sweet-smelling herb—lavender, cinnamon, the contents of a spiced tea bag—or put the perfume strips from magazines or a scented fabric softener sheet in the vacuum cleaner bag. The heat from the vacuum brings out the fragrance of the herb or perfume. It makes vacuuming a little more pleasant.

✳ **Prep the Brushes**

Go over the (unplugged) vacuum's brushes with a wet paper towel before you vacuum a carpet. It will help heighten its dirt-sucking power.

Finding Lost Beads

Necklaces break, containers of things fall over… it happens. And when it does, find a piece of old pantyhose (or use a knee-high stocking) and stretch it over the vacuum suction hose—you can keep it in place with a small rubber band.

Aim the hose at the little things on the floor, then turn on the vacuum and they will be sucked up against the pantyhose. Hold the vacuum hose over a shoebox or other wide, shallow container, and turn off the vacuum's power. The little things will fall into the box where they are easy to recover.

Changing Dust Bags

If you wait until the dust bag in your vacuum reaches its full capacity, you may notice a reduction in the vacuum's suction, and more dust in the room that you're supposedly cleaning. It's best to change the dust bag as soon as you can tell it's filling up. Check it every 3 or 4 times you vacuum—don't wait until it's bursting at the seams. (For bagless canister models, check them every other time the vacuum is used.)

To change the dust bag, spread out and spray a couple of newspaper pages with water. Put the vacuum on the wet paper and remove the old, filled dust bag. The loose dust will adhere to the wet paper.

Insert the new dust bag in the vacuum, fold up and discard the newspaper along with the old bag, and you're good to go.

Fighting Fleas

If you have a pet with fleas, your carpet may also have fleas. Fleas can be vacuumed up and continue living and multiplying in the vacuum's dust bag. If you're concerned that this may be happening in your home, place a commercial flea collar or a few mothballs in the dust bag to eliminate the problem.

Also, see the instructions for a do-it-yourself herbal flea collar on page 341 of "Care for Your Fuzzy Friends," Chapter 13.

WALLS

Walls are great. Without them, you would not know where a room starts and ends. Walls are there waiting for you to paint them, paper them, create wall arrangements or do any number of other things to make your living space a reflection of your taste and a happy place for you to be.

However you choose to decorate your walls, this section offers some basic cleaning, painting and wallpapering suggestions, which we hope will serve your walls well. Just keep in mind that you can always put on a new coat of paint or wallpaper if they don't work out.

> ✍ **NOTE:** It's not good to remove paint inadvertently while cleaning a wall, nor would you want to get rid of a stain and end up with a conspicuous light spot. So get testy! That is, test an inconspicuous part of your wall before you do a general cleaning or hone in on a smudge, stain or dirty area.

Cleaning Painted Walls

To prepare, it's important to protect the floor by putting down a fabric drop cloth…or an old bedsheet…or towels…or pieces of brown-paper bags…or newspapers. Don't use plastic drop cloths because they can get very slippery when they're wet.

Next, use a soft-bristled brush or a vacuum cleaner to get rid of any dust and cobwebs from the wall (especially in the corners or crevices, like near molding).

Clean off any marks from the wall (using our stain-removing tips—*see* page 12) in preparation for the overall washing.

Next, get 2 buckets. Fill one ¾ full with warm water, and add at least 1 tablespoon of liquid dish detergent (any other kind of soap or detergent may affect the color of the paint). Leave the other bucket empty.

Dampen a natural (better than nylon) sponge or sponge-mop or even a paint roller in the bucket with the soapy water, and wash the wall. As illogical as this sounds, always start at the bottom of a wall and work your way to the top. Trust the fact that it's easier to wipe off dirty streaks from a clean surface than from a wall that's dirty. Every so often, wring out the dirty water from the sponge into the empty bucket, then redip it in the soapy water.

> ✍ **NOTE:** Once you start, be prepared to wash the entire wall. Do not stop midway—when the wall dries, this will create a *tidemark*…a dirty line that shows where you cleaned and where you didn't. These types of marks can be difficult to remove.

After you've washed the wall, rinse it with a clean, damp sponge. Then dry the wall with a terry cloth towel. It's the best fabric to use for drying, and it has a minor loofah effect—so it will help to remove the last bits of gunk from the clean wall.

 "Dry" Clean Your Walls

Do you have terry-cloth sweatbands for your wrists, like tennis players use? If not, you can make wristbands by folding washcloths and securing them with not-too-tight rubber bands.

The wristband will help to prevent water from running down your arm while your hand is raised to wash the wall, even if you're wearing plastic gloves.

Cleaning Textured Plaster Walls

If you've stashed some small squares or swatches of leftover carpet in your junk closet or basement, dig 'em out—they are great to use to wash textured plaster walls (low-cut, thick piles generally work best).

In a pail, combine 1 quart of warm water with 2 tablespoons of liquid laundry detergent and 2 tablespoons of distilled white vinegar. Dip a piece of carpet in the solution and scrub the wall with the carpet square. It will get into the crevices and will clean the wall without scratching it. Wipe the wall down with a sturdy, wet sponge and dry it with a terry cloth towel.

Cleaning a Smoky Wall

If there's a smoker in the house, walls tend to get a dingy nicotine film—soapy water alone may not be able to cut through it.

Rather than subject your lungs to the strong fumes of ammonia, we recommend *trisodium phosphate* (TSP), which is available at most hardware stores. This ionic, water-soluble salt, used as a cleaning agent and degreaser, is also a food additive. That should be a good indication of how user-friendly it is. Follow the instructions on the package.

It's important to remember that, although TSP is safe, it can be *strong*. Wear protective gloves, goggles and even a nose/mouth mask for safety.

Removing Wall Stains

CAUTION: Once you decide which ingredient is necessary to get rid of a wall stain, test that ingredient on a small, inconspicuous area of the stained surface. By doing this, you'll make sure it's not going to create a new (and possibly worse) stain.

◆ For grease stains, pour some baby powder on a soft, clean cloth—no water necessary. Wait a few minutes, then rub a cloth on the spots until they fade away.

◆ A baby wipe should remove most crayon marks. You can also spritz them with WD-40, then clean with a paper towel.

◆ If there are marker marks on the wall, put some rubbing alcohol on a cotton puff and wipe the ink spots. The marker should come off and the paint or wallpaper should stay on.

◆ To remove ballpoint pen marks, spritz any type of hairspray on the mark, then blot it with a clean, soft rag.

◆ For pencil marks—as well as fingerprints—use a gum eraser (available at stationery and art-supply stores). If all you have is a pencil eraser, that's fine. To make sure it's clean, erase with it first on a blank piece of paper.

◆ If you took pictures off the wall and are left with the sticky remains of the masking or transparent tape, get out your blow-dryer. Set it on *low* and, in one hand, let it heat up the adhesive, while in the other hand, carefully use a knife to scrape up the tape goo.

If you don't trust yourself with the knife, then press a bit of transparent tape on the heated residue and pull it off. (Hopefully, you will remove all of the sticky stuff, and not add to it.)

Magic Dirt Erasers!

We would be remiss if we didn't mention a product that we use and love for wall clean-ups—Mr. Clean Magic Eraser (available at supermarkets and home-improvement stores).

Although these miraculous just-add-water sponges take off crayon, ink and grease stains, they may also remove dirt you didn't know was there. More often than not, you may have to clean the entire area so that there's not just 1 small yet conspicuous clean spot.

WALLPAPER

Putting wallpaper in a room is a great way to make a creative decorating statement. Depending on your choice of wallpaper pattern, texture and colors, it can coordinate or dominate …or simply become a low-profile background.

Want your room to look taller? Consider using wallpaper that has vertical stripes. Want your room to look wider? You guessed it—horizontal stripes. If you have a high ceiling and want the room to look cozier, consider adding a border near the ceiling. The room will appear smaller if you choose wallpaper with dark colors and large patterns.

Selecting wallpaper is the first and the most fun step. Next comes the work of prepping the walls and applying the paper. *Here are some tips that will help you get to the final step, when you can step back and admire the new look of your room…*

Removing Old Wallpaper

This process can get messy, so be sure to move your furniture to the middle of the room (or to another room), remove all curtains and window treatments, and cover the floor with a drop cloth, tarp, some old bedsheets or lots of newspaper.

◆ First perforate the old wallpaper (you can buy an inexpensive scorer at hardware and paint stores). Then mix equal amounts of hot water and distilled white vinegar. Saturate a sponge with the mixture and wipe it on the wallpaper. (If you prefer to use a paint roller and tray or a spray bottle, that's fine. It doesn't matter how the solution gets on the wallpaper as long as it's HOT going on.) Allow it to saturate the paper for 10 to 15 minutes, then you should be able to easily peel off the paper.

◆ If you would rather not be around the smell of vinegar, use 1 part liquid fabric softener to 2 parts hot water. Apply the solution to the wallpaper with a sponge, roller or spray. Then about 10 minutes later, start peeling.

Preparing the Walls

Take the time to thoroughly prep your walls before putting up wallpaper. It will help keep you safe, help ensure that the wallpaper adheres to the wall properly and will make future wallpaper removal a lot easier. *Let's start with safety…*

◆ After you remove the switch plates, cover electrical outlets and switches with pieces of masking tape to protect them from exposure to sanding, priming, paste and water.

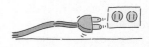

CAUTION: When the wallpaper is up, turn off the electricity in the room before cutting the excess wallpaper and cleaning around the electrical outlets and switches. You don't want there to be surging electricity when water and metal are involved.

◆ Before hanging wallpaper, be sure the walls are clean, completely dry and free of any residual paste, grease, mildew or other stains. Wait at least 1 hour after washing to apply new paper.

Use a spackling compound (available at hardware and home-improvement stores) to repair small nicks or cracks in the wall, then use sandpaper to make it smooth. It also helps to sand away small bumps or protrusions.

◆ Apply a good acrylic-based primer/sealer (get one that is specially formulated for wall coverings) to protect the wall surface from paste damage, and prevent the wall from absorbing moisture from the paste. Primer slows the paste's drying time and makes it easier to position and reposition the paper as you work with it.

Also, priming ensures that the wall and the paper will form a strong bond and adhere better. And in the future, when you're ready for another decorating change, the paper will be easier to remove, thanks to the primer.

✳ Ask the Expert!

The best advice we can give you—without devoting half of this book to wallpapering—is to buy wallpaper from a knowledgeable salesperson. Tell him/her exactly what kind of walls (such as painted, papered, drywall or new plaster walls) you want to cover.

The wallpaper person should be able to offer valuable guidance in terms of your specific wall preparation and wallpaper application, and also suggest the proper tools you will need for each step of the process. Take notes.

Applying Wallpaper Paste

Keep in mind that it's better for wallpaper paste to be too thick than too thin. Thicker paste will hold the paper in place better than thin paste.

You can test the paste by dipping the paste brush into it. Then, lay the brush on the back of the wallpaper. Leave it there for 1 to 2 minutes. When you pick up the brush, the paper should be stuck to it. Then you can just peel it off, knowing the paste is ready to use.

🕐 Clean as You Go

Keep a sponge and a bucket of clean water nearby. As you apply the paper to the wall, use the wet sponge to wipe off any globs of paste that land on the wallpaper.

The Case Against Seam Rollers

If you are applying embossed wallpaper, do NOT use a seam roller to seal the seams. The roller can crush the embossed pattern and give it a flattened look.

Even if you don't have embossed wallpaper, you may not want to use a seam roller. This type of roller seems to squeeze the paste out from under the paper.

★ Prevent Wallpaper Peeling

If your cooking heats up the kitchen…or your hot showers steam up the bathroom, you may want to take a precautionary step.

After you finish wallpapering the room, paint the wallpaper seams with clear varnish (available at paint and hardware stores). Doing this should go a long way in preventing the paper from peeling.

Creating a Wallpaper Patch

If you need to patch a section of wallpaper months—or even years—after you originally wallpapered a room, you will want that patch to be totally unnoticeable. But chances are, if you take a patch piece from the extra roll you put away when you first wallpapered, the piece will be brighter—and therefore more noticeable—than the rest of the wall.

To prevent that from happening, as soon as you hang your wallpaper, also tack a leftover piece of the paper in an out-of-the-way place—for example, on part of a wall that nobody can see…maybe behind a piece of furniture. Since it will be exposed to light and air, it will match your hanging wallpaper perfectly, if and when you need a patch.

⭐ **Make Note of It**

Write down all the details of the wallpapering job—for example, the wallpaper lot number, brand and name (go ahead and attach a sample), the store where you bought it, the price you paid, the size of each roll, the number of rolls you bought vs. the number of rolls you used, and the tools and supplies you needed to do the job.

Put the information in a computer document or attach it to something—in the back of a picture or on the bottom of a lamp—in the room that was papered. And make a note of where you put the note!

Using Leftover Wallpaper

Once you've saved enough wallpaper for patches that you may or may not need, think of creative ways in which you can use the rest of the leftover roll of wallpaper. *Here are some suggestions to get you started…*

◆ Line drawers and shelves.

◆ Let the pattern dictate shapes for you to cut out and use as place mats. Spray them with acrylic and set the table.

◆ If the paper is flexible, use it to cover books.

◆ Cover the mats on framed pictures in the wallpapered room.

◆ If the pattern lends itself, cut out appropriate designs and decorate furniture—such as cabinets, table tops and chair backs—with it. This usually works well with wallpaper in a child's room.

◆ You can cover kitchen windowsills with vinyl wallpaper.

◆ Use the wallpaper for scrapbooking activities.

Cleaning Washable Wallpaper

In a mixing bowl, combine ¼ cup of liquid dish detergent and 1 cup of warm water. Use a mixer to beat the solution until you get a stiff foam. Use the foam on a sponge or cloth to wash the wallpaper. The foam will clean the wallpaper without drenching it.

> ✍ **NOTE:** This tip is only applicable to wallpaper that is meant to be washed.

Cleaning Wallpaper Stains

◆ For stains on washable wallpaper, make a thick paste using 1 heaping tablespoon of either cornstarch or baking soda mixed with 1 teaspoon of water. It should be the consistency of oatmeal. Wipe on the paste, and wipe off the smudge with a clean cloth.

◆ For smudges and other unidentifiable spots on nonwashable wallpaper, use a gum eraser (available at stationery and art-supply stores). Make sure the eraser is clean before you gently rub it on the wallpaper. If the paper has a grain, rub with the grain.

◆ If there is a fresh grease mark on your wallpaper, blot off as much as possible with a clean paper towel. If the stain remains, cover it with 2 layers of plain brown paper from a grocery bag, and go over it with a warm iron. When the grease is transferred to the paper, use new pieces of paper. Continue doing this until the stain is gone.

◆ Gently rub a scrunched-up piece of fresh crustless bread—white or (seedless) rye—on the greasy stain. Think of the bread as an absorbent eraser with gluten, the substance that is said to be a cleaning agent.

◆ Use a soft brush to dust cornstarch or talcum powder on the grease spot. Let it stay on for 30 minutes, then brush it off. If it's not as clean as you hoped, repeat the process.

◆ To remove crayon marks from wallpaper, use a dry, fine-grade steel wool cleansing pad —the kind with soap in it. Gently rub the scribbles until they're gone.

◆ You can also dab on a dollop of non-gel white toothpaste to remove crayon marks. Leave it for 30 minutes, then wipe it off with a dry cloth.

Easier Kitchen Cleanup

If your kitchen is wallpapered and you have areas that are at high risk for stains (like behind the stove), cover the wallpaper in those areas with clear contact paper (available at paint, craft and some hardware stores). It's easier to clean contact paper than most types of wallpaper. Just be aware that it will look slightly different.

Cleaning Other Types of Wall Coverings

◆ Dyes in burlap-textured paper may run, so you don't want to clean it by wetting it. Instead, use an appropriate vacuum-cleaner attachment to dust it on a regular basis. If there's a stain, remove it by rubbing the spot with crustless white or (seedless) rye bread.

◆ As you may already know, grasscloth-textured paper is not the most durable paper to live with (especially if you have cats who like to scratch it!). It's not a good idea to place furniture—or anything else—against a grasscloth-covered wall. The grass will soon rub off and leave unattractive marks or bald spots. Dust grasscloth with a feather duster or, if you're brave and willing to take a chance, use a soft-brush vacuum-cleaner attachment on low suction.

PAINTING (Indoors)

Before starting any indoor painting project, it's important to make sure you are prepared. First and foremost, you need to use good paint—high-quality paint means the job will look better and last longer. When you're at the paint store, talk to the salesperson—he/she should be able to tell you which paint and tools are best for your specific job. *Then you're ready to get started...*

Preparing the Painter

◆ You can spare yourself the trouble of having to scrub your face and hands to remove any drips of paint—just cover up before you paint. Apply a thin layer of moisturizer... shaving cream...hair conditioner...petroleum jelly...or cold cream to any body parts that will be exposed to paint splatter.

◆ If you intend to wear glasses while you paint, cover each lens with a layer of plastic wrap. If you don't wear glasses, you may want to put on goggles to protect your eyes, especially if you are painting a ceiling.

◆ Cover your hair with a shower cap...swim cap...plastic bag...baseball cap...or paper bag. Or drape plastic wrap around your head to protect your hair.

◆ If you insist on wearing your watch while you paint, wrap plastic wrap around the face and band.

◆ Those dirty, should-have-been-thrown-out-years-ago sneakers are perfect to wear when painting. If you already threw away that pair, then put an old, stretched-out pair of socks over your new sneakers.

Since the socks will be slippery, especially on waxed floors, wear them only in the area where the painting is to take place. That area should have a cloth tarp or newspaper covering the floor, making it less slippery and, of course, protecting the floor from any paint splatters. Please, be careful!

◆ Even if you plan on wearing old, ratty painting clothes, you should cover them by wearing a big plastic trash bag with holes cut out for your head and arms.

When you're finished painting, throw the trash bag away and save the *clean* old ratty clothes for another messy job.

Painting Pointers

Here are a few things that you may want to consider before you paint…it never hurts to be prepared!

◆ While the light switch plate is off, make a note on the wall of the brand and exact color paint you're using, and the amount of paint it takes to do the room, so you'll know for next time.

◆ Sand the edges of any door that you are going to paint. This will help prevent eventual paint buildup, which can make the door hard to open and close. Be sure to wipe the sanded edges with a clean tact cloth (available at paint stores) to remove any debris.

◆ If you can't remove your doorknobs, cover them with plastic wrap, plastic sandwich bags held in place with rubber bands or aluminum foil.

◆ When you're going to paint cabinets or furniture and you take off their pull-knobs, fill the screw holes with matchsticks, toothpicks or cotton swabs so that they won't fill up with paint.

◆ Coat all door and cabinet hinges with petroleum jelly. It's a good lubricant, and you can easily wipe off any paint that gets on them.

◆ Before painting the ceiling, wrap a plastic bag around the chandelier to save yourself the bother of having to clean off paint splatters.

◆ Cover the blades of ceiling fans with plastic wrap or bags to prevent them being splattered with paint.

◆ Coat the edges around window panes with a bar of soap or a bit of petroleum jelly. It's also a good idea to cover the window panes with wet newspaper pages.

NOTE: Be sure to keep the newspaper pages or the soap or the petroleum jelly on the window panes until all the paint is completely dry.

◆ If you're not planning to paint the baseboard, use painter's tape (available at hardware and paint stores) to cover it. Once the paint is just about dry, remove the tape. When you see the paint-free baseboard, you'll be happy you used it.

Preparing the Room

◆ Remove the light switch plate—not to paint the space underneath it, but to protect it from unwanted paint.

⭐ **Waxy Tape Hint**

If you don't have any painter's tape available, then—as temporary protection when painting—rub a candle around the edges of a masking tape roll. The tape will be easier to remove, thanks to the candle wax, and it will also reduce the chance of the tape taking off old paint when it's removed.

Preparing the Tools

◆ Make sure there are no loose bristles in the brush. Run a brush comb through it a few times before you use the paintbrush.

◆ To revive an old stiff paintbrush that has hardened paint on it, heat some distilled white vinegar on the stove...once it's hot, pour it into a clean, empty coffee can. Cut an X in the can's plastic lid. Push the handle of the paintbrush through the X, then put the bristle end of the brush in the can. This will allow the brush to hang down in the hot vinegar without resting on its bristles. Let the brush soak for about 30 minutes.

    To finish the job, wash the paintbrush with warm soapy water. If the brush was in a really bad way, you may need to remove the loosened paint with a wire brush. Or you may need to buy a new paintbrush.

◆ If the brush is stiff but doesn't have much paint on it, add a capful of liquid fabric softener to a coffee can of hot water. Then push the paintbrush through the lid (as explained above) and let it soak until it's flexible— check it every 30 minutes. Rinse with clean water and let dry before painting.

◆ Line the paint tray with aluminum foil— that way, when you're finished painting, you can just throw away the foil. The tray will look like new, and it will be ready to be used again and again.

⭐ **Selecting the Right Roller And the Best Brush**

According to experts at Benjamin Moore & Co. (*www.benjaminmoore.com*), you should always use an applicator that is designed for the type of paint you're using. For latex paints, use a synthetic bristle brush or a shed-resistant roller with beveled edges to help prevent *lap marks*— lines formed where the paint overlaps.

Brushes that have natural bristles or high-quality Chinese bristles (known as *China bristle brushes*) and *phenolic-core* (treated cardboard) rollers are recommended for use with oil-based or alkyd paints. (Of course, most paint manufacturers have their own line of custom-blended brushes and rollers that are specifically made for use with their paints.)

Once you decide on the paint you're going to use, check the label on the paint can. In most cases, it will advise you as to the best kind of brush (such as natural or synthetic) or roller (including the pile height) to use. And chances are that the same paint company also makes the type of applicator you will need.

Preparing to Paint

◆ Enamel paint spreads more smoothly when it's warm. Fill a pot with hot water and put the enamel paint can in it. Once the paint has had a chance to warm up, start using it.

◆ Always stir your paint to adequately mix its compounds (even if the can was "stirred" where you bought it). Pick up a few complimentary wooden stirrers when you buy paint, or use a special paint-mixing drill bit (available at home-improvement stores). In a pinch, a food skimmer or draining tool does the job, but plan on thoroughly washing the utensil if you plan to reuse it—or, better yet, just toss it.

◆ After you open a can of paint, but before pouring it into a tray, put tape (masking or transparent) around the entire rim of the can. When you're finished painting, take off the tape and close the can. The rim of the can will be paint-free and the lid will not get stuck the next time you need to use the can of paint.

◆ If you're using spray paint, place the spray-paint can into a pail of lukewarm water. After 3 minutes, take it out and spray away. Warming the spray will produce a finer mist and a smoother-looking finish.

◆ If a can of spray paint seems to be clogged, turn the can upside down and spray it into a plastic bag for 2 or 3 seconds. (Be sure you're in a well-ventilated area.) That should clear the nozzle, and once again you'll be ready to spray away.

How Much Paint Do You Need?

One gallon of paint covers about 375 to 400 square feet. To find the total square footage of the room (not including the ceiling), multiply the perimeter of the room (the width of each wall, including doors that will be painted) by the floor-to-ceiling height.

For example: The room has 4 walls that are each 10 feet wide...4 x 10 = 40. If the floor-to-ceiling height is 8 feet, then 8 x 40 = 320 total square feet.

To find the number of gallons of paint needed for that room, divide the square footage by 375—in our example, that would be 320 ÷ 375 = 0.85, or less than 1 full gallon. (Be sure to account for the application of second or third coats of paint, if necessary.) To calculate the paint needed for the ceiling, multiply the length by the width of the room to get the square footage, then divide by 375.

If you don't want to fuss with the math, then take the measurements of the room(s) you want to paint and visit *www.glidden.com.* Click on "How-To," then "Paint Calculator"—the online calculator will do the math for you.

Paints That Let You Breathe Easy

A newly painted room can please the eye but offend the nose and lungs. If you want to avoid that too-familiar odor that accompanies most fresh paint jobs—or if you are decorating near infants, seniors, asthmatics or other people who have respiratory problems—consider using low VOC-emitting paints.

Volatile organic compounds (VOCs) are released by certain solvents, such as formaldehyde (used as a preservative), that are found in most commercial paints—these solvents are what causes odor. Benjamin Moore & Co. (*www.benjaminmoore.com*) was the first manufacturer to offer low VOC-emitting paints—its Eco Spec line contains no solvents, and therefore, it has virtually no residual odor. This line of paint was awarded certification from the GREENGUARD Environmental Institute (*www.greenguard.org*).

Other manufacturers also supply these paints, which are primarily used in hospitals, motels, schools and businesses that can't be easily emptied when a paint job is scheduled to take place. But low VOC-emitting paints are also recommended for residential painting, especially for those who may be sensitive to fumes. Figure on paying 10% to 20% more for this type of no-smell, fast-drying paint. It comes in the same finishes as other brands...and they are available in white and more than 1,000 custom colors.

Doesn't that thought make you breathe easier? *Ahhh...*

Painting Doors

Before installing a new door, be sure to paint all surfaces—including the bottom. This is especially important on new wooden doors that haven't already been primed or otherwise sealed.

If the door is already hung on its hinges, a toothbrush is great for painting the underside of the door.

White Paint That Never Yellows

Many experts believe that by adding a few drops of black paint to a gallon of white paint, it will keep from yellowing. WRONG!

We talked to sources at Benjamin Moore & Co. and also at Glidden. They told us that nothing keeps oil-based white paint from yellowing. If the painted room gets lots of sunlight, the ultraviolet rays will slow down the yellowing, but eventually, the paint will turn yellow. (However, by then, it may be time for another paint job.)

Instead, use latex (water-based) white paint, which will not yellow unless there is a heavy smoker in the house.

Painting Stairs

◆ If you want to paint the steps of a staircase to which people must have access, paint every other step. The next day, when the first set of painted steps are dry, go ahead and paint the other set of every-other steps.

◆ If people in your home can't manage climbing over every-other step, then put a strip of masking tape down the middle of each step. Paint one half of each stair, allowing people to use the unpainted half to get up or down the staircase. The next day, when the first half is dry, remove the tape, then paint the other half of the steps. (Be sure to let people know which half is wet and which is dry!)

Painting Closets

Consider painting the inside of a closet with white enamel paint. With or without a light in the closet, the white enamel should help you see the closet's contents more easily.

Painting Radiators

Paint adheres better to warm (not hot) metal. If you plan on painting the radiator, do it when the radiator is warm.

Painting Baseboards

Make it easy on your knees when painting a baseboard—borrow a kid's skateboard and sit on it. Merrily you'll roll along as you paint.

Painting a Small Object

When painting a small object, the first thing most of us do is to put down newspaper and work there. And then the object gets stuck to the newspaper. So forget newspaper! Use waxed paper instead.

If you don't have any waxed paper, then rub a candle on pieces of brown paper grocery bags, and use them when you paint objects and leave them to dry.

Easy Drip Catchers

◆ Attach a paper plate—use double-sided tape or glue—to the bottom of the paint can. All drips will stay on the plate, keeping the bottom of the paint can clean. The can will not stick to the floor, a ladder, a tarp, a table top or any other surface.

◆ Carefully cut a tennis ball in half with a sharp knife or scissors. Even more carefully, in the middle of 1 of the halves, cut a slit a little bigger than the width of the paintbrush handle. Stick the paintbrush handle through the slit and push it toward the bristles. The half-ball will catch drips from the brush when you raise your hand to paint overhead.

◆ Make a slit in the middle of a small paper plate or paper cup and push the paintbrush handle through it. It will act as a drip catcher (but you'll have to watch that the drips don't roll off the plate).

♦ To minimize paint smell, mix 1 teaspoon of peppermint extract or 1 tablespoon of vanilla extract into 1 gallon of oil-based paint. This solution will help reduce the strong, relentless smell of paint.

♦ To eliminate strong paint odors, the obvious thing to do is to open a window and air out the smell. But you may not want to open windows and run the risk of bugs and dirt coming in and messing up your newly painted walls. So keep the windows closed—instead, cut 1 or 2 big yellow onions into chunks. Put the chunks on dishes and place them around the room. They will absorb the paint smell.

By the way, don't keep the onions out for more than a day, or you'll need something to get rid of the obnoxious onion smell.

♦ Charcoal briquettes placed around the room will help absorb paint smells. So will a few plates or cookie trays filled with a layer of table salt.

 No More Wasted Paint!

If you have the most common kind of paint can, where the rim collects excess paint from your brush, carefully drill a few holes in the rim. The paint that comes off of your brush will go back into the can through the holes. When you put the lid on the can, it will cover the holes and keep the paint from drying out.

Dealing with Paint Problems

♦ If you have a *new* can of paint that has lumps in it, take it back to the store. If you have an *old* can of paint that has lumps, get a piece of screen from the hardware store—it should be about the size of the can. Put the screen on top of the paint and let it settle to the bottom of the can, taking the lumps with it.

♦ Sometimes, a can of paint that has been stored away for a while will develop a layer of "skin" on its surface. Get a large wide-mouthed jar (or a clean, empty paint can), stretch a piece of pantyhose across the mouth, and keep it in place with a rubber band.

For safety's sake, in addition to the rubber band, make sure the pantyhose stays secure by putting duct or masking tape around the can. Then carefully and slowly pour the paint from the can into the jar. You may have to pause for a few seconds to give the paint time to pass through the pantyhose. But in the process, you will be straining away the skin.

Straining paint through a screen will also work to get rid of the skin.

⭐ **Prevent Paint Skin**

Put the can of paint on a piece of waxed paper or aluminum foil, trace the can's circumference, then cut out the circle—it should be a tad smaller than your outline. Place the waxed paper or foil circle on the surface of the leftover paint, and put the lid on. The next time you're ready to use the paint, there will be no layer of skin on top...just the waxed paper or foil. Then remove it when you're ready to paint.

Saving Leftover Paint

♦ If you don't finish painting in a day, instead of cleaning the brush or the roller, just wrap it in aluminum foil, put it in a plastic bag and put it in the freezer. The next day, thaw out the brush or the roller at least 1 hour before you're ready to start painting again.

✎ **NOTE:** A wrapped paintbrush or roller can be stored in the freezer indefinitely.

♦ Put some paint in a small baby-food jar and keep it handy for minor touch-ups...the kind you can do with a cotton swab or a clean makeup sponge.

◆ With a magic marker, draw a thick line on the outside of the can that shows how much paint is left inside the can.

◆ Empty clean, plastic laundry-detergent bottles make great containers for leftover paint. They have a dripless pouring spout, a handy handle and if you close them tightly, the paint won't dry out in them.

🕐 Paint Color Keepers!

On a 3" x 5" index card, write the paint brand, color name and the room you used it in—you may even want to paint a color swatch on it. Then attach the card to the paint can or laundry-detergent bottle, sticking it in place with transparent tape.

While you're at it, paint an additional index card or dip half a popsicle stick in the paint. When it is dry, write the paint brand, color name and the room you used it in, so that you will have the color handy for matching and decorating purposes.

Cleaning Up After Painting

◆ Pour distilled white vinegar into a pot and heat it up (don't boil it). Then pour the hot vinegar into a pail or can, and soak your paintbrush or roller in it.

In 10 to 15 minutes when the vinegar has cooled off, take out the brush or roller and wash it in lukewarm soapy water, then rinse it in clear water. There shouldn't be any paint left in the roller or brush, and when it is dry…it will be good to go.

🅢 Keep Brushes Longer

You may want to rub a few drops of vegetable oil into the bristles of a clean, dry paintbrush. This will keep them soft and reusable.

◆ If paint splattered on your tile floor, warm up some distilled white vinegar in a pot on the stove, and sponge it on the tiles. Let it sink in for 1 to 2 minutes, then wipe it off with a clean cloth.

◆ Nail-polish remover will also do away with dry paint splatters on a ceramic tile floor. Dab it on the tiles, and rub it off with a clean, dry cloth.

> ✎ **NOTE:** These tile tips—hot vinegar or nail-polish remover—will also work for paint that has splattered on window panes.

◆ If you want to scrape dry paint specks off your windows, use the edge of a penny or a razor scraper.

◆ For skin-so-painted with latex paint, use Avon's Skin So Soft lotion to remove it. For oil-based paint, gently rub your skin with baby oil, olive oil or foam shaving cream. For a stubborn paint spot, dab it with a bit of nail-polish remover.

◆ If you get paint in your hair, rub the painted strands with a little baby oil or olive oil, then comb and shampoo as usual.

PAINTING (Outdoors)

Tom Silva, a member of the home-improvement team on the television program *This Old House*, says, "A good paint job protects the outside of your house like a thin, waterproof raincoat."

Mr. Silva also believes that a good paint job should last at least 10 to 15 years, depending on the location of the house and how well it is protected from the elements—such as sun, wind and rain. He suggests you follow 2 simple rules—prepare the surface well, and buy the best paint you can afford.

Here are more suggestions to get the job done efficiently…

When to Apply the Brush

The best time of day to paint outdoor surfaces is in the early afternoon, after the morning dew has completely evaporated.

Painting a Deck

It has been reported to us that it's best to paint a deck using a broom that has nylon bristles with "flagged tips" (these are essentially split ends, which is a good thing for broom or brush bristles to have). Using the broom is easier and more efficient than using a paintbrush.

⭐ **Repelling Insects**

Since bugs can't read a "Wet Paint" sign, add 1 tablespoon of oil of citronella (available at health-food and some hardware stores) to each gallon of paint, and stir it well. Your paint job should be bug-free thanks to the citronella.

Prepping Metal Surfaces

To reduce the possibility that paint will peel off a metal surface, wipe the clean, to-be-painted metal with a mixture of 1 part distilled white vinegar to 5 parts plain water. Let it air-dry, and then paint.

Painting Wrought-Iron Furniture

Dab paint on wrought-iron furniture with a regular kitchen sponge. You will be able to get the job done faster.

Painting Odd-Shaped Things

If you're painting unusual configurations, like intricate stair railings or wrought-iron gates, it may be easier to use your hand than a paintbrush. Put on a long plastic or latex glove and wrap an old hand towel around your hand. Keep it in place with rubber bands. Dip your fingertips into the paint, distribute it over the rest of your palm and then massage/paint the odd-shaped whatever. ■

■ **Products** ■

HANDy Paint Pail

Why did it take so long to come up with something so useful for the do-it-yourself painter? This pail holds up to 1 quart of paint, and it can be secured on a belt for hands-free use.

Source: Bercom, 877-464-1170 (or in MN, 952-448-2766), *www.handypaintpail.com*.

CHAPTER 2

Fantastic Furniture

When humans decided to settle in homes, giving up their nomadic lives, they began to make furniture. After all, they needed to sleep…to eat…and to kick back and relax in front of the TV.

Through the ages, people have continued making their own furniture. Recently, a man made news for furnishing his entire apartment with a bed, a corner desk, a table and chairs and a couch—all created from Federal Express boxes and packing supplies.

Chances are, you acquired your furniture through traditional means and simply want to know how to take care of it, so that you'll have it to enjoy for a long time. *Well, here's how…*

WOOD FURNITURE

We spoke with J. Michael Flanigan, owner of J.M. Flanigan American Antiques in Baltimore, Maryland. He is a fine-furniture expert who specializes in classic American furniture. After college, he spent 8 years repairing, restoring and conserving antique furniture.

Several of those years were spent at J.W. Berry & Son, a company that has done conservation work for almost every museum, historical society and historic home in and around Baltimore.

Mr. Flanigan is also the former administrator of the Kaufman Americana Foundation, where he oversaw the exhibition of the collection at the National Gallery of Art in Washington, DC. Since the close of the exhibit, Flanigan has been a private dealer and lecturer.

You may also know him as one of the guest appraisers on the popular PBS television program *Antiques Roadshow (www.pbs.org/wgbh/pages/roadshow)*. He graciously agreed to share his expertise with us.

And Flanigan's advice is thrilling. It turns out that all the time we were feeling guilty about not taking care of our 10-piece dining room set, we were in fact treating it right…by not treating it at all. *We want you, too, to know what to do—or what not to do—so here is advice direct from the expert…*

Flanigan's Furniture Philosophy

What's the best way to take care of furniture? Flanigan believes in an idea that was suggested by the late Daniel Patrick Moynihan, a revered

US Senator from New York—"benign neglect." Flanigan feels that if you leave something alone, it will be fine. In other words, you will cause no harm by doing *nothing* to your furniture.

The Best Way to Protect Furniture

Give fine wood furniture a good environment. That means keeping it out of direct sunlight. Also, keep the temperature relatively constant and without humidity fluctuating quickly or radically. *That's 99% of what needs to be done…*

The Other 1%—the Finish

Furniture comes with a finish. The finish is put on to protect the wood. The worst thing you could do for finished furniture is to put oils on it too often. If you want a little more sheen, put a small amount of beeswax on a soft cloth and massage it on your furniture once or twice a year. Buff it with a clean cloth, going with the wood grain. And that's it! Just beeswax once or twice a year.

If you have modern furniture, chances are it has a modern finish, such as a catalyzed varnish that you really don't have to wax…ever. Just dust the furniture when it gets dusty.

Thank you, J. Michael Flanigan!

✶ **Do-It-Yourself Furniture Polish**

For those of you who insist on polishing your wood furniture—regardless of what Mr. Flanigan advises—here are 2 formulas from which to choose…

◆ Mix ⅓ cup of distilled white vinegar with 1 cup of olive oil.

◆ Mix 1 cup of mineral or baby oil with 3 drops of lemon extract.

　Rub the homemade polish on the furniture with a soft, lint-free cloth, and then wipe it off.

Remove Polish and Dirt

If you watch *Antiques Roadshow*, you may know that many pieces of furniture go down in value (and price) because they've been cleaned, polished and/or refinished. Therefore, consider that you have been warned, once again, to practice "benign neglect."

To remove old polish and dirt, place 2 bags of black tea (such as Pekoe) in 1 quart of water and bring it to a boil. Once the tea cools to room temperature, dampen a cloth with the solution and wipe the furniture. Then buff it dry with a soft cloth. Hopefully, you will have gotten the furniture down to its original finish and will stop there.

Remove a Water Mark/ White Ring

A water mark or white ring is caused by moisture that's trapped between the finish and the wood. To get rid of the mark, the finish needs to be opened up so that the moisture can be released.

There is no way for us to tell you what will work best on your furniture. *Assess the level of damage, decide on a course of action and then proceed cautiously with 1 of the following…*

◆ Mix cigarette ashes with an equal amount of mayonnaise, butter or vegetable oil. Carefully rub the mixture on the water mark. Let it set for about 1 hour, then wipe it off. If the mark or ring didn't disappear, you may need to gently sand the mark with #000 (extra-fine) steel wool, and reapply the ashes and oil.

◆ Rub the ring with a dab of non-gel, plain white toothpaste on a damp cloth until the ring is gone. Then wipe and buff with a soft cotton cloth.

◆ For a major water mark, mix non-gel, plain white toothpaste with an equal amount of baking soda, then massage the mixture into the problem area. Then wipe and buff dry.

Removing Scratches

◆ On dark wood, fill in a scratch or nick with a paste made from a bit of cooled instant coffee mixed with 1 or 2 drops of water. Use a cotton swab to apply.

◆ Cover up a scratch on varnished wood by using an appropriately colored eyebrow pencil, shoe polish or crayon. You can also try rubbing a pecan, walnut, Brazil nut or peanut into the scratch.

◆ On mahogany, a little iodine will hide most scratches. Apply with a clean cloth or a cotton swab.

◆ If you have wrought-iron furniture that stays indoors, fill in scratches with black shoe polish. If the wrought-iron is subject to wet weather outdoors, rub a black crayon on the scratch and blend it in with a soft cloth.

★ Prevent Tabletop Scratches

Put small pieces of felt on the bottoms of lamps, vases and other decorative pieces that sit on top of furniture. It's easy to do—just attach the felt with plain white paste (school paste) or double-sided tape. Your tabletops will be better for it.

UPHOLSTERED FURNITURE

The furniture industry created a common cleanability code in 1969. The code is made up of 4 letters—W, S, W-S and X. Each letter stands for the recommended care and method of cleaning the specific fabric. The code assigned to each type of upholstery is usually found on the furniture label—check under a seat cushion or on the frame that the cushion sits on.

But here is a brief summary of each code, so that you can coordinate the code on your upholstered furniture with the cleaning suggestions that follow…

◆ **Code W**—Use water-based cleaning agents or foams only.

◆ **Code S**—Use only mild, water-free dry-cleaning solvents.

◆ **Code W-S**—This fabric may be cleaned with water-based cleaning agents and foams, as well as with mild, water-free dry-cleaning solvents.

◆ **Code X**—Do not use foam or liquid agents on this fabric. Vacuum or brush lightly to remove soil.

⚡ **CAUTION #1:** Before cleaning any upholstery, test a small, inconspicuous portion of the fabric to be sure the color stays the same and doesn't run, and that the fabric doesn't shrink.

⚡ **CAUTION #2:** Do not remove the cover from a foam cushion, even if it has a zipper that seems to be there for the purpose of removing the cover and throwing it in the washing machine. That would probably be a big mistake. Even if the cover doesn't shrink after being washed, it's almost impossible to get it on again properly. We know…we've tried. Also, chances are that once the covers are washed, they will not match the rest of the upholstery that wasn't washed.

Cleaning Upholstery (By Code)

Cleaner for Upholstery (Codes W and W-S)

In a big mixing bowl, combine 1 part mild laundry detergent with 4 parts water. Use a hand mixer or a whisk in the mixture and create as much foam as possible. Do one small, manageable section at a time. Brush on the foam, then wipe off the dirty foam with a spatula or an index card. The goal is to clean the fabric without drenching it. Next, blot it with paper towels.

Once you've cleaned every section of the entire piece of upholstered furniture, use a hair dryer to dry it thoroughly, or let it air dry. Be sure no one uses it before it's completely dry.

Remove Grease Stains
(Codes S and W-S)

Apply a layer of dry cornmeal to the stain, and let it stay on overnight. The next day, vacuum up the cornmeal—and the stain.

Remove Musty Smells (All Codes)

If your furniture smells musty or has the lingering scent of cigarette smoke, just sprinkle baking soda or natural clay kitty litter on the upholstery. After a few hours, vacuum up the baking soda or litter, and the smell should be gone.

Pick Up Pet Hair (Codes W and W-S)

Use a damp sponge, microfiber or chamois cloth to wipe the furry upholstery clean. You can also use a strip of sticky tape to pick up the hair.

Removing Candle Wax

Put ice cubes in a plastic bag and place the bag on top of the wax. Keep it there until the wax is frozen. Then break off as much of the frozen wax as possible. If all of the wax comes off—great. If not, cut pieces of paper from a brown grocery bag (make sure the pieces are print-free). Place a piece of brown paper on top

of the remaining wax. Then press over it with a medium-hot iron. After the paper absorbs some of the wax, place a new, clean piece of brown paper on it. Keep repeating the process until the wax is gone.

Even after the wax is gone, a wax stain may remain. If that's the case and you're brave enough to try something that may bleach out the stain, get some 3% hydrogen peroxide. Dip a sponge in the peroxide and gently sponge it on the stain. After 15 minutes, blot the stain with a dry paper towel. If the stain is lighter but still there, repeat the process again and again until the stain is gone.

Cleaner for Leather Upholstery

If there's a wax buildup on your leather furniture, rub it with stale beer…or a solution made from ¼ cup of distilled white vinegar combined with ½ cup of water. Then wash the leather with saddle soap (available at tack stores where saddles and other equine supplies are sold, as well as some shoe-repair stores) and water. Complete the job by buffing the upholstery with a soft cloth to bring out the leather's shine.

Cleaning Vinyl Upholstery

Oil from the human body and hair can stiffen vinyl and cause it to crack. That being the case, you should clean vinyl arm- and headrests fairly often if they get lots of use. Wipe them with a sponge that's been moistened with distilled white vinegar, or use a damp sponge sprinkled with baking soda. Follow that with a sponge dipped in a sudsy solution of water and a couple of drops of dish detergent. Then rinse and dry the vinyl.

WICKER (CANE) FURNITURE

By definition, *wicker* is anything that is woven—reeds, rush, willow...even paper. Most wicker furniture is made from the long, tough, slender stems of rattan climbing palms. *Cane* is the skin of the rattan pole and is used for certain parts of furniture—most often for seats—and for wrapping the joints of wicker furniture.

Now that you have a better understanding of what wicker furniture is, here's how to care for it...

Preventing Yellowing

If you have new natural-colored wicker furniture, sponge it down with a solution made from ½ cup of table salt mixed in 1 quart of warm water. Let it air dry.

Fixing a Sagging Seat

To firm up a sagging cane seat, turn the chair bottom-side up and sponge the seat's underside with hot water. The seat will shrink if you let it air dry, preferably in the sun.

DUSTING

The average American home generates about 40 pounds of dust every year for every 1,500 square feet of space. In only 1 ounce of that dust, there are about 40,000 dust mites, which may be the cause of many people's allergy problems.

A lot of dust comes into the house from the bottoms of people's shoes. It's a good idea to put rubber-backed, bristly mats near every door that opens to the outside world, and to make sure everyone does the *brush-brush-clean-your-shoes* dance before entering.

Here are some other ways you can deal with dust...

Inexpensive Dust Cloths

In addition to (or instead of) buying a microfiber dust cloth, recycle old pairs of cotton socks or gloves and use them to dust. Old, cut-up cotton T-shirts and discarded shoulder pads also make good dust rags. Snagged pantyhose and used fabric-softener sheets are excellent lint-free dust collectors. And they're all washable.

Shake That Dust Mop

To clean a dust mop easily and efficiently, put the dusty mop head in a plastic or paper bag, scrunch up the neck of the bag, hold it tight and shake it vigorously.

Dusting High-Ups, Unders and Behinds

Clean those hard-to-reach places with any or all of the following...

- **Broomstick**—Wind tape (transparent, duct, masking or any other kind)—sticky side out—around the end of a broomstick. Or put a net pouf or scrunched-up mesh onion bag on the end of the broomstick, securing it with string or rubber bands. You can then use the broomstick to clean cobwebs out of corners easily.

- **Long-handled automotive snow brush**—This long, slim brush is the answer for cleaning in and around a household radiator.

- **Yardstick**—Put a sock on it! Or wrap an old pair of pantyhose around it. Keep the sock or hose in place on the yardstick with string or rubber bands. Then you can dust high up, under or behind everything that is otherwise out of reach.

◆ **Golf club or hockey stick**—Wrap a cloth or hand towel around the head of a golf club or the blade of a hockey stick, and secure it with string or rubber bands. Both club and stick are perfect for dusting the tops of picture frames, high shelves, the tops of doors, near ceiling wall molding and the top of bookcases.

METALS

When young people talk about *metal*, they are usually referring to music—as in *heavy metal* or *rap metal*. But when we talk about *metal*, we mean the shiny *metallic* items in your home. *And if they're not shiny, here are some great ways to fix them up…*

Cleaning Metal Objects

Rule #1 for cleaning metals—*test, test, test!* Do not use any mixture or solution unless you try it first on an inconspicuous part of the metallic object. Wait a little while to see if anything unintended happens, such as discoloration, rust, tarnish or bubbling.

Also, keep in mind that cleaning some pieces may reduce their value. The appraisers on *Antiques Roadshow* have talked many times about how an item could have been worth thousands of dollars more…if only it hadn't been cleaned…if only it still had its natural patina. Don't let this happen to you!

If you have any doubt about cleaning a special *objet d'art*, seek the advice of a credentialed specialist at a museum, auction house or antiques gallery.

Great Use for Wine Corks
Most metals will shine like the sun if you rub them with cork.

Removing Tarnish

If you have a wood-burning fireplace (or know someone who has one), collect some wood ashes in a glass jar. Add 2 tablespoons of baking soda for each cup of ashes, then shake the jar until the ashes and baking soda are fully integrated.

When you are ready to clean a tarnished metallic object, take a scoop of the mixture and add enough water to form a mildly abrasive paste. Use a damp cloth to gently rub the paste on the metal. Use a soft cloth to wipe off the paste, then rinse and dry.

NOTE: Damp metal tarnishes quickly, so immediately after cleaning, dry the object thoroughly.

Silver

You are not the only person who appreciates the beauty and durability of silver. Silver has been mined for at least 6,000 years. It's easy to mold and shape. In fact, 1 ounce of silver can be drawn into 8,000 feet of thin…very thin…wire. For more information about this amazing ore, visit *www.silverusersassociation.org*.

Here are some ways to treat your silver as though it's worth its weight in gold…

Caring for Silver

◆ Put baking soda on a damp cloth and massage the silver with it. Then rinse and buff dry. Baking soda will remove tarnish and enhance the silver's patina.

Quick Silver Cleaner—and an Alternative

The following remedy is a popular cleaning method that cleans lots of silver pieces quickly and easily...

Line the bottom of a heatproof glass pan (Pyrex works well) with aluminum foil, shiny side up. Put the pieces of silver on top of the foil. Add 1 heaping tablespoon of baking soda, then pour in just-boiled water—enough to cover the silver items. In minutes, right before your eyes, the tarnish will disappear from the silver and end up on the foil. As soon as the silver is totally tarnish-free, rinse everything thoroughly, then buff the pieces dry with a soft cloth.

This easy and fast method magically removes the tarnish from silver—lots of pieces at once.

And although it works well, it may also remove dark accents in design crevices. That's not always a good thing. And it may also soften the cement of hollow-handled flatware. *Definitely* not a good thing. And, based on our experience, it may leave silver with a lackluster finish.

So, if you like luster...and the dark accents in design crevices...and you want to hang on to your flatware's hollow handles, then we have something that may be a better idea, especially if your silver pieces are heirlooms. *Try this...*

Rub each piece of silver with baking soda sprinkled on a moist, soft cloth. Then buff dry. It may take a little more elbow grease to clean your silver this way, but your heirlooms will be better off—and eventually, so will your heirs.

◆ Cut the hard ends off a banana peel, and purée the peel in a blender or a food processor. Then, using a soft cloth, rub the silver with the puréed peel. Wipe, rinse and buff dry with a clean soft cloth.

◆ Coat the silver with a thin layer of non-gel white toothpaste, and gently rub the object with a damp cloth. Once the tarnish is gone, wipe off all of the toothpaste, rinse and buff dry with a soft cloth.

◆ Got sour milk? Pour it in a glass pan and soak the tarnished silver pieces in it for 30 minutes. Then wash the silver with dish detergent, rinse and buff dry with a soft cloth. (Throw out the rest of the sour milk.)

⚡ CAUTION: Do not rub the silversmith's markings too hard. They will fade away, along with the value of the piece.

◆ Moisture causes silver to tarnish. So, whether you store or display your silver objects in a case, a credenza or a cabinet, add things that will help to absorb moisture, such as little pieces of blackboard chalk...a handful of uncooked rice...a few charcoal briquettes...or the small silica gel packets or drums that come in vitamin bottles.

◆ Exposure to moisture and air causes silver to tarnish. If you're not displaying your silver, store it in acid-free tissue paper or in specially treated tarnish-proof bags (available at some hardware and houseware stores). You can also look for bags that are made of *Pacific cloth* (also called *silvercloth*), which is available at some hardware, houseware or fabric stores, including Hancock Fabrics (*www.hancockfabrics.com* or 877-322-7427).

◆ Never let rubber bands or any rubber come into contact with—or even come close to—silver. The sulfur in the rubber can cause tarnishing and corrosion.

◆ Wrapping silver in newspaper is a no-no because the paper is acidic—it will cause silver to tarnish.

◆ Oak is an acidic wood. It's not a good idea to store silver in oak drawers or cabinets unless you wrap the silver or line the drawers with Pacific cloth or acid-free tissue paper.

◆ Plastic bags are better than nothing at all, but moisture can get locked in, and it will cause tarnishing. Find another way to store your silver.

✱ **Not Just for Special Occasions!**

If you have silverware, use it! The more you use it, the less it will tarnish, and the better the patina will be. If you're saving it for special occasions, make every occasion special by bringing out the good stuff.

Silverware—Dos and Don'ts

◆ According to the experts at Tiffany & Co., even though silver is dishwasher-proof, it's better to wash silverware by hand in hot sudsy water as soon as possible after use. Doing so will prevent food from causing tarnish stains. Rinse well in clear warm water, dry thoroughly (do not let silver air-dry) and put it away.

◆ Foods that contain sulfur, like eggs, and mild food acids, like those found in vinegar, mustard and salt, will make silverware tarnish and/or corrode faster than alkaline foods. That's not to say, don't eat those foods. It's just to emphasize—wash silverware as soon as possible after use.

◆ If you insist on putting silverware in the dishwasher, OK. Just don't put it in with stainless steel. An electrolytic action takes place when silver and stainless steel interact. The action causes pitting on the stainless pieces and leaves black spots on the silver.

Pacific Cloth/Silvercloth

Some smart cabinet and jewelry box manufacturers are now lining drawers with Pacific cloth (also known as silvercloth). If you have treasured silver, consider buying some Pacific cloth by the yard to line the drawer or wherever you keep your silver pieces. It is available at most hardware, fabric and housewares stores.

David W. Stevens, former owner of Stevens Paint and Wallpaper in Baton Rouge, Louisiana, agreed to share with us his method of applying a Pacific cloth lining...

"From my experience, doing one surface at a time works best. That way, you complete the job in manageable sections.

"When you cut each piece of Pacific cloth, overmeasure the cloth by an inch or so on all sides.

"Before applying the dry fabric, thin down white glue [school glue] with plain water. The glue should be thin enough to brush on but not so thin that it will soak through the fabric. Brush the glue on the surface area. Wait a few minutes until the glue is slightly tacky but not completely set.

"Keep the fabric taut—you don't want wrinkles as you lay it down—but don't overstretch the fabric. [*You may need someone to help you, especially if you're covering a sizable area.*] Once it's down, use something with a flat surface, like a spatula, to smooth it out completely. It can be problematic to turn corners with the fabric, so you may want to carefully trim the fabric in corners with a sharp razor blade, or you can have a little ruffle.

"Now that you have the basics, and you begin to work with the Pacific cloth, the best way to cover your space will become clear."

◆ Salt should not touch silver. Salt will make silver tarnish and/or corrode within no time. Be sure your shaker has a glass lining. It's also a good idea to remove the salt after each use, even if there is a glass lining.

Caring for a Silver Coffeepot or Teapot

◆ In between uses, keep the lid off and put lumps of sugar or a charcoal briquette inside. It will prevent the pot from developing a stale smell.

◆ To clean stains from the inside of a coffeepot, use fine steel wool that has been dipped in distilled white vinegar and table salt.

◆ To clean tea stains from the inside of a teapot, fill the pot with just-boiled water and ½ cup of washing soda (available at most supermarkets). Let the solution soak overnight, then rinse the pot and wipe it dry.

Caring for Silver Candlesticks

Remove wax by pouring just-boiled water over the candlesticks to melt off the wax. A hair dryer set on *hot* will also melt the wax. But be careful. You don't want to melt your fingers in the process!

Caring for Silver Jewelry

◆ Clean your silver jewelry by placing it in 1 cup of water. Add 2 Alka-Seltzer tablets and wait for the *plop, plop, fizz, fizz*. After 5 minutes, rinse the jewelry and dry thoroughly with a soft cloth.

◆ Tarnish on the posts of silver earrings may cause an ear infection. Prevent that from

happening by painting the posts with a tiny bit of clear nail polish—unless you're allergic to nail polish.

✳ Go Easy on Silver Plate
Treat silver-plated things as if they were solid silver, but with even more care—the coating on silver plate can come off if it is rubbed too vigorously.

Mixed Metals

If you have household objects or furniture details that are made from a "mixed metal" (such as brass, copper, bronze or pewter—*metal alloys* that are made from more than 1 type of metal), these pieces require special cleaning and care.

Caring for Mixed-Metal Objects

You can safely use this cleaning formula on most mixed metals. But please do a test spot first…just to be sure it's safe!

Mix 1 tablespoon of plain bleached or unbleached flour with 1 tablespoon of plain table salt. To that blended mixture, add 1 tablespoon of distilled white vinegar, and stir it all into a thick paste. Dip a damp sponge or cloth into the paste and rub it on the metal piece. Then rinse thoroughly and buff dry.

> ⚡ **CAUTION:** This formula should *not* be used on silver or silver plate. It will scratch the finish.

Cleaning Brass and Unlacquered Copper

◆ Put a few drops of Worcestershire sauce on a dry cloth and rub the tarnished object. It's said that the *ethanoic acid* in the sauce helps cut through the grime and tarnish. Once the brass or copper item is clean, rinse with warm soapy water and dry thoroughly.

◆ Make a paste by adding water to a powdered fruit juice like Tang. Rub it on with a damp cloth and wipe it off with a damp cloth. Rinse and buff it as you dry it with a soft cloth. (Rumor has it, this is what the US Navy uses to clean their brass.)

◆ Non-gel white toothpaste will act as a mild abrasive. Apply it with a damp cloth, gently rub the object, then rinse and buff dry.

◆ Dip a wedge of lemon into plain table salt, and clean the copper or brass item with it. The citric acid in the lemon helps dissolve the tarnish as the grains of salt scrub it away. Rinse thoroughly, then use a clean, soft cloth to buff it dry.

◆ Make a paste with plain table salt and distilled white vinegar to clean severely tarnished copper or brass. Be sure to rinse and buff dry.

Removing Bronze Patina

Corrosion can cause a thin greenish copper sulfate layer (*patina*) on some bronze pieces. It can be removed by making a paste with 1 tablespoon of baking soda and 1 teaspoon of lemon juice. Rub the paste on with a cloth, and keep rubbing until the green disappears. Rinse the piece thoroughly and buff dry.

You can also pour the baking soda straight onto cut lemon wedges and rub them directly on the bronze.

Cleaning Aluminum

◆ Use the juicy side of a lemon wedge to rub aluminum clean.

Aluminum or Stainless Steel? A Test

If you want to know what you are buying at a flea market—or what you already own—here's a simple test. Take a knife and carefully scrape along an edge of the item. If some of the metal flakes off, the piece is aluminum.

Cleaning Stainless Steel

◆ Gently rub any marked-up stainless steel fixtures and appliances with a used fabric-softener sheet from your laundry.

◆ Pour some club soda on a sponge to wipe stainless steel appliances clean. Be sure to dry them with a soft, clean cloth.

◆ If your stainless steel flatware is dull or streaky, pour a little baking soda on each utensil, add 1 or 2 drops of water and rub it shiny clean. Rinse and dry—you should be able to admire your upside-down reflection in a spoon.

◆ To clean a stainless steel teapot, just drop a denture-cleaning tablet into the pot, add warm water and let it stay that way for a couple of hours. Rinse thoroughly, and you're ready to make afternoon tea.

Caring for Stainless Steel Sinks

It's simple to clean a stainless steel sink. Just mix a little baking soda and water to create the mildest abrasive cleaner around. Use it to clean the sink without scratching it. Dry the sink thoroughly to prevent water spots and rust.

◆ To clean water spots from stainless steel, make a paste out of 1 part 3% hydrogen peroxide to 3 parts cream of tartar. Put it on the water spots, and when it dries, wipe it off with a wet sponge or cloth.

◆ Remove rust from your sink by rubbing the corroded areas with rubbing alcohol.

◆ Use distilled white vinegar on a damp cloth or sponge to get rid of your sink's unsightly rust and water spots. And, since the vinegar will brighten up the stainless steel, you may want to wipe the entire sink with it.

◆ When in doubt, use baking soda. Add water to baking soda to make a thick paste. Apply the paste on the stains and let it stay for 1 or 2 hours. Then, with a damp cloth, wipe off the paste and rinse the sink clean.

◆ If the hairline scratches in your sink really bother you, get rid of them by gently rubbing the entire sink with #00 (very fine) steel wool. Then buff the sink with a soft cloth.

◆ Once you're finished washing dishes, use a damp paper towel to wipe the sink. Then wipe it with a few drops of baby oil. The coating of oil will keep your stainless steel sink shiny and rust-free.

Cleaning Chrome

Just as there are different qualities of chrome, there are several chrome cleaners. Here's a selection, but it's up to you to test and determine which of them will get the job done.

◆ Use rubbing alcohol on a soft cloth or paper towel. If you don't have alcohol, you can use vodka to clean chrome.

◆ Baking soda on a damp cloth will get chrome clean. Wipe it on, then wipe it off with a damp paper towel.

◆ Rub a hard-to-get-off smudge with the shiny side of a scrunched-up piece of aluminum foil. After using foil on chrome, wipe the chrome

with a damp paper towel—you'll actually see the dirt on the towel.

When you scrunch up the foil, make sure there are no sharp points sticking out that might scratch the chrome.

◆ In some Chinese restaurants, the waiters pour leftover tea on the table to clean it. They know that strong black tea at room temperature is a good cleaner. You can use it on chrome to cut grease and add shine.

◆ Rub a damp and crunched-up piece of plain newspaper on chrome-trimmed glass fixtures or furniture, and clean the glass as well with the wet page. Both the chrome and the glass will be clean and lint-free.

◆ Remove rust stains from chrome by rubbing them with distilled white vinegar on a soft cloth.

Cleaning Pewter

◆ Use mild soapy warm water to wash off surface dirt. Rinse thoroughly to be sure there's no soap film left on the pewter.

◆ Use a large, outer leaf of a cabbage as you would use a cloth to rub the pewter clean. Then buff the pewter with a soft cloth.

◆ Boil eggs and keep the water. Once the water cools down, let the pewter sit in it for about 10 minutes. Rinse and buff dry.

◆ If a pewter object is badly tarnished, use #0000 (super-fine) steel wool dipped in olive oil and cautiously scrub off the tarnish. Then wash, rinse and buff dry with a soft cloth.

◆ Pewter items will take a lot longer to tarnish if they are kept in a glass enclosure and in a warmish place.

◆ Put baking soda on the stain. Then, with a cloth that's been moistened with vegetable or olive oil, gently rub the stain away.

◆ Remove wax by placing the candlesticks in the freezer long enough for the wax to freeze. Then flick it off.

⚡ **CAUTION:** Pewter has a low melting point. Do not EVER put pewter objects in an automatic dishwasher.

IVORY & BONE

How many animals can you name that are the source of ivory? Think about it for a minute…of course, you probably said elephant and maybe walrus. What about the elk, hippo and boar as well as sperm and killer whales? Ivory pieces are carved from the tusks and/or teeth of all those animals.

Now that you know where ivory comes from, here's how to take care of it…

Piano and Organ Keyboards

It's best not to keep the fallboard (the cover) over the keyboard. Let the piano or organ keys be exposed to air and light. The light helps prevent the keys from yellowing, and the air helps prevent warping.

Cleaning an Ivory Keyboard

Using a soft cloth, apply small amounts (you don't want any of it getting between the keys) of 1 of the following ingredients…

◆ Yogurt
◆ Milk
◆ Paste of baking soda and water
◆ Rubbing alcohol
◆ Non-gel white toothpaste
◆ 2 parts table salt to 1 part lemon juice

Carefully rub each key until it's clean, then wipe each with a clean, damp cloth.

If the keys are very yellow, mix equal parts of hydrogen peroxide and water. Use a damp sponge to apply the mixture. Give it some time to bleach the keys…about 10 minutes. Then wipe the keys with a damp cloth.

MARBLE

When limestone is exposed to the extremes of pressure or temperature, it undergoes a process known as *metamorphism*, and the limestone becomes crystal by nature, transforming into *calcite* or *dolomite*—the main materials in marble.

All you really need to know is that marble is considered to be an extremely sophisticated stone—used in art, architecture and for making home furnishings more beautiful. *That said, we're sure you want to know how to take care of it…*

Caring for Marble

Since marble is a porous stone and is at risk for holding stains, you may want to consider sealing it with a stone sealer (available at most paint and some hardware stores). If you do not have stone-sealer protection on your marble surface and you get a stain, it's important to tend to it as soon as possible. *You can try 1 of the following remedies…*

✍ **NOTE:** Be sure to test a small, inconspicuous spot first to make sure the cleaning solution won't damage the stone.

◆ For stains caused by beverages—such as coffee, tea or wine—mix 1 part 3% hydrogen peroxide to 4 parts water. Dip a cloth in

35

the solution and rub the stain, then wipe it quickly. If the stain doesn't go away, repeat the process.

◆ Make a paste by combining baking soda and equal amounts of water and lemon juice. Dip a cloth in the paste and rub the stain with it. Then rinse and dry.

◆ For non-beverage stains, spill table salt on them. After 1 or 2 minutes, brush off the salt and then spill some more. If the salt doesn't soak up the stain after 3 or 4 tries, then pour sour milk on top of the salt. The milk will keep the salt damp. Leave it that way for 2 or 3 days. Then use a damp cloth to wipe up the milky salt. Hopefully, there will be no trace of a stain.

> *(f)* **FYI: Slate Solution**
> You can also clean slate with the baking soda, water and lemon juice mixture. Dip a cloth in the paste and rub the slate with it. Then rinse with water and dry.

MIRRORS

Everyone has heard that old superstition about breaking a mirror and the 7 years of bad luck that supposedly follow. *If you buy into that, then you'll be happy to know that there are 3 ways to counteract that curse...*

◆ As soon as you realize that you broke a mirror, turn around 3 times counterclockwise. (Be careful not to step on the broken pieces of mirror. Now *that's* bad luck.)

◆ When it's dark out, light 7 white candles. At midnight, take a deep breath and blow them all out at once.

◆ Take a piece of the broken mirror to a cemetery and tap a gravestone with it.

Any of the above counter-curses should do it—or, rather, undo it.

Chances are you won't break a mirror, but you will need to clean the mirrors in your home. *Here are some suggestions that will help...*

Cleaning a Mirror

◆ Mix equal parts of distilled white vinegar and water in a bowl. Scrunch up a piece of (non-colored) newspaper, and dip it in the mixture. Wring it out, then wipe the mirror with it. Wipe the mirror dry with a soft cloth, soft paper towel or dry newspaper page. (Be sure to wear rubber gloves to keep the newspaper print off your hands.)

> ⚡ **CAUTION:** Do not spray water or liquid of any kind on a mirror. When moisture seeps into the edges and back of the mirror, the silvering gets spoiled...which causes dark spots.

◆ Wipe the mirror with a used, wet bag of black tea, then dry it with a paper towel or newspaper. The tea's tannic acid will leave the mirror sparkling clean.

◆ To get a lint-free shine, go over the mirror with a used sheet of fabric softener...or a dry coffee filter...or a pair of old pantyhose...or gift-wrapping tissue.

Creating Fog-Free Mirrors

◆ Apply a thin layer of glycerin (available at most drugstores) to the mirror to prevent it from fogging up in the shower.

◆ Before you shower, spray a dollop of foam shaving cream on a cloth and wipe the mirror with it.

◆ For longer-term defogging—2 to 3 weeks at a time—put a generous amount of foam shaving cream on the entire mirror and leave it there until the foam just about evaporates. Then wipe it off.

Removing Hairspray

Give your mirror the once-over with a cloth dampened with rubbing alcohol. Doing this will take off hairspray as well as any thin film that's left over from a cleaning agent, an aerosol product or from shaving cream.

Alcohol will evaporate on its own, which saves you the job of wiping it dry.

✳ **Mirror Touch-Ups**
- ◆ Most mirrors consist of 3 layers—a dark, protective bottom layer...a layer of metal (aluminum, silver or tin)...and a plain, glass top layer. If there are scratches in the metallic layer, and you can get to it, tape a piece of non-creased aluminum foil to the back of the metallic layer to hide the scratches.
- ◆ Put 1 or 2 coats of metallic silver auto paint on the scratched silver backing. Then seal the spot with clear shellac.

FISH TANKS

Keeping fish in an aquarium can be a wonderful, relaxing hobby. Fish tanks also make great conversation pieces! And it may surprise you to know that they don't take as much work to maintain as you might think. Actually, the bigger the fish tank, the easier it is to maintain. You won't have to change the water as often because the waste from the fish will stay stable longer.

When you buy a fish tank, look for the safety sticker on the glass (or ask someone at the fish and aquarium store). The sticker means that the tank has been tested for safety and has been caulked with a special silicon that will last for many years.

DID YOU KNOW?

The dirty water from a fish tank makes a wonderful organic fertilizer for houseplants.

Also—does your aquarium have a cover? A cover is a good thing. It helps prevent water from evaporating, and keeps your fish from leaping out.

Once you're squared away with a safe, covered tank, here's how to clean it...

Cleaning a Fish Tank

Put your fish in a temporary holding tank...put the tank's furnishings in a plastic shoebox...fertilize your plants (see above)...and you're ready to clean the tank. Soap or detergents of any kind may leave a residue that could be harmful to your fish, so get out the table salt instead.

Pour table salt on a sponge and pretend it's scouring powder. Once the tank is scrubbed clean, rinse it thoroughly and you're ready to set up the tank and move your fish back home. ■

■ Products ■

MAAS Polishing Creme for All Metals

Magic in a tube. We tested this creme on many household objects and had the most startling results with our grandmother's candlesticks. The silver was restored to what must have been its original beautiful patina, and it astounded us. The cleaning took some elbow grease (along with the polish) to remove the years of residue, but the outcome was worth it.

This creme restores and polishes just about all nonporous surfaces—all metals, fiberglass, Plexiglas, mirrors, crystal, ceramics, tile, porcelain, enamel, marble, linoleum, plastics, solid vinyl, polyurethane...and more. The results are long-lasting, too. Also available in a liquid.

Source: MAAS International, Inc., 630-654-4743, *www.maasinc.com.*

CHAPTER 3

The Best-Ever Kitchen Secrets

No room in the house declares "home, sweet home" more than the kitchen. It is the place where the food that sustains you and your family is stored, prepared and/or served. The kitchen is usually a warm, cozy room—and it always seems to be the busiest spot during a good party.

We hope the suggestions in this section help to keep your "kitchen, sweet kitchen" safe and clean, as well as providing ways for you to treat your appliances and dishes with the best care possible.

SAFETY

We don't want to frighten you with statistics concerning accidents that occur in the kitchen. But take our word for it—the numbers are high, the details are gruesome and (sadly) many disasters could have been controlled to minimize harm and damage...or even completely avoided. In many cases, all it would have taken was an ounce of prevention or some basic emergency-procedure information.

Please read through the following safety advice and take action now to prevent kitchen accidents—before you need to, but can't.

Fire

Every home should have a fire extinguisher on each level. It's important to know exactly where it is and how to use it! As soon as you bring a fire extinguisher into your home, go over all of the instructions with everyone who lives there. Have each person, including you, review the instructions thoroughly.

Then place 1 of the extinguishers in or near the kitchen—it should be in an easily accessible place. It's also a good idea to review the instructions each time you change the battery in your smoke detectors.

Statistics and our reasoning powers tell us that more fires start in the kitchen than any other room. *For safety's sake...*

- **NEVER** put out a grease fire with water. It will cause the grease to splatter, and the fire to spread quickly.

- **DO NOT** put a smoke alarm above the stove or kitchen sink. It will go off every time steam comes out of a pot or the hot-water faucet. You may get so annoyed with the false alarms that you disable the detector. Then, when you *really* do need it, it may not be working. The best spot for the smoke detector is right outside the kitchen.

◆ **DO NOT** douse flames in a pot or pan with water. Water will make the fire grow bigger. Instead, put a cover on the pot or pan, which will cut off the oxygen supply and smother out the fire.

◆ **DO NOT** keep a toaster under a shelf or kitchen cabinet. A little spark could pop up and ignite the wood above it.

◆ **DO** check the smoke alarm's batteries every month, and change them twice a year—the easiest way to remember is to do it when you change the clocks to and from Daylight Saving Time (if applicable in your area).

Distilled White Vinegar

As you may have noticed by now, we think distilled white vinegar is a great cleaning and disinfecting solution. *There are, however, a few cautions that need to be addressed...*

◆ **NEVER** combine white vinegar with ammonia or bleach of any kind (neither of these is ever recommended in this book). This combination creates a toxic gas, which can be harmful.

◆ **NEVER** use white vinegar on your teeth. It dissolves calcium.

◆ **DO NOT** use white vinegar on or around glued joints of furniture. It will dissolve most glues.

◆ **DO NOT** leave white vinegar on a metal surface. It may pit it.

◆ **DO NOT** sniff white vinegar, especially if you are sensitive to acidic fumes.

◆ **DO** clean up white vinegar with plain water. Vinegar is soluble in water, so if you get it on something, simply rinse it off with water (or neutralize it with baking soda), then clean up everything with a damp cloth.

Food Handling

How much time do you spend washing your hands before you handle food? Go through the motions of your typical hand-washing session, and you might be surprised at how quickly you do it. Maybe 4 seconds?

To be sure your hands are bacteria-free, the recommended amount of wash-up time is 20 to 30 seconds using warm, soapy water (and plain soap is often a better choice than the anti-bacterial type). If you sing the "Happy Birthday" song or recite your A-B-C's while washing up, your hands will spend the right amount of time getting clean. And don't rush through it! Finish the job by wiping your hands with a clean piece of paper towel.

Plastic Wrap in the Microwave

◆ Make sure the plastic wrap you use in the oven is labeled "microwave-safe." It's important that the plastic wrap does not come into direct contact with the food that you're cooking in the microwave—chemicals from the plastic can leach into your food.

◆ After zapping a plastic-wrapped dish, remove the plastic wrap and try to stay out of harm's way—fold back the plastic from the corner that's farthest away from you.

By doing this, you will avoid getting burned by the poof of scalding-hot steam that bursts out of the dish.

CLEANING BASICS

Don't you just hate it when you run out of a cleaning product—especially when you get that overwhelming urge to clean? We hope that doesn't happen to you, but if it does, there are suggestions in this section for several make-it-yourself substitutes.

And while you're here, there's helpful information on using some of the tools of the trade—sponges, steel wool, rubber gloves, our beloved baking soda and more. So don't let us keep you. Get to it!

Make-It-Yourself Scouring Powder

In a covered container, mix 1 cup of baking soda, 1 cup of borax powder (available at supermarkets and drugstores) and ¾ cup of table salt. Make it easy to use by keeping a portion of the mixture in a large salt shaker. Sprinkle some on whatever surface you need to scour, like sinks and bathtubs.

> **CAUTION:** Make sure you label the salt shaker clearly so that nobody mistakes the mixture for regular table salt! And be sure to keep the shaker in a cupboard along with your other cleaning supplies—out of the reach of children and pets. Borax can be dangerous if ingested.

Dish Detergent Mixture

In a plastic squeeze bottle, combine 1 part liquid dish detergent with 1 part distilled white vinegar and 3 parts water. Shake it a few times before using. The detergent cuts the grease, the white vinegar disinfects and helps clean, and the water acts as detergent-extender…making it last longer.

Dish Detergent Substitute

If you have a sinkful of dirty dishes and no dish detergent, use shampoo (make sure it's the non-conditioning kind) to clean them. If you have oily hair and use shampoo specifically formulated for it, all the better. It will cut right through the oily pots and pans and greasy dishes.

Steel Wool Tips

◆ After using a steel-wood pad, if there's still some scrub left in it, place it in a little plastic bag and store it in the freezer. It will stay rust-free. When you're ready to use it again, put it under warm water and it will thaw in a few seconds.

◆ To avoid getting metal splinters, wear rubber gloves when you use steel wool. If you don't have them, you can protect your fingers by cupping the steel-wool pad in the rind of a lemon, orange or grapefruit.

Deodorize and Disinfect Sponges

We don't mean to gross you out, but it's important to know that the average kitchen sponge contains more germs than the average toilet seat. The good news is that it's easy to disinfect the sponge.

◆ Each time you run your dishwasher, toss the sponge on the top rack and let it go along for the ride.

◆ Rinse the sponge and zap it (while it's still wet) in the microwave for 1 minute. (Be sure there aren't any metal fibers in the sponge.)

◆ Soak the sponge overnight in a solution of 1 cup of hot water, ½ cup of distilled white vinegar and 3 tablespoons of table salt. In the morning, rinse the sponge and use as usual.

Rubber Gloves

◆ If you're having a hard time taking off rubber gloves, hold your hands under cold water—they'll glide right off.

◆ Next time, before you put on the gloves, sprinkle a bit of baking soda or talcum powder on your hands or into the gloves.

◆ If a glove has sprung a leak and your fingers are wet after using it, throw the gloves away and put on a new pair.

 If your fingers are wet because water seeped into the gloves while you were wearing them, thoroughly dry the outside. Then, take each glove off by grabbing onto the cuff and pulling it over the fingers, turning the glove inside out. Let them air dry.

 When you're ready to wear them again, turn them right side out—and don't forget to sprinkle your hands or the gloves with a little baking soda or talcum powder.

Wrap It Up

◆ If plastic wrap gets unmanageable because of the way it sticks to itself, keep the box in the freezer. Cold plastic wrap will behave the way you want it to.

◆ If you have a hard time finding the beginning of the plastic wrap roll, take a piece of tape (any kind), and dab at the roll until it picks up the loose edge.

◆ If plastic wrap doesn't stick to the bowl or dish you're wrapping, dampen the outer edge of the bowl or dish, and then put the plastic wrap on.

◆ When aluminum foil touches acidic foods—tomatoes, onions, lemons—a chemical reaction takes place that can affect the taste of the food. Also, foil may rust when it comes in contact with salty foods. So, if you think a food is acidic or salty, use plastic wrap on it instead of foil.

A Freshness Test for Baking Soda

If not for baking soda, this book would be a pamphlet. In order for baking soda to perform to the peak of perfection, it must be FRESH.

 To test the powers of your baking soda, pour ¼ cup of distilled white vinegar in a little bowl, then add 1 tablespoon of baking soda. If it fizzes, it's fresh enough to use.

 If there is no reaction when the baking soda combines with the vinegar, forget it. Just pour the contents of the box down the drain. Stale or not, it's always good for the drain.

APPLIANCES

Yes, kitchen appliances—such as the toaster, microwave, blender, bread machine, mixer, juicer, food processor, can opener and coffee grinder—make life easier, but you still have to clean and maintain them…once you find room for them in your kitchen. Read through these suggestions, and they may make the job less formidable and the appliances more efficient.

CAUTION: When you're using any small kitchen appliance, pull the plug from the electrical outlet when you're done. It rarely happens, but if an electrical component malfunctions (or there is a power surge in your house) while an appliance is plugged in, it can burst into flames.

Cleaning a Can Opener

When it comes to cleaning, the single most overlooked item in the kitchen seems to be the can opener—electric or manual. Each time you use it, food particles are left behind. We're talking breeding grounds for germs here.

Wash your can opener with dish detergent after every use (if it's electric, be sure to unplug it first). If there's any dried-on food, clean it with a toothbrush or fuzzy pipe cleaner. As an added non-bacteria-spreading precaution, always wash (not just wipe) off the top of the can you're about to open.

✳ **Easier Can Opening**
If your can opener doesn't operate as smoothly as it should, run a piece of waxed paper through it a couple of times.

Cleaning a Blender

Let your blender clean itself...sort of. Once your blender is ready to be washed, fill it ⅓ of the way with just-boiled water. Add a few drops of liquid dish detergent and, when the water cools, toss in a couple of ice cubes. Put on the lid securely and blend for about 15 seconds on *high*. Then rinse and dry.

Cleaning a Toaster

If your toaster has a bottom door, open it and get rid of the crumbs. Then turn the toaster upside down over the sink and shake it. To get at any remaining crumbs, use a small food brush, or a compressed-air spray (available at art and computer stores. The spray is also good for getting the dust out of keyboards).

⚡ **CAUTION:** It might be common sense, but it needs to be said—before you clean a toaster, be sure to unplug it.

Cleaning Melted Plastic Off the Toaster

◆ If plastic wrap or the plastic bag from a loaf of bread gets melted on your toaster, here's what to do—first, wait for the toaster to cool. Then sprinkle baking soda on a damp cloth and rub off the plastic.

◆ Apply petroleum jelly on the melted plastic, and toast a piece of bread so that the toaster heats up. Then, rub off the plastic with a paper towel or cloth. Be careful not to burn your fingers.

◆ If the plastic seems stuck on for good, try nail-polish remover when the toaster is cool. It should take it off. The problem is, it may take the finish off as well. Test a tiny spot before you use it.

Cleaning a Drip Coffee Maker

Once a month—or whenever mineral deposits clog the coffeepot (you'll know because it will take longer than usual to prepare the coffee)—fill the water reservoir with equal parts of distilled white vinegar and water, and run it through the brew cycle. Then, using just plain water, rinse it out with another cycle.

Cleaning a Coffee Grinder/Mill

◆ Bitterness buildup from coffee residue will be scoured away when you run 1 cup of uncooked white rice through the grinder once a month. The grains of rice also help sharpen the blades.

◆ If you always use the grinder for coffee, and you occasionally use it for spices, be sure to clean out every morsel of spice before you go back to coffee. Do it by grinding 2 or 3 pieces of plain wheat bread.

Taste the last piece of ground bread to make sure there is no trace of the spice.

Cleaning a Waffle Iron

Nobody wants to clean the mess made by a waffle iron that won't let go of the waffles. To bring your waffle iron back to its *nonstick* condition, place 2 pieces of waxed paper where the batter goes, and let it heat up. Keep an eye on it, and as soon as the waxed paper turns dark brown, remove it. Your waffle iron should be good as new. Make yourself a waffle coming-out party!

Cleaning a Hand Mixer/ Electric Mixer

Make cleanup easier by spritzing the beaters with cooking spray before using them.

> **NOTE:** The only time you shouldn't spray the beaters with cooking spray is when you want to beat egg whites—the spray will prevent the egg whites from stiffening.

Cleaning a Food Processor

Once the food is in the work bowl, waiting to be processed, cover the bowl with a piece of plastic wrap. Then place the lid on top, and you're ready to go. Once the machine does its thing, take off the lid (which has remained clean), and throw away the splattered-on plastic wrap.

You still have to clean the bowl and the blades, but you won't have to bother digging out any food particles from the lid.

Cleaning a Microwave Oven

◆ In a microwave-safe glass bowl, squeeze in the juice of 1 lemon and add 1 cup of water. Place it in the middle of the microwave, and zap it on *high* for 1 minute. Let the bowl stay in the oven, with the door closed, for about 10 minutes. Then all the caked-on gunk will be loose and easy to wipe off. And the kitchen will have a great, citrusy scent.

◆ Clean and sanitize your microwave with a mixture of 1 part baking soda to 7 parts water in a microwave-safe glass bowl. Put the bowl in the oven, and set it on *high* for 2 minutes. Notice that the liquid turns to steam and coats the interior of the oven.

When it's finished, carefully remove the bowl, and wipe down the oven with a clean cloth or paper towels.

◆ If there's a dry, caked-on spill inside your microwave, cover it with a wet washcloth, then set it on *medium* for 20 seconds. Wait until the cloth cools before handling it, and then wipe up the loosened mess.

✳ Prevent Spills in the Microwave

If you're zapping something that may leave a messy splatter—such as vegetable soup or lasagna—put a paper plate or a piece of waxed paper under the dish to catch the splashes. Instead of having to clean the microwave, just throw away the paper plate or the paper.

You can also cover the open food container with a paper plate, coffee filter, or a piece of waxed paper or paper towel, which will help prevent the food from splattering.

Deodorize Your Microwave

Toss the peel of a lemon in a microwave-safe glass bowl, along with 1 cup of water, and zap it for about 30 seconds. (*See* "Cleaning a Microwave Oven" on this page, using the juice of the lemon instead of the peel.)

Microwave Facts

Microwave ovens were invented in 1946. A year later, the first commercial microwaves were sold. They were 5½ feet tall and weighed over 750 pounds. Each unit cost $5,000.

That's some mighty expensive popcorn!

Cleaning a Stove or Range

First, make sure the oven is off and cool inside. Then, use a wet sponge or wet cloth to wipe the inside of the oven. Next, before the oven surfaces dry, quickly sprinkle on baking soda. Leave it this way overnight. In the morning, wipe off the baking soda, along with the grease and grime.

Cleaning Spills Inside the Oven Or on the Stovetop

◆ If it's a *wet* spill (such as sauce, stew or gravy)…as soon as the food is out of the oven, carefully cover it with table salt. Remember—the oven will still be hot, so proceed with caution…and an oven mitt.

◆ If it's a *dry* spill (such as flour, sugar or ground coffee)…wet it with water and sprinkle on enough baking soda to cover it. Once the oven or stovetop is cool to the touch, you can scrape or scour off the spilled mess.

> ✪ **CAUTION:** Keep any type of oven cleaner away from the heating elements. Even baking soda can cause corrosion, which will result in a short-out.

Exterior Cleaner for a Gas or Electric Range

One guess as to what to use—you're right if you said baking soda. Sprinkle some on a damp sponge or cloth, then rub the outside of your range, rinse and dry.

Eliminate Oven-Cleaner Smells

If you are still using a store-bought, air- and lung-polluting aerosol oven cleaner, you can at least prevent the awful smell and smoke that happens when you turn on the oven.

Wet a sponge with distilled white vinegar, and wipe inside the entire oven with it. The vinegar neutralizes the lingering residual effects of the strong and irritating alkali from the commercial oven cleaner. It will also help prevent grease buildup.

Cleaning Burner Drip Plates and Burner Grates

Yes, that's what those removable, metal things on which you cook are called! To clean them, you will need a large pot that's *not* aluminum—glass or stainless steel will do. Put 1 quart of water in the pot, along with 1 tablespoon of baking soda. Put in the stainless steel or enamel burner drip plates and/or the cast-iron burner grates, and boil them for 5 minutes. Then remove them from the pot and let them cool. When each is cool enough to handle, rinse and wipe dry.

Unclogging Clogged Burner Holes

When spilled, caked-on food clogs the burner holes of your gas range, use a small, fuzzy pipe cleaner (available at art-supply stores) to clear the clogs. It's the perfect size for the job.

Cleaning an Oven Fan Filter

If you have an oven fan, chances are you have a greasy fan filter. It's easy to clean. Just take it out (that may be the hardest part), put it on the upper rack of your dishwasher, and let it go through a full wash cycle. (You may want to wash it by itself if it's really greasy.)

> ✎ **NOTE:** Pay close attention when you remove the filter from the fan, so you can reverse the procedure and put it back correctly once it's clean.

Cleaning a Broiler Pan

While the broiler pan is still hot, carefully sprinkle on some powdered laundry detergent —enough to cover the burned-on food. On top of that, place a wet paper towel. Leave everything for about 15 minutes. Then you should be able to scrape off the food easily.

Cleaning an Oven Rack

◆ Run very hot water in the bathtub—enough to completely cover the oven racks. Add ⅓ cup of liquid dish detergent and 1 cup of distilled white vinegar. Let the racks soak in the tub for at least 1 hour. Then scrub if necessary, rinse and wipe dry.

> If some stubborn caked-on crud refuses to come off, you can carefully scrape it away with a knife.

◆ If you want to save yourself the job of having to clean a dirty bathtub, then put the racks in a heavy-duty plastic bag with the water, detergent and vinegar. Fill the bathtub with hot water and soak the bagged racks in the bathtub for 1 hour.

Pretreatment for a Grill Rack

Spray the grid or rack with nonstick cooking spray before you heat the grill. It will keep food from sticking—which makes cooking easier and cleanup quicker.

Cleaning a Grill Rack

If there are lots of baked-on food and burned grease, take a sheet of heavy-duty aluminum foil and wrap it around the cooking grid (rack) —shiny-side down. Put it back on the grill, and turn up the heat for 12 minutes (give or take 1 or 2 minutes). Let the rack cool down, and when the foil is cool enough to handle, take it off the grill. The encrusted food should fall right off the rack.

✱ Foiled Again!

If the food doesn't come right off, crinkle a piece of aluminum foil into a ball and use it to clean the grill as you would use steel wool.

You can also do this if there's only a little bit of caked-on gunk on the rack.

Cleaning a Refrigerator

◆ To get your refrigerator clean and shiny inside and out, use (what else?) baking soda on a damp sponge or cloth.

◆ You can also wipe down the exterior surfaces of the fridge with a solution made from 1 part distilled white vinegar to 5 parts water—this will make everything extra-shiny.

✱ Butter Up Your Fridge

Want to clean behind the refrigerator? If you want to move something big and heavy, smear butter or other shortening on the floor right in front of the appliance. Then, with someone helping you, you should be able to slide the heavy appliance forward. Be sure to clean the floor when you're done!

Be aware that butter should NOT be used on marble floors—it can stain.

Cleaning Spills Inside the Refrigerator

If food spills are common in your refrigerator, spread a dishtowel on the bottom shelf to catch any drips. Instead of having to clean the bottom shelf every time there's a mess, you can just toss the towel in the wash.

Keeping the Drawer Liner Clean

◆ For easy cleanup (and to prevent messes), line the fruit/vegetable and meat drawers with old plastic place mats. You may have to cut them to fit, but considering how easy they are to wipe clean, it will be worth the effort.

◆ If you do not want to bother with cleaning place mats, line the drawers with some plastic wrap. Or use a few paper towels in the fruit drawer. They will help absorb moisture, which means the fruit will last longer.

Cleaning a Refrigerator Top

Relieve yourself of the very unpleasant chore of cleaning the top of the refrigerator—just line it with plastic wrap. But—unless you keep things on top of the fridge to hold down the plastic wrap—you may want to tape the sides of the plastic wrap to the refrigerator, to keep the plastic in place.

After a reasonable amount of dust-accumulation time, throw away the dirty plastic and rewrap the top of the fridge with fresh wrap.

✳ Put Jelly on the Racks

If the slide-out racks or trays in your refrigerator are not gliding as smoothly as they should, simply apply a thin layer of petroleum jelly to the edges—they'll whiz in and out.

Optimizing Refrigerator Efficiency

◆ The rubber piping (gasket) inside the door that seals the door should be clean, in good shape and attached properly. If it's dirty or not attached right, it will allow cold air to escape, which wastes electricity and could make your food spoil. Wash it regularly with soapy water, and dry thoroughly.

◆ If a refrigerator is level, it will use less electricity and run more efficiently than if it's a little off-kilter. Test out your refrigerator by placing an almost-full-to-the-rim glass of water on a shelf. Look at it while it's in the fridge—is the water level parallel to the rim, just as when you filled it? If the water is uneven—meaning, it swoops

Easy Refrigerator Deodorizers

Everyone knows about baking soda (we hope!). But do you know that you should keep the open box on the middle shelf in the back of the fridge for it to be most effective?

And when you put a new box in the fridge every other month or so, pour the contents of the old box down the drain while the hot tap water is running. The baking soda will help clean and deodorize the drain pipes.

Here are a few more suggestions for keeping your refrigerator odor-free...

◆ Dab a few drops of vanilla or lemon extract on a cotton ball and put it in a shot glass inside the fridge. Any unpleasant odor will be replaced with an appetizing scent.

◆ Cut a peeled, raw potato in half and place each half—cut side up—on a refrigerator shelf. When the surface of the potato turns black, cut off the top layer and use the clean sections to keep absorbing odors.

◆ Put an open container of natural clay kitty litter in the fridge. (But NEVER put kitty litter down the drain—it will clog.)

◆ A few plain charcoal briquettes will keep the refrigerator smell-free. And they're recyclable —after about 1 month, use a heavy stainless steel pot to heat them. In the heating process, the briquettes release the absorbed odors. When they've cooled off, put them in a container or on a plate and back on the job inside the refrigerator.

◆ When there is a particularly foul odor throughout the refrigerator, stuff a crumpled brown-paper grocery bag on each shelf. The paper will absorb any and all nasty odors. When each bag starts to smell bad, replace it with another until the awful smell is completely gone. (Of course, make sure that whatever caused the nasty smell is gone, too.)

◆ Put fresh coffee grounds in little bowls or in foil-laminated baking cups on each refrigerator shelf. The coffee will deodorize even the worst of smells within 1 or 2 days. Once the bad smell goes, so should the coffee grounds.

to one side of the glass and is not near the rim on the other side—you should adjust your refrigerator. It may only need a small piece of cardboard or a wooden shim to put the fridge on an even footing, but it could make a difference in your next electricity bill.

◆ For a refrigerator to operate at its best, don't overload the shelves—especially the top shelf. It is ideal for air to be able to circulate around each item in the fridge. (Yeah, right! Ideal, but not always very practical.)

◆ Keep leftovers in glass or plastic see-through containers so that you are reminded that they're there. Better yet, set aside a section of a refrigerator shelf for leftovers and eliminate soon-forgotten/long-hidden "UFOs"…*unidentifiable food organisms.*

◆ Putting uncovered food in the refrigerator uses extra energy—the refrigerator has to keep up with the moisture the uncovered food emits. So, when you put food in the fridge, put a lid on it!

Power Outage Guidelines

During a power outage, keep the refrigerator and freezer doors shut. If you can determine when the power outage began (check a clock that runs on electricity), you can figure out how long the food will be good. *As a general rule…*

◆ Food kept cold in an unopened refrigerator will last about 4 hours.

◆ Food in a full, unopened freezer will stay frozen for about 48 hours.

◆ Food in a semi-full, unopened freezer will stay frozen for up to 24 hours.

Cleaning and Defrosting A Freezer

◆ To get the inside of your freezer clean, wipe it with a sponge that has been dampened with rubbing alcohol.

◆ If your freezer needs to be defrosted regularly, try this before turning the freezer back on—wipe the interior surfaces with a light layer of glycerin (available at most drugstores), or give it a light spritz of nonstick vegetable spray. The next time you defrost, the excess ice will slide off easily.

❋ Very Cool Freezer Hints
◆ If your ice cube trays stick to the surface they're on, let them sit on pieces of waxed paper, and they will glide in and out smoothly.
◆ If there's a really bad food smell coming from your freezer, put ½ cup of freshly ground coffee on a plate, and place the plate in the freezer. In a day or so, the coffee will absorb the smell completely.
   An open box of baking soda may do the same thing and cost less than coffee.

Optimizing Freezer Efficiency

◆ Your freezer will work best if it's at least ⅔ full. But don't run out to the grocery store just to fill your freezer. Instead, put water in plastic bottles, bags or food containers, and use them to occupy the empty space.
   Keep in mind that water expands as it freezes, so leave a little expansion space in the containers.

◆ Put a label with the date and the contents on each food container you freeze. Do not delude yourself into thinking that you'll remember what you've frozen and when. We speak from experience.

◆ When you freeze food in a resealable plastic bag—the less air, the better. The trick to getting the air out is to insert a straw in the bag with the food. Close the bag as much as you can, except for the straw. Using the straw, suck out the air from the bag. Now this is the tricky part—quickly remove the straw and close the bag completely before air gets back in. Be sure to label the bag with the date and contents before you suck the air out of it.

◆ Do not wrap food that's headed for the freezer with reused aluminum foil. Crinkled foil can create little holes. Those holes will let air get at the frozen food and may cause freezer burn or spoilage. Splurge with a new piece of foil each time you wrap food for the freezer.

> **NOTE:** We take safe storage a step further by first wrapping the food in plastic wrap and then in aluminum foil.
>
> If you're wrapping single-serving items like burgers or hot dogs, wrap them individually for easier future separation.

Cleaning a Dishwasher

Believe it or not, even a dishwasher needs to be cleaned once in awhile. If you notice that your freshly washed dishes and glasses have a film on them, the time has come to clean the machine.

◆ Empty it out and place a dishwasher-safe bowl on the bottom rack. Add 2 cups of distilled white vinegar, and run the wash and rinse cycles only. When completed, open the door and let it air-dry.

◆ Sprinkle a few tablespoons of a lemon- or orange-drink powder (something like Tang will fill the bill) inside the empty dishwasher, then run the wash and rinse cycles.

◆ If there are tough stains inside the dishwasher that will not wash away with other methods, you should be able to rub them off with baking soda on a damp cloth. (How can we talk "cleaning" without bringing baking soda into the conversation?)

◆ Speaking of baking soda…sprinkle some on the bottom of the dishwasher before each use to enhance the cleaning power of your regular detergent.

◆ If your dishwasher has a musty smell—and it probably will if you keep it closed most of the time—empty it, then pour ¼ cup of lemon juice or 2 tablespoons of baking soda in the detergent dispenser. Let it run through the rinse cycle.

Dishwasher Performance Booster

If you've noticed that the ol' dishwasher just ain't what it used to be, the holes in the upper and lower spray arms may need unclogging.

Depending on the size of the holes, use an open safety pin…or an open paper clip…or pipe cleaners…or a knitting needle…or an ice pick to *carefully* clean them out.

If you can remove the spray arms (take out the racks and undo the hubcap that holds the arms in place), you can clean them more thoroughly. But please don't remove anything unless you're sure you can put it back without any problem. (We don't make house calls, and plumbers are expensive.)

✳ Better Washing with Detergent

◆ If your clean dishes and glassware often come out of the dishwasher with streaks and spots, you may have hard water.

Prevent the streaks by adding 2 tablespoons of baking soda to your regular dish detergent, or adding ¼ cup of distilled white vinegar to the rinse cycle.

◆ If you used too much detergent—or the wrong type of detergent—and the machine is spewing suds, add 1 capful of fabric softener. Let the washer run for a few seconds, then select the drain cycle. The softener will break up the suds and allow them to drain off.

◆ You can also liberally sprinkle table salt over the suds to disperse them. Then toss in a few dozen ice cubes. This will lower the water temperature, getting rid of more suds. If you still have a mess, soak up the rest of the water and suds with dry towels.

Cleaning a Garbage Disposal

Degrease the innards of the disposal unit every other month with 1 cup of baking soda. (Use the old baking soda from the refrigerator when you're ready to replace it.)

Turn on the hot water in the disposal and slowly pour in the baking soda. Let the water continue running for a minute or so after the soda is gone. It's easy and effective. Do it!

✳ Garbage In...Odors Out

◆ Don't throw out lemon peels—use them to deodorize your disposal and sharpen its blades. Put the peel from 2 small lemons or 1 large one, plus 10 ice cubes in the garbage disposal compartment. Turn on the water and run the disposal. The lemon will deodorize while the ice cubes sharpen the blades.

◆ You can just deodorize by pouring in ½ cup of table salt, adding hot water and running the disposal. It's like dermabrasion of the pipes.

◆ You can also mix 1 cup of distilled white vinegar with enough water to fill an average-sized ice cube tray. Once the cubes have frozen, grind them through the disposal and flush it with cold water.

◆ If you're going to be gone from home for a week or more, before you leave, pour ½ cup of baking soda down the disposal. But here's the trick—*do not run the water.* Let the baking soda stay in the disposal so that when you come home, you will have an odor-free sink.

POTS & PANS

The late author Susan Sontag once observed that "fewer and fewer Americans possess objects that have a patina...old furniture, grandparents' pots and pans—the used things, warm with generations of human touch, essential to a human landscape."

If you're lucky enough to have your grandparents' pots and pans—or if you have your very own collection—here are ways to take care of them as they develop that rich patina Ms. Sontag spoke of...

The following suggestions are reserved for more dramatic scenarios like burned-on gunk, scorches and discoloration, as well as for cast-iron and clay cookware.

★ Be Dishwasher Safe

It's safe to put anodized aluminum, stainless steel, enameled cast-iron and glass cookware in a dishwasher. But never put aluminum, copper or cast-iron cookware in a dishwasher.

Removing Stuck-on and Almost-Burned Food

◆ For most types of cookware, just fill the gunked-up pot or pan with water and 1 or 2 tablespoons of liquid dish detergent. Put the pot back on the stove, and bring the water to a boil. Then shut off the heat and let it soak until the water cools completely. Rinse out the water, and don't be surprised if the food comes out with it. Whatever is left should sponge off easily.

◆ To clean burned-on food from a cast-iron pan...fill the pan with water and 1 or 2 teaspoons of liquid dish detergent. Let it simmer until you see pieces of food starting to lift off the bottom. Then wait until it's cool enough to touch, and scour off whatever didn't come completely loose. You may want to reseason the pan again. (*See* "Caring for Cast-Iron Cookware" on pages 50–51.)

◆ To loosen food stuck on an enamel pot, mix 2 tablespoons of baking soda with 2 cups of water, bring it to a boil and let it boil for 10 minutes. Once the water cools down, scrape off the food and wash the pot.

Cleaning Burned Pots/Pans

◆ If the burn is moderate—meaning, not easy to clean, yet not burned to a crisp—put about 2" of water in the pot and bring it to a boil. Once it starts boiling, cover the pot and let it boil for another 5 minutes.

As soon as it's cool enough to touch, scour off the burn. If it doesn't come right off, add a few tablespoons of baking soda and/or distilled white vinegar. Give it a few minutes to sink in and scour again.

◆ For moderate burns, boil 1 cup of cola in the pot, wait for it to cool and then you should be able to scrub off the burn.

◆ If the burn is severe…fill the pan halfway with water. For a small pan (up to 7" in diameter), add ¼ cup of baking soda…for a big pan (8" or larger), add ½ cup of baking soda. Bring it to a boil, then watch as it continues boiling. The burned pieces should float to the top.

If it doesn't happen within a reasonable amount of time, chances are it's never going to happen because the pan was scorched beyond salvation. Sorry!

◆ If you really love the pan and are willing to try *anything* to save it, fill it with mud—from your yard or a garden-supply store—and keep it that way overnight. The next day, use the mud to scrub the pan (look out for rocks and small stones!). This remedy may not work, so you should go in knowing that it is very iffy. *Iffy* it works, though, you'll be glad you tried it.

⭐ **Burn-Stopping Secret**
Before you fill a double-boiler with water, put a few glass marbles in the bottom half. Then set it up as usual. If the water level gets too low, the marbles will start to make noise. Their clatter will be a loud and clear warning for you to add more water, which will prevent the pan from burning.

Caring for Aluminum Pots

◆ To remove stains…fill the pot with enough water to cover all of the stains. Then gently boil the peel of an apple or some rhubarb stalks…or slices of grapefruit, lemon or orange…or slices of tomato. After about 5 minutes, take the pot off the fire, spill out the water, dispose of the food, wash the pot with a little liquid dish detergent, rinse and dry.

◆ To clean up a blackened pot…put 1 teaspoon of cream of tartar (available at the supermarket's spice or baking section) and 2 cups of water in the pot. Boil the mixture for about 3 or 4 minutes. Then wash and dry as usual. That should get rid of the blackened area.

Caring for Stainless Steel Pots

While rainbows are beautiful, you don't necessarily want them on your pots. Rainbows on stainless steel pots will disappear if you rub them with a drop of olive oil.

Caring for Cast-Iron Cookware

◆ Even though cast-iron cookware is an excellent source of dietary iron, you don't want food that tastes like cast iron. And it won't if you season the pot or pan before you cook with it for the first time. Seasoning it will also help prevent food from sticking to the pan.

Season it by rubbing on a thin layer of vegetable or mineral oil with a soft cloth or piece of paper towel. Then put the pan in a 250°F oven for 2 hours, until it's smoky and blackened.

◆ To remove rust from your cast-iron cookware, mix sand (available at hardware stores, nurseries, pet shops…and the beach) with enough vegetable oil to form a thick, gritty paste. Smear the paste on the rusty portions of the cast-iron pan. Then scour it with steel wool. When the rust is gone, wash the pan thoroughly and reseason.

⭐ **Rust-Free Cast Iron**
Moisture causes rust. To absorb moisture when any piece of cast-iron cookware is not being used, let it sit on a coffee filter.

Caring for Clay Cookware

⚡ **CAUTION:** Clay cracks. Do not wash it in the dishwasher. Do not scrub it with steel wool. When a piece of clay cookware is very hot, do not put it on a cold counter.

Soak the cooker with warm water and 1 to 4 tablespoons of baking soda, depending on the size of the smelly, stained clay piece. Let it stand for a few hours, then rinse thoroughly and dry.

⭐ **Add Paper to Clay**
Line a clay cooker with parchment paper to prevent food from staining its porous surface.

GLASS & CRYSTAL

G lass is mainly made of *silica* (sand). When Englishman George Ravenscroft added lead oxide to the glass composition, he created a highly refractive (more sparkly) and softer glass that's easier to cut. And so, in 1676, lead crystal was born.

It's NEVER a good idea to clean crystal pieces in a dishwasher. They may crack or chip, and they may lose their sparkle. So always be sure to handwash your good glass and crystal pieces. *Here are some other ways you can clean glass and crystal...*

Caring for Glassware

We fill an empty plastic liquid dish-detergent bottle with 1 part dish detergent, 1 part distilled white vinegar and 3 parts water, and shake it a few times.

We use this solution daily—a little on a sponge—to do the dishes and glasses. It's a winning combination that leaves everything clean and sparkling, and lasts a long time.

⭐ **Best Way to Clean Up Broken Glass**
When you break a glass, the first thing to do is put on shoes if you're barefoot. Then put on rubber or latex gloves. Start the cleanup by picking up the bigger pieces and putting them into a trash bag.
    To collect all of the tiny scattered slivers of glass, carefully use wet paper towels. Also, check the bottoms of your shoes for little shards of embedded glass. If you have a vacuum cleaner handy, a final suck-up is a good idea.

Glass-Breaking Celebration

Whenever a glass broke at our home, we'd all yell "Mazel tov!" as though it was a good thing. And we thought it was, because of the custom of breaking a glass at the very end of a Jewish wedding ceremony. The custom comes from several different traditions...including a medieval belief that making loud noises will ward off evil spirits. (Ringing church bells comes from the same era and idea.)

So, if and when someone breaks a glass, take it as a sign of good luck and the banishment of evil spirits—you will make the glass-breaker feel less guilty for the little accident.

⭐ **Unstick Drinking Glasses**
Don't you hate it when your stacked glasses stick together? Submerge the bottom glass in hot water, which will expand it...then pour ice-cold water in the top glass, which will contract it. Once you have the hot-and-cold thing happening, you should be able to pull the glasses apart easily.

51

◆ When you are washing glass dishes in hot water, always put them into the water *sideways*. This will prevent them from cracking due to expansion (from heat) and contraction (from cold).

Caring for "The Good Crystal"

◆ We're talking about the tumblers and stemware and serving pieces you only take out for company…special company…and on special occasions. To clean these irreplaceable treasures, fill a basin or the sink with a 3:1 combination of hot water and distilled white vinegar.

 NOTE: For crystal that is really grimy or filmy, use 3 parts hot water to 2 parts distilled white vinegar.

Once all the crystal is clean, rinse and dry each piece with a lint-free cloth. Your best bet in terms of *lint-free* is a linen towel, or a cloth made of least 25% linen.

✳ Protect Your Breakables
When you wash glasses in the sink, line it with a fluffy towel or a rubber mat in case a piece of crystal slips out of your hands.

◆ If your crystal has ornate and deep decorative etching, clean it with an old-fashioned shaving brush. If you do not have a brush lying around, they're available at The Art of Shaving Shops (nationwide, *www.theartofshaving.com*). You can also use a big makeup brush (used for rouge or powder, available wherever cosmetics are sold). These brushes are stiff enough to get into the dirt-collecting crevices, but are also soft enough to not damage the crystal.

◆ To repair hairline scratches on your crystal, put a dab of non-gel white toothpaste on a cloth and rub the scratches. The mild abrasive paste should smooth out the glass without a trace of a scratch. Rinse and wipe dry.

◆ If you don't use your crystal for long periods of time, consider covering each piece with plastic wrap. Then, the next time you take out the good stuff, each piece will be spotless and ready to use.

Cleaning Crystal Vases

◆ If you're reading this, it means that you don't have a bottle brush with which to reach the bottom and sides of your narrow-necked vase. Hopefully, you do have 2 or 3 tablespoons of dry, uncooked rice (either short-grained white or brown rice), and about ¼ cup of distilled white vinegar.

Put the rice and vinegar in the vase, and then use a circular motion to shake it. The idea is to have the vinegar clean as the rice scours—without scratching the crystal.

◆ If your vase has caked-on crud on the inside, measure the amount of liquid it will hold, then mix 2 parts strong black tea to 1 part distilled white vinegar to fill it. Let the mixture stay in the vase overnight. The next day, spill out the solution and wash the vase with regular dish detergent. Rinse, dry and bring on some fresh flowers!

◆ Fill the vase with just-boiled water, then toss in 2 Alka-Seltzer tablets and let the citric acid and sodium bicarbonate bubbles scour your vase clean. Rinse as usual and dry.

CHINA

As you probably guessed, china dishes originated in the country of China, but it is now produced in many countries throughout the world. *China* generally refers to hard, white, translucent pottery. When it has a soft glaze, it is known as *porcelain*. This glaze can be produced in many different colors and designs, but purists tend to prefer it in white or ivory.

If you have fine china, it's important to wash it by hand. The heat from the dishwasher's drying cycle may do damage.

For more suggestions on how to wash china, *see* the remedies under "Caring for Glassware" on pages 51–52.

★ Keep China Safe

◆ If you are going to stack your fine china dishes, put a coffee filter or a paper plate between each piece. Doing so will prevent damage to the dishes' decorated surfaces.

◆ Every thrift shop has china teapots with chipped spouts. Prevent your teapot's spout from chipping by keeping a toilet paper tube over it, especially when it's in storage or during a household move.

You can also cut off the thumb from a big, thick, old glove and put it over the spout.

Seek and Thou Shalt Find

Are you missing a cup or saucer from your collection of good china? Will 1 dinner plate complete the set you inherited from your grandmother?

You may be able to fill in discontinued patterns of fine china, silver or crystal pieces from Replacements Ltd. Visit them at *www.replacements.com* or call 800-737-5223.

Cleaning Stains

For coffee, tea and most other stains, any of the following tips should work...

◆ Sprinkle baking soda on a damp sponge or cloth, and rub the cup or saucer.

◆ Rub the stain with white non-gel toothpaste, then rinse thoroughly with warm water.

◆ Fill the stained cup with warm water, drop in a denture-cleaning tablet and let it stay overnight. The next morning, wash, rinse and dry as usual.

◆ For a tough tobacco stain, mix a few drops of water with 1 tablespoon of table salt, then stick a cork in it. Use the salted cork to rub away the stain.

★ Cook Away Cracks with Milk

Put a cracked china cup or plate in a pan and pour in enough whole milk to cover it—and then some. Let it simmer on the stovetop for 45 minutes. That allows enough time for the milk protein (casein) to do what it needs to do, which is to fill in the fissures. When the time is up, take the china off the stove and let it cool. Then rinse and marvel at the restored piece.

CORNINGWARE

This kitchenware classic was developed by a company whose history dates back to 1851, and which has made contributions that have affected—and continue to affect—our lives on a daily basis.

For instance, in 1880, Corning provided the glass for inventor Thomas Edison's first lightbulb. By 1915, Corning had developed its Pyrex heat-resistant glass tableware. And in 1957, Corning's innovative glass-ceramic technology made the production of CorningWare possible.

With such a rich history, it pays to keep your CorningWare looking its best.

Cleaning CorningWare

You can remove grease and stains by pouring ¼ cup of distilled white vinegar and 1 teaspoon of liquid dish detergent in the piece of CorningWare. Fill the rest with hot—but not boiling—water. Let it stand for about 5 minutes, then wash and rinse it out.

EVERYTHING *AND* THE KITCHEN SINK

While researching this section, we were so amazed to discover that many of the kitchen accessories and appliances that are considered to be *modern* conveniences have actually been around since the 1800s.

How much do you know about the things that help you prepare food on a daily basis? See if you can select a kitchen item from the following list that was NOT invented in the 19th century—electric mixer, toaster, potato peeler, pressure cooker, waffle iron or coffee grinder.

If you said "pressure cooker," you are right. It was not invented in the 1800s. It was invented by French physicist Denis Papin—in 1679!

Well, enough fun and games. *Here are some hints to help you keep your kitchen tools in good shape and working well...*

Cleaning a Porcelain Sink

To remove yellow stains from a porcelain sink, make 1 of 2 pastes—either add lemon juice to borax powder (available at supermarkets and drugstores)...or add 3% hydrogen peroxide to cream of tartar (available at supermarkets).

For both pastes, use a ratio of 1 teaspoon of the dry ingredient to ¼ teaspoon of the wet ingredient—the paste should be the consistency of soupy oatmeal. Rub the paste into the stained sink with a clean, dry washcloth. Let the paste dry, then wipe it off with a wet cloth or sponge and rinse the sink.

Unclogging a Sink Drain

If your drain is starting to back up, it may be clogged. First, pour 1 cup of baking soda down the drain. Then, in a pan, warm up 1 cup of distilled white vinegar, and pour *that* down the drain. Wait about 10 minutes, then let the hot water run for a minute.

Preventing Clogged Drains

◆ If you have used coffee grounds, pour a little bit down the drain, then let the hot water run for a minute.

◆ Mix ½ cup of salt in 1 quart of hot water, then pour the salt-water solution down the drain. Do this every other week, and it should prevent grease buildup and deodorize as well.

Hang Your Hat—or Rings

If you normally wear rings, a watch, a bracelet or any other jewelry that shouldn't be worn while cooking or cleaning, it's good to have a safe, reliable place in the kitchen where you can stash it.

Put up a hook large enough to hang a watchband on (or whatever jewelry you wear on a regular basis). Position it near enough to be convenient when you start to work in the kitchen, but out of harm's way when the stove, microwave, dishwasher or garbage disposal are in use. Putting up that little hook will be something you wish you had thought to do years ago.

✳ Weigh In More Accurately

Check the accuracy of your food scale by putting 9 pennies on it. If the indicator points to 1 ounce, the scale is accurate.

Nothing to Sneeze At

Instead of having plastic produce bags taking up lots of space in a drawer waiting to be recycled, or floating around loose in a cabinet, pack them into an empty tissue box.

If you do not want to use the cardboard kind, look for a plastic tissue dispenser that matches your kitchen.

Cute Cookie Cutter Creation

Use some ribbon that matches your kitchen's color scheme to string together your cookie cutters. If you have a lot of them, tie together the ends of the ribbon to make an attractive cookie-cutter wreath—hang it on a hook as a decoration in your kitchen.

Of course, if you just have a few and don't want them on display, you can hang the ribbon on a hook inside a cabinet.

 ### No More Rust Rings

Cans stored for a long time on a kitchen shelf or counter may sometimes leave rust rings. To prevent this, place small lids—such as from plastic containers of yogurt, cottage cheese, butter/margarine, etc.—under the cans as coasters. You'll never have to deal with a rust ring on your shelf or counter again.

Removing Jar Labels And Glue

◆ Remove a label from a jar by first rubbing regular (not reduced-fat) mayonnaise, butter or cooking oil into the label. Then soak the jar in very hot water. After about 10 minutes, peel off the label.

◆ If the label or price tag is off, but a sticky glue spot remains, massage vegetable oil or peanut butter into the spot until all the glue is gone. Clean the jar with soap and water.

Jar Opening Made Easy

◆ To open a stubborn jar, put on a pair of rubber gloves. Then, get a good grasp, and twist the lid counterclockwise.

◆ Put a thick rubber band around the lid of the jar and another rubber band around the middle of the jar. Grasp a band with each hand, and twist the lid counterclockwise.

◆ Turn the jar upside down and let the hot tap water run over it for about a minute. Then turn it right-side up, put on rubber gloves and try to open it.

◆ Vacuum-sealed jars are often hard to budge, but they may be opened with the help of a small screwdriver. Slip the tip of the screwdriver under the edge of the lid and turn it a little to allow air to seep in and unseal the lid. It should open easily.

◆ If you're dealing with a jar of something sticky—such as honey, maple syrup or jam—after it's opened, rub a coat of petroleum jelly lightly over the rim of the jar and the screw part of the lid. The jar will be easy to open from then on.

Make Life Easier for the Chief Bottle Washer

After rinsing out a bottle or jar, turn it upside down and shake it in a circular motion, creating a whirlpool effect.

The air rushes in, the water rushes out and your bottle-rinsing time is cut in half. This saves both time and water.

One to Grow On

Use a terra-cotta flowerpot as a lovely kitchen caddy for spatulas, wooden spoons and other utensils that don't fit in silverware holders.

Flowerpots are inexpensive, come in a variety of sizes and, if you're craftsy, you can have fun decorating them.

Starchy Protection

To prevent light grease stains from messing up your beautiful new pot holder or oven mitt, just spray it with spray starch. You won't need to wash the pot holder very often, but each time you do, spray it after each washing. The starch forms a coating that protects the potholder or mitt—it prevents the oil from seeping through the fabric.

Washing Wood Salad Bowls

It's important to remember that wood is porous and may absorb some dish detergent. If you don't want to wash your mouth out with soap when you eat dinner, then don't wash wood food bowls with detergent!

Instead, rinse out the bowls with plain water, then wipe the inside with a light coating of cooking oil on a paper towel.

✪ Instant Apron!

It's easy to make a homemade apron that's a CUT above the rest! Here's an easy and inexpensive way to cover up in the kitchen (it can also be used as a smock for painting or any other messy job).

Just take a big plastic trash bag and cut out about 12" to 15" along the center of the sealed edge (this is where your head goes through). On the side edges near the head hole, cut a few inches to make holes for your arms to go through. Pull the bag over your head, insert your arms and *voilà*!

Stacking Cookware

Get a few cardboard boxes and use them to cut out circles that fit inside the bottoms of your nonstick cookware.

To prevent one pot's outer bottom from scratching another pot's inner surface, be sure the cardboard circles are in place before you stack one pot on top of another.

You can also use big plastic lids (like those from a set of Tupperware) as pot coasters instead of the cardboard.

✱ Junk Drawer Safety

Keep a pulled cork on the end of a corkscrew, especially if the corkscrew is loose in a drawer with other things you often seek out.

Cleaning a Garbage Can

Clean the garbage can with ½ cup of distilled white vinegar mixed with 1 tablespoon of liquid dish detergent and 2 cups of hot water. Rinse well and wipe dry or air dry. Then sprinkle a thin layer of borax powder (available at supermarkets and drugstores) on the bottom of the can.

Doing this should inhibit the growth of bacteria and mold, and will also prevent the dreaded reeking garbage can. Resprinkle the borax about once a month, and use the vinegar solution every 6 months—or at the first sign of a garbage smell.

Taking Care of Kitchen Knives

◆ To sharpen a knife, find a coffee mug with an unglazed rim on the bottom, or turn a terra-cotta (clay) flowerpot upside down. Hold the knife at an angle and run the blade (starting at the knife's handle) down the bottom of the mug or flowerpot.

Then turn the knife over and do the same thing to the other side of the blade. Repeat the procedure until the knife is as sharp as you want it to be. Just be careful!

◆ To sharpen a small knife blade, slide it back and forth on a matchbox's strike panel.

◆ If you have a set of knives that are kept in a wood container, that's good. But if you have knives floating around in a kitchen drawer, that's not so good. But you can make easy sleeves for the knives—just flatten a few empty paper towel rolls, fold over 1 end and close it off with tape or a staple. Insert the knife into the open end, with the blade side pointing away from you (toward the closed end of the sleeve). The sleeves will protect the knife blades as well as your fingers.

◆ To remove rust on a good kitchen knife, cut an onion and rub the cut onion on the blade several times. If all the rust doesn't come off, stick the knife into the onion and let it stay that way for about 1 hour. Then rinse and dry the knife and throw away the onion.

Taking Care of Scissors

◆ To sharpen a pair of scissors, fold a piece of aluminum foil in thirds, then cut it with the scissors at least a dozen times. Then cut a piece of paper and see if the scissors' blades are sharper. If they *still* aren't as sharp as you want them to be, take another piece of foil and do it again. If they <u>still</u> aren't sharp enough, then take a sheet of fine sandpaper and cut it up.

If, after you've cut foil and sandpaper several times, the scissors STILL aren't as sharp as you want, consider buying a new pair of scissors.

CAUTION: Sandpaper sharpening is not recommended for a good pair of sewing shears. Always have them sharpened by a professional sharpener.

◆ Scissors that stick might have some gooey residue from something they cut, such as tape or glue. Clean the scissors' blades with rubbing alcohol on a cotton ball. If doing that doesn't unstick them, rub the blades with an emery board.

◆ If the scissors stick after the blades have been cleaned, they may need to be lubricated. But you don't want to put oil on scissors because the oil will stain everything you cut.

Instead, use the natural oil on your fingers. Gently massage the blades—being careful not to cut yourself—until the blades move more smoothly. (If you have dry skin, you may be busy rubbing your scissors for the next year or so.)

Caring for a Cutting Board Or Butcher's Block

◆ To sanitize your plastic cutting board or your wood butcher's block, coat it with a light spray of distilled white vinegar, followed by a light spray of hydrogen peroxide. Let it sit for 10 minutes, then rinse and dry thoroughly.

NOTE: Most bacteria cannot survive without moisture. Keep all surfaces in the kitchen dry...especially cutting boards and butcher's blocks.

◆ To remove a stain from your plastic cutting board or wood butcher's block, sprinkle table salt on it, then rub it with a wedge of lemon or lime. Rinse and dry. The salt draws out the grease and acts as an abrasive, while the lemon/lime helps bleach out the stain.

◆ Cuts in a wood cutting board? Well, uh, *yeeeah*. But those cuts can be home to germs. Every now and then, smooth away the cuts with a piece of fine sandpaper.

◆ To remove a strange smell from your wood board or block, rub it with a piece of lemon. Rinse. Dry. Sniff. No smell!

NOTE: These suggestions also apply to caring for a wood rolling pin.

Caring for All Types of Countertops

◆ If you border on obsessive-compulsive when it comes to having your countertop and other kitchen surfaces clean and disinfected, keep 2 spray bottles handy—fill 1 with 3% hydrogen peroxide and the other with distilled white vinegar.

Lightly spray your counter with the peroxide, and wipe it clean. Follow up with a light spray of the vinegar, and wipe it clean. Then relax, knowing that your countertop and other kitchen surfaces have been treated with antiviral, antifungal as well as antibacterial agents.

◆ Food stains on your nice, clean countertop can be eliminated with a sprinkle of baking soda. Just add some water to make a paste and, after a few minutes, rub off the stain with a damp cloth.

◆ For coffee or tea stains, rub the countertop with a piece of lemon rind.

◆ How many times has the purple ink from a stamped-on price stayed on your countertop? Rub off the ink with rubbing alcohol or the inside of a piece of lemon rind. If the alcohol or the lemon doesn't do it, try nail polish remover. Then wipe with a damp cloth or sponge.

NOTE: If you have any hesitation about using nail polish remover on the surface of your counter, either don't use it...or test a tiny can't-be-seen-area before using it on the whole countertop.

✳ Make More Space!

When you need more counter space for a party or special occasion, set up an ironing board. Make sure it's secure and won't tip over, then cover it with a nice tablecloth to make it look more festive.

Or, open a kitchen drawer and put a cutting board, cookie pan or serving tray on it.

Cleaning a Grater

◆ How yucky is it to clean a grater, especially after grating cheese? Instead, grate a piece of raw potato and let it do the cleanup for you.

◆ Running cold water on the grater will harden the cheese, making it easier to clean off. Hot water melts the cheese on.

◆ If you're into *zest* (the outermost part of a lemon or orange) and frequently grate rind, set aside an old toothbrush to use as your grater cleaner.

🕐 "Grate" Cleanup Advice

Spray the grater with nonstick cooking spray before you use it. It will take the yuck out of cleanup.

Cleaning a Thermos

◆ Fill the thermos about 2" from the top with warm water, then add 2 tablespoons of baking soda. Put the top on and shake vigorously. Then rinse and dry.

◆ If the thermos is really dirty, add equal parts of baking soda, cream of tartar and lemon juice—enough to fill about ⅓ of the thermos. Put the cover on and shake vigorously, or use a bottle brush to scrub with the mixture. Then rinse and dry.

✳ Sweeten Your Thermos

If you don't use your thermos for long periods of time, store it with 1 white-sugar cube or with 1 teaspoon of white sugar (make sure the thermos is clean and dry and that the top is screwed on *tight*!). The sugar will stop any stale odors before they start.

What's That Smell?

◆ To freshen up a stinky metal or plastic lunch-box, moisten a slice of bread with distilled white vinegar and let it stay in the lunchbox overnight. The next morning, throw away the soggy bread, wash out the lunchbox with warm soapy water, rinse and dry thoroughly —then load it up with your child's sandwich and fruit.

◆ Depending on the size of the plastic container you want to de-skunk, put in anywhere from 1 to 3 tablespoons of baking soda. Add hot water to the brim, cover the container and let it stay that way overnight. The next morning, rinse and dry. Instead of baking soda, you can also use ¼ to ½ teaspoon of mustard powder.

◆ Crinkle up a page of black-and-white newspaper, put it in the smelly plastic container, cover it and let it stay that way overnight. The next morning, take out the paper, wash, rinse and dry.

✳ **Keep Smells from Sticking**
Line a container with plastic wrap before you put in foods—such as cheese, peanut butter, salami, sour pickles or tuna fish—that might leave lingering smells.

Removing Stains from a Plastic Container

Apply a little lemon juice on the stain, then let the container sit in the sun for a couple of hours. Then wash, rinse and dry.

✳ **Contain Your Stains**
If you have stain-causing leftovers—such as to-mato sauce, curry or chili—lightly mist the container with nonstick cooking spray before putting in the food. The *lecithin* in the spray acts as a re-pellent to stain-setting pigments.

Cleaning a Highchair Tray

You can wipe off food splatters on your baby's highchair with a bit of baking soda sprinkled on a damp cloth or sponge.

To disinfect the eating surface (tray), just wipe it down with antiseptic mouthwash (such as Listerine).

And while you're at it, you can wipe down teething toys this way, too. ■

■ Products ■

Touchless Trashcan
Whoever thought that we'd get excited about a trashcan? Fair warning—if you see this product in action, you'll want to own it.

Why? It's a sleek, stainless steel can with a brushed-chrome silver finish and a black lid that opens and closes automatically. You do not need to touch anything...you do not have to step on anything. You just hold your hand over the Smart-Chip, and technology does the rest (and it can operate manually, if you choose). The unit uses four "D" batteries (not included), which last for about 3,600 openings...or 6 months at 20 openings a day.

Source: iTouchless Innovation Housewares & Pro-ducts, Inc., 800-660-7978, *www.touchlesstrashcan.com.*

Talking Timer
If you need to keep to a schedule or remember when to take the baking dish out of the oven, this device can help you. It's both a clock and a timer, and it's smaller than a deck of cards.

A female voice announces the time and counts down (for example, "One minute remaining..."), and counts up, too. The timer has 6 different alarm sounds. It has a waistband clip, a magnet and a stand so you can use it anywhere.

If you can set a digital watch, you can follow these simple instructions.

Source: Dynamic Living, Inc., 888-940-0605, *www.dynamic-living.com.**

*The company has a free monthly e-mail newsletter that offers ideas and tips to make living at home a little easier.

CHAPTER 4

The Best-Ever Food Secrets

Whether you are a gourmet chef or you need a map to find your kitchen, we hope there are lots of helpful ideas here that will make food preparation a delicious, safe and successful experience.

FOOD A TO Z

Anybody who is into food should enjoy reading this A-to-Z listing—and hopefully, you will learn a lot in the process. If you're not a food person, then instead of overwhelming yourself by reading through ALL of this information, we suggest that you just look up the foods you intend to use—everything is arranged alphabetically for your convenience. That way, you'll be able to use the appropriate information when you're in the supermarket or in your kitchen.

Apple Cider

Before drinking fresh apple cider, find out if it has been pasteurized. Unpasteurized cider has been linked to food poisoning from bacteria, such as *salmonella*, *E. coli* and *listeria*. If you aren't sure about the jug of apple cider in your refrigerator, boil it for 1 full minute before drinking it (of course, make sure it has cooled first). Better safe than sorry!

Apples

◆ Apples will keep for weeks in a cool, dark place. Your refrigerator's fruit bin is perfect as well as your basement or garage. And it seems to be true that 1 bad apple spoils the rest. So, if there's room, don't let the apples touch each another, just in case 1 of them is bad.

◆ To keep cut apples from turning brown, try these suggestions…

　◆ Dunk the cut pieces in a mixture of ¼ teaspoon of salt and 1 pint of water.

　◆ Spritz citrus juice—either lemon, orange or grapefruit—on the cut apple pieces.

　◆ Cover cut apple slices with apple juice and refrigerate them for about a half-hour. They won't turn brown, and the juice will make dry, flavorless apples crunchier and tastier.

◆ To prevent a mess when baking apples, there are 2 ways to prevent pressure from building in the apple's core…

   ◆ Remove ½" of peel around the middle of the apple and then bake it.

   ◆ Make 8 shallow slits around the apple before baking it. The slits will allow steam to escape, which prevents the rest of the peel from splitting.

◆ If you sprinkle the apple's bare midriff (or the 8 slits) with lemon juice, the citric acid may help stop the breakdown of proteins that can cause a mealy texture.

Asparagus

◆ Once you get these spears home, cut about ½" off the bottom. In a tall drinking glass or small vase, stand the bunch upright in about 1" of water. Cover them gently with a plastic bag, and refrigerate until they're ready to be used.

◆ Our instinct tells us to open the *top* of a can. But when it comes to canned asparagus, open the *bottom* of the can. That way, the spears will slide out, leaving the delicate asparagus tips intact. Hey, you'll have tip-top tips.

Avocados

◆ Avocados ripen best when kept at room temperature. The cold air in the refrigerator can turn them black.

◆ If you want an avocado to ripen quickly, place it in a brown paper bag along with an apple slice, a banana peel or a tomato. Keep the bag closed, but check often so that the avocado doesn't get overripe and turn into mush.

◆ If you only use ½ an avocado, keep the pit in the remaining half, then lightly brush lemon juice on the open side. Cover it with plastic wrap and refrigerate. (The same goes for guacamole—add some lemon juice, cover and refrigerate to keep it fresh.)

Avocado Bravado

The avocado is a great source of heart-healthy monounsaturated fat, which helps increase the body's absorption of antioxidants known as *carotenoids* (nutrients that help reduce the risk of cancer and cardiovascular disease).

And, as if that wasn't enough, avocados are also loaded with dietary fiber and other healthy stuff like folate and vitamin K. And they taste great!

Bacon

◆ When you bring home the bacon (literally), roll the package lengthwise, and put a rubber band around it to keep it that way.

Then refrigerate it. When you're ready to use it, the bacon slices will be easier to separate.

■ Recipe ■

Bacon Sticks

To create a will-be-gobbled-up-in-seconds treat, you'll need 1 package of prebaked, store-bought bread sticks and 1 pound of low-sodium bacon (also works with soy bacon or turkey bacon). Adding 1 cup of Parmesan cheese is optional.

Wrap ½ slice of bacon around each bread stick, barbershop-pole style. Line up the sticks on a broiler pan and put them in the oven at 325°F for about 30 minutes, or until the bacon is crisp.

When you take them out of the oven, roll them on paper towels to blot them. Here comes the optional part—you can then roll them in the Parmesan cheese. With or without the cheese, they're scrumptious.

◆ Rinse the slices in cold water before frying, and they won't curl in the pan.

◆ If you throw a few celery leaves into the pan along with the bacon, the grease will stay in the pan instead of splattering.

◆ To minimize the shrinkage of the bacon, do not preheat the skillet. Just plop in the bacon and let it cook over a medium flame.

Bananas

◆ To ripen bananas, poke holes in a brown paper bag, then put the bananas and 1 ripe apple in the bag. It should speed up the ripening process of the banana before you peel it. Check often so that you use the banana and the apple before *ripen* turns to *rotten*.

◆ If you brush an unpeeled banana with lemon, orange or pineapple juice, it won't turn brown …for a while.

◆ Forget the myth about not putting bananas in the refrigerator. If you put a ripe banana (with the peel) in a sealed jar or a plastic bag, getting out as much air as possible, and then put it in the fridge, you'll slow down the ripening process.

NOTE: If you use this method, the peel will turn yucky brown, but the banana itself will be banana-color and delicious.

◆ Here's how to make a yummy frozen snack— peel a ripe banana, cut it into 1" to 2" pieces, wrap it in aluminum foil and put it in the freezer. When you want to eat the banana, just take off the foil and eat it like any frozen dessert.

◆ If you have a powerful blender or juicer, put several pieces of frozen banana into it, and whip up a surprisingly good banana custard.

Bay Leaves

Make it a snap to remove the bay leaves from your sauce, soup or stew by putting them in a tea ball (available at kitchen specialty stores). The holes let the flavor out, but keep the herb contained inside.

Beans

We love beans, but we hate the intestinal gas they create! These suggestions range in effectiveness from partial flatulence prevention to totally gas-free. The only way to know which works best for you is to put them to the test… when you're dining alone.

◆ Soak dry beans overnight in a pot of water along with ⅛ to ¼ cup of apple cider vinegar. The next morning, thoroughly rinse the beans, put fresh water and 1 or 2 tablespoons of apple cider vinegar into the pot, and cook the beans as usual.

◆ Soak dry beans overnight in water with 1 teaspoon of fennel seeds (tied up in a piece of cheesecloth). The next morning, take out the seeds, spill out the water and cook the beans as usual in fresh water. During the cooking process, toss in a few pieces of raw peeled potato. When the beans are done, remove the potato pieces.

◆ If you want to add salt when you're cooking beans, add it when they are almost finished cooking. If you add salt too early, it will impede the beans' softening process. Ah, so that's why it takes forever for the beans to get done!

◆ While beans are cooking, pour in ½ can of cola to the water. Wouldn't you think that carbonated soda would *add* gas? It's good to know it actually *prevents* gas. Kitchen magic—that's what we're talking about.

◆ Avoid boil-over mess by adding 1 tablespoon of olive oil to the beans' cooking water.

◆ Keep weevils away from your supply of dry beans—put a dried hot pepper in the container in which the beans are stored.

Beef

◆ When you're grocery shopping, make the meat counter your last stop—that way, whatever you buy will stay cold as long as possible. Also, put the meat into a plastic bag so that if there's any dripping or leaking of the raw meat's juices, the other food in your cart and grocery bag will be protected.

◆ Marinate meat in a self-sealing plastic bag. This disposable container distributes the marinade evenly and there's no cleanup needed. After the marinating is done, simply throw away the bag.

◆ Let steak or ribs marinate in cola for 3 to 4 hours before cooking. The results are a more tender and tasty meat treat.

◆ A marinade made from distilled white vinegar will destroy bacteria as it tenderizes meat. Use ½ cup vinegar on a 4- to 6-pound roast. If you use herbs in your usual marinade, add them to the vinegar. Let it marinate overnight, and then prepare the meat without draining or rinsing it.

◆ The tannic acid in tea makes meat tender and juicy. Add 2 teabags (without the strings or tabs) of Pekoe black tea to the pot roast pot and cook as usual. Remove the teabags when the roast is done.

◆ It's tough to reheat a roast without drying it out. The idea here is to moisturize the roast as it reheats. Start by wrapping washed lettuce leaves around the roast, and wrap aluminum foil around the whole thing—pinch it closed.

Heat the oven to 425° to 475°F and put the roast in for 2 to 10 minutes (depending on the size of the roast). By flash-heating it, you get the meat warm without overcooking it.

◆ Put raw beef in the freezer for about 15 minutes, and it will be much easier to cut the slim slices needed for a stir-fry.

◆ If you don't have a sharp knife—or you're not comfortable using one to cut thin strips of beef—use kitchen scissors to get the job done safely.

Also see "Thermometers/Cooking Temperatures" on pages 99–100 for guidelines on cooking beef properly.

Beef (Ground)

◆ Use a strainer (with a close weave) to rinse cooked, crumbled ground beef under hot water. By doing this, you will actually be able to wash away up to 50% of the fat.

◆ If you do not want to rinse your cooked ground beef, you can also use paper towels to blot off a lot of the excess grease and fat.

◆ Make a package of ground beef easy to stack in your freezer. Take the meat out of the package and put it in a plastic freezer bag, then flatten it with a rolling pin. When you want to use it, the flattened-out beef will thaw quickly.

> ✎ **NOTE:** Cut the label off the original meat wrapping and attach it to the new freezer bag so that you know what it is and when you got it.

◆ Put patties in the freezer for about 3 minutes right before you put them on the grill. It will help them keep their shape from grill to bun to mouth.

◆ Before piling on the raw patties to be grilled, cover your platter with plastic wrap. Then put the patties on top of it. Once you've transferred the patties to the grill, remove and discard the plastic wrap. You can now use the clean platter for the finished product...the grilled patties. This way, you have to wash the platter only once, and you save a trip inside to get another platter.

◆ Before broiling or grilling, poke holes in the center of the burgers, which will let in the heat—they will cook surprisingly fast. How do you think White Castle is able to fill orders as quickly as they do? It's all about poking holes in the patties.

◆ Cut slices of white and yellow American cheese into 3" x ¾" strips. (If you're into soy cheese, you can use white Swiss or American and yellow cheddar.) Weave these strips (3 white and 3 yellow) into a checkerboard pattern and plop it on top of the burger for the last minute of grilling time. It's a creative way to serve cheeseburgers.

✳ Healthier Beef Alternatives

For those of you who want to cut down on your intake of high-cholesterol foods and/or reduce your intake of fat, replace traditional ground-beef products with *textured vegetable protein* (TVP), soy crumbles or cooked bulgur. All are available at supermarkets and health-food stores.

While you're there, check out the wide variety of beef substitutes in the form of burgers, nuggets and steaks. Be adventurous. You may actually enjoy eating these meat alternatives. (For starters, we recommend Sunshine Burgers, found in the refrigerated section.)

Meatballs with a Twist

Put a new ingredient in an old standard—meatball hors d'oeuvres. When making the meatballs, start with a little chunk of something—sautéed mushroom, pitted olive, cheese, dried apricot, grape tomato or come up with something even more creative—and pack the meat around it, forming the meatball.

Then cook, grill, broil or fry the meatballs as usual. *Ahh*, but there will be nothing "usual" about them! Guests will love tasting and comparing the fillers in these meatball hors d'oeuvres.

If you want to stick with the standard meatball, but want them perfectly moist, place a small ice cube in the middle of each before cooking.

◆ For easier meatloaf mixing, put the ingredients in a sturdy, resealable plastic bag and zip it closed. Then knead the outside of the bag, thoroughly blending the ingredients together. Then unseal the bag, plop the meat out into the meatloaf pan and discard the bag. Everything—especially your hands—will stay clean. And no concerns about raw-meat contamination.

◆ When making meatloaf, place 1 or 2 slices of uncooked bacon on the bottom of the pan. This will prevent the meatloaf from sticking, and it will add a little more flavor.

Also see "Thermometers/Cooking Temperatures" on pages 99–100 for guidelines on cooking burgers properly.

❈ Make Extra-Tender Fruity Beef

Many people are sensitive to *monosodium glutamate* (MSG), a substance that is commonly used in cooking as a meat tenderizer. Fortunately, MSG is not the only tenderizer available. *Papain* is an enzyme found in papaya that can help tenderize meat. Let the meat sit in papaya juice (available at grocery stores) in the refrigerator for 3 or 4 hours. Then blot the meat dry and prepare as usual.

Berries

OK, so you got a ton of berries for a bargain price. Instead of eating all of these little beauties so quickly that you can't look at them anymore—freeze them.

If space allows, the best way to do this is to spread them on an ungreased cookie sheet. Cover the sheet with plastic wrap, and freeze the berries for about 20 minutes, until they're frozen solid. Then put them in a plastic freezer bag, and seal it closed with as little air in it as possible. This freezing system will prevent the berries from squishing and sticking together.

Bread and Biscuits

◆ Aluminum reflects heat, so line your breadbasket with foil, then cover the foil with a napkin. The bread will stay warmer longer.

◆ When mixing the dough for whole-wheat bread, add 1 tablespoon of lemon juice. The bread will rise higher and be lighter, and you won't taste the lemon.

◆ About 5 minutes before your bread finishes baking, brush the top with distilled white vinegar—this will make the loaf shine.

◆ To enhance the rising time of your bread's yeast, run the dishwasher on its hot cycle, and dry it with a towel. Then place the bowl of bread dough in the dishwasher. Within no time, it should rise.

◆ To make stale bread fresh again, spray it with a bit of water or milk and wrap it in aluminum foil. Put it in a 350°F oven for about 8 minutes, and the bread should taste as though it just came out of the oven…for the first time.

◆ If you want to freshen a stale loaf of Italian or French bread, follow the steps above, then carefully open the foil and leave the bread in the oven for another 3 to 5 minutes.

◆ When a recipe calls for stale bread, but your bread is fresh, put the slices in the toaster on the lowest setting—this will dry out the bread. Let it cool for a few minutes, then it will be stale enough for the recipe.

◆ If you like your biscuits to be crusty, space them out on the baking sheet. If you like soft-sided biscuits, line them up next to each other with the sides touching. For browner biscuits, lightly spray the tops with butter-flavored cooking oil.

Bread Crumbs

◆ When you want to prepare your own bread crumbs and don't have any stale bread, lightly toast slices of fresh bread. Cut them in pieces and toss them into the blender or food processor.

◆ If your loaf of bread is frozen, you can grate it into crumbs.

◆ Consider seasoning the bread with your favorite dried herbs and/or powdered spices. But be sure to do a taste test before mixing anything into the entire batch of bread crumbs.

◆ For every cup of bread crumbs called for in a recipe, use ¾ cup of cracker crumbs.

> **Great Use for Cereal**
>
> Instead of bread crumbs, consider using oatmeal or instant mashed potatoes (ground in the blender) as a filler for meatloaf and veggie burgers.
>
> You can also use any whole-grain flaked cereals (unsweetened, of course) or soda crackers (also ground in the blender) as a substitute for bread crumbs in stuffing or as a casserole topping.

Brown Sugar

See "Sugar" on page 98.

Butter

◆ It takes only seconds for butter on the stove to go from *good* to *gone*—as in burnt and no longer usable. The secret to sautéing butter and not scorching it is to add a little olive oil.

> ✍ **NOTE:** Olive oil contains healthy monounsaturated fats, so consider using just the olive oil and forget the butter altogether.

◆ When your cookie recipe calls for butter, do not melt it…especially in a microwave. The melted butter will make the cookies flat and greasy. Soften butter at room temperature. If it's cut into small pieces, it's easy to blend.

◆ Use a cheese grater to shred your too-hard butter, making it easier to work with and more blendable.

◆ For your next dinner party, serve a bowl of butter balls instead of putting out sticks or individual pats of butter. Simply place a melon ball cutter in very hot water for about 5 minutes.

While it warms up, prepare a bowl of cold water with lots of ice cubes in it. Then, when the melon ball cutter is hot, scoop out the butter balls from a large container of butter, and drop each of them in the bowl of ice-cold water. Keep the balls cold in the refrigerator until you're ready to put them on the table for your guests.

Buttermilk

◆ An alternative for buttermilk in a recipe is to use the same amount of plain yogurt.

◆ Or you can mix 1 tablespoon of lemon juice into 1 cup of regular milk, and let it stand for 10 minutes before using—this is the equivalent of 1 cup of buttermilk.

> ✍ **NOTE:** Instead of putting lemon juice in the milk, you can use 1 tablespoon of distilled white vinegar. Let it stand for 10 minutes before using it in your recipe.

Cabbage

◆ To wash away any small insects that may be nestled between the cabbage leaves, fill a basin or sink with cold water, add 2 or 3 tablespoons of distilled white vinegar, and soak the cabbage for 10 minutes. Then rinse the cabbage with plain water and use those lovely, bug-free leaves.

◆ To remove leaves easily, freeze the head of cabbage. Once it's completely frozen, take it out of the freezer, and let it thaw completely. The leaves will be soft and easy to pull apart.

◆ Any of these suggestions may eliminate—or at least reduce—the smell of cabbage's volatile sulfur compounds…

  ◆ Add a stalk of celery to the cooking pot.

  ◆ The minute you begin cooking cabbage, toss a walnut—with the shell still on—into the pot.

  ◆ Add a pinch of baking soda to the cooking water.

  ◆ While the cabbage is cooking, place a heel of bread on top of it.

  ◆ Add ½ lemon to the cooking water once it starts boiling.

Cake

◆ Believe it or not, there is a fat substitute for some (not all) cakes. It works best with recipes that include *wet* ingredients, such as milk or fruit. Just substitute an equal quantity of applesauce or other fruit purée for the oil, butter or margarine called for in the recipe.

Smart Sauce Idea

Buy small snack-packs of applesauce, and use them as you need them. It's more efficient than having a big, open jar of applesauce taking up space in your refrigerator.

◆ An easy and efficient way to mix dry ingredients is to put them together in a plastic bag and *shake-shake-shake*.

◆ When mixing nuts and/or dried fruit, put them in a plastic bag, add a little flour and shake the bag so that the ingredients get fully coated with flour. When added to the cake batter, these coated pieces will be distributed evenly instead of sinking to the bottom.

◆ Is it done yet? If you don't have a toothpick —or if a toothpick isn't long enough to test whether or not the cake is ready to take out of the oven—use a strand of uncooked spaghetti to get the job done.

◆ To prevent your cake from sticking to the serving plate, sprinkle the cake plate with powdered sugar before setting down the cake. Now you're ready to cut and serve!

Cake Frosting

◆ You want to cover a cake with plastic wrap, but don't want it to stick to the cake's icing. Just spray the inside of the plastic wrap with a nonstick spray before covering the cake.

◆ If you're a big fan of the chocolate–peanut butter combination, just mix 1 tablespoon of creamy peanut butter into chocolate frosting. Because of all the good-for-you fats that peanut butter contains, it's a healthy addition... not to mention how delicious it tastes.

◆ If you don't want to frost a cake, you can decorate it with the help of a paper doily. Here's what to do...after the cake has cooled, center a doily on top of the cake and sprinkle powdered sugar on it. Be sure all the openings

in the doily's pattern are covered with sugar. Then gently lift off the doily to reveal a lovely, lacy design on the cake.

NOTE: If you are so inclined, use a piece of paper to cut your own lacy pattern and decorate the cake with it.

◆ The secret to slicing a frosted cake easily and neatly is to dip the knife in hot water before you make the first cut.

Candy

◆ If you make your own candy, do it on dry days to get the best results. Candy made on rainy or damp days won't set properly—this is because sugar blots up humidity.

◆ When preparing to boil homemade candy, butter about 1" around the inside of the top of the pot. This will help prevent liquid from boiling over.

Cans

Before opening a can of soda or soup or beans, rinse the top with water and then dry it off. This quick, easy step can help prevent undesirable bacteria from getting into the can when you open it.

Carrots

Put the crunch back into raw limp carrots by letting them soak in some ice water for about 30 minutes.

Cauliflower

◆ Soak a head of cauliflower in salted ice water with the florets facing down for at least 30 minutes. Any little bugs that have taken up residence will float out.

◆ To maintain cauliflower's bright white color, cook it with 1 tablespoon of distilled white vinegar...or a little lemon juice...or some milk added to the water.

Caviar

With this section, we're straying from the practical and introducing the extravagant. It's meant for those who want to try caviar for the first time, as well as for those of you who have had a long-running *roe-mance* with this delicacy. *Here are a few suggestions to help you select, store, serve and eat these salted sturgeon eggs...*

◆ There are several high-profile types of Russian caviar, with *beluga* being considered the best (it's the most expensive). There is also the fine-flavored *osetra*...as well as *sevruga*, whose eggs tend to clump together...and the almost-extinct *sterlet sturgeon*. The choice is up to you, your budget and the availability of these precious little glistening eggs.

When you're ready to splurge, keep in mind that caviar connoisseurs generally agree that *pasteurized* caviar—which is not refrigerated and is sold in vacuum-packed jars—cannot begin to compare to the taste of fresh caviar.

> **NOTE:** Caviar on crackers is sinful...in a bad way. According to some food mavens, crackers are too crisp for the tender fish eggs. Then again, there are some beluga buffs who wouldn't eat it any other way.

◆ Caviar should be served simply with *crème fraîche* (a cultured cream with the texture of a rich cream cheese, but with a taste that is more tart, like a fine yogurt) and fresh handmade *blini* (yeast-risen buckwheat pancakes)—both tend to be available at specialty gourmet shops that also sell caviar.

◆ The top 3 most traditional potables paired with caviar are champagne (chilled), vodka (chilled) and dry white wine (cool).

◆ Caviar is delicate and perishable. Read all of the labels on the packaging before serving.

◆ Take caviar out of the refrigerator 10 to 15 minutes before serving. If it's going to be on a buffet table and may not be eaten for a while, keep it in its original jar or tin, and wedge that container into a bowl of crushed ice.

◆ Once the caviar container has been opened, finish it within 2 to 3 days.

◆ *Never* use a metallic spoon for scooping out, serving or eating caviar. The metal will taint the taste, giving it a horrid, unsavory flavor. The utensils of choice should be made from mother-of-pearl, bone or tortoise shell. The spoons are usually available wherever caviar is sold. (Of course, if you've spent too much money on the caviar, *crème fraîche* and *blini*, it's perfectly fine to use plastic spoons.)

Celery

◆ Peel the stalks with a vegetable peeler to get rid of the strings and minor boo-boos. The peeled-off strips of string are wonderful for decorating dishes of prepared food. Peel a celery stalk, and you'll see what we mean.

◆ If you want to dice up celery, use a pair of kitchen scissors and you won't have to peel it or deal with the string thing.

◆ To revive wilted celery, place the rubbery stalks in a bowl or pickle dish with ice water and a few slices of raw potato. In about 1 hour, the stalks should be nice and crisp and ready to serve.

◆ You can also cut about ⅛" from the bottom of the stalks, stand them up in a tall drinking glass or small vase that is filled with cold water, and let them stay in the refrigerator for a couple of hours.

◆ When you buy celery that still has its leaves, put the entire bunch in a plastic bag and keep it in the refrigerator…leave the leaves on until you're ready to use the stalks. If you buy celery that's been trimmed, put the stalks in aluminum foil. They should keep fresh in the refrigerator for weeks.

Cheese

◆ To prevent a chunk of cheese from getting moldy, place it in a resealable plastic bag along with 1 or 2 cubes of sugar (try to squeeze any excess air out of the bag). The cheese should stay fresh longer, and the sugar deters mold.

◆ You can also dampen a piece of cloth with apple cider vinegar, wrap it around the block of cheese, and seal it in a plastic bag. The acid in the vinegar will help prevent the growth of mold.

◆ Keep shredded cheese in an airtight, resealable bag in the freezer—where no mold can grow.

◆ If the cheese has mold, cut off a 1" square around the moldy area, and you can safely eat the rest.

◆ To prevent cheese from hardening, coat the exposed edges of the cheese with a thin layer of butter—the moisture from the butter will prevent the cheese from getting hard and inedible. Wrap and store the buttered cheese in the refrigerator. When you're ready to eat the cheese, just wipe off the butter…or not.

◆ Bring out the full flavor of your favorite hard cheese by putting it in the microwave. Nuke it for about 10 seconds on a high setting or 15 seconds on a medium setting.

◆ To prevent grated cheese from sticking to the bowl you're grating it into, lightly coat the bowl with flour.

◆ Before you cut or grate a block of cheese, put the wedge in the freezer for about 20 minutes. This will prevent it from clinging to the knife or the grater.

◆ If you're grating just a little bit of cheese, spray the grater with a nonstick vegetable spray. The spray helps prevent the cheese from sticking to the grater, but not for long (you may have to reapply).

◆ Once you open a container of cottage and/or ricotta cheese, you can do 1 of 2 things to prolong its staying power—either transfer the unused portion to a glass jar with a screw-on lid and refrigerate…or, after you've opened the container, close the lid securely and store it upside down in the refrigerator.

◆ It's not a good idea to zap cream cheese in the microwave—it can melt. Instead, put the cream cheese in a resealable plastic bag and zip it closed. Then dunk it in warm water for about 4 minutes…until it's soft and workable.

◆ If you're counting fat grams and want an alternative to cream cheese, line a strainer with a coffee filter and place it over a bowl. Fill the center of the filter with plain, low-fat yogurt. Cover it with plastic wrap and refrigerate it.

C **FYI: Yummy Creamy Yogurt**
Yogurt cream is delicious mixed with any number of things, including fruit, honey, vanilla extract, almond extract, carob powder, cocoa powder, flaxseed and wheat germ. Or, you can add herb seasonings and use it as a healthy dip for vegetables.

About 8 hours later, most of the moisture will have drained out, and the yogurt should have a spreadable consistency like cream cheese.

Cheesecake

◆ If the surface of your cheesecake is cracked—or just not presentable enough to serve to guests—spread an attractive and delicious topping of fresh fruit…or pie filling…or 1 cup of sour cream mixed with 1 tablespoon of sugar…or shaved shards of chocolate.

> ✎ **NOTE:** To make chocolate shavings, use a vegetable peeler on a chocolate bar. And try to make your shavings from dark chocolate—it's healthier than milk chocolate.

◆ Unflavored dental floss will cut a cheesecake better than most knives. Take a piece of floss that's a few inches longer than the diameter of the cake. Hold an end in each hand, and hold your hands as far apart as possible, making the floss taut. Then cut the cheesecake in half. Slide the floss out from the bottom of the cake. Now that there are 2 halves, you can cut slices—1 at a time—using the same method.

Chicken

◆ The "use by" or expiration date on a package of chicken is there for your safety. Abide by it unless you freeze the chicken. And even then, be sure to note the date you put the chicken in the freezer. If the freezer is set at 0°F, chicken can be frozen for 9 months to 1 year. If you've already cooked the chicken, either eat it or freeze it within 1 or 2 days.

◆ Always thaw a chicken in the refrigerator …in its original package…on a plate on the lowest shelf. This will help the chicken retain its moisture and reduce the possibility that it will grow harmful bacteria, while the plate will catch any juices that may trickle out of the packaging.

◆ Do not put raw chicken alongside any food that is usually eaten raw, such as salad greens or fresh fruit.

◆ Wash everything that touches raw chicken —such as your hands, the cutting board, knives, counter, plates—with hot, soapy water before handling any other food.

◆ Raw chicken skin is usually slippery. To remove the skin easily, grab hold of it with a paper towel and give it a firm pull. *But…*

◆ If possible, leave the skin on the chicken—there's a membrane between the skin and meat of a chicken that keeps moisture in and fat out while it's cooking. So, for juicier, more flavorful chicken, remove the skin *after* it has been cooked.

◆ For crispier and more delicate fried-chicken coating, add about 1 teaspoon of baking soda to the batter.

◆ For extra-crispy fried chicken, add 1 rounded tablespoon of cornstarch for each cup of flour used.

Also see "Thermometers/Cooking Temperatures" on pages 99–100 for guidelines on cooking chicken properly.

Chili

Have a chili party and impress your guests by hollowing out crusty loaves of whole-grain bread and using them as the chili bowls. Put the chunks of bread that are taken out of the hollowed loaves in a breadbasket on the table —your guests can use them to dip in the chili. They can also eat the chili-soaked bowl once the chili is gobbled up.

Chocolate

◆ If a recipe calls for unsweetened squares of chocolate and you don't have any, you can substitute 3 tablespoons of powdered cocoa and 1 tablespoon of shortening for every square needed.

◆ When baking chocolate-based cakes, cookies or bread, use cocoa powder instead of plain flour to dust whatever needs dusting—the work surface, the rolling pin, the pan, etc.

◆ When you have cookies or cake or any dessert that would be more complete with some chocolate design on top, use chocolate chips. Put the chips in a heavy-duty resealable plastic bag and zip it shut. Dip the bag in a pot of very hot water (about 140°F) and keep it there for a few minutes…until the chocolate feels soft.

    Carefully dry the outside of the bag, and cut a tiny hole in a bottom corner of the bag. Now you're ready to squeeze out the chocolate and do your creative dessert decorating.

> ✎ **NOTE:** You will probably want to practice on something *other* than the cake until you get the feel for it, and can coordinate your concept with your execution.

Chopsticks

If you sometimes have problems using chopsticks efficiently, bind them together with a rubber band set just above the halfway point. And then bring on the vegetable lo mein!

Coconut

◆ Select a coconut that sounds like it's full of liquid. When you're ready to open it, take out a hammer and a big nail or screwdriver. Place the nail or screwdriver on 1 of the 3 small, hairless black eyes or indentations on the coconut. Then tap the top of it with the hammer, piercing the eye. Ouch! Repeat the process on the other 2 eyes, and pour the liquid into a bowl.

◆ A coconut has a natural fault line. If you have a feel for these things, you may be able to crack the coconut open by using a hammer to tap around the widest part until there's a crack in the shell. Then continue turning and tapping the coconut on that fault line to make a clean break.

◆ Instead of depending on your *Survivor* abilities, you may want to put the coconut in a 375°F oven for 20 minutes. Take it out and let it cool for about 5 minutes. Then put a towel on top, and tap on it with a hammer until the coconut breaks.

◆ Instead of putting the coconut in the oven, try this—after you've pierced the eyes and purged the liquid, put it in the freezer for 1 hour, then cover it with a towel and tap on it with a hammer to break it open.

◆ Whichever method you use, you still have to pull the meat away from the shell with your hands and a screwdriver. It's dirty work, but it's worth it. The coconut meat will keep fresh in the refrigerator for about 5 days.

Coffee

◆ If you have ground coffee or coffee beans, but don't use them often, keep them in a tightly sealed container in a cool, dark place (like your kitchen pantry). By keeping air out, the coffee will retain its strong flavor. (As a last resort, you can also store coffee in the freezer.)

◆ If you gotta have that "cuppa joe" and you're out of filters, you can use 2 paper towels or 1 thick paper napkin instead of a filter.

◆ Before brewing ground coffee, try spicing it up with a pinch of cinnamon or a couple of drops of almond or vanilla extract.

◆ Freeze leftover coffee in an ice cube tray. Then you can use it to cool *hot-hot-hot* coffee…or to make iced coffee…or to add great flavor to eggnog.

Condiments

For a fun and colorful way to serve condiments (especially at a backyard barbecue), try this—hollow out a red bell pepper and fill it with ketchup…hollow out a yellow bell pepper and fill it with mustard…hollow out a green pepper and fill it with relish. Serve with a spoon.

Cookies

◆ Refrigerate your cookie dough. After about 30 minutes, the dough should be easier to work with. If it's still too sticky to manage, slowly knead in 1 or 2 tablespoons of flour.

◆ Before scooping up cookie dough with a spoon, dip the spoon in milk or olive oil to coat it. That way, the dough will glide off the spoon onto the cookie sheet.

◆ If you use your hands to shape the cookies, keep wetting them with cold water to prevent the dough from clinging. Better yet, spray your hands with cooking spray.

◆ When you're preparing peanut butter cookies, use a plastic fork to flatten them. The batter will not stick to plastic.

◆ If your kitchen is like most counter-scarce kitchens, and you need more space to cool your cookies, set up the ironing board. Put the cookies on paper plates and put the paper plates along the ironing board.

◆ Cookies will stay moist if you put a slice of apple in the container with them.

◆ Cookies will stay soft if you put a slice of bread in the container with them.

◆ Cookies will stay crisp if you crumple up a piece of tissue paper and place it on the bottom of the cookie container. Keep the cookies on top of the tissue and be sure the container stays closed—except when you're taking out a crisp cookie.

◆ To get neat, smooth squares when making cookie bars, use a pizza cutter to do the job.

Cookie Sheet

◆ Consider using parchment paper instead of greasing a cookie sheet. Not only will you save yourself the job of cleaning the cookie sheet, but the cookies will bake more evenly on the parchment paper. Plus, it's easy to transfer the finished product to the cooling rack.

◆ Also consider taping some parchment paper to the work surface on which you roll out the cookie dough.

Cooking Spray

Hold the pan (or whatever you're going to spray) over the kitchen sink, then spray. This will prevent you from spraying a slippery spot on the kitchen floor, and the overspray in the sink will get washed away.

You can also spray over the open door of your dishwasher to achieve the same effect.

Corn

◆ Don't consider buying a cob of fresh corn unless it has husks—nature's freshness seal. The husks should be moist (rather than dried out) and bright green, with a little brown tassel on top. The kernels should feel full and plump.

> **NOTE:** Do not remove the husks until you are ready to prepare the corn for eating.

◆ As soon as you've taken off the husks, remove the silk threads by wiping them off, in a downward motion, with a damp paper towel.

◆ Do not add salt to the water when boiling corn—it will toughen the kernels. If you want to enhance the corn's natural sweetness, add 1 tablespoon of sugar or 1 or 2 packets of sugar substitute to the cooking water.

Cornstarch

If you've run out of cornstarch and need it for a recipe, use double the amount of flour instead.

Crackers

If your crackers are soggy, spread them out on an ungreased baking sheet, and put them in a 250°F oven for 15 minutes. Let them cool before serving the crispy treats.

Cranberries

Many recipes call for cranberry halves, which prevents whole cranberries from bursting while they're cooking. To halve them quickly, use a cutting board that has a gutter, line up the berries and cut them in half with a long knife.

> **NOTE:** Since the fresh-cranberry season is short—just November and December—buy them in season and freeze them. That way, you'll have the luxury of eating them all year-round.

Crumbs

Put whatever you want to turn into crumbs (such as cookies, crackers, nuts) in a resealable plastic bag. Make sure it's closed securely. Then roll over it with a rolling pin until the contents are as crummy as you want them to be. Use as much as you need, and then refrigerate the remaining crumbs in the plastic bag.

Cucumbers

If you keep cucumbers in the vegetable bin on the bottom shelf of your refrigerator, you're doing the right thing. It's the warmest place in the fridge. When cukes get too cold, they get mushy.

Cupcakes

◆ Do you love chocolate cupcakes with cream inside? Here's how to do it yourself—use a drinking straw to poke a hole in the middle of the top of each cupcake (when cool).

Then fill a clean plastic bag with vanilla frosting and cut a tiny hole in 1 corner of the bag. And now for the fun part—carefully pipe in the frosting from the bag into the hole in the cupcake.

> **NOTE:** If you want the cream to come as a surprise to the eater, place a chocolate chip...or a raisin...or a piece of walnut on top of the cupcake to hide the cream hole.

◆ About 3 or 4 minutes before the cupcakes are ready to be taken out of the oven, put a marshmallow on top of each. Then watch as the cupcakes finish baking with their instant frosting. Remove them from the oven when the melted marshmallows are just slightly brown.

◆ Once the cupcakes are out of the oven and cool, place a small chocolate-covered mint on top of each, and zap it in the microwave for a few seconds. Take out the cupcake and spread the melted chocolate mint around, just as you would spread frosting.

Deodorizers for the Kitchen

Whether you want to cover up cooking smells or create a fresh, appetizing scent in the kitchen, here are some suggestions…

◆ Keep a small bowl of leftover coffee grounds on the counter. They will help absorb cooking smells.

◆ In a pot, combine ½ cup of lemon juice, 1 cup of water and 3 or 4 whole cloves and/or a few cinnamon sticks. Let it simmer on your range for about 20 minutes…enough time to freshen the air in your kitchen.

◆ If it's cool outside, and you don't mind heating up your kitchen a little—and your smoke detector won't go crazy—preheat your oven to 300°F. With the oven door open a little, bake 1 whole (unpeeled) lemon for 15 minutes (poke a few holes in it first).

◆ If you like the lemon scent, but don't want to do the open-oven-door thing, slice up 1 whole lemon, put it in a pot of water and let it simmer on the stove for about 15 minutes.

◆ Put 1 teabag (make sure there's no metal staple), 2 teaspoons of cinnamon or another favorite spice and 1 cup of water in a microwave-safe bowl. Nuke it on *high* for 2 minutes. Then open the microwave door and wait a few minutes before removing the scented bowl and setting it on the counter.

◆ If you prefer a room spray, you can prepare your own. It will be healthier than commercial chemical sprays and also more economical. Combine 2 cups of distilled water (available at supermarkets), 2 cups of rubbing alcohol and 3 drops of natural lemon oil (available at health-food stores) in a large spray bottle. Shake it until the mixture is completely blended, and then it's ready to freshen the air.

Eggplant

◆ Choose an eggplant that's heavy for its size…or 1 that seems heavier than others that are the same size. To tell if an eggplant is ripe, gently press its flesh. If the dent bounces back and disappears, the fruit is ripe. If the dent stays a dent, the eggplant is too ripe.

On purple eggplants, look for smooth, taut skin that's glossy. If you're looking for white eggplant, discard any that seem to have a tinge of yellow.

◆ When you buy an eggplant in summer, during the fruit's peak season, it will be less bitter and have a thinner skin than when you buy it off-season.

◆ To take the bitterness out of a mature, out-of-season eggplant, chop or slice it and put it in a colander in the sink…or in a strainer over a bowl…or on a cooling rack on a baking pan. Sprinkle all of the eggplant pieces with table salt and let it stay that way for 1 hour. Then rinse well and pat dry before sautéing, grilling or baking.

NOTE: The salt causes the release of the fruit's bitter juices, and it also helps keep it from absorbing excess oil.

Eggs

◆ As soon as you select a carton of eggs, open it and turn each egg. Make sure the egg moves within its little cubbyhole. If an egg doesn't move, it may be cracked and the leaked egg has glued to the carton. Or it may mean that it's stuck to the carton because of the dripping of another egg. In any case, you want a carton in which all of the eggs move freely when you turn them.

If a recipe (for example, Caesar salad) calls for a raw egg, be sure to use an egg that has been pasteurized (heated)—or do not use an egg at all.

> ⚡ **CAUTION 1:** NEVER eat a raw egg! The main risk is *salmonella*, a bacterium that can contaminate eggs through microscopic imperfections in their shells. The only way to kill the bacteria is through adequate heating.

> ⚡ **CAUTION 2:** NEVER use an egg that's cracked. Even if it's not oozing, just the fact that it has a crack means it could be contaminated with bacteria.

◆ Every hour that a carton of eggs is left out at room temperature is said to be equivalent to a week stored in the refrigerator. With this in mind, when you come home from the market, put those eggs in the fridge ASAP!

◆ Do not wash eggs before refrigerating them… not that we think you would. But keep them in their original carton, not in the refrigerator door's egg section. It's too warm there, and there's too much shaking going on each time the door opens and closes.

◆ Stored properly in the egg shelf of the refrigerator, fresh eggs will keep for up to 5 weeks.

◆ If your eggs have been in the fridge for a while, you may want to test their freshness. To do this, place each raw egg in a pot of water. If the egg floats, it's rotten. If it stands on its pointy end, it's 10 to 14 days old. If the egg tilts, it's about 3 or 4 days old.

You want an egg to sink and lie on its side. That means it's fresh—any fresher, and a live chicken will be walking out of your kitchen.

◆ When a recipe calls for 1 or more eggs but doesn't specify the size, use *large*—this is the recipe standard.

◆ You need not have egg-separation anxiety if you have a little funnel. Place the funnel in a glass, then crack the egg over it. The egg white will glide into the glass and the yolk will (hopefully) stay in the funnel.

◆ If you want to separate eggs, do it as soon as you take them out of the fridge. They're harder to separate when they're warm.

◆ To get best results when you are whipping egg whites, whip them in a glass or metal bowl at room temperature.

> ✎ **NOTE:** If you think the whites are whipped enough, turn the bowl over slowly…if the eggs start to slide out, turn it back and whip some more. If the eggs stay in the bowl when inverted, they're whipped enough.

◆ When a raw egg falls on the floor, discard the eggshell first, then pour table salt over the egg and wait about 5 minutes, until the salt soaks up the egg.

We tried it, and the salt does make for easier cleanup. There's no drippy, gooey slime to contend with. You might have to use a lot of salt, though, and you also have to be careful not to step in the spill during the 5-minute wait.

◆ We discovered an easy way to retrieve a piece of eggshell that falls into the bowl of eggs—just use a larger piece of eggshell to get the little piece of shell out of the bowl. The larger shell attracts the little shell, almost like a magnet.

> ⚡ **CAUTION:** Wash your hands thoroughly after touching raw eggs or eggshells to reduce the risk of spreading harmful bacteria.

◆ When making deviled eggs, put all of the ingredients—egg yolks, onions, mayo, etc.—in a resealable plastic bag. Close the bag and knead it—this blends the ingredients from the outside.

Then cut a small tip off 1 bottom corner of the bag. Line up the empty hard-boiled egg whites, and fill them by squeezing the yolk mixture out of the bag through that little hole. Just throw away the empty plastic bag to clean up.

◆ If you want float-off-your-plate omelets or scrambled eggs, stir in a pinch of cornstarch before cooking.

◆ Eggs should not be frozen in their shells.

◆ Uncooked whole eggs (out of the shell) can be frozen for up to 1 year if you beat them lightly, pour them into a freezer-safe container and seal it tightly. Don't forget to label the container with the number of eggs it contains, and the date they were frozen. To thaw the eggs, let cool water run over the container, or leave it in the refrigerator overnight.

CAUTION: Use frozen whole eggs as soon as they're thawed, and only in dishes that are thoroughly cooked.

Then again, all eggs should be thoroughly cooked before eating.

◆ Raw egg whites can be frozen the same way as whole eggs, except you should not beat them first. Just pour them directly from the shell into a container.

◆ You can also freeze egg whites in an ice cube tray—but be sure to put the tray into a resealable plastic freezer bag to prevent spills. And don't forget to label the bag with the number of egg whites it contains and the date they were frozen.

◆ Thaw egg whites the same way you thaw whole eggs (at left). If you are going to beat the thawed egg whites, keep them at room temperature for about 30 minutes after thawing, and they will have better volume.

◆ To store raw egg yolks, put the yolks in a container, fill it with cold water, put a tight lid on the container, and refrigerate it. The yolks should stay fresh that way for several days.

◆ Wondering whether an egg is raw or hard-boiled? This question comes up more often than you would think…especially when preparing eggs for holidays like Easter or Passover. The secret is to spin the egg. A raw egg will wobble, and a hard-boiled egg will spin.

Blood Spots on Eggs

Blood spots, also called *meat spots*, are found on less than 1% of all eggs produced. Contrary to popular belief, these tiny spots do not mean that the egg was fertilized. The spots are caused by the rupture of a blood vessel on the surface of the yolk. And, according to the American Egg Board (*www.aeb.org*), from both a chemical and nutritional standpoint, these eggs are fit to eat.

As an egg ages, the blood spot gets diluted as the yolk absorbs water from the *albumen* (the gooey egg white). While that's probably more information than you need to know, the ironic significance is this—a blood spot in an egg is an indication that the egg is fresh.

Eggs (Hardboiled)

◆ To prevent an egg from cracking during the hard-boiling process, first carefully puncture either end of the egg with a clean pin or thumbtack. Then gently place the egg in the water to boil.

◆ You can also add 1 tablespoon of distilled white vinegar to the water to prevent cracks. If the egg does crack, the vinegar should keep it from creeping out of the shell.

◆ Another crack-prevention idea is to cover the eggs with water in a yet-to-be-covered pot that has a tight lid. As soon as the water comes to a rolling boil, turn off the heat, cover the pot with the tight lid, and let it sit for 12 minutes. The eggs will come out hard-boiled and uncracked.

◆ Hard-boiled eggs that are overcooked tend to take on a greenish hue. To avoid this, place the egg in a pot, cover it with water, bring it to a boil, then set the timer for 12 minutes. When the buzzer rings, take the egg off the stove, then drain and rinse under cold water until the egg is cool.

◆ To peel a hard-boiled egg, gently roll it between your palm and your kitchen counter, making hairline cracks in the shell. Then hold the egg under cold running water and, starting at the large end, carefully pull off the shell.

◆ Do not freeze hard-boiled whole eggs or egg whites. When you defrost them, they're tough and watery.

Substitute Egg Poacher

Remove both ends of a tuna can, and wash it thoroughly. Put some water into a skillet... when the water starts to simmer, place the can in the skillet and then crack an egg into the can. Within no time, you'll have a perfectly poached egg.

Eggs (Substitutes)

◆ If you buy into the "no yolks because of the cholesterol" theory, substitute 2 egg whites for each whole egg called for in a recipe.

◆ If you're baking a cake and you're short 1 egg, mix 1 teaspoon of distilled white vinegar with 1 teaspoon of baking soda. Add this to the cake recipe to make up for the missing egg.

◆ For a recipe other than a cake, try this when you're minus 1 egg—use 1 teaspoon of cornstarch in its place.

Extracts

When your recipe calls for a small amount of vanilla, almond or any other extract, don't risk pouring straight from the extract bottle. Use a separate dropper (available at kitchen-supply stores) so that you can control the exact extract amount needed.

Prevent Foodborne Illness

Every year, an estimated 76 million Americans get sick because of foodborne illness, and more than 5,000 people die from it. But those numbers could be lowered if people heeded the "2-hour food rule."

Basically, food that is exposed to the open air for longer than 2 hours will grow bacteria to harmful levels. So at a party or a picnic—or wherever you serve food—keep track of the amount of time the food has been out of the refrigerator or oven. And after 2 hours, wrap the food properly and put it in the refrigerator or freezer.

Also, when a platter is empty (or almost empty) and you want to refill it, DO NOT just dump new food on top of the old food—in fact, don't even put new food in the empty-but-used platter. Each time you want to set out new food, wash the platter before you refill it, or serve the new food on another clean platter.

Fish

◆ To determine the proper cooking time for your fish, lay out the whole fish, fish fillet or fish steak. Pinpoint the thickest part of the fish, and then measure it with a ruler. For each inch of thickness, figure on 10 minutes of cooking time.

◆ Thaw frozen fish in milk or in 1 cup of nonfat dry milk mixed with 3 cups of water—this will remove the freezer taste, and the fish will cook up as though it was just reeled in.

◆ Neutralize the fishy smell of fresh fish by restoring its pH balance. You can do this by soaking fish fillets in a mixture made from 4 cups of water and 2 tablespoons of baking soda. Let the fish soak for at least 10 minutes. Then rinse under running water, and bake, broil or sauté.

◆ If there's a frying-fish smell when you're frying fish, add 1 teaspoon of peanut butter to the pan to eliminate the smell. The peanut butter will also add an interesting taste.

> ⚡ **CAUTION:** If you're preparing peanut-butter fish for guests, be sure none of them has a peanut allergy.

◆ Fish-cooking smells can be absorbed—just place a small bowl of distilled white vinegar or fresh coffee grounds near the stove or wherever the fish is being prepared.

◆ If your fish fillet gets a little too blackened, it's minced parsley to the rescue! It's the go-with-everything herb that will cover up the whoopsies...and it tastes good, too. When cooking for company, always keep a stash of parsley on hand.

◆ After your fish is prepared, get rid of the fishy smell by washing the pan with distilled white vinegar.

◆ When you open a can of sardines, salmon or tuna and it has a strong fish-oil smell, drizzle distilled white vinegar on it. Let it stay that way for about 5 minutes, then spill it out. Chances are, the too-fishy taste will be gone too.

Flour

◆ If you keep your flour in bins without labels and you keep forgetting which is plain and which is self-rising—taste them. Plain flour is tasteless...and self-rising is a little salty because of the baking powder in it.

◆ Once you open a bag of flour, it's on its way to tasting stale. OK, it probably won't happen for a few months, but if you transfer the flour from the bag to an airtight container and keep it in a cool place, it will stay fresh for YEARS. The *coolest* place, the freezer, will keep it super-fresh as well as bug-free.

◆ To keep flour handy, fill a large salt shaker or an empty, clean spice container with flour and keep it in the freezer. When you need just a little bit for dusting or coating, it's easier to reach for the freezer-shaker instead of opening a sack of flour or the airtight container it's stored in.

◆ If you keep flour in a canister, also keep a clean, new powder puff in with it. Whenever you need to dust a surface—or lightly coat something—the powder puff will do the job.

Flour (Substitutes)

◆ *All-purpose flour*—You can use 1 cup plus 2 tablespoons of cake flour for each cup of all-purpose flour.

◆ *Cake flour*—Use 1 cup less 2 tablespoons of all-purpose flour for each cup of cake flour.

◆ *Self-rising flour*—Combine 1½ teaspoons of baking powder with ½ teaspoon of table salt, and fill up the rest of the cup with an all-purpose flour. Make sure it's level.

Fruit

◆ The use of pesticides to kill bugs on produce has become a big concern for many people. However, until organic fruits and vegetables are more affordable and readily available, you may have to remove the pesticides yourself at home.

Jay "The Juiceman" Kordich recommends this method—clean your sink and fill it with cold water, then add 4 tablespoons of salt and the fresh juice from ½ of a whole lemon. This will make a diluted form of hydrochloric acid.

Soak most fruits and vegetables for 5 to 10 minutes...leafy greens, 2 to 3 minutes...strawberries, blueberries and all other berries, 1 to 2 minutes. After soaking, rinse the produce thoroughly in plain cold water and dry each piece. Now, it's pesticide-free and ready to eat!

◆ Another way to remove pesticides is to soak your fruit in a clean sink or basin with ¼ cup of distilled white vinegar. Then, with a fruit/vegetable brush, scrub the fruit under cold water. Give it a final rinse, dry it and it's ready to be eaten.

◆ You can also mix 1 teaspoon of baking soda with 1 cup of plain water, and wash the produce with the solution. Then rinse and dry.

◆ And a final pesticide-removal suggestion— in a sink or basin of cold water, add ¼ cup of 3% hydrogen peroxide. Wash the fruits and vegetables in it, then rinse with water and wipe dry.

◆ According to the United States Department of Agriculture (USDA), fruit should be ripened at room temperature. *When it is ripe and refrigerated, you can plan on it staying edible for the following amounts of time...*

◆ Apples—1 month
◆ Apricots, bananas, grapes, nectarines, peaches, pears, plums—3 to 5 days
◆ Berries and cherries—2 to 3 days
◆ Citrus fruit—2 weeks
◆ Cranberries and melons (except watermelon)—1 week
◆ Watermelon—3 to 5 days

◆ Many fruits—including apples, pears, peaches, avocados and tomatoes—will ripen faster in a brown paper bag. The paper bag helps the natural fruit-ripening gases do their job.

NOTE: If you're very eager for your fruit to ripen, put a banana in the bag with it. The banana's gases will speed up the ripening process.

◆ When you refrigerate fresh fruit, the ripening process stops.

Fruit (Dried)

If you need to cut up dried fruit, make this sticky chore easier by freezing the dried fruit for 45 minutes. Then spray a kitchen scissors with nonstick vegetable spray or dip the scissors in flour before cutting the dried fruit.

NOTE: If you insist on using a knife to cut dried fruit, spray it with cooking spray or dip it in flour to help prevent sticking.

❋ Quick Funnel

If you need a funnel and don't have anything handy, cut a 20" piece of heavy-duty aluminum foil, fold it in half and then roll the double thickness into a cone shape. Cut off the pointed end, and it's ready to be used as a funnel that's perfect for filling bottles.

Garlic

- There are several ways to peel individual cloves of garlic. *Choose the method that works best for you...*

  - Put the clove on its side, and smack it with the bottom of a large can. Or put the flat side of a wide knife's blade on top of the clove. Make a fist and quickly pound the blade, or press down on the blade with the heel of your hand.

  - Immerse the clove in a bowl of cold water for 20 minutes.

  - Put the clove in hot water for 5 seconds.

  - Microwave the clove for 20 seconds.

- To remove the odor of garlic from your hands, use a piece of silverware (stainless steel works fine) like a bar of soap, and wash with it under cold water. Or wash your hands and rub the stainless-steel faucet at the same time.

- To remove the smell of garlic from your breath, mix a touch of sugar in a little lemon juice and swill it around your mouth, then swallow it.

- When a recipe calls for both fresh garlic and fresh ginger, work with the garlic first, then ginger. The ginger will remove the garlic smell from your hands, utensils and cutting board.

Gelatin

- When preparing gelatin, add 1 teaspoon of distilled white vinegar for every 4 cups of liquid—this way, the gelatin will stay firm longer than usual.

- Do not add kiwi or fresh pineapple to gelatin...not unless you want it to be runny. The enzymes in both fruits keep gelatin from setting properly.

Roast Your Own Garlic

Roasted garlic is a versatile treat. You can use it as a healthy spread (and butter substitute) on bread...or as a paste in sauces, soups, grain dishes, dips and dressings. It's easy to prepare.

Start with a large head of garlic. Flake off the outer layers of skin, but leave the peels on the cloves intact. Cut off about ¼" of the pointed tops so that the individual cloves of garlic are exposed, while the head of garlic is still intact.

Place the head of garlic in a small baking dish, with the cut side up. Drizzle about 1 tablespoon of olive oil on the cloves. Cover the dish and let it bake in a 400°F oven for about 30 minutes, until the cloves feel soft when pressed.

Let the head get cool enough to handle. Then use the tip of a small knife (or a fork) to remove the softened garlic from each clove. Or, you can simply squish out the garlic and discard the skins.

Roasted garlic will keep for 1 week or longer if you refrigerate it in an airtight container.

NOTE: You can also roast garlic in the microwave. Prep the head of garlic the same way as for oven-baking.

Then place the head in a small, deep, microwave-safe dish, along with 2 tablespoons of water. Cover the dish with microwave-safe plastic wrap, and cook it on *medium* for 7 to 7½ minutes.

Then remove the garlic from the microwave and let it stand for 10 minutes before taking off the plastic wrap. Use the garlic the same way you would use it if it were oven-roasted. *Bon appétit!*

Garbage Bowl

When you're preparing food, keep a large bowl on the counter and use it for food scraps and waste. It will help keep things neat during the food-preparation process, and it will save you from making countless trips to the garbage can.

Ginger

◆ Fresh gingerroot can last indefinitely if it's stored in sherry and sealed in a covered jar in the refrigerator. The ginger will not take on the taste of sherry, but the sherry will taste like ginger. Use both the ginger and the sherry to cook with—and to drink.

◆ You can also store a piece of fresh gingerroot in the freezer. When you want to use it, just lop off a piece and grate it. It's so much easier to grate frozen ginger than ginger that's at room temperature (or even refrigerated).

Glass

If you break a drinking glass—or anything made of glass—put on rubber gloves, then pick up the shattered pieces with a few slices of bread. It's thicker than paper towels and it's also safer to use.

Once you think you've cleaned up all of the glass, throw out the bread and carefully go over the area using the hose attachment of your vacuum cleaner.

Grapes

◆ Wash and dry bunches of grapes, then freeze them for a yummy cold snack.

◆ For your next party, add frozen grapes to the punch bowl in place of ice cubes. You will have a lovely garnish, and they will not dilute the punch.

◆ On a hot day, take frozen grapes out of the freezer, lightly sprinkle them with confectioner's sugar and serve them as an unusual, refreshing and sensual snack.

Grater

◆ Before grating lemon, lime or orange zest, wrap 2 layers of plastic wrap around the grater. Then when you grate the fruit, the zest will stick to the plastic wrap, not the grater. When you're done, gently remove the plastic wrap from the grater and shake the zest onto a plate.

✳ **Zest Conversion**
One medium lemon should provide about 1 tablespoon of zest.

◆ When a recipe calls for grated zest, only grate the thin outer layer…the colored portion of the fruit. The white pith will give the dish a bitter taste.

★ **Protect Your Digits**
Nobody wants grated finger in his/her food. Go to a sewing-supplies store and get thimbles that fit the fingers that are in jeopardy each time you use the grater.
    With the thimbles in place, you will be able to grate faster and more completely. And no more leftover stubs of potato, carrot or cheese!

Gravy

◆ To remove fat that's floating on top of gravy, blot it up with a piece of dry bread.

◆ You can also remove fat by putting the gravy in a container in the freezer for about 30 minutes. After that time, the fat will have formed a solid layer on top, and you can easily spoon off the fatty layer.

◆ When adding wine to gravy, cook it for about 10 minutes longer than usual—doing this will boil off the alcohol, but not the flavor of the wine in your gravy.

Greens

Here's a great way to keep collard greens, kale, mustard greens, lettuce and other salad greens fresher longer—keep them in a covered container in the refrigerator, along with a piece of stainless-steel silverware. (If you don't think this will work, try it for yourself and see.)

Hair Dryer

Yes, keeping a hair dryer in the kitchen is a good idea. It can help you dry just-washed salad greens...soften too-frozen ice cream...set icing on a cake...dry a big water splotch you got on your blouse right before your guests are due to arrive...and probably a dozen more useful things that you'll think of when the dryer is within reach in the kitchen.

Ham

Due to their high salt content, leftover ham and other cured meats do not freeze well. Wrap sliced ham tightly in plastic wrap, then cover it with aluminum foil and freeze it for no more than 1 to 2 months. Leftover ham can generally be kept in the refrigerator for 3 to 5 days.

Herbs (Fresh and Dried)

◆ Before using any herb, crumble it by rolling it around in the palms of your hand. Doing this will release the herb's flavor—not just in your hand, but for the dish it's going into.

◆ Freeze fresh herbs by washing and cutting them into pieces that are small enough to fit in an ice-cube tray compartment. Once the entire tray is filled with pieces of herb, carefully add a little water to each compartment.

Then it's ready for the freezer. Once the herbs are completely frozen, transfer these cubes from the tray to resealable plastic freezer bags. Label the bag with the name of the herb. Then, when a recipe calls for that herb, figure on 1 ice cube yielding 1 teaspoon of it. To defrost the cube, just put it in a small strainer and run hot water over it.

◆ Add dried herbs to what you're cooking about 30 minutes before the dish is done. To help the fresh herb keep its color and flavor, add the herb 10 minutes before you turn off the heat.

✳ **Herbal Plate Decoration**

Spread the rim of each dinner plate with a light, even coating of margarine. Select an herb that goes with the entrée, chop it finely and sprinkle it on the margarine, creating an herbal border around the plate. Put your entrée in the middle of the plate, add your side dishes and serve.

◆ If your recipe is not specifically written for microwave cooking, keep in mind that *fresh* herbs tend to be milder when microwaved, so you may want to *increase* the amount you use. And the flavor of *dried* herbs is heightened in the microwave, so you may want to *decrease* the amount you use.

◆ To make fresh herbs into dried herbs, place them on a paper towel and cook them in the microwave on high for about 1 minute. When dry, store them in labeled resealable plastic bags. They should retain their flavor for up to 1 year.

DID YOU KNOW?

You can keep lettuce fresh in a resealable plastic bag with a piece of almost-burnt toast. When the toast gets soggy, replace it with another piece.

Lettuce should stay crisp in the fridge for a couple of weeks this way.

◆ Here's a helpful guideline—when a recipe calls for a fresh herb, but you want to use a dried herb instead, use ⅓ the amount. So, if the recipe says to use 1 tablespoon of fresh basil, use 1 teaspoon of dried basil.

Of course, the reverse is also true. If the recipe calls for 1 teaspoon of dried basil, use 3 times as much (1 tablespoon) fresh basil.

Honey

◆ If your jar of honey has crystallized, reliquefy it by putting the jar in a bowl filled with very hot water. Let it stand for about 5 minutes, then stir until it's the consistency of honey.

◆ You can also remove the lid and put the uncovered, metal-free jar or container in the microwave and heat it on *medium* for 10-second increments. Stop the microwave as soon as the honey is liquefied.

◆ Always store honey in a dark place at room temperature.

Jelly/Jam

Transfer jelly or jam to a clean squeeze bottle to make it more manageable for young children.

Juice Boxes

In hot weather, when you plan on packing a juice box in with lunch, freeze the juice box overnight. Pack the frozen juice box in with lunch in the morning, and by the time lunch rolls around, the juice should be thawed to a slushy consistency.

NOTE: As a bonus, the frozen juice box will keep the rest of the lunch contents cold.

Ketchup

◆ *Shake, O shake the ketchup bottle...none will come, and then a lot'll.* Insert a straw into the bottle of ketchup—all the way to the bottom—and then remove it. Doing this lets in air, which breaks the vacuum and helps the ketchup come out quickly.

◆ To get the last few splurts out of the almost-empty ketchup bottle, try this—first make sure the cover is tight on the bottle. Then get a good, strong grip of the neck of the bottle and swing it in a circular motion. Every last drop will come to the top.

Kiwi

◆ To ripen a kiwi quickly, put it in a brown paper bag with a banana or an apple. Close the bag and let it stay that way overnight. The banana or apple's ethylene gas will help ripen the kiwi quickly.

◆ If you want to peel a kiwi quickly, first slice off the top and bottom of the kiwi. Then insert a teaspoon or tablespoon (depending on the size of the fruit) between the flesh and the peel. Gently turn the spoon around the inside of the kiwi, which will separate the flesh from the peel.

Smart Way to Peel Kiwi
It helps to use an egg slicer to peel kiwi quickly and evenly.

Lasagna

◆ If you don't want to cook the lasagna noodles before you start layering the pan, add more liquid in the form of tomato sauce, and a little more cheese. How much more sauce and cheese? We wish we could tell you, but there are so many variables, that the only way to know is by using your own judgment.

So, if you're a courageous cook, layer the pan with the uncooked lasagna noodles, add extra sauce and cheese and hope for the best. (You may not want to have dinner guests the first time you try this method.)

◆ If your lasagna tends to stick to the aluminum foil with which you cover it, try this—spray the foil with nonstick cooking spray *before* you cover and bake the lasagna. Or, check the supermarket for nonstick aluminum foil.

Leftovers

Never put hot leftovers right into the refrigerator—doing so requires the refrigerator to use extra energy to cool the food, which makes it less efficient. Instead, place leftovers in shallow containers (with the lids securely fastened) and set them out on your counter until they reach room temperature.

> **NOTE:** The leftovers will cool faster in the shallow containers, which means there's less of a chance that harmful bacteria will grow, and the food will stay safely edible for a longer period of time.

Lemons and Limes

◆ When all you need is a squirt of juice, don't dry out the entire lemon or lime by cutting it open. Just puncture the peel with a toothpick and squeeze out the little bit you need. Then put a piece of masking tape over the hole…or cover the fruit with plastic wrap…or put it in a resealable plastic bag.

◆ You can also take the lemon/lime out of the refrigerator, and when it's reached room temperature, use your palm to roll it back and forth on a hard surface. This will break the fruit's inner membranes, and you'll get close to twice as much juice that way.

◆ If you can't wait until the lemon is at room temperature, let hot water run over it for 1 minute, then do the palm-rolling thing.

◆ To get the most juice out of a lemon (or lime), jab it with a fork, then microwave it for about 15 seconds on medium power. Juice as usual.

◆ For fresh-squeezed juice, it's best to use an old-fashioned and low-tech juice reamer (the kind with the conical-ridged center). But if you don't have a reamer, try this—cut the lemon/lime in half and then stick a fork in its center, where the conical-ridged center of the reamer would go.

◆ Turn the fork around and around in the center of the lemon that you're holding in your palm. Then turn the fork in the opposite direction, until no more juice comes out. Repeat the entire procedure with the other half of the lemon.

◆ When a recipe calls for the juice of 1 lemon, figure that you'll need to use 2 to 3 tablespoons of lemon juice.

Lemon (Substitutes)

When a recipe calls for lemon juice and you don't have any, you can substitute equal amounts of lime juice or white wine.

Lentils

One of the oldest cultivated crops in the world, lentils may be dusty and have tiny pebbles mixed in. There are no shortcuts when it comes to sorting and cleaning them…start by spreading them out in a single layer on a cookie sheet. Pick out and discard the pebbles as well as any shriveled or discolored lentils.

Transfer the remaining lentils to a bowl of water. Clean the beans by swishing them around with your hand. Throw out all the ones that float to the top. Transfer the rest to a strainer and rinse them under running water. Then 1 more transfer…to a pan for cooking as usual.

Lettuce

◆ To make lettuce last longer, take it out of its plastic bag and store it in a brown paper bag—this will allow moisture to escape, and the lettuce will last longer. But do NOT store lettuce with apples, pears or bananas. Their ripening gases will cause the lettuce to turn brown and yucky.

◆ Soak limp lettuce leaves in ice-cold water with a splash of lemon juice. After about 15 minutes, they will be crisp again.

Marshmallows

◆ It's best to store marshmallows in your freezer—put them in a plastic container with a tight-fitting lid. They will stay fresh and not mush together.

◆ When you open a bag of marshmallows and don't seal them closed again, they will get hard and stale.

   If that happens, put the hardened marshmallows in a resealable plastic bag along with 2 slices of very fresh bread. Seal the bag closed and let it stay like this for a few days…until the marshmallows are soft again.

✷ Phenomenal Pumpkin Pie Topping

Put a layer of marshmallows on the bottom of a pie crust, and pour the pumpkin pie filling on top of it. Bake the pie as usual, and keep checking it—you'll want to witness the moment when the marshmallows make their way to the surface of the pie, where they will form a tufted topping.

Measuring Spoons/Cups

◆ Spray measuring spoons with cooking spray before you measure a sticky ingredient. Then go ahead and scoop up the molasses or peanut butter or chocolate syrup. Each will glide right off the sprayed spoon.

◆ You can spray a measuring cup with cooking spray before you pour in a gooey ingredient, or you can line the cup with a piece of plastic wrap and spray the wrap with cooking spray. That way, after you've poured in the honey or whatever, you can simply discard the sticky plastic wrap and rinse out the cup.

◆ Is it hard to read the faded markings on your measuring cup? Carefully repaint the lines and numbers with bright-red nail polish.

◆ To be super-organized, measure all of the recipe's dry ingredients first, then measure all of the wet ingredients. Put everything in its own little dish or bowl…in the order you'll need it for the recipe. That way, you will be able to use the same measuring utensils several times over, without having to wash and dry them for each measured ingredient.

 Makeshift Measuring Cup

Clean, empty yogurt containers make good measuring cups. Filled almost to the top, a 4-ounce container = ½ cup…a 6-ounce container = ¾ cup…and an 8-ounce container = 1 cup.

Milk

◆ Buy milk in a cardboard carton or in a jug that's opaque. See-through (translucent) containers let light seep in. That can cause milk to spoil…especially if it stands out on the sidewalk in hot weather, waiting to be brought into the supermarket.

◆ Keep containers or jugs of milk on a shelf inside the refrigerator, not in the door. The door keeps opening and closing, exposing

Common Kitchen Measurements

A dash of liquid = A few drops
3 teaspoons = 1 tablespoon
½ tablespoon = 1½ teaspoons
1 tablespoon = 3 teaspoons
2 tablespoons = 1 fluid ounce
4 tablespoons = ¼ cup
5⅓ tablespoons = ⅓ cup
8 tablespoons = ½ cup
8 tablespoons = 4 fluid ounces
10⅔ tablespoons = ⅔ cup
12 tablespoons = ¾ cup
16 tablespoons = 1 cup
16 tablespoons = 8 fluid ounces

⅛ cup = 2 tablespoons
¼ cup = 4 tablespoons
¼ cup = 2 fluid ounces
⅓ cup = 5 tablespoons plus 1 teaspoon
½ cup = 8 tablespoons
1 cup = 16 tablespoons
1 cup = 8 fluid ounces
1 cup = ½ pint
2 cups = 1 pint (16 ounces)
2 pints = 1 quart
4 quarts (liquid) = 1 gallon
8 quarts (dry) = 1 peck
4 pecks (dry) = 1 bushel
1 kilogram = approximately 2 pounds
1 liter = approximately 4 cups or 1 quart

the items in the door to warm air from the kitchen. The cool air inside the refrigerator remains more constant.

◆ When boiling milk, rinse the pot with cold water right before you pour in the milk. That little step will prevent milk from scorching and sticking to the pot.

◆ Put a clean marble or stone in the pot to prevent milk from boiling over. Just be sure to remove the marble or stone before pouring the milk!

◆ Also, don't ever let milk come to a rolling boil. Turn off the heat as soon as little bubbles form around the edge.

Milk (Substitutes)

For baking or cooking...

◆ Substitute 1 cup of whole milk with 1 cup of skim milk plus 2 tablespoons of (melted) unsalted butter or margarine.

◆ Substitute 1 cup of whole milk with ½ cup of evaporated whole milk plus ½ cup of water.

◆ Use ¼ cup of dry whole milk plus ⅞ cup of water in place of 1 cup of whole milk.

Muffins

◆ To avoid over-baking your muffins, take them out of the oven when they have a few minutes left to bake. They'll finish baking on their own, outside of the oven.

◆ Instead of using the milk that's called for in a muffin recipe, use the same amount of plain yogurt or buttermilk. Also add ½ teaspoon of baking soda for each cup of milk you're replacing. These muffins are so light, they will practically float out of the pan!

- If, after you've poured the muffin batter into the baking tin, there are empty compartments, fill them halfway with water. This will prevent the tin from smoking or warping while baking.

- Muffin mavens advise against cooling muffins in their pans. They say that the bottoms will get soggy. Instead, take the muffins out of the oven and put the pan on a wire rack...let the muffins sit there for 10 minutes. Then take the muffins out of the pan, and put them on the rack until they have finished cooling. When muffins have been allowed to cool this way, they are less likely to fall apart.

- Use a clean shoehorn to help you take warm muffins out of the tin easily.

- If the muffins are stuck to the pan, spread a wet towel out on your work surface. Then put the hot muffin pan on the wet towel. After 1 to 2 minutes, you should be able to pop out the muffins without any problem. But next time, consider baking the muffins in paper baking cups.

Mushrooms

- To keep fresh mushrooms fresh, keep them in a basket or in an open brown paper bag in the refrigerator. Dried mushrooms should be stored in an airtight container.

- Do not wash or soak fresh mushrooms in water. The mushrooms are sponge-like and they will absorb the water. This will make them watery and tasteless.

    Instead, clean them with a damp cloth, or gently scrape them with a paring knife. OK, if stubborn dirt is clinging to a mushroom, you can rinse them with water. Just be sure to dry them thoroughly. Also, cook

them immediately or the water will cause them to decay.

Nuts

- Keep Brazil nuts and other hard-shelled nuts in the freezer. Frozen nuts are generally much easier to crack.

- Soak shelled walnuts in salted water overnight, and they'll be a cinch to crack.

- Hot water makes pecan shells more porous and creates air pockets, making them easy to crack. Here's how to do it—place pecans in a microwave-safe container, cover them with water and zap them on high for about 3 minutes. Then take the pecans out of the water and, once they're cool, their shells should be easy to crack.

> **NOTE:** You can also soak pecans in a covered pot of just-boiled water for about 15 minutes before cracking them.

- When a recipe calls for *unsalted* nuts, but the ones you have are salted, cook the *salted* nuts in boiling water for 2 minutes. Then drain them and spread them out on an ungreased baking sheet. Bake them in a 200°F oven until they're dry...no more than 5 minutes. Then continue on with your recipe and your unsalted nuts.

- To skin almonds, first boil a pot of water. Then put the shelled almonds in a strainer and plunge the strainer into the water. After a couple of minutes, take the almonds out of the water. When they're cool enough to handle, pinch the lower portion of each almond and watch it slip right out of its skin.

Toasting Nuts

Toasting brings out the full flavor of nuts. And it's easy to do. Start with nuts that are shelled and about the same size. *Then decide whether you want to toast them in the oven or in a skillet...*

◆ *Oven*—Spread the nuts in a single layer on a baking pan and cook them at 400°F for 7 to 10 minutes, or until the nuts start to turn golden. Halfway through the toasting, carefully rotate the nuts by shaking the pan.

◆ *Skillet*—Place nuts in a single layer and put the skillet over medium-high heat. Stir or shake the nuts while they're toasting for 5 to 7 minutes, or until they start to turn golden. Always aim for *golden*. Toasted nuts taste best if they're not darker than light brown.

◆ Macadamia nuts are a real treat. Because they're pricey, people tend to buy a jar and dole out the nuts over a period of time. But that's *not* a good idea. These nuts turn rancid rather quickly. Make sure the lid is on the jar tightly, keep it in a cool place, and eat them sooner than later!

Oil

◆ If the new bottle of cooking oil you open has a foil seal, cut a small slit in it—instead of removing it completely. The slit will give you more control over the amount of oil you pour...and should eliminate any extra drips or the occasional spill.

◆ To make a bottle of cooking oil easier to use, transfer it to a clean, empty mustard bottle—you know, the kind you squeeze.

◆ Lids from plastic containers—such as yogurt, cottage cheese or margarine—can be used as coasters for bottles of oil. Using them will save you from having to clean oil drips off your countertops and cupboard shelves.

◆ Before heating oil, add 1 tablespoon of distilled white vinegar to the frying pan. It will help cut down on the amount of fat absorbed by the frying food, and the food will taste less greasy.

 Quick Oil Absorber

If you spill oil on the floor, pour some flour on the spill. Wait 1 or 2 minutes for the flour to absorb the grease, then clean it all up with a few paper towels.

Oil (Substitute)

Cut the number of calories and fat grams in your baked goods by using the equivalent amount of apple sauce instead of oil (in other words, 1 cup of oil equals 1 cup of apple sauce).

 Smart Sauce Idea

Buy snack-packs of apple sauce, and use them as you need them. It's more efficient (and less wasteful) than keeping a big, open jar of apple sauce in your refrigerator.

Onions

◆ When you cut a raw onion, a compound called *propanethial-s-oxide* is released in a vapor. When the vapor comes into contact with a person's eyes, it is converted into a form of sulfuric acid. No wonder it causes stinging and tearing!

To slow down the enzymes that cause this unpleasant chemical reaction, put onions in the freezer for 15 minutes—or in the refrigerator for 1 hour—before you have to cut them. *But if you don't plan ahead, here are some other suggestions...*

- Work with the onion under cold running water, or fill a basin with cold water and submerge the onion while you cut it.

- Wear a pair of safety goggles while working with onions.

- Try to breathe through your mouth instead of your nose.

- Burn a candle in the area where you are cutting. The tear-causing vapor from the onion is drawn to the heat source from the flame, and it will burn off some of the noxious fumes.

- Bite on a slice of bread and have the rest sticking out of your mouth to absorb the tear-making fumes.

- Here's a great way to peel onions quickly—and it's particularly useful if you have a lot of small onions to peel. Soak them in just-boiled water for a few seconds. Then soak them for another few seconds in cold water. The skins should slip right off.

- Let's suppose you want to use a milder and sweeter-tasting onion in your salad, but all you have is a regular, strong yellow onion. Slice the yellow onion and soak it in cold water for 30 minutes, along with 1 teaspoon of distilled white vinegar. The pungent acid will dissipate in the water, and the onion will have a milder, sweeter flavor.

- You can also make an onion sweeter this way—cut it into thin slices and put them in a bowl, then pour just-boiled water over them. Let the slices stand for 2 to 3 minutes, then drain and refrigerate until the onion is cold…and sweet.

- If your onions are sprouting *and* it's springtime *and* you have a garden—plant them! Or plant them in a flowerpot and place them in a sunny window. Use the green stalks in recipes the same way you would use scallions.

- If you bought onions in a mesh bag, keep them in that bag so that the air can circulate around them. If you bought the onions loose, keep them in the leg from an old, clean pair of pantyhose, knotted on the open end.

- You can get the onion smell off your hands by rubbing them with table salt, then rinsing and drying your hands.

- Another way to remove the onion smell is to squeeze a dollop of regular non-gel toothpaste in your palm, then distribute it over your hands. Then wash off the toothpaste under running water and dry your hands. There shouldn't be a hint of the onion smell left.

Onion (Substitute)

When a recipe calls for 1 small onion, it's equivalent to ¼ cup of chopped, fresh onion. You can substitute it for 1 to 2 tablespoons of instant minced onion…or 1 tablespoon of onion powder…or 1⅓ teaspoons of onion salt.

Pancakes

- Here's a simple way to make your pancakes super-light and fluffy—instead of using the milk or any other liquid called for in the recipe, use the same amount of seltzer or club soda (at room temperature). The carbonation bubbles will cause the pancakes to rise higher and stay airier.

  Be sure to use all the batter you make as soon as you prepare it. Batter made with seltzer or club soda doesn't have staying power.

◆ If mornings are hectic and you welcome all the time-savers available, then prepare pancake batter the night before (but not with seltzer or club soda!). Put the prepared batter in a squeeze bottle (clean out and reuse an empty ketchup or mustard bottle), and keep it in the refrigerator. It will be good to go in the morning.

 Prepare Perfect Pancakes!
Put batter in a clean plastic squeeze bottle or a turkey baster, and you will have an easy time forming perfect pancakes.
   While you're at it, have some fun with it ...make odd-shaped pancakes, or pancakes in the shape of big letters for the names of the people who will be eating them.

◆ For very decadent pancakes, use eggnog instead of the milk (or any other liquid that's called for in the recipe). It's a real once-in-a-blue-moon treat.

Parsley

◆ When your parsley has wilted, cut off ½" from the stems and let them stand in the refrigerator in a glass of ice-cold water for 1 to 2 hours.

◆ When you are serving food or spices that stay on the breath—such as garlic, onions or curry—garnish the food with parsley. It looks nice and, if your guests eat it, it will help freshen their breath.

✳ Paper Towel Alternative
When you need to wipe up a spill and there are no paper towels handy, reach for a couple of coffee filters.
   You may be thinking, "Chances are, I'd sooner have paper towels within reach than coffee filters!" This is probably true most times, but on the off-chance that you've run out of paper towels and you spilled something *right near* where you keep coffee filters, you'll know what to do.

Pasta

◆ Pasta won't stick together if you add 1 tablespoon of olive oil (or any vegetable oil) to the water while it's cooking.

◆ Always add the pasta *after* the water starts boiling. If you add the pasta before the water boils, it will slow down the boiling process... which causes the pasta to clump together.

◆ To avoid having the pasta water boil over, coat 1" of the inside top of the pot with olive or vegetable oil.

◆ When steam from the just-served, hot pasta condenses, there will be a puddle pooling on the plate. To prevent the puddle, wait a few minutes until the pasta stops steaming before putting it on the plate.

★ Better Pasta Storage
If pasta is a real passion for you, invest in a spaghetti canister for proper storage. They are available at some supermarkets as well as kitchen and cookware stores.

◆ Why don't spaghetti boxes close on their own without having to be taped shut? When you have uncooked spaghetti, transfer it from the original box to a clean potato-chip can.
   This kind of can is tall enough to hold spaghetti, and when it's closed, it's airtight. Store in a cool, dry place.

⚡ CAUTION: Do not put uncooked pasta in see-through (plastic or glass) containers. Exposure to light contributes to the breakdown of the vitamin content that's in fortified pasta. Stored in airtight, non-see-through canisters in a cool, dry place, fortified pasta will retain its benefits for up to 18 months.

Peanut Butter

Natural peanut butter (available at supermarkets and health-food stores)—which is made only from peanuts (no sugar or other additives...and no preservatives—nothing to interfere with the wonderful peanut butter taste)—has a layer of oil on top. *The oil should not be spilled off!* It's necessary to make the solid portion spreadable and even more delicious. The oil should be mixed in before the jar is refrigerated.

The best way to do that is to leave the jar on its side for a few days before you want to open it. Then the mixing process will be fairly easy. Just mix it until the oil is fully integrated into the solid portion, and refrigerate it.

 Keep PB Fresh Longer
Once you open a jar of natural peanut butter, store it upside down in the refrigerator. It will stay fresher longer.

Peppers

When preparing stuffed bell peppers—especially if you're going to serve them to guests—have them look their best even after they soften during the cooking process. Just place them in muffin tins and they will keep their shape.

 Smart Pepper-Baking Hint
If there are empty compartments in the muffin tin, fill them halfway with water to prevent the tin from smoking or warping in the oven.

Pepper Shaker

To keep the holes in a pepper shaker from getting clogged, toss in a few whole black or white peppercorns. Doing this seems to make the pepper taste fresher, too.

Pies

◆ Custard-type pies, including pumpkin pie, should *always* be refrigerated...even if that means rearranging everything on the shelves

to make room. Left out at room temperature, pies can grow dangerous bacteria.

◆ To prevent the juice from oozing out of a pie and making a mess in the oven, stand a 4" piece of uncooked macaroni in the middle of the pie while it's baking.

Piecrust

◆ When a pie recipe calls for 1 tablespoon of ice water, instead use 1 tablespoon of distilled white vinegar—this will make a crispier crust.

◆ For a flakier piecrust, substitute the same amount of sour cream or plain yogurt for the liquid called for in a pie recipe.

◆ Before you put the pie in the oven, dip a pastry brush in cold water and lightly paint the crust with it. The crust will become nice and flaky.

Pineapple

When you're cutting a whole pineapple, wear oven mitts to hold on to it more securely.

Pita

Here's an easy way to cut open a pita—heat it in the microwave for about 20 seconds, long enough for it to puff up. Watch it every second, though, and as soon as it looks like a blowfish, stop the cooking.

When you open the microwave door, the pita will unpuff almost entirely. Even so, it should be easy to cut the pita neatly along the edge without tearing into the middle of it.

Make Your Own Pita Chips

Preheat the oven to 350°F. Cut each large pita into 16 triangles—first, by cutting the pita in half, then by cutting each half in half, then cutting each quarter in half. That leaves you with 8 double triangles. Now, turn them into 16 single triangles.

Put them on a tray and bake them at 350°F until they're crisp…about 5 minutes. Let them cool, then you can use them for dips…or spray them lightly with vegetable spray and sprinkle on your favorite seasoning(s). They're great with a little garlic powder.

Hands-Free Phone

When you're involved in food preparation, it's usually inconvenient to answer the telephone. You can solve that problem the same way that professional chefs do—keep a small plastic bag next to the phone. Just put the plastic bag over your hand, and you'll never miss another call. Plus, your phone receiver will stay clean.

Popcorn

◆ If you air-pop popcorn and want to add salt, garlic powder or any other seasoning, lightly spray the popcorn with vegetable spray first to help the seasoning adhere to the popcorn.

◆ If you use a hot-air popcorn maker, preheat it to get the very best results.

◆ An hour before popping corn, sprinkle a little warm water on the kernels. Or keep your popcorn kernels in the freezer. Either way—warm water or freezer—your popcorn will be fluffier and have fewer duds.

CAUTION: Never leave the kitchen when popping popcorn. It can scorch and burn unexpectedly.

◆ If you don't have an air popper, but you do have a microwave, you can still prepare fresh popcorn. Put ¼ cup of popcorn kernels in a lunch-sized brown paper bag. Fold the top over twice and secure it closed with tape. Microwave the bag on high power until you hear the kernels finish popping…they usually take anywhere from 1½ to 4 minutes.

◆ When the popcorn is done popping, carefully open the bag…facing away from you. Then put the popcorn in a bowl, and add salt or curry or any seasoning of your choice. You can also drizzle melted butter on it. Stir and enjoy!

Prevent Popcorn Pain

Don't you hate biting down on an unpopped popcorn kernel? *Ouch!* Here's a way to prevent that from happening ever again. After you've popped the corn and it has cooled, transfer it to a resealable plastic bag. Cut a small hole in 1 bottom corner of the bag, and shake it over the sink—the duds (unpopped kernels) should all fall out of the hole.

Potatoes

◆ To store potatoes, keep them in a cool, dark place with a piece of fresh gingerroot. Both will stay fresh longer.

◆ If you peel potatoes and you don't want to use all of them, put the leftovers in a bowl. Then add 1 teaspoon of distilled white vinegar and enough cold water to cover them completely. Put plastic wrap across the top of the bowl and refrigerate. The peeled spuds will stay good this way for 2 to 3 days.

◆ Keep the skins on the potatoes while you boil them. The skins help hold in the flavor and the nutrients. Also, potatoes are easier to peel once they've boiled.

◆ If you do peel the potatoes before you boil them—and you want them to remain firm and whole and white—add 1 tablespoon of distilled white vinegar or white wine to the water. The vinegar or wine will help form a light skin on the potatoes, which will prevent them from falling apart when you work with them.

Potatoes (Baked or Mashed)

◆ After scrubbing and puncturing the potato skins, stand the spuds in a muffin tin and they will bake quickly.

⭐ **Smart Potato-Baking Hint**
Be sure to fill any empty muffin compartments halfway with water to prevent the tin from smoking or warping while baking.

◆ Get an aluminum nail—they are specifically made for baking potatoes, and are available in some supermarkets, cookware stores and hardware stores. Then, starting at the top of the potato, stick the nail in through the center, lengthwise.

Bake the potato in a 400°F oven for about 35 minutes (the nail shaves off about 20 minutes of baking time), directly on the oven rack. When it's crisp on the outside and tender on the inside, it's done. Oh yes, don't forget to take out the nail before serving.

⚠ **CAUTION:** NEVER put a potato in the microwave if you've used the nail or the muffin-tin cooking method.

◆ Brown-skinned russet and Idaho potatoes are the same, and they are said to make the fluffiest, creamiest mashed potatoes. To make them extra-fluffy, add a pinch of baking powder as you mash them. The powder mixes with the heat and forms tiny air pockets.

Rice

◆ Have your white rice stay white by adding 1 teaspoon of lemon juice for each quart of water used to cook the rice.

◆ To prevent a messy boil-over when making rice, add 1 teaspoon of butter or oil to the cooking water.

◆ Prevent rice from getting mushy and clumping together—add 1 teaspoon of lemon juice for each quart of water used to cook the rice.

◆ Instead of preparing rice with water, substitute a delicious rice "go-with"—try onion soup…or vegetable or beef broth…or miso soup…or low-fat chicken soup…or tomato juice. Experiment. You may discover a wonderful new dish.

◆ OK, you've cooked the rice, but you're not ready to serve it…you want to keep it warm, but you don't want it to get sticky. So, here's what to do—take a few sheets of paper towel, stretch them across the top of the pot and then put the lid on it.

The towels will absorb the condensation that accumulates on the lid. This will prevent it from dripping back into the rice, which is what would make the rice too sticky…and the rice will stay warm.

◆ When reheating rice, put it in a microwave-safe bowl and place an ice cube on top of the rice. Cover the bowl with plastic wrap, and puncture a few holes in it to allow the release of steam. Heat the bowl on high power for about 90 seconds per cup of rice. The rice should taste as though you just cooked it for the first time.

Rolls

◆ Here's a great way to freshen stale rolls—put them in a small, brown paper bag, moisten the bag with water and put it in the oven (preheated to 300°F). When the bag is dry—in just a few minutes, so don't leave the kitchen—take out the bag and remove the rolls. They should taste like they did when they were baked the first time.

◆ Another way to freshen stale rolls is to lightly spray them with water and wrap them loosely in aluminum foil. Then put them in the oven (preheated to 350°F) for 10 to 15 minutes. Keep watch because it could take less than 10 minutes to reheat the rolls.

> ✎ **NOTE:** If you're warming croissant-type crusty rolls, put them in the oven uncovered and on a piece of foil.

◆ If you want to warm rolls in the microwave, first wrap each in a dry paper towel. The towel will absorb moisture and the rolls will not come out soggy.

◆ If you are serving warm rolls, place a piece of aluminum foil under the napkin in the serving basket. The foil will help the rolls retain their heat longer.

🕐 Efficient Recipe Holder

If you are always collecting recipes, there is a unique, organized and efficient way to keep them protected—get a large Rolodex (available at office-supply and stationery stores) and put the recipes on cards in plastic sleeves.

This is more user-friendly than a cookbook because the page won't turn while you're preparing a recipe. The Rolodex recipe card stays in place.

If your recipes are pulled from magazines or printed on sheets of paper, put the pages in plastic holders in a 3-ring notebook.

Salads

◆ The drier the salad ingredients, the better the dressing will coat them. To dry your rinsed salad greens efficiently, use a salad spinner (available at kitchen-supply stores). Put a few paper towels in the spinner along with the wet greens, and they'll dry even faster.

◆ If you want to prepare a salad in advance, place a saucer or plate face-down on the bottom of the salad bowl, covering as much of the bowl's bottom as possible. Then prepare the salad in the bowl. Water from the rinsed salad greens will drain off and slide down the sides of the plate to the bottom of the bowl. The plate will keep the salad stuff from sitting in water and getting soggy.

◆ Tossing a big salad can be messy, but not if you toss all of the salad ingredients into a big plastic bag. Hold the top closed and shake the bag until everything's perfectly integrated.

◆ Control portion size and neatness by giving your guests individual salad bowls with the salad already in them. Put the remaining salad in a bowl on the table so that guests can help themselves to more.

Salsa

If your salsa is too intense, mix in a few drops of vanilla extract. It tames the heat, making it seem less spicy.

Salt

◆ Highly salted foods—also highly spiced foods and foods with vinegar, as well as highly acidic foods, such as tomatoes—have an adverse reaction with aluminum foil. They cause the food to be damaged and the foil to rust.

◆ If a dish is over-salted, gradually add ½ teaspoon of distilled white vinegar and ½ teaspoon of sugar to the food. Do a taste test, and if it's still too salty, add another round of vinegar and sugar. Keep tasting and adding until the saltiness has been neutralized.

◆ An easy way to reduce saltiness in over-salted stews, soups or sauces is to add a potato. Just peel a raw potato, cut it into about 6 pieces and put them in the pot with the over-salted food for the last 10 minutes it needs to cook. As the potato gets soft, it will absorb some of the salt. When the dish has finished cooking, discard the potato. If it's still very salty, discard the dish.

◆ Most everyone knows that putting grains of raw rice (about 10 of them) in a salt shaker will soak up moisture and prevent the salt from clumping up. But you may not know that the grains of rice should be replaced once a year.

◆ If you don't want to bother with the grains of rice, mix 1 tablespoon of cornstarch into a 1-pound box of salt. The cornstarch will keep the salt clump-free.

◆ Kosher or coarse salt has large grains and requires a shaker that has larger holes. A cheese shaker (available at kitchen-supply stores) works well.

◆ To keep kosher salt from caking, add a few dry beans to the shaker. The beans will absorb moisture, and they won't fit through the shaker's holes as grains of rice would.

Sandwiches

Two things usually make a sandwich soggy— the dressing (such as ketchup, mayonnaise and/ or mustard)…and the wet add-ons (such as lettuce, tomato, pickles and/or cucumber). Instead of smearing the dressing on the bread, which is what gets the soggiest, smear it on the main ingredient (the meat, cheese, fish, veggie patty).

★ **Smart Sandwich Prep**

If your sandwich needs to be prepared hours before it will be eaten, wrap the wet things separately. Then, when it's time to eat, assemble the sandwich.

Sausage

When a recipe calls for loose or bulk sausages and you only have link sausages, just remove the casings. Do this by using a knife or kitchen scissors to slit the casing lengthwise from top to bottom, and then peel it off.

Seafood

◆ Refrigerate any seafood you buy as soon as possible. If you have not eaten the seafood within 48 hours, freeze it. Depending on what type of fish it is, it should keep frozen for no more than 6 months. Don't forget to label it with the date of purchase. (Fresh crab and lobster should NOT be frozen.)

◆ For fresh-tasting shrimp, consider buying them frozen, since most shrimp are frozen at sea. Right before you want to cook them, thaw the shrimp by running cold water over them for a few minutes. They will taste fresh, as though you just got off the shrimp boat with them.

◆ To get the fullest flavor from shrimp, prepare them with their shells on. If the shells are already off, then simmer the shrimp in beer for a real taste treat!

Shortening

Measuring out shortening can be a messy job, and don't you hate washing the greasy measuring cup? A standard-sized ice cream scoop holds ¼ cup of shortening—use it to plop out the amount of shortening called for in a recipe. With the scoop, cleanup seems easier.

Shortening (Substitute)

In a never-ending effort to cut calories and fat grams, we found a good way—instead of using butter or lard—to substitute ⅓ less vegetable oil. If a recipe calls for 3 tablespoons of butter, use 2 tablespoons of vegetable, canola, olive or coconut oil instead.

✳ Removing Kitchen Smells

◆ **Burned food**—Wet a large towel with plain water, and imitate a cowboy swirling a lasso for a couple of minutes...until the smell is gone. If there's smoke in the air from the burned food, wet the bath towel with distilled white vinegar instead of water and start lassoing. Be careful not to knock any knick-knacks, mugs or dishes off nearby shelves.

◆ **Plastic container**—Crumple a sheet of newspaper and stuff it into the plastic container. Then put the lid on and let it stay that way for a few days. When the time is up, remove the newspaper and wash the container with soap and water. Rinse and dry.

You can also make a paste from baking soda and water, and rub the inside of the container with it. Let it stay that way overnight. The next morning, rinse and dry the odor-free container.

Soup

There are several ways to help remove some of the fat from soup. *Use whichever method is most appropriate...*

◆ Wash and dry 1 or 2 lettuce leaves. Once the pot of soup is done cooking, place the lettuce leaves on the surface of the soup. Within a couple of minutes, the leaves will be coated with fat. Remove and discard them.

◆ Add 1 raw egg white on the top of soup that's in a pot. As the soup cooks, all the fat will be collected by the egg white. Then, just scoop out the egg. Bye-bye egg...and bye-bye fat.

◆ If you have fatty broth, strain it through a paper coffee filter.

◆ If time permits, refrigerate the soup. A layer of fat will form on top, and you can simply scrape it off with a spoon.

◆ If you can't wait for the soup to cool in the refrigerator, put 6 ice cubes into the soup pot. They act like fat magnets. In seconds, grease solidifies around the cubes. Use a slotted spoon to remove the fatty ice.

Chances are, you will need to warm up the soup again before serving it.

◆ When you need to thicken soup, the standard thickeners—flour, cornstarch, or arrowroot—can add lumps to the soup. Experiment by using a more creative thickener, such as crustless bread crumbs...or quick-cooking oatmeal...or leftover cooked oatmeal. Mashed potatoes (or instant potato flakes) also make a good thickener.

> ✎ **NOTE:** If you insist on using flour, cornstarch or arrowroot as a thickener, mix it with a liquid (such as water, broth or wine) before adding it to the soup. This will prevent it from getting lumpy.

Sour Cream (Substitute)

◆ As a substitute for 1 cup of sour cream, combine 1 cup of cottage cheese, 1 teaspoon of distilled white vinegar plus ¼ cup of skim milk in a blender.

◆ You can also use plain yogurt as a substitute for sour cream—the amounts are equivalent. If you use the yogurt in cooking, add 1 tablespoon of cornstarch to each cup to prevent it from separating.

Spices

◆ Red spices—such as chili powder, cayenne pepper and paprika—lose their color and potency faster than other colored spices. It's best to keep them refrigerated to help prevent loss of color and flavor.

> ✎ **NOTE:** Most spices will keep their flavor even longer if they're kept in the freezer.

◆ If storing spices in the fridge or freezer is not convenient or practical, then keep them in airtight containers in a cool, dark place—far away from the stove.

◆ The conventional wisdom says that spices should be replaced 1 year after they've been opened. Unless you regularly use a large quantity of a specific spice, it's a good idea to buy the smallest available size. Date the jar the first time you open it, so that you will know when to replace it.

◆ When you cook using spices that are not meant to be eaten (such as bay leaves or whole cloves), put them in a metal tea ball or in a piece of cheesecloth tied with string. Then drop them into whatever you're cooking. When the soup or stew is done, fish out the tea ball or cheesecloth, and then discard the contents.

◆ Whether you pour your spices into a shaker or a measuring spoon, do it over a small piece of waxed paper. When the inevitable spill happens, just fold the piece of waxed paper and pour the spice back into its container.

Spinach

◆ This may not come up too often, but we thought it was interesting enough to mention—a *carbon-steel* blade will cause discoloration to spinach leaves, but a *stainless-steel* blade will not. So, now you know which knife to use next time you cut fresh spinach.

◆ When cooking spinach, use a stainless-steel pot. An aluminum pot will give the leaves a metallic taste, and they will also turn a dark, dismal color.

Spray Bottles

It's a good idea to keep several small spray bottles in the kitchen. If you know that they're there, we're sure that you will find many uses for them. The next time you want to moisten, mist, coat, sprinkle or spritz something, you'll be glad you have a spray bottle handy.

Squash

It's generally hard to cut into a butternut or acorn squash—but it's easy if you use a serrated knife. Try it yourself and see.

Also, when you slice squash (or any other round, awkwardly shaped food), do it on a non-skid cutting board or plastic mat to reduce the chance that you'll inadvertently cut yourself.

Strawberries

◆ Want to cut washed strawberries quickly? Use an egg slicer to do it.

◆ Frozen strawberries will stay good up to three months. First, spread the unwashed strawberries on a baking sheet and put them in the freezer. Once they are frozen solid, transfer them to a resealable plastic freezer bag and put them back in the freezer. (Don't forget the label with the date they were frozen.)

Stuffing

◆ It's best not to cook stuffing inside a turkey. When stuffing is in the bird, heat penetration is reduced. And if the inside temperature doesn't reach at least 180°F, bacteria can survive in the innermost part of the turkey and the stuffing. To make sure the meal is as safe and healthy as possible, cook the turkey and stuffing separately.

◆ Here's a unique way to cook prepared stuffing—fill clean coffee cans with the stuffing, cover the cans with aluminum foil and bake for about 2 hours at 350°F.

> **NOTE:** You can store leftover stuffing in the coffee can—just cover it with the can's plastic lid and put in the fridge.

Sugar

◆ When you check labels for the food's sugar content, you may not see the word "sugar" listed. But that doesn't mean the food is sugar-free. There are other words to look for—*dextrose, fructose, lactose, maltose* and *sucrose* are all forms of sugar. Other sugary sweeteners include corn syrup, honey, maple syrup and molasses.

◆ Keep sugar on your table in a large shaker. This will make it handy for sprinkling on food.

◆ Clean and dry a plastic 1-gallon milk jug, and use it to store granulated white sugar. The closed container will not attract bugs, the sugar will not clump up and the jug's handle makes it easy to pour.

◆ If you store sugar in a canister, keep a chopstick inside it. It will come in handy each time you want to level off a measuring cup.

◆ Put a couple of saltine crackers in the sugar container to help prevent the sugar from lumping up.

Sugar (Brown)

◆ If you can wait a day or so for brown sugar to unclump, then place a few slices of apple in the bag, box or jar of sugar. Close it tightly and wait.

> **NOTE:** A slice of fresh bread or a few marshmallows will also help to keep brown sugar unclumped.

◆ If you're in a hurry, put the brown sugar on a rimmed baking sheet and bake it at 225°F for 5 to 10 minutes—until it's soft enough to mash down and be normal consistency.

◆ If you're in a really big hurry, put the brown sugar in a microwave-safe bowl, cover it with plastic wrap and poke a few holes in the plastic. Zap it on high power for 30 seconds. Then test it to see if it is unclumped. If not, let it go for another 30 seconds.

◆ To prevent brown sugar from hardening in the first place, try this—after opening a package of brown sugar, put in a strip of orange zest (about 1" wide and 3" long) or a few prunes. Close up the package securely, then store it inside a resealable plastic bag in your cupboard or pantry.

◆ You can also prevent brown sugar from hardening by keeping the package in a resealable plastic freezer bag in the freezer.

Sugar (Brown, Substitute)

Use 1 cup of white sugar plus 2 tablespoons of molasses in place of 1 cup of brown sugar.

> **NOTE:** If you substitute brown sugar for white sugar when baking, the baked goods may be a little moister and have a slight butterscotch taste. What could be bad?

Sugar (Confectioners', Substitute)

In a blender, combine 1 tablespoon of cornstarch plus 1 cup of granulated sugar. Blend at high speed until it's a fine powder consistency. It's not an exact copy of the real thing, but it comes close.

Sweet Cream

If you have sweet cream that's just starting to turn sour, but you're intent on using it anyway, you can bring back the sweetness by adding a pinch of baking soda.

Tacos

Tacos can be messy to eat, but not if you use a coffee filter as a holder. Once you try it, we're sure you'll agree…it's neat.

Tea

◆ When preparing water for tea, turn off the heat as soon as you see little bubbles forming— *before* the water comes to a rolling boil. This prevents oxygen from being boiled out of the water, which would result in flat-tasting tea.

◆ For a slightly spicy taste, stir a cup of hot tea with a cinnamon stick.

◆ If you made a pot of tea and have some left over, freeze it in an ice cube tray. Then use the tea cubes when you make iced tea—they won't dilute the flavor.

Thermometers/Cooking Temperatures

There are several types of meat thermometers available. Before using a thermometer, make sure it's accurate. To test it, boil water and pour a few inches into a glass. Then submerge the thermometer in the water. The temperature should read 212°F. If it does, then you know that the thermometer is accurate. *Here are some general guidelines for cooking meat…*

◆ **Beef roast**—The thermometer should be inserted into the side of the roast, with the stem reaching the center. For a medium-rare beef roast, cook until the thermometer reads 145°F.

◆ **Chicken**—The thermometer should be inserted into the thickest part of the thigh, away from the bone. The chicken is properly cooked when the thermometer reads 180°F.

◆ **Hamburgers**—The thermometer should be inserted into the side of the burger, so the stem reaches the center. Cook until the thermometer reads 160°F.

◆ **Pork roast**—The thermometer should be inserted into the side of the roast, with the stem reaching the center. Remove the roast from the oven when the thermometer reads 155°F, and then let it stand, tented, until the thermometer goes to 160°F for medium.

◆ **Steaks**—The thermometer should be inserted horizontally, into the side of the steak so that the stem reaches the thickest part, not near fat or bone. For medium-rare, the thermometer should read 145°F…for well done, the reading should be 170°F.

◆ **Turkey**—The general rule when cooking a whole defrosted turkey is 25 minutes for each pound at 325°F. When a turkey reaches an internal temperature of 180°F, it is considered done.

> ✎ **NOTE:** If the turkey doesn't have a little button that pops up—and you don't have a meat thermometer—make a discreet incision between the bird's back and thigh. If the juice that seeps out is clear, it's time to *gobble-gobble* the cooked turkey.

Tomatoes

◆ To ripen tomatoes quickly, place them in a brown paper bag with a banana or a couple of apples. The ethylene gas emitted by the banana or apples will help the tomatoes ripen.

◆ Tomatoes have ovary walls and when you cut into them, the pulp and juice tend to slosh out. But if you slice a tomato vertically—from the top of the stem down to the bottom of the fruit—the slices will stay firmer, which will keep your sandwich drier. Also, vertically cut tomatoes will not dilute salad dressing from the excess juice.

◆ If you want to peel fresh tomatoes, here's a simple way to get the job done—dunk the tomatoes in just-boiled water for about 30 seconds, then in cold water for another 30 seconds. The skins will practically fall off!

Tomato Sauce/Paste

◆ Most cooks know to add 1 teaspoon of sugar to sweeten acidic-tasting tomato sauce. But a more nutritious way to get the same result is to add 1 whole carrot to the sauce during the last 30 minutes of cooking. The natural sugar from the carrot will offset the tomatoes' acidity. Before serving the sauce, remove the carrot…or not.

◆ Does anyone use an entire can of tomato paste at once? Use what you need, then put the rest in a small resealable plastic bag. When you're spooning it into the bag, make note of the total number of tablespoons that are going into the bag. Flatten out the paste to about ¼" thickness and freeze it. Then, whenever a recipe calls for 1 or 2 tablespoons of paste, just break off an appropriate-sized piece.

> ✎ **NOTE:** Remember to label the bag of paste with the number of tablespoons it contains as well as the date you put it in the freezer.

Tuna Salad

Oops! Too much mayonnaise in the tuna salad? Soak up the excess mayo by mixing in some breadcrumbs.

Turkey

◆ There are basters (available at some supermarkets or at cookware and hardware stores) that separate the fat from the juice. Be sure to baste with the juice and discard the fat.

◆ You can also baste turkey by soaking a large piece of cheesecloth in melted butter or olive oil, and then covering the turkey with it. This way, the bird will baste itself.

Remove the cheesecloth during the last 30 minutes of baking so that the skin can brown.

◆ For nonstick roasting, let clean celery stalks be your roasting rack, preventing the turkey from sticking to the bottom of the pan.

Line the bottom of the roasting pan with the stalks, and place the turkey on top of them. The gravy will drain to the bottom of the pan and, once the turkey is cooked, it will lift out easily.

◆ When you want to transfer the turkey from the roasting pan to the serving platter, insert a long-handled wooden spoon in each end of the turkey (top and tail), and it will lift out easily.

Also see "Thermometers/Cooking Temperatures" on pages 99–100 for guidelines on cooking turkey properly.

✳ **The Place to Talk Turkey**

The turkey specialists at the United States Department of Agriculture (USDA) are available to answer cooking questions from 10 am to 4 pm (Eastern time), Monday through Friday, excluding holidays—except Thanksgiving. They also have recorded information that is available 24 hours a day.

The toll-free Meat & Poultry Hotline is 888-674-6854. Or you can visit the USDA's Food Safety and Inspection Service Web site at *www.fsis.usda.gov.*

Turnips/Turnip Greens

◆ While cooking turnips, add 1 teaspoon of sugar to the water to help prevent that unappetizing turnip-cooking smell.

◆ When cooking turnip greens, always use a stainless-steel pot. An aluminum pot will give the greens a metallic taste, and it will also turn the greens a dark, dismal color.

Vegetables

◆ Always store fresh vegetables in your refrigerator (preferably, in the lower fruit/vegetable bin) to keep them crisp and fresh. *The United States Department of Agriculture (USDA) recommends these optimum storage times for fresh vegetables...*

  ◆ Asparagus, beans (snap or wax), cauliflower, celery, cucumber, eggplant, green peppers, salad greens and tomatoes—1 week

  ◆ Beets, carrots, parsnips, radishes, rutabagas and turnips—2 weeks

  ◆ Broccoli, brussels sprouts, greens (spinach, kale, collards, etc.), okra, green onions, peas and summer squash—3 to 5 days

  ◆ Cabbage—1 to 2 weeks

  ◆ Corn—Eat as soon as possible

◆ As soon as you bring home root vegetables—such as carrots, beets, ginger, potatoes, parsnip, radish, turnip, yam, jicama, horseradish, rutabaga—cut off their leafy tops. If you leave the leaves on, they will rob the roots (the edible part) of their nutrients. And then what's the point of eating your veggies?

◆ To revive wilting greens, gather them in a bowl filled with ice-water plus 2 or 3 tablespoons of lemon juice. Cover the bowl with plastic wrap and put it in the refrigerator. Wait about 1 hour for your greens to perk up again.

Vinegar

Food that contains vinegar (such as vinaigrette dressing, cucumber salad or coleslaw) should not be served on painted plates. The vinegar may leach out the lead from the plates, and that can be dangerously toxic, especially to children. If you have any question about the plates you use, buy a lead-testing kit (available at home-improvement stores) and check them out.

Water

If your water filter is out of kilter, get out the vitamin C! A pinch of vitamin C powder—or a tiny piece of a vitamin C tablet added to a glass of water right before you drink it—will eliminate any chlorine taste and smell.

Watermelon

Here's a yummy, healthy treat for the summer! Remove the seeds from a chunk of watermelon, and purée the melon meat in the blender. Transfer the puréed pulp into popsicle makers and put them in the freezer. These watermelon pops make a thirst-quenching treat on a hot day.

Whipped Cream

◆ One cup of heavy or whipping cream will provide 2 cups of whipped cream.

◆ To speed up the process of turning heavy cream into whipped cream, chill the bowl, beater and cream before you start whipping—and/or add a pinch of salt or ¼ teaspoon of lemon juice to the cream.

Yogurt

While this is not a cookbook, we wanted to share a quick and easy, satisfying and nutritious dessert recipe. *We'll give you the basics in the hope that you will take it from there and turn it into a treat to suit your specific taste...*

Start with 6 to 8 ounces of plain low-fat yogurt, 1 level teaspoon of carob powder (or 1 teaspoon of unsweetened cocoa powder) and 1 to 2 teaspoons of sugar (or 1 packet of artificial sweetener).

NOTE: Instead of carob or cocoa powder, you could add your favorite flavor of gelatin. For example, lemon tastes great with yogurt. Have fun experimenting. Add little bits at a time and taste as you go. It's easier to *add* more sweetener than to...well, you know.

The Legend of the Zucchini Fairy

Have you ever opened your front door and seen a basket of fresh-grown zucchini waiting there? You probably wondered where it came from—perhaps your neighbor with the lovely garden and the green thumb gave you some overflow from his/her bumper crop. Well, we have a secret to share with you—you've been visited by the Zucchini Fairy!

So pull out the recipe book and make some stuffed zucchini, zucchini quiche or *ratatouille*...and maybe invite your neighbor over for dinner, anyway.

Mix all the ingredients until they reach a marvelous *mousse* consistency. For a little extra pizzazz, add a few drops of almond extract.

Zucchini

Size *does* count. In zucchini's case, the smaller the vegetable, the more flavorful. Look for zucchini that's 2" to 8" in length. They can be stored in a plastic bag in the refrigerator for up to 4 days, but it's best to use them the same day you buy them. ■

CHAPTER 5

Loads of Laundry Care

Today's average family generates approximately 50 pounds of laundry every week. If you are the person who gets stuck doing the wash, and there are kids around, get them to help you. Turn sorting, folding and putting away into a race. Time them and keep track of their performances. Encourage them to beat their own records. If you don't have children, you won't have nearly as much laundry, but it's still not always a fun job.

In any case, we hope the following solutions will help make cleaning your clothes easier, faster and more efficient.

WASHING MACHINES

We owe a debt of thanks to William Blackstone of Bluffton, Indiana…in 1874, as a birthday present for his wife, he built a machine that removed and washed dirt from clothes. That was the first washing machine designed for home use.

In 1908, the first electric-powered washing machine was introduced by the Hurley Machine Company of Chicago, Illinois.

And it just got better and better from that point. We've certainly come a long way from pounding clothes with a rock by a stream.

If you're in the market for a new washing machine, you may be interested to know that front-loading machines use 40% to 60% less water…30% to 50% less energy…and 50% to 70% less detergent than top-loading models.

If you're keeping the washing machine you have, here are some tips for making your machine perform at its peak.

> **FYI: Heavier Than It Looks!**
> A normal-sized load of wash is approximately 6 pounds of dry laundry. Who says doing chores isn't exercise?

Maintaining a Washer

Built-up detergent residue may be preventing your washing machine from doing its best. At the start of each month, clean out that residue by letting your machine run without laundry, but with a cup of distilled white vinegar.

Prevent Residue Buildup

Vinegar is not strong enough to harm fabric, but is strong enough to dissolve the alkalies in soaps and detergents. Get rid of detergent residue with each load you wash by adding 1 cup of distilled white vinegar at the start of the washing machine's final rinse cycle.

> ⚡ **CAUTION:** If you use chlorine bleach in your wash, do not add distilled white vinegar. The combination will produce vapors that are extremely dangerous.

as we know that a colorfast garment won't run (see "Test the Colorfast Claim" on page 105), then we're lenient when it comes to mixing light and bright colors.

> **DID YOU KNOW?**
>
> **S**oils can travel from one garment to another in the washing machine. That being the case, you should always separate heavily soiled clothes from not-so-soiled clothes.

LAUNDRY SORTING & PREPPING

Doing a little bit of preparation *before* starting a load of wash will save you lots of work afterward. *Here's what to do…*

Sort Socks in the Hamper

Collect the plastic caps from gallon-sized jugs of spring or distilled water or from milk containers. Carefully cut an "X" in the middle of each cap. Place these cut caps wherever sock-wearers tend to take off their socks—in the bathroom, bedroom, den, etc.

Each time a pair of socks is taken off, the wearer should push a small part of the 2 socks through the cut in the cap, which can then be tossed in the hamper.

Just think of the results…each pair of socks will stay together through both the washer and dryer cycles—no sorting necessary, and no more missing socks.

Know Your Colors

There are 3 color categories—whites, pastels and darks. You may be someone who insists on separating clothes according to color. As long

Delicates vs. Indelicates

It's always a good idea to separate delicate fabrics from heavier garments that would not get as clean with the gentle cycle.

Lint Producers

Fabrics like terry cloth and chenille produce lint. It's wise to put linty robes, towels, blankets and spreads in a separate load.

But if you insist on throwing these items in with the rest of your wash, add 1 cup of distilled white vinegar in place of fabric softener. The vinegar will help prevent the lint from attaching to other clothes in the machine. (You also might want to invest in a lint roller to clean your clothes.)

Sorting Things Out

- Zip all zippers closed. Hook all hooks. That will prevent zippers and hooks from snagging or attaching to other items in the wash.

- Remove all items from pockets, particularly tissues. You don't want tiny bits of tissue all over every item in your wash.

- Button the cuffs of a blouse or shirt to the front of the garment. It will keep it from tangling in the washing machine.

- To machine-wash your delicates, put them in a pillowcase, tie it closed and then toss it in the machine.

- If you turn clothes inside out, it can help reduce wear-and-tear on them. Knits, permanent-press and quilted fabrics may have less fading and pilling, and corduroy won't pill, gather lint or flatten out.

- If you don't turn pants inside out, then at least pull the pants' pockets inside out. They will dry much faster that way.

- If you're washing a garment that has a drawstring waistband, make a knot or sew a bead or button at both ends of the drawstrings to prevent them from disappearing into the waistband during the washing process.

- If you have a drawstring that needs restringing, tape one end to a chopstick—or attach an end to a long safety pin—and patiently push the string through. Be sure you have a knot, bead or button at the other end.

Going to the Laundromat

Lighten your trip to the laundromat by putting each wash load in a pillowcase, along with 1 cup of powdered detergent, instead of lugging a big box or bottle with you. Empty the pillowcase plus detergent into the washer, and you're ready to go.

Disinfect a Laundromat Machine

If you are troubled by the thought of who used a public washing machine before you, you can disinfect the machine and your clothes by adding ½ cup of mouthwash to the wash cycle.

Colorfast Garments

If clothing is labeled as "colorfast," it means that the colors should not run or fade from washing or wearing them.

There has been an occasional instance when we didn't realize that a garment was NOT colorfast, and we threw it into the washing machine with other clothes. When that happens, you have to be flexible. If a red shirt turns your white towels pink, consider changing the décor of your bathroom. Better yet, follow the advice here and you won't have a problem with non-colorfast clothes.

Test the Colorfast Claim

If the care label says "colorfast," chances are the colors will not run. But if the label doesn't address this (or it says "do not use detergent" or "wash only in cold water"), you can test a garment's colorfast-ability before throwing it in with other clothes.

Test: Take a clean, white, wet washcloth, and rub an inside seam of the colored item with it. If the white cloth becomes stained, the garment is not colorfast. Which means that if you throw it in with light-colored clothes, everything will come out the color of that garment.

The good news is, once you've discovered that a garment is not colorfast, you can then lock the color so that it won't run or fade. *To do this, keep reading...*

Make a Garment Colorfast

Fill a basin with 1 gallon of water and 1 teaspoon of Epsom salt (available at drugstores). Soak the non-colorfast garment in the basin overnight. The next day, wring out the garment, then thoroughly rinse it with a mixture of ¼ cup of distilled white vinegar mixed with 1 gallon of water. Let the garment dry.

Next, do the colorfast test again, rubbing the wet, white washcloth on an inside seam. When none of the color comes off, you can then consider the garment colorfast.

HARD WATER

Hard water is water that contains salts—such as calcium and magnesium—that limit the formation of lather with soap. If you have hard water, there may be an easy solution.

Does This Apply to You?

If your clothes don't seem to be getting clean, it may mean that you have hard water.

Test: Add ½ teaspoon of detergent to a 1-quart jar filled with warm water. Close the jar and shake it vigorously. If it doesn't get real sudsy—or if the suds that are there just disappear quickly—then, we hate to be the people who tell you, but you've got hard water.

Hard-Water Remedy

Did you think we were just going to leave it at that? *Of course not…*

Clean out a few empty, plastic detergent jugs…big enough to hold more than ½ gallon of water. In each jug, combine 4 ounces of washing soda (a natural detergent booster and freshener, available at supermarkets) with 2 ounces of borax powder (a chemical compound used as a cleansing agent and water softener, available at supermarkets and drugstores) and ½ gallon of warm water. The water must be *warm* for the washing soda and borax powder to completely dissolve.

CAUTION: The solution that's in the jugs should be labeled clearly and kept with your other clothes-washing supplies—out of reach of children and pets.

To soften the water, add 1 cup of the solution to the wash water, along with your regular laundry detergent—every time you do a wash. This *solution* is the solution!

DETERGENT

Powder…liquid…with bleach …for whites…for colors… for black clothes…with fabric softener…allergen-free—decisions, decisions, decisions. We may not help you decide exactly which product to use, but we will give you some hints for getting your clothes their cleanest.

Use the Right Stuff

For best results, adhere to the manufacturer's recommendation for the proper amount of detergent to use—based on the size of the wash load. Remember, when it comes to detergent… more is *not* better.

Avoid Overload

Oops! Did you spill in too much laundry detergent? Quick—add 2 tablespoons of distilled white vinegar…or a capful of fabric softener…or 3 tablespoons of table salt to the water. Any of these additives will deactivate the extra suds.

Get a Brightness Boost

In addition to your regular detergent, pour ½ cup of baking soda into the load. Clothes should come out smelling fresh and looking cleaner, since the baking soda helps get rid of soap residue.

Keep Children's Clothes Flame-Retardant

Children's clothing is required by law to be flame retardant. But be sure to use a phosphate detergent to launder children's clothing. The label should clearly state that the product contains phosphates. If you use a detergent with a label that says, "contains no phosphates," the fabric may lose its ability to be fire-resistant.

If you use a non-phosphate detergent, boost the flame-retardant property of the fabric by adding 1 cup of white vinegar to the cold rinse water. Let the clothes soak in it for 30 minutes before continuing as usual with the spin cycle.

Detergent Extender

If you must do a wash, but you don't have enough detergent, add ¼ cup of baking soda to make up the difference. You may be so pleased with the results, you'll start doing every wash this way!

Detergent Substitute

In an emergency, when you *must* do a wash and you don't have any laundry detergent (or baking soda), use shampoo…that is, if you have shampoo. About ⅓ cup will do a full load.

🖎 **NOTE:** In case you were wondering, dishwashing liquid is NOT a good idea as a laundry-detergent substitute.

The amount of liquid that is needed to launder clothes clean would create enough suds to float the Titanic.

Bleach Substitute

Instead of using harsh bleach, try one of these safer, gentler—and more effective—alternatives. Use ½ cup of lemon juice…or 1 cup of distilled white vinegar…or 6 ounces of hydrogen peroxide (make sure the label says 3% hydrogen peroxide) in your wash.

WASHING INSTRUCTIONS

As of July 1997, the Federal Trade Commission (FTC) allows apparel manufacturers to use symbols instead of written washing instructions on the care labels of garments. So the American Society for Testing and Materials (ASTM) developed a simple system…for details, visit the Web site of the Soap and Detergent Association, which publishes "Fabric Care Language Made Easy," a listing of the symbols and their meanings. The page is at *http://cleaning 101.com/laundry/fabricsymbols.html.*

And see the following for more helpful washing instructions…

Dry-Clean Only…or Not

In our experience, many clothes that are labeled "Dry-Clean Only" can actually be washed at home. If you're willing to take a chance with your silk nightgown, chiffon wraparound, cashmere vest, angora scarf or lace bustier, put a few drops of clear dishwashing liquid into a basin of cold water and add the garment.

Swish around the water so that the detergent can do its job. Then gently rinse the suds out, shake off the excess water and let the garment dry flat on a sweater-drying rack or on a clean white towel.

Permanent-Press Clothes

If your permanent-press clothes need an energy boost, pour in 1 cup of powdered milk during the rinse cycle. This should give the clothes more body and help bring them back to their original shape.

> ✎ **NOTE:** Rinsing with powdered milk helps to remove chemicals, so it can be helpful to people who have allergies. Double-rinsing is recommended.

Silk and Other Fine Washables

◆ You can wash washable silk with shampoo. But make sure its first ingredient is water, *not* oil. Silk is a delicate fabric that must be treated gently. Don't wring it out. Instead, let it drip-dry, and keep it out of direct sunlight.

◆ To clean your other fine washables, add 1 tablespoon of hair conditioner to a sink or basin full of water. After 10 minutes of soaking, gently rinse the garment and drip-dry.

> Think about it…the amino acids in hair conditioner make hair clean and soft, so they should make your delicate garments clean and soft as well.

Wool

Some interesting wool facts…

◆ Sheep are sheared (shaved) once a year for their soft woolen fleece.

◆ One pound of wool can be spun into 20 miles of yarn.

◆ A woolen sock was found buried on the banks of a river in England. The sock was perfectly preserved and estimated to be about 1,000 years old.

> Here are ways to take care of your woolens so that they'll last—well, maybe not 1,000 years, but for as long as you enjoy wearing them.

Resize Snug Sweaters

Shampoo and hair conditioner soften and loosen knit fibers, which allows them to return to their original size. If your wool sweaters have become too snug, shampoo can help bring them back to their original size.

Put a couple of capfuls of shampoo—or ⅓ cup of hair conditioner—in a sinkful of warm water. Add your tight sweater, and let it soak for about 10 minutes. Then lay it flat on a towel. While it's still wet, reshape it by holding each side and pulling the sweater, making it larger. Pull it even in this way—both sides at the same time—all around the sweater.

Shrink Stretched Sweaters

Don't you hate it when a turtleneck looks more like a hippo neck? When this happens, it's easy to shrink a sweater's stretched-out neck, cuffs and waist back into shape.

Dunk the sweater in a sink filled with hot water. Shake off as much water as possible, then blot the sweater with a clean, dry towel. Once the sweater is no longer dripping wet, dry the stretched-out part(s) with a blow-dryer set on *hot*.

> ⚠ **CAUTION:** Do *not* touch a wet sweater with a plugged-in dryer.

Remove and Prevent Pilling

◆ Turn the garment inside out when washing. Although there's no guarantee, doing this will go a long way in helping to prevent *pilling*—the formation of those unattractive balls of fabric on the surface, which is caused by abrasion from wear and washing.

◆ Put wool clothes in a pillowcase, tie the case closed with ribbon or string, and then wash.

◆ A wig brush—the kind with the little plastic balls at the end of the bristles—helps to depill wool clothes. Brush gently while constantly changing directions.

Soften Your Sweater

If a sweater is stiff or rough, wash it with your usual detergent plus 1 teaspoon of olive oil to soften the wool. Add the oil *after* the washer has filled with water.

Prevent Itchiness

If you are super-sensitive to wool, add 1 or 2 tablespoons of glycerine (available at drugstores) to a warm-water wash. Doing this should make the garment become less scratchy on your sensitive skin.

Avoid Moth Holes

If you suspect that moths have invaded your wool clothes, you can kill the eggs—just place the garment in a plastic bag, seal it closed and put it in the freezer for 24 hours. Then launder as usual.

Drying Sweaters

See "Speedy Sweater Drying" on page 113.

Whites

Whiter than white. That's what some laundry products—or their advertising agencies—promise. We don't know what it means, and we certainly aren't going to promise it, but we can tell you that the following ideas should work wonders to lighten and brighten your whites.

Hung Out to Dry

This suggestion may not be practical for most apartment dwellers, but for house owners—get out the clothesline. Hang your white clothing and linens outdoors to dry, and take advantage of the sun's bleaching power.

Cold Weather Clothesline

◆ To prevent wet clothes from freezing when hung outside to dry, pour ¼ cup of table salt into the last rinse cycle. (The salt will also help brighten your wash.)

◆ To prevent clothes from freezing onto the clothesline, sponge the clothesline with distilled white vinegar before you hang out the clothes to dry.

Lemony Fresh

In a basin of just-boiled water, add the juice of a small lemon. Let your white clothes soak for at least 30 minutes, then launder them as usual. For super-grungy sweat socks or other very soiled whites, let the clothes soak overnight before laundering.

An Aspirin a Day...

Dissolve 5 adult aspirin tablets (325 milligrams each) in a basin of hot water, and soak your white clothes in it. When you're ready to do the wash, pour the contents of the basin in the washing machine—the clothes along with the aspirin-water. The aspirin helps to remove perspiration stains.

Bright-White Maintenance

Add 1 cup of distilled white vinegar during the washer's rinse cycle to wash away soap residue, which is often the yellow-causing culprit.

Get Out the Yellow

Wash your clothes as usual until the last rinse cycle. Then dissolve 1 tablespoon of borax powder (available at supermarkets and drugstores) in 16 ounces of hot water, pour it in the machine and continue laundering as usual. This will remove any yellow dinginess in your clothes.

Boost for Whites

Fill a basin or sink with warm water and add ¼ cup of powdered, automatic dishwasher detergent. Add your socks, underwear or whatever else needs whitening. Swish them around, and let the garments soak for 1 hour.

Wring out the sopping clothes—enough to get them to the washing machine without making a mess—and then launder as usual.

Colors

People wear colored clothes for many reasons —because the colors enhance their skin tone and make them look good…cheery colors make them happier…or maybe the clothes don't show dirt as much. Whatever the reason, even if the dirt doesn't show, colored clothes need to be cleaned. *These hints will help…*

Set Bright Terry Cloth

The first time you wash those new towels, or that flashy bathrobe, pour in 1 cup of table salt along with your detergent, and it will set the color.

Perk Up Deep Colors

When colored fabrics start to fade, add 1 cup of table salt to the wash to help restore the color's original vibrancy.

Get Black Clothes Blacker

When doing an all-black wash, add 2 cups of strong, brewed black tea or coffee into the washer during the rinse cycle.

Jeans

Only a teenager, an immigrant tailor named Levi Strauss designed a pair of coveralls out of canvas. His target market for these coveralls was the miners in San Francisco during the 1850s. Those men were tired of their trousers wearing out and welcomed the change of clothes.

Some 10 years later, Strauss switched from canvas to a softer fabric—denim. To help decrease the appearance of soil stains, he dyed the denim dark blue. And, as they say, the rest is history.

Levis, dungarees or jeans…no matter what you call them, here's how to care for them.

Soften the Fabric

Soften jeans by tossing them in the washing machine with your usual detergent plus ½ cup of table or rock salt. You may need to double-rinse them.

Prevent Fading

Although the current trend is the more faded, the better, there are still some people who like a fresh, strong denim look. *Here's how to keep that look…*

Before you wash them for the first time, soak the jeans for 1 hour in a mixture of 2 tablespoons of table or rock salt and 1 gallon of cold water, or ½ cup of distilled white vinegar in 2 quarts of cold water.

After the soak, turn the jeans inside out and run them through the washing machine as usual, using a cold-water setting.

> **NOTE:** To prevent streaking and fading, always wash your jeans turned inside out.

Other Fabrics

Sheets and baby items—such as diapers, blankets and changing-table pads—all require special treatment because they come into contact with your delicate skin. *Here are some ways to make these items more comfortable and cleaner…*

Get Sweet-Smelling Sheets

To enjoy a special sensory treat at bedtime, add a small amount of your favorite bath salts during the rinse cycle when you launder your sheets.

Cleaner Baby Diapers

If you're using cloth diapers and the baby keeps getting diaper rash, separate the diapers from the rest of the laundry, and add 1 cup of distilled white vinegar during the rinse cycle.

In general, when washing any items the baby has soiled, it's smart to add 1 cup of distilled white vinegar during the rinse cycle. Vinegar is great at breaking down uric acid and puts the laundry's pH in balance. Your baby's clothes, sheets and blankies will all come out clean, soft and smelling good.

 It's Easy to Change

Use a pillowcase for a baby's changing-table pad cover—it's easy to put on and take off. When it gets dirty, you can easily throw it in the washing machine.

Plastics

Since 1976, plastic has been the most used material in the modern world. Plastics is a major industry, and plastic can be found in all or part of many products that are used in our daily lives…for example, clothing, televisions, cars, computers, packaging and even body-part replacements.

Here's how to care for the plastic products (excluding the body-part replacements) that we have come to depend on…

Tablecloths, Mats, Curtains

If a plastic item is machine-washable, add a couple of bath towels to the wash with it. The towels will help buff and scrub the plastic clean.

When drying plastic, put the towels in the dryer with it, and let the dryer run for only a few minutes so that the plastic item doesn't melt. It should come out practically wrinkle-free.

Floor or Bath Mats (Rubber and Vinyl)

Toss the mat in the washing machine along with a couple of bath towels. The towels will help scrub the rubber or vinyl mat.

Do not put rubber or vinyl in the dryer. Use another towel to wipe the mat dry or hang it on a clothesline.

Curtains (Dacron and Nylon)

After you launder as usual, soak the curtains—1 panel at a time—in a basin or sink filled with at least 1 cup of Epsom salt (available at drugstores) and 1 gallon of water (the ratio should be 1:1 for each gallon of water needed). Let each panel soak for about 5 minutes, and then hang them up. They should dry wrinkle-free.

NOTE: Be sure to put something on the floor underneath the wet curtains—such as a towel on top of a plastic shopping bag— in order to catch the dripping water.

DRYERS & DRYING

If you're still using an old clothes dryer, you may want to consider replacing it with a new model. Newer dryers have better insulation and use much less energy.

The newest clothes dryers on the market do not have the yellow Energy Guide label that helps you compare similar models, nor do they have the ENERGY STAR label (provided by the US Department of Energy and the Environmental Protection Agency)—this is simply because there's now very little difference in energy use from model to model.

Regardless of the age of your dryer, here are some ideas for how to make it perform at its very best…

 ### Cut Down on Drying Time

◆ The more crowded the dryer, the more wrinkled the clothes—and the longer it takes them to dry. Consider dividing a big wash load into two drying cycles.

◆ Cut drying time considerably by tossing in a dry hand towel with each dryer load. The dry towel will keep absorbing water from the wash, then dry quickly and continue to absorb more water.

Lint Catcher

Cut an old pair of pantyhose in half, and tie 1 side in a few knots. Then toss it in the dryer to collect lint.

Wash-and-Wear

Do your so-called "wash-and-wear" clothes need ironing? If they do—and you don't feel like getting out the iron and setting up the board—just throw the garments in the dryer with a damp towel, and let it run for about 10 minutes. Make that—wash-*and-dry*-and-wear!

Safer Dryers

A friend of ours, artist Bon Gordon, drew our attention to the fact that dryer sheets create a film over the dryer's lint-screen mesh. This film can cause the heating unit to burn out or—even worse than that—catch fire. You can't see the film, but it's there.

The dryer repairman told Bon the best way to keep a dryer working well for a long time—and to lower your electric bill—is to wash the lint filter with hot soapy water and an old toothbrush at least every 6 months.

Test your lint screen by running water over it. If the water runs through, then it's as clean as it needs to be. But if the water collects on it, prepare some hot soapy water and get a toothbrush…and then get busy cleaning the filter.

Drying Delicates

Give your hand-washed scanty undies a drying head-start by swirling them around in a salad spinner (you might want to designate a spinner just for this purpose). Once the excess moisture is removed, they'll dry a lot quicker when you hang them up.

Drying Wet Sweaters

If you don't use a drying rack for your wet sweaters, then consider the ol' pantyhose trick to avoid shoulder *pupkees*. (That's our family's word for those stretched-out, epaulet-type of shoulder bumps that result from hanging wet—and sometimes dry—sweaters on hangers.)

Take a pair of clean pantyhose and thread the legs through each arm of the sweater—1 leg in 1 arm, and the other leg in the other arm.

Bring the waist of the pantyhose up through the sweater's neck.

If you use a clothesline, attach clothespins to the waist and each of the 2 feet. If you want to use a hanger or a hook, tie the 2 pantyhose feet together, forming a loop, and then put it on the hanger or hook. This method puts no stress on the shoulders.

Speedy Sweater Drying

After you hang up your sweater to dry—or before you spread it out to dry—cut a brown paper bag down the seams, crinkle it and stuff it into the sweater. The paper stuffing will speed up the drying process.

Revive Stored Woolens

When you take sweaters and other wool clothing out of storage, throw them in the dryer with a couple of fabric-softener sheets. Dry on low heat for 30 minutes. The sheets absorb odors and the dryer action fluffs up fibers. The wool items will come out looking and smelling good.

Try to Be Static-Free

Crinkle up a piece of aluminum foil, and toss it in the dryer with your clothes. It will help eliminate static cling.

> ⚡ **CAUTION:** Do not include sheer fabrics, silks or delicates that can get snagged on the aluminum foil.

Down-Filled Drying

◆ After washing a down-filled item—such as a coat or comforter—put it in the dryer along with 3 or 4 tennis balls. The balls will do a good job of fluffing up the down item. (They will also do a good job of waking up anyone who is taking a nap.)

◆ You can also put new life into an old, flattened-out feather or down pillow by letting it toss and turn for 10 minutes in a warm dryer with 3 or 4 tennis balls and a fabric-softener dryer sheet.

Unwrinkle Your Sheets

When you take a bedsheet out of the washing machine, shake it out a bit, then fold it before you put it in the dryer. The folded sheet will dry faster and come out less wrinkled.

Slipcovers

◆ After you've washed a slipcover and tossed it in the dryer, do not wait for it to finish the drying cycle. Instead, remove the slipcover while it's slightly damp. Put it back on the furniture, and let the material finish drying as it conforms perfectly to whatever it's covering. Use a hairdryer set on low heat to dry any lingering wet spots.

Be sure that people and pets keep off the just-washed-and-still-drying slipcovers.

◆ Once you've washed and dried a cushion's slipcover, it's usually difficult to put it back on the foam cushion...especially if the cover has shrunk a little. To remedy this problem, put the foam cushion in a dry cleaner's plastic bag, cut off the excess plastic, then slip the cover on the plastic-covered cushion.

This makes all the difference in getting it on. And if someone accidently spills something on the cushion, the spill won't go through to the pillow.

FABRIC SOFTENER & STARCH

Many fabric softener sheets have chemicals that eliminate static cling in the dryer, help soften clothes and make them somewhat wrinkle resistant, and produce a fragrance that makes clothes smell fresh. The down side is that the chemicals used in the production of the sheets may cause allergic reactions in people who are sensitive to them.

But don't fret! There are all-natural (chemical-free), nontoxic dryer sheets available. They cost about $20 and are reusable for about 500 loads of wash (which means that by using them, you can save money in the long run). One company that sells them is Nirvana Safe Haven, based in Walnut Creek, California (800-968-9355 or *www.nontoxic.com*).

Another company that produces excellent hypoallergenic, reusable fabric softener sheets (which also work wonders at removing pet fur from laundry) is Gaiam…877-989-6321, *www.gaiam.com*. Just type "static eliminator" in the product search box for more information.

However, if you do use regular, commercially produced fabric softeners, here are some helpful hints…

Suffering Sneezes?

An allergic reaction—possibly even an asthma attack—can be caused by fabric softeners when they are used on bedding and clothing.

If you (or someone for whom you do the laundry) are sensitive in this way, you may want to skip the softener.

⑤ Save on Softener!

◆ Buy liquid softener instead of expensive fabric-softener sheets. Dilute the liquid with water and pour 2 capfuls of the mixture on a clean washcloth, then toss it into the dryer with your wash load.

◆ If you don't want to use liquid softener, hair conditioner will also work—just use the same directions as above.

Less Cents and Less Scents

During the last rinse cycle, add ¼ cup of distilled white vinegar. It's a good and inexpensive fabric softener, and it will make your colored washables more vivid. It will also help eliminate bacteria, mold and fungus.

The wash will not smell like vinegar…but it won't have a nice, fresh-air fabric-softener smell, either.

★ Smart Hint for Towels

Do not use fabric softener when washing your kitchen towels—they will be more absorbent and your plates don't care if they feel rough.

Starch

Starch is a complex carbohydrate that is mostly found in corn, potatoes, wheat and rice. For laundry use, starch is commonly prepared as a white, tasteless powder (but don't ever ingest laundry starch!). It is used to help clothes (especially shirt collars) retain their stiffness and shape.

If you run out of store-bought starch, you can make your own…

Make a Super Spray Starch

To prepare a super spray starch, you'll need a bowl, cornstarch, cold water and a 16-ounce fine-mist spray bottle.

For a light starch, combine 1 tablespoon of cornstarch with 2 cups of cold water in the bowl. For a heavier starch, use 3 tablespoons of cornstarch in the same amount of cold water. Mix well—making sure that the cornstarch is completely dissolved—then transfer the mixture from the bowl to the spray bottle.

To use the starch, shake the bottle, then spray the garment and iron immediately.

SMELLS

According to the Sense of Smell Institute in New York City (*www.senseofsmell.org*), the average human being is able to recognize approximately 10,000 different odors—and tell where the odor is coming from because a nose can smell directionally. This is all the more reason to keep your clothes smelling clean and fresh. *Here are some tips for common scents…*

Steam Out Cigarette Smoke

If you've spent time in a smoke-filled room, chances are your clothes will reek from it. To get rid of the odor, fill a bathtub with steamy hot water and add 1 cup of distilled white vinegar. Carefully hang the smoky garment so that the steam envelops it.

Use a padded hanger so that the garment doesn't get *pupkees* (those unwanted epaulet-type shoulder bumps—*see* "Drying Wet Sweaters" on pages 112–113). If you don't have a padded hanger, you can pin shoulderpads around the ends of a hanger to avoid getting the pupkees.

Booze for Cigarettes

Fill a plastic spray bottle with 1 ounce of vodka and 3 ounces of water. Mist-spray the smoky garment and hang it up to dry. The booze mixture should help to neutralize the cigarette-smoke smell. But you may still smell like a saloon.

Just Like New…

If you have a new washable garment that has an unpleasant chemical finish or dye smell, add ½ cup baking soda to 1 gallon of water in a sink or basin, and presoak the clothing for at least 2 hours.

After soaking, toss the clothing into the washing machine and wash as usual. During the rinse cycle, add ½ cup of distilled white vinegar.

> **NOTE:** This de-smelling process will also work if you (and your clothes) have been sprayed by a skunk.

Hinder Hamper Smells

Cut off the foot part of a pair of clean pantyhose and fill it with baking soda or kitty litter. Tie the open end closed and keep the soda- or litter-filled foot in your hamper. It will absorb moisture and help prevent stinky mildew from building up. Refresh the baking soda or kitty litter every month.

* Hamper Freshener

In addition to—or instead of—the baking soda in a stocking, sprinkle a little baking soda on clothes that you put in the hamper each day. The hamper won't smell, and when you do wash the clothes, the baking soda will make them softer and smell fresher.

Scentsational Gym Bag

Place a fabric softener sheet in the bottom of a gym bag. This will help mask the smell of sweaty clothes and sneakers—and you'll know when it's time to put in a new softener sheet.

Managing Mothballs

If you store clothes in mothballs, let them air out for several hours when you first take them out. Then toss the clothes in a warm dryer for about 15 minutes. You may want to add a fabric-softener sheet, but check the information on the softener box to make sure the softener won't stain the clothes.

Tablecloths, Mats, Curtains (Plastic)

If a plastic item doesn't lose that yucky plastic smell soon after being unwrapped and out in the open, then help it along by soaking it in a sink with ½ cup of baking soda.

    If the item also needs softening, add ½ cup of distilled white vinegar to the baking-soda water. Let it soak for 3 to 4 hours, then rinse and air-dry.

CLEANING NON-CLOTHING ITEMS

If it's time for spring cleaning or you're expecting your in-laws for a visit, there are many things that perhaps you didn't think need cleaning… but they do. *Try these suggestions…*

Artificial and Dried Flowers

- Dust delicate blossoms with a hair dryer set on the lowest heat.
- If a hair dryer set on the lowest heat is too strong for fragile dried flowers, you can use an empty turkey baster, spray bottle or atomizer to gently blow away the dust.
- Wash plastic flowers in warm water with a mild detergent, then dry them thoroughly.

Once they're clean, help them stay that way by putting 1 or 2 coats of clear nail polish on the flowers.

Shake Yer Stems

If you want to clean sturdy fabric flowers, take a plastic or paper bag (big enough to hold the flowers), and pour in 1 cup of table salt. Hold the flowers by the stems and put the blossoms into the bag. Hold the neck of the bag closed around the stems, then *shake, shake, shake*, giving the salt a chance to clean the flowers.

    When you take the flowers out of the bag, do it over the sink (or outside) and shake out all the salt that stayed on the flowers. The flowers should be clean and their colors fresh and bright.

Children's Toys

If a stuffed toy isn't machine washable, you can "dry-clean" it by placing it in a plastic bag and sprinkling in some baking soda or cornstarch. Shake the bag enough to evenly distribute the powder. Then seal the bag, and let it stay that way overnight. The next day, open the bag over the sink, shaking out most of the powder. Brush or vacuum off the remainder.

Removing Dust Mites

Those wonderful stuffed toys—which take up more room in the bed than the baby—are a breeding ground for dust mites. They can trigger allergic reactions, including asthma attacks.

    Get rid of dust mites by placing the stuffed toy in a plastic bag and putting the bag in the freezer for 24 hours. Do this once a week with a child's most played-with stuffed toys, and there may be a noticeable difference in the child's health and well-being.

Cleaning Vinyl Toys

Use a damp sponge and some baking soda to wipe vinyl clean. Then rinse and dry.

Cleaning Hard Plastic Toys

Combine 1 tablespoon of liquid dish detergent with ¼ cup of baking soda to form a paste. Put the paste on a toothbrush and brush away the dirt. Use a clean, moist sponge to wipe the plastic clean. This works especially well on dolls with plastic faces.

STAINS A TO Z

STOP! PLEASE READ THIS BEFORE CONTINUING TO LOOK FOR A STAIN SOLUTION.

The stain removers described in this section are effective. That is, they've worked for the people who have passed them along to us.

Not knowing the extent of the stain and the quality of the fabric in question, we strongly recommend that—before trying any of these suggested stain removers—you test it on an inconspicuous area of your garment to prevent making a messy spot worse.

Thank you—now please continue…

The Simple Solution For UFOs

Before we get to specific kinds of stains, here's a basic formula for what we refer to as "UFOs"—"Unidentified Filthy Oooooh…where did I get this spot?"

Invest in a new spray bottle, so that you can prepare this mixture and always have it on hand when you discover a UFO.

Combine 1 cup of filtered, spring or distilled water with 1 cup of rubbing alcohol and 2 teaspoons of liquid dish detergent (the stuff that breaks down the oil on dirty dishes) and you're good to go. Spray a bit to pretreat or spot-clean a UFO. Whatever you do, go ahead and launder the garment as usual.

> **NOTE:** The UFO solution can be used on many different stains. But, when in doubt, try it first on a small, inconspicuous area of the stained garment.

- The packaging on denture cleansers promises to dissolve tough stains. True, they don't necessarily mean food stains on clothing, but we've tried it and it worked 2 out of 3 times. If you like those odds and you have a stained garment, it's worth a shot!

  Get a clean container (we used an empty, plastic shoebox), fill it with warm water and drop in 2 or 3 denture tablets. Leave the garment soaking for about 15 minutes—the same amount of time recommended for soaking dentures. When the time is up, launder the clothing as usual.

- If you find an unidentified stain on your furniture's upholstery, sponge it with distilled white vinegar and let it set for 15 minutes. Then wash the area, following the manufacturer's instructions.

> **CAUTION:** Check the upholstery's label for cleaning instructions (and do a spot test) *before* trying this suggestion!

⭐ Cold Water Rules
Do not use hot or even warm water to get rid of a stain…not unless you want to set the stain permanently. Cold water will go a long way to prevent the stain from staying there forever.

Baby Formula/Milk

◆ Do not reach for the bleach to treat a baby-formula stain—it will set it. Instead, for colored clothes, use unseasoned meat tenderizer. It has an enzyme that breaks down the protein in baby formula and milk.

◆ After rinsing the garment in cold water, rub it in the tenderizer, completely covering the stain. Let it stand for 1 hour and then wash as usual.

◆ For whites, saturate the formula/milk spot with lemon juice, and leave it in the sun for 30 minutes, then wash as usual.

Ballpoint Pen

See "Ink" on page 121.

Barbecue Sauce

See "Tomato Sauce, Ketchup, Chili or Barbecue Sauce" on pages 124–125.

Beer

Wash out beer suds in warm soapsuds.

Blood

◆ If it's a small stain, and it's your blood, spit on it. The enzymes in your saliva should dissolve the stain.

◆ Do not use hot water on a bloodstain. It will set the stain. Instead, put the bloodied fabric in cold salted water—use 2 tablespoons of table salt for each cup of water. Strong salt-water breaks down the proteins that bind blood to fabric fibers.

◆ Let cold water run over the bloodied fabric. Then make a paste with unseasoned meat tenderizer and cold water, and put it on the stain. Let it sit and, after about 30 minutes, rinse off the tenderizer and wash the garment as usual.

◆ Try using 3% hydrogen peroxide to fizz away the stain. (Don't forget to test the fabric first.) Pour it on the blood, then rinse and wash the garment as usual.

◆ For a bloodstain on upholstery, cover the stain with a paste of cornstarch and water. Let it dry, then brush or vacuum it clean. If the stain is lighter but still there, repeat the procedure a second time.

> ⚠ **CAUTION:** Check the upholstery's label for cleaning instructions (and do a spot test) *before* trying this suggestion!

Candle Wax

See "Chewing Gum" on this page.

Canvas

If you want to clean canvas, sailcloth or some other heavy material, use a gum eraser (available at office- and art-supply stores). It may not make the fabric spotless, but it should be better than it was.

Chewing Gum

◆ Put a few ice cubes in a resealable, plastic produce bag, and place it on top of the gum stuck to your garment. Leave the ice-bag in place for 15 minutes. Or, place the gummy garment in a plastic bag and stick it in your freezer for 1 hour.

Gum shrinks and hardens when it gets cold, making it easy to peel away from fabric.

◆ Using a toothbrush and the white of 1 egg, scrub the section of fabric that has chewing gum stuck to it. After you remove as much of the gum as possible, let it stand for 30 minutes. Then flick off the rest of the bits of gum and launder as usual.

◆ Place a piece of waxed paper over the sticky spot (waxy side down), and go over it with a warm iron. The gum should adhere to the waxed paper and you should be able to peel it right off.

◆ Dip any gummy or sticky fabric in lemon juice and keep it there for about 5 minutes. Then rinse with warm water as you scrape off the stickiness.

Chili

See "Tomato Sauce, Ketchup, Chili or Barbecue Sauce" on pages 124–125.

Chocolate

Make a paste with borax powder (available at supermarkets and drugstores) and water—you can also use meat tenderizer and water—and rub it into the stain. Let it stay that way for 1 hour, then brush it off and launder as usual.

Cigars and Cigarettes

See "Tobacco" on page 124.

Coffee or Tea

◆ If you promise to be *very* careful, then consider this remedy for taking a coffee or tea splotch out of white fabrics.

Stretch the stained area over an empty bowl or pot, and keep it in place using a rubber band. Then put the bowl or pot in the bathtub (it's safer than the sink). Boil a full kettle of water.

From a height of about 2 feet—here's where you have to be careful!—pour the boiling-hot water through the stained fabric into the bowl. Then launder as usual.

◆ If you have a coffee or tea stain on colored fabric, soak the area in distilled white vinegar. Then launder as usual.

◆ For stains on white cotton, linen or lace—first dampen the stained area with warm water. Spread out the garment in a sink or basin. Drop 2 denture-cleaning tablets in ½ cup of warm water. Pour the fizzing liquid on the stain, and let it stay that way for 30 minutes. Then launder as usual. **Remember, this is for *white* fabric only.**

◆ When dining out, don't just let the stain sit there because you're embarrassed. In fact, you will gain everyone's respect when you show them that you know exactly what to do. And this is what to do—moisten a clean napkin with seltzer or club soda and gently wipe the stained fabric.

◆ If seltzer doesn't do the trick, rub table salt on the spill, and let it stay that way for 15 minutes. Then wipe it off. Needless to say, launder the garment as soon as you get home.

If the stain remains and the garment requires a trip to the dry cleaner's, send the bill to the klutz who caused the spill.

Cola

Pour distilled white vinegar on the spot, then launder as usual. The secret to getting out a cola stain completely is to put vinegar on it as soon as possible...within hours (not days) after saying, "Oops! I spilled cola on my shirt."

Crayons

◆ Rub a few drops of liquid dishwashing detergent into the crayon marks, and then launder the clothing as usual.

◆ Lay the cloth stain-side up on a stack (8 to 12 sheets) of paper towel. Spray the stained area with WD-40 lubricant, and let it set for 3 to 5 minutes. Turn the cloth over and spray the other side, letting it set for another 3 to 5 minutes. Then launder as usual.

Deodorant Stick

If you accidentally get a bit of deodorant on a dark-colored shirt, use a clean pair of pantyhose to wipe it off. Those nylon fibers work like some kind of magic eraser.

Fruit, Berries and Fruit Juice

◆ If you spill grape juice on your shirt or drop a blueberry on your pants (at home or at a restaurant), first gently wipe the stain with cold water. Then, as soon as possible, prepare a kettle of boiling water. Stretch the stained area over an empty bowl or pot, and keep it in place with a rubber band.

   Then put the bowl or pot in the bathtub (it's safer than the sink). From a height of about 2 feet, pour the boiling-hot water through the stained fabric into the bowl. Then launder as usual.

◆ If you can act quickly, soak the stained area in distilled white vinegar, and then launder the garment as usual.

◆ If you get a fruit stain on a tablecloth or linen napkins, douse the spot with powdered laundry starch, and let it stay on for 3 to 4 hours. Then launder as usual.

Glue

If glue gets on your clothes in the middle of an arts-and-crafts project, this is one time you may want to come unglued.

   Simply place your shirt, smock or apron in a sink or basin filled with water, and add 4 tablespoons of distilled white vinegar. Let the garment soak for 1 to 2 hours...until the glue dissolves, and then launder as usual.

Grass

◆ If the stain just occurred, and you can get home quickly, squeeze out a portion of white, non-gel, non-whitening toothpaste and apply it to the stain. Work the toothpaste into the fabric until the grass stain is gone, and then launder the clothing as usual.

◆ You can also soak the stained area in distilled white vinegar, and then launder as usual.

◆ If the grass stain is old and set, cover it with rubbing alcohol and let it soak for 10 to 15 minutes. Rinse out the alcohol with warm water, and launder the clothing as usual.

Gravy

◆ For a major mess, sop up as much of the gravy as possible with napkins or towels. Then cover the stain with cornstarch...or flour...or baking soda...or table salt...or artificial sweetener. Once dinner is over and your company leaves, brush off whatever you put on the stain, and rub laundry detergent into the stain. Launder as usual.

◆ For a minor gravy stain, dissolve the gravy's starch by soaking the stain in cold water for 30 minutes. Then launder the clothing as usual.

Grease

◆ Absorb the grease by rubbing cornstarch, talcum powder or chalk into the stain. Let it stay that way for 15 minutes, then whisk off the powder. If the stain is gone, great. If it's still there but smaller than it was, repeat the process. If there's no change, then try the next remedy.

◆ Soak the grease stain in cola for 15 minutes. It should help loosen the grease. Then launder the garment as usual.

◆ Attention all you mechanics—if you're doing a greasy-clothes wash, pour a 1-liter bottle of cola in the washing machine along with the laundry detergent.

◆ Dish detergent cuts the grease on pots and pans, and it will do the same thing on fabric. Pour a little on the greasy spot, then launder the garment as usual.

◆ If you get a grease spot on your new couch, rub table salt on the stained upholstery as soon as possible. Give the salt at least 30 minutes to absorb the grease, then brush or vacuum the salt away.

> ⊘ **CAUTION:** Check the upholstery's label for cleaning instructions (and do a spot test) before trying this suggestion!

Gum

See "Chewing Gum" on pages 118–119.

Ink

◆ If you get an ink spot on colored fabric, soak the stained area in milk, or sponge it out with milk.

◆ You can also douse an ink stain on colored clothes with rubbing alcohol. Let it stay that way for 5 minutes, then launder as usual.

◆ For ink stains on white clothing, combine 2 tablespoons of lemon juice with 1 teaspoon of table salt. Rub the mixture into the stained area, and then let it dry in the sun.

◆ If you get purple ballpoint pen on your white shirt, apply a dollop of foam shaving cream, and let it sit for a few minutes. Dab it off with a clean cloth, and the mark should be gone.

◆ For all fabrics, spray a 2-second spritz of hairspray on the ink mark, then launder the clothing as usual.

◆ Wet a cloth with vodka and rub the ink stain. It should make the permanent marker a temporary marker.

Ink Remover—The Formula

If our simple solutions do not effectively take out an ink stain, you may want to try the following formula...

In a bowl, combine 1 tablespoon of milk, 1 tablespoon of white vinegar, 1 teaspoon of lemon juice and 1 teaspoon of borax powder (available at supermarkets and drugstores) in a bowl. Put the stained area of the garment between 3 or 4 thick sheets of paper towel.

Dip a sponge in the mixture and pat it on the towel that's covering the stain. (You want the liquid to reach the fabric, but you don't want to put it directly on the stain.) After about 3 minutes, try sponging the stained area with cool water. Repeat the entire procedure until the stain is completely gone. When it is, launder the garment as usual.

Ketchup

See "Tomato Sauce, Ketchup, Chili or Barbecue Sauce" on pages 124–125.

Kitchen Curtains

To prevent stains from splatter and dust, starch your kitchen curtains before you hang them.

For simple spray-on starch instructions, *see* "Make a Super Spray Starch" on pages 114–115, or buy a box of starch in the supermarket and follow the package directions.

Lipstick

◆ Use a slice of white bread to blot off as much lipstick as possible, then launder the clothing as usual.

◆ Wet the lipstick-stained clothing with water, then rub on a little bit of dishwashing liquid. Thoroughly rinse the garment, and launder as usual.

◆ Brush white, non-gel, non-whitening toothpaste on the lipsticky clothing, and launder as usual.

◆ For lipstick marks on a cloth napkin, put several layers of paper towel under the stained area. Wet a clean cloth with rubbing alcohol and press down on the stain. Do that a few times to blot up as much of the lipstick as possible. Then launder the napkin as usual.

Makeup (Foundation)

◆ If there's a little smudge of makeup on your clothing, you may be able to make it disappear by rubbing the mark with a balled-up slice of white bread or stale rye bread.

◆ For a major makeup smear, cover the stain with baking soda. Then brush the area with a wet toothbrush. Keep adding baking soda and wet-brushing until the stain is gone.

Mildew

Put buttermilk in a basin and soak the mildewed fabric in it overnight. The next day, you can launder the garment as usual.

Milk

Meat tenderizer is effective on most fresh protein-based stains. Pour meat tenderizer on the wet milk stain. Let it stay that way for 1 hour,

then brush off the residue and launder the clothing as usual.

Mud

Rub the mud-stained fabric with a slice of raw potato. Soak the garment in cool water for 15 minutes, then wash as usual.

Oil

◆ Drip a few drops of shampoo-for-oily-hair on the stained fabric. Let it set for 15 minutes and then launder as usual. Shampoo for *oily* hair…think about it.

◆ You can absorb a fresh oil spill with baby powder. Cover the soiled spot with a few shakes of powder. Let it set for a few minutes, then brush it off and wash the garment in warm water.

◆ If you get an oil spill on leather, clean it by covering the spot with cornstarch. Let it stay that way overnight. The next day, wipe the area clean with a dry cloth.

Perspiration

◆ For stains on cotton or polyester clothing, add 1 cup of white vinegar to a sink or basin filled with warm water. Soak the garment for about 1 hour, then launder as usual.

◆ For sweat stains on wool, mix ¼ cup of salt with 1 quart of cold water. Soak the garment in the mixture for about 30 minutes, and then launder as usual.

◆ If the wool still has a perspiration smell, mix 1 cup of water with 1 teaspoon of distilled white vinegar and gently sponge it on the sweaty areas. Let it stay that way for 1 hour, and then launder as usual.

Pillowcases

To help prevent stains caused by hair oil and face cream, lightly starch pillow cases.

For simple spray-on starch instructions, *see* "Make a Super Spray Starch" on pages 114–115, or buy a box of starch in the supermarket and follow the package directions.

Plastic Tablecloth

See "Vinyl or Plastic Tablecloth" on page 125.

Red Wine

As soon as possible once a spill happens, cover it with table salt or artificial sweetener. Then after dinner—or at least within 24 hours of the spill—brush off the salt or sweetener, and rub the clothing under cold water.

If the fabric is cotton, a cotton blend or permanent press, dab some distilled white vinegar on the fading stain, and launder as usual.

Ring Around the Collar

◆ First, check the ingredients in your shampoo. If the first ingredient is *water* rather than *oil*—that's good. Then look for *ammonium lauryl sulfate* in the list of ingredients. That's the ingredient that will help break down an oil stain.

Once you know that you have the right shampoo in hand, rub a few drops of it on the ring-around-the-collar (RATC) stain. Or you may want to brush it on with an old, clean toothbrush. Let the shampoo set for about 30 minutes, then wash the shirt thoroughly in warm water.

◆ If you don't have the right shampoo (to make the RATC solution), make a paste of baking soda mixed with distilled white vinegar. Massage the paste into the collar ring, then launder the shirt as usual.

◆ To prevent ring-around-the-collar on a clean, white shirt or blouse, sprinkle baby powder on the inside collar before you iron. The powder prevents the shirt from absorbing the wearer's body oil.

◆ In addition, you can use rubbing alcohol or witch hazel to clean off any oil or dirt from your neck before you put on clean, white, collared clothing.

Rust

◆ To remove rust stains from most colored and non-delicate fabrics, make a paste using equal amounts of table salt and cream of tartar (available in supermarkets) mixed with hot water.

Work the paste into the stain and let it sit for 15 minutes. Then launder as usual. For delicate fabrics—such as silk, satin, lace or organdy—proceed with caution...test the paste on an inside seam to be sure.

◆ On white clothing, douse the rust spot with lemon juice and leave it in the sun for a couple of hours. Then launder as usual.

> **ⓒ FYI: How Clothing "Rusts"**
> If you're wondering why rust stains pop up on clothing, it may be because you hung a garment on a metal hanger, and the garment or the hanger was wet.
>
> Or, if you have hard water in your house and use bleach, the bleach's chlorine can leach iron out of the water, which contributes rust stains. Rusty pipes could also be at the root of the problem.

Scorches

The following remedies should work for all colors and most fabrics.

For delicate fabrics—such as silk, satin, lace or organdy—proceed with caution. Test the solution by first testing an inside seam with the ingredient you plan to use…just to make sure it doesn't worsen the problem.

♦ If you scorch the garment you're ironing, rub the scorched spot with an ice cube as quickly as possible. Most of the time, the scorch will disappear.

♦ Moisten a clean white cloth with distilled white vinegar and place it on top of the scorched area. Then cautiously iron it using a warm iron. Keep checking to make sure the scorch is disappearing, not getting worse.

♦ Take a piece of yellow onion and rub it on the scorched area. Make sure the onion juice soaks into the fabric. Let it stay that way for a couple of hours, then launder as usual.

♦ Mix equal parts of 3% hydrogen peroxide and water. Sponge it on the scorch and let it set for about 30 minutes. Then launder as usual.

Shower Curtain Liner

Put the shower curtain liner in the washing machine, along with 2 or 3 bathroom towels and start it going on *warm*. Then add ½ cup laundry detergent and ½ cup baking soda, and let the machine run its course.

The towels act as scrub brushes, removing soap scum and mildew from the liner. During the final rinse, add 1 cup of distilled white vinegar. When you take the clean-as-new liner out of the washer, hang it in the shower to dry and toss the towels in the dryer.

Suntan Oil or Lotion

Knead a little liquid laundry detergent into the stained area of clothing, then let cold water run forcefully through it.

Tea

See "Coffee or Tea" on page 119.

Tie Stains

If you are one of those men who is always staining his tie, you should consider making your ties stain-resistant. To do this, simply spray your neckwear with an upholstery guard (available at most hardware stores and some supermarkets).

Tobacco

Add ¼ cup baking soda to the wash along with your laundry detergent. It should help get out cigar and cigarette stains (not burns), and it will also take out any lingering smell.

See "Smells" on page 115 for more suggestions on getting rid of a tobacco smell.

Tomato Sauce, Ketchup, Chili or Barbecue Sauce

♦ Quick—get the shaving cream! Squirt a blob of plain, foam shaving cream on the saucy stain. Then wet a sponge with warm water and work the cream into it. Let the garment dry, and then launder as usual. The shaving cream's deionized water and alcohol should help dissolve a tomato sauce–based stain.

◆ Dip the stained area in cold water and then rub it with glycerine. Let it stay that way for 30 minutes, then wash it in warm water. If you can still see the stain from what you had for lunch, sponge it with 3% hydrogen peroxide, then rinse in cold water.

Urine

Babies and puppies are prone to pee-pee accidents on clothes, sheets, rugs, etc. This type of stain calls for soda water. Wipe the area with a sponge that's been dipped in soda water, then launder as usual.

If the urine is on a mattress or mattress cover, moisten the spot…this time with plain water. Work in enough borax powder (available at supermarkets and drugstores) to cover the stain, let it dry, then vacuum or brush it clean. You can launder the mattress cover as usual.

Vomit

This is possibly another form of "the hair of the dog that bit you"…sponge vodka on the stain, scrub it with a brush, and then launder as usual. This remedy can be used for bedding and removable slip covers or upholstery, as well as for clothing.

Vinyl or Plastic Tablecloth

Make a paste from 1 teaspoon of cream of tartar and ¼ teaspoon of lemon juice, and rub the stain with it. Let it stay that way for 15 minutes, then brush off the dried paste and rinse the tablecloth clean.

IRONING

At the end of the 1800s, women would iron their family's clothes using heavy irons that were heated near an open fire or on the stove. As you can imagine, the handles became red-hot and hands were burned. So…back to the drawing board.

Next came wooden handles and brass hotboxes that were fueled by charcoal and placed in the body of the iron, then lit. OK, so they sometimes caught on fire or simply exploded. Gas irons were the new-and-improved models to replace them. Talk about dangerous…! And this went on well into the 20th century.

We're telling you all this so that you'll appreciate the sleek and SAFE irons of today and will regard ironing as a pleasant chore…a task that might be made a bit easier and more efficient with the following hints.

Prepping Your Clothes

Dampen your clothes with warm water—rather than cold—which will help to make ironing faster and more efficient.

★ **Frozen and Fresh-Pressed**

If you have already dampened your clothes but have to put off ironing them, put them in a plastic bag and place the bag in the freezer.

Doing this prevents mildew, and when you are ready to iron, you won't have to redampen them. You may have to thaw them out a bit, but otherwise they're good to go.

Supercharge Your Iron

Place one sheet of aluminum foil—uncoated, shiny side up—between the ironing board and the fabric ironing-board cover. As a result of the foil reflecting the heat from the iron, the ironing gets done faster and better.

All the Right Moves

Go with the grain of the fabric, using a back-and-forth motion to iron. A circular motion may stretch the fabric.

Keep the iron in constant motion without rushing. After completing a section of the garment, lift the iron and wait about 10 seconds… enough time to let the press set.

CAUTION: Do not iron stained clothes. The heat from the iron can set the stain permanently.

Shine Prevention

Dark cottons, linens, rayons and silks should all be ironed inside out. Cover delicate fabrics with a sheet of tissue paper and use a cool iron.

Velvet and Velveteen

Do not iron directly on velvet or velveteen. Instead, use a pressing cloth (available at most supermarkets and hardware stores). Wet the pressing cloth, place it on the velvet and start ironing. Expect to hear a sizzling sound.

NOTE: For a pressing-cloth substitute in a pinch…cut a panel out of a brown, paper grocery bag, moisten it and use it as you would the pressing cloth.

Ironing Sleeves

Slide a small rolled-up towel into the sleeve, and you may be able to iron it without creating a terrible-looking sleeve crease.

 Use a Broom to Sweep Up

To avoid sweeping the floor with clean clothes that you're ironing, use spring-type clothespins to shorten the hanging-down factor of shirt or blouse sleeves, full-skirt hems, tablecloths and scarf ends.

Pucker Prevention

Iron your cuffs, collars and hemlines on the underside first, gently pulling and stretching the fabric away from the iron.

Unsticking the Iron

If the underside of your iron is sticky, wait until it's cool (very important!), then put some baby powder on a cloth and coat the iron's bottom. Once it's coated with powder, turn on the heat and watch the powder disappear.

At this point, the iron should no longer be sticky. It should glide over silks and other delicate, catchy, clingy fabrics. To be sure, test the iron on an inconspicuous part of any delicate garment that needs to be pressed.

Scorch Prevention

If you don't want to risk scorching a special, potentially scorchable garment, carefully iron the item between 2 pieces of aluminum foil.

Pleats

You can use spring-type clothespins, bobby pins or the old hair-setting clips to hold pleats in place at the waist and/or hemline. Once you have ironed most of the pleats, just remove the

STEAM-IRON CARE

Cleaning the Water Tank

If you use a good ol' steam iron, you may need to clean out the built-up mineral deposits, which can create stains on clothes.

Mix ½ cup of distilled white vinegar with ½ cup of water (use distilled water if possible) and fill your iron with it. Let the iron steam until all of the liquid is gone. Once it cools down, rinse the iron's tank with water, and refill it with water. This time, shake the water through the steam holes. Before using the steam iron on wearable clothes, test it on an old cloth.

> ⚠ **CAUTION:** Do not put your face or your hands in the path of the escaping steam.

Cleaning the Holes

When the steam iron is cold and unplugged, dip a small, fuzzy pipe cleaner in distilled white vinegar to clean its holes.

Mineral Deposit Prevention

◆ Here's a really easy way to prevent mineral deposits from forming—before ironing, put distilled water in the iron's water tank.

◆ If you do not use distilled water, then each time you finish ironing, while the iron is still warm, empty the water tank. Any remaining moisture will evaporate, thanks to the iron's heat. And, as long as there's no water left in the tank, there will be no mineral deposits —and no damaging spots on clothes.

Clean Off Starch

To clean starch off the bottom of an iron, heat the iron and then run it over a piece of aluminum foil several times.

Filling a Steam Iron

Prevent water spills by using a turkey baster to fill the steam iron's water tank.

holders and complete the job by ironing the waist/hemline.

Create a Permanent Crease

Put distilled white vinegar in a spray bottle. Lay out the pant leg on the ironing board, arranging the crease exactly where you want it. Spray the crease with the vinegar, then iron it. Let it set for several seconds and do the other side, then the other leg.

Buttons

Always iron *around* buttons, never *over* them. Otherwise, they may melt...they may break... they may discolor.

NO-IRON NEEDED

Humorist and author Erma Bombeck once said, "My second favorite household chore is ironing. My first being hitting my head on the top bunk bed until I faint."

If you agree with Erma, here are some ways to avoid dealing with the iron...

Pants

After washing, hang your pants by the ankle end, not by the waist. The wet weight of the pants hanging down will take out most, if not all, of the wrinkles.

Vinyl Tablecloths, Shower Curtains, Shelf Paper

Set a hair dryer on high heat and hold it about 8" away from the wrinkled section of a vinyl tablecloth, shower curtain or shelf paper.

While the hair dryer is on, pay close attention. When the plastic seems soft and pliable, shut off the dryer and use your hand to smooth out the wrinkles.

Sheer Curtains

While your washable sheer curtains are in the wash, dissolve a packet of unflavored gelatin in a cup of boiled water, and add it to the final rinse cycle.

The protein in gelatin has a relaxing or softening effect on the fabric, doing away with wrinkles. (If only it worked that way with skin!)

Ribbons

When you have to wrap a gift and the piece of ribbon you want to use is creased, don't bother to take out the iron and set up the ironing board. Instead, carefully run the wrinkly ribbon over a clean, warm lightbulb.

Sheets

◆ Nobody likes to iron sheets. But you don't really have to if you take them out of the dryer promptly—while they're still warm— and put them right on the bed. They'll look and feel freshly ironed.

◆ If the sheets are cool by the time you make the bed, put them back in the dryer for a few minutes with a clean, damp washcloth. When the sheets are warm again, make the bed as soon as possible.

✳ Folding Fitted Sheets

If you have warm, hardly wrinkled, fitted sheets that you want to put away neatly, we're hoping this helps.

There are a few ways to fold fitted sheets, but none of them seem simple when you read the instructions. (If only this book came with a video!) The secret is to work with the sheet as you read the instructions and, sooner than later, you'll figure it out...or discover an even better way of folding the fitted sheet (in which case, please let us know!). *Here goes...*

Begin with the sheet inside out, then spread it on a bed with the pocket-sides up. (Tall people can do the folding while holding the sheet up in front of them. We find it easier to work with the sheet while it's on a flat surface.)

Place each hand in each of the top corner pockets. Bring your right hand to your left, and fold the corner pocket in your right hand over the 1 in your left hand. If you did it correctly, the corner on top will be right-side out.

Keeping your left hand in place, use your right hand to reach down to the remaining 2 corner pockets and tuck the corners into each other. Next, fold these corner pockets over the first 2 that are in your left hand.

All 4 corner pockets should now be tucked inside one another and the sheet should be folded in quarters. (Bonus points if you got it right on the first try!)

Put the sheet on the bed again, and fold the pocketed side over the flat part of the sheet. Now you should be able to fold it neatly to the size you want it to be without any elastic corners jutting out.

Pantyhose

◆ Strengthen the fibers of new pantyhose by soaking them in a basin of saltwater—about 4 quarts of warm water to ¼ cup table salt— for 15 minutes. Rinse them with cold water. It should make them more run-resistant.

◆ Picture yourself wearing your favorite sheer, black pantyhose. How unsightly is a run or a snag? Help prevent that from happening by lightly spritzing hairspray on the pantyhose as soon as you put them on. Hairspray stiffens the fibers, making them less vulnerable to average stocking abuse.

Keep Your Freshly Ironed Clothes Smooth

◆ Roll silk scarves around the empty cardboard tube from a roll of paper towel, plastic wrap, aluminum foil or gift wrap.

◆ Take a paper towel tube and cut a slit all the way across lengthwise. Slip the slitted tube on a hanger and hang any just-ironed linen or delicate article of clothing that's likely to crease.

◆ Hang 1 or 2 towel rods on the inside of your linen-closet door. It's perfect for storing tablecloths and keeping them wrinkle-free.

◆ When you rinse out your pantyhose, add a drop of liquid fabric softener to the water. The softener will lubricate the fibers, which is said to make them last longer.

Washing Hose

If you do not have a zippered laundry bag made for hosiery, this is a good alternative—put the pantyhose that need to be washed in the cut-off leg of an old, unusable pair of pantyhose (so if you get a bad run in your hose, don't throw them away—keep them for future uses!). Be sure to knot the top to keep the pantyhose from falling out and flailing around while in the washing machine.

Three for the Price of Two

Buy 2 of the exact same pair of pantyhose. When the leg of 1 pair gets a run, it still has 1 good leg. Set the run hose aside and wear the second pair. When the leg of the second pair gets a run, it still has 1 good leg.

Now, cut off the legs with the runs (and use them for machine washing!). You'll be left with 2 panty parts and 2 good legs. You can then wear them as a third, run-free pair of pantyhose.

SHOES & BOOTS

Before you criticize someone, you should walk a mile in his/her shoes. That way, you will be a mile away when you criticize him—plus, you will have his shoes! (Let's just hope they're nice ones.)

Here are some great ways to take care of all your shoes...

> **NOTE:** Several of the hints that follow recommend that you polish, rub, massage or lightly coat your shoes or boots with a *soft* cloth. If you have an old, clean T-shirt that you're tired of wearing, cut it up and use it to spiff up your shoes.

Shining Shoes and Boots

If you do not have a commercial shoeshine product, you may want to use one of these—Coppertone Sunscreen (the SPF number doesn't matter)...lip balm, such as ChapStick...or a light coat of floor wax or furniture polish. With any of these, wipe the shoes dry and then buff them with a soft cloth.

Mold and Mildew

Mix enough fresh or bottled lemon juice with table salt, and use this mixture to wipe down a pair of shoes. You can use a soft cloth to wipe them clean. This will eliminate any surface mold and mildew.

Extend the Life of Shoes

◆ Take your new shoes to a shoemaker or shoe-repair shop, and have him/her add a thin piece of rubber to the sole of each shoe. The shoes may feel more comfortable, you'll be a teeny bit taller, you'll have more traction (especially in rainy weather and on slippery pavement) and the shoes should last longer.

◆ Human feet have 250,000 sweat glands. It's no wonder then that the sweat from an average pair of feet amounts to about ½ pint daily. *Phew!*

With that in mind, it makes sense that 3 pairs of shoes worn alternately will last as long as 4 pairs of shoes that are not worn on a rotating basis. So, let the shoes you have on now air out for at least 24 hours before wearing them again.

◆ Cedar shoe trees are ideal for absorbing moisture and helping shoes keep their shape. Shoe trees are available at the Container Store (888-CONTAIN, 800-733-3532 or *www.containerstore.com*. Second best—stuff your shoes with a bit of newspaper.

Scuff Marks

◆ Prepare a paste made from baking soda and water—about 1 tablespoon of baking soda to 1 teaspoon of water. Use a clean cloth to apply the paste, and wipe off the scuff marks.

◆ Get a gum eraser (available at stationery and art-supply stores)—it is a very effective scuff-mark remover.

Dark Leather

Dip a soft, clean cloth in some lemon juice and rub it on your shoes or boots. Then buff it with another soft, clean cloth. The juice should make the dark leather glisten.

White Shoes (including Leather)

◆ Use an old toothbrush to scrub a little bit of white, non-gel toothpaste on your white leather shoes. Wipe off any excess.

◆ If the toothpaste didn't work on those stubborn scuff marks, cover them with correction fluid (such as Liquid Paper or Wite-Out). Afterward, you may want to polish the shoes to even out the color.

◆ If you don't have any correction fluid, rub the leather shoes with a piece of raw potato and then polish them. The potato will help the polish go on smoothly and the polish will cover the scuff marks.

◆ If you really love those old, dingy, used-to-be-white leather shoes and want to make them look like new, spray them with a couple of coats of semigloss white spray paint. Be sure to let them dry thoroughly between each coat.

◆ If you get grass stains on white leather shoes, rub the stains with molasses and let it set overnight. Next day, use regular soap and water to wash the molasses off the shoes. Your shoes should be white again and grass stain–free.

◆ Get your baby's white shoes clean—just use a bit of baking soda on a damp cloth and wipe off the dirt. Then rinse the shoes with another damp cloth and buff them dry.

Black Shoes

Touch up scrapes and nicks with a black permanent marker or India ink. Desperate times call for desperate measures—on occasion, we have even used mascara and liquid eyeliner.

Gold or Silver Shoes

Use white non-gel toothpaste on a toothbrush to brush away scuff marks. You may need to wipe off any excess paste.

Suede Shoes

Dip a clean sponge in glycerine (available at drugstores) to rub out grass stains. Be sure to test a tiny, inconspicuous spot on the shoes first.

Salt and Grease Stains on Leather and Suede

To remove salt and/or grease stains, a conservator at Toronto's Bata Shoe Museum (*www.batashoemuseum.ca*) recommends mixing a solution made from 1 cup of water and 1 tablespoon of distilled white vinegar. Dip a soft sponge in the vinegar-water, and gently wipe the stains off the leather or suede shoes.

This mixture will also remove salt stains and grease stains from suede. (Be sure to test an inconspicuous section of the suede before working on the stain.)

 Keep Your Boots Salt-Free

If you live in Salt Stain Country (meaning, anyplace that spreads salt on snowy, wintry roads and sidewalks), and you wear leather boots on a regular basis, here's a smart suggestion…

Smear petroleum jelly on a soft cloth and keep it in a closed container. Put the container in a closet or cupboard near the door you use to enter and leave your home. Each time you go out, give your boots a light once-over with the jellied cloth. Do the same thing when you come back in. Your well-nourished boots will never have salt stains.

This solution may also work on boots made from synthetic materials and imitation leather— but we can't guarantee it. Test a small, inconspicuous area before coating the entire boot.

Salt Stains

If you've been walking on wintry streets, you can wipe salt stains off your shoes with a piece of raw potato.

Wet Shoes and Boots

Let shoes or boots dry naturally, away from direct heat and out of the sun. You can speed up the drying process by stuffing them with newspaper (which will absorb odors, too).

When leather shoes or boots are completely dry, rub them with a piece of raw potato, then polish them.

Once-Wet-Now-Dried-and-Stiff Shoes

To recondition stiff leather footwear that got wet and then dried in direct heat, wipe them down with warm water and massage them with a little castor oil.

Buffing Shoes

Scrunch up a lint-free coffee filter and use it to buff your leather shoes.

Waterproofing Shoes… Sort Of

First, polish your leather shoes or boots…and then add a light coating of floor wax.

Let's put it this way—it's better than nothing, but we wouldn't recommend you try this on your pricey pair of Manolo Blahniks.

Patent Leather

Use a soft cloth dipped in a small amount of petroleum jelly, almond oil or baby oil to clean and shine patent leather shoes. Once you have gently massaged the oil into the leather, buff it with a soft, dry cloth.

Applying a bit of Pledge or Windex will also do the trick.

Shoe Polish Reviver

Some shoe polishes have a tendency to get hard. Make sure the bottle of polish is tightly closed, then place it in a bowl of hot water and let it stay submerged for about 5 minutes. After that, it should be liquid again.

Keeping Tall Boots in Shape

When you're ready to put your tall boots back in the closet, slide an empty, clean and dry 1- or 2-liter plastic bottle into each leg.

Safer Shoes

◆ New shoes, which have smooth soles, can cause you to slip and slide on slick surfaces, especially rain-soaked streets. To gain some traction, you can put a few small pieces of masking tape on the soles and heels of those new shoes.

◆ To help prevent baby shoes from sliding, lightly roughen the soles of the shoes with sandpaper or an emery board.

Squeaky Shoes

One of the many uses for the lubricant WD-40 is to take the squeak out of shoes. Spray it on the spot where the sole and heel meet, then enjoy your quiet steps (just don't walk on carpet immediately—wait for the WD-40 to dry).

Deodorizing Smelly Shoes

◆ You can prevent odor buildup by not wearing the same shoes every day. Give them at least 24 hours to freshen up.

◆ To deodorize a pair of shoes, put half of a scented fabric-softener or dryer sheet in each shoe and leave it overnight.

◆ Spread a few tablespoons of baking soda in your shoes and leave them overnight. In the morning, shake out the shoes over the sink or garbage can, and notice how great they smell.

◆ Take a pair of pantyhose, cut off the feet (at the ankle), then fill each foot with standard clay kitty litter and close it with a rubber band, ribbon or a twist-tie. Stick the litter-filled stocking feet in your smelly shoes and let them sit overnight. As you might imagine, kitty litter is a very effective absorbent.

◆ Place your shoes in a plastic bag (either separate or together) and put them in the freezer overnight. The cold temperature will kill any odor-causing bacteria. (Talk about *cold* feet...!)

◆ Crumple up a small piece of black-and-white newspaper and stuff it in your smelly shoes. The carbon in the newsprint absorbs odors.

Foolproof Storage

Put that old Polaroid or new digital camera to good use—take a picture of each pair of shoes that you own. Then tape, staple or glue the photo to the front of a box, identifying which shoes are kept in that box.

This system will make your shoe-storage more efficient. And you will save lots of time rummaging through boxes, looking for the shoes you want to wear.

Loosen a Tight Spot

To temporarily ease a shoe's tight spot, put rubbing alcohol on the inside part of the tight area.

Shopping for Shoes

Your feet tend to be 1 size in the morning and, as the day progresses, they get a little bigger. So it's a good idea to shop for shoes as late in the day as possible. That way, you'll be sure to buy shoes that will ultimately be more comfortable —day and night.

Cleaning Sneakers

◆ Give your white leather or canvas sneakers the once-over with a wet scouring pad and soap. Then dampen a sponge with a bit of lemon juice, and wipe the sneakers clean. (Windex also works.)

◆ To help your sneakers stay cleaner longer, once they are washed, allow them to dry, and then give them the once-over with spray starch. It will help them resist future dirt and grime.

Shoelace Maintenance

◆ If you're tired of having to retie your (or your child's) shoelaces, clamp a "claw clip" (the kind girls use in their hair) on the knot in the middle of the bow.

> **NOTE:** Because these clips come in many styles and colors, you may want to color coordinate them with your shoes or clothes.

◆ Shoelaces will stay tied if you dampen them before tying.

◆ The plastic tip of a shoelace is called an *aglet*, and these little pieces are prone to breaking and wearing out.

　　To structure a new aglet, simply dip the aglet-less end of the shoelace in colorless nail polish. As it's drying, use tweezers to shape the end into a point, then let it dry completely before retying your shoes.

Shoes on Ice—How to Make Tight Shoes Bigger

Everyone has a pair of killer shoes…the shoes that were most likely bought on sale and/or impulse. You don't wear them much because they're too tight, but you won't throw them away because you love them. Help is here!

First, you'll need 4 plastic produce bags, the size that you get at the local fruit stand or in a supermarket's produce aisle. Make sure the bag has no holes or rips, then place 1 bag in each shoe, pushed all the way down into the toe area.

Next, pour water into the plastic bag so that the shoe area is filled with the plastic bag of water. Then seal each bag securely so that there's no chance of water spilling out. Put each shoe into 1 of the other empty plastic produce bags, and close it securely with a twist-tie.

Let's review: You put a water-filled, plastic bag in each shoe. And each shoe is in another plastic bag. Right? *OK, let's continue…*

Place both shoes (plastic bags and all) in the freezer and keep them there for 24 hours. Now here's the secret—as the water inside the shoes turns to ice, it expands, which stretches the shoes!

The next day, when you remove the shoes from the freezer, take them out of the plastic bag and let them thaw for a while, until you can easily remove the bag with the frozen shoe-cicle.

The shoes may have expanded ½ to 1 full size. But if the shoes are still not loose enough, repeat the process.

> **NOTE:** We've been told that this solution also works on boots. Of course, you may have to empty out your freezer to make room for them.

◆ You can also create a new aglet with transparent tape. Wrap a piece of tape tightly around the frayed end of the shoelace. If you can do this so that the tip comes to a point, so much the better.

◆ If you need to replace your shoelaces, measure the ones that came with the shoes and look for the same size replacement. Or just look at the shoe and count the number of *eyelets* (openings) that the shoelace goes into on both sides, and then multiply that number by 3.

So, for example—say your sneaker has 10 eyelets (5 shoelace openings on 1 side... and 5 on the other). Then 10 x 3 = 30, so you will need 30" shoelaces for those sneakers.

LEATHER ACCESSORIES

Leather has always been fashionable in this country. In fact, many Native American tribes lived in tepees made from cow leather and wore clothes and footwear that were made from leather. And why not? Leather looks good, it's warm and it's durable. *Here are some tips for making it even more durable...*

Liven Up Leather Luggage

Dampen a cloth with an egg white and then lightly coat the leather with it. Wait a few minutes, then wipe off the egg and buff the leather with a soft cloth.

Remove Scuff Marks on Luggage

Wipe the scuff marks off your best leather luggage with a dab of lemon extract (available at

supermarkets) using a clean washcloth. Then wipe off any excess extract.

> **FYI: Extract...Defined**
> In case you're wondering, an extract is the distilled or evaporated oil of a food or plant, which is usually dissolved in an alcohol base.

Stains on Leather Gloves

You can erase practically any stain from your nice leather gloves with a gum eraser (available at stationery and art-supply stores).

For an oil stain on a pair of leather gloves, pack cornstarch on the spot and let it sit overnight. Whisk it off the next day with a soft brush or your hand.

Dirt on White Kid Gloves

Rub a bit of flour into the dirt, then whisk it off with a soft brush or your hand.

HATS

We've all heard the expression "mad as a hatter"—historically, hatters DID go mad from inhaling the mercury used in the process of making felt hats. But mercury is no longer used, and hatters are no longer mad. (Here comes the segue for this section...)

But if you're mad about hats, here are some ways to take care of them...

Clean and Brighten

In a clean, dry container, combine 1 cup of cornmeal with 1 cup of table salt. Cover the container and shake it until the ingredients are combined. Then, using a soft hairbrush, brush your felt hat.

With your hand, diligently work the cornmeal-salt mixture into the hat, then let it stay that way for a few minutes. Brush your felt hat again—removing all of the mixture this time—and you'll have a tip-top topper.

Revitalizing Your Hat's Nap

Use this hint only if you have a felt hat that looks like it has seen better days, and if you promise to be super-careful.

Boil water in a teapot, and when the steam starts pouring out, lower the heat so that the steam trickles out at a steady pace. Then, *using extreme caution*, hold the hat over the steaming spout, rotating it, and allow the steam to reach every inch of the hat. When you're done, let the hat air-dry and gently brush it with a soft hairbrush. (Easter Parade anyone?)

Drying a Beret

After you've washed your beret, help it keep its proper shape by letting it dry on a Frisbee or a dinner plate.

Wash Your Caps

Washing machines tend to be tough on baseball caps...so use the dishwasher instead. The cap will come out clean, and it will also retain its shape.

SEWING

Whether it's a torn hem or it's a popped button, our aim here is to keep you in *stitches*—ba-da-DUM! And these suggestions should help.

Needles and Pins

◆ Use a bar of soap or a thick candle as a pincushion. When you take a pin or needle out of the soap or candle, it should glide through the fabric with the greatest of ease.

◆ If you didn't do the soap or candle thing, and you have oily hair, carefully (*very* carefully) rub the needle or pin through your hair and see if that helps it glide through the fabric.

◆ Keep a magnet handy (you may want to glue it to the end of a yardstick), and use it at the end of a sewing session to attract any stray needles and pins.

◆ To sharpen the tip of a pin or needle, rub it with an emery board.

◆ Make a pincushion by stuffing a little drawstring bag or plastic bag with plain (no soap) steel-wool pads. Each time you stick pins or needles in or out, you'll be sharpening them.

Thread

◆ Dip the end of the thread in nail polish and let it dry. The dry thread will be stiff and easy to put through the eye of the needle.

◆ Squirt a bit of hair spray on the end of a piece of thread—this will stiffen it and make it easier to use.

◆ As soon as you've threaded the needle—but before you knot the bottom—sew through a fabric-softener sheet. This will make the thread behave better as you sew with it.

◆ Keep threads from unraveling and tangling by putting a rubber band around each spool of thread. Be sure to tuck the loose thread end under the rubber band to hold it in place.

135

Hems

Measuring and Marking

Whether you use a ruler to measure the number of inches to turn up a hem, or a yardstick to mark the inches from the floor to the hemline, make the marking process easier by placing a rubber band around the exact line on the ruler or yardstick.

No-Pins Pinning

Paper clips or spring-type clothespins can be more convenient than pins when pinning up a hem…and you cannot prick yourself with a clothespin.

Hemming Jeans

If your jeans are too long and you're not into the style of having shredded hems, consider an easy way out. Rather than dealing with the difficult chore of denim hemming (say that 3 times fast!), turn up each hem, iron the folded edge, and then put on duct tape.

Duct tape now comes in many colors, so you can match the tape to your jeans or other clothing…not that anyone will see it. The duct tape should stay stuck on your clothes through many washings.

Emergency Hemming

You pull an innocent-looking thread and half your hem comes down…or you get your heel caught in your hem, making that section of hem hang down. When these mini-emergencies occur, you can do a temporary repair, depending on what's available.

Double-sided tape is great, but chances are, you'd sooner have needle and thread around. There's always a quick fix with duct tape, safety pins or staples. If you're going to staple a hem, be sure to do it so that the open side of each staple is on the outside, rather than next to your skin where it can scratch you or snag your socks or hose.

✳ The Ghost of Hemline Past

If you lengthen a hemline and don't want the previous hem to show, here's what to do—on the underside of the fabric, gently sponge distilled white vinegar on the old crease.

Fold the garment where you want the new hem to be, place a damp cloth over the fold, then press it with a hot iron. The old hemline will disappear, the new hem will be nicely set.

Basting—Just Thread Once

If you work off a spool of thread when *basting* (using long stitches to temporarily hold fabric layers or seams in place until the final sewing is completed…at which time the basting stitches will be removed), you won't have to stop to rethread your needle. This may be one of those "Hey, why didn't I think of that?" moments.

✳ Waistband Expander

When your favorite skirt has gotten a bit too tight around the waist, get a piece of 1"-wide elastic. Determine how many inches you need to extend the waistband and cut the length of the elastic accordingly.

Then using a button that's the same size as the button that's already on the waistband, sew it on 1 end of the piece of elastic. On the other end of the elastic, cut a buttonhole-size slit. The waistband button goes through that slit, while the button on the elastic goes in the original buttonhole.

Of course, it may be easier to just go on a diet than to bother with all of this!

Sewing Machines

◆ It's important to keep your sewing machine well-oiled. It's also important to make sure the oil doesn't stain the fabric you're sewing. So, after each oiling, treat a few sheets of paper towel as if they're fabric, and stitch some rows until you're sure that all of the excess oil has been absorbed.

◆ To prevent the sewing machine pedal from sliding around on a hardwood floor, place the pedal on a computer mouse pad or on a drink coaster.

◆ To sharpen a sewing-machine needle, take a sheet of fine sandpaper and stitch a few rows of thread.

◆ For more accurate sizing, be sure to iron pattern sections *before* laying them on the fabric. A wrinkled pattern piece can change the size of a garment.

Buttons

◆ Double-over your thread before threading a needle. Next, using a big-eyed needle, thread it, then double the thread again and knot it.

Think of the time you'll save. You'll be sewing with 4 strands of thread and will only have to go through the buttonhole a couple of times to secure the button in place.

✳ Sewing Buttons on Thick Fabric

Do you know how, on some jackets or coats, it looks as though the buttons are falling off, but they really aren't? A bit of slack is purposely put between the button and the garment—it allows the garment to lie flat when buttoned.

Here's how to create that slack between the button and the fabric—first, anchor the thread starting from the underside. Pull the needle through the fabric and sew 2 tiny stitches on top of each other. Then place the button over the stitches and place a toothpick or kitchen matchstick on top of the button. Bring the needle up through 1 hole, over the toothpick and down through the other hole.

Repeat the "up, over and down" 2 or 3 times, ending under the button. Discard the toothpick and wind the thread around the underside of the button a few times. Push the needle through the fabric, make a couple of stitches, then knot and cut the thread.

◆ Dab a little glue or clear nail polish on the thread in the middle of each button and it will be less likely to pop off—no matter how much you eat for dessert.

◆ Children's clothes and some types of work clothes often test the endurance of buttons. However, you can sew buttons on with dental floss, and they'll pass the test with flying colors (and no cavities!).

◆ When sewing 4-holed buttons, first sew 2 holes as though they were the only holes on the button. After you finish off these 2 holes with a knot, then sew the other 2 holes.

That way, if the thread on 2 of the holes tears or comes loose, the other 2 holes (which were sewn separately) will keep the button from falling off.

◆ If you need to reattach a popped button and there's no needle and thread around, see if you can find a twist tie, like the kind used to close loaves of bread, garbage bags or supermarket produce bags.

Let water run on the twist tie for a few seconds and remove the paper. If it's a plastic twist tie, cut off the plastic. The object here is to use the piece of wire. Thread it through the button's holes and twist it closed.

◆ To guard against cutting or tearing a garment when removing a button, slip a comb under the button. Then slide a knife, razor or box cutter between the button and comb to cut the thread.

◆ This is just plain ol' common sense—store buttons in a glass jar or plastic case so that you can see what you have.

◆ String all the same-color buttons on a long piece of dental floss...or put sets of buttons on big safety pins.

Zippers

◆ Replace a zipper's missing pull tab with a silver, gold or any other appropriately-colored paper clip.

◆ Squirt a small puff of foam shaving cream on your finger and spread it over the teeth of the stuck zipper. The cream should lubricate the area, allowing you to unzip the problem.

Patches

◆ To prevent a patch from shrinking after it's been sewn on a garment, wash the patch fabric before attaching it.

◆ Before sewing on a patch, attach it in place with a straight pin or a few dabs of water-soluble liquid glue (such as Elmer's). The patch will stay in place while you stitch it on. And the glue will wash away when the garment is laundered.

◆ If you want to cover a hole with an iron-on cloth patch, be sure to place a piece of aluminum foil under the hole. It will keep the patch from sticking to the ironing-board cover.

◆ How's this for *irony*? To remove an iron-on patch, just iron it with a hot iron—it will peel right off.

✱ Padded Patch for Work Pants

This is a good idea if you're doing any on-your-knees cleaning, gardening or just crawling around on the floor.

Take that old, comfortable-but-less-than-flattering pair of pants out of the thrift-store donation bag. Sew a patch on each knee, leaving the top side of the patch open...as though you've sewn a pocket on each knee.

Then, in each pocket, place a sponge...or a substantial shoulder pad...or a piece of foam rubber. These protective pads are easy to remove and will make a big difference in your on-the-knee cleaning or gardening endurance.

Pockets

At the first sign of a pocket wearing thin (you know that thin, threadbare feeling), reinforce it with iron-on tape (available at sewing-supply and crafts stores). ■

■ Products ■

Oliso Steam Iron with Auto-Lift

You'll want this iron if you have arthritis, carpal tunnel syndrome or any other pain-in-the-wrist condition. This is the first major innovation in iron design in over 60 years. And innovative it is.

Imagine—a handle senses your touch and lowers the iron onto the fabric. When you release the handle, it lifts the iron to protect the fabric. Therefore, you don't keep lifting the iron and standing it on its end. You won't burn the garment you're ironing (or your hand or arm), and the iron won't topple over. This smartly designed iron is safe, efficient, fun to use and it can cut down your ironing time by as much as 30%.

The Oliso Steam Iron is available at retail stores throughout the country. You may find it at Hancock Fabric Stores, as well as select Ace Hardware stores and online at Amazon.com or other online sources.

Source: Oliso, 800-899-5157, *www.oliso.com*.

Color Grabber

A terry-cloth panel lets you wash colored and white fabrics together. It helps both colored and white clothes keep their vibrancy. When you toss this item in with your wash load, it grabs hold of and absorbs loose dye and grime.

Color Grabber starts out white, then changes—getting darker and darker with each wash load...proof that it does absorb the dye from clothes. It's available at supermarkets across the country.

Source: Carbona, 866-227-2662, *www.carbona.com*.

CHAPTER 6

Head-to-Toe Magic

In the wise words of Parisian designer Coco Chanel—an influential fashion icon in the early part of the 20th century—"I don't understand how a woman can leave the house without fixing herself up a little—if only out of politeness. And then, you never know, maybe that's the day she has a date with destiny. And it's best to be as pretty as possible for destiny."

If you're concerned with *destiny*, or you just want to know how to take care of yourself and your belongings, you're on the right path and page. There are lots of useful suggestions here—for men as well as for women—that will help to make you even more perfect than you already are.

SKIN CARE FOR YOUR BODY

Skin is the human body's largest organ. The average adult's skin measures 19 square feet and weighs about 9 pounds. The thinnest sections of skin are on your eyelids…the thickest are on your palms and the soles of your feet.

The average person sheds about 1½ pounds of skin particles every year. That means, by the time you're 70 years old, you will have lost a little over 100 pounds of outer skin! Those shed skin particles get replaced with another coat of skin about once a month.

That may be more than you need to know. So let's move along to all that you may want to know about taking care of your skin.

Bumps Remover

Do you have lots of tiny bumps on the backs of your arms? They are clogged pores. To unclog them, mix together 2 tablespoons of sugar, 1 teaspoon of lemon juice and 5 drops of vegetable oil. Rub the blended mixture on your bumpy skin in a circular motion for about 1 minute on each arm. Rinse off with warm water.

The citric acid in the lemon unclogs the pores as the abrasiveness of the sugar sweeps away dry skin and the oil moisturizes the area, making your arms nice and smooth.

Soften Dry Elbows

Cut a lemon in half and drizzle a few drops of baby oil on each half. Stand over the sink and

139

put an oily lemon half over each elbow (1 at a time!)—then squeeze and twist the lemon like you are juicing it. Put the lemon halves on a table and place your elbows in them. Stay that way (if you can) for 30 minutes. Then rinse and dry your newly cleaned and smoother elbows.

All-Natural Underarm Deodorant

Fill a clean, empty face-powder container with baking soda, and apply evenly under your arms using a powder puff or blush brush. The alkaline nature of baking soda balances pH levels to neutralize odor.

Power Up Your Deodorant

If you have a real perspiration problem and feel more secure using a commercial deodorant, you can boost its power by applying baking soda over it to absorb additional moisture.

♦ If you've run out of deodorant, you can use antiseptic mouthwash or apple cider vinegar to neutralize odor. Just dampen a washcloth, and pat it on your armpits.

Underarm Stain Prevention

If you are wearing a light-colored shirt or blouse—and you don't want to let 'em see you sweat—stick a self-adhesive mini-pad (panty liner) on the inside armpits of your garment.

If profuse perspiring is a major problem for you, ask your doctor about Botox injections. They are now the standard treatment to help reduce sweat production.

Prevent Body Odor

Baths made with apple cider vinegar help fight off unfriendly bacteria and fungal overgrowth that may cause body odor.

A couple of times a week, pour 2 to 4 cups of apple cider vinegar in with your hot bathwater and take a nice soak for at least 10 minutes. Then either rinse off under the shower or just dry off...and trust that the smell of vinegar will disappear within 30 minutes.

For body odor prevention, it's best to use pure, unprocessed apple cider vinegar, which is available at health-food stores.

Temporary Varicose Vein Treatment

After taking a warm bath or shower, soak a few washcloths in witch hazel and wrap them around your legs, covering the veins. Sit with the towels on—with your legs extended—for 5 minutes.

Witch hazel has astringent and vasoconstrictive properties, which will temporarily lighten the appearance of varicose veins and help reduce inflammation.

SKIN CARE FOR YOUR FACE

According to writer Cynthia Ozick—"After a certain number of years, our faces become our biographies." How true it is. *Here are some hints to help make your face a best-seller...*

Firming Facial

Chocolate is rich in copper, an essential nutrient for the skin-firming connective tissues.

Mix 1 heaping tablespoon of unsweetened cocoa powder with enough heavy cream to form a paste. Apply it to your clean, dry skin and leave it there for 15 minutes. Then lick it off...*just kidding*! Rinse it off with lukewarm water and a washcloth, then pat dry.

Skin Beautifying Mask

Peel a ripe peach, remove the pit and pulse the fruit in a blender with 1 tablespoon of brandy. When it's a purée consistency, smooth it on your damp face. Relax and leave it on for 20 minutes. Then rinse it off with lukewarm water and pat dry. (Throw away any leftover purée.) This mask should unmask a radiant complexion.

DID YOU KNOW?

Peaches are rich in vitamin A and, when applied topically, the fruit helps protect skin against bacteria that causes pimples and blemishes. Vitamin A also builds *collagen* (the elastic fibers in skin), which helps to improve your skin's elasticity, tone and texture.

Cleansing Mask

Want to look pretty in pink? Apply a thin layer of Pepto-Bismol to your face. Leave on until it dries completely, then rinse it off with warm water and pat dry. The claylike mineral in Pepto-Bismol (and similar products) is *bismuth subsalicylate*, which acts as a cleansing agent and helps draw out the skin's impurities.

Unclog Pores

Boil 2 cups of water in a pot, then add 2 chamomile teabags. Cover the pot and let the teabags steep for 7 to 10 minutes. Put a towel over your head and hold your face about 12" above the uncovered, steaming tea. Stay that way for about 7 minutes. Then rinse your face with cool water and pat dry.

Chamomile has properties that help unclog pores, making them look smaller and your complexion look better.

Face and Neck Toner

Each time you yawn, use the opportunity to tone your face and neck muscles. Inhale deeply as you yawn and open your mouth as wide as it will go. As you exhale, stick out your tongue and roll your eyes upward.

Oily Skin Balancer

Use witch hazel as a balancing agent. Dab it on your face with a cotton ball first thing in the morning, last thing at night and anytime you feel your face is feeling oily.

Exfoliation Scrub

Mix 1 teaspoon of sugar with a few drops of champagne—enough to form a paste. In circular motions, apply the mixture all over your face and neck, then rinse it off with lukewarm water and a washcloth, then pat dry.

The enzymes that are in champagne's tartaric acid, along with the abrasive quality of the sugar, should do a super job of exfoliating your skin.

Make Pimples Disappear

◆ Dab the blemish with regular (non-gel) toothpaste...or lemon juice...or milk of magnesia. Leave it on overnight to dry out the eruption.

◆ Zap the pimple with eyedrop solution—dab it on throughout the day to make the pimple less noticeable as it heals. Eyedrops contain the capillary constrictor *tetrahydrozoline*, which makes redness disappear.

◆ Apple cider vinegar dabbed on with a cotton ball several times during the day will also dry out an oily pimple and should make it disappear within a day or so.

141

◆ Make a paste using equal amounts of cornstarch and rubbing alcohol—½ teaspoon of each should be enough—and put it on the pimple to dry it out.

Combating Age Spots and Freckles

Grate half of a medium-sized onion onto a piece of cheesecloth, then squeeze the juice into a small bowl. Mix in 2 teaspoons of distilled white vinegar and 1 tablespoon of 3% hydrogen peroxide. Using a cotton swab or cotton pad, lightly dab the solution on your spotty skin and let it dry. Do this in the morning and evening.

If you don't see results in 1 or 2 weeks, then you may have to learn to love your age spots and freckles.

> **CAUTION:** Keep hydrogen peroxide away from your eyes. Also, be aware that hydrogen peroxide tends to lighten any body hair with which it comes in contact.

Skin Slougher for Dry, Chapped Lips

◆ Mash 2 fresh strawberries with ½ teaspoon of honey. (If you have lips like Angelina Jolie, you might want to double the recipe.) Spread the goo on your lips and wait 5 minutes for the strawberries' fruit acids and the honey's healing enzymes to do their thing. Then wet a washcloth with warm water and clean off your lips.

◆ Form a paste by combining 3 drops of lemon juice with 1½ teaspoons of baking soda. Use a soft, dry toothbrush to brush the paste across your lips.

Once all of the dead skin cells have been scrubbed away, rinse and dry your lips, and then smooth on some castor oil or petroleum jelly.

◆ Puncture a vitamin E gel capsule, squeeze out the oil and mix it with ¼ teaspoon of sugar and a few drops of vanilla extract. Work it into your lips and let it stay on for 5 minutes. Then clean it off with a clean, wet washcloth.

MAKEUP

Retired fashion designer Calvin Klein spent many of his workdays dressing the world's most beautiful women. According to Mr. Klein—based on his years of experience working with supermodels—"The best thing is to look natural...but it takes makeup to look natural." Here are some makeup tips that will help you look your best, naturally.

Lipstick

After applying lipstick, glide an ice cube over your lips. The ice will set the color and prevent it from bleeding, melting or smudging.

> ★ **Find Your Perfect Color**
> Before you apply lipstick, purse your lips together for about 30 seconds. When you stop, look at the color of your lips. That's the shade to match for your most natural lipstick color.

Do-It-Yourself Lip Gloss

Dig out the clump that remains from your favorite tube of lipstick, and put it in a small microwave-safe glass bowl along with an equal amount of petroleum jelly. Zap the bowl on *high* for 10 seconds at a time, until the mixture is melted. In between zappings, stir it with a toothpick. While it's still warm, transfer your new lip gloss to an empty gloss container (available at drugstores).

Prevent Eye Shadow Buildup

Brush translucent powder on your eyelids before applying powder eye shadow. If you use cream-based shadow, apply a bit of translucent powder over it. The translucent powder will set the eye shadow so that it won't collect in the crease of your lid, and the color will last a lot longer.

Eyeliner Protection

Typically, eyeliner pencil lead is soft and breaks easily. And when you sharpen it, there goes half the pencil.

Try this—put the pencil in the freezer for about 10 minutes, and sharpen it right before using it. The cold temperature hardens the pencil, which prevents the tip from breaking off in the sharpener and makes it easier to apply.

Keep Eyelashes Curled Longer

If you are used to using an eyelash curler—they can be tricky, you know—follow up by applying waterproof mascara. The waterproof formula contains synthethic components that will lock the curl in place.

Babyish Makeup Removers

◆ To remove eye makeup, just lather up a couple of drops of tear-free, hypoallergenic baby shampoo in a wet washcloth and softly dab each of your eyes. Then gently rinse the eye area with water. No mess. No sting. No liner. No mascara.

◆ Just as baby shampoo works for removing eye makeup, so do baby wipes for removing face makeup...even if it's waterproof. Baby wipes are especially good to use if you have sensitive skin.

◆ Mix 1 teaspoon of nonfat dry milk powder in 1 cup of warm water. Use the mixture on a washcloth to remove makeup. Then rinse and dry.

Makeup Touchups

◆ If you carry a small purse and don't have room for a makeup case, dip a cotton swab into whatever makeup you may need to refresh your face—eye shadow, concealer, lip gloss, blush, etc.—and place each swab in its own little resealable plastic bag. A few little plastic bags will take up very little space, and will help you look your best day and night.

◆ You want to wear that sleeveless gown to a special occasion, but you have a big black-and-blue bruise on your arm. If you have Caucasian skin, you can cover up the mark with the right color makeup—yellow!

Yellow counteracts blue tones, so it becomes an effective bruise concealer. Use your finger to pat a yellow-based stick foundation (Wet 'n' Wild is a brand to try) over the mark, then put some face powder on a makeup sponge and gently press it over the spot to set it.

Eyebrow Taming

Take an old, clean toothbrush, give it a spritz of hairspray, then brush it over your brows. The brush will put the hairs in place, and the spray will keep them there.

After each use, clean your brow toothbrush with hot water.

HAIR

A little less than 70% of the American population have dark hair...and only 15% have blond. About 65% of us have straight hair, while 25% have wavy hair, leaving only 10% with hair that's curly.

On average, hair grows ½" each month—a little less in February, of course. Your hair grows fastest when you're in love...probably because your hormones are jumping for joy.

The average person loses about 70 hairs a day—more if you are sick, anemic, malnourished...or the love of your life leaves you.

Statistics like these are interesting, but they aren't going to help you take care of your hair. *However, these suggestions may...*

Hair Color and Dye

◆ Joseph Caron, color director at the Mark Garrison Salon in New York City, adds 2 packets of Sweet 'N Low to hair dye. The artificial sweetener neutralizes the acidity of the dye's ammonia, which helps prevent scalp irritation.

The sweetener can also be used with any at-home dye as long as it contains ammonia—read the label carefully.

◆ The standard advice to prevent hair coloring from getting on your face is to apply petroleum jelly near your hairline. Our experience is that the jelly gets in your hair. So while it prevents the dye from staining your skin, it may also prevent the dye from coloring some of your strands.

So forgo the jelly. If dye gets on your skin, wipe it off immediately with a moist paper towel. For hard-to-remove dye stains, rub a little non-gel toothpaste on the spot, then wash with soap and water.

The Color Boosters...

To boost your hair color, try an all-natural, homemade enhancer. First, boil 1 quart of water. Fold over a piece of cheesecloth—it should be large enough for you to add the ingredient that matches your hair color—and tie the cheesecloth closed with the ingredient inside. Remove the boiled water from the fire, add the cheesecloth and let it steep for 10 minutes.

Blondes: 3 tablespoons of dried chamomile

Brunettes: 3 tablespoons of fresh, bruised rosemary sprigs (bruise them by crumpling in your hand)

Auburn redheads: 1 chopped beet

Orange redheads: 1 chopped carrot

While the cheesecloth is steeping (and cooling), shampoo and rinse your hair as usual. Discard the cheesecloth bag and use the warm, color-enhancing liquid as a next-to-last rinse over your hair. The last rinse should be 1 quart of cool water.

Use this treatment once a month to add vibrancy to your hair color in a healthy, non-chemical way.

Redhead and Brunette Luster

After shampooing, rinse your hair with 1 cup of cool, brewed black coffee, then rinse with plain water. It should make your red or brown hair more lustrous.

Solutions for Chlorine-Damaged Hair

Try these remedies *after* you hit the pool…

◆ If your blond hair tends to turn green after swimming in a chlorinated pool, wash the chemicals out of your hair with club soda… lots of it.

◆ Dissolve 1 adult aspirin (325 milligrams) in 1 cup of warm water and massage it into your hair. Let it sit for 5 minutes, then shampoo. Rinse thoroughly.

Fresh Water Protection

Before you expose your lovely locks to the harsh chemicals in a pool, saturate your hair with fresh water from a shower, hose or faucet. Drenching your hair with plain water helps to block the absorption of chlorine.

Dry Shampoo

Sprinkle talcum or baby powder in your hair, massage it into your scalp and then brush it out thoroughly and completely. Your hair will be cleaner than it was, and it will smell nice, too.

Hair Volumizers

Use a hair volumizer *after* shampooing and towel-drying your hair…

◆ In a spray bottle, dissolve 1 teaspoon of table salt in 8 ounces of warm water. When the water is room temperature, spray your entire head of hair. The salty water adheres to hair strands and increase their diameter, making your hair fuller and ready to be styled.

◆ Combine ¾ cup of water with ¼ cup of beer. Dip a cotton ball into the mixture and dab it on your hair, starting at the roots. The yeast in the beer is said to expand each strand, giving the appearance of a fuller head of hair.

◆ Mix equal amounts of Epsom salt (available at drugstores) and deep hair conditioner in a pan and warm it. Then when the mixture is still warm but cool enough to touch, work it into your hair. Let it stay that way for 15 minutes, then rinse.

Hair Thickener

A deficiency in mineral salts is believed to be a common cause of thinning hair. Studies show that mineral-rich apple cider vinegar improves the overall health and volume of hair.

Drink 3 teaspoons of apple cider vinegar in a glass of water right before a meal or first thing in the morning. Do this daily for a few months, and you should see your hair thicken up.

✪ Thicker Hair Bonus

In addition to thicker hair, don't be surprised if weight control or even weight loss seems easier while using the vinegar remedy.

Freeze Frizz

◆ If you wake up with out-of-control frizz and have no gel to tame it, take an ice cube and run it over your hair. It's a *cool* way to calm down frizz.

◆ Buy great-smelling fabric-softener sheets to run over your hair from top to bottom. *Cationics*, the softening ingredients in the sheets, lubricate hair and counteract the static that causes flyaways and the frizzies.

A Nutty Way to Care for Hair

Coconut oil (available at health-food stores) contains *lauric acid*, which helps do wonderful things for hair—it moisturizes, detangles, deflects the sun's damaging UV rays and prevents color-treated hair from fading.

Rub a dab of coconut oil between the palms of your hands, then smooth it over your hair. It's been used by women in tropical areas throughout the world for ages.

Shine On

Add 1 tablespoon of baking soda to your regular portion of shampoo—your hair will have a natural-looking shine and bounce.

Combat Oily Hair

◆ Add 2 tablespoons of Epsom salt to a bottle of your regular shampoo. Shake it thoroughly to dissolve the salts. Then, *every other time* you shampoo, massage your roots and scalp (the oiliest areas) with the Epsom-salted shampoo. (Yes, this means you'll need to rotate between 2 bottles of shampoo—1 plain and 1 salted.)

◆ Bend your head over the sink, and massage a handful of coarse (kosher) salt into your scalp. Let it stay there for about 5 minutes, then stand on newspaper or in the bathtub or shower, and shake or brush the salt out of your hair. The salt absorbs excess oil and destroys bacteria.

◆ Combine equal parts of plain water and apple cider vinegar in a spray bottle and keep it in the shower. After shampooing, spray the solution on your hair and comb it through. Wait 2 minutes, then rinse.

Vinegar's acetic acid is said to boost your hair's ability to stay oil-free, plus it will restore fullness and shine.

Soften and Moisturize Dry Hair

◆ Put a dollop of sunscreen on your palm, rub your hands together, evenly distributing the lotion, and then massage it into your hair. The lotion in the sunscreen will moisturize and soften your hair and, as a bonus, the sun protection factor (SPF) will protect your hair against the sun's damaging UV rays.

◆ Cut a leg off an old pair of clean pantyhose, and turn it into a cap. Pull it over your head with your hair tucked in, and knot the top of the hose to stop it from dangling around.

Leave the cap on for about 30 minutes …enough time for the nylon to smooth the waves and for your body heat to tame the dry ends. When you remove the cap, your hair should be calmer and softer looking.

Herbal Dandruff Remover

Dandruff may be caused by an overgrowth of yeast on the scalp. Tea tree oil has antiseptic properties that can neutralize that yeast, doing away with the dandruff.

Add 5 drops of tea tree oil (available at health-food stores) to your regular amount of shampoo—but not dandruff shampoo. (Dandruff shampoo may actually remove protective oils from your hair and skin.) Some prepared shampoos made with tea tree oil are also available.

> ✎ **NOTE:** Tea tree oil has a pungent antiseptic scent that may take getting used to. When you open the bottle and take your first whiff, keep in mind that it will be diluted in your pleasant-smelling shampoo. And, after shampooing with it, you should rinse thoroughly.

 Mouthwash Stops Dandruff!

Twice a month, rinse your hair with antiseptic mouthwash to help prevent mild cases of dandruff.

Do not use this remedy if you have cuts or abrasions on your scalp—it may be irritating.

Combat an Itchy Scalp

Before you shower, work ¾ cup of lemon juice into your scalp. Wait 5 minutes, then rinse and shampoo as usual.

The lemon's citric acid helps slough off dead skin cells and kill the bacteria that clogs sebaceous (oil) glands, allowing the release of moisturizing scalp oils that will put an end to the itching.

Homemade Conditioners

◆ A classic conditioner is real mayonnaise—about ½ cup—massaged or combed into damp hair. Wrap your head in a towel and stay that way for 20 minutes. Then shampoo your hair as usual and wash the towel.

◆ If your hair seems damaged from commercial products…or the sun…or just neglect, you may want to try this deep conditioner—mash ½ avocado (which is rich in vitamins A and E) into ½ cup of real mayonnaise, and massage or comb the mixture into your damp hair.

Cover your hair with plastic wrap and stay that way for 20 minutes. Then shampoo, rinse and know that you did something good to help restore the health of your crowning glory.

Restore Bounce and Highlights

Add 1 teaspoon of champagne to 2 tablespoons of your regular amount of shampoo. Work it into your hair, washing and rinsing as usual. (You can also rinse with a bit of champagne after shampooing.)

The bubbly should help give your hair body and bounce, and the tartaric acid in champagne will bring out your hair's natural highlights—especially if you are blonde.

An End to Split Ends

Before going to bed, apply a coat of olive oil to the bottom 2" to 3" of your hair, and put on a shower cap. Leave it on overnight and shampoo as usual the next morning. Then say "Arrivederci!" to dry, brittle ends!

If sleeping with a shower cap is not for you, then apply the olive oil and shower cap first thing in the morning on a day when you don't have to go out. Wait 8 hours before shampooing.

All-Natural Styling Gel

Store-bought styling gels tend to be sticky and some make hair look as though it needs to be washed. Aloe vera gel (available at health-food stores and many drugstores) is a less sticky, chemical-free, effective alternative.

Get Big, Bouncy Curls

Hooray—here's a lovely use for those empty cardboard toilet paper tubes. Wrap a section of damp hair around a tube (you may want to cut the rolls in half, depending on the length and thickness of your hair), and keep them in place with bobby pins or hair clips. When your hair (and the paper tubes) is dry, take out the tubes and unfurl your curls.

Avoid Too-Short Bangs

If you want to avoid too-short-bangs, keep a serious face when you're in the beautician's chair. A big smile raises your forehead, which may lead the stylist to lop off an extra ½".

Hairspray

◆ If you don't want your walls, fixtures and floor or carpet to have sticky hairspray buildup, then step into the shower to spray your hair.

Chances are your shower is used daily and the spray residue will be easily rinsed away.

If you need to see your handiwork, attach a small hand mirror to a shower wall with tile adhesive.

✳ Breathe Easier

Hairspray usually contains a small amount of toxic chemicals and inhalants. Hold your breath when you use it, and your lungs will thank you.

◆ To unclog a sticky hairspray nozzle, dunk the clogged nozzle in rubbing alcohol and let it soak for 2 minutes. Rinse it under hot water and dry it, then you should be ready to spray away.

◆ Researchers at Purdue University in West Lafayette, Indiana, suggest this recipe for homemade hairspray—chop 1 lemon (for dry hair, use 1 orange). Place the chopped fruit in a pot with 2 cups of water. Boil the brew until half of the initial amount remains. Let it cool, then strain out the fruit…and pour the remaining liquid into a spray bottle (if it is too sticky, add more water). Store the bottle in the refrigerator until you need to give your hair a sticky spritz.

NOTE: Refrigerated, this homemade mixture will be good for about 1 week.

If you don't want to refrigerate the spray, you can add 1 ounce of rubbing alcohol as a preservative, and the mixture will keep for up to 2 weeks.

Get Rid of Sticky Buildup

Pour 6 tablespoons of flat beer in 1 cup of warm water. Get in the shower and pour the mixture through your hair. It should rinse away buildup from hair gel, mousse, spray and any other commercial product. Then rinse and shampoo as usual.

Removing Gum

◆ Ask someone how to get gum out of hair, and the answer is usually "peanut butter." Yes, it works, but it's still peanut butter that you're using. The truth is, almost any oil-based product—baby oil, cooking spray, petroleum jelly, etc.—will work just as well and may be easier to shampoo out.

◆ Make a paste with baking soda and water—start with 1 teaspoon of baking soda and add ¼ teaspoon of water…more water if you need it. It should be the consistency of runny oatmeal.

Work the paste into the gummed hair, and keep at it until all of the gum is removed. Once the gum is gone, shampoo as usual.

Tear-free Tots

Put a pair of swim goggles on your child and have a *Finding Nemo* or *Little Mermaid* adventure. The eyes will stay soap- and sting-free, and the experience will be more fun for both of you. Bath time will change from teary eyes to cheery eyes!

Hairbrush and Comb Cleaner

Put a leg from a pair of old pantyhose over the hairbrush's head, pushing it down so that all the bristles poke through the hose. Then yank off the hose, taking with it the clinging hair and dust from the brush. *Now you're ready for the second cleaning procedure…*

Fill a basin with warm water and add 4 tablespoons (¼ cup) of borax powder (available at supermarkets and drugstores), and 1 tablespoon of liquid dish detergent. Let your brush and comb soak in the solution for about 15 minutes, then rinse and dry the comb…let the brush air-dry.

Prevent Blow-dryer Burnout

Moisten a cotton swab with rubbing alcohol and use it to wipe the blow-dryer's vents (make sure the dryer is unplugged first!).

Remove dust this way once a month to keep your dryer performing at its peak. It will also keep your hair dust-free.

Improvised Diffuser

When you don't want your blow-dryer spewing out blasts of air at your hair, but you don't have a diffuser attachment, put a sock on it. A clean sock put over the end of the dryer for a few minutes will let heat through gently…which will allow you to create a variety of hairstyles.

Curling Iron Cleaner

Styling products often build up on a metal curling iron, which makes its curling power less effective. When the iron is cool and unplugged, clean it with a paste made from baking soda and water—start with 1 tablespoon of baking soda and 1 teaspoon of water. Wipe it off with a damp cloth, then dry with a soft, clean cloth.

TEETH

Children have 20 first teeth. Adults have 32 teeth. Just like fingerprints, everyone's set of teeth is unique, even those of identical twins. In this section, we offer all kinds of helpful suggestions to take care of your extra-special set of choppers.

Remove Stains Between the Teeth

Dip a strand of unwaxed dental floss in 3% hydrogen peroxide for about 30 seconds, then floss with it. (However, if you've smoked for 20 years and have nicotine buildup, please don't expect this to make much of a difference.)

Prevent Teeth Stains

It is said that many celebrities keep their teeth white and stain-free by drinking coffee, tea and red wine through a straw. Although it might raise eyebrows at the dinner table, it really *does* help prevent stained teeth.

Good to the Last Drop

If you think you've squeezed every last bit of toothpaste out of the tube—think again. Place the tube in a glass of hot water for 1 or 2 minutes. As the heat makes the tube expand, it will release any paste stuck on the sides, and you should be able to get 2 or 3 more squishes out of it.

Quick Toothpaste Substitute

When you run out of your regular toothpaste, make a paste with baking soda and water—use about 1 teaspoon of baking soda and ¼ teaspoon of water.

Brush extra gently at the gum line because the baking soda can be irritating. And don't forget to stop at the store to buy more toothpaste.

Simple Cleaners for Dentures Or a Retainer

◆ Mix equal amounts of distilled white vinegar and filtered or spring water (you don't want your dentures turning green from the chlorine in regular tap water), and put the solution in a clean cup. Soak your dentures or a retainer overnight, and get ready for some clean choppers!

◆ Dissolve 2 teaspoons of baking soda in 1 pint of filtered or spring water. Then drench a clean washcloth and wipe the dentures or the retainer. Rinse and wear.

BAD BREATH

If you occasionally suffer from bad breath—and you know it's not a symptom of gum disease (visit your dentist to be sure)—these suggestions may help you make your mouth fresh and sweet-smelling...

Homemade Mouthwash

Cinnamic aldehyde—the naturally occurring chemical compound in cinnamon that's responsible for its wonderful smell—also helps eliminate odor-causing bacteria in the mouth.

Boil 2 cups of water, then add 5 or 6 pieces of cinnamon stick (available at supermarkets) and let it simmer for 5 minutes.

Once it's cool, strain out the sticks and pour the liquid into an empty bottle. Use it as you would use any commercial mouthwash.

Tea for Sweet Breath

Make your after-dinner drink black tea (such as Pekoe). Researchers at the University of Illinois at Chicago reported that the plant chemicals *catechins* and *theaflavin* are released from black tea leaves during the brewing process. These compounds help shut down the digestive

enzymes that trigger odor-producing bacteria in the mouth.

Odor Buster

After eating onion, garlic or anything else that stays on your breath, dip your toothbrush in a small amount of distilled white vinegar and brush your teeth as well as your tongue. This should help clean your breath and may even help whiten your teeth.

HANDS

Without thinking twice, draw a circle in the air with your left hand. If you drew the circle clockwise, chances are you're left-handed. More men are left-handed (12.6% of the male population) than women (9.9% of the female population).

But no matter which handedness you are, both hands should be cared for. *Here are some great ways to do that...*

Reverse Roughness and Dryness

Olive oil is an effective moisturizer. Massage some into your hands and give it time to sink in. (You may also want to put on a pair of rubber or latex gloves to avoid getting oil stains on whatever you touch.) After about 30 minutes, take off the gloves and wipe the oil off your soft, moisturized hands with a dry paper towel.

Soften and Exfoliate

Add 1 teaspoon of sugar to a dollop of baby lotion and rub it over your hands. The lotion softens and moisturizes, while the abrasive sugar exfoliates. This is an effective combination that will leave your hands looking and feeling good.

Cracked Skin Healer

Puncture a vitamin E gel capsule, squish out the oil and rub it on your hands. Do this twice a day—especially in cold weather when the hands tend to be dry and get painful cracks.

Pain-Easing Solution

If your hands are feeling achy, try this solution. In a bowl, combine 3 cups of hot water, 3 tablespoons of witch hazel and ½ cup of Epsom salt (available at supermarkets). Dip your hands in the solution for about 5 minutes…enough time for the magnesium sulfate in the mixture to penetrate and ease the pain in your joints.

Cleaning Grimy Hands

◆ Clean grease, grime or any other dirt from your hands by rubbing on a bit of solid vegetable shortening (such as Crisco) or margarine. Wash with soap and water to clean off the shortening or margarine.

◆ You can also knead some Play-Doh in order to de-grime your hands.

Odor Remover

If your hands have an unpleasant, lingering smell from bleach or any other strong, chemical cleaner, wash them with lukewarm water and some non-gel toothpaste. The mildly abrasive consistency of the paste will scrub off the nasty scent molecules from your skin's surface.

NAILS

If you've ever gotten a black-and-blue nail, you may have wondered how long it would take to grow out. Generally, fingernails grow from the root to the tip in about 6 months. Toenails take 2 to 3 times as long.

The medical community regards fingernails as a mirror of a person's general health. Doctors and nurses can see clues to conditions like asthma, improper nutrition and stress—just by looking at a patient's fingernails. So it's important to skip the polish and faux tips when you go for a medical examination.

If you look at your nails and are not happy with what you see, the following remedies are right at your fingertips…

Speedy Grower and Strengthener

Studies show that women who drink 8 ounces of soy milk daily have longer and stronger nails after 1 week.

In addition to soy milk—or instead of it—consider rubbing a tiny dab of non-gel fluoride toothpaste on each fingernail at bedtime. *Fluoride* is said to help nails grow faster and stronger. (You may want to use this fluoride treatment on the nails of just 1 hand first, to see if it really works for you.)

Brighten and Strengthen

Ginger ale contains *monopotassium phosphate*, a natural bleach and strengthening agent. Soak your nails in a glass of ginger ale for 10 minutes, and then rinse. Do this daily for at least a week, or until your nails look nice and bright.

Yellow Stain Remover

◆ The same abrasive and bleaching properties in tooth-whitening toothpaste can also work on nails. Squeeze out a portion of the paste on an old toothbrush and scrub your fingernails with it. Then wash it off and marvel at the difference.

◆ Soak nails for 15 minutes in a combination of ¼ cup lemon or lime juice and ½ cup water. The citric acid in the lemon/lime juice is a mild bleaching agent that will lift out the yellow stains, especially after you've taken off dark nail polish.

◆ Mix 3 tablespoons of baking soda with 1 tablespoon of 3% hydrogen peroxide. Use a cotton swab to wipe the mixture on top as well as underneath each nail. Wait about 5 minutes, then rinse your stain-free fingernails with warm water.

Shine Up Those Nails

Massage a few drops of olive oil into your nails, then use a tissue to buff them until they're oil-free and shining.

Ridge Remover

In a microwave-safe bowl, combine 2 parts of olive oil to 1 part lemon juice. Zap it for about 20 seconds—just until it's warm, not hot. Work the solution into the bottom part of each nail (where the nail meets the cuticle).

Spend 1 minute on each fingernail every day. You can refrigerate leftover solution, and microwave it again the next day.

Massaging the oil into the fibrous material that runs across the nail will help smooth the ridges and strengthen the nails. Give it a chance…be consistent…and do it daily.

Nail Polish and Manicures

It is said that nail polish was invented in China about 5,000 years ago, during the Ming Dynasty. The most popular colors at that time were red and black.

The Chinese polish was made from a combination of beeswax, egg whites, gelatin, vegetable dyes and Arabic gum. The modern-day form of nail polish is made from a refined version of automobile paint. *Here are some suggestions that will help you get the most out of your manicure and/or pedicure…*

Nonstick Nail Polish Cap

When you open a new bottle of nail polish, put a thin coat of petroleum jelly around the bottle's neck to prevent it from sticking all the other times you're going to use that polish.

Yellowing Prevention

Before you go out in the sun, apply a thin layer of lip balm—the kind that contains sunscreen—to your nails. It will block the sun's rays from yellowing your polish.

And while you're at it, put some balm on your lips, too!

Revive Old Nail Polish

If your nail polish has gotten thick and gloppy, let the bottle sit in hot water for about 5 minutes, and it should be good as new.

Fizz Away Your Polish

When your regular nail polish remover doesn't do a perfect job and there are traces of color left, try this—fill a cup with plain water and drop in 1 denture-cleaning tablet. Once the tablet dissolves, soak your nails in the solution for about 10 minutes.

The tablet's bleaching agents should leave your nails looking like a clean canvas, ready for the artist's brush and paint.

Get a Neater Manicure

Before you polish your nails, use a cotton swab to apply a thin layer of petroleum jelly to the skin around your nails. That way, you won't have to bother taking off the nail polish that dried on your skin while you were giving yourself a manicure.

✱ **Secret to Slimmer Fingers**
When you polish your nails, leave a thin unpolished line of space on each side of your nail. By applying polish just down the center of your nails, the illusion of narrower nails is created—which, in turn, makes your fingers look longer and slimmer.

Longer-Lasting Manicure

A clean, oil-free nail surface will help polish stay on longer. Try this—wipe your nails with a cotton ball or pad soaked with witch hazel. Witch hazel (available at health-food stores) is an astringent cleanser, and its salicylic acid helps to remove oils.

Prevent Chips

Every couple of days, polish *underneath* the edges of your nails to strengthen the tips—which are extremely vulnerable to chipping and breaking.

Emergency Nail File Substitutes

♦ If you're away from home and really need a nail file, desperate times call for desperate measures—go to the nearest bathroom and file your snagged fingernail on the grout (that's the usually rough mortar or plaster used between sections of ceramic tile).

♦ If grout is out, then look around for a book of matches. You can file your nail on the abrasive emery-board-like panel on the back (where you strike the match).

FEET

 There are 52 bones in your feet, which is ¼ of all the bones in your body. The average person uses those foot-bones to take about 6,000 steps a day. It's time to step up to the task of taking good care of your feet. *These suggestions can help…*

Eliminate Foot Odor

Boil 2 quarts of water, then steep 5 bags of black tea in it until the tea is cool enough to transfer to a basin (you can also divide the tea between 2 plastic shoe boxes). Soak your feet in the liquid for 10 minutes, then rinse and dry thoroughly.

Tannic acid, the natural astringent found in black tea, neutralizes and absorbs sweat, destroying the moist breeding ground for odor-causing bacteria.

✱ **Socks and Soda Solution**
Before putting on socks, apply a thin coat of baking soda on your feet to keep them dry. This will also keep them smelling fresh.

Fix Up Your Hot, Tired Feet

♦ Boil 2 quarts of water and add ¼ cup of baking soda. When it's cool, pour the liquid into a basin (or divide it between 2 plastic shoe boxes). Then soak your feet for about 10 minutes. Rinse and dry thoroughly.

◆ Mix 4 tablespoons of mustard seed into 2 quarts of just-boiled water. When it's cool, pour the mixture into a basin (or divide it between 2 plastic shoe boxes).

Soak your feet for about 10 minutes, enough time for the *sinigrin,* an important compound in mustard, to stimulate blood flow in your tired tootsies. Then rinse and dry thoroughly.

Flaky Skin Scrub

Strawberries, with a little help from oil and salt, work wonders to slough off dead skin cells, so you can say good-bye to dry, flaky feet.

In a blender, combine 1 cup of sliced strawberries, 2 tablespoons of olive oil and 2 teaspoons of coarse (kosher) salt. Pulse the mix until it has a pulpy consistency. Then gently massage it into your feet, especially on the heels where skin is usually the flakiest. Let it stay on for about 2 minutes, then rinse with warm water and dry thoroughly.

Treating Blisters

Dip a cotton swab in 3% hydrogen peroxide and dab it on the broken blister. The antiseptic properties of the peroxide help heal the blister quickly while preventing infection.

 Minty-Fresh Feet

If you don't have 3% hydrogen peroxide on hand to treat a blister on your foot, use antiseptic mouthwash.

Blister Prevention

When you get a new pair of shoes that you plan to wear without socks or pantyhose, swipe the inside of the shoes' heels with a stick of clear underarm antiperspirant/deodorant. The waxy silicone in the deodorant creates a barrier that stops the blister-causing friction.

The woman who told us about this remedy claims she has no blisters, no pain and odor-free feet. Sounds good to us, but you be the judge.

SHAVING

If you've ever wondered when and why women started shaving under their arms, we have the answer—the May 1915 issue of *Harper's Bazaar* magazine featured a model wearing a sleeveless evening gown. For the first time in fashion, a woman's bare shoulders and hair-free armpits were exposed.

Along with the start of media advertisements, a savvy executive at the Wilkinson Sword Company (which makes razors and razor blades) mounted a campaign to convince women that their underarm hair was unhygienic and unfeminine...and most women have been shaving their armpits ever since.

If you are intrigued by shaving apparatus and barbershops from bygone eras, consider a trip to The Ed Jeffers Barber Museum in Canal Winchester, Ohio. It's the only museum of its kind in the world, and it's free to the public (by appointment only). For more information, call Zeke's Barber Shop at 614-833-9931 or visit *www.edjeffersbarbermuseum.com.*

If you'd rather skip the museum and move on to super shaving tips, keep reading...

Shaving Cream Substitutes

These suggestions work for both face and legs...

◆ Shave in the shower and use a thin layer of hair conditioner (or shampoo that has conditioner in it) instead of shaving cream.

Let it soak in for a couple of minutes, enough time for the steam of the warm shower and the ingredients in the conditioner to soften the hair and moisturize your skin, resulting in a close shave and no razor burn.

◆ You can also use hand or body lotion as a substitute for shaving cream. And you may like the results well enough to stick with it from now on!

Aftershave Substitutes

◆ If you're traveling and you forgot to pack your aftershave lotion, check to see if your hotel room has a mini-bar. If you're willing to pay for great skin, open a bottle of vodka and splash it on. It will be a refreshing aftershave, and an interesting anecdote to tell people when you describe your trip and the expensive aftershave you used.

◆ If you're at home and you run out of aftershave, you could, of course, use vodka—but perhaps you'd rather save that for company. Instead, mix equal parts of apple cider vinegar and witch hazel (both available at supermarkets and health-food stores).

The concoction should do wonderful things for your complexion, and you may not want to go back to using a commercial aftershave product.

Shave Legs Less Often

Studies show that the *serine protease inhibitors* in soy milk decrease the size of the hair shaft and reduce the rate of hair growth.

Right after shaving and drying your legs, drench a washcloth with soy milk and wipe your legs. Do not rinse it off. Just let your legs air dry.

If researchers are right, not only should you have to shave less often, but the hair growth itself may be less dense. (Of course, if you notice your leg hair getting thicker, stop using the soy milk right away.)

✳ Cutting It Closer

To get a really close shave, shave your legs first thing in the morning. At the end of the day, legs are slightly swollen from being up and around, making it hard for the razor to cut hair as short as in the morning.

Prevent Razor Rust

Put some vodka in a cup and soak your safety-razor blade in it after shaving. The vodka will disinfect the blade and prevent it from rusting.

Prevent After-Waxing Redness

After you have your eyebrows, upper lip or bikini area waxed, dab the area with some eyedrop solution. Eyedrops contain a capillary constrictor, *tetrahydrozoline,* which makes redness disappear.

If you have the waxing done at a salon, you'll be ready to leave there and greet the world without anyone knowing that you were just waxed.

PERFUME & COLOGNE

The comedian Rita Rudner once said—"To attract men, I wear a perfume called New Car Interior." Hey, whatever works! *And whichever perfume you choose to wear, here's how to make the best of it...*

Shelf Life of Scents

The shelf life of perfume is about 12 to 14 months…and the shelf life of cologne is only about 6 months. So don't save your scents for special occasions. You deserve to make every day a special occasion by indulging yourself. You're worth it!

Is It for You?

◆ If you're looking to buy perfume, the best way to tell how a scent will react on your skin is to spray it on the inside of your wrist. Then shop around for a while. About 20 minutes later, take a whiff of the fragrance on your wrist to decide whether or not you like it. Yes? Go back and buy it.

◆ If you can't wait around for 20 minutes, take a few sample cards of the scents you think you'll like—the cards are usually on the fragrance counter, or ask a salesperson to get you some.

Once you're home, brew some non-flavored, regular or decaf coffee. In between sniffs of each fragrance, cleanse your nose's palate by smelling the used coffee grounds. That way, you'll be able judge each perfume sample on its own merit without the scents blending together.

Increase Staying Power

There's no need to keep reapplying fragrance throughout the day and night—just put a light layer of petroleum jelly on your pulse points (wrists, back of knees, behind the ears, etc.), and then apply your perfume or cologne over it.

The stickiness of the jelly will attract fragrance molecules and lock them in. Just be sure you want the scent with you around the clock.

Tone Down Fragrance

You can tone down a too-strong perfume or cologne by adding some vodka—just dab a little at a time to your pulse points until the fragrance is as mild as you want it to be.

Recycling Bottles

Put open, empty perfume or cologne bottles (or the fragrance cards from magazines) in your underwear drawer or linen closet. The aroma will gently infuse your things.

JEWELRY

Most people know their birthstone…and many women own a piece of jewelry with their special stone. *Here's a list to check to make sure you're right…*

January: Garnet
February: Amethyst
March: Aquamarine and bloodstone
April: Diamond
May: Emerald
June: Pearl, moonstone and alexandrite
July: Ruby
August: Peridot and sardonyx
September: Sapphire
October: Opal and pink tourmaline
November: Citrine and yellow topaz
December: Blue topaz and turquoise

For more information—such as descriptions, legends, symbols and more—about each birthstone, visit *www.about-birthstones.com. And for more information about caring for your jewelry, simply keep reading…*

Watch Scratch Remover

If your watch has a scratched plastic (not glass) face that's covering the dial, dip a cotton swab in some nail polish remover and rub it over and over and over the face. Keep rubbing until the scratches are gone.

Safe Way to Clean Pearls

Pearls are said to be "the queen of gems and the gem of queens." With that in mind, you should treat them royally.

Never use an ultrasonic cleaner, ammonia, harsh detergents, an abrasive cleaner or an abrasive cloth on pearl jewelry—you may end up with just a strand of beads. The pearl's outer coating (called the *nacre*) is extremely delicate and can wear away. The calcium carbonate in pearls can dissolve from body heat or the skin's oil. To keep your pearls intact, use a soft, lint-free cloth to wipe them as soon as you take them off.

If you need to wash the pearls, use a solution made from mild soap (such as Ivory Snow) and plain water. A spokesperson for the Cultured Pearl Information Center suggests rinsing the pearls 3 times more than you think you have to, just to be sure that all of the soap is removed from the drill holes. Be sure to let the pearls air-dry before putting them away.

Use Caution with Pearls

◆ Hairspray and perfume both contain alcohol, which can damage pearls. Spray your hair and apply perfume at least 5 minutes before you put on your pearl earrings, necklace, bracelet, brooch or ring.

◆ The same goes for hand cream, body lotion and makeup. Wait until they're completely absorbed and/or dry before putting on your pearl jewelry.

◆ Exposure to direct sunlight for a long period of time will cause the protein in pearls to turn yellow. Be sure to keep them in a cool, dark, SAFE place.

◆ It's best to keep pearls in a box or pouch. They can get scratched if they rub up against other jewelry.

✳ Keep Pearls Around

The silk or nylon cord that holds your strand of pearls can wear out. The Cultured Pearl Information Center recommends a fine pearl necklace that is worn a few times each week should be restrung every 6 months...pearls worn a couple of times each month should be restrung once every year.

Pearls of Wisdom

You may have heard that the more often you wear your pearls, the better they will look. Although it's a lovely thought, it's a fact that body oils are not the best thing for maintaining—nor improving—the natural luster of pearls.

Many years ago (before cultured pearls came into existence), only super-rich aristocrats could afford strands of rare and prized natural pearls. Believing the myth that wearing pearls enhanced their patina, these wealthy matrons would have their maids sit for hours at a time, several times a week, wearing the pearls. (All that money, and what they really needed was a copy of this book to set them straight!)

Safe Way to Clean Diamonds

Soak diamond jewelry in a small bowl filled with warm sudsy water, or equal parts of distilled white vinegar and warm water.

While the jewelry is soaking, brush each piece with a soft toothbrush. Rinse the jewelry under warm running water. Then pat it dry with a soft lint-free cloth.

Diamonds Are Forever

◆ A diamond is the hardest natural substance in the world, and it will last forever...give or take a few years.

◆ The word *diamond* comes from the ancient Greek word *adamas,* which means *unconquerable.* The Greeks thought of diamonds as the "tears of the gods."

◆ The tradition of wearing a diamond engagement ring on the fourth finger of the left hand dates back to ancient Egypt. It was believed that the vein of love ran from that finger directly to the heart.

CAUTION: If your jewelry has emeralds, opals, turquoise or pearls in addition to diamonds—*do not* use vinegar!

Opals and turquoise are both porous stones. Just wipe them with a chamois cloth. Emeralds chip easily. They should be cleaned only by a professional jeweler.

In addition, it's not a good idea to wear gold jewelry when swimming in chlorinated water. The gold may react with the chlorine, causing the jewelry to become brittle and break. Think twice before wearing your beautiful gold chain when you're going in the pool.

Remove a Ring Without the Sting

◆ If your finger has become swollen and you can't take off your ring, wet your finger and put 1 or 2 drops of liquid dish detergent (or soapy water) above and below the ring. It will lubricate your finger so the ring can slide off easily.

◆ Soak your hand in a bowl of ice water. Doing this will shrink your swollen finger enough to allow you to remove your ring.

◆ Coat your finger with mayonnaise, olive oil or butter and slip off the ring.

Untangling a Chain

Put the knotted chain on a piece of waxed paper. Sprinkle some talcum powder on the tangle. Then, with a needle or straight pin in each hand, work at untangling the knot(s).

Storing Jewelry

◆ Take a wooden hanger and screw in hooks (the kind used to hang drinking cups) along the width, about 1" apart. This will keep your necklaces tangle-free and easy to see.

◆ You can also use a tie rack as a neat way to store your necklaces.

◆ Keep your earrings paired up and organized in empty ice cube trays or egg cartons.

◆ Keep pierced earrings together by sticking the posts through the holes of a button.

◆ Store and display your bracelets and watches on the branches of a coffee-cup tree.

◆ With a tie knot, tie an unused necktie on your closet rod, and use the tie to hold pins and tacks. You can even push through pierced earring posts. It's a neat way to hold the jewelry and to see things at a glance.

Easy Bracelet Fastening

Instead of going around in circles trying to fasten your bracelet, tape 1 end of the bracelet to your wrist, then simply fasten the clasp. It's so easy when you know how. (Of course, don't forget to remove the piece of tape once the bracelet is fastened!)

Temporary Replacement for Pierced Earrings

Most pierced earrings are made up of the ornament, the post and the *friction nut* (the back part that holds the post to the earlobe). If you lose the friction nut, then you have to take off the earring or, chances are, you'll lose the ornament and post.

If you want to continue wearing the earring, find a pencil with an eraser at the end. Break off a small piece of the eraser, and use the post to make a hole in the middle of the eraser piece. Put the earring post back in your lobe, and attach the eraser as the new, temporary nut. Once you get home, replace the eraser with a real friction nut (available at jewelry stores).

Costume Jewelry

Does your neck or wrist or earlobes or finger change color every time you wear a certain piece of costume jewelry? The solution is to paint colorless nail polish on the jewelry—wherever it touches your skin.

If you are sensitive to regular nail polish, use a hypo-allergenic brand of clear polish.

Cleaning Costume Jewelry

Mix 1 teaspoon of baking soda with 1 cup of warm water, dip a soft cloth in the solution and gently clean the jewelry.

> ⚡ **CAUTION:** When cleaning costume jewelry, do not use distilled white vinegar or any other cleanser that might undo the glue bonds.

EYEGLASSES

Many historians believe that the first eyeglasses were invented in Italy around 1284. Throughout the 1300s, eyeglasses became a symbol of wealth and power, since only the rich could afford this luxury.

In 1456, Gutenberg invented the printing press, which made books available...and which created a market for reading glasses. Gradually, eyeglasses became an important part of everyday life for even the most common people.

If spectacles are part of your daily life, here are ways to care for them...

Cheers to Your Specs!

If you're at a bar and you want to see who's paying for your drink, clean your eyeglasses with a little vodka on a soft cloth.

Fog Prevention

Smear a tiny dollop of foam shaving cream or a drop of liquid dish detergent or non-gel toothpaste on both sides of your eyeglasses, and wipe it off with a soft cloth (or you can just spit on them, the way scuba divers do).

Doing this leaves a very thin, invisible coating on the lenses...which will help fend off moisture...which will prevent the glasses from fogging up each time you come out of the cold or while cooking.

Fast Fix for Scratches

If your glasses' plastic lenses are scratched, spray Pledge furniture polish on both sides of the lenses. Rub the polish in, then wipe it off with a soft cloth.

Temporary Screw Replacement

◆ If you lose 1 of those tiny screws that hold your glasses together, you can fix it temporarily. Here's what to do—thread a piece of dental floss through the holes that the screw goes through. Then knot the floss and cut off the excess. Dental floss is strong and should hold your glasses together until you can replace the screw.

◆ If you don't have dental floss, take a twist tie (like you use to close garbage bags), and peel off the outer paper or plastic. Thread the thin little wire through the screw holes of the eyeglasses, and twist it closed.

   Cut off any excess wire so that it will be safe to wear the glasses until you can replace the screw.

◆ Of course, you can always use a nerdy-looking small safety pin (or a toothpick...or a wooden match) to keep your glasses together until you can replace the screw.

Loose Screws Sink Ships

◆ If you can do delicate work with a tiny screwdriver, then unscrew the screws on each side of the glasses ¾ of the way. Apply a coat of colorless nail polish to the threads of each screw, and then tighten them. This procedure will prevent the screws from getting loose again.

◆ If the screws are popping out and you don't have a tiny screwdriver, press a pencil eraser against each screw and turn the pencil (remember—lefty-loosey, righty-tighty). The eraser is non-slippery, so it will provide enough traction to get the screws out. Apply clear nail polish to the heads of the little screws and then tighten the screws back into place with the pencil.

Do-It-Yourself Magnifier

◆ When you want to read a price...or look up a phone number...or see what time it is on your watch, but the type is too small to see without your glasses, try this—make a fist, leaving a small hole between your palm and pinky. Bring your fist up to your eye, look through that small hole and focus on the number you want to read. For some unknown reason, the small channel of light entering your eye clears the vision.

◆ You can also puncture a small hole in a piece of paper with a pen point. Hold the paper hole to your eye, focus on the number and see it come into view—large and sharp.

CLOTHING

Whether you're a slave to fashion...or you base your fashion taste simply on what doesn't itch, there are ways you can wear clothes easier and have them look better. *Check out these hip suggestions...*

Clothing Storage

◆ If your closet space and storage space are both limited, store out-of-season clothes in empty suitcases.

NOTE: No matter where you store your out-of-season clothes, if they are machine washable, wash them before packing them away. It will help prevent a moth infestation.

◆ Clothing fibers need to breathe, so do not hang them in plastic bags, especially those you get from the dry cleaner's. If you want to cover any of your garments, use old, clean pillowcases. Just cut a hole in the top to accommodate the hanger.

◆ Shoeboxes—either cardboard or plastic—that are lined up side by side in your dresser drawers will help keep underwear, socks or pantyhose reasonably neat, and make specific items easy to find.

Fragrant Mothball Substitute
To repel moths when storing clothes, use whole cloves (the kind used when making a citrus pomade or preparing ham). Wrap a handful of cloves in a piece of old pantyhose, and tuck them in with your winter woolens. They will serve the same repellent purpose as efficiently as mothballs, but they smell much better.

If you're feeling particularly protective of your special cashmere sweaters or other woolen garments, store the cloves with the sweaters in large glass jars.

Hide Cellulite

If your thighs and tush have cellulite, stay away from clingy, too-tight clothes. In other words, let your clothes stay away from you. Rub a fabric softener sheet over your dimpled flesh and inside the clothing that will touch it. No cling...no cellulite show-through.

Swimsuit Shopping Made Kinder

Shopping for a swimsuit is an ordeal for most women. Before you head for the mall, put on a pair of pantyhose that are a couple of shades darker than your skin tone. You'll boost your self-esteem with your legs looking their suntanned best when you're in the changing room.

Zippers

◆ If the teeth are properly aligned, but the zipper doesn't go up and down smoothly, rub

the teeth with a bar of soap or a candle. It should make a difference.

◆ Also, you can try rubbing the teeth with a pencil. The graphite should help the zipper glide more easily.

> **NOTE:** It's best to use the pencil only on dark-colored clothes. You may not want to take the chance of graphite smudging on light-colored garments.

◆ If your skirt or dress zipper unzips when it shouldn't, coat the teeth with a little spritz of hairspray once it's in place. The stickiness of the spray should keep the zipper zipped—until you're ready to unzip it.

Pantyhose

◆ Consider buying pantyhose 1 size larger than usual. The less stress put on the hose, the longer they will last.

◆ Got a run in your pantyhose? When you take them off, put a dot of red nail polish on the waistband. From then on, you'll see at a glance that this pair of pantyhose should only be worn under slacks, where the run will not show.

Lingerie Camouflage

If you don't want your underwear to show through the white shirt or pants you're wearing, put on a bra, slip or panties that matches your skin color.

Create Cleavage

◆ *If you wear a B-cup bra...*loosen the straps on your bra until they can't be any looser. Then, while wearing the bra, bring the straps together at the nape of your neck and pin them with a safety pin. If this trick created the cleavage you were hoping for, take off the bra, sew the straps together securely and remove the safety pin.

◆ *If you wear a C-cup (or larger) bra...* for an uplifting experience, attach a wide barrette to your bra straps—it should be in the middle of your back. This will improve your posture and your bustline without the reminder to keep your chest out and shoulders back.

FOOTWEAR

You think you have a lot of shoes? Imelda Marcos, wife of deposed Philippine president Ferdinand Marcos, once had 1,500 pairs of shoes in her shoe room. Yes, she had a *shoe room!* And if you feel guilty about splurging on a recently purchased pair of shoes, just think about the $665,000 that was paid at auction for 1 of the 8 pairs of ruby slippers made for Judy Garland to wear in *The Wizard of Oz.*

Now that your shoe collection is in its proper prospective, here are some ideas on how to wear them more comfortably.

Keep Shoes On

If your slingbacks aren't adjustable and they keep slipping off, find a shoemaker and have him/her put a half-pad beneath the shoe's inner-sole liner. That half-pad will make the whole difference. It will push the front of your foot backward, tightening the slingback strap enough to keep it from slipping off your heel.

Put on Boots

If your boots don't have zippers, a plastic bag can help you get them on easily. Place a closed plastic bag into the boot, with the bottom of the bag reaching into the boot's foot area and the top of the bag hanging out over the top.

Hold the top of the bag and the top of the boot with both hands, then slide your foot along the plastic and into the boot. Once your foot is in the boot, pull out the bag.

✳ Easy Way to Slip on Shoes
If you don't have a shoe horn, use a large spoon or a narrow, thin spatula. (Run it through the dishwasher after you get your shoes on!)

Foot Note

If you're *really* head-over-heels about footwear... over 10,000 shoes are housed at the Bata Shoe Museum in Toronto. This unique museum celebrates the style and function of footwear. Exhibited artifacts range from Chinese bound-foot shoes and ancient Egyptian sandals to chestnut-crushing clogs and a collection of celebrity shoes.

For more information, call 416-979-7799 or visit *www.batashoemuseum.com.*

HANDBAGS

We know that the first handbag dates back to ancient Egypt—hieroglyphics depict purses attached to "girdles" and fastened at the waist. Jewels and embroidery usually embellished the bag, and these decorative touches indicated social status—the richer the person, the more complex the bag.

Times may have changed, but you can still tell a lot about a woman from the handbag she carries. *For example...*

◆ Bulky, oversized bags tend to be used by down-to-earth, low-maintenance women.

◆ Designer handbags, which often cost more money, are often associated with high-maintenance, confident women.

◆ Cigar-box purses are for women who like to stand out in a crowd. They tend to be comfortable with themselves and very independent—don't try to tell them what to do!

◆ Leather bags with buckles and zippers signify a "bad girl" image—these women are unleashing their wild side. They tend to act before they think and are always up for a good time.

◆ Bright-colored handbags in pink, purple and bright green indicate women who are fun, friendly and easy to approach. They can start a conversation with complete strangers.

◆ Black and brown handbags may represent women who are more reserved. They can be shy at first, but open up after a while.

The purses we carry often become an extension of ourselves—and sometimes an extension of our home office. Writer Anita Daniel once said, "Every woman's handbag is a lost-and-found department in itself." With that in mind, we hope you'll *find* these handbag hints helpful. Hmmm…now where did I put my keys?

Perk Up a Straw Bag

Bring last year's straw bag back to life by dusting it off and then coating it with hairspray (do this outdoors or in a well-ventilated room).

Your bag will take on a whole new shine. This trick also works on straw hats!

Nonslip Shoulder Strap Solution

It's so annoying to carry a purse with a shoulder strap that keeps slipping off your shoulder. Try this—sew a BIG button on your jacket or coat…under the collar…on the side you usually carry your bag. Use the button as a hook to keep the slippery strap in place.

> **NOTE:** For this solution, try to find a button that matches the color of your jacket, so that it will blend in.

Pen Holder for Your Purse

You should always carry around something to write with (what would happen if the battery ran down on your Palm Pilot or your BlackBerry?). But instead of having pens or pencils floating around loose inside your purse, put them in a plastic toothbrush holder.

The holder is easy to find in a crowded bag, and it will also prevent a pen from accidentally losing its cap and making marks inside the bag's lining. (If you already carry a toothbrush in a holder in your purse, be sure to label the containers accordingly.) ■

■ Products ■

E-Pen™ Electrolysis System

With patience and persistence, this system will remove hair safely and permanently. And it's a lot less expensive than going to an electrologist. Unlike the needle system of electrolysis, this unit treats many hairs simultaneously. Most important, there is no pain, scarring or pitting.

It comes with simple, detailed instructions and includes everything you need to customize the treatment. It also has a soft carrying case.

Source: www.epenelectrolysis.com.

T3 Tourmaline Featherweight Ionic Hair Dryer

The T3 is a bit of a splurge, but it can save you time and money at the hair salon. Tourmaline, a semi-precious gemstone, is said to produce more negative ions than any other substance. The ions make water evaporate more quickly.

We don't really know about negative ions, but we do know that the T3 leaves our hair smooth, shiny, frizz-free and damage-free.

Source: T3 Micro, Inc., 866-376-8880, www.t3tourma line.com.

Lite-E-Nuff Key Light

Be safe and stop scratching the keyhole of your door. This small key-ring accessory fits over any key and aims a small, powerful beam of light wherever your key points. It also helps you open your car or house door quickly instead of fumbling in the dark.

Source: Miles Kimball, 800-546-2255, www.miles kimball.com.

Magnetic Clasp

If you've ever struggled to clasp a favorite necklace, this clever item makes it easy to be self-sufficient. In a few seconds, you can convert your hard-to-hook necklace or chain into a simple, secure, no-problem-to-put-on-and-take-off magnetic clasp. The 2 brass magnetic clasps come with gold or silver plating.

It works for bracelets, too.

Source: Miles Kimball, 800-546-2255, www.miles kimball.com.

Jewelry Clasp

When you're tired of chasing your slippery bracelet around your wrist, trying to clasp it, this 6" clip—which is as simple as it is helpful—will hold the fastening ring in place while you close the clasp.

Source: Miles Kimball, 800-546-2255, www.miles kimball.com.

CHAPTER 7

Better Bath Basics

On the TV show *Family Feud*, the question was, "Which room in your house do you most hate to clean?" And the #1 answer was, "The bathroom!" While we don't have any magic solution for avoiding the ongoing chore of bathroom cleaning and maintenance, we do have some helpful hints on how to get satisfying results without too much work.

For starters…José Carreras, a member of the world-renowned "Three Tenors," says that he never sings in the shower, but he does occasionally sing in the bathroom. He notes that bathrooms usually have the best acoustics. If you like to sing, do it while you work. It will make you feel a lot happier as you get the job done.

TOILET

According to the World Toilet Organization (*www.worldtoilet.org*), the average person uses the toilet 2,500 times each year—that's about 6 to 8 times a day. And it will probably come as no surprise that women generally take 3 times as long as men to use the toilet.

With all that use, it's no wonder the toilet needs cleaning. *Here are some hints that will have your bowl gleaming as you flush with pride…*

Cleaning the Bowl

◆ For basic cleaning, just toss 2 or 3 tablespoons of baking soda around the bowl, then scrub with a toilet brush and flush.

◆ If you want a deodorizer and disinfectant as well as a cleaner, pour ½ cup of distilled white vinegar around the bowl, with or without the baking soda. Let it stay for a few minutes, then scrub with a brush and flush.

Bowl Brightener

Every now and then, pour a 1-liter bottle of cola—flat or fizzy, regular or diet—into the bowl. Let it stay there for an hour or so, then flush and notice how the porcelain sparkles.

Cleaning Toilet Rings

◆ A ring in the toilet bowl is usually because of hard-water buildup. Make a paste of borax powder (available at supermarkets and drugstores) and a few drops of lemon juice. Wet the bowl by flushing the toilet. Then smear the paste on the ring with a sponge or plastic knife. Let it stay there for a couple of hours. Then scrub with a toilet brush and flush the toilet again.

◆ Wet a pumice stone (available at drugstores) with a bit of water, and then gently rub the toilet ring with the stone. Wetting the stone is important because a dry pumice stone will scratch the porcelain surface.

Basic Stain Removers

◆ Toss a couple of Alka-Seltzer or denture-cleansing tablets into the toilet bowl. Once the fizzing stops, scrub the stains with a brush and flush.

◆ If you have some Tang fruit juice powder, sprinkle ⅓ cup of the powder in the bowl. Leave it there for a few hours, then scrub with a brush and flush.

◆ If the stains are too tough for even Tang or denture cleanser, empty a few vitamin C capsules, or mash vitamin C tablets into a powder and drop it in the bowl. Let it stay that way for a few hours. Then scrub with a brush and flush.

Toilet Seat

You can clean and disinfect the toilet seat by using this simple formula. In a spray bottle, add ½ cup of distilled white vinegar, ½ cup of plain water and 15 drops of tea tree oil (available at health-food stores). Shake the bottle, then spray both sides of the toilet seat. Wipe the seat dry with a clean cloth.

The slight vinegar smell will disappear, leaving the unusual, fresh scent of tea tree oil.

FYI: Keep a Lid on It

When you flush without closing the toilet seat lid, a polluted plume of water vapor and bacteria spews out of the flushing toilet bowl. The polluted water particles waft around the bathroom and eventually land. If there are toothbrushes out in a nearby cup or holder, they will be a landing strip for some of those particles.

Toilet Tank

The parts inside a toilet tank—including the flush valve and the ballcock—are constantly submerged in water and are used many times each day. There's a lot of wear and tear on these parts and, even though they're fairly easy to replace, you want them to do their job properly for as long as possible. *The following suggestions should help that happen...*

Cleaning the Tank

◆ Once a month, before you go to bed, pour half of a 1-pound box of baking soda into the toilet tank. The next morning, when you flush the toilet, the tank—and the bowl, too—should be nice and clean.

◆ Drop in a couple of denture-cleansing tablets. Wait 1 hour for them to stop fizzing, then start cleaning and flush.

Tank Leak—A Test

If you suspect that water is leaking from your tank to the bowl, test it by putting a few drops of food coloring in the tank. If, after flushing, the water in the bowl turns the color of the food coloring, it's time to call a plumber to repair the leak.

Overflow Prevention

If, after you flush, the water is rising higher than it should, quickly turn on the cold water in the sink as well as in the bathtub or shower. The cold water coming through the pipes will cause a vacuum that will suction the water in the toilet down the drain.

Commit this tip to memory. It's a great thing to know, especially when you go to somebody else's home.

Clogged Toilet

If you have a minor clog and no plunger, try squirting about 2 ounces (4 tablespoons) liquid dish detergent in the bowl. Give it at least 15 minutes to work its magic, then flush. (Keep in mind the overflow prevention method, above.)

DID YOU KNOW?

The cleanest toilet in a public rest room is usually in the stall *closest* to the door. It tends to be the least used.

BATHTUB

Bathing began as part of a magical and religious ritual. Then, thanks to the ancient Romans' regard for physical cleanliness, luxurious public baths were built and became the rage. By 300 AD, there were more than 900 bath houses in Rome. Gradually, people realized the health implications of public bathing and, what started as a social event soon shifted to a personal experience in the privacy of a person's home.

Today, it seems as though we've come full circle. While a shower is for getting clean, a bath is a magical, relaxing indulgence…it's almost a religious experience. *But whatever the reason for using your bath, here are ways to make it the best it can be…*

Cleaning the Tub

◆ The best time to clean the tub is right after someone has taken a shower or bath, and the room is warm and humid. Get rid of the grime before it has a chance to cake on.

◆ When cleaning the tub, kneel on a couple of sponges or shoulder pads. Your knees will be glad you did.

◆ Try this for an easy cleanser—sprinkle baking soda around the tub, then wet a washcloth with distilled white vinegar and scrub, then rinse.

If you do this once or twice a week, chances are there will be no need to *scrub*. It will be more like "just wipe it down." Plus, it's great that you are not using harmful chemicals or drain-clogging cleansers. *And your bathtub is so clean!*

Bathtub Rings

To prevent bathtub rings, do not use any bath preparations (such as gels, bubble bath, salts, pearls, etc.) that contain oils.

But what if you don't use them, and you still have a ring around the tub? Then, as you're filling the bath, add ½ cup of baking soda to the running water. After the bath, let out the water, and there should be no ring around the tub.

As a bonus, the baking soda soothes, softens and conditions skin.

✱ **Remove a Ring with Hose!**
If you forgot to add the baking soda and the bathtub still has a ring, get a pair of old, clean pantyhose, cut off a leg, scrunch it up and use it to rub off the ring.

Chlorinated-Water Stains

◆ Put a few paper towels on the water stains, then pour distilled white vinegar on the towels. Let it stay that way for at least 30 minutes, until the towels are almost dry and the stains are gone.

◆ If the stains are stubborn and the vinegar alone doesn't make them disappear, sprinkle baking soda on the stains and wipe them away with the moist paper towels.

Discolorations

◆ Cover the discolored spots with lemon juice —enough to cover the spots—and let it stay there for about 30 minutes. Then sprinkle about 1 tablespoon of baking soda on a wet washcloth and scrub the discolored spots.

◆ If you're still seeing spots, take 1 tablespoon of cream of tartar and add a few drops of 3% hydrogen peroxide—just enough to make a paste. With an old toothbrush, rub the paste into the discolored spots and then let it dry. When it's dry, rinse it clean.

Rust Stains

◆ Does the can of shaving cream leave a rust ring in the bathtub or on the sink? Paint the bottom rim—the part that touches the sink or tub and leaves the ring—with colorless nail polish. Let it dry thoroughly and then give it a second coat.

◆ Mix 1 teaspoon of table salt or cream of tartar with ¼ teaspoon of lemon juice to make a paste. Put the paste on a soft cloth and rub the rust stain away. (Then be sure to paint colorless nail polish on the bottom of the can that caused the rust ring.)

Cleaning Bathtub Mats

If you have a rubber or vinyl bathtub mat, throw it in the washing machine with a load of towels. The agitating towels will scrub the mat clean.

> **CAUTION:** Do not put a rubber or vinyl bath mat in the dryer.

Removing Nonslip Bathtub Appliqués

◆ Put 1 cup of distilled white vinegar in a pan and heat it up. Once the vinegar is hot, soak a sponge or cloth in it, then use tongs to plop it on top of the appliqué. When it cools to room temperature, take it off…the sponge or cloth *and* the appliqué.

> **CAUTION:** Although distilled white vinegar should be safe for all shiny surfaces, check with the manufacturer before you use it—especially if you have a new bathtub that's made of fiberglass, Plexiglas or any other modern material.

◆ Cover the appliqué with a piece of aluminum foil. Then zap it with a hair dryer set on *hot*. The idea is for the heat to melt the glue that's causing the appliqué to stick. After 1 or 2 minutes, you should be able to peel it off.

◆ Dunk a straight-edged razor blade (it may help to use a blade holder) in liquid dish detergent and *very carefully* scrape off the appliqué. Keep redunking as you progress.

If some of the appliqué adhesive remains on the bottom of the tub, use nail polish remover to clean it off.

Cleaning Whirlpool Tubs

It's important to prevent soap scum and anything else that might build up and clog the jets of the whirlpool. Once or twice a year, pour 1 gallon of distilled white vinegar into the water and run the whirlpool.

SINK

O nce considered utilitarian, bathroom sinks are now available in a wide range of colors, materials, shapes and sizes to match any décor. So if you want to wash your troubles down the drain, be sure to choose the right sink for the job.

Cleaning the Sink

See "Cleaning the Tub" on page 167.

Fixing a Faucet Drip

◆ If you can't stop the faucet from dripping, you might need to replace the washer (a flat, rubber disk that prevents leakage). Any hardware store should have them—be sure to ask a knowledgeable salesperson for instructions.

◆ Until you replace the washer, you can at least stop the drip from getting on your nerves... just place a sponge or washcloth in the sink, directly underneath the faucet.

◆ If you can still hear the *drip...drip...drip*, then wrap a towel around the faucet and keep it in place with a rubber band or piece of string. Or, just take the string and tie it around the spout—the water will run down the string noiselessly.

SHOWER

T he average in-and-out-in-5-minutes shower uses almost 20 gallons of water... compared with 37 gallons for the average bath. Obviously, showering is a good way to get clean *and* save water. You can save even more water by showering "The Navy Way."

Because of the scarcity of fresh water on ships, sailors are taught to turn on the shower just long enough to get wet. Then they turn off the shower, quickly soap up and scrub, and turn the shower on again to rinse off. Fast and efficient!

Whether you "Go Navy!" or shower any other way, here are some helpful hints to increase your shower power...

Cleaning the Showerhead

◆ If you aren't getting enough shower power, it may be that mineral deposits (hard-water buildup) are clogging the showerhead and minimizing the spray.

Do you have a totally metal showerhead that can be safely detached from the pipe and then put back? If so, remove the showerhead, put it in a big pot with ½ cup of distilled white vinegar and 1 gallon of water. Boil it for about 15 minutes. Then, when the showerhead is cool enough to handle, reattach it and...have a nice spray!

◆ If the showerhead is not all metal—or if you cannot detach it from the pipe—pour about 1 cup of distilled white vinegar in a small, leak-proof plastic bag. Put the bag over the showerhead and secure it in place with a thick rubber band or piece of string. Let it stay that way overnight.

In the morning, remove the bag, scrub the head with an old toothbrush, rinse with clean water and enjoy your power shower.

Cleaning Glass Shower Doors

◆ While you're still in the shower, pour a little shampoo on a washcloth and wash the doors. Rinse them with the shower's spray. After you're out of the shower and finish drying yourself, wipe the shower doors dry with your used towel.

◆ That takes care of the inside-the-shower shower doors. Clean the other side—the outside —of the shower doors with 1 part distilled white vinegar to 3 parts plain water. Dampen a cloth with the mixture and wipe down the doors, then dry them with a few paper towels or a dry cloth.

◆ For really grimy glass shower doors—either inside or outside—pour some full-strength distilled white vinegar on a washcloth or sponge, and go over the doors with it. Wait 5 minutes, then rub a corner of the door with the cloth or sponge.

If the grime comes off easily, finish the job. If the scum and film don't come off, sprinkle a bit of baking soda on the cloth or sponge, and scour the doors until they're clean. Then rinse with plain water and dry with a clean cloth.

Keeping Shower Doors Clean

Once your glass shower doors are nice and clean, pour a few drops of baby oil on a soft cloth and apply a light layer of the oil to the doors. This will keep them free of soap scum, hard-water deposits and dirt for weeks at a time.

Cleaning Shower Door Tracks

Stuff up the drain holes in the door track with wadded-up pieces of paper towel or aluminum foil. Then trickle in distilled white vinegar so that it covers the entire bottom of the track. Let it stay that way for 30 minutes.

Then remove the paper or foil plugs and rinse the track with water. Wipe it with a clean cloth or paper towel to dry.

✱ **Smooth-Sliding Secret**
Apply a light coat of petroleum jelly to the track—this will keep your shower doors gliding smoothly.

Cleaning a Plastic Shower Curtain

◆ Before you hang up a brand-new curtain, fill the bathtub with a few inches of water, then add 2 cups of table salt. Put in the new curtain, and let it take a saltwater bath for about 10 minutes. Shake off the water, dry with a clean cloth and then hang up your mildew-proof curtain.

◆ If the curtain has been used for a while and it has some mildew or soap scum on it, check to see if it is machine washable—lots of plastic curtains are nowadays.

If so, just toss it in the machine along with 2 or 3 towels. Add your regular laundry detergent and 1 cup of distilled white vinegar. The towels act as buffers against the machine's agitation, and they will scrub the curtain clean.

As soon as the curtain is machine-clean, it should be mildew-free, soft and pliable—dry it with a cloth and rehang.

◆ If your curtain is not machine washable, you can clean it with a cloth or sponge dipped in distilled white vinegar.

✳ Slip-Sliding Away

If the curtain doesn't glide open and close as smoothly as you would like it to, coat the rod with a thin layer of baby oil or petroleum jelly, or rub it with a bar of soap.

Replacing Shower Curtain Rings

The next time you buy plastic shower curtain rings, consider buying 2 sets instead of just 1. That way, if a ring breaks (as plastic rings often do), you will have extra replacement rings handy, and you won't have to buy and change an entire new set of rings.

TILE & GROUT

Have you ever noticed that the interior walls of many highway tunnels are tiled? According to the International Bridge, Tunnel & Turnpike Association (*www.ibtta.org*), ceramic tiles have 2 big advantages—tiles are easy to clean (think of the constant fumes, dust, tire particles, and exhaust in a tunnel)...and tiles are durable (having to withstand grime, vehicle emissions, water leakage, temperature changes, artificial light, sunlight and vibrations).

Compared to the abuse tiles take in a tunnel, cleaning and maintaining your tiled bathroom should be a piece of cake...or a cake of soap...or all of the hints that follow...

Cleaning Solutions

◆ Wet a sponge with distilled white vinegar, wipe it over the tile and grout and then use an old toothbrush to scrub it. Rinse everything clean with plain water.

◆ Mix 1 part borax powder (available at supermarkets or drugstores) with 2 parts baking soda, then add enough water to form a thick paste. Dip an old toothbrush in the paste and scrub the grout and tile. Rinse it clean with plain water.

◆ Do you have an old-fashioned typewriter eraser at home—the kind that's round and has a brush attached? If so, rub the eraser on the grout, then brush away the eraser particles. (Aren't you glad you kept that eraser all these years?)

◆ The grungiest grout is usually underfoot between floor tiles. If you want to get the grout back to its original color and are willing to work hard to do it, stock up on sandpaper.

> ✎ **NOTE:** If fine (150-grit) sandpaper doesn't do the job, kick it up a notch and use medium (100-grit) sandpaper.

Cut the sandpaper into 2" strips. Sand the grout with a folded piece of the sandpaper strip. It's a tedious job, but if there's a big difference in the way it looks, and you love it, then keep it up!

Once you complete the sanding, wipe the floor clean. You may also want to apply a coat of tile sealer (available at hardware and paint stores).

Mold and Mildew

If you suspect a major mold problem is developing in your home or office (the first clue is that you feel sick only when you're in that moldy area), visit the Mold-Help Organization's Web site (*www.mold-help.org*) for more information, including an inexpensive method of mold testing.

In this section, we offer solutions for dealing with mild cases of mold and mildew...and ways to prevent a major problem.

Preventing Mold and Mildew

◆ Moisture is the primary cause of bathroom mold and mildew. To combat excess moisture, open the bathroom door right after you shower or bathe. Better yet, if you have an exhaust fan, turn it on right *before* you jump in the shower.

◆ When you're done bathing, wipe down the shower walls with a clean, dry cloth or towel. It should only take a minute or so, and it will save you the trouble of cleaning away mold and mildew later on.

◆ After you step out of the shower, close the shower curtain to help prevent mold and mildew from growing in the folds. (You may first want to wipe down the shower walls with a towel or cloth.)

◆ If you are going to be away from home for some length of time, leave an open bag of natural clay kitty litter in the bathtub (or put an old box top filled with litter in the bathroom). The litter absorbs excess moisture and helps prevent mildew.

◆ Hot showers or baths produce moisture that can cause mold and mildew. Absorb some of the excess moisture by keeping a few charcoal briquettes in the bathroom.

Preventing a Steamy Bathroom

Before you run a bath, fill the tub with about 1" of cold water—and *then* add the hot water. Doing this should prevent "steamy bathroom syndrome," which may stop mold and mildew from developing.

Remove Mold and Mildew

Add 1 cup of lemon juice and 1 cup of table salt to 1 gallon of hot water. Use this solution to wipe the moldy and/or mildewed areas thoroughly.

Then rinse with plain water, and dry with a clean cloth.

Cleaning Chrome Fixtures

◆ Clean anything made from chrome with distilled white vinegar or rubbing alcohol, dabbed on a cloth or sponge. Then dry and buff the chrome with a soft cloth.

◆ Fabric-softener sheets—before or after they've been used—give chrome a great shine.

DRAINS

There are 2 kinds of drains—clogged and unclogged. The remedies that follow should work like magic to clear your drain without harmful fumes, harsh chemicals or—the best part—an expensive plumber.

Clean and Deodorize

Once a month—or anytime there seems to be an unpleasant smell coming from 1 of the bathroom drains—pour 1 or 2 cups of baking soda down the drain. Follow by flushing it with hot tap water.

Fixing Clogged Drains

◆ If the water in your bathroom sink or tub isn't draining as quickly as it should, chances are there is a tangle of hair that needs to be cleaned out. It's a simple yet disgusting job, but someone's gotta do it. You'll want to wear rubber gloves and have a plastic bag handy.

Twist and pull out the pop-up stopper. Remove the hair and put it in the bag. Then clean the gunk off the metal tube with

1 tablespoon of baking soda or 1 ounce of distilled white vinegar on a sponge. Then replace the stopper and see how quickly the water goes down the drain.

◆ Pour 1 cup of baking soda down the clogged drain of your shower or bathtub. Follow that immediately with 1 cup of table salt, then ½ cup of distilled white vinegar.

If there is foaming and fizzing and gurgling—that's good. Let the ingredients continue working their way through the sludgy clog, while you boil 2 quarts of tap water and set a kitchen timer for 15 minutes.

When the timer goes off, carefully and slowly pour the boiled water down the drain. Then let the hot tap water run for a minute.

If the drain isn't completely unclogged, repeat the entire procedure again.

◆ Toss 3 Alka-Seltzer tablets down the drain and add 1 cup of distilled white vinegar. Wait 3 minutes, then run the hot water.

Clog Prevention

Use a hair catcher over the drain every time someone showers or bathes. They are inexpensive and available at most hardware and drugstores—even some supermarkets.

Hair catchers generally come in 2 sizes, so measure the diameter of your drain before you go shopping.

SOAP

The innovative and influential artist Pablo Picasso once said, "The purpose of art is washing the dust of daily life off our souls." In that vein, we say, "The purpose of soap is washing the dust of daily life off ourselves." *Here are some very helpful ways to make the most of your bars of soap…*

Preventing Messes

◆ Keep a sponge on the soap dish and place the soap on the sponge. The sponge will absorb all of the soap's drippings. (You may want to forget about the soap dish and just use a sponge instead!)

◆ Place a small, waterproof object—the plastic cover from a prescription-pill bottle, or the round plastic core of a used-up roll of transparent tape—and keep it on the soap dish. Place the wet soap on top of the object, which will enable the soap to dry without soap mush getting stuck to the dish.

Soap Slivers

◆ Instead of discarding that last little sliver of soap, paste it onto the new bar of soap. Just suds up the new bar, and stick the sliver on top. The 2 soaps will dry as 1 bar.

◆ You can recycle slivers of soap by making slits in a bath sponge. Then stick the slivers into the sponge and enjoy a wonderfully soapy bath or shower.

Soap Life Extension

Keep a bar of soap unwrapped for a month before you use it—the air-exposed soap will harden and, once you start using it, it will last longer than usual.

If the unwrapped soap is scented, let it sit in your linen closet. It will make everything smell nice.

FRESHEN UP

Our sense of smell is closely linked to our sense of well-being. Get a whiff of a pleasant scent, and we want to stick around. This section includes easy, healthful ways to keep the bathroom fresh and at its best, especially when *female* company is coming (women have keener senses of smell than men).

Safe and Natural Room Deodorizer

In a spray bottle, add 2 cups of distilled water (available at most supermarkets), 2 cups of rubbing alcohol and 3 drops of natural lemon oil (available at health-food stores). The lemon oil may seem pricey, but a 1-ounce bottle may last you a year or more.

A few sprays of the mixture will freshen the air without exposing you to the toxic risk of chemicals that are typically used in many commercial air fresheners. Inhaling certain chemicals has been linked to headaches, sinus infections and even asthma attacks.

Fresher Clothes Hamper

Sprinkle baking soda on the bottom of the hamper...or keep an open box in the hamper...or in some inconspicuous place in the bathroom. After a couple of months, change the box and pour the baking soda down the drain.

When Company Is Coming

◆ Right before your company is due to arrive, apply 1 or 2 drops of vanilla, almond or lemon extract (available at health-food stores) on

a bathroom light bulb. Turn on the light as you walk out. When the bulb heats up, the pleasant fragrance will permeate the air.

You can also give the warm bulb a spritz of your favorite perfume.

◆ Light scented candles to help eliminate odors and to create a more romantic or festive atmosphere.

> **NOTE:** If you haven't followed our other cleanup suggestions, soft candlelight can cover a multitude of sins. Just be sure the candles are in secure holders and placed in safe areas, away from children and pets.

Extra Towels

If you have counter space in your bathroom—and you want to have extra towels on hand for you or for guests—get a freestanding wine rack (available at household-supply stores). It's perfect to hold rolled-up towels.

Bathtub Toys

Get a mesh bag (available at most hardware and household-supply stores) to hold kids' favorite bathtub toys, and hang it on the tub's faucet. When not in use, the mesh bag will allow the toys to drain and dry. Besides, it's a neat way to keep them tidy and out of the way.

Guest Amenities

To make guests feel comfortable, hang a shoe bag over the bathroom door and fill the pockets with items they might need—for example, bars of soap, washcloths, body lotion, shampoo, a hair dryer, combs and brushes, hair ornaments, gel, mousse, toothbrush and toothpaste...even a rubber ducky. ■

■ Products ■

Starfish Bath Alarm and Temperature Sensor

This item is wonderful for people who are not able to gauge water temperature accurately because of *neuropathy* (a disorder of the nerves).

This adorable Starfish Alarm helps put an end to bathtub overflow and accurately checks the water temperature. Features an LCD readout in either Fahrenheit or Celsius—your choice.

Batteries included...as well as free shipping from England.

Source: Byretech Ltd., +44 (0) 1527-522-522, *www. byretech.com.*

Aquasana Shower Filter Systems

Removes chlorine, enhances pH balance and removes synthetic chemicals and volatile organic compounds from your water. Easy-to-install filter comes with a cartridge that filters up to 10,000 gallons. You can expect to save 20% to 25% on your water and water-heating expenses.

With chlorine filtered out and pH balance improved, your skin and hair will feel softer and healthier. The health benefit of no longer inhaling chlorine or absorbing it through your skin is far-reaching. Good for your health...and your pocketbook. What more could we ask?

Source: Aquasana Factory Direct. *www.aquasana.com.* 1-866-NOBOTTLE.

CHAPTER 8

All-Around-the-House Hints

Beloved 18th-century author Jane Austen knew what she was talking about when she wrote, "Ah! There is nothing like staying at home for real comfort."

Although we do not want to encourage couch potato-ism, we do want you to thoroughly enjoy your home, both inside and out, each day of the week and every season of the year. With that in mind, we hope our suggestions help you with the basic maintenance and care of your humble abode.

INSIDE THE HOME

Instead of sitting in front of the TV or computer for the next few minutes, take a tour of your home with a pad and pen in hand. Pretend that the person or people who live there hired you to improve their living conditions. Look at each room as though you're seeing it for the very first time. Jot down all of the things that need fixing, moving, redecorating, reorganizing...whatever can be done to make it a more comfortable, convenient and attractive living space.

At the end of the tour, if you have a list of changes, set up a room-by-room schedule, and do what needs to be done within a reasonable amount of time—without putting pressure on yourself. (We're sure you'll find lots of ideas in this book to help get you through the list.)

If you couldn't think of any ways to improve your living conditions, it means 1 of 2 things—either everything is exactly the way you want it, which is great (and rare!)...or you couldn't be objective enough to see the need for improvement.

Regardless, we suggest that you check out the suggestions offered here for ways to organize everything that needs organizing...and to care for things you have.

★ What's in Store at Your New Home

◆ If you've just moved into a new home, ask the previous owner for the names of stores where certain household accessories were bought—such as tile, light fixtures, paint/wallpaper, carpeting, countertops, appliances and whatever else came with the house that may need repairing or replacing at some point down the road.

◆ If you had the house built for you, ask your contractor for the names of stores that he used as resources for your new home. You'll be happy you have the information—if and when you need it.

HOME OFFICE

Just about everyone seems to have a home office these days, whether it's a separate room, a computer work station or the dining room table.

Here are some helpful hints to help you organize your space and manage your clerical work more efficiently...

⭐ Increasing Accomplishments

Studies have shown that making lists encourages productivity. Tack a to-do list up in your office. Once you've completed something on the list, put a line through it with an orange highlighter.

The color orange stimulates the involuntary nervous system. It should make you feel more alert and competent.

Pens and Pencils

◆ When you can't find your usual pencil sharpener, use a vegetable peeler instead. It's safer and more efficient than using a pocketknife.

◆ Store pens in a cup with the point down. They will last longer (and poke you less) than if they're stored with the point up, or lying down in a drawer.

◆ When a marker has just about had it, dip the tip in distilled white vinegar for a few seconds. Instead of diluting the ink, the vinegar will help bring out the marker's last drop of color.

🕐 Better Business Cards

Before filing a business card, write pertinent information on the back of it so that when you come across it a few months or years from now, you'll know exactly who this card belonged to...where you met the person...and what you may have had in mind when you took the card. The more details you can jot down, the better.

Paper Shredder

To sharpen a paper shredder, take 2 pieces of aluminum foil about the size of an 8½" x 11" sheet of paper, and put them 1 at a time through your paper shredder. That should make the shredder's blades as sharp as new.

💲 Recycle a Slinky

Use an old Slinky on your desk to hold things like mail, CDs, Lotto tickets waiting to be checked or checks waiting to be deposited.

Correction Fluid Extender

If your bottle of correction fluid is too gooey to use, add 1 or 2 drops of nail polish remover. Shake the bottle vigorously until it sounds like there's liquid sloshing around.

🕐 Easier Trash Cleanup

Put several liners in the wastebasket at once. When the basket is full, take out the trash in the top liner, leaving the liner underneath already in place.

Dry-Erase Board Cleaner

If you pick up the wrong marker—it's indelible instead of dry-erase—and write on the dry-erase board, try erasing the mark with some rubbing alcohol or non-dairy powdered creamer, such as Coffee-mate. Add a little of the powder on a damp cloth and wipe the board clean.

✳ Easy Tape Starter

Here's a great way to save time in finding the beginning of an already-started roll of tape—just place a toothpick under the end each time you finish using it.

Packing and Shipping Hints

Keep this tip in mind when you're packing and shipping books or any other printed material (as well as CDs, DVDs and video or audio cassettes)—the US Postal Service (USPS) offers a low "media mail" postage rate.

You can determine domestic and international postage rates online at *http://ircalc.usps. gov* or by calling 800-275-8777. Then compare the rates with UPS (*http://wwwapps.ups.com/ ctc/request* or 800-742-5877)…as well as Federal Express (*www.fedex.com/ratefinder/home* or 800-463-3339).

Before you check out the cost of shipping a package, it's important to know the package's weight, its measurements and the sender's and recipient's ZIP codes.

Here are some other ways to help you wrap the package…

 Filling for the Birds

When packing a box to mail, use non-buttered air-popped popcorn to fill in spaces. It's inexpensive, weighs practically nothing, it's good for the environment and it does the job.

You may want to add a note from you, the sender, to the recipient—"This popcorn used for packing is safe for birds to eat."

Dealing with Packing Peanuts

As soon as you open a package and see those polystyrene packing peanuts sitting there—just waiting to attack you—rub your hands with an unused fabric-softener sheet. The peanuts will not cling to your fingers, and you'll be able to throw them away easily.

FYI: Reuseable Peanuts

Although polystyrene packing peanuts are not recyclable, they are reusable. Oregon State University has a program where they will pick them up and redistribute them. If you're near OSU, call them at 541-737-2856 or fill out a service request at *http://recycle. oregonstate.edu/pickup.cfm*.

You can also call the Plastic Loose Fill Council's Peanut Hotline at 800-828-2214 —they will tell you which businesses in your area are willing to accept used polystyrene packing peanuts.

Sealing/Unsealing Envelopes

◆ Lick the problem by *not* licking the envelope. Instead, use a glue stick or a small sponge and some water. It's fast, easy and sanitary.

◆ How many times have you sealed an envelope—and then realized that you forgot to enclose something…usually the whole reason you needed the envelope in the first place!

Place the sealed envelope in the freezer for about 3 hours. When you take it out, slip a knife under the flap and you should be able to open it neatly, then repackage it and reseal it.

Mailing Photos

Next time you use a new light bulb, keep the cardboard sleeve that the bulb was in. When you mail a photo, just slip it in the sleeve. It's the perfect protection for the photo (provided the sleeve and photo are compatible sizes).

LIGHTING KNOW-HOW

How many readers of this book does it take to change a lightbulb? Just 1—you. That is, if you have a lightbulb that needs to be changed and if you turned to this page for advice. Well, go to it…and light up your life.

✳ Quieter Fluorescent Bulbs

The buzzing sound of a fluorescent lightbulb can be extremely annoying. Before buying a fluorescent bulb, discover how much noise it will make by looking at the bulb's box.

For a quieter bulb, look for the letter "A" on the box. Noisier bulbs have the letter "B" (as in buzzing) on the box.

Halogen Bulbs

When you acquire a halogen light fixture, chances are there will be a sticker on it that tells you that you need to use a specific type of bulb. Before you buy a halogen fixture, check it out with the salesperson…so that you know *exactly* what you're buying and what you will need in the way of replacement bulbs.

Halogen bulbs are generally more expensive than regular lightbulbs, but you make up the price because these bulbs are more energy efficient than regular incandescent bulbs.

Of course, halogen bulbs should *only* be used in halogen-approved fixtures. And never touch the bulb when it's on, or right after it has been turned off. Hot! Hot! Hot! *A few more cautions you may not know…*

◆ Always turn off the power source before removing, inserting or cleaning a lightbulb.

◆ DO NOT use halogen bulbs in close proximity to fabric, paper or any other combustible material.

◆ DO NOT look at the lit bulb for any length of time. It can be damaging to your eyes.

◆ DO NOT touch the halogen bulb's surface or inside reflectors with your bare hands—oils from your skin can shorten the life of the bulb. Wear clean, lint-free cotton or latex gloves or a lint-free cloth to install, clean or remove a halogen bulb.

◆ Any dirt, oil or lint that's on the bulb can also cause hot spots, resulting in lamp failure. If you notice dirt of any kind, turn off the electrical power. When the bulb is cool, put on gloves and clean the bulb with rubbing alcohol and a lint-free cloth.

🕐 Spare Fuse-Box Fuses

Tape an extra fuse on the inside of the fuse box. When a fuse gets blown and needs to be replaced, you'll have a new one right where you need it.

GETTING ORGANIZED

According to the National Association of Professional Organizers (*www.napo.net*), Americans are busier and more stressed than ever before, and they are looking for ways to better organize their lives—sometimes to the point of obsession.

There's no need to obsess! There are stores galore that cater to everyone's organizing needs—Bed, Bath & Beyond, Lowe's, Home Depot, and the Container Store as well as discount stores, such as Target, Kmart and Wal-Mart.

Before you head out to the nearest mall, check out the following suggestions…they will show you how easy it is to begin organizing the disorganized things in your life. Once you start—and get the satisfaction of organizing a few small things—you will want to continue. And before long, you will be well on your way to having an orderly and organized home.

Storing Manuals, Guarantees And Warranties

Invest in a 3-ring, loose-leaf binder. Every time you buy something that comes with an owner's manual or instructions, punch holes in the paperwork and store it in the binder. Also, staple the purchase receipt and any guarantee or warranty (as well as replacement reorder instructions) to the item's manual.

If you ever need the proof of purchase …or you have a question about using the item …or need a replacement part—you will have all the information organized in the binder without going through a frantic sweat-and-search routine.

Of course, you should keep the binder in a special, within-sight and within-reach place so that you *always* know where it is.

Storing Take-out Menus

◆ Instead of having take-out menus floating all over your house, paste a manila envelope to the inside cover of the telephone book, and keep them in there.

◆ If you want to keep menus handy, put the menus in a large photo album that you can keep near the kitchen telephone (or wherever is most convenient).

When it's time to get take-out, flip through the pages until you reach the menu that whets your appetite and make your call.

✳ Terrific Take-out Tip

Always put the date you got the menu right on the front of the menu. As prices and dishes change, you'll be able to keep tabs on the most recent menus of your favorite restaurants.

Storing Posters

Keeping posters flat seems better than rolling them up—and keeping them flat and protected seems best. Measure your posters, then get 2 pieces of clean cardboard from an art-supply or stationery store—you can also cut them out

of large cartons. But be sure that the cardboard pieces are larger than the posters.

Lay the posters between the 2 pieces of cardboard, put white tissue paper between each poster, and tape the sides closed. You can store about 6 posters this way.

Put the cardboard holder behind any piece of furniture that's against a wall and big enough so that none of the cardboard can be seen. Or slip the cardboard holder under a bed. Just remember where you hid it in case you want the posters.

★ The "What's Where" Book

It's a good idea to keep a "What's Where" notebook, especially if you are in the habit of putting lots of stuff away, then forgetting exactly where you put everything.

Of course, you must remember where you keep the "What's Where" book. How about keeping it on a bookcase or in a bedside drawer?

BOOKS

Francis Bacon—a prominent 17th-century statesman, philosopher and essayist—believed some books are to be tasted, others to be swallowed, and some few to be chewed on and digested. Of course, he didn't mean that *literally*…and certainly not by silverfish—those fast-moving little insects that feed on the starchy material in book bindings.

Here are some helpful ways to keep your books (including this book!) in good condition, so that you're the only living thing feasting on the pages.

🌀 Sticky Bookmark

It's so easy for a bookmark to slip out of a book, especially if it's the laminated kind. If you don't want to lose your place in the book you're reading, use a Post-it note instead.

You can either stick it directly on the page where you've stopped reading...or adhere it to the inside cover of the book—then, each time you stop reading, write the page number where you stopped on the Post-it note. It's an inexpensive, reusable and efficient bookmark.

Preventing Mustiness, Mildew and Silverfish

◆ Lack of circulating air around books encourages mustiness, mildew and silverfish. Resist the urge to stuff your books into the bookcase, and instead give them a little room to breathe by limiting your books to 1 layer per shelf, with enough room to add just 2 or 3 more books—but don't!

It also helps if you can keep books close to the front of the bookcase shelves, which lets more air get to them. Remember—no books behind books.

◆ If you're a real book lover, you may run out of bookshelf space and may have to store your excess books in cartons. Wrap a few charcoal briquettes in cheesecloth or in an old sock, and put it in the box along with the books. This helps to prevent mustiness and mildew. Store the carton in a cool, dry place, which will also help to keep your books in good condition.

Removing Mustiness

◆ Put the odorous tome in a brown paper bag, and fill the bag with crinkled pieces of plain (non-colored) newspaper, or 1 cup of natural clay kitty litter. Close up the bag, securing it with a rubber band.

After a couple of days, open the bag, take out the book and check to see if the smell is gone. If it isn't, replace the newspaper pages or kitty litter with a fresh supply, close the bag tightly again, and let it stay that way for 2 more days. Repeat this process until the book is odor-free.

◆ You can also place the book in a frost-free freezer overnight. In the morning, the musty smell should be gone.

★ Best Book Duster!

Use a clean (never used) paintbrush to dust your books.

Removing Mold or Mildew

If you have a moldy or mildewed book that you treasure, and you have the patience to do a tedious job, try this remedy...

Get a soft toothbrush, and gently brush off the mold or mildew from each affected page. Then sprinkle cornstarch or baking soda between the dirty pages, and let it stay that way overnight.

The next morning, use a new, clean toothbrush to gently brush out the cornstarch or baking soda. The book may not be as good as new, but it will be a lot better than it was, and you will have stopped it from getting worse.

HOME ELECTRONICS

The home-shopping channel *America's Store* recently projected that the average American household will spend approximately $1,250 on consumer electronics this year. And that's just for batteries! (Only kidding.)

Actually, $1,250 seems conservative to us, considering all of the new and smaller versions of electronic gadgets that we see advertised on a daily basis.

Whether you're the first on your block to have the latest *whatever*, or you're happy hanging on to the older models of electronic products you've finally mastered, here are some ways to take care of them so that they will keep working for you.

Cleaning a Telephone

◆ Dampen a soft cloth with distilled white vinegar and wipe the telephone clean. Be sure to thoroughly clean the handset, earpiece and mouthpiece, where most germs congregate.

◆ For hard-to-reach areas around the buttons, use a cotton swab that's been dipped in distilled white vinegar. The smell will disappear in a few minutes.

Caring for a Computer

◆ Get the dust out of the keyboard crevices with a can of compressed air (available at hardware and art-supply stores).

◆ A hair dryer on *cool* can clean the keyboard.

◆ If the keys are the kind that don't pop off, you can use a portable vacuum cleaner on the keyboard.

◆ Use swabs moistened with water or rubbing alcohol to get at those hard-to-reach places. Lint-free (foam) swabs are best.

◆ If there's something stuck between 2 keys, press Silly Putty on it. When you peel off the Putty, the piece of dirt should come out with it. What? You don't have Silly Putty? *You can make your own using either of the following recipes…*

   ◆ In a cup, put 2 tablespoons of white glue. In another cup, dissolve 1 teaspoon of

Epsom salt in 1 teaspoon of water. (Don't worry if it doesn't dissolve completely.) Add the Epsom-salt liquid to the glue, and stir until it's the consistency of Silly Putty. Store the mixture in a plastic bag or other airtight container.

◆ Combine 1 cup of white glue with ½ cup of liquid starch. Stir until you have Silly Putty. Store the mixture in a plastic bag or other airtight container.

◆ An occasional swipe with a fresh baby wipe will work well to clean the computer's screen, keys and mouse.

◆ Wipe the monitor screen with a used fabric-softener sheet. The sheet helps repel dust by eliminating static cling. (You can also use this to dustproof your television screen.)

Cleaning a Spill on the Computer

Quick—turn off the computer! As soon as the power is off, turn over the keyboard to help prevent the spilled liquid from saturating circuits. Spread out paper towels in a dry area and shake the keyboard over them.

With the keyboard upside down, lift it high enough to clean it out with a microfiber or cotton cloth, and dry it as best as you can with paper towels. Once that's done, leave the keyboard upside down for at least 12 hours…even longer is better.

Meanwhile, check your newspaper for computer sales, because if it doesn't work when you plug it in again, you're going to need to buy a new keyboard.

⭐ **Preventing Spills**
The key is to never eat or drink when you're working at your computer. Obviously!

Conserving Battery Power on a Laptop

◆ If you're not using your wireless card or the DVD player, switch them off.

◆ Use the battery until it's dead. Charge the battery completely, never partially.

◆ It's best to use and charge the battery at room temperature, definitely not in extreme heat or cold.

◆ Read the laptop manual and follow the suggestions for using your laptop's automatic function to save your work.

Keeping Computer Cables Neat

If you have an old telephone around—a unit you'll never use again—and it has a coiled cord, cut off the cord and gather up the messy computer cables. Wrap the coiled cord around the cables to keep all those loose wires together. It's so much neater to have 1 line of cables than several strands floating about.

If you don't have an old corded phone, you can also buy coiled telephone cord at the hardware store.

Keeping Electrical Cords Neat

Loose cords from extension cords and appliances can be kept together neatly—just thread the cords through a cardboard paper-towel or toilet-tissue tube.

✳ Clean Up Cord Clutter
Write the length of each extension cord and the appliance it fits on the storage tube as well as in the "What's Where" book (*see* page 180).

Electrical Connections— A Handy Guide

If you have several things (computer, printer, fax, speakers, etc.) plugged into a wall outlet or surge protector, take a picture of how the connections are set up.

Take a few photos—from the front, back and sides—so that if something gets undone, or if you have to move the equipment, you will know exactly what needs to go where.

★ Dial, Switch or Knob Markings
When dial markings fade or are rubbed off by constant use, repaint those hard-to-see dials, switches or knobs with red nail polish.

Caring for Batteries

Battery manufacturers agree that refrigerating *alkaline* batteries—which are the most common household batteries—is not necessary or even recommended...and freezing alkaline batteries is definitely NOT recommended.

However, it IS a good idea to store alkaline batteries in a cool, dry place. They should retain 90% of their power while stored at room temperature, for a shelf life of 5 to 7 years.

Rechargeable batteries—either NiMH (nickel-metal hydride) or NiCad (nickel-cadmium)—lose their charge when kept at room temperature for a few days. If you store them in the freezer, they will retain 90% of their charge for several months.

When you take them out of the freezer, though, you will have to wait until they reach room temperature before using them.

✍ **NOTE:** Always read and follow instructions diligently when using batteries and electronics equipment.

Caring for CDs, DVDs and Other Media

It seems like only yesterday that people were listening to music on the radio and watching films in movie theaters—and there were no other options. But today, people have a choice as to how they want their entertainment— either at home or in a public setting.

And technology is moving faster than ever—film reels and videotapes are being replaced by digital video disks (DVDs)...compact disks (CDs) have replaced record albums and audio tapes...and everybody seems to be connected to an iPod.

Here are some suggestions on how to care for your video/audio stuff...at least until it becomes obsolete.

◆ DO NOT touch the surface of a CD. Use only the outer edge and the center hole when you need to handle it.

◆ *NEVER* wipe a CD in a circular motion. It can—and most probably will—cause micro-scratches. If you do not have a CD-cleaning kit (available at electronics and music stores), then wipe the disk gently with a soft, water-dampened, lint-free cloth. Start in the center and work your way to the outer edge. Fight the urge to wipe in a circular motion.

◆ If the CD still skips after you wiped it with a dampened cloth, then combine 2 tablespoons of baking soda and 2 cups of water in a spray bottle. Shake well and spray the disk lightly. Then, with a dry, soft cloth, wipe it from the center outward in straight strokes.

◆ There's a rumor going around that peanut butter will clean CDs. We consulted with technicians and couldn't find anybody who thought this was a good idea. Eat the peanut butter yourself, and use baking soda and water on the disks. Just be gentle and use extreme care.

Storing CDs

Don't throw out cardboard shoe boxes. Paste attractive, room-matching contact paper on them and use them to store your CDs.

If you use clear (see-through) plastic shoe boxes, you can see which CDs are stored inside without opening them up.

Cleaning DVDs

Handle DVDs the same way you handle CDs... carefully. And NEVER wipe a DVD in a circular motion. Use a soft, cotton cloth or chamois to wipe the disk from the center straight toward the outer edge.

If the DVD is dusty, use an air puffer (available at art-supply and photography stores) to blow off the dust.

If a DVD has a somewhat heavy accumulation of dirt, rinse it with water. Remember— no rubbing or scraping. Pat dry with a cotton cloth. Do not use paper products, including lens paper, to wipe a DVD. They're too scratchy.

✳ **Preserving Videotapes**

You may be using DVDs now, but you're probably holding on to stacks of old VHS videotapes. It's important to store videotapes away from stereo speakers, which create a magnetic field that can actually erase the tapes.

Cleaning an Audio Cassette Recorder

It's important to clean the *play, record* and *erase* heads of your tape recorder. Cleaning will keep the heads free of dust and dirt that builds up (mostly from flakes that come off magnetic tape). If you use the recorder often—4 or 5 times a week—clean the heads about once a month using denatured alcohol on a cotton swab. The manual that came with the cassette player should have an illustration, showing you the exact location of the heads...or bring it to

the store where you bought it and ask a knowledgeable salesperson for guidance.

Cleaning a Camera

◆ Use the soft, lint-free cloth with which you clean your glasses to clean your camera lens.

◆ Every time you change the batteries in your camera, clean all the contact points with a good, clean pencil eraser.

Cleaning Photos

After passing around traditional photo prints, you may want to clean off any fingerprints before putting them into an album. Lightly moisten a cotton ball with rubbing alcohol and gently wipe off the smudges. The isopropyl in the alcohol cleans off the oily residue that is left behind from people's fingers.

Test a tiny corner of the photo before you begin the cleaning process. Proceed with caution and care.

Unsticking Stuck Photos

You can separate photos that are stuck together by working a piece of dental floss between them. There's no guarantee that 1 or both of the pictures won't get damaged, but it's the best separating method we've come across.

 Safeguard Photos
Keep irreplaceable prints, disks of digital photos and copies of treasured family films/videotapes in a fireproof box.

AIR CONDITIONERS & HUMIDIFIERS

Think about it...air conditioners and humidifiers create man-made weather. The commercial use of air conditioners has changed the way we live, work and play—especially in Sunbelt cities like Miami, Houston, Phoenix and Las Vegas.

After World War II, air conditioning became a more common feature in the average American home. It was for the millions, not just the millionaires. *Here are some hints to help you chill out...*

Cooling a Room Efficiently

If your air conditioner is not doing its job as effectively as it should, and you have a furry pet, check the AC's filter. The animal's loose hair may be causing a blockage. Clean the filter often (according to the manufacturer's instructions) and, while you're at it, vacuum the air conditioner case as well as the area around it.

If you don't have a pet, you may have to call a repair service, or resort to using a fan. If you do that, put a bowl of ice cubes in front of the fan—the room's temperature will drop at least 10 degrees in a short amount of time. The ice increases the cooling output of your fan by 100%—especially if it's a stationary fan parked right behind the ice cubes.

Unclogging a Humidifier

If you use regular tap water to fill your humidifier, the water's mineral deposits will build up and eventually clog the machine.

If that has already happened, fill the humidifier bowl with warm distilled white vinegar, and let it soak for a couple of hours. Also, soak the *impeller* (rotating rod) in a jar with warm vinegar for the same amount of time. Then rinse and dry both parts. Be careful not to get the motor wet.

To prevent clogs, use only distilled water (available at supermarkets and drugstores) to fill your humidifier.

WINDOWS

Our mother used to say to us it was a sin to have dirty windows and not let the sunshine come in. *So all you sinners, atone— and here's how...*

Preparing to Clean Windows

If you have curtains, here is a way to prevent them from getting messed up while your windows are getting clean.

Without taking them off the rod, drape each panel on a hanger, then hang the hanger on the curtain rod—the panels on the right side of the window should, of course, be hung on the right side of the curtain rod. The panels on the left side of the window should be hung on the left side of the curtain rod. (We're sure you would figure that out for yourself.)

☼ Easy Window Cleaner

Combine 1 cup of distilled white vinegar with 3 cups of warm water. (If your windows seem extra grimy or greasy, add either 2 tablespoons of rubbing alcohol or 2 tablespoons of pulp-free lemon juice.)

Then, dip a scrunched-up piece of plain newspaper (no colored ink) into the mixture, squeeze it until it stops dripping, then use it to clean the window. (Be sure to wear rubber gloves so that the newsprint doesn't get on your hands.) Then dry the window with some dry pieces of scrunched-up plain newspaper.

✳ Better Window Washing

The key to getting clear windows is to use either a squeegee, pieces of scrunched-up plain newspaper (no colored ink), dry coffee filters, a clean blackboard eraser or any of the new microfiber cleaning cloths—they are available at supermarkets and hardware stores.

Window Cleaner And Primer

Mix ½ cup of cornstarch into 1 gallon of warm water. Dip a coarse washcloth into the solution, wring it out and use it to clean the window. Then dry the window with paper towel or plain newspaper.

After doing this a few times, the window should be primed, and all you'll need to clean it in the future is a dry cloth.

Window Caulking Needed? A Test

If your air conditioner and heater don't seem as effective as they should be, your windows may be to blame.

To test for air leaks, go outside and stand in front of the window in question with a plugged-in hair dryer. (You'll need an extension cord or a battery-operated dryer.) Meanwhile, have someone standing inside the house hold a lit candle in front of the window.

Turn on the hair dryer and hold it near the window, opposite the candle on the inside. If the flame flickers because of the air coming from the dryer, then you'll know that the window needs caulking.

✳ Up, Down and Side to Side

When you wipe your windows, clean up and down on the inside, and from side to side on the outside. That way, if you do see a streak that you want to wipe away, you will know which side it's on.

Cleaning High Windows

If windows that need cleaning are too high for you to reach, get a water gun and a long-handled squeegee. Fill the water gun with a cleaning solution and spray it on the window pane, then squeegee it off. It's safer than climbing up on a stool or ladder…and it's more fun, too.

Cloudy Means Clean

If you clean your windows on a bright, sunny day, they will dry quickly, leaving those dreaded streaks. The answer? Clean windows on an overcast day so that they will dry more slowly, giving you more time to wipe them.

Preventing Window Frost

When freezing temperatures are in the forecast, dot the inside of your window with glycerin (available at drugstores), then use a cloth to spread the dots into a thin layer that covers the entire window.

Glycerin's moisture-binding ability helps prevent warm, moist air from seeping out and forming moisture on the outside window pane, which then freezes, causing the window to become frosted.

A Breath of Fresh Air

If you can't open your window because of the freezing cold weather, use a hair dryer to defrost it open along the edges. (But why do you even want to open your window if it's freezing cold outside?)

Windowsill Cleaner

Combine equal amounts of rubbing alcohol and water, then wet a soft cloth with the solution. Use it to wipe the sill clean.

Be sure to test a small area of the sill to make sure it's safe. DO NOT use this remedy on bare metal.

Keep Sills Dust-Free

To prevent dirt, paint the windowsill with high-gloss paint or clear polyurethane. Both will help prevent dust from sticking and are easy to clean.

Cleaning Window Screens

Before you wash the screen, vacuum up the dirt that's sitting there. Then you can get any leftover dirt by pressing a sticky lint roller over the screen's surface.

After vacuuming or lint-rolling, you may not need to wash the screen after all.

Cleaning Venetian Blinds

◆ Dust the slats with your hands—just cover them with either cotton socks or gloves.

◆ If the blinds need more than dusting, you can disassemble them, then wash them in the bathtub or hose them down outside on your porch.

◆ Keep the slats cleaner longer by giving them the once-over with fabric-softener sheets to help repel dust.

CEILING FANS

In 1882, Philip Diehl invented the first electric ceiling fan… and it was *fantastic*. Diehl spent years improving his original model, and by the late 1920s, the ceiling fan was part of the décor and ventilating system of just about every public eatery—from elegant dining rooms to bawdy speakeasies.

If you have a ceiling fan, you're part of the ongoing history of this remarkable invention. *Here's how to take care of it…*

Dusting

Prevent the dust from flying all over the room by using a damp sponge instead of dry dust cloth to clean your fan's blades.

Smart Fan Use for Warm and Cool Months

You probably read the instructions when the ceiling fan was being installed. But if you're new to ceiling fans, you might not know that you can reverse the direction of the blades.

You may wonder, "Why would I want to do that?" Changing the direction of the blades helps circulate warm air during the cold months, which may cut your annual heating bills by about 10%.

When the blades are turning in a clockwise direction, they push the air against the ceiling and down the walls. The warm air gets recirculated without creating a cooling wind.

During cool months, turn on the fan and make sure the blades are rotating *counterclockwise* (the warm-weather setting). Turn off the fan and get a safe ladder—you need to reach the middle section of the ceiling fan. There's a switch that's located on the side of the section that houses the motor. Flip the switch to the opposite setting.

Once you've carefully climbed down off the ladder, turn the fan to its lowest setting. Check that the blades are now rotating *clockwise*. If they are, you're set for winter.

Be sure to reverse the switch and have the blades rotate counterclockwise during the hot summer months...or whenever you want to feel a cool breeze.

FIREPLACE

Comedian Ellen DeGeneres once said, "Go to bed in your fireplace—you'll sleep like a log." Although you shouldn't take Ellen's advice literally, you may want to follow through with some helpful hints to make your fireplace cleaner, prettier, safer and more efficient.

Read All About Substitute Firewood

If you want to light your fire but have no firewood (and it's too cold to go out and get some), finish reading your daily newspaper.

Then tightly roll up a couple of the plain (not colored) papers, and tie them securely with twine or wire. Use the paper-rolls in place of real or fake logs.

CAUTION: NEVER burn colored newspapers or magazines in the fireplace. The inks and dyes used to make them contain lead—and that lead can be inhaled. This can be very dangerous, especially for children and pets.

Feeding the Fire Efficiently

By opening the window that is closest to the fireplace, the fire will use oxygen from outside, instead of taking it from inside the rest of the house. You only need to open the window an inch or even less.

Make a Scented Fire

♦ Spread the rinds from an orange or lemon on paper towels, and let them dry out overnight.

When the rinds are thoroughly dry, toss them on the fire to create a lovely citrus aroma.

◆ If you are not into a citrus scent, you could instead toss in a few pinecones for a more woodsy fragrance.

★ **Grate Idea!**
If your fireplace has grates instead of andirons, you may be able to reduce the amount of smoke the fire emits—just place a brick under each leg of the grate.

Managing Soot

◆ Before lighting the fire, toss a handful of plain table salt on the logs (real, fake or made from newspaper). The salt will help to loosen soot from the chimney, and it will also give the fire a bright, yellow flame.

◆ If you don't eat a lot of potatoes, make a deal with a restaurant that serves french fries, and have them save the potato peels for you.

Put the peels on paper towel, and let them dry overnight. When the peels are dry, you can burn them in your fireplace. They burn with a gusto that sends the soot up and out of the chimney.

◆ If you're a tea drinker, tear open steeped, moist tea bags and sprinkle the tea leaves over the sooty fireplace remains. If you're a coffee drinker, you can use moist coffee grounds on the soot.

The tea leaves and coffee grounds help prevent the ash particles from flying up into the air when you clean up the soot.

✳ **Soot Smell Absorber**
After you've cleaned the ashes from the fireplace, fill a pan or a paper plate with baking soda and place it in the fireplace. Leave it for a day or so, and it will absorb the smell of soot.

Cleaning Glass Fireplace Doors

Use a wet sponge to rub on some wood ashes. Then use a clean sponge to rinse off the glass... along with the dirt.

Cleaning the Hearth

If you can regularly clean the soot marks off the hearth (the area surrounding the fireplace), the soot won't become ingrained and hard to clean off.

For light soot marks, dust them away with a vacuum cleaner attachment or a brush. For soot stains that can't be removed that way, try a gum eraser (available at office- and art-supply stores), or scrub them with a stiff brush and plain water.

For stains that don't scrub off that way, wet a sponge or brush with distilled white vinegar and go at it. Then, rinse the spot well with plain water.

EVEN MORE HINTS...

If you've ever needed to know how to keep your magnetized cabinets closed...or how to see if things are level...or get back something you loaned out, here's how...

Cabinet Magnets

Do you have the type of cabinets that are held shut with a magnet in the corner? Do you have a wrestling match with your cabinet door each time you want to open it? If the magnet is too strong, just put a piece of transparent tape over it. The door will stay closed, yet opening it will be a lot easier.

On the Level...or Not

If you want to know if an object is standing level, use a measuring cup that has the same measurement markings on each side. Put water in the cup—enough to reach 1 of the marks.

Stand the cup on the object in question. If the water hits the same exact mark on each side of the cup, then the object is level. If the water level is different on each side, then the object is lopsided.

The Return of Your Stuff

At last, a good use for the return-address labels you get from charities! Put a label on each item of yours that friends or family may borrow. Let it remind the borrower to whom it should be returned.

What comes to mind? A stapler? A bottle of correction fluid? A bottle of nail polish? Tupperware containers? An umbrella? A tape dispenser? A videotape? A DVD? A book? Power tools? You bet!

CLOSETS

If you have used your closets as dumping grounds for stuff you do not want anyone to see, it's time to go through that stuff...then sell or donate to charity the things you don't need, and organize the things you still value and use.

There are stores that specialize in storage and organizational products—closet stores have do-it-yourself kits that will help you reconfigure closet space for your specific needs. But before you can know what you *need*, you have to know what you *have*. Keep in mind that less is best.

Here are some suggestions to help you thin out the stuff in your closets...and to use the space more wisely. After you've done the initial thinning and organizing, you'll be able to determine whether or not a trip to a closet shop would be helpful.

Closet-Clutter Reality Check

Keep track of which clothes you wear—and, more importantly, which clothes you don't wear—using this simple method. First, start each new wardrobe season by hanging your clothes in the closet with all of the hangers' hooks facing you.

Then, each time you wear and wash an article of clothing, put it back with the hook facing into the closet. At the end of the season, you will be able to tell at a glance which garments were not worn simply by the way the hanger hooks are facing.

Now comes the decluttering part of this process. To thin out your wardrobe, select give-aways from the clothes that are on the hangers with hooks still facing you...the clothes that you didn't wear at all. And then, take it a step further. Review the clothes you DID wear and didn't like. Take them to a thrift shop and let them make other people happy.

Making Hangers Glide

◆ Rub your closet's clothing rod with a piece of waxed paper and your hangers will move along the rod smoothly and easily.

◆ Hardware stores have inexpensive plastic rod covers that come in a variety of colors.

The covers make it easy to slide hangers back and forth on the closet rod.

Extra Hanging Space

◆ Place a shower-curtain ring on the neck of a hanger, and then you can hang another hanger on it.

◆ Always hang your clothes facing the same direction—that way, there's less space between clothes. So, you'll have more hanging space, and your closet will look neater.

Hanging Accessories

If you have some extra shower-curtain hooks around, slip them on the closet rod, and use them to hang purses, belts or ties…or tote bags filled with stuff that would otherwise be floating around loose in the closet.

Shelves Made Easy

If you wish you had shelves in a roomy closet, visit a thrift shop or unpainted furniture store and look for an inexpensive bookcase.

Put the bookcase inside your closet—you will have your shelves and none of the bother of putting them up.

Entryway Closet Convenience

If you have a guest closet in your entryway, hang a shoe holder on the inside door. To store accessories that you may need before going outside—such as scarves, gloves, hats, sunglasses—assign compartments of the shoe bag for each of those things.

You can also store pet accessories in the shoe bag, such as your dog's leash or winter jacket, as well as a small flashlight.

Removing Moisture and Musty Smells

◆ Keep a few open boxes of baking soda somewhere in the closet.

◆ Put natural clay kitty litter in a shoe box or pie tin, and leave it on the floor of the closet…but NOT if you have a cat who has access to the closet.

If it's a walk-in closet and you don't want to step on the litter, put it in the leg of an old pair of pantyhose, knot it closed and hang it in a corner.

◆ Use chalk…or charcoal briquettes…or cedar chips to freshen your musty closet. Put them in a pie tin on the floor or hang them in an old pair of pantyhose.

> ⚡ **CAUTION:** Do not let cedar chips come into direct contact with your clothes. They can cause fabrics to yellow.

Protecting Clothes

If you have louvered or slatted closet doors, you can keep your clothes dust-free and moth-free by covering the openings—just tape sheets of waxed paper on the inside of the doors.

Storing Blankets

If you're like everyone else, your closet space may be limited. Instead of taking up room storing blankets, put them on the floor under the beds on which they're used. That way, you save space in the closet, and it makes it easy to get to them on a cold night.

Sweet-Scented Moth Repellent

Ever make an orange-spice pomander ball? If not, here's your chance. *Start by gathering the following ingredients…*

1 ounce ground orrisroot (available at some herb stores…or from Elizabeth Bradfield, *www.soapmoldsnmore.com* or 858-452-8980)

1 ounce ground cinnamon

½ ounce ground nutmeg

2 feet of ¼"- to ½"-wide ribbon (non-silky ribbon, such as grosgrain, works best)

1 thin-skinned orange (the peel stays on)

1 box of whole cloves

Combine the orrisroot, cinnamon and nutmeg in a bowl and set it aside.

Take 1 foot of the ribbon and cut it in half. Then tie 1 strip around the orange and knot it on top. Do the same thing with the other strip of ribbon, so that the 2 strips criss-cross the orange. (If your ribbon is silky, you may want to stick a pushpin in on each of the strips to keep them from slipping.)

Next, stick the cloves all over the orange —but not in the ribbon. Then place the clove-stuck orange in the bowl with the spices, gently rolling it around. Let it sit in the bowl for about 5 days, turning it occasionally.

After 5 days, take the orange out of the bowl, hold it over the sink and, using a hair dryer set on a low and cool setting, blow off any excess spices. Now the pomander ball is ready to be hung in the closet.

Attach the remaining ribbon to the pomander ball, and hang it from the closet rod. This scented moth repellent will last for years.

> **NOTE:** For a spicy-scented moth repellent, cut the leg off a clean, old pair of pantyhose and fill the foot with crushed peppercorns. Knot it closed, and hang it in the closet.
>
> It smells better than mothballs and does the job as well.

DO-IT-YOURSELF SECRETS

If you are (or want to be) a do-it-yourselfer, here are the top 10 categories of tools you should have to help you with most loving-hand-at-home projects…

◆ Claw hammer

◆ Level

◆ Pliers (tongue and groove long-handled pliers, needle nose, medium-sized locking pliers and slip joint)

◆ Screwdrivers (3 standard sizes and 3 sizes of Phillips head)

◆ Adjustable wrenches or 1 complete set of small-to-large wrenches

◆ Utility knife (average-sized and heavy-duty)

◆ Retractable, metal tape measure (make sure it's at least 12' long)

◆ Small all-purpose saw

◆ Small drill

◆ Safety goggles

You'll also need an assortment of nails, screws, nuts and bolts, electrical, masking and duct tape, sandpaper and glue.

As you get more and more into do-it-yourself projects, you will get a better idea of which tools you use most, and which need upgrading. At some point, you may want to treat yourself to a power saw or a sander…or whatever will make your workshop more complete. The main thing is to know what you're doing before you do it. *Be careful.* Oh yeah, and have fun!

Cleaning Rusty Tools

Author Robert Hughes once remarked, "A determined soul will do more with a rusty monkey wrench than a loafer will accomplish with all the tools in a machine shop."

As far as we're concerned, you can either get the rust off that monkey wrench or prevent it from rusting. *Just follow the advice below…*

◆ If you have a tool that is so rusty you're ready to throw it away, give it a final chance to unrust. Get a container—most tools will be able to stand in a wide-mouth jar—and fill it with apple cider vinegar. Put the rusty tool in, and let it marinate overnight. The next day, clean the tool with a cloth. It should be rust-free and usable again.

◆ You can also use sandpaper to take rust off a tool. Start with a fine grade, and if it doesn't work, use coarse sandpaper.

◆ Try getting rid of the rust with a moistened steel wool pad. If that doesn't work, you may have to replace the tool with something new…at least you know you tried.

⭐ **Keep Tools from Rusting**

To prevent rust, keep pieces of chalk or a few charcoal briquettes in your toolbox. This chalk or charcoal will absorb the excess moisture that causes rust.

If you don't use a toolbox, prevent rust from forming by cleaning your tools with steel wool, then applying a thin coat of petroleum jelly.

Removing Nuts, Bolts And Screws

◆ If you want to remove a nut, bolt or screw, but it won't budge, do the unexpected and try turning it to the right, tightening it a bit. If it gets tighter, chances are you can then undo it by turning it to the left.

◆ Pour a little cola on the culprit, wait 1 to 2 minutes for the soda to eat into the rust, then have a go at it.

◆ Distilled white vinegar, iodine or 3% hydrogen peroxide may help loosen a rusty nut, bolt or screw. Dab it on with a cotton ball and let it soak for about 5 minutes before turning it…yes, to the left.

 The Answer to "Which Way?"

When you need to remember which way to loosen or tighten a nut, bolt or screw, try this—"righty tighty, lefty loosey."

Tightening Loose Screws

◆ If the screw is just a little loose, dip it into a bottle of clear nail polish (or coat the screw's hole with a just-dipped nail polish brush). Let it set for a minute, and then screw in the screw.

This remedy is especially helpful if the screw is attached to a knob, like on a dresser drawer.

◆ Take a twist-tie from a loaf of bread, fold it over, then cut the unfolded, open ends so that the tie is the length of the screw's hole. Place the V-shaped end of the twist-tie into the hole, then put in the screw.

If there's not enough room for the screw, cut the twist-tie in half, reinsert only 1 side of the twist-tie in the hole, and then reinsert the screw.

◆ If the hole has gotten much too large for the screw, soak a piece of cotton ball in white glue (such as Elmer's) and stuff it into the hole. Let it stay that way until it dries—at least 24 hours—then screw in the screw.

Creating New Screw Holes

You can close up a large screw hole and start over—just get a little carpenter's glue or wood putty (available at hardware stores), a wooden golf tee (available from your neighbor, the golfer), a hammer and a saw.

Dip the tee in the glue or putty, hammer the tee into the screw hole and let it dry overnight. Then saw off the part of the tee that's jutting out of the wall, sand it flush, and you're ready to create a new hole for a screw or a nail.

Keeping Screws, Nails, Nuts and Bolts Together

When you take something apart, don't risk losing any of the hardware, especially if you will need to put the object back together again. As you remove them, stick all of the nails, nuts, bolts and screws on a thick piece of tape.

It's a good idea to stick the parts on the tape in the same order that you remove them (you may also want to write down the order as a backup).

Dealing with Drywall

◆ If you're putting up a shelf or a mirror or a towel bar, you'll want the solid backing of studs (the vertical 2' x 4' boards behind finished walls) to hang them securely.

If you do not have a battery-powered stud finder (available at hardware stores), you can use an electric razor. Plug it in and move it on the wall as though you were giving it a shave. When the razor passes over a stud, the sound will change from a hollow hum to an up-front buzz. Once you have found a stud, there should be another stud 16" or 24" away.

◆ When you know the exact spot on the drywall that you plan to hammer in a nail, place a piece of masking or transparent tape there. It should help prevent the plaster from chipping off as the nail goes in. Once the nail is in the wall, gently and slowly peel off the tape so that the paint and plaster continues to stay intact.

Hammering Made Painless

If the nail in question is in an awkward spot and it's difficult to hold in place while you hammer (or if you hit your finger more often than the nail), the answer to the problem is a strip of clay (available at crafts and toy stores). Stick the clay on the wall, and let it hold the nail for you. Once you've nailed the job, peel off the clay.

 Hit the Nail on the Head

If you rub the head of your hammer with fine sandpaper every so often, it will help prevent the hammer from slipping off the nail and hitting your finger or the wall.

Using a Screwdriver

◆ To keep a screwdriver from slipping off the head of the screw, rub chalk on the end of the screwdriver before using it.

◆ Before screwing in a screw, screw it in and out of a bar of soap. The soap-coated screw should then screw into your target easier. (Easy for us to say, we know.)

 Shine a Light

If you need to use an electric drill in a dark area, tape a small flashlight (such as a penlight) to the side of the drill to make the work more visible…this will make it easier and safer to do the job.

Fixing Squeaky Hinges

If the hinges on a door or cabinet are *squeeeeeaking*, just dab a bit of petroleum jelly or foam shaving cream on the noisy part, or spray the hinges with nonstick vegetable spray.

Keep opening and closing the door until the jelly or spray works its way in and thoroughly lubricates the hinges.

Making Drawers Glide

Go over the tracks or runners of a drawer with a bar of soap or some leftover candle wax, and they'll practically open and close by themselves.

Smart Sandpaper Substitute

When a small job requires sandpapering, it may be more efficient to use an emery board than to try to maneuver a piece of sandpaper in a tiny or hard-to-reach place.

Fixing a Sticky Door

◆ Find the exact spot that causes the door to stick, then sandpaper it down a little at a time until it no longer sticks.

◆ If the bottom of the door is rubbing, wedge coarse sandpaper between the floor and the door, and open and close, open and close, until the trouble spot is sanded down.

NOTE: To make sure you sand the door and not the floor, staple a piece of thin cardboard on the bottom of the sandpaper—it should rest on the floor while the coarse sandpaper is up against the bottom of the door.

Hiding the Dark Marks

If there are annoying little marks throughout your home, consider covering them up with liquid correction fluid. Even though the white fluid may be whiter than most kitchen sinks or bathroom tiles, it will cover up a dark ding and make it a lot less noticeable.

If the surface on which you apply the cover-up is shiny, dab a little colorless nail polish over the correction fluid.

NOTE: In addition to white, Liquid-Paper correction fluid comes in several colors, such as ivory, blue, green, pink, ledger buff and canary yellow.

You can also get a matching paint sample from your local paint or hardware store.

PEST CONTROL

Would you believe that 95% of all the animal species on Earth are insects? Scientists have discovered over 1 million species, and there may be 10 times that many insects that haven't been named yet.

One out of every 4 animals on the planet is a beetle of some kind. (There are about 500,000 different species of beetle.) Social insects—such as ants and termites—make up about 20% of the total animals in the world.

We've given you these insect facts, not to gross you out, but to make your insect-control challenge seem minor when you realize that millions of insects can exist in 1 single acre of land. *And here are some solutions…*

Repelling Flying Insects

Many insects with wings are repelled by the smell of basil. If you're into growing herbs, be sure to feature basil in your herb garden, and you won't have to shoo-fly any flying insects.

If you don't grow your own basil, buy a bunch at the grocery store or flower shop…you can dry them by clumping 3 or 4 stems together with string or a rubber band. Once you have a bunch of clumps, hang them upside down in a place that's well-ventilated but that's not in direct sunlight.

When the leaves are dry, crumble them into small muslin bags or pieces of cheesecloth, and hang them all around your home, or wherever you suspect flying insects enter or where they like to hang out.

Battling Fruit Flies

◆ When you set out a bowl of fruit for company, just make sure your guests are not fruit flies—to repel these pests, just put a few sprigs of mint around the fruit bowl.

◆ If you have fruit flies hovering around the garbage can or your bunch of bananas, set out a small plastic container filled with a mixture of 1 tablespoon of apple cider vinegar, 6 drops of liquid dish detergent and ½ cup of water. The bugs will fly in, but they won't fly out.

Fighting Silverfish

◆ If silverfish are making their way through your books and important papers, clear out those shelves or boxes and thoroughly vacuum the entire area. Also vacuum the books and papers.

◆ If you have books that need special care, seal them in plastic bags and put them in the freezer for 4 days, time enough to destroy any insect infestation.

◆ Before putting your books and papers back on shelves or in boxes, get 1 of the following (or create a mixture of several)—dried lavender leaves, bay leaves, wormwood, tansy, mint leaves, cinnamon bark.

Silverfish hate all of these pungent smells and tend to be repelled by them. Put the leaves in muslin bags or in cheesecloth, and tuck them into the shelf corners. (The bags can also be used in the kitchen to repel silverfish.)

◆ If silverfish are in your kitchen, remove all utensils from drawers and food from the cabinets. Wash the drawers and cabinets with very hot water and dry it all with a blow-dryer set on *hot*, especially along the wall edges. The hot water and blow-dryer will help eradicate silverfish eggs.

◆ If you've had a severe silverfish infestation, wipe the cabinets and drawers with a potent lavender oil. That should keep them away for about a year.

◆ If you see a silverfish scooting across your bathroom floor, boil a pot of water, and carefully pour it down your bathtub and sink drains, which will hopefully destroy their hiding place. Then vacuum all of the room's corners and crevices.

When you remove the bag, it's best to do it outdoors. Once the bag is out of the vacuum cleaner, be sure to tape it closed, put it in a plastic bag, tape that bag closed and then discard everything.

NOTE: When using the vacuum cleaner to get rid of insects, spill 1 cup of table salt on the floor and vacuum it up. The salt will help kill insect eggs and larvae that may be *inside* the vacuum cleaner bag.

Removing Bugs from Grains And Beans

◆ Place a dried chili pepper in the container with your dry grains or beans, and you will not be bothered by weevils.

◆ Weevils and meal worms are repelled by the scent of mint. Fresh mint leaves or strong-smelling dry mint leaves will keep the bugs away.

A stick of mint-flavored chewing gum in with flour or spaghetti will also get the job done. Each time you open a new bag of flour or package of spaghetti, put in a new stick of peppermint gum.

Dealing with Ants

Figure out the ants' main points of entry—windowsill, doorway, baseboards—and sprinkle those places with any of the following...

◆ cayenne pepper

◆ chili powder

◆ cinnamon

◆ sage

◆ whole cloves

◆ bay leaves

◆ cream of tartar

◆ salted cucumber peelings

◆ dried peppermint leaves or peppermint oil

◆ distilled white vinegar

◆ lemon juice and peel—mix it with water and wash the kitchen floor

◆ baby powder

◆ uncooked white or brown rice

You can also sprinkle the above items in food pantries, cupboards, cabinets or any other place you've seen ants scurrying around.

Rousting Out Roaches

There are various ways to get rid of roaches. The most successful methods use 1 of 3 ingredients—baking soda, borax powder or boric acid (which is a key element in most commercial roach products). The idea is to get the roaches to eat the bait, then go back to the nest and die. *Here is a selection of ways in which each of the 3 B's can eradicate a roach infestation...*

Combating Carpenter Ants

Black and red carpenter ants are found in woody environments. While they do not bite unless provoked, it's not fun to have them crawling around, chewing up your house or furnishings. *To combat these destructive pests, brew up this recipe...*

Carpenter Ant Bait

> 3 cups water
> 1 cup sugar
> 4 teaspoons boric acid powder
> several jar lids (shallow enough so ants can crawl in)
> wads of cotton batting

Heat water in a pot and then add the sugar and boric acid powder. Stir to dissolve. Place a wad of cotton on a jar lid, and soak the cotton with solution. Place lid in the area frequented by ants, and keep the solution replenished until ants disappear.

The ants are attracted to the sweet sugar ...and, because they will take it to their nests to share it with other ants, the deadly boric acid will reach ants you can't even see.

Source: Department of Conservation, Augusta, Maine.

> **⚡ CAUTION:** Boric acid is toxic. Use extreme caution when you're preparing this bait...wear rubber gloves and protect your eyes, nose and mouth with goggles and a mask...wash the pot thoroughly when you're done. Keep this bait out of reach of all people and pets.

◆ Combine equal parts of baking soda and confectioners' (powdered) sugar, and sprinkle the mixture wherever roaches hide and walk. The sugar will attract them and the baking soda will kill them (in a way that's too gruesome to explain).

Combating Roaches

The measurements for this popular roach-exterminating recipe seem flexible (no 2 sources agree), and since none of the roaches have lived to complain, it must work. *Here's our version...*

Roach Bait

¼ cup cooking oil or bacon drippings
¼ cup sugar
8 ounces boric acid powder
½ cup flour
½ cup chopped onions

Combine the oil and sugar in a pot. Mix in the boric acid powder, flour and onions. The idea is to form soft dough. You may need to add a little more oil.

Shape the soft dough into small, marble-size balls and place them in open plastic sandwich bags (the bags help keep them moist longer). Distribute them around your home, in the corner seams of your windows and doors, tiny floor or wall cracks or wherever roaches enter, as well as their favorite hangouts—kitchen cabinets, drawers, under the sink and other dark, damp areas.

When the dough get hard as a rock, whip up a fresh batch of bait balls...unless, of course, the first batch wiped out the problem completely.

> **CAUTION:** Boric acid is toxic. Use extreme caution when you're preparing this bait...wear rubber gloves and protect your eyes, nose and mouth with goggles and a mask...and be sure to wash the pot thoroughly when you're done. Keep this bait out of reach of all people and pets.

> **NOTE:** You can also prepare a non-toxic version of this recipe with baking soda instead of boric acid powder.

◆ Combine 2 tablespoons of flour with 4 tablespoons of borax powder (available at most supermarkets) and 1 tablespoon of cocoa powder. Spoon it out on plastic lids and leave this lethal blend in cabinets...under the sink ...on a kitchen counter...or wherever you've seen the cockroaches crawling.

◆ Use the recipe at left—and please be aware of the caution.

OUTSIDE THE HOME

Have you devoted a lot of thought and attention to the outside of your home? Well, now may be the time to start—or improve on what you've already done. Make the great outdoors safer in cold weather and more pleasant in warm weather. *Here are some ideas on what you can do...*

De-icing the Sidewalk, Steps, Driveway, Patio

◆ If the sidewalk or patio that needs de-icing is near your garden, DO NOT use rock salt. The salt will leach into the soil and poison it. Instead, use natural clay kitty litter, sand or granular fertilizer (dry, tiny pellets that are natural or synthetic...available at garden-supply stores).

◆ Distribute a dusting of baking soda. It will melt the ice and help prevent slipping. And you don't have to worry about it eating away at the outdoor ground covering, or the soles of your shoes. (And if it gets tracked into the house, it may even help clean the floor.)

◆ When your wooden deck is iced over, get out the cornmeal. A sprinkling of it will provide traction without damaging the wood or harming your garden.

Safer Concrete Steps

Mix ½ cup of clean sand into a can of paint, and paint the concrete steps with it. The sand in the paint will offer some traction when the steps are icy or wet.

If you are going to paint the steps, consider painting them white so they're easier to see on dark nights, especially if your outside light burns out.

Snow Shoveling Made Easier

◆ Right now—no matter what the weather is in your part of the country—put a coat of floor wax on your snow shovel. It will help prevent a metal shovel from rusting, and when it comes time to use it, the snow will glide on and slide off.

◆ If you've neglected to do the floor-wax coating, and you have to use the shovel now, spray it with nonstick vegetable spray. Once it dries completely, get out there and start shoveling.

Removing Moss

If you have a brick or stone walkway, this remedy should get rid of any moss overgrowth. In a spray bottle, combine 2 tablespoons of rubbing alcohol and 1 pint of water. Spray the moss with the solution, then rinse it away with a hose.

Removing Stains on Concrete

If any of the concrete on your property has grease stains, drench it with liquid dishwashing detergent. Let it stay that way for about 1 hour. Then pour just-boiled water on it. If the stain isn't completely gone (and it probably won't be), repeat the process once or twice more.

Removing Storm Windows And Doors

Spray metal window and door frames with nonstick vegetable spray to make this putting-up and taking-down seasonal chore much less of a *pane in the glass.*

Unlocking Door Locks

If your key doesn't go in and out of the lock smoothly, any of the following should help...

◆ Spray the key with nonstick vegetable spray and, before it dries, insert it into the keyhole a few times.

◆ Dip a powder puff or a cotton ball in talcum powder and smack it on the keyhole. The idea is to have a bit of powder coat the inside of the keyhole.

◆ Rub the serrated side and the underside of a key using a soft lead pencil. (It's not actually *lead,* it's *graphite.*) Then transfer the pencil's graphite from the key into the keyhole by putting the key in the lock and moving it back and forth until the key comes out clean.

Unsticking Outdoor Bulbs

Moisture, pollen, dust, dirt and pollution all conspire to make it practically impossible to remove an outdoor lightbulb from the socket shell. If you lightly coat the threaded base of the bulb with petroleum jelly *before* you screw it in, when it comes time to remove and replace the bulb, unscrewing it will not be a problem.

 Ladder Safety

If a household chore has you mounting a ladder on soft earth, make it safer by putting each leg of the ladder in an empty coffee can, which will help stabilize the ladder, making it safer.

If possible, have someone hold the sides of the ladder steady while you climb up. (To be even safer, hire an insured contractor to do the chore for you.)

Cleaning a Plastic Kiddie Pool

Dissolve 4 cups of baking soda in 2 gallons of hot water. When the water is still warm (but not hot enough to melt plastic), pour the solution into the plastic pool. Swish it around with a clean sponge, then pour out the solution and rinse the kiddie pool with clear water.

Create an Outdoor Dolly

Buy an old skateboard at a yard sale, thrift shop or from a teenage neighbor, and use it to cart around heavy or awkward things, such as moving your full garbage can to the curb or relocating big potted plants.

Make sure the skateboard is stable before you move anything, especially on an incline.

Cleaning a Swimming Pool

You'll have a cleaner pool if you keep a tennis ball floating in the water. The ball *serves* to absorb body oils. Don'tcha just *love* it?

Cleaning Plastic Patio Furniture

◆ Spray the plastic furniture with foam shaving cream and let it stay that way for 5 minutes. Use a soft brush or a coarse sponge to wipe the dirt away. Then hose it down.

◆ After wiping the dust and dirt off plastic, wood, or metal furniture frames—not chair seats or any other parts that come in contact with people's skin—buff the frames with liquid car wax. It will protect your furniture from pollution, bird droppings and anything else that may cause erosion.

◆ Protect and clean your white resin patio furniture when there's a big storm brewing. (A small detail we didn't mention yet—you need to have a swimming pool for this tip.)

Put the furniture in the pool and it won't blow away. When the storm is over and you take out the furniture, each piece will be sparkling clean, thanks to the chlorine in the water.

Cleaning Patio Umbrellas

While you're at the auto-supply store buying liquid car wax, pick up some cleaner for a convertible car top. It will go a long way in cleaning and giving your sun-beaten patio umbrella a revitalized look.

Using an Outdoor Grill

◆ Before you fire up the grill, lightly coat the racks with vegetable oil or a nonstick spray. Meats and vegetables will slide off easily.

◆ Toss some fresh herbs on the coals—rosemary, basil, sage or a few bay leaves work well. As the coals get hotter, the scent of the herbs will subtly flavor the food. The herbs will also permeate the air with the promise of good eats.

Grilling Safety!

Keep antibacterial wipes close by to clean your hands after handling raw meat.

◆ When you're finished barbecuing and the grill is still warm, sprinkle baking soda on it. Let it stay that way overnight. The next morning, wipe it clean, then rinse and dry.

Handling a Garbage Can

◆ Sprinkle about ½ cup of borax powder (available at supermarkets and drugstores) on the bottom of the garbage can to help prevent mold from growing.

◆ If you have a severe fly problem around your garbage can, line the bottom of the can with a light coating of powdered dishwasher detergent. The smell of the soap will repel the flies. And when you want to clean out the can, just add water and rinse.

◆ To keep the flies away, dip a sponge in oil of lavender (available at health-food stores), and wipe the inside of the can and lid with it. Do this after every garbage pick-up.

◆ If neighborhood dogs or cats insist on dining out at your garbage can, sprinkle black pepper around the can. They should stop coming over for take-out.

Tie Up Loose Lids

You can prevent the lid of the garbage can from flying away on a windy day—just get some rope or wire and tie the lid to the garbage can handle.

Dealing with Outdoor Pests

In addition to the millions of insects crawling around, there are pigeons in just about every city in America. Their droppings deface and hasten the deterioration of statues, buildings and walkways…mar windowsills and terraces…and make fire escapes dangerous. Pigeons' nests, along with their droppings, can clog drain pipes and air vents. Pigeons are also known to carry or transmit disease.

Then there are rodents. We have several good suggestions for getting rid of these vermin, but we can't bear to write about them. If you want to learn more, visit *www.kness. com/rodents.html* for insights into ridding your home of mice, rats and squirrels.

Meanwhile, here are a few bearable ways to solve your outdoor-pest problems…

Ants

Place the legs of your picnic table in paper cups that are filled halfway with water. Ants can't swim! If they crawl up the sides of the cup, they will fall into the water—and it will be no picnic for those ants.

Bees, Yellow Jackets and Wasps

◆ Put your yellow jacket away to keep yellow jackets away. These flying stingers are attracted to bright, warm colors, such as yellows, oranges and reds. Instead, use a pale pastel color scheme at your next outdoor shindig—perhaps a soft blue or green for the plates, napkins and tablecloth—and wear an outfit to match.

◆ Set your table with several fabric-softener sheets. They will keep away bees and yellow jackets as well as ants.

◆ Sculpt a sandwich-size brown paper bag into the shape of a beehive, and hang it somewhere along the air path outside your home where bees and wasps travel. The bag should mislead the flying pests into thinking there is already a hive on your property.

The theory is that bees and wasps avoid hives that are not their own. They do not want to be confrontational because it would turn into war.

If the bag needs help keeping its shape, fill it with polystyrene packing peanuts, or blow up a balloon and put it in the bag.

Cats

You can prevent cats from using a children's sandbox as their outdoor litter box—just pour distilled white vinegar around the box every month or so.

Flies

What's good for the sandbox (*see* "Cats," above) is also good for the pool. Pour distilled white vinegar around the sides of your pool, and it should help keep flies from hanging around. The smell of vinegar will disappear in no time.

Mosquitoes

A popular mosquito repellent is the mosquito coil. The coiled, clay-like material sits on a stand and is burned. It releases a pleasant odor that is very repellent to flying pests. Each coil burns for about 2 hours.

But many of them contain a potent lung carcinogen. Studies show that burning 1 coil could be the equivalent of smoking more than 100 cigarettes. Not good!

You may be better off with a couple of harmless mosquito bites…or, you may want to try the following suggestions to deal with those little buggers.

◆ Drink 2 teaspoons of apple cider vinegar in a glass of water. The smell of vinegar, emitted in your normal perspiration, will repel the mosquitoes, whose sense of smell is about 10,000 times better than ours.

◆ Dab 1 or 2 drops of lavender oil (available at health-food stores) on pulse points—including the inside of your wrists, inside your elbows, behind your ears and in back of your knees—when you know you're going to be in a wet, marshy or mosquito-infested area. The oil is a great repellent—and it also makes a lovely perfume.

> ### 🄲 FYI: The Problem with Citronella
> First used in 1882, oil of citronella is the classic mosquito repellent. Most popular in candle form, the citronella creates fumes that will repel mosquitoes—but only if they fly within the fumed air space.
>
> Because the candles' smoke emissions are not evenly spread out, some of the mosquitoes are bound to get through.

◆ Since mosquitoes enjoy taking up residence on top of tall weeds and grass, give your lawn and yard a crew cut—keep it trimmed down, especially during mosquito season.

◆ Mosquitoes lay eggs in standing water, such as in open-ended rain barrels, wheelbarrows, bird baths and kiddie pools. To prevent mosquitoes from breeding, put 2 tablespoons of olive oil in the water.

Avoid attracting mosquitoes by dumping any standing water—especially in overturned garbage can lids.

⭐ **Pest-free Picnic**

When you're having a picnic, barbecue or any other kind of outdoor gathering, put portable, battery-powered fans around the area (at least 2). Place 1 facing the center of the party, and 1 aimed at the food table.

The fans will keep flying insects (such as mosquitoes, bees, wasps, flies and gnats) away while keeping your guests cool.

Pigeons

Glop up the pigeons' landing strip—the railing or ledge of your terrace, balcony or patio—with petroleum jelly or powdered chalk. Those substances should make it uncomfortable for them and, with any luck, they will fly away...never to return.

Rodents

◆ Use steel wool to plug up every big and small hole that leads into your home (or any structure on your property). Stuff steel wool in all the cracks around gas and water pipes and around electrical outlets...even in the hole for your TV cable lines. Rodents do not like to chew through steel wool.

◆ Mice hate the smell of peppermint. Put a few drops of oil of peppermint (available at health-food stores) on cotton balls, and place them wherever you think the critters may visit—the garage, a workshop, a storage shed, a porch, etc. This is also a good reason to have mint plants planted in and around your home.

◆ If you have a cat, put some of his/her used cat litter in plastic containers. Put the containers wherever you suspect the mice will play when the cat's away. The cat's urine scent should make the mice run for their lives.

◆ Another use for baking soda...rodent repellent. Sprinkle baking soda liberally around your property and garage.

✍ **NOTE:** Although baking soda is generally safe, it's better to keep kids and pets away from the area you sprinkled.

⭐ **Humane Rodent Trap**

Forgive us, but we can't bear researching and writing about trapping and killing rodents. While the thought of having them around is absolutely revolting to us, the thought of killing them is even worse.

If you have a rodent problem, and you do not want to use the popular commercial killing products on the market, contact Arbico Organics. This Tucson, Arizona, company offers humane traps. Visit their Web site at *www. arbico-organics.com* or call 800-827-2847 to ask questions or request a catalog.

◆ If you have greenery that's attracting mice, here's a solution that will repel them—in a 1-gallon jug of water that's almost full, add ½ cup of non-detergent soap powder and 1 tablespoon of Tabasco sauce. Mix it well, then pour some of the solution into a spray bottle.

Generously spray the tops and undersides of the leaves that are a magnet for mice, and the problem should disappear...along with the mice. ■

■ Products ■

Gorilla Glue

The company bills this product as "The Toughest Glue on Planet Earth." You'll get no argument from us. This product bonds wood, stone, brick, concrete, ceramic, metal, plastic laminate and more...lots more. It is 100% waterproof and not affected by sun, rain, snow and extreme hot or cold temperatures...it can also be sanded, stained and painted.

Gorilla Tape

The company bills this as "The Toughest Tape on Planet Earth"—notice a pattern here? This incredibly strong tape bonds to things ordinary tapes cannot, including brick, stucco, wood and more.

Source: The Gorilla Glue Company, 800-966-3458, *www.gorillaglue.com**.

* Visit the company's user-friendly site for creative product uses and project ideas.

Gripping Stuff!

Here's a whole family of incredibly useful products. They are removable, reusable, repositionable, nontoxic and they eliminate the need for pushpins, tape and messy putty. They are fun to use...practically addictive.

This Gripping Stuff! is polyester felt with a special adhesive that allows you to press it on practically anywhere and peel it off—repeatedly. It comes in many sizes, several colors and makes an instant bulletin board.

Poster Pads let you hang up posters without tacks or nails. You can also snip off a little piece of the *stuff* and use it to turn any piece of paper into an adhesive note.

The *Memo Strip* is good for putting notes around your computer monitor.

Put *Gripping Stuff! For Cards* around your doorframe, and display your birthday or holiday cards on it.

There's also a *Dry-Erase Board and Pen* that wipes off with a cloth.

You can find these products at stationery, crafts and hardware stores as well as most supermarkets nationwide. Ask for it by name...or if you can't remember the name, just ask, "Do you have any of that gripping stuff?"

Source: Gripping Stuff International, + 44 (0) 20-8979-3585, *www.gripping-stuff.com*.

CHAPTER 9

Great Greenery Solutions

Many people can appreciate the magnificence of a garden, but have you ever thought of the real value of creating and/or tending your own? Mike Steven, a former researcher and lecturer in landscape studies at Australia's University of Western Sydney, worked on a project titled "The Congruent Garden: An Investigation into the Role of the Domestic Garden in Satisfying Fundamental Human Needs."

After interviewing gardeners on the importance of gardening in their everyday lives, Mr. Steven concluded that gardens have the potential to satisfy 9 basic human needs—leisure, subsistence, protection, affection, understanding, participation, creation, identity and freedom—along with 4 existential states—being, having, doing and interacting.

While satisfying the gardener's personal needs, the garden also increases property value. And that's not all. According to the US Department of Energy, properly placed shade trees can help lower your annual utility bills by shading windows and walls in the summer, and acting as windbreakers in the winter. Indoor gardens—or even just a single houseplant—can improve the quality of the air and nurture the soul by bringing nature as living sculpture into our homes.

If plants are living sculpture, then consider yourself the artist-in-residence who will care for your indoor and/or outdoor garden. In this section, we provide tips to help you develop a green thumb simply, safely and economically.

In the words of the innovative landscape architect Thomas D. Church—"When your garden is finished, I hope it will be more beautiful than you anticipated, require less care than you expected and have cost only a little more than you had planned."

TOOLS

Garden tools date back thousands of years. We heard it through the grapevine that the first woody plant—which actually *was* a grapevine in Armenia—was pruned by man around 6000 BC. (We can only imagine the crude pruning shears used then!) Spades made of bronze were used in China in 1100 BC, and the ancient Romans used iron spades and shovels.

Fast-forward to the middle of the 14th century when, thanks to iron-smelting technology, tools were made lighter in weight and more shapely. Then take another leap forward to the mid-17th century when gardens became the rage, and gardeners wanted to be well-equipped to both plant and prune. The industrial revolution had begun, and steel and alloys were used to make tools lighter, more precisely shaped and more durable.

Enterprising manufacturers met the needs of gardeners with a wide range of tools—including pruning and hedge shears, cultivating forks and trowels...just about every nonmechanical gardening tool that is still used today.

We bet you never thought that your gardening tools had their *roots* in the 14th or 17th centuries. Also, we bet you can find some helpful tips on organizing and caring for those tools if you'll just keep reading.

Organizing Tools

◆ Make room on your garage or shed wall to hang a clear-plastic shoe bag—the kind that has 12 or 16 or more shoe compartments. It's a great way to keep your gardening tools and gloves in 1 convenient place.

◆ Tired of misplacing your tools while you work in the garden? Get some bright, fluorescent (meaning, day-glo colors) spray paint or tape, and put some on the handles of your garden tools.

If you tend to garden after sundown, add strips of glow-in-the-dark tape (available at hardware stores and most crafts stores) to the tools' handles. The time you've saved looking for the implements will be extra time spent gardening.

NOTE: If you take a portable phone outside with you to the garden, add a piece of day-glo tape to the receiver so you can find it quickly.

◆ Use an old golf bag to store rakes, spades and hoes. You can get an inexpensive bag at a yard sale or a second-hand sporting goods store. When you decide to use your garden tools, is there any better way to drag them around than in a golf bag? Well, yes...have your *caddy* drag them around.

✳ Tools Rule!

When planting and harvesting, a ruler often comes in handy—to calculate distances when planting seeds or bulbs...or to measure how deep seeds should be planted...or at what height they should be harvested.

So, turn the handles of your tall tools into rulers. Account for the number of inches from the tip of the tool to the start of the handle and, at the start of the handle, mark off and number each inch with a waterproof pen. Measure each of your small tools as well, and assign it a number for its length in inches.

Use colorful poker chips to mark the measured spots where you plan to plant.

Caring for Rusty Tools

◆ Pour some dry sand into a big bucket until it's about ¾ full. Then pour motor oil...or machine oil...or mineral oil...or even used cooking oil...evenly over the top. For every gallon of sand, use about 1 pint of oil.

To clean a rusty tool, stick it in the sand several times, then wipe it with a soft cloth or paper towel. The sand cleans the tool...the oil coats it and prevents moisture from rusting the metal.

You may want to store your tools in the bucket just for the night, but you can even keep 'em there for the winter.

◆ If you keep your garden tools in a toolbox, toss in moisture absorbers, such as some loose rice...or activated charcoal...or pieces of chalk ...or mothballs. Doing so will help prevent your tools from developing rust. Also, make sure that your tools are clean and not caked with soil before storing them.

Tool Case and Seat, All in 1

Put a large plastic bag in a big (5-gallon) plastic bucket. Then fill the bag (and the bucket) with your tools, gloves, bulbs, seeds, bottle of drinking water and cell phone, and take the bucket to the garden.

Once you've reached the patch of garden you plan on tending, empty the contents of the plastic bag onto the ground. Then turn the bucket over, have a seat and get to work.

Sanitizing Tools

◆ If you've had sick plants, your garden tools may be infected with the plants' disease. Kill the problematic bacteria by thoroughly washing the tools with soap and warm water. Wear rubber gloves while doing this task.

> **NOTE:** Don't forget to wash your gloves, gardening shoes and any other clothes that may have had contact with the ailing plants.

◆ If you want to use something stronger than soap and water to sanitize your tools, soak them in 1 gallon of water mixed with ¾ cup of bleach. Rinse the tools thoroughly with plain water before using them again.

Make Your Own Scooper

Take an empty plastic detergent bottle...or a bleach bottle...or spring water bottle—the size depends on how big or small you want the scooper to be—and thoroughly wash it out with plain soap and water.

Then, with the handle in your left hand, use regular kitchen scissors to cut from the bottom of the right side of the bottle. Cut in a diagonal to the left side about 1" under the handle and go around to the other side, and then diagonally down to the bottom. (Cut in the opposite direction if you're left-handed.)

It may sound complicated, but when you follow these instructions, you'll see exactly how easy it is to create a terrific scooper that can be used to scoop seeds, fertilizer, mulch...and whatever else needs scooping.

Caring for Hoses

◆ Do not store a hose where the sun will shine down on it. The sun's heat will dry it out. Also, keep a hose away from any kind of heating source, like a furnace or outdoor barbecue.

◆ If the hose has sprung a little leak, instead of using glue or tape to repair it, try this fix— heat up the tip of an ice pick or Phillips-head screwdriver, and gently touch the rubber around the hole in the hose with the hot tip of the tool. It should seal the hole closed.

Used Hose Uses

If your garden hose has sprung several leaks and is beyond repair, you can recycle it by poking more holes into it and turning it into a sprinkler (also called a "soaker hose") for your lawn or garden.

You can also cut up an old hose and use it to brace newly planted trees—it will protect their bark.

GLOVELESS GARDENING

 Gloves will help protect your hands from getting cuts, splinters and blisters. They will also help keep your nails clean.

Even though it's a good idea to wear gloves when gardening, many gardeners prefer to remain bare-handed while they commune with nature. *Here are a few suggestions for you gloveless gardeners, so that you don't get too "down and dirty"...*

Ensuring Clean Nails

Right before you start to garden, scratch a wet bar of soap with your nails. Make sure that a bit of soap gets under each fingernail. Doing so will prevent soil from getting under your nails.

Soil under the nails is hard to clean, whereas soap can be easily washed and nail-brushed away as soon as you've finished gardening.

Blister Prevention

Moist hands blister easily. When your hands get sweaty from working with a shovel or hoe, rub your palms with some soil to help keep them dry and blister-free.

Infection Prevention

It's not unusual for a person working in the garden to get a scrape…a scratch…a nick…a gash…or an insect bite. However, you don't have to run into your house to tend to every little abrasion.

The answer is to take a small spray bottle of full-strength distilled white vinegar outside with you whenever you garden.

Spritz the minor wound with the vinegar—which will help prevent it from becoming a major infection—then cover the boo-boo with a bandage until you go indoors and can clean and dress it properly.

Sweeter Soap Secret

After gardening, add 1 teaspoon of sugar to your soapy lather, and wash your hands with it. The sugar acts as an abrasive to clean away grass and garden stains.

Garden Lime Neutralizer

Garden lime—which is used to raise the *pH level* (the measurement of acid/alkaline) of soil, and to add calcium or break up heavy clay soil—can dry out your hands and make them look like alligator skin.

Whenever your hands have been exposed to lime—even a little of it—pour some distilled white vinegar on them. After 1 to 2 minutes—once the vinegar has had a chance to neutralize

the lime—rinse your hands with plain water. (And next time, you might want to wear gloves when you work with lime.)

Easy Knee Protection

Knee pads will add to your gardening endurance. To make an affordable pair, take your most comfortable work pants and sew on knee patches, leaving the top side of each patch open—as though you've sewn a pocket on each knee. (For proper placement of the patches, be sure to get into "gardening position" to determine exactly where the pants bend at the knee. Kneeling on something damp will help "mark the spot.")

In each knee-pocket, place a sponge…or a substantial shoulder pad…or a piece of foam rubber. If you have a couple of extra computer mouse pads, you can use them as knee cushions, too.

You can also put on an old pair of pantyhose and line up foam rubber pads (or thick sanitary napkins) at the knees. If you're uncomfortable being seen in this getup, put on a pair of work pants over the pantyhose.

SOIL

Soil is a mixture of organic material plus very small mineral and rock particles. It plays a vital role in the way plants grow because of its relationship to the roots. The roots gather moisture and fertility, and use soil as a storehouse for food elements and water. Roots also make use of soil to anchor plants and hold them in place. The bottom line is—the healthier the soil, the healthier your garden.

The soil of a famous French vineyard is so prized that the vineyard workers must scrape it off their shoes before they leave work each night.

Here are some ways you may be able to improve the quality of your soil and make it shoe-scraping good…

Testing Your Soil's pH

The pH level is the measurement of acid or alkaline. Many plants need acidic soil to thrive. Some types of acid-loving plants and bushes are roses, azaleas, gardenias, rhododendrons, English holly and camellias. Other plants need alkaline soil to thrive. Some alkaline-loving plants and bushes are lilacs, mimosas, bougainvilleas, common garden petunias and bird of paradise flowers.

To learn about your soil, perform 1 or both of these simple tests, and take the results into consideration when planning your garden...

◆ Take 1 tablespoon of wet garden soil and sprinkle a pinch of baking soda on it. If it fizzes, gurgles or effervesces, the soil is *acidic* and its pH is under 5. To raise it, add lime.

◆ If nothing happened, test 1 tablespoon of wet garden soil with ½ teaspoon of distilled white vinegar. If there's fizzing, gurgling or effervescing, then the soil is *alkaline*. The more excited the fizzing, the higher the soil's pH level. To lower it, add sulfur.

Supplementing Your Soil

Some gardeners will not sow their crops until they've enriched the soil with Epsom salt. It is said to help grow stalks stronger, leaves greener and blossoms more substantial. It also makes plants less vulnerable to disease.

Sprinkle about 1 cup of Epsom salt over every 100 square feet (or 10' x 10' patch) of garden. Of course, use a smaller amount if your garden is smaller.

SEEDS

The word "magic" aptly describes a seed. Seeds can be planted many ways. For example, gravity causes heavy seeds to simply fall off the plant and onto the soil. Very fine seeds just blow away on the wind. Some seeds are covered with hooks that catch on the fur of animals passing by and are eventually rubbed off on the ground. Some pods burst and toss their seeds out over a wide area. And, of course, there's the gardener who lovingly plants seeds with his/her own hope and hard work.

Here are some suggestions to make planting those seeds a more fruitful mission...

✳ Fertility Test for Large Seeds

In order to weed out any seeds that may be infertile, fill a bowl with tepid water and empty the seeds into it. The fertile seeds will sink to the bottom of the bowl...the duds will float. Just strain them out and discard.

Dump the Clump

Tiny seeds have a tendency to clump together, which is not a good way to plant them. Prevent them from clumping by mixing the seeds with sand (bags are available at nurseries, pet shops and most hardware stores). Make sure the sand is moist.

Put the clump-free mixture of seeds-and-sand (4 parts sand to each part seeds) in a large salt shaker and sprinkle it over the soil. The even distribution of seeds will produce plants that grow better and stronger.

✳ Create Your Own Seed Tape

You will need seeds, waxed paper, transparent tape and a landscaping plan. Once you decide which seeds are going to go where, then you're ready to prepare seed tapes that will help carry out your landscaping vision.

On a piece of waxed paper, put the seeds in a straight line that's as wide as the tape you're going to use. Then place the sticky side of the tape over the seeds, picking them up off the waxed paper.

After finishing the first row, put it aside, and continue the process until all of the seeds are on lengths of tape that you then can arrange according to the way you want them planted. Then plant them—tape and all!

Storing Leftover Seeds

The next time you finish a jar of vitamins, keep that little, moisture-absorbing silica gel packet that came in it. They are good to use when storing seeds.

Put any leftover seeds in a jar along with the silica gel, close it tightly and keep it refrigerated until next year. It's best to keep the jar in the fridge—a cool, bug-free environment. Most seeds will stay viable for 2 or 3 years.

Or you can store leftover seeds in empty, airtight, light-free 35mm film canisters.

> **NOTE:** Be sure to label the jar clearly so you know which seeds are which.

Caring for Seedlings

◆ To start seedlings, use plastic pots—they will retain moisture better and longer than clay pots. Of course, that doesn't mean that you have to go out and buy them. Recycle empty (and clean) margarine tubs, cherry-tomato or berry containers, or nursery cell packs. Any wide, flat plastic container will do.

◆ Gently brush your hand over seedlings several times a day to get them used to air movement, which will help them grow strong and hardy. Sound a little far-fetched? Tell that to the commercial growers who do this in their own greenhouses.

WATERING

Water, which makes up approximately 90% of most plants, is used to carry nutrients from the roots to all parts of the plant. Water also provides elements used in making plant food.

Watering incorrectly is the #1 killer of plants. So, even though there are no hard-and-fast rules for correct watering—a lot depends on air temperature, soil conditions, the types of plants and their stages of development—these suggestions may help you get it right.

Watering Your Lawn And/or Garden

◆ Do your plants and lawn a big favor and water them early in the morning. That way, the moisture is absorbed before the hot afternoon sun has a chance to evaporate it.

As for watering at night…don't do it! Leaving leaves and grass wet overnight makes them vulnerable to fungal diseases.

> ★ **Protect Your Plantings**
> Water plants, shrubs and flowers around the base—not over the leaves. Wet leaves can get burned by strong sunlight.

◆ Watering often, but a little at a time, can weaken plant or grass roots and causes them to grow upward instead of downward. A better idea is to water more thoroughly and less frequently, as evenly as possible, and never faster than the soil can absorb.

◆ The grass will tell you when it's thirsty by starting to wilt. Look for a change in color—from bright green to a drab blue-green.

◆ If you do not trust your eye for color, then ignore the "Keep Off" sign and step on the grass. If the imprint of your foot stays in the grass longer than a few seconds, get out the hose and start watering.

◆ It's also a good idea to water the grass thoroughly after fertilizing, so that the nourishment gets down to the roots—instead of sticking to the lawnmower blades.

FERTILIZING

Just as humans require vitamins and minerals, plants do as well. Fertilizer is plant food, helping plants and lawns meet their nutritional needs. Nitrogen, phosphorus and potassium are the 3 most needed nutrients, which are often referred to as *macronutrients*. There are other nutrients that plants need in small amounts, and they are often referred to as *micronutrients*.

Here are ways to help feed your plants all the nutrients they need…

Using Natural Fertilizers

◆ Pelletized horse feed (available at farm-supply stores or wherever horse-care products are sold) is an inexpensive organic fertilizer.

The pellets of crushed grains and molasses will supply your plants with much-needed NPK—the chemical symbols for *nitrogen*, *phosphorus* and *potassium*. Lightly sprinkle the pellets over the soil, or put some in your planting holes.

◆ If you do not have cats, consider this Native American method of fertilizing—gather unused fish parts (heads, tails, innards, etc.) and keep them in the freezer until you're ready to do your planting.

When it's time, defrost the fish parts, then dig holes deeper than you need for planting and bury the fish. Cover the parts with soil, and then plant as usual. The fish dissolve easily, and the plants will absorb the many nutrients they offer—such as calcium, phosphorus, sodium, potassium and iron.

For some other fertilizing suggestions, *see* "Popular Garden Plants A to Z" on pages 219–227.

⚡ **CAUTION:** Do not let fertilizer come into direct contact with seeds or plants. Feed the soil *around* the plant, not the plant itself.

LAWNS

If you want your lawn to look as nice as your neighbor's, just wait until it snows. *But seriously, folks…if snow is not in the forecast, here are some ways to take good care of your lawn and make it look its best…*

Mowing the Grass

◆ Mow often—a couple of inches at a time and no more than ⅓ the total blade length—rather than waiting until the grass is as high as an elephant's eye. It's less stressful for the grass. Besides, the short, unseen, leftover clippings do not have to be bagged, and they will eventually decompose and return valuable nutrients to the soil.

How High the Grass?

It's beneficial for grass to be at least 3" high. It shades the soil and helps prevent it from drying out. It also shields weeds and crabgrass from the sunlight, so they have less of a chance to grow.

◆ For the cleanest cut, it's best to mow when it's cool and the lawn is at its driest—typically, in the late afternoon or early evening.

◆ Do not mow the lawn when it's wet. Mowing with wet-grass conditions—such as morning dew—will spread turfgrass disease pathogens, which already exist on your lawn.

Aeration—What, Why, When and How

As time goes by, the soil under your lawn becomes compacted. This is not a good thing. Soil compaction reduces the absorption of water and makes it hard for the grass roots to grow.

Aeration, which is loosening or puncturing the compacted soil, does the lawn a world of good. It increases the availability of water and nutrients, and enhances oxygen levels. It helps produce new shoots and roots that fill up the holes in the lawn, and makes the grass fuller, more dense and better looking. It reduces water runoff, increases the lawn's drought tolerance and improves its overall health.

If you have cool-season grass such as Kentucky bluegrass, aerate in the fall. If your lawn has a warm-season grass, such as carpetgrass, aerate in the late spring or summer when these types are actively growing.

No matter what kind of grass you have or when you aerate, choose a mild day when the soil is moderately moist and does not stick to your shoes. If the soil is too wet and messy, aerating may further compact the soil, which is exactly the opposite of what you want it to do.

Aerate your lawn as often as necessary. One way to test it is to stick a screwdriver in the soil when it's moist. If the screwdriver meets with little or no resistance, you probably don't need to aerate the lawn. If the screwdriver has a hard time making its way into the soil, chances are you need to aerate.

There are many kinds of aerating gadgets available at garden-supply stores and on the Internet, but you may not need any of them if you have spiked golf shoes or soccer cleats. Put them on and start walking on your lawn, especially when you mow. It's good exercise for you and great for your grass.

◆ Each time you mow the lawn, start at a different place. That way, you won't keep rolling over the exact same lanes, which means you won't be making permanent tire ruts in your lawn.

◆ To prevent grass from sticking to the mower's blades, spray the blades with nonstick cooking spray before you begin.

🕐 **Best Time to Rake**
Do not rake right after it rains. Wait until the leaves are dry and weigh half as much as when they're wet.

WEEDS

 **H**ave you ever heard the expression "One year's weed …seven years' seed?" Well, it seems to be true. There's your garden without weeds. No weeds. No weeds. You cultivate the soil, make conditions right for the seeds to germinate—and then suddenly you have weeds! That's because weed seeds may remain viable for at least 7 years.

You could do 1 of 2 things—either you learn to love 'em. Some weeds (such as morning glories) have beautiful flowers…and some are edible, such as dandelions, purslane and chickweed. Plus, most weeds offer shelter to beneficial insects. Or, if you can't love 'em, you can get rid of 'em. *Here's how…*

Eliminating Garden Weeds

The following solutions are all safe, environmentally friendly weed killers…

◆ In a spray bottle, combine 1 quart of water and either 1 ounce of distilled white vinegar or 1 ounce of gin, plus 1 capful of baby shampoo. Spray the weeds until they're soaking wet. After a day or so, the weeds will turn brown, shrivel up and then die.

◆ Give weeds a killer shower with 5 tablespoons of liquid dishwashing detergent mixed in 1 quart of water.

◆ Prepare a mixture of 1 tablespoon of rubbing alcohol for each cup of water, and put the solution in a spray bottle. Take aim and drench the unwanted plants.

◆ This pet-safe formula consists of 2 quarts of distilled white vinegar, 1 teaspoon of liquid soap and ½ cup of orange oil (available at some health-food stores or garden-supply stores). Put the mixture in a spray bottle and drench the weeds with it.

CAUTION: When using weed killers, be certain to spray *only* the weeds, not any of the plants you want to keep.

✳ Spray in the Box

Use this tried-and-true gardener's trick to kill *only* the weeds you want to get rid of and not your prized petunias.

Take an appropriate-sized box, carton or foam cooler (something with a top that opens), and cut off the bottom. Place the box over the weed, open the top, spray, then close the top for a few seconds. Doing this will keep the weed-killing spray from reaching surrounding plants.

If you have more weeds than desirable plants, cover the desirables with boxes to protect them, and just spray the exposed weeds.

Pulling Garden Weeds

If you want to do away with the weeds in your garden, get out there right after it rains. That's when you'll have the easiest time yanking the weeds out of the ground. Of course, if you don't want to wait until it rains, you can wet the soil yourself with a garden hose.

Low-Tech Weed Eaters

If you're a weed hater and an animal lover, consider getting a goat to do your weeding for you. Better yet, there are *weeder geese* that eat grass and young weeds, but stay away from certain cultivated plants. All you need are 2 to 4 geese per acre of row plantings. (Check your town's by-laws before buying geese.)

In addition to the geese being weeders, they are also manure spreaders and cultivators, continually adding fertilizer and organic matter to the soil. And their work ethic is unequaled. Geese work from daylight to dark, 7 days a week, feasting on grass and weeds as soon as new growth appears. Now you'll understand the bumper sticker that says— "Honk if you believe in *geeses*."

If you want more information about these weeders, contact the world's largest rare-breed hatchery, Murray McMurray Hatchery in Webster City, Iowa. Visit their Web site at *www.mcmurrayhatchery.com* or call 800-456-3280 or (in Iowa) 515-832-3280.

✳ Working on the Rim

If you're weeding, trimming or planting along the rim of a paved surface (such as your driveway), take the strain off your legs and back by sitting on a skateboard. This will make it easier to gradually roll along.

Eliminating Patio or Sidewalk Weeds

Personally, we think it's charming to see a feisty plant pop up through sidewalk cracks or in between patio stones. Then again, we don't have a patio, and any greenery seen on the sidewalks of New York City is generally appreciated. *But if you're not charmed by pavement weeds and want to get rid of them, these solutions may help...*

◆ Pour distilled white vinegar on the weeds—enough to get them good and wet—but don't hose it off. Let it stay there, and in a couple of days the weeds will be dead. Vinegar will also get rid of patio moss.

◆ For immediate results, boil ½ cup of table salt in 1 quart of water, and then pour the *hot-hot-hot* liquid onto the weeds. This will also work on patio moss.

★ Make Weeds Stay Away

To prevent weeds from growing in the first place, sprinkle table salt or baking soda into the patio/sidewalk cracks.

PLANT & GARDEN PESTS A TO Z

Garden pests? Oh, you can bombard them with pesticides—chemicals that the pests may not have developed tolerances to—but they generally smell bad, are unhealthy for you (and other living creatures), and they tend to be expensive.

Our goal is to protect your plants from pests with inexpensive remedies that will do the job, but will not harm you, any other beneficial garden organisms or the environment. So what are you waiting for? Bug off!

✳ Plant Ugly Flowers

There are flowers and vegetables that are not attractive to bees. If you want a bee-free garden, consider planting chrysanthemums, forsythia, daffodils, tulips and/or lilacs.

The bees will also stay away from certain vegetables that are generally harvested before they flower—such as carrots, Jerusalem artichokes, beets, cabbages and lettuce.

Ants

While most ants are harmless, nobody wants them crawling all over plants. *This "smear campaign" is an efficient, nontoxic deterrent...*

For an indoor plant, smear petroleum jelly on the base of the plant's pot. Petroleum jelly smeared on the stems of outdoor plants will keep ants and most other insects from crawling up.

Bees and Wasps

Chances are, if you refrain from shooing those flying insects away with your hand (which presents a threat to them), they will refrain from stinging you.

It's just hard to trust that fact and to ignore your instincts when they're buzzing around you. *Try using these deterrents instead...*

◆ One of the most popular bee, hornet or wasp zappers is hairspray...super-hold works best. Just point and shoot.

◆ Our cousin keeps her screenless windows open in summer, and when an occasional bee flies in, she kills it by spritzing it with Windex.

◆ We heard from a man who uses a spray can of WD-40 lubricant to zap any stinging bugs that get in his workshop.

◆ A spray bottle filled with vodka can also be an effective exterminator.

> ✎ **NOTE:** If it's a matter of *spray* or *be stung*, then *spray*. But please keep in mind that ⅓ of the foods you eat—either directly or indirectly—depends on pollination by bees. And wasps are an important part of the ecosystem and help control garden pests. So, you may want to think twice about ending their productive little lives.

Birds in the Garden— Pro or Con?

Birds are beautiful and fun to watch. They do the gardener a big favor by eating unwanted insects. However, they may also eat just-planted seeds, or pick at ripening tomatoes.

One school of thought is that if there is a birdbath and a birdhouse in the yard, then birds won't bother with the plants. Another school of thought is that you should attract the birds with a birdhouse and birdbath in the winter, but take them away during the spring/summer growing season. That way, the birds won't come around and eat plants growing in your garden.

Birds or no birds? You decide.

The best way to prevent birds from getting into your garden is to cover plants with netting (available at garden-supply stores). You can also program your sprinkler system to go off at set intervals—a sudden burst of water should scare off the birds.

But if you love having these fabulous feathered creatures flying around, give them the creature comforts—a birdbath regularly filled with fresh water and a birdhouse or feeder. *Here are some catering suggestions…*

◆ Stock the birdhouse with uncooked oats. Birds love 'em.

◆ Freshly popped, plain popcorn—without butter or salt—is a real treat for birds.

◆ Mix 1 part peanut butter with 5 parts cornmeal, then divide it and shape it into fat hockey pucks. Place each puck into a mesh (onion) bag. Tie the bags closed and hang them outside…wherever you want birds to come and feed.

◆ Save the seeds from summer melons, such as honeydew or cantaloupe, and let them dry out. Birds love to feast on them, so put them out in a bird feeder…or wherever birds can snack safely.

◆ Robins and bluebirds will flock to wherever you lay out a tray of raisins.

◆ Some of the many red- and orange-shaded flowers that will attract hummingbirds include columbine, coral bells, flag iris, lily, petunia, scarlet sage, trumpet honeysuckle and verbena.

Keep Bees Away

◆ Wear neutral-colored clothes to keep bees away from you. Orange? Green? Red? Purple? **No!** Beige? Gray? **Yes!**

◆ Wearing perfume or scented hairspray is another no-no.

Birds

If the birds are feeding on your newly planted seeds or ripening fruit, and you want to get rid of them, tie flashy Mylar or tinsel-type strips (available at crafts stores) on posts and stakes throughout the garden. The shiny, flailing tinsel will frighten away most feathered pests.

Cats

◆ To deter cats from wandering around your garden, mince a few garlic bulbs and scatter the little pieces everywhere. (Pieces of citrus peel and eucalyptus oil also work.)

◆ If the garlic smell is too pungent for you, mix up a cat-repellent solution—use 2 tablespoons of mustard powder, 1 tablespoon of cayenne pepper, 2 tablespoons of flour and 2 cups of water. Pour the mixture into a spray bottle and spritz it around vegetable patches, flowerbeds and the border of your yard.

◆ If a cat has his eye on your birdbath, get out the distilled white vinegar and spray it on the birdbath's base. The smell of the vinegar should repel the cat and neutralize the cat's urine, which he uses to mark his territory.

◆ To keep your cat(s) from snacking on your indoor houseplants, place small pieces of citrus rind—lemon, lime, grapefruit or orange—on the soil.

◆ A non-odoriferous method of keeping your cat from turning your indoor plants into a playground is to place pine cones…or pebbles…or aluminum foil…or seashells…or marbles… around the plants. The rule to follow is—without harming the plants, cover up the soil and the cats will not want to dig in.

Deer and Other Animals

◆ At the risk of grossing you out, go to your local beauty salon and ask for a bag of human hair. Then cut the legs off a few pairs of old pantyhose, stuff the hair into each foot and knot them closed. Attach them to the trees and bushes near where the deer have been feeding.

When deer, rabbits or any other neighborhood animals pick up the scent of the human hair, they should be frightened off. Wouldn't you be?

You will have to replace the hair after it rains, but hopefully by then, the animals will no longer come around…and you will no longer need the hair to chase them away. (Human urine is also an effective repellent.)

◆ Wrap aluminum foil around young tree trunks, and keep the foil in place with rope or heavy cord. That should stop deer from taking a bite out of the tree's bark.

◆ Hang scented car air fresheners on trellises, trees, shrubs, bushes and fence posts—anywhere the deer and the antelope play on your property. The smell—especially mint—will chase them away.

◆ Hang deodorant soap (not the perfumed bars) in trees and on bushes. Drill a hole in the middle of each bar of soap, and use an "S" hook on a wire to attach each bar (almost like you're hanging Christmas ornaments). Put the soap about 4' off the ground. Use a few in each tree or bush.

> **NOTE:** To prevent the soap from bubbling up your garden and disappearing when it rains, you may want to use a wax-coated paper cup for each bar of soap.
>
> Poke a hole in the bottom of the cup, and thread the wire through it so that the upside-down cup covers the soap. Then hang it that way in the tree.

◆ Deer and most other animals will not walk on bubble wrap. Place sheets of it around your garden, holding the corners in place with rocks, big flowerpots or stakes that you put in the ground.

◆ If you have old CDs that you can't use anymore, tie a string through the center hole of each, and attach them to bushes and trees. The shiny glint and constant movement from the CDs will scare off most animal trespassers.

◆ The smell of mothballs will repel many unwanted animals (including dogs, cats, squirrels and snakes) from munching on your garden greenery. Spread mothballs around plants and shrubs.

◆ If you find the mothball smell too offensive, scatter some cayenne pepper on the soil, or sprinkle a little directly on the plants.

Dogs

As you may already know, when dogs frequently urinate on the lawn, it can cause yellow burn marks. To bring back the grass to the way it should be, mix 1 cup of baking soda into 1 gallon of water, then saturate the peed-on area with this solution every 3 days.

The baking soda neutralizes the urine's acidity, which restores the grass back to normal—it also deodorizes the area so that the dog will not recognize it and mark the same spot again. (Is that why "Spot" is such a popular name for dogs?)

Insects

Certain critters can be the pestiest of pests. *Aphids* are plant lice—soft-bodied, pear-shaped insects that are less than ⅛" long and are most commonly green, yellow or black. *Whiteflies* (insects that look more like tiny moths than flies) are found on citrus fruit and just about any plant. And *red spiders* (also known as spider mites) are the bane of bonsai and ornamental plant growers.

These effective suggestions should help you to squash them…

◆ Aphids and whiteflies are attracted to the color yellow. So get a few yellow index cards, smear them with petroleum jelly and place them on the soil near where there is an aphid or whitefly infestation.

The idea is that the bugs will land on the cards and get stuck in the jelly. Later, when the cards are full, put on gloves and carefully discard them.

◆ A yellow pan filled with soapy water will attract most flying pests and then drown them.

◆ If you see aphids on your plants, mix ½ cup of powdered milk with 1 quart of warm water and put the solution in a spray bottle.

Spray the plants' leaves thoroughly. As they dry, the aphids will die.

◆ This potent formula should get rid of spider mites, whiteflies and aphids…in a blender, purée 3 cloves of garlic and 2 teaspoons of Tabasco sauce. Add 1 pint of plain water and 2 tablespoons of liquid dish detergent. Strain the mixture into a spray bottle and spritz the infected plant's leaves.

◆ If the plants in your garden suffer a plague of insects, plant garlic and/or onion throughout your patches. You can also stick a peeled clove of garlic in the soil of each plant that seems to attract bugs. Don't be surprised, though, if you end up with a crop of garlic!

◆ Most insects, including aphids, despise the smell of mint. If you don't grow mint, then get some mint leaves at the grocery store and spread them around your garden.

> **CAUTION:** If you plant mint, be warned that it grows without mercy! To prevent it from overtaking your garden, plant it in its own container. And be sure to keep it trimmed back—live mint will often root wherever it touches the ground.

Moles

Most gardening experts believe that a commercial mole trap is the best way to rid your garden and lawn of these burrowing little critters. We're sure that is so, but the thought of then having to dispose of the trapped animal is enough to have us try something that will just chase the pest away. This remedy is a *chaser* that takes advantage of the moles' intense dislike of noise.

To discover the mole's run, imagine a line between 2 molehills. Dig down at a spot along this imaginary line until you locate the run. See if you can get a portable radio to blare

217

down there. If not, drop in the little mechanical movement from a musical greeting card. (They seem to go on playing forever.)

If this doesn't work, there's always the trap. Check your local garden-supply store, or search the Internet for "wildlife control supplies."

Rabbits

◆ Having a "bad hare day"? Stop rabbits from enjoying a salad in your garden. Wet down the leaves of your vegetable plants and sprinkle ground cayenne pepper on them.

◆ Hare today and seedlings gone tomorrow? Protect your seedlings by sprinkling baby powder on them. Rabbits hate the smell of baby talc. Other deterrents include used kitty litter, mothballs and human hair.

Raccoons, Woodchucks And Gophers

◆ If you're really desperate to get rid of any raccoons—especially when your vegetables (such as corn) are almost ripe—invest in 2 or 3 portable radios. Set them on different talk-radio stations, put them in plastic bags to protect them from the elements and leave them in your garden. The surround-sound effect will scare the raccoons away.

Remember, it must be *talk* radio only—*music* might actually encourage those masked bandits to stay for dinner and dancing.

◆ Nobody wants gopher or woodchuck holes in his/her garden or lawn. In a blender, put all the cloves from 3 bulbs of garlic, a few chili peppers and 3 cups of water. Blend thoroughly and transfer the mix to a jar.

Pour some of the solution into each hole…then, put a hose down the hole and let the water push the strong mixture deeper

into the hole. This formula will help you get rid of gophers or woodchucks for good.

Slugs and Snails

Collect any clean and empty tuna cans and use them to set traps for beer-loving critters (we're referring to slugs and snails, of course!). Since you don't want the slugs in your garden, scatter the cans around your garden. Dig shallow holes, or carefully press the cans—open side up—into the soil so that the rim is level with the ground. In the early evening, fill ⅔ of each can with beer. The next morning, you will be able to dispose of cans of slugs that died happy.

Squash Bugs

If you grow squash, cucumbers or pumpkins, keep squash bugs away by placing strips of heavy aluminum foil under the vines. The foil will help keep the soil moist and block sunlight, which will keep weeds from growing. It may also speed up the crop-ripening time.

Squirrels

If you have a *bird* feeder and don't want it turned into a *squirrel* feeder, then try coating the metal feeder pole with petroleum jelly. (Suddenly, the old Simon & Garfunkel song came to mind—"Slip Sliding Away.")

PLANT & GARDEN FRIENDS

Almost 90% of all the world's plants rely on insects (such as bees) to spread their pollen and perpetuate the plant species. *So, before you pick up that fly swatter, you may want to know about a few helpful garden insects…*

Beneficial Bugs

◆ Praying mantids gobble up aphids, mites and scale insects. Pray that you have these critters in your garden.

◆ Ladybugs—also known as lady beetles or ladybirds—are attractive assets in your garden. They devour aphids, scale insects and other plant-eating pests. During the average ladybug's lifetime, it destroys 5,400 aphids. Let's hear it for the ladybugs!

✱ **Buy Your Bugs**
If there are no garden ladybugs in your area, they are available on-line. A package of 300 costs about $3.85. Check out *http://gardening zone.com*.

Butterflies

Who wouldn't want butterflies in their garden? These *flying flowers* are especially drawn to red, scarlet, purple and blue blossoms.

If you want to extend a butterfly invitation, plant any or all of the following flowers and herbs—cornflower, aster, dill, morning glory, verbena, mint, globe thistle, goldenrod, lilac, pansy, parsley, shasta daisy, sweet marjoram, zinnia, sage and (wouldn't you know?) butterfly bush.

POPULAR GARDEN PLANTS A TO Z

Talk about popular! Tomatoes are by far the most popular garden plant, with almost 90% of all home gardeners growing this delectable red fruit. According to a survey reported by Heirloom Seeds (*www.heirloomseeds.com*), the next 9 most popular home-grown vegetables in the US and Canada are (in order of their popularity)—peppers, cucumbers, onions, beans, lettuce, carrots, sweet corn, radishes and cabbage.

No matter which plants are your favorites, and whether or not they're among the top 10, here are some ways to add to the life and beauty of all of your plants.

African Violets

Grow bigger and heartier plants by feeding them an iron supplement—simply stick a few nails in the soil around them, and enjoy the lovely results.

Azaleas

These acid-loving plants will love you if you give them an occasional bracer. Once a month, fill your watering can with 2 tablespoons of distilled white vinegar in 1 quart of water to promote bloom growth and color.

The same mixture is also great for rhododendrons and gardenias.

✎ **NOTE:** In case you are wondering, of all the colors the plant comes in, white azaleas stay in bloom the longest.

Beans

See "Legumes (Beans and Peas)" on page 222.

Bulbs

◆ Before planting bulbs, protect them from burrowing insects and rodents by dusting them with medicated baby powder.

◆ After you dig up your cold-vulnerable bulbs, apply medicated baby powder all over them to prevent rot and fungal problems when you put them into winter storage.

Cabbage

◆ Keep animals from snacking on cabbage by sprinkling a little cayenne pepper on the plants as they grow. Remember to resprinkle with more pepper after it rains.

◆ You can also trickle a little milk mixed with water on the cabbages to protect them from cabbage worms.

◆ After cutting off the first mature head of cabbage, leave the rest of the plant as is. Chances are, a few more small heads will grow in the same place.

Cacti and Other Succulents

In addition to keeping moths away, mothballs or camphor flakes added to your potting mix will help prevent mealybug problems in the roots of cacti and other succulents.

Be sure to plant the mothballs only in clay pots—they may ruin plastic pots.

Carrots

Mix your carrot seeds with some coffee grounds. The seeds will have more substance and be easier to work with. Another plus is that coffee grounds will add nitrogen and other nutrients to the soil as they break down.

Also, the coffee grounds will be a deterrent to root maggots that might otherwise eat some of your carrot crop.

Climbing Plants

Give climbing plants something creative to hang on to. Simply take a large, no-longer-used umbrella and remove the fabric from it, then drive the handle into the ground and open the umbrella so the spokes are extended.

At the base of the umbrella, plant clematis or wisteria (in a sunny location)…or honeysuckle or morning glory (in partial shade)…or any other climbing plant you like. Then watch the blooms turn the bumbershoot frame into an unusual trellis.

Corn

When it comes to harvesting corn at its prime, the window of opportunity is limited to a few days. Start testing the ears about 2 weeks after the corn silk can be seen, to make sure that you don't miss those few days.

To test for ripeness, peel back the husk enough to see about 2 inches of kernels. Press a kernel with your fingernail until you split the skin and juice comes out. If the juice is milky, the corn is ripe—so start picking. If the juice is watery, put the husk back in place and give the corn a few more days. If the juice is gooey, the corn is getting too starchy. Of course, that won't happen to you—the ripeness test is the *ear*mark of a good corn grower.

Corn tastes best when picked, cooked and eaten all on the same day. Writer and humorist Mark Twain once said—not entirely in jest—that folks should just set up kettles in their cornfields, build a fire under them and shuck the ears of corn directly into the boiling water. Really, that's not a bad idea if you want the tastiest corn!

In general, the best time of day to pick corn is late in the afternoon, when the sugar content is at its highest.

Cucumbers

Coddle those cucumber seedlings by giving them the warmth they love. If you don't mind the look, place an old rubber tire around each plant. The tire keeps in heat during the day and releases it at night.

Harvesting Popcorn

Popcorn seeds are completely different than the regular corn-on-the-cob (sweet corn) seeds. Do not plant any variety of popcorn in the same garden as your sweet corn. The quality of the sweet corn will be diminished once it is cross-pollinated by popcorn.

If you do grow your own popcorn, be sure to let the kernels dry in the garden as long as possible. Don't harvest them until the kernels are hard and the husks are completely dry.

After harvesting them, remove the husks, put the ears in mesh bags, then hang them in a warm, dry, well-ventilated place. When you've tested a few kernels by popping them—and they taste good—then it is time to remove all of the kernels from the ears.

The easiest way to do it without using and bruising your thumbs is to hold 1 ear in each hand and rub them against each other. The kernels will knock each other off the cobs. Then store the kernels in jars with tight-fitting lids—this will keep moisture in and bugs out.

One of the most popular products that's in Paul Newman's philanthropic line of all-natural foods is *Newman's Own OldStyle Picture Show Microwave Popcorn*. Newman's experience is that *small* kernels yield tastier popcorn—the bigger the corn pops, the more dissipated the taste.

Eggplants

If you would rather have 4 big, impressive eggplants per plant instead of lots of little unimpressive ones, then read on…

As soon as you see 4 fruits starting to plump up, pinch off all the other flowers as well as the buds. In doing so, the eggplants that may come along later will not have enough time to amount to anything before the season ends, and most of the plant's energy will go into producing the 4 beauties.

To help nourish this fruit-bearing plant, occasionally treat it to a magnesium and sulfur drink—1 tablespoon of Epsom salt (available at supermarkets and drugstores) dissolved in 1 gallon of warm water.

Ferns

For a fantastic fern fertilizer, finely chop 3 to 5 raw oysters and work the pieces into the soil. Your ferns will love it!

Forsythia

Once a forsythia bush blooms, it should be pruned. To revitalize mature forsythias, remove ¼ to ⅓ of the oldest (largest) branches at ground level. Do this every other year. New shoots will come up from the ground and bloom in subsequent years.

Geraniums

Geraniums are thirsty plants that require lots of water (but make sure the roots don't sit in water). After preparing your morning coffee, rinse off the coffee grounds, and put them on top of the soil surrounding the geraniums. The grounds become a marvelous mulch that helps keep in moisture.

Herbs

Fresh herbs are most flavorful when harvested right before their flowers open.

Hollyhocks

When you've finished drinking your beer, add a little water to the can, bottle or glass, swish it around and water your hollyhocks with it.

The yeast in the beer will help the plant rise to new heights—in addition to its usual watering, of course.

Hydrangeas

Pink or blue, it's up to you. Grow a particular variety of hydrangea bush in acid soil, and the flowers will be blue...grow another type in alkaline soil, and you'll have pink flowers.

So, to enhance the pink, add *dolomitic lime* (available at garden-supply stores) to your plants several times a year to help raise the soil's pH to about 6.0 to 6.2.

For blue hydrangeas, lower the soil's pH to 5.2 to 5.5. You can do this by adding a solution made from 1 tablespoon of *aluminum sulfate* (available at garden-supply stores) per gallon of water, and use it to water the plants (make sure the plants are at least 2 years old) throughout the growing season.

> ⚡ **CAUTION:** Water the plants thoroughly before applying this aluminum solution, and be warned that too much can burn the plants' roots. Talk to a knowledgeable salesperson at the garden store to get more information.

Kale

If you're new at gardening and don't want to run the risk of crop failure, plant fail-safe kale seeds. The vegetables are beautiful, healthy and very easy to grow in just about any kind of soil.

Legumes (Beans and Peas)

Right after you pick the first crop of legumes, use a hand mower to mow the plants down to about 3" from the soil.

That way, you will have another crop to harvest before the end of the season.

> ⚡ **CAUTION:** Do not plant members of the *allium* family—such as garlic or onions—in or around a pea patch. They may inhibit the growth of peas.

Lettuce

Grow lettuce in a shady patch of your garden. If you keep the lettuce cool as a cucumber, it will mature without any bitterness...but then again, wouldn't we all?

Lilac

After a lilac bush blooms, it should be pruned. To revitalize an older bush, remove entire dead branches at ground level and all weak or broken branches. Cut back the healthy stems to 1' to 2'.

Then start taking care of the bushes by watering and fertilizing them regularly. The lilacs may take 1 to 2 years to rebloom, but they're worth the effort!

Melons

Put melons on a pedestal while they're growing, and they'll happily ripen early. To do so, place each melon on an empty coffee can that has been turned upside down and pressed into the soil. The metal attracts and holds on to heat from the sun, which is a ripening agent.

Onions

Before you plant onions, save up several days' worth of used coffee grounds and let them dry out. When it's time to plant, spread a layer of the coffee grounds on the bottom of each row of onions. Doing so will help prevent worms from getting at your onions.

Perennials

Perennials are meant to grow back year after year. But a premature thaw, followed by a deep freeze, can be the end of your perennials.

If you put a layer of hay, shredded leaves or grass clippings on the ground over your perennials, it will keep the ground frozen and

Good Advice for Allergy Sufferers

According to Clifford Bassett, MD, an allergist at Long Island College Hospital in Brooklyn, New York, seasonal allergy sufferers should avoid planting chrysanthemums, privet, palm and mulberry trees, juniper and cypress, as well as Bermuda, fescue and perennial rye grasses.

Allergy-prone gardeners will do better planting hydrangeas, viburnum, begonias, bulbs like tulip and iris, dogwood trees, azaleas, boxwood, daisies, geraniums, pansies, petunias, sunflowers and zinnias.

It's best to garden on low pollen–count days, and also when it's damp or rainy...and in the evening, if possible. Also, be sure to eliminate all weeds from your garden.

And the last bit of advice to help you keep allergic reactions at bay—before entering your house, always remove all of your gardening clothes...dust off your shoes...and don't forget to clean your glasses.

prevent a premature thaw. Do this after the first frost, but before it gets *really* cold. And then you'll be able to enjoy these bloomin' plants for many seasons to come.

Petunias

If you smoke, scrub up like a surgeon before working with petunias. These sensitive plants are extremely susceptible to the *tobacco mosaic virus*, a disease that can be spread by cigarette, cigar or pipe smoke.

Poinsettias

These traditional winter holiday plants can be enjoyed all year 'round if you give them plenty of sun in the winter, and nondirect sunlight in the summer. Poinsettias like sun but not heat. They need moderately moist soil...water thoroughly whenever the soil feels dry to the touch.

Potatoes

If you're going to plant potatoes, start eating lots of canned soup, and save the cans. Turn them into protective cylinders by taking off their lids and bottoms.

Then press each soup-can cylinder into the soil around each young potato plant. Not only will the can shelter the young plants from the wind, it will also protect them from cutworms, grubs and other pests.

Pumpkins

If you want a pumpkin to grow really big, cut off all of the blossoms except 2. Then all of the pumpkin's energy will go into pumping up its size, rather than nourishing lots of blossoms.

Radishes

To invigorate your radish plants, serve them a monthly tonic made from 1 tablespoon of apple cider vinegar in 1 gallon of water. They'll thrive on the trace minerals that the apple cider vinegar has to offer.

Raspberries

The best time to pick ripe raspberries is after the morning dew is gone, simply because dry fruit is less perishable.

Gather the raspberry harvest in wide, shallow containers so that these delicate berries aren't piled up on each other. Piling up means *mush* on the bottom.

Roses

◆ Every rose grower should know the secret to a healthy and beautiful rose crop—banana peels! The peels are rich in calcium, magnesium, phosphorus, potash, sulfur, sodium and silica…so they make a great fertilizer.

Save the banana peels or air-dry them until they're crispyish and crumblyish. Figure on using about 3 peels per rosebush—cut the peels into small pieces and bury them around each bush, a few inches deep into the soil.

◆ Nourishing your rosebushes using Epsom salt (available at supermarkets and drugstores) will help strengthen the color of the flowers. During the first and third weeks of May and during the first and third weeks of June, feed your up-and-coming bushes according to their height—1 teaspoon of Epsom salt per foot—worked into the soil around the stems.

For a mature rose bush, sprinkle ½ cup of Epsom salt on the soil around it. You may also notice that the plants blossom faster due to the magnesium in the Epsom salt, which helps boost their rate of growth.

◆ As the day progresses, rose stems stock up on food manufactured by the leaves. By the time evening rolls around, the stems are at their most hale and hardy. That's the best time to cut the flowers—they, too, will be hale and hardy. If you cut roses in the morning, before the stems have had a chance to bulk up, they will not have as much staying power.

◆ The best way to cut roses is to look for the uppermost 5-leaflet branch and cut the stem above it. By doing this, you can be sure of the abundant regrowth of more roses. Cut below that branch and the new shoot may be flowerless.

◆ Thorns help the rose plant drink water. If, in the process of removing the thorns, you tear, peel or damage the bark, you will impede the amount of water that makes its way up to the flower. A damaged stem will shorten the life of the rose.

If the thorns on the rose are a thorn in your side, buy a de-thorning tool (available at garden-supply stores) and follow the instructions. You may wound a few flowers until you become a proficient de-thorner, but stick with it.

◆ When you're pruning roses or any thorny plant, use kitchen tongs to hold the branches out of your way—this will prevent the thorns from pricking your fingers and/or scratching your arms.

✳ Sun- or Shade-Loving Produce

◆ If a section of your garden is bathed in sunlight, consider growing corn, melons, peppers and/or tomatoes. They thrive in the sun.

◆ If a section of your garden doesn't get much sun, consider growing lettuce, pumpkins and/or spinach. They thrive in the shade.

Tomatoes

◆ Protect your seedlings from the cold air by planting them during the afternoon—the warmest part of the day. (And protect yourself from the sun with a hat, sunglasses and sunscreen.)

◆ Consider including carrots, lettuce, nasturtiums, chives, onions and parsley in the tomato patch. Any or all of them can help prevent disease, stimulate growth and enhance the flavor of the tomatoes.

◆ Another beneficial addition to the patch is dill. It will keep away pests, such as hornworms. French marigolds will ward off whiteflies and rabbits. Sagebrush will stimulate tomatoes to produce a pest-repelling chemical. Asparagus will help deter any *nematodes* (including pinworms, hookworms and roundworms), while tomatoes will help repel the asparagus beetle.

★ Protect Your Tomatoes!

Do not grow cabbage, fennel, kohlrabi or potatoes near your tomato patch. *The Moosewood Restaurant Kitchen Garden* (Ten Speed Press) suggests that you won't be doing any of the plants a favor—they will attract pests that will attack tomatoes.

◆ Lower the acidity of the tomatoes, and they'll taste sweeter. To do that, sprinkle baking soda around the plants and work it into the soil.

◆ To prevent blossom-end rot, mix a packet of powdered milk with water (follow package directions), and feed it to your plants. Or use crushed oyster and crab shells (available at garden-supply stores)—follow the directions on the package and sprinkle the powder around the plants.

The milk and shells both contain calcium, which will keep the plants healthier and help produce juicier tomatoes.

◆ According to Cornell University researchers, gently petting tomato seedlings every now and then produces short, stocky plants that are more desirable for transplanting. Start stroking the plants when they are 2½" tall, and continue until you're ready to transplant them.

◆ If you smoke cigarettes, find the strength to stop…at least while you're in the garden. Tomato plants are susceptible to the *tobacco mosaic virus*, a disease that can be spread by cigar, pipe and cigarette smoke. (It's always a good idea to wash your hands before you start to garden.)

◆ It can happen! You can save tomatoes from a frost. The first thing to do is to pick them—no matter how green they are. Wrap each tomato in 3 layers of newspaper and they will eventually ripen.

If you can't pick them, cover the plants with a clean, empty milk jug—cut the top off and place it over them. It will make an effective shield.

◆ Instead of throwing out that shabby old bra, use it to support *zaftig* tomatoes. Brace the tomato plant by tying it to 2 wooden stakes. Then attach each end of the bra to each stake, making sure the cups are positioned under 2 large tomatoes.

The bra will give the plant the extra support it needs, and prevent it from collapsing under the weight of the plant's oversized love apples.

★ Black or White?

If you have a choice as to which color bra to use, black will attract more sun and should be used *before* the tomatoes ripen…a white bra should be used for ripe tomatoes, during the last days before picking.

◆ When you're cleaning your garden in autumn and you come across unripe tomatoes, pull out the plants—roots and all. Then shake off the dirt and hang the plants upside down in your basement or garage. Believe it or not, the tomatoes will ripen on the vine. Think of it, fresh tomatoes at Thanksgiving!

◆ You have 2 options when it comes to planting tomatoes. You can help them grow either by getting *over* them or getting *under* them.

Over: If you're concerned about providing moisture and warmth to the plants, spread black plastic over the soil. Then cut out holes in the plastic and plant the plants through them.

Under: Wad up some newspaper and set it on the bottom of each planting hole. The paper will absorb water as it trickles through the soil, and the roots can make use of it throughout the hot, dry summer.

Another "Under": Sprinkle 1 teaspoon of Epsom salt on top of the newspaper in the planting hole. The magnesium sulfate in the Epsom salt will help the plant grow more and bigger tomatoes.

Tulips

Protect bulbs from rodents by planting them in metal cylinders. Gather large cans—such as those from fruit or vegetable juice—and use 1 can for each bulb.

Remove the contents and the top and bottom lids of each can, and wash inside the empty can. Press each clean cylinder into the soil until the rim is ground level. Take out ⅔ of the soil, place the bulb inside and replace the soil around the bulb up to the rim.

This can system is an *uncanny* way of keeping animals away from the bulbs while allowing rain to reach them.

Safe Way to Handle Poison Ivy

If you discover poison ivy on your property, **DO NOT** burn it. You don't want the plant's oil to get into the air that you breathe. Instead, put 1 ounce of vodka and 2 cups of water into a spray bottle, then saturate the poison ivy plants with it. Oddly enough, even though you're spraying it with a liquid mixture, the alcohol in the vodka helps to dehydrate and kill the plants.

If you don't want to waste your good vodka on the misery-causing greenery, put on gloves and uproot the plants, then leave them on the ground to dry out in the sun.

As soon as you've done the deed, clean all your tools thoroughly in a solution made from ¾ pound of table salt mixed with warm, soapy water. When you take off your gloves, turn them inside out and dispose of them. Be careful and make sure that the gloves or oils do not touch your skin.

You should also *carefully* remove any clothes that came in contact with the poison ivy. If you do not want to throw away the clothes you were wearing, then you can wash them in the washing machine—but separately from other clothes.

Be sure to wear disposable rubber gloves when handling the clothes. And use 1 ounce of liquid dish detergent rather than laundry detergent—it's better at breaking up *urushiol*, the poison ivy oil. Run the washing machine's rinse cycle twice after you take out the clothes.

> **CAUTION:** Urushiol oil is sticky and can stay on clothes and cause new rashes—even years later.

Also, while wearing the disposable rubber gloves, scrub your boots or shoes with warm, soapy water (use 1 capful of liquid dish detergent in 1 gallon of water). Leave the footwear in the sun to dry.

Vegetables

◆ While *pantyhose on plants* doesn't sound very practical, it does seem to provide protection to the vegetables that tend to attract harmful bugs. (We hope by now that you know to NEVER throw away old pantyhose!)

Snip off the feet of the pantyhose and cover each growing vegetable with a foot. Use a rubber band or string to secure it in place. The nylon fabric will let the sun and air get in and will keep the bugs out. Also, as the veggie grows, the hose will stretch.

◆ If you find it hard to plant your veggies in straight rows, use 2 wooden stakes and a ball of string to lead the way.

Insert 1 stake in the ground where you want the row to start, and put 1 stake where you want the row to end. Tie the string on 1 stake, then stretch it across to the other stake. The string is your straight line. Follow it as you distribute your seeds.

TREES

Trees are the longest living organisms on Earth. You may have heard that you can calculate a tree's age by its rings. Ahh, but do you know that those rings also provide precise information about environmental events, such as volcanic eruptions…and that the study of these rings is called *dendrochronology*?

If you plan on planting a tree—or if you already have a few trees on your property—you may find some suggestions here that will help them live long and grow tall.

Planting Trees

Over the life of a tree, its roots can be far-reaching. With that in mind, plant the tree so that its roots will not come in contact with (and do damage to) your house's foundation—no matter how old the tree gets or how big it grows. Make sure any tree is planted well away from sidewalks and sewer pipes and/or septic tanks.

Once you find the right spot for the tree, project into the future. Envision the tree mature and all grown up. Is it shading your driveway so that your car stays cool in the summer? Or is the sap from the tree messing up your car? Is the tree blocking the sunlight from your garden? Are the tree's fruits falling off and possibly attracting hungry critters?

Think about it before you plant the tree so that you won't have any regrets down the road. (Hey, perhaps *that's* where you should plant the tree!) As a general guideline, most trees should be planted 7–15 feet away from your home.

When you finally find the perfect place to plant a tree, be sure the drainage is good. Test the drainage by digging a hole in the exact spot you plan to plant the tree, and fill it with water. Check on the hole about 10 hours later. If the water has completely drained out, that means drainage is good and you can start planting.

★ Line the Tree Hole

Any young tree that you're going to plant will need all the help it can get. Start by lining the hole that's been dug for the tree with baking potatoes. They will help provide moisture for the young plant.

As the potatoes decompose, the tree will benefit from their nutrients. *This spud's for yew!*

Apple Trees

◆ Before it's apple-blossom time, collect empty gallon jugs (like from milk or spring water). You'll need 1 jug for each apple tree. You'll also need 1 quart of distilled white vinegar, 1 quart of water, 1 cup of sugar and 1 banana peel for each tree.

Combine all of the ingredients in each jug *in the order they're listed*. Then hang a filled jug in the middle of each tree (and be sure to leave off the cap). Put the jugs in place *before* the apple blossoms open, and this will ensure worm-free blossoms.

◆ There are 2 ways to check if apples are ripe enough to harvest. First, take an apple off the tree with a clockwise twist. If it comes off easily, the apple is ripe.

If you have to keep twisting until it finally lets go of the tree, give the rest of the apples more time to ripen.

Another way to check for ripeness is by the color of the apple's seed. If it's dark brown, then the apple is ripe…if it's pale tan or white, the apple is not quite ripe.

Other Fruit Trees

◆ If your fruit trees have been barren, the soil may need boron, a nutrient found in borax. Sprinkle about 1 cup of borax powder (available at supermarkets and drugstores) around the base of each tree right before you give it a thorough watering.

◆ Or you may just need to smack your trees around…*really*. To do this, take a rolled-up newspaper and hit the tree with it, up and down the trunk.

The idea is to loosen the vessels that carry sap to the leaves and buds. According to the wisdom of folklore, it's best to whip fruit trees in early spring, by moonlight.

HOUSEPLANTS

A nice addition to any room is a splash of color—courtesy of plants and indoor flowers. These decorative accents can lend a feeling of hominess to your living space. Here are some ideas that will help you make your household greenery thrive. *But first, an important warning…*

> **CAUTION:** We would be very remiss—especially if there are children and/or pets in the home—if we didn't make readers aware of the fact that several common house and garden plants are poisonous (and potentially lethal) when ingested. *Read on…*

All parts of philodendrons, rhododendron, azaleas, laurels, dieffenbachia, elephant ears and buttercups are toxic…as are the seeds and pods of wisteria…the leaves and flowers of lily-of-the-valley…the bulbs of autumn crocus, hyacinths, narcissus and daffodils…the leaves of foxgloves, the berries of jasmine and mistletoe…and the leaves and branches of oleander.

In fact, the beautiful oleander bush that's grown indoors and outdoors throughout the country is so potent that ingesting a *single leaf* can kill a child. Even using oleander twigs to spear meat that's roasted over a campfire can (and has) proven fatal. While this sounds like material for a fictional murder mystery, it shouldn't be taken lightly in real life.

If you want to check out a plant that you would like to bring into your home—or a plant that's already there, visit *www.yardener.com/AvoidingPoisonousPlants.html*.

Or call the US National Poison Hotline at 800-222-1222. When you dial this number, you will automatically be linked to the poison center in your local area. The operator will look up the plant in question in a comprehensive database and tell you all that you need to know about its toxicity. This service is free, and it's available 24 hours a day, 7 days a week.

New Plants

A gardener at The New York Botanical Garden told us that April is generally the best month to bring home new houseplants. The reasoning is that the light becomes stronger and the days become longer in the springtime, which means better conditions and fewer problems for plants.

Cuttings

If a friend offers you cuttings of plants that you admire, ask him/her for a raw potato along with the cuttings. Cut off a chunk from one end of the potato, and make holes in it with a chopstick or ballpoint-pen cap. Gently insert the cuttings into the holes. Then put the potato with the cuttings in a bag or box, and they should stay safe and moist during your trip home.

Once the cuttings are home, you should mist them with a solution of ¼ teaspoon of 3% hydrogen peroxide to 2 cups of water. This will serve to help prevent them from getting a fungal spore infection.

Live-Long-and-Prosper Plants

If you haven't had much luck with plants due to your unintentional neglect, start over with those that require very little care. Select from Devil's ivy, snake plants, corn plants, Chinese evergreens or begonias. And, this time, don't forget to water them!

Clean Means Sunny

Up to twice as much beneficial sunlight will stream into your home through windows that are clean as opposed to windows that are dirty.

See Chapter 8, "All-Around-the-House Hints," pages 186–187, for easy and effective ways to clean windows.

Sun-Loving Plants

If you have a particularly sunny room, plants such as jade, coleus, cacti and *orchids* should all thrive there.

> ✍ **NOTE:** The secret of growing orchids successfully is to keep them in a room that's heated to between 75°F and 85°F during the day and 60°F and 65°F at night.
>
> Many orchids will remain bloomless unless they live with the temperature variation of 15°F to 20°F between day and night.

Shade Plants

You can grow healthy plants in a room without sunlight streaming in the window—and even without a window—as long as you have the right types of plants. Pothos, ferns, peace lilies and prayer plants do not require a sunbath to be hale and hardy. Just be sure to keep them watered properly or placed in a shady and humid area (such as the bathroom).

Potting

◆ Have you ever dissected a disposable diaper? Well, now's your chance. Cut open a diaper (any brand/absorbency will do), remove the polymer flakes and mix them into the potting soil. Since the flakes absorb 300 times their weight in liquid, they will keep plant soil nice and moist. The polymer also stores nutrients, which will gradually feed the plant.

◆ When it comes to pots for flowering plants, bigger is *not* better. For the health of the plant, use a pot that will keep the roots close together rather than spread out.

Pot Liners

◆ Instead of lining the bottom of your pots with rocks or pebbles, use polystyrene packing peanuts. They are good at retaining moisture—so you may not have to water plants as often—and they weigh next to nothing. That can make a big difference when you have to lug around a large potted plant.

     It's an especially good idea to use the packing peanuts in hanging plants because of how weightless and absorbent they are.

◆ Line the inside of the pot with a coffee filter or with the leg piece from an old pair of pantyhose. Then add the soil and the plant. The drainage hole will let the water out, and the pantyhose acts as a filter to keep the soil in.

Enhancing the Sun

◆ Plants that need lots of light—but do not get enough—usually look weak, gangly and yellowish. If you have sun-worshipping plants like geraniums, jade plants, ficus and cacti, line the windowsill near them with aluminum foil. The foil will enhance the reflection of the sun.

◆ Get a cardboard box big enough to house your plant(s). Cut off the top of the box and 1 of the sides. Then line the inside of the box with aluminum foil—shiny side out. Put the plant(s) inside the box and then place it near the window.

> ✍ **NOTE:** The foil-lined box is better than the foil-lined windowsill because the plants in the box will be surrounded by reflected sunlight and will grow straight up—while the plants near the windowsill will be leaning toward the source of light—the window. If the cardboard box appears unsightly, cover the outside with attractive contact paper (self-adhesive vinyl).

Use Plants to Clear the Air

In 1989, the National Aeronautics and Space Administration (NASA) conducted extensive (and expensive) research during a 2-year study. The scientists found a list of common, attractive and easy-to-grow houseplants that can dramatically reduce toxic chemical levels in the home. One plant will generally remove up to 87% of the toxic organic pollutants in a 100-square-foot area—increase the air-cleaning with even more plants.

Putting plants in each room may go a long way in eliminating problems like sore throats, stuffy noses, headaches, nausea, teary eyes and even acne—all of which may be caused by indoor contaminants that come from drapes, carpets, insulation, paint, household cleaning products, paper towels, tissues, plastics…really, almost everything. *Take this list with you when you shop for air-cleaning plants…*

◆ Golden pothos
◆ Peace lily
◆ Spider plant
◆ Chinese evergreen
◆ Boston fern
◆ Rubber plant
◆ English ivy
◆ Bamboo palm
◆ Weeping fig (*Ficus benjamina*)

> ⚠ **CAUTION:** The ficus tree or shrub is sensitive to gas leaks. If all of the leaves suddenly fall off your ficus plant, open your windows, then call the gas company to test your gas lines. Do not ignore what may be a warning that could save lives.

Misting

Plants should be misted several times a week to make up for the low humidity level in most homes. This is especially important during dry winter months.

Brush the Fuzzies

Do not mist plants that have fuzzy-surfaced leaves, including cacti. Clean the *fuzzies* with a soft brush instead. A clean, new makeup brush or a baby's hairbrush both work well.

Watering Houseplants

◆ Overwatering is the leading killer of houseplants. Know when to water a plant by sticking your finger about 1" into the soil. If the soil feels dry, then it's time to quench the plant's thirst.

◆ Water your plants in the morning, when they begin to wake up. It's when they will best absorb water.

◆ Watering often, but a little at a time, can weaken the roots. Instead, water plants thoroughly once every week—or whenever the soil feels dry to the touch.

◆ Plants prefer lukewarm or room-temperature water because it's easier for them to absorb. But ice-cold or boiling-hot water—NEVER!

Enriching Elixirs

◆ Gelatin is a great source of nitrogen. Dissolve 1 envelope of unflavored gelatin in 1 cup of just-boiled water. Then add 3 cups of tap water and—when it cools to room temperature—use the mixture to give your plants an energy boost once a month.

◆ Water from boiled pasta or potatoes has a high starch content and makes an excellent plant fertilizer. Let the water cool to room temperature before using it.

◆ After you hard-boil an egg, douse your plants with the protein-enriched water. Wait until the water is lukewarm before you use it.

◆ Whenever you steam or cook vegetables, save the excess water as a vitamin-filled treat for your plants. Let the water cool to room temperature before using it.

◆ If your plants aren't doing well, they may be sensitive to the chlorine gas in your city or town's water system. Instead, let tap water sit in the watering can overnight (which will allow most of the gas to escape), then use it to water your plants.

Also, when it snows, gather a few handfuls of fresh powder in a bucket, let it melt and warm up to room temperature, then water your plants with the gas-free water.

◆ If you maintain a fish aquarium, save the old water every time you change it, and feed the nutrient-rich water to your plants. They will thank you by thriving.

◆ Alkaline-loving houseplants, especially African violets, always appreciate a dairy boost. Instead of throwing away an empty milk carton, fill it halfway with tap water and water your plants with it.

◆ Dissolve 2 tablespoons of Epsom salt (available at supermarkets and drugstores) in 1 gallon of warm water to quench your plant's thirst. Epsom salt (magnesium sulfate) provides the plant with magnesium.

Do this once a month, and you'll see your plant revive and thrive, and it will become more resistant to disease.

◆ Used coffee grounds enrich the soil with nitrogen. In addition to being a good chemical-free fertilizer, the grounds will also make the plant undesirable to any cats you have roaming around.

Once a week, scatter 1 tablespoon of the moist, used coffee grounds onto the potted plant's soil.

Flowering Plants

◆ To make a young plant grow into a full-bodied plant (instead of a tall, scrawny plant), pinch off the growing tips of the stems. This will wake up the lower-down dormant buds.

> **NOTE:** You can do the same tip-pinching with vines, but never pinch a palm or any other 1-point-of-growth plant.

◆ When a flowering plant starts to wither, gently remove the dead flowers so that the plant doesn't waste its energy on them.

Luminous Leaves

◆ Water your plant with sodium-free seltzer water or club soda that has gone flat. Make sure the fizzy stuff is at room temperature. This drink will help brighten the color of your plants' leaves.

◆ To make the leaves of a plant appear their greenest, gently massage each leaf with castor oil or mineral oil.

◆ Use a soft cloth and wipe plant leaves with Cool Whip or milk (make sure it's at room temperature). *Sodium caseinate*, the natural protein in dairy, is said to be an effective cleaner for plant-cell walls.

◆ Mix ⅛ cup of baking soda into 1 quart of lukewarm water, and then use it to wash 1 leaf at a time.

◆ Add a few drops of liquid dish detergent to 1 quart of lukewarm water, then wash each leaf. Not only will the plant be clean, it will also repel bugs.

◆ If the leaves of your plant are yellowish and yucky instead of bright and beautiful, try giving them an iron boost. Soak a steel-wool pad or some metal nails in a tin can filled with water overnight. Then you can use the heavy-metal water to supplement the plant's iron deficiency.

✳ The Sound of Music

Research suggests that playing music for your plants can help them flourish. Not all music, though…according to some experiments, *rock* music killed the plants, and *classical* music helped them thrive.

Hanging Plants

◆ Do not water hanging plants by putting ice cubes in them. It may be easier that way, but your plants will hate you for it. They prefer lukewarm or room-temperature water.

◆ If you place a potted plant inside a hanging basket, put a pair of baby or adult diapers (such as Huggies or Depends) under the pot to absorb the excess water that can leak from the drainage hole.

Once the pot is in the basket, it will look fine, but forget this suggestion if you have a hanging pot *without* the decorative basket—nobody wants to see a plant wearing a diaper.

◆ To prevent floors and carpets from getting wet each time you water a hanging plant, forget the silly superstition about opening an umbrella indoors…just turn the open umbrella upside down, and place it on the floor under the pot you want to water.

Let it stay there during and after the watering, until all of the excess water has dripped out of the pot's drainage hole. Then you can empty and rinse out the umbrella, or move it along to the next hanging plant you want to water.

◆ Put a shower cap or plastic bowl cover on the bottom of the pot or basket to catch the excess water. Secure it in place with a tight, thick rubber band around the cap or cover.

FIRST AID FOR PLANTS

All sorts of plants and green growing things can get weak, sick or injured. If you ever thought about taking a class to learn CPR—*Caring Plant Resuscitation*—you may want to start here with some useful treatments.

"Planti-Aging" Cure

If you have a frail, old plant that needs a boost, try this solution—twice a week for 3 months, before you water the plant, give it about ⅛ cup of Geritol (available at drugstores).

Within a month, you should see healthy, new leaves sprouting up. Of course, if your plant seems worse, suspend the treatment.

Infections

When you *know* your plant has a viral or fungal infection, and you want to treat it yourself, these remedies are worth a try...

◆ Combine 1 gallon of warm water with 1 cup of molasses. Once the molasses completely dissolves, transfer it to a trigger-spray bottle and spray the infected plant. The plant will be nourished by the sugar, while the sulfur that is in the molasses should help destroy the fungi.

◆ If your plant is ailing and you suspect that it has some kind of leaf infection, combine 1 tablespoon of baking soda, 1 tablespoon of dishwashing liquid and 1 gallon of water.

Put the mixture in a trigger-spray bottle and spray the infected plant, including the underside of the leaves.

Mealybugs

If you see little white cottony masses on your plant's leaves and stems, those are mealybugs. Soak a washcloth in soapy water and wipe off the mealybugs. Or get them with a cotton swab that has been dipped in rubbing alcohol.

Once the plant is clear of the bugs you can see, check the plant pot carefully—including the underside—for mealybug egg masses. (You'll know the whiteish, gooey clump of eggs when you see it.) Get rid of the eggs the same way you got rid of the bugs—with a warm, soapy washcloth or rubbing alcohol.

---

⑤ Create a Basic Pesticide

If you see insects in the plant's soil, add a few drops of liquid dishwashing detergent to warm water, and use it to water the plant. It will put an end to anything in the pot that crawls.

WHILE YOU'RE AWAY...

If you're traveling for vacation or a business trip, you don't want to worry—or even think about—your plants withering away at home. *Here are a few ways to keep them alive and well while you're out of town (for up to about 2 weeks)...*

◆ Place plastic trash bags on the floor of your bathtub. Put big towels on top of the bags and pour water on the towels until they're completely wet. Check each plant to make sure it has a drainage hole at the bottom of its pot, and bring it into the bathroom—then set it on top of the towel.

Right before you leave the house, give the plants a thorough watering, kiss them good-bye and *bon voyage*!

◆ For a clever method of letting gravity help water your plants, you'll need a stool or a chair, a bucket of water, a plastic drop cloth and several long strips of ½" cotton rope or unwaxed cotton wicking (available at craft stores)—1 strip for each plant—and ample space in your living room (or wherever you keep your plants).

Put the plastic drop cloth on the floor and set your plants on top of it. Place the stool or chair close to the plants, and then put the bucket of water on the chair. Take a strip of wicking or rope, drench it and bury 1 end of it deep in the soil next to the plant. Place the other end of the strip in the water bucket. Do this with each strip and each plant.

> ✎ **NOTE:** If you have delicate, rare, exotic plants that need special care, you should probably not rely on any of these methods. Instead, ask a neighbor who has a green thumb to stop by and tend to those unique plants while you're away.

CUT FLOWERS

There is an old Lithuanian saying—"The seed is hope; the flower is joy." What a sweet sentiment. With that in mind, here are some ways to cut and keep your flowers—and in doing so, prolong your joy.

Cutting Live Flowers

◆ Take a bucket of lukewarm water with you to the garden, along with a pair of garden or pruning scissors, or a sharp knife. (A dull scissors or knife can pinch the flower's stem closed.) Always cut flowers on a slant. Then, as soon as you cut each flower, put it into the water bucket.

◆ Venture out into your garden to cut flowers during the coolest parts of the day—early morning or late evening. The flowers will stay fresh longer.

◆ Tightly closed buds may never open in a vase, and fully bloomed flowers will not last long. So pick the buds that are about to open or have just opened.

◆ As soon as you bring the flowers indoors, cut each stem again on a slant while keeping it under water. That way, the flower will drink in water, not air.

◆ After you put your slant-cut flowers into a vase filled with lukewarm water, be sure to remove all of the leaves that are below water level. This will keep them from poisoning the water.

Life Extenders (General)

◆ Most tap water contains minerals that make it *alkaline*. And alkaline water has a hard time moving through cut flower stems. This means that the life of cut flowers in a vase will be shortened because the flowers do not get the hydration or nutrition they need to thrive…and survive.

To overcome this challenge, simply lower the pH of the water…or *acidify* it. You can do this by adding 1 part of non-diet lemon–lime soda (such as Sprite or 7UP) to 3 parts of water in your flower vase. The citric acid in the soda helps lower the pH, and the sugar in the soda gives the flowers an energy boost.

> ✎ **NOTE:** You can avoid the pH problem altogether by using distilled water (available at supermarkets and health-food stores) in your flower vase, instead of tap water.

◆ Protect flowers from harmful bacteria that cause stems to rot by adding ½ teaspoon of antiseptic mouthwash (such as Scope or Listerine) for every quart of water in the vase.

◆ For every quart of water in the vase, add 2 tablespoons of distilled white vinegar and also 2 tablespoons of sugar. The vinegar helps prevent the growth of bacteria and the sugar gives the flowers nourishment.

◆ Hydrogen peroxide is another preventive measure against stem-killing bacteria. Add 1 teaspoon each time you refresh the water.

◆ As soon as cut flowers start to wilt, reach for a can of aerosol hairspray. Hold the can about 1 foot away from the underside of the leaves and petals, and spray in an upward direction. The glycerin and the *acrylates* (a class of acrylic resins) found in commercial hairspray should help the flowers survive another few days.

◆ To revive wilting flowers, dissolve 1 or 2 regular adult aspirin (325 milligrams each) in ½ cup of warm water, then pour it into the vase.

◆ One last-ditch effort before you ditch the flowers—in warm water, cut the stems again on a slant.

◆ To freshen flowers, put the tired-looking flowers in a closet an hour or so before daytime guests are due to arrive. When you bring them out—and don't forget to bring them out—they will perk up when exposed to the light of day. (Obviously, don't try this at night!)

◆ Apples, pears and bananas emit ethylene gas that is harmful to most flowers. Do not place cut flowers near a bowl of fresh fruit. And do not refrigerate flowers if you have fruit in the refrigerator.

◆ For short-stemmed flowers…arrange them in a container with sand that's been saturated with lukewarm water. They will thrive.

Life Extenders (for Specific Cut Flowers)

Use these helpful suggestions as soon as you bring cut flowers inside the house from the florist or garden…

◆ **Carnations**—Add a capful of boric acid (available at drugstores) to the water, and then you should be able to enjoy having them around for a few extra days.

◆ **Chrysanthemums**—Prolong them by adding about 1 tablespoon of sugar to the water.

◆ **Daffodils**—Before you add daffodils to a floral arrangement, put them in a vase half-filled with lukewarm water. Within a couple of hours, after they've released their saplike fluid (which can be harmful to other flowers), empty the water out of the vase, rinse off the daffodil's stems with lukewarm water, and then they can be safely included in a vase with other flowers.

◆ **Gardenias**—Be very gentle with these sweet-scented blossoms. Their petals bruise easily. Floating in a bowl, gardenias make an elegant centerpiece.

◆ **Marigolds**—Add 1 teaspoon of sugar or empty a couple of activated charcoal capsules (available at health-food stores) to the water to help prevent these beautiful flowers from reeking.

◆ **Roses (and other woody-stemmed flowers)** —Place them in a vase with hot (not boiling) water. That way, the stems will expand, making it easier for water to zoom up to feed the buds and blooms.

Also, roses seem to love salt. Add a pinch of table salt to their water, and they'll stay fresher longer.

◆ **Tulips**—These flowers will keep growing, even once they're cut. After 2 or 3 days, you may need to move them to a taller vase to keep the stems from falling over.

Or throw a few pennies into the vase. The copper seems to keep the blooms from opening too wide and drooping.

Daily Care

Out with the old, in with the new...water, that is. If your vase fits under the sink faucet, let lukewarm water run until the new water replaces the old.

If the vase is too big for the sink, use a turkey baster to suction out the old water before replacing it with fresh lukewarm water. Also, be sure to keep the water level just below the rim of the vase.

As the days go by, keep removing any flowers and leaves that have wilted.

✱ **Hue Knew?**

If you have white or very light-colored flowers, add food coloring to the water they're in. As they absorb the colored water, the flowers will become a muted version of that new color.

Flower Arranging

◆ When a flower has a long, thin stem that can't stand up straight, help it by sticking the stem in a plastic drinking straw.

Magical Words

In the wonderful words of author and landscape designer Barbara Damrosch—"I don't think we'll ever know all there is to know about gardening, and I'm just as glad there will always be some magic about it!"

◆ Put transparent tape across the mouth of the vase, crisscrossing it according to the size of the vase and the amount of flowers you intend to put in the arrangement.

The tape will make it easier to do the arranging because it will hold the flowers in place.

◆ To lengthen stems that are too short for a vase, stick each in a plastic drinking straw, and then cut them to the proper length for the vase.

◆ If the flower stems are too thick to fit into plastic drinking straws, then layer the bottom of the vase with marbles or a crumpled piece of aluminum foil.

◆ You know those mesh bags that onions come in? Wad up a bag and place it on the bottom of your vase, then arrange the cut flowers—just stick the stems through the holes in the mesh. ■

■ Products ■

Self-Watering Globes

If you forget to water your plants regularly—or if you are going away for a few days—these spheres will do it automatically. The hand-blown, colorful spheres are truly beautiful and available in different sizes.

After watering your plant as usual, fill the sphere with water (about ¾ cup) and place it (stem first) into the soil. Your plant will draw water as needed and thrive longer. *www.orchidlight.com.*

Garden Kneeler/Sitter

We find new uses all the time for this handy item—it can be a kneeling device or a seat. Two durable, thick-foam cushions take the torture out of staying on your knees for long periods, and sturdy steel arms help when getting up off your knees.

Source: Improvements, 800-634-9484, *www.Improvements catalog.com.*

CHAPTER 10

Easy Holiday & Party Plans

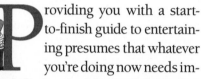

Providing you with a start-to-finish guide to entertaining presumes that whatever you're doing now needs improvement. And that's not right (and that's also a whole other book).

We're taking it for granted that you are already a great and gracious host or hostess who's always looking to add to your repertoire of ways to please your guests.

So, although we're sure that you could teach us a few things, we hope that you will discover some helpful tips to enhance your next dinner party, romantic rendezvous, luncheon, backyard picnic, family get-together, holiday celebration or any other special event that's made extra-special because you're in charge.

INVITATIONS

Receiving a creative invitation in the mail is the beginning of the fun for the people who are invited to a party or special event. Be sure that each invitation you send to your guests has all of the pertinent information they need to know—the reason for the event, date, time,

location (with directions, if necessary) and RSVP contact information and "respond by" date.

Invitations are the first thing that people see, and they can set the overall tone for your party or gathering. *Here are a few ideas to get you thinking of attention-getting invitations…*

◆ Print the invitation on T-shirts.

◆ Make jigsaw puzzles out of the invitations.

◆ Use a permanent marker to write every invitation on a blown-up balloon (you may want to enlist a helper to hold each balloon while you write on it). Let the air out of the balloon, then put it in an envelope and mail 1 to each person you're inviting.

Be sure to include in the envelope a separate piece of paper with your phone number and directions to your home.

> **NOTE:** If you need help with the directions you provide, check out *www.mapquest.com* or *http://maps.google.com*. (If you're not on-line at home, take advantage of the free Internet connection at any public library.)

If your potential guests have e-mail and Internet access, send them electronic invitations. You can either design an attractive e-mail and write something clever yourself, or use a free e-vite service, such as *www.evite.com*.

PLACE CARDS

Place cards are used to determine the seating arrangement of the guests, and where you place the place cards can signal the failure or success of a dinner party. Since you, the host or hostess, control who sits where, you can arrange people however you think best—for example, the big (and loud?) talkers should sit next to the good listeners, and 2 feuding relatives should be seated at opposite ends of the table—or at different tables.

In addition to arranging people in the best possible way, place cards serve another important purpose...they help remind people of their tablemates' names. (Doesn't everyone seem to be having a hard time remembering names these days?)

When we recently attended a private business dinner at the famed Four Seasons restaurant in New York City, we noticed that each place setting had a tent-shaped place card with the name of the guest printed on BOTH sides of the card. *Very clever.* That way, you can see the names of the people sitting across the table from you, as well as the names of people seated on either side of you—and they can all see your name as well.

Here are some fun place card ideas...

◆ For moderate-sized parties, blow up balloons and write your guests' names with a permanent marker or nail polish (you may want to enlist a helper to hold each balloon while you write on it). Then attach the named balloon to the chair as a unique place card.

◆ Put a fresh (or artificial) rose across each place setting with the guest's name written with metallic ink on a leaf. (If the flower doesn't have leaves, use an adhesive address label—just wrap it around the stem.)

◆ Bicycle nameplates serve as novelty place cards that can be taken home as souvenirs.

If you need to invite 2 people with the same name, use a permanent marker to write in a last name or initial.

◆ Buy miniature picture frames and put each guest's name in a frame—they make great keepsakes. It would be even more fun if you had a photo of each guest to put in the frame.

✳ Fun Photo Place Cards

This is a great idea if you have a digital camera, a printer and a helper (cohost, relative, spouse or close friend)—as each guest arrives, you or your recruited assistant will take a photo of him/her. Then print out the photo, cut out the face, frame it and place it at the appropriate place setting.

◆ For a pasta party, use a permanent marker to write each guest's name on a piece of uncooked lasagna. Place the pasta on each dinner plate setting.

On a buffet table, identify the food in each dish by writing the information on pieces of uncooked lasagna that you then place in front of the appropriate dish.

◆ Buy a rubber stamp (available at crafts stores) that's appropriate for the occasion or that tells guests they are in your home (for example, your initial in an elegant font). Also buy an ink pad in a stand-out color.

Fold an unlined 3" x 5" index card in half (tent style) and stamp it, then write the guest's name on it to make your own creative, personal placecards.

NAPKINS & NAPKIN RINGS

Creative and interesting napkins and napkin rings are a good way of adding personality to your table setting. *Here are some unique suggestions...*

◆ If you're not using cloth napkins, give paper napkins some personality by stamping them with the same rubber stamp you used on the place cards.

◆ If you're baking bread, make an extra portion of dough and use it to make napkin rings. Roll out the dough in 8"-long strips. Use 2 strips entwined to form a circle for each ring. Bake them at 350°F until golden-brown, and when they're cool, set the table with these edible treats.

Barbara, our neighbor and generous friend, shared this idea with us—she uses 3 strips of dough, braids them, makes them napkin-ring shaped and bakes them (also at 350°F until golden-brown). Her napkin rings match the top of the challah (braided bread) she uses on the Sabbath table.

◆ Remember those candy dots on long strips of paper? Many candy stores still carry them, and they make adorable napkin holders, especially for a dessert table or a grown-up's birthday celebration dinner. Each holder requires about 8" of dots-paper, wrapped around the napkin. Close the ends of each strip with double-sided tape.

You can also tie the napkins with long strings of black or red rope licorice.

◆ Make napkin rings from empty tubes of toilet tissue or paper towel (depending on the thickness of the napkins you plan to use). Cover the tubes by pasting on paper that matches your table or room décor. You can use construction paper, wrapping paper, left-over wallpaper, last season's sample wallpaper books (available at your local paint store) or even newspaper—try the comics.

Once the tube is covered, cut it crosswise into equally sized pieces—about 1½" wide. If you use solid paper to cover the tubes, you can also decorate them with stickers, sequins and ribbon—or stamp them to match your rubber-stamped napkins and even your place cards.

We recently set a dinner table with a solid red tablecloth, napkin rings covered in black-and-white magazine excerpts with thin red ribbon tied around them, white linen napkins and white dinnerware. *Dahling, it looked mahvelous!* Conversations started immediately as dinner guests read their napkin rings and shared the articles.

TABLE DECORATIONS

Decorating your table is like putting on sparkling pieces of jewelry after you are dressed—it completes the whole picture. *Here are some decorative ideas that are gems...*

Fruit-Flavored Fun

This simple idea is attractive and smells good, too. Cut a citrus fruit (lemon, lime, orange, etc.) in half. Remove the pulp* and put a votive candle in the middle of the shell. Surround the candle with cranberries to hold it in place.

You can use several oranges, grapefruits, lemons or limes as a centerpiece, or you can space them out around the table.

*Choose the fruit according to its color and scent as well as which fruit pulp you can use in the meal.

To help you decide on which fruit to use, you should know about the results of a recent study conducted by Alan R. Hirsch, MD, neurological director of The Smell & Taste Treatment and Research Foundation in Chicago. According to Dr. Hirsch, "In the presence of the smell of pink grapefruit, women appear [to men] to be 6 years younger than their real age."

A Festive Touch

Scatter some confetti on the table. You can make your own with a hole puncher or paper shredder, or you can buy packages of confetti in a variety of colors and shapes (available at crafts and stationery stores). Use a disposable tablecloth, and cleanup will be a breeze.

Centerpiece Enhanced

Whatever your centerpiece—flowers, leaves, fruit, candles—place it on a mirror to create the illusion that you have twice as many flowers, leaves, fruit or candles. Candles will be especially dazzling because of their reflection in the mirror.

> ### ✆ FYI: Enhance Sparkling Conversation
> Think low and wide for your centerpiece. If a floral arrangement is on the tall side—beautiful as it may be—conversation across the table will be blocked, along with your guests' view.

Tablecloth Substitute

For something a little different, use a colorful bedsheet with a great design as a tablecloth. (No, not a fitted sheet.)

Anticipation Preparation

Before her company begins to arrive, Caroline (our neighbor and a gracious hostess) fills an average-sized vase with water, and leaves it in an out-of-the-way place in the kitchen.

Then, if 1 of the guests brings flowers, Caroline is able to quickly put the bouquet into the vase, place it in the living room and continue hostessing.

Glass Dinnerware Extraordinaire

If you have clear glass dinner plates—or a set of clear glass plates and a set of solid colored plates—and you want something unique (and don't mind washing twice as many dishes), then this idea is for you.

Use 2 plates per setting—the clear plate laid on top of the colored plate. In between the 2 plates, press fresh flowers and leaves...or fresh herbs...or make a collage of photos, special announcements/news clippings, or birthday, anniversary or holiday cards...or use a printed or solid napkin to match the tablecloth...or whatever else will fit between the plates. It's your dinner party and your plates, so use your imagination for a memorable idea that will have everyone talking.

> ### ✳ Traditional (and Practical) Food Service
> It's traditional for food to be served from the left side of each guest. Because most people are right-handed, they generally tend to gesture more with their right hand.
> Therefore, it's safer for food to be served from the left side, so that a plate or serving dish will not be knocked out of the server's hand by any of those right-sided hand gestures.

CANDLES

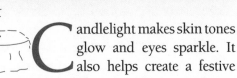 Candlelight makes skin tones glow and eyes sparkle. It also helps create a festive atmosphere. And doesn't food just taste better when eaten by candlelight? These suggestions will help you handle each candle safely, efficiently and imaginatively.

Lighten Up with Carbs

When you want to light several candles at a time, first light the end of a strand of dry spaghetti. Use it to go from wick to wick to wick.

Relighting a Candle

Before relighting a candle, trim the candle's wick to ¼" in length. The candle will burn longer and without smoking.

Drip Prevention

◆ Beeswax candles do not drip. If your candles are not beeswax, and you don't want them to drip when lit, prepare some saltwater—use 2 tablespoons of table salt to 2 cups of water —and let the candles soak in the solution for about 4 hours. Then dry the candles thoroughly. When lit, thanks to the saltwater soaking, the candles should be dripless.

◆ Keep candles in the freezer for several hours before lighting them. The candles will burn longer and hardly drip, if at all.

Candle Holders

◆ If your candle is a little too big for the holder, dip the last inch of the candle in hot water and keep it there until the wax is soft enough for you to squeeze it and make it thinner so that it will fit into the holder.

◆ Before inserting a candle, lightly spray a holder with cooking spray to help prevent melted wax from sticking to it.

Candle Holder Alternatives

◆ Use apples that are flat on the bottom and won't topple over. Core each apple carefully and insert a candle.

◆ Mini-pumpkins and gourds make colorful candle holders, especially at Halloween and Thanksgiving dinners. Cut out the top, scoop out the inside, then insert a candle.

◆ Using teacups and saucers to hold votive candles, floating candles or tea lights can add a feminine touch to a table setting.

> **NOTE:** Tea lights are the candles that are shorter than votives and used in fondue sets, chafing dishes and butter warmers.

◆ Candle holders made from uncooked artichokes will add soft light and panache to your buffet or dinner table. Cut a thin slice off the bottom of the artichoke, so that it stands up straight. Trim the sharp points off the leaves and scoop out the middle and place a votive candle there. If you want some glitz, spray paint the artichokes gold.

◆ If you don't have holders for candles on a birthday cake, use a few gumdrops as colorful holders. You can also use them to spell an appropriate word or name on the cake.

◆ Insert birthday candles in mini-marshmallows and put the marshmallows into the cake. You may wind up with waxy marshmallows, but you'll also have a cake that's free of wax…and that's the whole idea.

✳ Bright Birthday Ideas!

◆ Consider using fuzzy pipe cleaners instead of candles. They're colorful, stiff enough to stand up straight, burn brightly thanks to their metal core, and your cake will stay free of candle wax.

◆ Let everyone get a chance to blow out a candle. Give each guest an individual cupcake or miniature cake with a candle on it. This is especially nice at kids' birthday parties.

Votive Candles

◆ Pour 1 ounce of water on the bottom of each votive holder to prevent the candle's heat from cracking the glass.

◆ Before putting a votive candle in the holder, rub the bottom of the candle with petroleum jelly. When you want to remove the candle, just turn the holder upside down and out it will slide.

◆ Put 6 drops of liquid soap in the votive holder and fill it halfway with hot water. Let it soak for 20 minutes, and you should be able to pop out the wax along with the metal wick holder.

Candle Cleaner

Wipe the surface of a decorative candle with a clean piece of pantyhose to remove dust and fingerprints and to restore its shine.

Candle Storage

Keep your long candles out of harm's way by storing them in cleaned-out, tall potato chip cans (such as Pringles), or paper towel tubes with aluminum foil on both ends and held in place with rubber bands. If you're on a low-carb diet and no longer have use for your spaghetti canister, it's perfect to hold a few long tapers.

ALCOHOL & OTHER BEVERAGES

There's a popular toast that sums up this topic—"If all be true that I do think, there are 5 reasons we should drink. Good friends, good times, or being dry, or lest we should be by and by, or any other reason why." So, with that in mind, here are some hints to quench your thirst for potable knowledge.

Wine

Writer and world traveler Ernest Hemingway thought wine to be the most civilized thing in the world. *Here are some civilized ways to treat it…*

Corks Away!

When tiny pieces of cork break off into the bottle, pour the wine through a fine strainer or sieve, or through a coffee filter. Pour the wine into a lovely decanter or other decorative serving bottle, preferably crystal.

Quick Chill for White Wine

Salt keeps ice colder longer. Put ice in a bucket or pail, and mix salt in with the cubes. Then put in the bottle of wine to chill.

White wine kept in a bucket of ice and water will chill faster than if the wine is in a bucket of ice *without* water.

Drip-Free Wine Pouring

Just as you finish pouring a glass of wine—right before you are about to lift it away from the glass—give the bottle a slight twist. The drip will roll around the bottle's lip and disappear,

instead of ending up on the tablecloth or on someone's lap.

Wine Recycling

◆ Save leftover wine for recipes that call for wine. To keep the wine's flavor longer, add 1 teaspoon of vegetable oil to the bottle and put it in the refrigerator.

◆ Freeze leftover wine in ice cube trays. You can then use the cubes anytime for recipes or in wine coolers.

Cool Idea for Hot Coffee

Freeze leftover coffee in ice cube trays and use it to cool *hot-hot-hot* coffee...or to make iced coffee...or to add great flavor to eggnog.

Better Wine Storage

Remember the 2004 film that featured people who are passionate about wine? The name of the film is *Sideways*—which is the best way to store bottles of wine, especially pinot noir.

If a bottle is stored sideways, the wine is always in contact with the cork. (A wet cork expands to form a tighter seal. Exposure to air can spoil wine.)

If you keep several bottles of wine in your house, a wine rack is a wise investment.

Amount to Buy

When you're having a party and want to figure out how many bottles of wine to buy, start with the number of people who have accepted your invitation. Then consider how much your guests will drink—how many may limit themselves to 2 or 3 glasses, and how many will nurse 1 glass all evening? Once you have that number, figure on 5 glasses of wine per average bottle. OK, now you do the math...and the ordering.

Champagne/Sparkling Wine

Dom Pierre Perignon, the 17th-century Benedictine monk who is credited with the invention of champagne, was quoted as saying, "Come brothers, hurry, I am drinking stars." *Here are some tips to help you reach for those stars...*

Proper Amount of Bubbly

According to the Comité Interprofessionnel du Vin de Champagne (*www.champagne.us/index. cfm*), for a champagne aperitif at cocktail hour, 1 bottle (*see* "Champagne Equivalents" on page 244) should serve 3 or 4 guests. When serving a meal, count on 1 bottle for every 2 or 3 people.

For the traditional champagne toast to the bride...or the birthday honoree...or the retiree... or the newly promoted someone—1 bottle can usually be stretched to serve 6 to 10 people.

Proper Way to Open a Bottle

Also according to the Comité Interprofessionnel du Vin de Champagne, begin by slanting the champagne bottle at a 45° angle away from guests. Then, with a thumb on the cork, untwist and loosen the wire muzzle. Grasp the cork firmly, twist the bottle slowly and let the pressure help push out the cork. Allow a light and merry pop.

Service Preparation

Refrigerate champagne for no longer than 2 to 3 hours before serving. Overdoing it in the fridge may weaken the champagne's taste and its bouquet.

The Coolest Way to Chill

If the opportunity presents itself—and we're talking snowstorm here—chill the champagne in an ice bucket filled with snow.

Champagne Equivalents

When you serve champagne, figure there will be about 4 ounces per serving. If you're using champagne for a toast, figure on 2 ounces for each guest. *The following can help you place your champagne order...*

Split	2	4-ounce servings
(½ pint)	4	2-ounce servings for a toast
Half	4	4-ounce servings
(1 pint)	8	2-ounce servings for a toast
Bottle	8	4-ounce servings
(1 quart)	16	2-ounce servings for a toast
Magnum	16	4-ounce servings
(2 quarts)	32	2-ounce servings for a toast
Jeroboam	32	4-ounce servings
(4 quarts)	64	2-ounce servings for a toast
Rehoboam	48	4-ounce servings
(6 quarts)	96	2-ounce servings for a toast
Methuselah	64	4-ounce servings
(8 quarts)	128	2-ounce servings for a toast
Salmanazar	96	4-ounce servings
(12 quarts)	192	2-ounce servings for a toast
Balthazar	128	4-ounce servings
(16 quarts)	256	2-ounce servings for a toast
Nebuchadnezzar	160	4-ounce servings
(20 quarts)	320	2-ounce servings for a toast

Graceful Pouring

Fill each flute about ⅓ of the way, then begin again at the first glass, doubling the amount so that each glass is appropriately ⅔ full.

By pouring champagne ⅓ at a time, you allow the fizzing to subside, which prevents the bubbly from bubbling over.

Ice Cubes

Who would think there's a lot to learn about ice cubes? You just put water in a tray, and put the tray in the freezer. Ahh, but there's so much more. *See for yourself...*

Preventing Fizz Overflow

If you want a glass of soda with ice, first rinse the ice cubes with cold water before putting them in the glass. The rinsing changes the surface tension of the ice and prevents the soda from fizzing over.

Storing Ice Cubes

When you want to accumulate ice cubes in your freezer, keep the extra cubes in a brown paper bag. It helps prevent them from sticking to each other and becoming a big frozen blob.

Get Frozen Faster

Just-boiled water freezes faster than cold water. The reason is that hot water evaporates faster than cold water, so there's less water to freeze. Also, the evaporation process creates an air current over the ice cube tray, and this creates a cooling effect—similar to blowing on a spoonful of hot soup. If you don't believe us, try it and see for yourself.

Clear and Not Cloudy Cubes

Fill your ice cube trays with distilled water (available at most supermarkets and grocery stores). This will make extra-clear cubes that look like crystals dancing in your drinks.

Floral Ice Bowl

For you artsy and ambitious hosts and hostesses, this is something special—a beautiful floral ice bowl in which to serve a dessert (such as berries or ice cream), a colorful side dish (such as cranberry relish) or anything else in your recipe repertoire that needs to be served cold. If you have the time—and room in the freezer—this floral ice bowl can be a spectacular addition to your table.

To create this bowl made of ice, you'll need 2 freezer-proof glass or aluminum bowls of the same shape, but one of the bowls should be about 2" smaller than the other. You'll also need an assortment of edible flowers (*see* "Colorful Ingredients," below) or slices of citrus fruit, herbs or confetti.

Pour 1" of cold tap water into the larger bowl and stand it flat in the freezer. After a few hours, start checking to see if the water in the bowl is completely frozen. (The amount of time it takes depends on your freezer and the size of the bowl you use.)

When the water in the bowl is completely frozen, take the bowl out of the freezer. Place the smaller bowl inside the larger bowl, perfectly centered on the ice. Tape the bowls together to hold them in place—you don't want them to shift positions.

Pour water into the space between the 2 bowls, until it's halfway up the sides. Drop the flowers, herbs, citrus slices or confetti into the water, all around the perimeter of the bowl. You may want to use a pencil or chopstick to push down the decorations.

Put the bowls back in the freezer, again on level ground. When the water is frozen solid, remove the bowls from the freezer. Take off the tape and gently separate the bowls. If they won't budge, run tepid water over the outside of the larger bowl until the ice bowl is released.

Once it's dislodged, put the ice bowl back into the freezer until it's time for your party. Chill a glass plate or tray, and serve the ice bowl on it so that dripping water from the melting ice will collect on the plate.

Colorful Ingredients

Surprise your guests with pretty and tasty ice cubes in their drinks. Before you fill your ice-cube trays with water, put a single mint leaf…a strawberry…a raspberry…a maraschino cherry…or a few edible flowers—such as Johnny Jump-ups, nasturtium, violets, roses or borage (available at specialty-food stores)—in each cube compartment. If you're serving alcoholic drinks to adults, you may want to prepare ice cubes that contain cocktail onions or olives.

Substitute Ice Cube Tray

Wash the bottom half of an empty plastic egg carton, fill it with water and then put it in your freezer.

Keeping Punch Cool

The larger the ice cube, the slower it melts. A few days in advance of your party, make 2 big ice cubes. You can do this by cutting off the tops of milk or juice containers, washing them, filling them with water and putting them in the freezer.

NOTE: The large cubes will take hours to freeze. It's a good idea to leave them overnight. If you have a hard time removing the ice from the container, run some tepid water over the bottom of the container.

When the punch is made, put 1 of the large ice cubes in a punch bowl, and then add the punch. This will keep it cool…for a long time. Use the other big ice cube for the punch bowl refill.

 NOTE: If you feel that a big ice cube will water down the beverage, add an extra amount of whatever ingredient makes the punch punchy.

◆ Another option is to prepare big or small ice cubes made with juice—the same juice that goes into the punch—and use them to keep punch cool without diluting it.

Other Beverages

If your tastes go beyond wine and champagne, we offer several suggestions on how to make your adult beverages even more sophisticated.

> **✱ Keep It Cold**
> Fans of chilled vodka know to drink it in small glasses with stems so that their hands won't warm up the vodka.

Keep Beer from Getting Flat

Whether you're drinking a bottle of beer at an outdoor barbecue or an indoor card game, place a wooden matchstick across the mouth of the bottle to keep your suds from going flat.

The next time you host a party, you may want to provide matchsticks with the beer.

Prevent Spills When Serving Drinks

If you're taking several drinks from the kitchen out to the dinner table, deck chairs or backyard picnic table, carry them in a clean muffin tin. Most glasses (such as tumblers), coffee mugs and beer bottles will fit in the muffin holders of an average-sized muffin tin.

Vodka on Ice

For those of you who have a dramatic flair, this is a creative and exciting way to serve chilled vodka…in an ice bucket made of ice. *Here's what to do…*

You will need either a metal champagne bucket, a large metal can or a plastic bucket —it should be large enough to hold the vodka bottle with some space on all sides.

Fill the bucket with water. Place a vodka bottle in the middle, and add pretty, freezable things—such as lemon, lime and orange slices …flowers and leaves…berries and grapes—to float around the sides of the bucket. This will become a decorative mold.

Place the bucket in the freezer and let it stay overnight. The next day, make sure that it's frozen solid when you take it out. Unless your freezer is exceptionally cold—we're talking cryogenics-laboratory cold—the vodka in the bottle will not freeze.

When you're ready to serve, get the decorative mold out of the container by carefully holding the bucket sideways under warm running water—but don't let the water go over the top of the bucket!

Once the mold is released from its container, put it on a rimmed plate with an absorbent towel underneath to catch the water as the ice melts. The mold is now your ice bucket!

Keep Drinks Cool at an Outdoor Party

If you're hosting a casual backyard party, a great way to keep soda, beer and bottled water cold and available to your guests is to fill a small kiddie pool with lots of ice. Then just add the drinks.

246

PICNICS

 It's glorious to eat outside on a lovely day and get in touch with nature. *To enjoy your outing even more, here are a few ideas to perk up a picnic and have it be less messy…*

◆ When you're going on a picnic, take along a paper or cloth table covering. Picnic tables can be very unsanitary. Also bring a container of premoistened baby wipes. They make great napkins for messy kids of all ages.

◆ Bring a big plastic garbage bag with you, and use it for trash so that you leave the picnic area as clean as when you arrived.

◆ Most picnics consist of free-for-all food laid out on a blanket or table. Consider, instead, preparing individual lunches for each person at the picnic.

If the picnic-goers are your immediate family, then you will know exactly what each person would like in his/her picnic lunch box. This separate-lunch system frees everyone up to eat when they want to—not just because the food is out there, sweltering in the sun.

◆ If you are going to picnic in an area where there are wildflowers growing, bring along an empty coffee can. Once you get to the picnic grounds, pick some flowers, put them in the coffee can and fill the can with water…or sand…or soil…or pebbles. Then put the floral arrangement on your picnic table or blanket for all to enjoy nature's beauty.

THEME GATHERINGS

You don't have to wait until it's someone's birthday or a holiday to throw a party. Select a theme, think it through, make your plans and let the festivities begin! *Here are a few suggestions to help your creative juices begin to flow…*

◆ Have a slumber party that's just for grown-ups. Why should kids have the only fun? Eat pizza, bake cookies and stay up late watching scary movies.

◆ Invite friends over for a Clothing-Swap Party. Everyone has clothes that he/she is willing to trade for something that fits better or is more comfortable or more flattering. This is an especially good idea for women whose sizes tend to change more frequently.

◆ Have a Bring-and-Bid Party. Guests bring items that you auction off. It can be a fundraiser for charity or just for fun.

◆ Start your own Book Club or DVD Club. There are many Web sites available to help guide you. (To get started, try *www.ehow.com/how_6181_start-book-club.html.*)

◆ Anyone can celebrate New Year's Eve, Easter or Labor Day. Be innovative and find an underplayed or obscure holiday and build a theme party around it. The fourth Sunday in July is Parents Day. June 5th is World Environment Day. August 26th is Women's Equality Day. Getting inspired? September 13th is Defy Superstition Day.

One of the most unusual, educational and fun parties we ever attended was on November 2nd—it was a birthday celebration in honor of the 11th president of the United States, James K. Polk.

GUEST TREATMENT

It's tricky when guests visit—you want to make them feel at home, but you don't want them to stay forever. *Here are some ideas that may make their visit a happy—but not overly long—stay...*

Putting a Guest at Ease

According to the theory of *neuro-linguistic programming* (NLP), you will make a person feel accepted and interesting if you mimic (pattern) his/her body language while talking to him.

For example, if your guest sits with his legs crossed at the ankles, cross yours at the ankles. If he sips his drink with his pinky extended, you do the same thing.

Just do it in moderation, and be sure not to pattern that person's nervous twitch—or you might wind up with a punch in the nose.

Getting Rid of Dinner Guests

When your guests have outstayed their welcome around your dinner table, you can get rid of them without being rude. Simply place your hands—fingers together, palms down—on the table in front of you, as though you were about to stand up. Your guests may subconsciously pick up on that cue and assume that the party's over. This subliminal signal should have them on their feet, grabbing their coats and thanking you for a wonderful evening.

If the hand signal doesn't work, then start to yawn. Within seconds, everyone else will start yawning and realize that the party's over.

Welcome a Sleepover Guest

A lovely way to welcome an overnight guest is to leave a goody bag on the bed or dresser. Fill the bag with gender-appropriate sleepover items, such as 1 or 2 magazines (in keeping with your guest's interests), a sweet treat, some night cream, a scented candle and holder, a sleep mask, a packaged toothbrush and a little card wishing your guest "pleasant dreams."

TAKING PICTURES

Writer Eudora Welty said, "A good snapshot stops a moment from running away." Make your photographs the most treasured memories they can possibly be. *These hints may help...*

Set Up Your Shot

The day before you plan to use the camera, check the batteries. If the camera is not digital, be sure you have film. Clean the lens with a lint-free cloth. You may also want to snap a few pictures, just to test that the camera is in good working order.

If your batteries die unexpectedly, rub both ends with a clean pencil eraser—you may be able to get a few more shots.

✳ Making Memories

If you're hosting a party, buy a few disposable cameras for your guests to use during the festivities.

Positioning the Camera

Hold the camera at the subject's eye level, even when the photos are candid and the subject is not staring into the camera lens. That eye-level angle will create a personal and inviting feeling that pulls the viewer into the picture.

Be prepared to stoop all the way down when photographing young children.

Souvenir Photos

◆ The next time you're hosting a party, use your digital camera to take a picture of every guest at your gathering. If you have a printer at home, you can give each guest a souvenir print just before he/she leaves.

◆ If the occasion calls for you to send a thank-you note, paste a fun photo on the front of a blank card and write your note inside.

◆ Take photos of your friends at a party or social gathering. The next time you invite them over for a dinner party, put their photos in little frames and use them as place cards.

HOLIDAYS

We're probably all in agreement that the holidays have gotten to be way too commercial. But when you think about it, putting aside the in-your-face marketing aspects, the holidays are a wonderful time to celebrate being with the people you hold dear.

It's a time to talk about the good old days… to eat more than you should…to exchange gifts …to play catch-up…and to promise that you'll get together more often. Holidays are a time for making happy memories.

So here are some hints to enhance a handful of national holidays, in the hope of helping you create those happy memories while you celebrate a specific time of year.

New Year's

Although the exact date may vary depending on where it's celebrated, New Year's is the most universally observed holiday in the world. It's filled with traditions, rituals and resolutions that may be in 1 year and out the next. But many believe that there is *magic* in the air on New Year's. It's a time to be with family and friends, and a time for letting go of the old and embracing the new.

For your next New Year's celebration, add some foreign flavor to the festivities by incorporating customs from other countries. *Here are some from which to choose…*

Good Luck from Around the World

According to folklore from across the globe, there are certain food and home traditions that are supposed to bring good fortune into your life for the next 365 days. These traditions come with no guarantees, just with every good wish for a most wonderful New Year.

◆ **China**—The color red is the Chinese symbol of good luck and happiness. Paint your front door with a new coat of red paint or hang a red banner.

Although Chinese families have a feast for the New Year, food is prepared on the last day of the old year. On New Year's Day, all knives are put away for 24 hours to prevent anyone from cutting himself/herself, which is believed to cut the family's good luck for the New Year.

◆ **England/Wales**—When the clock starts to strike midnight, open the back door of your house and then close it. You will be releasing the old year, along with all of its misfortune. Then, on the 12th chime of the clock, open the front door, which welcomes in the New Year with all of its good luck.

◆ **France**—Good health and good fortune will come to those who eat a stack of pancakes on New Year's Day.

- **Italy/Sicily**—Good luck will come to those who eat lasagna on New Year's Day, but Sicilians warn you to stay away from macaroni or any other type of noodle on the first day of the year.

- **Japan**—This good luck tradition comes from the Japanese practice of *feng shui,* which is the positioning of objects based on the patterns of *yin* and *yang*...this is believed to create a flow of positive and negative effects.

    Buy a yard of tiny, white tree lights to symbolize stars. Bunch the string of lights loosely in a clear glass vase. Place the vase in the southwest part of your living room.

    When it is dark outside, just before 12 midnight on New Year's Eve, light the lights. This will ensure that you invite lucky stars into your life and have a fresh start for the new year.

- **Norway**—Prepare rice pudding and hide 1 whole almond in the bowl. Dish out the pudding to family and friends on New Year's Day. The person who gets the almond is assured of major wealth.

- **Peru**—Eat 12 grapes to mark the New Year. A 13th grape must be eaten to assure good luck.

- **Puerto Rico**—At 12 midnight, children throw pails of water out of a window in the belief that doing so rids the home of evil spirits.

- **Spain**—At 12 midnight, eat 1 grape with each toll of the clock, which will assure that you have good luck each month of the year.

    If you don't have a clock that chimes, get out your grapes and follow the countdown on television.

- **Switzerland**—On New Year's Day, let a drop of cream land on the floor to make sure you have a rich New Year.

- **United States** (Southern states)—Eating a dish of hamhocks and black-eyed peas on New Year's Day is thought to bring luck and prosperity. Some people add a dime to the peas for an extra bit of luck (just try not to eat the dime).

    Salad greens—such as kale, collard greens, spinach and mustard greens—symbolize folding money, and they are often eaten along with the black-eyed peas.

St. Valentine's Day

According to the Society of American Florists, the Chocolate Manufacturers Association and the National Confectioners Association, US consumers purchase approximately 189 million roses and more than 36 million heart-shaped boxes of chocolate for Valentine's Day each year.

Sure, it's easy to go out and splurge on something nice that your loved one(s) wouldn't buy for themselves. But we think it's a better idea to top off your store-bought gift (or replace it) with a *priceless* loving-hands-at-home gift. *Here are a few ideas...*

The Gift That Keeps Giving

Prepare a booklet of coupons for your mate and/ or someone you love. Decide on the number of coupons—1 for each year you've been together, 1 for each month of the year, 1 for each day of the week—and come up with doable things that will make the person happy.

The coupons could range from personal pleasures to practical chores—from a 30-minute back massage to washing the car. This gift's true test—wouldn't *you* like to get a booklet of coupons from someone special?

Love, Sweet Love

Chocolate contains *phenylethylamine* (PEA), which some scientists believe releases the same chemicals in the brain that induce the euphoria we feel when we are in love.

So bring on the chocolate! Bake some fudgy chocolate brownies, a chocolate cake or prepare chocolate pudding—whatever it is will be extra-sweet because you made it.

Easter

'Twas Easter Sunday.
The full blossomed trees
Filled all the air with fragrance and with joy.
Henry Wadsworth Longfellow used those words to express his feelings during this springtime holiday. We hope your Easter is filled with joy. *As for the air being filled with fragrance, consider the following suggestions so you can help make it happen...*

Easter Flowers

Flowers always make a home more festive and usually more fragrant. For a colorful, Eastery way to display the daffodils, irises, tulips, lilacs and hyacinths in bloom during this season, put the flowers in an appropriate-sized vase and fill it with water. Then put that vase in a larger, clear-glass vase. Fill the space between the 2 vases with jelly beans. Colorful and Eastery, don't you think?

✳ Sweet Decorating Idea

If you are using artificial flowers, use only 1 clear-glass vase for the flowers—and use the jelly beans in place of water.

Easter Centerpiece

If you want a beautiful, sugar-coated fruit-and-flower centerpiece, gather the following ingredients, and then set aside some time to be your most creative self.

> Spring flowers
> About 6 pounds of fresh fruit (coordinate the selection of fruit with the color of the flowers)
> 1 cup of apple jelly
> 1 cup of water
> Superfine sugar
> Pastry brush
> Waxed paper
> Flat basket, platter or tray
> Big doilies (optional)

1. Cover your work surface with waxed paper. Wash and dry the fruit and put it on the waxed paper.

2. Mix 1 cup of apple jelly with 1 cup of water until the jelly liquefies. You may have to zap it in the microwave for 20 to 30 seconds to get the apple jelly to dissolve completely.

(If you do heat it, let the liquid cool before continuing.)

3. Using the pastry brush, give the fruit a once-over with the apple jelly mixture.

4. Pour the superfine sugar on a small plate and roll the moist fruit around in it. If you don't want the fruit covered with the sugar, you can just sprinkle the sugar on the fruit instead of rolling it. (But we think *more* sugar looks better.)

5. Let the sugared fruit dry thoroughly. If possible, let it stand overnight, uncovered, on the counter.

To make your seasonal centerpiece, use a decorative basket, platter or tray, and build a beautiful mound of sugared fruit. Intersperse the flowers.

Optional: Line the basket, platter or tray with doilies.

✎ **NOTE:** A centerpiece like this can be created anytime throughout the year—for every occasion. Just use the loveliest seasonal fruit and flowers you can find.

Easter Place Cards

◆ Put chocolate Easter bunnies at each place setting. Attach a name tag on each bunny with a ribbon that matches your tablecloth.

◆ Use hard-boiled eggs as place cards. Cut out strips of construction paper or cardboard (about 1" x 5"), and write a different guest's name on each strip. Form a circle, overlapping 1 end of the strip on top of the other, and glue or tape it to stay that way. Use this as an egg stand and place 1 at each table setting.

✳ Egg-stra Special Place Cards

◆ Write your guests' names on the eggs with crayon, then dye them with food coloring or egg dye.

◆ If you have extra time and the talent, you can also decorate the eggs to resemble each guest.

Independence Day (4th of July)

Independence Day, the original American holiday, was first celebrated on July 4, 1777. And we Americans have been celebrating our country's birthday ever since with parades, parties, picnics and pride.

For many, displaying the American flag is a time-honored tradition. If you want to get in on the action, the National Flag Foundation (*www.americanflags.org*), the foremost authority on US flag etiquette, offers this advice on how to do it right. *For example…*

◆ **Lapel pin**—Position the flag pin on the left side, over your heart.

◆ **Indoor flag**—If you hang the flag on a wall, do not tack down the bottom edge. A flag should hang as freely as possible.

◆ **Outdoor flag**—When it's raining, cotton or wool flags should not be left outside. Water weighs them down, preventing them from flying properly. If a flag cannot be illuminated at night with a spotlight, porch light or streetlamp, take it down at sunset.

◆ **On a car**—The flag should be firmly attached to the right bumper (this means your right side when you are behind the wheel).

All flags should be displayed upright, with the stars on the upper left side. When flags become tattered or frayed, it's respectful to remove and replace them immediately.

Decorations

Red, white and blue are the patriotic colors of the day. Decorate with streamers, banners and balloons, tablecloths, napkins and place settings, all in those colors.

◆ Get a blue vase and fill it with red flowers (roses, zinnias, scarlet salvia or dahlias) and white flowers (phlox, Queen Anne's lace, cosmos or chrysanthemums).

◆ When the sun goes down, add some atmosphere to an outdoor gathering by lighting many festive red, white and blue votive candles and placing them on tables and surrounding surfaces.

◆ Create a patriotic centerpiece. Fill a tray with things that represent to you the greatness of this country. A few things that come to mind are an apple pie, a bottle of Coca-Cola, a baseball and maybe even a DVD of *Yankee Doodle Dandy*.

Once the goodies are on the tray, trim it with an American flag and red, white and blue streamers.

Food for the 4th

◆ Serve a patriotic appetizer—cherry tomatoes, a creamy white cheese and blue corn chips.

◆ Prepare red, white and blue desserts using strawberries, blueberries, vanilla ice cream and/or whipped cream in between.

◆ Hollow out half of a watermelon, leaving 1" or 2" of the red fruit. Then add scoops of vanilla ice cream and sprinkle with blueberries.

◆ Whip up white frosting and spread it on brownies or cupcakes, then top it off with red, white and blue sprinkles.

Halloween

According to the National Retail Federation (*www.nrf.com*), sales of Halloween cards, decorations, costumes and candy was more than $4.75 billion in 2009 (nearly $57 per person). It's everyone's favorite holiday!

The majority of the money is for candy, but it's not just for kids. The National Confectioners Association (*www.candyusa.com*) claims that 90% of parents admit that they sneak goodies from their children's Halloween trick-or-treat bags.

Here are some tricks to help you make this Halloween a treat...

Perfect Pumpkin Presentation

◆ Use an ice cream scoop to clean out the pumpkin's pulp. It's a fast and easy way to do it.

Then use a drywall knife (available at home improvement stores) to carve your pumpkin—it provides better control than a kitchen knife.

◆ Nobody wants a moldy jack-o'-lantern. In a spray bottle, combine 2 parts lemon juice to 1 part water, and spritz the carved pumpkin inside and outside to prevent mold.

◆ If you're putting a candle in a scooped-out pumpkin, first sprinkle in a little cinnamon and nutmeg, so that when the candle burns, the air will smell as though you're baking a scrumptious pumpkin pie.

◆ Draw or paint a face on your pumpkin instead of carving it. Then, after Halloween, you can cut it up and use the pumpkin meat for baking pies or bread.

Eerie Lights

◆ Replace some of your regular lightbulbs with black-light bulbs (available at hardware stores). White and light-colored objects will seem to have a spooky glow.

◆ To create a creepy Halloween atmosphere, replace a few of your regular lightbulbs with green bulbs.

Halloween Costumes

With just a little imagination and some stuff around the house, you (or your child) will be all dressed and ready for the holiday. You may want to use 1 of these suggestions...or perhaps they'll inspire you to come up with something even more original.

◆ **Static Cling**—Wear a gray sweat suit and use doubled-sided tape or safety pins to attach the things that usually cling when taking clothes out of the dryer—such as socks, a fabric-softener sheet, a washcloth, underwear, etc. Brush your hair so that it's a static mess, and spray it to stay that way.

◆ **Castaway**—Shred the bottoms of an old pair of khaki pants or shorts. Wear them with a seen-better-days T-shirt. If you're a man, don't shave for a few days...if you're a woman, fix your hair as though you haven't put a comb through it for weeks. Man or woman, carry a volleyball named Wilson.

◆ **Woodstock Survivor**—Wear a dirty, old tie-dyed T-shirt, your torn jeans, old sneakers, a bandanna around your head, several strands of love beads and wire sunglasses. Groovy, man!

◆ **Junk Drawer**—Wear a black sweat suit or a black leotard and tights, and pin on the stuff found in a junk drawer—odd pieces of string, a used-up tape dispenser, coin wrappers, buttons, etc.

◆ **Movie Theater Floor**—Wear a black sweat suit or black leotards and tights. With double-sided tape or safety pins, attach empty candy wrappers, chewed gum, popcorn pieces, empty soda cups, ticket stubs, straws, etc. And wear a popcorn bucket as a hat.

Halloween Party Treats

◆ Serve apple cider in a punch bowl along with floating "hands" and "eyeballs." To make the hands, fill rubber or latex gloves with water, close them tightly at the top with twist ties or rubber bands and put them in the freezer the day before Halloween. When the hands are frozen solid and you're ready to put them in the punch bowl, carefully peel off the gloves.

The eyeballs can be made from peeled red seedless grapes.

◆ For more gore, prepare popcorn and bloody it up—mix red food coloring into melted butter, and drizzle it over the popcorn.

◆ Who wouldn't want a cup of worms in soil? It's easy to prepare for a Halloween party, and you don't have to dig 'em up from your garden. *Here's what to do...*

Make chocolate pudding and refrigerate it for a few hours. Spoon out individual portions into clear plastic cups. Don't smooth it out—just sprinkle some cocoa powder or crushed chocolate cookies on top so that it really looks like soil. Then place a few gummy worms in each cup.

Put the cups in the refrigerator until it's party time.

Thanksgiving Day

The first Thanksgiving was celebrated in 1621 to commemorate the harvest that was reaped after a harsh winter. In 1789, US President George Washington declared Thanksgiving a holiday. In 1863, President Abraham Lincoln was looking for ways to unite the country during the divisive Civil War, so he declared the last Thursday in November as a day of national thanksgiving. Now it's traditionally observed on the 4th Thursday in November.

According to humorist Erma Bombeck, "What we're really talking about is a wonderful day set aside on the fourth Thursday of November when no one diets. I mean, why else would they call it *Thanksgiving*?"

Here are some tips to help make this diet-free day something extra-special...and another reason to give thanks.

Centerpiece de Résistance

Also called a "horn of plenty," a *cornucopia* is traditionally a goat's horn that is overflowing with an abundance of fruit, vegetables and flowers. This signifies the wealth of the fall harvest at Thanksgiving time.

Enjoy creating a magnificent and meaningful cornucopia basket centerpiece, overflowing with a selection of the season's harvest—such as apples, dried ears of corn, tomatoes, carrots, peppers, pumpkins, artichokes, pomegranates, gourds, mixed nuts, cranberries, leaves, pine cones and flowers. You can buy cornucopias at craft stores, or wherever big selections of baskets are sold.

You can also make and bake your own edible cornucopia (*see* below). But before you start gathering the necessary ingredients, take into consideration the size of your table, the size of the cornucopia (check the measurements) and the available space in your freezer...especially if you plan to make this more than a few days in advance.

If we haven't scared you away by now, then forge bravely ahead. Enjoy the process—and then the praise!—as the finished product enhances your holiday table.

To fill the cornucopia, place it on a large tray, platter or flat basket. That allows you to move it easily in case you need to make room on the table for food that's being served. You can decorate the tray or basket with artificial leaves.

Cornucopia Centerpiece

3 11-ounce containers of soft breadstick
    dough
1 egg, beaten with 1 tablespoon of water
pastry brush
heavy-duty aluminum foil
standard aluminum foil
wire-mesh cornucopia (optional, available
    at crafts stores and some florists)

1. Preheat your oven to 350°F. Lightly spray a cookie sheet with nonstick cooking spray.

2. If you have a wire-mesh cornucopia, cover it with heavy-duty aluminum foil, skip the next step and go directly to step 3.

If you don't have a wire cornucopia, tear off a 30" x 18" sheet of heavy-duty foil. Fold it in half so that it's 15" x 18". Roll it diagonally to form a hollow cone about 18" long, with a diameter of 5" at its widest (the cornucopia's opening). Fasten the end with clear tape. Stuff the cone with crumpled regular foil until the form is solid. Bend the tail of the cone up and then down at the very end.

3. Spray the outside of the cone with the nonstick cooking spray and place it on the cookie sheet.

4. On a work surface, open and unroll the first container of breadstick dough. Separate the breadsticks. Begin the wrapping process with 1 breadstick around the tip of the cone.

5. The beaten egg with the tablespoon of water is the glaze that acts as glue. Brush the end of the second breadstick with glaze and attach it by pressing it to the end of the first breadstick.

Continue spiral-wrapping the cone with the breadsticks from all 3 containers, slightly overlapping the dough. Stop when there are 6 breadsticks left.

6. Pinch 3 breadsticks together at one end and then braid them. Then pinch the other 3 breadsticks together at one end and braid them.

7. Brush the glaze around the opening of the cornucopia and gently press on the braid. Brush the entire cornucopia with the glaze.

Optional: Sprinkle on sesame seeds.

8. Bake for 45 minutes or until the bread is a rich brown. (If you notice that a part of it is darkening too much, carefully cover that part with a piece of foil.)

When it's done and you take it out of the oven, leave it on the cookie sheet. Put the cookie sheet on a wire rack to help it cool. When the cornucopia is completely cool to the touch, gently remove the foil.

Consider using straw, excelsior or raffia —artsy stuffing that is available at crafts stores and florists—as filler for the cornucopia. They will support the fruits and vegetables you put inside (also, you won't have to use as much produce if you have filler). Keep in mind that waxy-skinned fruits and vegetables (eggplant, cucumbers, apples, pomegranates, turnips and bell peppers) last longest without refrigeration.

This cornucopia is edible, but chances are, your harvest arrangement is going to be so beautiful that nobody would dare take a bite out of your horn of plenty. In fact, you may want to preserve it and use it again next Thanksgiving, or throughout the year. In that case, spray it with shellac or clear enamel, or a spray acrylic lacquer (available at art-supply, hardware and paint stores).

If you choose not to preserve the cornucopia with shellac, you can bake and freeze it up to a month before the big day. Just make sure that the baked cornucopia is completely cool, leave the foil inside it and then wrap the outside airtight with foil. Now it's ready for the freezer.

NOTE: If you haven't given the cornucopia enough time to fully defrost, you can still decorate the table with it...even if it's partially frozen.

Thanksgiving Place Cards

◆ Use the fall harvest or foliage to hold place cards—for example, cut a slit on top of an apple or a miniature pumpkin, and stand a name card in the slit...write each guest's name on a leaf using a paint pen...wedge a place card into a pinecone or hot-glue it on.

◆ Here's a more schmaltzy way of saying, "sit here"—get a few small paper bags, and use a magic marker to write something on the bag that shows your appreciation of the guest.

Include his/her name so that the bag also serves as a place card.

For example, you could write—"I'm thankful for you, (guest's name)"...or, "You're a blessing, (guest's name)"...or, "You grace my table, (guest's name)." When you're done with the writing, add a few pieces of candy to the bag, tie it up with some colorful ribbon and place it on your table.

Thanksgiving During-Dinner Amusement

You and your guests can talk about your gratitude in a fun way around the table. Have the person whose name is first alphabetically begin telling something that he/she is thankful for, starting with the letter "A." The next person at the table continues by telling what he/she is thankful for, starting with the letter "B." And so on around the table and through the alphabet.

Keep it going through the alphabet—twice or more if your guests are enjoying it. When you do stop, tell everyone that this will give them some idea of the countless blessings in our lives for which we should all be thankful.

Thanksgiving End-of-Dinner Game

Here is a fun memory game to play around the table. The mental exercise may help keep people awake at the end of a high-carbohydrate, sleep-inducing meal.

Have the first player start by saying, "At the first Thanksgiving dinner, the Pilgrims ate turkey." Go around the table—the next player must repeat the sentence and add another dish. For example, the second player might say, "At the first Thanksgiving dinner, the Pilgrims ate turkey and cranberry sauce." The game continues with each player repeating the Pilgrims' menu and adding a new item to it.

When a player makes a mistake, he/she is eliminated. The game continues until there is only 1 player left. Give the winner a chocolate turkey…and a nap.

Thanksgiving After-Dinner Turkey Trot (for children)

◆ Play some lively music, get out the camera and ask the children to move like different types of turkey—for example, happy turkey, scared turkey, adorable turkey, goofy turkey, sad turkey, big turkey, jerky turkey, tough turkey, baby turkey, tired turkey, etc.

◆ Hold an "Act Like a Turkey" contest. Each participant has to go through the motions and sounds of a turkey. Be prepared with prizes for all, for fun distinctions including "loudest turkey," "cutest turkey," "most authentic turkey," "turkey most likely to be kept as a pet," "most outrageous turkey," and any other turkey title that comes to mind.

Chanukah

No matter how you spell it—Chanuka, Channukah, Hanukah, Hannukah, Hanika, Kaneka or Khanukkah—this happy Jewish holiday is the "Festival of Lights." It is celebrated for 8 days beginning at sundown on the 25th day of Kislev, a month in the Hebrew calendar. Chanukah

---

■ Recipe ■

The most traditional oil-laden Chanukah dish is potato latkes (*latkes* is the Yiddish word for *pancakes*). Our mother's latkes were the greatest. Mom never measured the ingredients she used—it was as though she was divinely guided. Through trial and error, we did our best to re-create our mother's recipe.

Lilly's Luscious Latkes

Yield: About 12 latkes

2 pounds (about 6 medium-sized) potatoes
1 medium onion
1 large egg, beaten
salt and pepper to taste
vegetable oil for frying

1. Peel each potato and then put it in a bowl of cold water.

2. Coarsely grate the potatoes and onion using a grater or a food processor.

3. Place the grated potatoes and onion in a fine-mesh strainer or clean dish towel and squeeze out all of the water over a bowl that is big enough for the whole latke mixture. The potato starch will settle on the bottom of the bowl. Carefully pour out the water, leaving the starch, and then mix in the grated potatoes as well as the onion and the egg. Add salt and pepper to taste.

4. Coat a griddle or nonstick pan with a thin layer of vegetable oil and warm it over medium heat.

5. Flatten about 2 tablespoons of the potato mixture in the palm of your hand and then place it on the griddle. Use a spatula to flatten it even more. Let it fry for a few minutes until it's golden. Flip the pancake over and brown the other side.

6. Remove and let each latke drain on paper towels, or use a cut-open brown paper bag (which is what our mom used).

usually falls sometime during November or December.

Chanukah is meant to be an uplifting holiday of renewed dedication and faith. Although it commemorates a victory and celebrates a miracle, the loud-and-clear message of Chanukah is "never lose hope."

Traditional Food

The ancient miracle of Chanukah occurred in 165 BCE. It had to do with a little bit of oil—there was not enough to burn for more than 1 day, yet it *miraculously* burned for 8 days and nights. So an important part of the Chanukah celebration is eating foods cooked in oil.

Latke Cooking Hints

◆ Several latke mavens we know recommend using Yukon gold potatoes for a more buttery batch. But ordinary baking potatoes are fine—russets, Idaho or Oregon. However, NEVER use red-skinned bliss potatoes. They will make the latkes gummy.

◆ Press the water out of the grated potatoes and onion before you mix in other ingredients—doing so makes for a firmer, crispier latke.

◆ Put the potato starch back into the mixture to add real potato flavor.

◆ For frying, use canola, peanut or another vegetable oil. These lighter-tasting oils will ensure that the full flavor of the latkes won't be overpowered by the taste of oil.

◆ You can freeze the latkes, then crisp them in a preheated 350°F oven for about 10 minutes.

Chanukah Party Ideas

Chanukah is a great time to spend with people who *light up your life*. Hey, that's an appropriate phrase to use when sending out e-mail (or snail-mail) Chanukah party invitations.

In addition to lighting Chanukah candles and serving food (and plenty of it), you may want to plan some entertainment before and after the meal, or anytime during the festivities. *Here are a few suggestions…*

◆ In some families, gift giving is a part of the Chanukah holiday. If it is in yours, have a grab bag. Ask your guests to bring 2 gifts—1 for a child (if children are going to be at your gathering) and 1 for an adult. You may want to set limits on price. Or tell your guests that the gifts must be homemade…or have a Jewish theme…or they must be made of paper. Be sure to have a big basket or box in which to collect the wrapped gifts. You also may want to prepare some extra gifts in case some people didn't bring any.

Game Time with Gelt

After dinner, ask everyone to open his/her sack of gelt, and take out the chocolate coins. Then challenge all of your guests to a game of "Go Know!"

You go first. Start the game by saying "I have never _____" (fill in the blank). *Some examples…*

◆ I have never gone horseback riding.

◆ I have never had a pedicure.

◆ I have never talked into a microphone.

◆ I have never had a passport.

Anyone who *has* done what you have *never* done has to give you a gelt coin. After everyone has had a turn saying "I have never _____," the person with the most coins wins. Or, you can keep going, eliminating players as they run out of gelt coins. The player who ends up with all the coins wins.

When you feel the time is right, pass around the container with the gifts and give everyone a chance to take something.

- If you and your guests are musically inclined, make copies of various song sheets and have a sing-along.

- Decorate the dinner table with Chanukah *gelt* (money)—the chocolate-wrapped-in-gold-foil candy that comes in gold net sacks (available at some supermarkets, card, candy and kosher stores). Attach a name tag on each bag, and use them as place cards on your table.

Christmas

Some popular holiday traditions—such as the yule log, carolers singing from house to house, parades, the giving of gifts, church processions and holiday feasts—can trace their origins back thousands of years to Mesopotamia, an ancient region of southwest Asia. Over the years, those traditions have evolved into the holiday we know as Christmas.

In the words of clergyman and positive thinker Norman Vincent Peale—"Christmas waves a magic wand over this world, and behold, everything is softer and more beautiful."

Here, to help you perform your own kind of magic, are some tips to brighten up this special holiday season.

Christmas Tree Care

Christmas trees are grown in all 50 states, and an average-sized tree (7 to 8 feet tall) takes 7 to 10 years to mature. More than 100,000 people are employed in the Christmas-tree industry, making it possible for you to have a tree for the holiday.

Your job is to select a wonderful tree, take care of it and enjoy it.

Fireproofing Your Tree

- The Department of Risk Management and Safety at the University of Arizona (*risk. arizona.edu/healthandsafety/holidaydecorations.shtml*) strongly recommends that cut Christmas trees should be treated with a flame-retardant solution (the trees can be either sprayed or dipped).

  The recipe is 9 ounces of borax powder, 4 ounces of boric acid, 1 gallon of water and ½ teaspoon of low-sudsing laundry detergent.

> **CAUTION:** Keep borax powder and boric acid away from children and pets. Both are harmful when ingested.

- The most important fire-retardant is water. Give your tree plenty of water daily. The first time you water it, make it hot water—about 80°F. The warm temperature helps open up the tree's circulatory system, enabling it to draw up the water more easily. After that, use lukewarm water.

  The average tree will consume up to 1 gallon of water per day.

Quick Freshness Test

If you're buying a balsam fir, gently bend a needle between your thumb and forefinger. If the tree is fresh, the needle will break.

If you're buying a pine tree, the needle should not break if the tree is fresh.

For any species, if the tree is fresh, the needles will stay on the branch and not fall off if you touch them.

Treats for the Tree

- The first time you water your tree, use hot water—about 80°F. After you're done watering, add 2 ounces of antibacterial mouthwash to the water to prevent the growth of any unwanted bacteria.

◆ Give the tree a pick-me-up by adding 1 ounce of maple syrup to the water. The syrup's sugar feeds the tree. It seems to make the pine needles a more vibrant green, and they may last longer, too.

Tree Decorations

Whether you use all, some or none of the same ornaments each year on your tree, the following tips and suggestions may inspire you...

◆ Use a used fabric-softener sheet to wipe glass Christmas ornaments. They will get clean and also repel dust while on the tree.

◆ If you want to decorate your tree with strings of popcorn, air-pop the corn a few days before the stringing. Stale popcorn is a lot easier to work with than fresh popcorn—it's tougher and holds together better. Besides, fresh popcorn is too tempting to eat.

Christmas "Family" Tree

Decorate a tabletop Christmas tree with photo ornaments. Make small color copies of your favorite family photos. Mat them with red and green construction paper. You may want to put photos in the center of stars or other shapes. Punch a hole in each mat and thread a red, green or gold ribbon through it and attach each one to the tree...the "family" tree.

Write Down a Christmas Tradition

Write out note cards that say wonderful things. Place them in small red envelopes (in some Asian countries, red is believed to be the color of good fortune and happiness). Then, attach them around the Christmas tree with paper clips, small clothespins or clamps.

Tell every guest that comes into your home to select a red envelope. The uplifting message will make the person feel hopeful, happy and glad he/she stopped by.

Here are some examples of what the cards could say...

◆ All of your dreams will come true in the New Year.

◆ Your dazzling personality makes the sun shine brighter.

◆ Many memorable adventures are in store for you.

◆ Your creative ideas will soon pay off.

◆ Expect the best because you are the best.

◆ Your kindness will soon be rewarded.

House Decorations

At the risk of sounding like a Christmas card— let the spirit of the holiday season bring you joy outside and inside your home. Start by surrounding yourself with festive decorations. *Here are some suggestions...*

◆ As soon as you hang your holiday wreath outdoors, spray the ribbons and bows with super-hold hairspray. It will help keep the wreath clean and crisp. Just be sure to hang the wreath in a place where it cannot be rained on, OK?

◆ This is a great way to decorate windows— first, mix equal amounts of Epsom salt (available at drugstores) with stale beer. A little

Proof That Santa Claus Was Here!

This idea requires stencils of a pair of men's boots and flour in a sifter. Are you getting the picture? Place each boot on a big enough piece of cardboard—you can use the thin cardboard that comes from the cleaners in a man's shirt, or use a manila file folder. Then outline a right boot and a left boot, and cut out the insides of the outlines. You will now have cardboard stencils of a pair of boots.

Once the wee ones have visions of sugarplums dancing in their heads, figure out the path Santa would take from his entrance into the house (a fireplace is, of course, ideal) to the Christmas tree. Place both stencils on the floor, creating Santa's first 2 footsteps inside your home, and sift the flour over each (it should look like snow from his boots).

Gently and slowly lift each stencil, and dump the excess flour into a paper bag. Now you're ready to create Santa's next 2 footsteps. Keep repeating the footstep process all the way to the tree, then back again to the fireplace (or other point of entry/exit).

The flour will vacuum up in seconds the next morning. If you have a rug or carpeting, you may want to use baking soda instead of flour. The baking soda will actually help clean the rug!

> ✎ **NOTE:** This suggestion may not be a practical Christmas surprise if you have pets roaming around the house.

goes a long way, so start with ¼ cup of each. Then use a clean sponge to apply the mixture to a small area of the window you want to decorate.

As you work with it, you'll get a feel for the frost-and-snow effects you can create.

Give the small section a chance to dry. Then you'll be able to complete the job…knowing what to expect, what you want and how to achieve it.

When the holiday season is over, wipe off the faux frost with warm, soapy water. A vacuum cleaner will be helpful to clean up the powdery residue.

◆ In the middle of your dining room table, make an arrangement of small, gift-wrapped packages nestled in holiday greenery—such as fir sprays or holly. Coordinate the colors of the wrapping paper and ribbon to match the tablecloth and napkins. The packages may or may not be real gifts for people seated at the table. If they are, you may want to hand them out after dessert.

The Best Christmas Gifts

Oren Arnold—novelist, journalist and humorist—provides this advice…"To your enemy, forgiveness. To an opponent, tolerance. To a friend, your heart. To a customer, service. To all, charity. To every child, a good example. To yourself, respect."

And, according to writer Burton Hillis— "The best of all gifts around any Christmas tree [is] the presence of a happy family all wrapped up in each other."

Kwanzaa

If you think that Kwanzaa is an ancient African celebration—think again. The holiday was first established in 1966 for the African-American community as a way to celebrate their heritage and to reinforce positive community values.

Kwanzaa is the Swahili word for "the first," referring to "the first fruits of the harvest." The holiday lasts from December 26th through January 1st.

Meaning of the Kwanzaa Candles

The 7 candles that are used in the holiday *kinara* represent the *Nguzo Saba*, which means "7 principles" in Swahili. These values are central to the celebration of Kwanzaa—they help to build and reinforce family, community and culture among African-Americans as well as Africans throughout the world.

1. *Umoja oja* (Unity)—fostering togetherness for the family and the community.

2. *Kujichagulia* (Self-Determination)—building our lives in our own images and interests.

3. *Ujima* (Collective Work and Responsibility)—being responsible for our failures as well as our victories and achievements.

4. *Ujamaa* (Cooperative Economics)—sharing wealth and resources and building financial security.

5. *Nia* (Purpose)—discovering each person's ability to put his/her skill or talent to use.

6. *Kuumba* (Creativity)—building and developing our creative potential in order to improve the world.

7. *Imani* (Faith)—believing in ourselves, developing the family and the community, and controlling our own destiny.

For more information on the traditions and celebration of this wonderful holiday, visit the official Kwanzaa Web site at *www. officialkwanzaawebsite.org/index.shtml.*

Traditions

This is a new and evolving holiday, which means it's an opportunity for you to create traditions. *Here are a few suggestions to start you thinking about how you can participate and celebrate…*

◆ Prepare a fun video with the people around you, and send copies to relatives and friends who can't be with all of you for the holiday.

■ Recipe ■

If you want to bring something special to your Kwanzaa Feast, consider tossing together this colorful dish we created…

Confetti Salad

> 2 15-ounce cans whole-kernel corn, drained
> 1 15-ounce can black beans, rinsed and drained
> 12 scallions, chopped
> 1 small red onion, chopped
> 1 green bell pepper, chopped
> 1 red bell pepper, chopped
> 1 avocado, peeled, pitted and cut in small chunks
> 1 4-ounce jar pimentos, chopped
> 12 black olives, pitted and chopped
> 4 medium tomatoes, seeded and chopped
> 1 cup fresh cilantro, chopped
> 3 cloves garlic, peeled and finely minced
> ½ teaspoon salt
> ¾ cup Italian salad dressing (or any other dressing you prefer)

1. In a big salad bowl, combine all of the ingredients except the Italian dressing.

2. Mix about ½ cup of the dressing into the salad, then taste the salad. Continue adding more dressing, a little at a time, until the salad tastes great. If you need more than ¾ cup, add more.

3. Chill until ready to serve.

◆ Make resolutions and set goals. Then during next year's Kwanzaa, take out the list and see how many resolutions you've kept and how many goals you've reached.

◆ Ask your holiday guests to bring some form of African culture—such as a book, a poster, a statue—and have "show and tell."

Decorations

Use an African motif to decorate your home for the holiday. The Kwanzaa colors are black, red and green. Trim your home with balloons, streamers and flowers in those colors, and include them in the traditional holiday candleholder (called a *kinara*) with 1 black, 3 red and 3 green candles (*see* page 262 for an explanation of the candles' meaning). Also, use African-design fabrics as a tablecloth and napkins.

The Kwanzaa Feast (Karamu)

The purpose of this special event, held on December 31st, is to bring the celebrants closer to their African roots. It's a time for culture, tradition, food and festivities. It is usually held at a church or community center. ■

■ Products ■

Vacuum Wine Saver

Save money and save wine with this fantastic product...it has a reusable rubber stopper to reseal the bottle, ensuring that the wine stays fresh and flavorful. It works by slowing down the oxidation process—so you don't have to polish off the entire bottle in one evening. The bottle can be opened and resealed as many times as it takes to finish the wine. The Vacuum Wine Saver is made from stainless steel and is sold throughout the country.

Wine Server Crystal

Lets you pour wine easily without spilling a drop. Not only does this special device prevent dripping, it also returns any excess wine back into the bottle. The high gloss transparent material gives the server a crystal appearance. Fits most wine bottles.

Source: Vacu Vin Inc., 704-882-3521, *www.vacuvin.com.*

Chocolove

Linking *chocolate* with its natural companion *love,* each Chocolove bar resembles a love letter, addressed and affixed with a stamp that declares its cocoa content. Waiting on the inside of the wrapper is a romantic love poem.

Chocolove was the first US company to specify its chocolate's cocoa content on the front of its bars (that was in 1995). Bars range from 77% cocoa content in the Extra-Strong Dark Chocolate bars to 33% in the Milk Chocolate bars. Premium Belgium chocolate is used, but Chocolove bars are made in the US—produced in small batches to ensure quality and freshness.

Chocolove is available nationwide at select specialty retailers, gourmet grocers and natural food stores as well as online.

Source: Chocolove, 888-CHOCOLOVE (246-2656), *www.chocolove.com.*

Celebrations—The Jewish Museum Design Shop

1 East 92nd Street (next door to the Museum)
New York, NY 10128
212-423-3333

This store specializes in finely crafted ceremonial objects to commemorate the holidays and other joyous occasions. *http://shop.thejewishmuseum.org.*

CHAPTER 11

Car & Travel Smarts

Americans love their cars! But before we get to the helpful stuff, we thought you might like to know some intriguing facts about your home-away-from-home. First of all, for those of you who think that cars are a guy-thing, think again—the next time it rains, say "thank you" to Mary Anderson, who patented windshield wipers in 1905. In fact, in 1923 alone, women patented more than 170 automobile-related inventions, including the carburetor, a clutch mechanism and an electric engine starter.

A woman is also responsible for helping to make safety belts and air bags mandatory equipment in all cars. That woman is Elizabeth Dole, who was US Secretary of Transportation from 1983 to 1987. Mrs. Dole was also the first person to propose installing a third rear brake light in all automobiles.

According to the National Insurance Crime Bureau (*www.nicb.org*), approximately 1.2 million vehicles in the US are stolen annually—that's 1 car almost every 30 seconds. And at least 21% of car owners do not lock their car doors, which makes thieves' jobs a lot easier. (Of course, you're part of the 79% who *do* lock their car doors, right?)

So buckle up, lock up and take the time to check out some information that will keep you safe and happy behind the wheel.

CAR SAFETY

Car manufacturers and the US government want you to be safe in your car. Sturdier construction, air bags, antilock brakes and stricter seat belt laws have all contributed to improved driver safety on the road. But the biggest contribution is up to you, the person behind the wheel—you are responsible for doing everything within your power to monitor the safety of the car you drive.

Please read through this section and consider ways you can use the information to keep yourself and your passengers as safe as possible.

Baby on Board

The safest place in a car is the center of the back seat. According to the American Academy of Pediatrics (*www.aap.org*), babies who weigh less than 20 pounds should ride facing backward in a car seat that has been properly secured in the middle of the back seat.

When you purchase a car seat, read the manufacturer's instructions and cautions *thoroughly* to be sure that you understand every word before using the product.

Once the baby weighs more than 20 pounds, the car seat and baby should ride facing forward, also in the middle of the back seat.

Pumping Gas— A Shocking Revelation

There have been stories about some gas station fires, involving mostly women. After starting the nozzle to fill the gas tank, a woman often gets back into the car to get her purse. When she slides out of the car, the fabric of her clothes rubs against the seat upholstery, creating static electricity. When the woman touches the gas pump's nozzle again, the static electricity sparks can ignite the free-floating gas fumes.

Whether or not this is an urban legend, here's how to prevent it—after sliding out of the car, discharge the static electricity from your body by touching something metal— your door handle, hubcap or the car itself— *before* you touch the gas nozzle. Or better yet, stay outside of the car to pump your gas.

Buckle Up *Everyone*

A study from the University of Tokyo concluded that, in an accident, the driver and any front-seat passengers (who are buckled up) are 5 times more likely to be seriously injured if back-seat passengers are not wearing their seatbelts.

Think about it. In a rear-end crash, the back-seat passengers tend to be flung forward with a great deal of force. According to the Japanese study, 80% of front-seat injuries could be avoided if back-seat passengers were strapped in.

For your own safety, as well as for the rest of the passengers, the car shouldn't start moving until everyone has his/her seatbelt buckled.

Steering

If you took driver's education classes as a teenager, you were probably taught to hold the steering wheel at the 9 o'clock and 3 o'clock position or the 10 o'clock and 2 o'clock position—both of these combinations allow you to have control to turn the wheel more freely.

Eileen Beetar, an instructor with the AAA Driver Improvement Program, suggests holding it at 8 o'clock and 4 o'clock. You may have slightly less control of the wheel, but this position keeps your arms out of the way of the airbag in the event of a collision.

> **CAUTION:** Never hold your arms *across* the steering wheel, such as at the 1 o'clock and 3 o'clock position. It's bad form for steering control, and the airbag could potentially break your arm(s) during a collision.

Driving in Fog

Since it's difficult to see oncoming cars when you're driving in a thick fog, keep your window open. Chances are, you'll *hear* the cars coming toward you before you can *see* them.

COLD WEATHER CURES

Prepare for winter weather before it arrives. Go to your local service station and make sure that your car is in good working order. *Here's a basic checklist…*

- Antifreeze
- Battery
- Brake fluid
- Brakes
- Defroster
- Emergency flashers
- Exhaust system
- Fuel
- Heater
- Ignition
- Oil
- Radiator
- Tires (air pressure and wear)
- Windshield wiper fluid (wintertime mixture)

Once your car is in tip-top shape for the cold months, you will have prepared yourself to *weather* whatever hazardous road conditions may come your way.

The following hints should pull you through the little nitty-gritty challenges that come with the cold…

Stuck in Snow

Carry around 4 strips of old carpet, measuring about 1' x 4'. If you get your car stuck in the snow, take the strips out of your trunk and place a strip under each tire for traction.

What? You don't have carpet strips in your trunk? If desperation sets in, use the floor mats from inside the car, and put them under your tires to provide traction. Or keep a bag of clay kitty litter in your trunk—putting some under the tires will provide traction in the snow.

Frosty Windshield Prevention

- When you park your car outdoors overnight, spread a large plastic trash bag or sheet of plastic over the front windshield. Secure it under the windshield wipers and/or by shutting the doors on the edges of the bag(s). If you don't have plastic bags, you can also use brown paper bags, which will be held in place by the windshield wipers.

The next morning, when you remove the bag(s), there will not be any frost or ice on the windshield.

Put little plastic or paper bags over your side mirrors to keep them frost-free, too.

- Before leaving your car outside overnight, combine 6 cups of distilled white vinegar with 2 cups of water, and drench a cloth with the solution. Then use the cloth to give the windshield and other windows a good once-over. (You can also pour the solution into a trigger-spray bottle and spritz it all over the glass.) The next morning…come out to find frost- and ice-free windows.

Use the solution on your side mirrors so that they, too, will be frost-free.

- If snow is coming, and your car is going to be out on the street all night, pull up your windshield wipers and coat the windshield with sulfuric compounds.

Does that sound extreme? In other words, cut an onion in half and rub the glass with the onion's cut surface. The coating will prevent the formation of ice on your windshield. Don't forget to onion-up your side mirrors.

Defrosting the Windshield

- If you did not prevent your windshield from frosting with our tips (above) and you don't have a proper ice scraper, use a plastic dustpan—it will do the scraping job without scratching the windshield.

- If you don't have a plastic dustpan to use as a scraper, pour some cola on a cloth and rub off the icy buildup.

> ⊘ **CAUTION:** If cola splashes on the car, wipe it off quickly. You don't want it eating through the paint.

Frozen Door-Lock Prevention

- Don't let the frost get in. Cover the door locks with magnets…thin, flat ones are best (available at hardware or crafts stores). You may not want to tempt the neighborhood kids by using the big, novelty magnets from your refrigerator—although they would work, too.

- One of the most popular of the more than 2,000 uses for the lubricant WD-40 (available at hardware stores) is to spray it in the car door or trunk lock *before* it gets cold—this will prevent the locks from freezing. But you can also spray the locks after they've frozen to defrost them.

- Coat the rubber gaskets around the doors with vegetable oil or petroleum jelly to prevent cold weather from freezing them shut.

    You can also use a bit of vegetable oil or petroleum jelly to prevent your trunk from becoming frozen shut.

Opening Frozen Door Locks

- If your locks are already frozen, light a match and carefully stick your car key in the flame. Keep it there long enough to get hot but not long enough to burn your fingers. Then quickly put the key in the lock and turn.

- Do they say you're full of hot air? Prove it. Take a plastic drinking straw and put it over the lock, then blow through it and into the lock. After a few minutes, the lock should be warm enough to open.

FUEL ECONOMY

Everyone wants to save money on fuel. The US Department of Energy has a Web site (*www.fueleconomy.gov*) that may help you learn what would be the most fuel-efficient vehicle to meet your needs. *Meanwhile, here are some suggestions that may show you how to save some money with the vehicle you have…*

Keep Windows and Sunroof Closed

Driving with all the windows and/or sunroof open—especially when you're zooming down the highway—causes wind drag, which slows down the car and decreases fuel efficiency by about 10%.

Keep Tires Properly Inflated

You can improve your vehicle's gas mileage by about 3% by keeping the tires properly inflated. Using the recommended tire pressure (specified in your vehicle's owner's manual) will also allow the car to handle better and will help prevent flats.

> **DID YOU KNOW?**
>
> **U**nderinflated tires wear out faster. So that is another reason to check your tires' air pressure regularly—at least once a month. Be sure to check your spare tire, too.

Penny for Your Tires

Learn when it's time to replace your tires by putting Honest Abe to work. While holding a penny on the words *In God We Trust*, insert it into the tire's tread. If the top of Lincoln's head cannot be seen, that tire is fine. However, if Lincoln's hair is sticking out, your tire is worn down and probably needs to be replaced.

Less Is More Cost-Efficient

◆ Except for a spare tire and other emergency equipment, don't use your trunk as a storage bin. Driving around with extra weight decreases your car's fuel efficiency.

◆ While you're at it, take off the roof rack when it's not being used. The added weight adds drag on the engine, causing it to use more fuel.

Cruising Speed

Since most gas is consumed when you hit the pedal to accelerate, it's best to select a speed and maintain it.

Keep in mind that every 5 miles per hour (mph) you drive over 60, you add approximately 21 cents to the cost of a gallon of gas (depending on current prices). More important, slower speeds can also help keep you safe.

> **NOTE:** It's also important to not accelerate and brake suddenly. Try to use even, gentle pressure to accelerate and slow the car—especially in stop-and-go traffic—which will improve your fuel efficiency.

Cheapest Gas Prices

Not all, but many gas stations raise their prices from Friday to Sunday when the demand is greatest. Instead, gas up on Tuesday, Wednesday or Thursday to avoid the jacked-up prices over the weekend.

Get More Gas for Your Buck!

◆ Fill up your tank in the early morning or late at night. Gasoline expands with heat, so if the outside air temperature and the car's gas tank are cooler, you end up getting more for the same price.

◆ Visit the Web site *www.gasbuddy.com* and enter your ZIP code or the ZIP code of the area to which you're traveling. You'll be given a list of local gas stations, along with their current gas prices.

Car Battery

The main job of a car battery is to start the engine. If the battery is in bad shape, chances are the car won't move. But a well-maintained battery should last anywhere from 2 to 5 years.

Here are some suggestions that will help you maintain your battery...so that it stays in good working order for more like 5 years than 2.

Battery Corrosion

◆ Slowly add plain tap water to 1 cup of baking soda until it becomes a paste. Then, using a small paintbrush, apply the paste to the car battery posts (also called terminals) to help neutralize corrosion (also known as rust). Leave the paste on for 1 hour, then clean it off with a damp cloth.

◆ Fizz away the corrosion by pouring a can of cola over the terminals. Since the phosphoric acid in cola can dissolve a nail in about 4 days, it should be able to bubble away dirt and rust in no time. After it's done bubbling, wipe the terminals clean with a fresh, moist rag, and towel dry.

> **CAUTION:** If cola splashes on the car, wipe it off quickly. You don't want it eating through the paint.

Prevent Battery Corrosion

◆ Smear petroleum jelly on the battery terminals before attaching battery cables. This will help prevent corrosion.

◆ Using regular transparent tape, attach a copper penny to the top of your battery. The penny may corrode, but the electrodes should remain clean.

Battery Recharge, Then Recycle

According to television actor Richard Karn—the knowledgeable sidekick on the television show *Home Improvement*…and author of *Handy at Home* (St. Martin's)—many batteries can be recharged up to 1,000 times. Once a battery cannot be revived anymore, it should not be thrown in the trash. The battery can explode if the trash is incinerated.

Karn suggests that you recycle it at 1 of the more than 30,000 recycling centers throughout the country. To find the center nearest you, visit *www.call2recycle.org*, or call the toll-free number, 1-800-8-BATTERY or 877-2-RECYCLE.

NOTE: For those of you who are brave enough to tinker, we suggest that you visit *www.icarumba.com*.

This site offers a Reference Library that deals with everything you ever wanted to know about car repair, including testing the battery, recharging it, what to look for when buying a new battery and installation.

Caring for a Fan Belt

The fan belt is the traditional term for what is known now as the *drive belt*. There are 2 kinds of drive belt—V-belts and serpentine belts. Their job is to provide power to engine-mounted accessories like the air-conditioning compressor, the power-steering pump and air-injection pump.

The chances of a drive-belt problem rise dramatically after the car has been driven for 3 years or 36,000 miles for a V-belt…and 50,000 miles for a serpentine belt.

Have your drive belt checked every time the oil is changed, to make sure that it is properly tightened and in good shape.

Belt Moisturizer

If your car's engine has a dry fan belt, smear a bit of petroleum jelly on the inside edges of the belt, then start the car and let the engine idle for 2 or 3 minutes. The jelly will recondition the belt, help grip the pulleys better than commercial lubricants, and do away with squeals and slippage.

Buying a Used Car?

Get the car's *vehicle identification number* (VIN)—it's stamped onto a small metal plate and is attached to the driver's side of the dash where it meets the window—and then invest about $40 in a CARFAX Vehicle History Report—go to *www.carfax.com*.

As they say on their Web page "…[this is] the first step to protecting yourself against buying used cars with costly hidden problems."

Some car dealers may offer this information for free. Be aware that repair/accident information that was never officially reported may not appear in the CARFAX summary.

CAR COMFORT

Fine-tune your driving experience with ways to make it more comfortable to get and be behind the wheel. *These suggestions may help…*

Shade Against a Hot Seat

When you park your car in the sun on a hot day, open an umbrella and leave it on the seat. When you return to the car and sit behind the wheel without burning your backside, you'll be glad you did that umbrella thing.

Smoother Antenna

If your car's radio antenna doesn't slide up and down easily, you can gently rub it with a piece of waxed paper.

Sun Visor Trapper Keeper

Clamp a few big clothespins to the sun visor on the driver's side of the car. If you don't have clothespins, you can also put a thick rubber band around each side of the visor.

Then when you have directions...or a map...or toll tickets...or parking stubs...or a pen and paper...or your shopping list...or your Weight Watchers Points–system page...or anything else you may want to reach for while in the car, clamp it to the visor with the clothespin or slide it under the rubber band.

CAR CLEANING

In 1913, Richard Spikes invented the automatic car washer (and, in that same year, Spikes also invented automobile directional signals). In 1955, Dan Hanna, known as "The Father of the Modern Carwash," convinced his mother to mortgage the family home to finance what was to become Hanna Enterprises, a famous, innovative car wash manufacturing company.

Thanks to Spikes and Hanna, you can use your appropriate directional signal and drive into a car wash to have your car cleaned. *And*

thanks to our suggestions, you can learn to keep your car cleaner and spiffier in several ways...

Bugs Off

◆ Before a long car trip, spray vegetable cooking oil on the car's clean bumper, grille and hood. The bugs you pick up along the way will wash off easily, and the spray won't damage the car's finish.

◆ If you forget to spray and the car gets covered in bugs, scrunch up a mesh onion bag or shower sponge, pour on some baking soda and wipe off the splattered bugs. Clean up with a damp cloth.

✳ **Pantyhose Power!**

Instead of using rags and sponges, dip an old pair of clean pantyhose in warm sudsy water. Use the hose to wash away any dirt and dead bugs on the car's exterior.

Cleaning Windshields

◆ If you get bugs splattered on your windshield, mix 1 tablespoon of liquid dish detergent with 1 pint of water, and pour it on the windshield. Then use a mesh onion bag or shower sponge to scrub off the bugs. Finish the job by wiping the windshield with a clean cloth.

◆ Prepare your own windshield cleaner in an empty gallon-sized spring water or milk jug. Add 2 tablespoons of liquid dish detergent, 3 cups of rubbing alcohol and fill the rest with water. Pour 1 or 2 tablespoons on a clean cloth and wash the windshield with it. Rinse clean with plain water.

◆ To remove haze from the windshield (inside or out), dip a clean cloth in distilled white vinegar and wash the windshield. Rinse off the vinegar with plain water, then wipe dry. The windshield will be haze-free and showroom clean.

◆ Use a blackboard eraser (available at art-supply and stationery stores) to clean steamed-up windows. It's easy, fast and does the job without leaving streaks.

◆ Wipe the insides of your car's windshield (and windows) with a little gel shaving cream to help prevent them from fogging up. Apply, let dry and then rub off with a clean cloth.

Cleaning Wipers

◆ If your windshield wipers have caked-on gunk, clean the blades with rubbing alcohol. The alcohol will clean the blades and also prevent ice from forming on them.

◆ You can also use a piece of extra-fine sandpaper to clean gunk off windshield wipers. Bend the sandpaper in half, and run it along the edge of the wiper. (This also helps keep the wiper blades fresh under normal circumstances.)

Fixing Nicks, Chips And Scratches

◆ If your windshield gets a little nick, a tiny hole or a small scratch, you can patch it up with a few dabs of colorless nail polish.

Be sure to let the polish patch dry thoroughly before using the windshield wipers.

◆ Buy a box of Crayola® Crayons that contains the same color crayon as your car. Carefully work the crayon into the scratch to fix it.

◆ If you don't intend to get a matching-color crayon or have a scratch professionally touched up...then, as soon as you see the scratch, apply clear nail polish. This will prevent the nick, chip or scratch from rusting and getting worse.

Cleaning Tree Sap

◆ Don't let sticky sap cake on—clean it off your car as soon as possible. Slather the sap with mayonnaise and let it sink in for a few minutes. Then rub the mayo and sap off with a soft, clean cloth. Finish the job by washing the car.

◆ You can also pour a bit of rubbing alcohol or even WD-40 on a soft, clean cloth and gently work at cleaning off the tree sap.

Cleaning Bird Droppings

Bird droppings contain harsh acids that can burn through your car's paint. The secret to cleaning up—and saving your car's exterior—is to take action as soon as you spot the plop.

◆ Pour on some seltzer and let it bubble up. Once the bubbling stops, wipe the area clean with a microfiber (available at supermarkets and hardware stores) or cotton cloth.

◆ Since time is of the essence when it comes to cleaning off bird droppings, you might want to keep some special wipes in the car to deal with roadside cleanups (it's easier than taking a bottle of seltzer with you).

One product that was recommended to us is a quick detailer. It's available in soft, paint-safe wipes. Travel Pack Speed Shine Wipes fit in your glove compartment and are perfect for cleaning those messy bird hits before they etch your paint.

For more information on these helpful wipes, contact Griot's Garage (a catalog that offers car-specialty products) at 800-345-5789 or *www.griotsgarage.com*.

Howzabout Those Headlights?

Don't be that person who cleans the car but forgets about the all-important (and often grimy) headlights. Mix 1 cup of distilled white vinegar in 1 quart of water and, as a mild abrasive, add 1 tablespoon of cornstarch. Use a sponge to wash the headlights with the solution, then rinse with plain water. You'll see the light!

Bye-Bye Tar

◆ Spritz your car's tar stain with laundry prewash spray, and let it sink in for 1 to 2 minutes. Then wipe it clean with a soft cloth.

◆ If you don't have any prewash spray, you can dab on a dollop of mayonnaise, keep it there for a couple of minutes, then wipe it clean with a soft cloth.

Grease Away

Had a tailgate party and got some of the barbecue grease on the car? Whether the mess is from food or grease your car picked up at the service station, wipe it off with a baby wipe. If it's gentle enough for a baby's skin, you can trust that it won't damage your car's paint job.

Amazing Trunk Extender

When you leave that yard sale and put your oversized purchase in the trunk, you may need to secure the trunk lid for the trip home. If you don't have rope, twine or a bungee cord— pantyhose to the rescue! Keep an old pair—as well as rope, twine or bungee cords—in the trunk to tie down the trunk lid.

Removing Decals and Bumper Stickers

◆ Time to remove the old campaign sticker? The college decal? The bumper sticker that once seemed so funny—but isn't anymore? Saturate a cloth with distilled white vinegar and cover the sticker with it.

　　Give the vinegar at least 30 minutes to soak through and dissolve the glue. Then peel off the sticker or gently scrape it off with an expired credit card. If some glue

When Your Car Needs Repair...

If your car needs a repair that isn't covered by the manufacturer's warranty, go to the dealership and ask to read the Technical Service Bulletin. This document describes the manufacturer's authorized repairs, and it may include a repair your car needs that was caused by other defects or problems your car model has had.

　　If you have a newer car, you can also save yourself a trip to the dealership by visiting *www.mycarstats.com/auto_tsbs/Auto_tsbs.asp*. This Web site has Technical Service Bulletins and Car Reports for 1990–2010 model cars.

still remains, you can rub it off with a bit of vegetable oil.

◆ If you have a portable hair dryer...or 1 with a long extension cord from your house to your car...or if you keep your car in a garage and there's an electric outlet, then you may want to use the hair dryer to loosen the sticker's glue.

　　Set the dryer on *high* heat and blow it over the sticker for a couple of minutes, until you're able to easily peel off the sticker. If some glue remains, rub it off with vegetable oil or WD-40.

Cleaning Vinyl or Cloth Upholstery

To clean vinyl or cloth upholstery, use unscented baby wipes. Dry the vinyl with paper towel, and let the cloth upholstery air-dry.

NOTE: *This cleaning tip is NOT for leather upholstery.* Instead, use saddle soap (available at tack stores, where saddles and all other equine supplies are sold, as well as some shoe repair shops) on leather or leatherette upholstery.

GARAGE FLOOR & DRIVEWAY CLEANUP

Bet those oil and grease stains bother you every time you drive in or out of your garage or driveway. So why let them remain? *Now is the time to do something about them, and here's how...*

Wiping Out Oil or Grease Stains

◆ To start the cleaning process, turn 1 or 2 cups of standard clay kitty litter into powder. Pour the litter on a piece of cloth or a dish towel. Bring the 4 ends of the cloth together so that the kitty litter is enclosed and won't fall out, then hammer the cloth until the litter gets powdery.

Cover the oil stain with the powder, put a piece of cardboard on top and step on it. Make sure the kitty litter powder works its way into the stain—you may even want to brush it in with a scrub brush. Let the powder sit there for 1 to 2 hours. Then sweep up or vacuum up the powder.

◆ Pour cola on the stain and let it stay on overnight. The next day, mix ⅓ cup of liquid dish detergent with 3 cups of plain water, and rinse the stained area with the soapy water. Then hose it down with plain water.

◆ If you don't want to use cola, then drizzle liquid dish detergent on the stain. Let it sit there for about 10 minutes, then pour some boiling-hot water over it. When it cools, scour the area with a stiff scrub brush and hose it off.

◆ Sawdust (available at home improvement stores) also makes a great oil absorber.

Changing Oil

Check the owner's manual for your car's oil-changing schedule. It may be a lot less often than your mechanic suggests. For example, instead of every 3,000 miles, it may only be necessary every 5,000 miles or more.

Stain Prevention

Get the goop before it stains the garage floor. Place a piece of cardboard under the vulnerable areas, like where your car drips oil or where you park your lawn mower.

An even better idea should be obvious—get your leaky car fixed!

GARAGE PARKING

If you still park your car in your garage...then good for you for not taking up the space with clutter overflowing from your home. *To fully enjoy the luxury of this perfect place to house your car, here are a few suggestions...*

X Marks the Perfect Spot

Pull your car into the garage and park it just the way you like best. Then wrap some string around a tennis ball and hang it from the garage ceiling, positioning the ball against the windshield—the ball should be at your eye level when you're sitting in the driver's seat.

The next time you pull into the garage, the tennis ball will touch your windshield—and that's the signal that you've made it to the perfect spot.

Prevent Dings

If you need to pull in close to the garage wall, protect the front-end of your car from dings by hanging a couple of old tires on the wall or nailing carpet remnants to the wall.

This lining will help prevent dents and scratches if you misjudge the distance from your front bumper to the garage wall.

Finding Your Car

Make your car a standout in a crowded parking lot by tying a Day-Glo or any brightly colored ribbon to the radio antenna.

Cleaning Your Hands

The proclamation that was issued for Clean Hands Week (*www.cleanhandscoalition.org*) in September 2005 stated that the role of hand-washing in America has been overlooked and undervalued. *Well, we are doing our best to value clean hands, especially those made dirty from car care...*

◆ If you get grease or oil on your hands after working on your car, rub a little olive oil on the greasy/oily areas, then wipe your hands with a paper towel. Follow up by thoroughly washing with soap and water.

◆ If you are at a service station and your hands are dirty after pumping gas or from touching something greasy, clean your hands with a baby wipe. Yes, you should keep a box of baby wipes in the car.

CAR SMELLS

Everyone loves that new-car smell, but it doesn't last long—especially if you have smokers, children and pets as passengers. *Here are some ways to clear the air and keep your vehicle smelling fresh...*

Cigarette Smoke

Stick an unused citrus-scented fabric softener sheet under the driver's seat. It will help to eliminate smoke odors and replace them with a fresh, clean smell.

Also, the scent of citrus has been known to keep people more alert than usual. Replace the softener sheet every couple of weeks.

Bad-Smell Neutralizer

A pet has an accident in the car...a child gets sick...someone has too much to drink—you get the idea. There's a *baaaaaaad* smell in the car! Put a shallow bowl of distilled white vinegar on the car's floor, both in front and in back. Then close the windows and lock up the car for the night.

In the morning, the offensive smell should be gone. Remove the bowls, then open the doors and windows for a few minutes so that any lingering vinegar smell will also disappear.

Sweeten the Air

If there are ashtrays in your car that are not used—particularly those in back—fill them with some pleasant-smelling potpourri (available at crafts stores as well as herb and health-food shops).

You can also put unused dryer sheets under the seats, or place fragrant sachets in the seat corners.

CHECKLIST OF CAR SHOULD-HAVES

While it's true that driving around with extra weight decreases your car's fuel efficiency, it's also true that there are some things you should have with you at all times—for your safety and in case of an emergency. *Keep these items handy in your car and/or garage…*

◆ Cell phone and cell-phone car charger

◆ Carpet strips for traction

◆ Sand or kitty litter for traction

◆ WD-40 for frozen locks

◆ Plastic straw to unfreeze a lock

◆ Rope, twine, bungee cords and/or pantyhose to tie down the trunk

◆ Umbrella to prevent a hot seat or to keep you dry when it rains

◆ Blackboard eraser to clean fogged windows

◆ Unscented baby wipes to clean hands after pumping gas

◆ Pack of chewing gum in case there's a small leak or puncture that needs plugging up

◆ A few plastic trash bags with head and arm holes cut out to use as emergency raincoats for you and your passengers

◆ Funnel—store-bought or improvised by cutting a liquid laundry detergent bottle in half and removing the cap—necessary for an emergency infusion of motor oil, antifreeze or water

◆ Small container of motor oil

◆ Aerosol can of Fix-a-Flat

◆ Travel Pack Speed Shine Wipes for bird droppings

◆ Two roadside flares

◆ Safety matches

◆ Jumper cables to start a dead/low battery

◆ Flashlight and fresh batteries (or flashlight that doesn't require batteries)

◆ Thermal blanket(s)

◆ Bottled water—for yourself or an overheated radiator

◆ Packages of dried fruit, crackers, protein bars and/or nuts

◆ Small hand shovel

◆ Spare tire

◆ Jack

◆ Lug wrench

◆ Work gloves (in case you have to shovel or change a tire)

◆ Ice scraper and brush for your windshield and windows

◆ Small fire extinguisher

◆ Tire chains (depending on the weather in your area)

◆ Pen and paper

◆ Money (keep an emergency $20 in the glove compartment)

◆ Tissues/napkins/paper towels

CAR TRAVEL

Although driving may be a relaxing way to travel, it is definitely not a mindless activity. Stay alert and stay defensive—it will take you a long way in staying safe.

If you want to improve your skill as a driver, consider learning how to drive a race car. You will have the chance to practice accident-avoidance maneuvers and skid recovery in a controlled environment. Besides, it promises to be lots of fun.

One of the premier schools is Skip Barber Racing School LLC. It offers high-performance driving instruction, with classes in 5 locations nationwide. For more information, call 866-932-1949 or visit *www.skipbarber.com.*

Until you sign up for racing school, here are some suggestions that will help make the going easier and enhance your good time behind the wheel...

Packing Clothes

Keep your clothes on hangers, then put them in clothing bags, dry-cleaning bags or even large plastic trash bags. Spread out the bags in your trunk, placing them on top of any other luggage you've packed. The clothes will stay wrinkle-free, and unpacking will be a cinch.

Pillowcase Smarts

If you plan on taking a pillow for comfort in the car, put a few pillowcases on each pillow. When the top pillowcase gets dirty, you can take it off and use it as a laundry bag for dirty clothes. When the second pillowcase gets dirty, take it off and put it in the first pillowcase that has become a laundry bag.

Directions on Tape

Go over a map to plan out your trip or use an on-line map-and-directions service, such as *www.mapquest.com* or *http://maps.google.com.* Once you have your route figured out, record the directions on a cassette recorder.

When you're on the road, pop the tape into your cassette deck and hit the *play* button when you're ready for the next direction. It may be easier than reading directions on paper while you drive.

If your car doesn't have a cassette deck, bring along the recorder you used to make the tape. Just make sure its batteries are in good working order before you leave home.

NOTE: Always bring along a set of directions on paper (and copies of all necessary maps), just in case technology fails you.

Traveling with Pets

Pull into a rest area at least every 2 hours to let your pet take a potty break, have a drink of water (and maybe some food) and get some exercise outdoors—a walk for 10 minutes or more is ideal. The exercise will be good for *your* road-weary body, too.

Cleaning Pet Hair

When pet hair is all over the seats of your car, put on a rubber glove and rub the upholstery with it. The hair will cling to the glove. Take off the glove by turning it inside out, and discard it along with the pet hair.

TRAVEL FUN & GAMES

Here are some ways to distract the young and the restless from asking those inevitable questions, "Are we there yet?" and "How much longer?" Incidentally, these games are also fun for the not-so-young-but-still restless.

Create a Trip Travelogue

All it takes is a cassette recorder (the same recorder you may be bringing to play the directions that you recorded) and a few blank audio tapes.

Let each passenger take a turn talking about his/her experience of the trip...the things that he's seeing out the window…a description of the place you stopped for a meal…funny incidents that happen along the way. The tape will be a real vacation keepsake.

 "Award-Winning" Vacation Videos
A video recorder is even more fun to bring on a trip. Have family members pretend that they are filmmakers doing a documentary or newscasters reporting on an important event.

Geography—A Classic Game

One person names a place—city, state or country. The last letter of that place is what the next person has to use as the first letter of another place.

Example: Cincinnati (ends with an "i"), then Indiana (begins with an "i" and ends with an "a"), then Armonk. The next person has to name a city/state/country that starts with a "k."

When a player is stumped, he/she drops out. Continue the game until only 1 player is left…or just quit playing when you're all geographied out.

A Game of Questions

Start with 2 players. One asks a question. Every question has to be answered with a question.

When 1 of the players messes up by not asking a question, he/she is out and is replaced by the next player, who starts a new conversation by asking a question. The winner is the player who is still asking questions after everyone else has been eliminated.

Example:

Player #1: "Are you going on vacation?"

Player #2: "Would you like to come with me?"

Player #1: "Would you mind if I go with you?"

Player #2: "Would I ask you if I minded?"

Player #1: "Can you please tell me where you're going?"

Player #2: "Wouldn't you rather be surprised?"

Player #1: "Don't you remember that I dislike surprises?"

Essence—A Game Of Perception

One person pretends to be someone that everyone in the car knows either personally (like a relative or friend) or knows of (like a famous celebrity). The player who is "it" tells whether the person he's pretending to be is male or female, living or dead.

The other players take turns asking a question that will establish the essence of the person. *Sample questions…*

◆ If you were a flower, what kind of flower would you be?

◆ If you were a magazine, what magazine would you be?

◆ What color would you be?

◆ Which American city would you be?

◆ What article of clothing would you be?

◆ What kind of car would you be?

◆ What snack would you be?

The game ends when someone correctly guesses the identity of the "it" player. Then the correct guesser gets to be "it."

Watch What You Say— A Gotcha! Game

Come up with any 2 common words, such as "how" and "that," or "it" and "yes." Player #1 starts a conversation by making a statement about any subject…the trip he/she is taking… the weather…a favorite television show—anything. Player #2 must carry on the conversation without using the 2 no-no words.

Players get eliminated when they say either of the 2 words—the more players, the more fun. The winner is the last player remaining.

Story Time—A Game Of Imagination

You may want to turn on the cassette recorder for this game—1 person starts telling a story and stops a few sentences into it. The next person picks up where the first player left off. Keep the story going as long as possible.

If the story is any good, transcribe the tape and get a literary agent to represent it!

GENERAL TRAVEL

Whether you're traveling for business, pleasure or both…if you're going by plane, train, bus, boat, camel, camper or car…if you're staying at a motel, hotel, hostel, lodge, chalet, castle or camping grounds…off season or in season…alone, with a tour group or with family or friends—there's valuable information that can help make your trip the best it can be.

Travel Planning

"Without leaps of imagination, or dreaming, we lose the excitement of possibilities," said feminist journalist Gloria Steinem. "Dreaming, after all, is a form of planning."

Many people consider the planning stage of a trip to be as much fun as the trip itself. So we hope these suggestions help you plan the most exciting trip possible.

Airfare Prices

Generally, most major airlines offer bargain prices on Tuesdays and Wednesdays as well as Saturday mornings. Fares tend to be highest on Mondays and Fridays. Discounted rates are most often given on midday and late-night flights, but hardly ever during morning and evening business-commuting hours.

Hotels—Bargain Prices

Several hotel chains offer low-low prices on rooms that would otherwise go unoccupied. It's very last minute, and you'll find these bargains only on the Internet.

If *short notice* is not your way of planning a trip, there are also lots of bargains on the Internet for advance reservations. But always read the fine print and confirm the deal with the hotel directly. *When you're ready to start looking, check out these sites…*

◆ **Priceline**—*www.priceline.com*

◆ **Radisson**—*www.radisson.com*

◆ **Quikbook**—*www.quikbook.com*

◆ **hoteldiscount!com**—*www.hoteldiscount.com*

Before the Trip…

Travel light! When in doubt, leave it out! You don't want to lug around unused or unwashed clothing. Nor do you want to have to be dependent on porters, cab drivers or other travelers for lifting and carrying your overstuffed luggage. Give lots of thought to what you *really* need to take, keeping in mind that packing light can add to an enjoyable time.

Packing Styles

There are several different packing options to consider when it comes to proper packing. Read through our suggestions—keeping in mind the kind of clothes and accessories you will be taking with you when you travel—and decide which packing style will work best for you.

No matter how you decide to pack, be sure to button buttons, zip zippers, tie ties, snap snaps and buckle buckles before putting your clothes into the suitcase.

◆ This packing order should keep the creasing down to a minimum—first, lay out jackets…then shirts/blouses and pants/skirts… followed by jeans—all folded in half across the length of the suitcase. Shoes go in the corners.

◆ Instead of folding clothes, roll them. It doesn't take up any more room in a suitcase, and your clothes will be less creased when you unpack. If you have clothes on hangers, put plastic dry-cleaner bags over them and, yes, roll them up.

◆ If having wrinkle-free slacks is your priority, fold them in half and stretch out the top half in the bottom of your suitcase, and let the bottom half (the legs) hang over the side of the suitcase. Then pack the rest of your clothes on top of the slacks in your suitcase. (It's starting to sound very confusing, but if you do a dry run as you read these instructions, it will make sense.)

Once your clothes are packed on top of the slacks, cover the clothes with the legs of the slacks that have been draped over the side of the suitcase.

This method of packing will eliminate the creases in pants that are packed after being folded in half at the knees.

◆ For an overnight stop at a hotel, you may want to have your nightgown handy, and for that morning swim, you may want your bathing suit easy to reach. It would be nice to not have to search for those garments, messing up the other clothes you packed so neatly.

The solution is to pack your clothes in the order in which you will need them, with the ones you will need first on top in your suitcase.

◆ An editor at Fodor's Travel Publishing suggests folding shirts, pants and skirts in half lengthwise, and then stacking or rolling them from the bottom up.

✳ Pack to the Proper Capacity

A suitcase that's *appropriately* full—rather than emptyish or overstuffed—will help minimize the creasing of clothing.

Packing Suggestions

Before you begin to pack, think about what you'll need on your trip and write out a packing list. Then, as you pack, check off each item as it goes into the suitcase.

Once you've finished packing, pack the list in the suitcase so that you can recheck everything when you pack to go home.

◆ If you don't have a toothbrush holder, find an empty plastic pill bottle—you know, those little amber containers that you keep because you think they just might come in handy someday. Well, today's the day!

You'll want a pill bottle that has a childproof cap—a soft-plastic cap inside the hard-plastic cap. Pluck out the soft-plastic cap. Then, using a knife or box cutter, carefully cut about a ¾" slit in the cap. Push the handle of the toothbrush through the slit and put the head of the toothbrush into the pill bottle. Move the cap down, closing the pill bottle with the toothbrush inside its new, clean, covered holder.

◆ Put your underwear in thin plastic bags, and stuff your shoes with them. It will use suitcase space wisely and help your shoes keep their shape. You can also stuff your shoes with socks. *Or you can…*

◆ Put socks *over* your leather shoes (just make sure they're clean first). Doing this will prevent them from getting scratched inside a super-stuffed suitcase.

◆ All expert packers seem to agree that belts should not be rolled up. They should line the perimeter of the suitcase.

◆ If you're into necklaces, you know how easily the chains tangle. Open the clasp and thread 1 end of the chain through a plastic straw, then bring the 2 ends together. Close the clasp the way you would if the chain was around your neck. *Ta-da!*

 Pack Bring-Alongs

Pack a couple of large plastic garbage bags in your suitcase. You'll find many uses for them, including as a waterproof layer in your suitcase, a laundry bag for dirty clothes or as an impromptu raincoat.

If there's room, take a few different-sized bags. Chances are, you will use them in ways you may not be able to anticipate. They come in handy for carrying leftover food from a restaurant, for leaky bottles or for wet shoes and bathing suits.

You may also want to take a lightweight, fold-up bag that opens to become an extra piece of luggage, especially if you like to shop for clothes and souvenirs when you travel.

Preparing Medication

◆ Buy a thermal-insulated lunch bag in which to keep your medication cool, especially if you're traveling when the weather is hot.

◆ Bring an extra supply of necessary medication—about 3 days' worth—before traveling.

And get a note (and duplicate prescriptions) from your doctor for all medications and health gear, such as syringes, glucometers, lancets, blood pressure monitors and inhalers.

✳ Fly Through Airport Security

Be sure to have a doctor's note for anything that might delay you in getting through airport security, such as metal plates or pins, artificial limbs, a pacemaker, etc.

Copy Credit Cards and Personal Documents

Photocopy 2 sets of all your important identification and travel documents—such as your passport, driver's license, travel tickets, credit cards and traveler's checks—and anything regarding your health and medication.

Make sure that credit card cancellation instructions and phone numbers are included. Keep a set filed away at home and carry a set with you in a safe place.

✳ And Just to Be Safe…

When copying your identification and documents, you may want to copy a third set and leave it with a hometown contact person.

In general, it's a good idea to give your travel itinerary (with flight numbers, hotel contact information, etc.) to someone at home, just in case of an emergency.

Preparing Snail Mail

If you plan to send "wish you were here" postcards to all your friends and family, write or type their names and addresses on self-stick labels to take with you. And if you're traveling within the US, don't forget to bring postcard stamps.

Power Outage Protection

The following tip doesn't prevent a power outage, but it lets you know if something happened while you were away…

Before you leave on your trip, put a few ice cubes in a resealable plastic freezer bag and leave it in the freezer. When you get back home, check to see if the ice cubes are still shaped like cubes and not a frozen puddle.

If it's a solid puddle, it means there was a power outage and the food in your freezer thawed and refroze. And if that's the case, you should throw away that food.

Prevent a Musty Home

A house can smell musty if it's been closed up for a while. Before you go away on a trip, place small bowls of distilled white vinegar in each room. The vinegar will keep the air fresh, so you'll breathe easier when you get home.

Prevent Bathroom Mildew

Buy a big bag (it's not expensive) of clay kitty litter. Pour it into a big, flat box. The top of a cardboard storage box (about 25" x 15") is perfect. Place the box top in your bathtub and pour some kitty litter into it. It will absorb moisture and prevent mildew while you're away.

First-Night-Back Bliss

Before you leave home, plan for your return! You'll have traveled all day and you'll be tired—the last thing you'll want to do is to change the linens on your bed. Here's what to do—before you leave on your trip, place an unused fabric-softener sheet between the flat and fitted sheets of your bed.

The porous material of the dryer sheet absorbs moisture, keeping the linens nice and crisp. The scent from the dryer sheet will also leave your bed sheets smelling fresh and clean. All of this should ensure that you settle easily into slumber upon your return.

Light Up the Place

Light timers (inexpensive and available at hardware and discount stores) installed near the front and back windows of your house will give the impression that there is life and activity inside a home (especially if you keep the curtains drawn).

Noise can further enhance the illusion of people at home. You can use the same light timers to turn on radios and/or television sets.

Luggage—Ship Ahead

There are companies that will pick up your luggage, golf clubs, skis, gifts for the grandkids (and whatever else you want to take on your vacation) and deliver it all to your destination—just about anywhere in the world.

This service will save you the hassle of dragging stuff through airport check-in and security lines. Before you get excited about this, though, keep in mind that luggage-shipping services are *expensive*.

But if you're still interested, check out these companies…

◆ **Luggage Express**—866-744-7224 or *www.us xpluggageexpress.com*

◆ **Skycap International**—877-775-9227 or *www.skycapinternational.com*

You can also use Federal Express, UPS, DHL or even the US Postal Service to send the luggage, but you would have to box or shrink-wrap everything you send yourself. The ship-ahead services handle all of that.

Plants

Don't forget to plan for your plants! *See* "While You're Away" on pages 233–234 of Chapter 9, "Great Greenery Solutions."

During the Trip...

In the earlier section on packing (*see* pages 279–280), we advised you to pack light...so you definitely don't want to take this book with you! Instead, read through our suggestions, take notes or commit the information to memory, and then be on your way—knowing when to take your medication...how to keep track of your finances...how much to tip...and finding your hotel.

Taking Medication

If you will be crossing time zones, you may wonder exactly when you should take your medication. Most drugs that are meant to be taken once a day build to steady levels in the body, so discrepancies of a few hours shouldn't matter. But if you take medication(s) several times a day, consult with the prescribing physician and get specific instructions before your trip.

Credit Card Expenditures

Write down everything you buy as you buy it. Include a description of the item, the date/time, the price, the credit card used, the store name—all the details.

We know you're on vacation and you don't want to have to do clerical work, but this running tally can give you an overall picture of your finances, help prevent you from going over your budget (and perhaps your credit limit) and keep you from being charged for items you did not purchase. Be sure to keep the list with you in a secure place.

High-Tech Gear

Place a sticker with contact information—the name and number of a relative or friend, or the address and number of your travel destination, hotel or office—on a cell phone, laptop, iPod, BlackBerry, digital or video camera...or any other high-tech equipment you are traveling with.

If you lose it or leave it somewhere, a person with a conscience and a kind heart can return it to you. (You may also want to add the word "Reward" to the sticker.)

Tipping

Based on advice from several travel experts, we came up with a few tipping guidelines. These ranges are generally accepted, with the exception of an unusual circumstance that requires someone doing something above and beyond his/her job description—for example, a cab driver brings your luggage into the hotel...a waiter packs your leftover food in a doggie bag...a maid gives you extra towels or soap. In that situation, show your gratitude by tipping an amount that would make you happy if you were the person being tipped.

Here are tipping ranges for some common travel services...

- **Airport porter or skycap**—$1 to $2 (or the equivalent in foreign currency) per bag.

- **Taxi, limo, shuttle or van driver**—15% of the total fare.

- **Valet parking attendant**—$1 to $2.

- **Driver of a courtesy shuttle**—$1 to $2 (or the equivalent in foreign currency) per bag if he/she helps with the bags.

- **Hotel doorman**—Opening the door, nothing.
  - If the doorman brings your luggage into the hotel, $1 to $2 (or the equivalent in foreign currency) per bag.
  - If the doorman hails you a cab, $1 to $2 (or the equivalent in foreign currency).

- **Bellman**—Taking your bags to your room, $1 to $2 (or the equivalent in foreign currency) per bag.

- **Hotel maid**—$2 to $5 (or the equivalent in foreign currency) per night. Tip daily because maids often rotate. Put the money in an envelope marked "Housekeeping" and leave it on your pillow.

- **Tour guides**—Check with the tour company to see if the tip is already included. If not, give 10% to 15% of the tour price.

- **Restaurant tipping**—Food server, 15% to 20% of the food bill (before tax)…coat check, $1 (or the equivalent in foreign currency)…cocktail service, 15% to 20%…maître d', nothing unless he seats you when the restaurant is full and you didn't have a reservation—then give him at least $10 (or the equivalent in foreign currency)…wine steward, 10% of the wine bill (before tax)…restroom attendant, $1 (or the equivalent in foreign currency).

Be aware that in many European and Asian countries, the tip is included in the lunch and/or dinner bill.

Invaluable Tipping Tip!

When tipping, be prepared. Have lots of singles (or the equivalent in foreign currency) handy. Giving the exact tip amount is easier than asking someone to make change.

Hotels

As soon as you arrive at your hotel, take a matchbook…or a piece of hotel stationery…or a pen that has the hotel's address and telephone number on it, and throw the item in your pocket or purse.

Once you leave the hotel, if you need to contact the front desk for any reason, you can just look at the matchbook, stationery or pen and get assistance.

TRAVEL SAFETY

Knowledge is power! Before you leave home, contact the US Department of Transportation (*www.dot.gov/citizen_services/index.html* or 202-366-4000), a government agency that provides travel warnings and safety alerts for domestic and international travel. You can also contact another agency, the National Transportation Safety Board (*www.ntsb.gov* or 202-314-6000), to find out if there have been any accident reports or travel delays issued for your flight, train, highway route or cruise.

If you are traveling outside of the United States, research the areas you plan to visit (and *see* page 287 for detailed safety information). There are tourist guidebooks available for just about every place on Earth, and there are Web sites that have all the information you will need to have a safe journey.

So don't be lazy—do your homework before you walk out the door. And ALWAYS put safety first. *In the meantime, here are some other ways to stay safe…*

Money Smarts

If you're in the habit of keeping your wallet in your pants pocket—don't! It's much safer to carry your wallet or billfold in a jacket's breast pocket. (This is a good idea even if you don't travel outside of your hometown.)

Prevent Hotel Break-ins

Pack a small rubber doorstop in your bag. Once you're in your hotel room for the night, lock the door and wedge the doorstop under your room door from the inside. It may give you peace of mind and a better night's sleep.

Safer Water Bottle

When on vacation, touring and sightseeing, it's common for people to take along a bottle of drinking water, especially during hot weather. Fine—good idea.

What's *not* a good idea is to keep refilling the same water bottle. In fact, it's a terrible idea! According to the International Bottled Water Association (*www.bottledwater.org*) most plastic water bottles are not intended for multiple uses. The necks of the bottles are too small for soap and water to thoroughly clean them. Bacteria thrive in these made-to-be-disposed-of bottles.

Also, these bottles are not designed to stand up to commercial dishwashing. The heat, and even the detergents, used to wash the bottles can degrade the plastic and cause chemicals to leach out into the water you drink. Some of those chemicals may be carcinogenic.

It's important to start every day with a new bottle of water, keep it away from direct sunlight and discard it at the end of the day. Or, you can get a sturdy, *high-density polyethylene* (HDPE) bottle, the kind you can buy at a sporting goods or outdoor store (Nalgene is a good brand).

These bottles are meant to be reused, they can be easily washed, and they are not affected by the sun's heat nor by hot water and detergents.

Let There Be Light

If you wake up in the middle of the night to go to the bathroom, it can be confusing or just plain scary to be in a strange room in the dark. Before you leave home, pack a nightlight and/or a flashlight. Plug in the nightlight before you go to bed, and keep the flashlight on the night table next to the bed.

You *Can* Take It with You!

If you're traveling abroad, remember to take all the equipment—batteries, adapter, transformer or converter—needed for your electrical items. Most foreign countries use different types of currents.

Common Sense

◆ When traveling abroad or in touristy sightseeing areas, keep a low profile. Do not wear expensive or ostentatious clothes and jewelry, and don't flash around a stuffed billfold.

◆ Before you venture out, talk to the hotel concierge about the city, and ask him/her which areas are unsafe for tourists.

AIRLINE TRAVEL

According to the Transportation Security Administration (*www.tsa.gov*), air travel in the United States has never been safer. Besides continually bolstering security at the nation's airports, the TSA is always looking for ways to refine processes that improve customer service at checkpoints.

Visit the TSA on-line for up-to-date rules and information about items that are allowed and those that are prohibited on board aircraft. Their site also has details about transporting special items and other travel considerations. *But first read the rest of this section to help you prepare for your flight…*

Luggage Allowances

Regulations regarding allowable luggage size and weight may vary with each airline. Most carriers allow only 2 carry-on bags, and they may charge extra for oversized luggage (generally, anything weighing more than 50 pounds).

Always contact the airline (or check its Web site) before your trip to confirm its specific luggage guidelines.

Better Packing

◆ Do not wrap gifts before you leave. Chances are, the packages will be torn open when your bags go through airport security.

Instead, measure, cut and pack wrapping paper and ribbon, along with a roll of transparent tape. Or buy those items at your destination.

◆ If you're traveling by plane, leave some room at the top of each bottle (of lotion, tonic, cough syrup, shampoo, etc.) you pack. Changes in air pressure may make contents expand, causing a leak in a bottle that is filled to the brim.

◆ Be sure to pack in your carry-on bag all medications, an extra pair of glasses, a change of clothes and anything else you might need for health or emergency reasons.

Share a Suitcase
If you're traveling with your mate, family or friend(s), pack a change of clothes in someone else's suitcase and pack an outfit of theirs in your suitcase. That way, if one of your suitcases gets lost, you'll each still have something to wear.

Luggage Identification

◆ Make your luggage easy to spot. Tie a stand-out ribbon (a loud plaid or a Disney print) or a piece of brightly colored, braided wool around the handle.

Or, wrap glow-in-the-dark electrical tape around the handle. Not only will it be easy for you to identify your luggage, but if someone takes it by mistake, he/she should

see the ribbon, wool or tape and realize that it's not his.

◆ Name tags on the outside of luggage can fall off. Airline personnel know to check inside lost luggage for identification information. For that reason, put an index card with your name, address and home and cell phone numbers in a small plastic bag and pack it in your suitcase. You may also want to include the contact information at your destination.

You may also want to include the name and number of a relative or friend who is not traveling with you—it should be someone who can be contacted in case your luggage is found and you can't be reached. You know, the "hometown contact" we mentioned in "Copy Credit Cards and Personal Documents" (*see* page 280)…the person who also has your personal information and travel itinerary. (Of course, check with him/her first to make sure it's OK to put personal information in your luggage.)

More Comfortable Airplane Travel

◆ Request seats over the wing, and you will enjoy the least bumpy ride on the plane. Also, the exit seats located over the wing have extra legroom. To sit in exit-row seats, you must meet Federal Aviation Administration (FAA) criteria—be over the age of 15, able-bodied and able to lift at least 50 pounds, so that you can assist passengers and crew in the event of an emergency.

NOTE: For comfort, avoid seats that are in front of exit rows—for safety reasons, they do not recline.

Seats located behind *bulkheads* (the partitions that divide the plane into compartments) also offer plenty of legroom. The downside is that on some planes, these seats are often close to the food/drink station and restrooms, which can be busy, crowded and/or noisy.

The safest seat? According to a study by the aircraft manufacturer Boeing, there is no evidence that any single part of an aircraft is safer than another.

To get the seats you want, check the airline's seating chart before making your reservation. Select and request specific seat numbers. When placing the reservation, check and recheck to make sure you are asking for the exact seat(s) you want. It often helps to book your reservation as early as possible, before the seat(s) are taken. Also, a great on-line source for seating details is *www.seatguru.com*.

◆ If you are traveling with a baby, during take-off and landing, feed him/her a bottle of his favorite drink. The constant swallowing can help equalize ear pressure, making the baby more comfortable…which will make you more comfortable…and make everyone around you more comfortable.

◆ Ladies, save the high heels for dinner parties, night clubs or the office—not for airplane travel. Chances are that you will never have to exit via the emergency slide, but if you do, high heels can be a real impediment.

Heels can also be impractical when going through airport security checkpoints or if you have to make a quick connection between flights. Wear flat-soled, slip-on shoes to get around quicker and easier.

Water on Airplanes

The US Environmental Protection Agency (EPA), which is responsible for water quality, conducted tests on airline drinking water. According to their findings, water on airplanes may be contaminated with harmful bacteria.

The agency said that it would take steps to improve the situation, but until it does, it's important to avoid anything dangerous that you may potentially be exposed to on planes. *And be aware of these suggestions…*

◆ Bring your own water with you in a clean, *high-density polyethylene* (HDPE) bottle—the kind sold at sporting goods or outdoor stores (Nalgene is a good brand).

◆ If you don't bring your own water onboard, ask the flight attendants if they have commercially bottled water. If that's not available, ask for sparkling water, seltzer or club soda.

✳ Quench Your Thirst

It is said that the air in the cabin of an airplane is drier than any of the world's deserts. That being the case, it's extremely important to keep hydrating yourself…wisely.

A sensible guideline is to drink an 8-ounce cup of water for each hour of air travel.

◆ Avoid airline drinks that must be made with water, such as coffee, tea and lemonade. And, for the drink that you do choose, ask whether the airline makes its own ice cubes onboard. (Many airlines get ice elsewhere…from safe sources—but it's important to ask.)

FOREIGN TRAVEL

You are about to embark on an adventure, leaving your home soil. *With that in mind, here are some profound thoughts and advice from fellow international travelers…*

◆ **James Michener** (American author)—"If you reject the food, ignore the customs, fear the religion and avoid the people, you might better stay home."

◆ **Seneca** (ancient Roman philosopher, dramatist and statesman)—"Travel and change of place impart new vigor to the mind."

◆ **St. Augustine** (1st-century bishop)—"The world is a book, and those who do not travel read only a page."

◆ **William Least Heat-Moon** (Native American author)—"When you're traveling, you are what you are right there and then. People don't have your past to hold against you. No yesterdays on the road."

We wish you a safe, happy and memorable trip and hope that the following information helps you every step of the way…

International Travel Warnings

◆ Before you travel abroad, check the Web site of the US Department of State, the Bureau of Consular Affairs, at *http://travel.state.gov*. It lists conditions abroad that might affect your safety and security.

The Web site also offers several links to requirements for Americans traveling overseas, including information on passports, visas, immunizations and other medical information.

If you don't have access to the Internet, you can call American Citizen Services at 888-407-4747 to obtain more information.

◆ The Association for Safe International Road Travel (ASIRT) is a nonprofit, humanitarian organization that provides travelers with reports on road safety and driving conditions in more than 150 foreign countries.

Take advantage of this incredible service by calling ASIRT at 301-983-5252, or visiting their Web site, *www.asirt.org*.

US Representatives

When you arrive in a foreign city, find out the location and telephone number of the closest US embassy (*www.americanembassy.com*), consulate or mission. Contact the American Embassy for the names and numbers of English-speaking doctors and of the best local hospitals. Keep the information handy in case of emergency.

Electrical Appliances

Most foreign countries use a different type of electricity. So, when you're traveling outside the US and you're taking along electrical appliances, you will probably need some or all of the following…

◆ Plug adapters
◆ Transformer
◆ Converter
◆ Batteries
◆ Rechargeable batteries
◆ Battery charger

Chances are, a good guidebook for the country you plan to visit has specific information. But double-check with the country's official visitors' site, your travel agent or an electrical-supply store.

Money

◆ Before you leave home, exchange some of your cash for the currency of the foreign country you're going to visit. But do not use an international airport's bank or currency exchange window if you don't have to. They are hangouts for thieves who are watching and waiting for tourists to exchange big bucks.

Thomas Cook, authorized dealers in foreign currency exchange, has more than 50 locations throughout the world. Chances are, no matter what your foreign exchange need is, you'll find help at a Thomas Cook location. For more information, visit *www. thomascook.com.*

◆ Exchange rates fluctuate. The only way to know if you are getting the best exchange rate is to know what the *current* currency rate is. You can do that by visiting the Universal Currency Converter at *www.xe.com/ucc/*—it has up-to-date rates and information.

◆ If you are going to travel to several countries and encounter more than 1 foreign currency, pack a few resealable plastic bags in your handbag or travel kit. Assign a plastic bag to each currency so that the currency of 1 country doesn't get mixed in with the currency of another country. By keeping each currency separate, you will eliminate the chances of currency confusion.

Water and Food Precautions

Contaminated drinking water is the leading cause of health problems for travelers. Bacteria, such as *E. coli, cholera* and *salmonella,* are most often responsible for water-borne illnesses, and they can cause anything from a mild upset stomach to a serious (even fatal) bacterial disease.

Therefore, DO NOT take any chances. Instead, take every precaution possible. When you're traveling outside of the US, drink only bottled beverages. If you have a stove or hot plate, drink water after it has been boiled for 3 to 5 minutes. Remember that ice cubes made with local tap water can also be contaminated. Play it safe and do not drink anything that contains ice cubes.

While you're at it, eat only fruits that you yourself peel, and order only well-cooked foods.

Pack Washcloths

If you are traveling outside of the US, bring along a package of disposable cloths (like Handi-Wipes) just in case your hotel, motel, bed-and-breakfast or castle doesn't provide washcloths. You may be surprised to find that many places don't offer this amenity—simply because it's not part of their culture.

Also, be sure to bring along liquid hand sanitizers and/or sanitary wipes to keep hands clean while flying or sightseeing.

Contact Lens Caution

When traveling out of the country, be sure to bring your own sterile contact solution and eyedrops. You do not want your contact lenses anywhere near tap water—especially water that might be contaminated.

HOME AGAIN!

You've just come home after a wonderful vacation. You check your snail mail, your e-mail and your phone messages. You water your plants and then relax a little. After grabbing something to eat, you start to unpack. Once that's done, you're ready to put away the luggage. *Phew!*

All that for this tip—toss a fabric softener sheet into each piece of luggage before you store it away. This will leave a fresh, clean smell for the next time you use it.

So when's the next vacation? ■

■ Products ■

We found so many clever, magical products that make travel safer and more efficient than ever before that we almost want to jump on a plane ourselves!

We surveyed many products and found that, unlike our other chapters, we can recommend 1-stop catalog shopping. Magellan's offers a wide array of travel products—really, everything you can think of…and some you probably hadn't thought of. We especially suggest that you look at the variety of personal security pouches in which you can stash your valuables.

Here are some other favorite Magellan products that will help you travel well…

EarPlanes

Avoid that awful pain in the ear with these ear filters, tested by US Navy pilots. They relieve air-pressure discomfort and reduce harsh noise naturally, without drugs. They are safe, soft, made of hypoallergenic silicone and disposable.

Children suffer the most from ear pain caused by changes in cabin pressure. EarPlanes are available for children from 1 to 10 years of age, as well as for adults.

EarPlanes are also good for elevator rides in high-rise buildings!

No-Jet-Lag

This product gets great reviews. Our favorite comment—"No jet-lag. No kidding." This natural, homeopathic product has been proven effective for all the symptoms of jet lag, including sleeplessness.

It's safe for all ages, can be used with other medications and has no side effects. Each packet contains 32 pleasant-tasting chewable tablets—enough for about 450 hours of flying time.

Also available at some drugstores and on-line.

Ultra Soles

Ultrathin soles protect your feet from athlete's foot, fungi, mold and other bacteria, as well as from sharp objects. Use the soles anywhere you don't want to walk barefoot while traveling, like the cabin of an airplane or a hotel hallway.

They also help prevent potential slips in hotel showers, campground facilities or any other damp/moist surfaces.

SteriPEN

The money you will save on bottled water will pay for this product tenfold. SteriPEN is a portable water purifier that uses proven ultraviolet (UV) technology to kill viruses (such as *hepatitis* and *poliovirus*), protozoa and bacteria (including *E. coli* and *salmonella*). Purifies up to 16 ounces of water at a time. Easy to use and lightweight. Requires 4 AA batteries.

Source: Magellan's, 800-962-4943, *www.magellans.com*.

Door-Jamming Alarm Security Bar

Wedge this anti-break-in device under almost any doorknob. If the door opens, a loud siren goes off—this sound alerts you and most likely scares off the intruder. It takes a 9-volt battery (not included).

This alarm is great for travellers who want to feel more secure in a hotel or motel room.

Source: Improvements, 800-634-9484, *www.improvementscatalog.com*.

CHAPTER 12

Our Favorite Folk Remedies

You may wonder—what's a health chapter doing in a book of household hints? Well, we believe that the most important part of any home is the people who live there. You can't take care of your house and physical surroundings if you haven't taken care of yourself—and the people you love—first.

We're providing a collection of practical, safe and effective health remedies that are easy and simple enough to use every day—and many of the necessary ingredients can be found in your kitchen. In this section, we've included old and new ways to help you feel better physically and emotionally, organized by condition in alphabetical order.

We've been collecting folk remedies for more than 2 decades. And where do we get them? From *folks*, of course! Can you trust that they're safe? All of the remedies we share with our readers have been reviewed (for safety) by a medical doctor. Do we know that these remedies work? Well, they worked for the people who shared them with us—so we're hoping they'll work for you, too.

We do, however, caution you to heed the CAUTION at right…really!

CAUTION: Before you use any of these remedies to treat yourself or somebody else, please check with your health care professional. This is *extremely important* if you have ANY existing health problems, including—but not limited to—cancer, liver or kidney disease, diabetes, high blood pressure, ulcers, bleeding disorders or a compromised immune system.

Even natural remedies can have side effects, so if you notice a reaction after trying a particular treatment, stop using it immediately and consult your doctor. If you have allergies, be very careful about ingesting any of the foods and/or herbs that are recommended, or applying certain topical treatments—for example, ingesting royal jelly or applying honey can cause a serious reaction if you are allergic to bee venom.

Also, if you are taking any medications —including prescription and/or over-the-counter drugs, vitamins or other homeopathic remedies—be aware that certain herbs or natural treatments may interact with them. If you notice any kind of reaction, stop using the remedy immediately.

So, if we haven't stressed it enough— just to be on the super-safe side, be careful and *consult your doctor before trying any of these treatments.*

CONDITIONS A TO Z

Acne

At least 3 out of every 4 people in the US have had acne at some point in their lives, making it the most common skin disease. The myth is that it's caused by dirt. In fact, acne is a disorder caused by the action of hormones on the skin's oil glands (sebaceous glands), which leads to plugged pores and outbreaks of lesions (pimples).

According to the American Academy of Dermatology (*www.aad.org*), frequent washing does nothing to prevent these outbreaks. Over-washing is actually irritating, and excess irritation can worsen acne. A washcloth can aggravate this situation further. So use your bare hands to wash gently, and only wash twice a day.

Here are some suggestions to help clear up the condition...

◆ First, wash your face with a mild soap—as it removes dirt, oil, makeup, sunscreen and/or moisturizer, it will not remove your skin's natural *acid mantle*—the protective layer on your skin's surface.

Mix the juice of an average-sized lemon (about 2½ tablespoons) with 1 teaspoon of dark brown sugar. Then gently apply the mixture all over your face. Let it stay that way for 20 minutes. Rinse with lukewarm water and pat dry. Do this twice a day for at least 2 weeks, and you should see the acne clear up.

◆ To speed the healing along, mix 1 tablespoon of honey with 1 tablespoon of unfiltered apple cider vinegar (available at health-food stores) in 1 cup of hot water. It may be tough to do, but try to drink this solution 2 to 3 times a day.

★ Powerful Pimple Prevention

To prevent acne, moisten a cotton ball with some unfiltered apple cider vinegar (available at health-food stores) and dab it on. Do this after a shower or washing your face with mild soap or another gentle cleanser. *Be careful not to get any of the vinegar in your eyes!*

Excessive cleansing can destroy your skin's acid mantle—the oily layer on the skin's surface that protects the skin from bacteria and other environmental impurities. Vinegar helps restore the skin's natural pH balance (the acid mantle) while it acts as an astringent to help tighten your skin's connective tissues.

In just a few days, your complexion should look healthier.

Allergies

If you have a runny nose, sore throat and/or itchy eyes, you may be suffering from seasonal allergies. These allergies generally occur when your body overreacts to the pollen from trees, weeds, flowers or crops.

When the pollen count is sky-high and you dread going outside, dab the inside of your nostrils with a little sesame oil. It can help stop the irritation and allergic reaction that is caused by breathing in environmental or seasonal allergens.

Arthritis

According to the US Centers for Disease Control and Prevention in Atlanta (*www.cdc.gov*), arthritis is among the leading diseases in the United States. Approximately 70 million Americans are affected by arthritis—which has over 100 different forms. *Arthritis* is actually a catchall term that refers to many types of inflammation of (and pain in) the joints.

Here are some remedies that could help spell *r-e-l-i-e-f*...

◆ Eat a serving of gelatin daily, either sugar or sugar-free. The amino acids are believed to help restore cartilage and make a difference in the flexibility of your joints. It takes time—about 3 months—to notice an improvement, so try to stick with it.

◆ Check your jars of mustard and curry and you will see that turmeric is 1 of the ingredients. Turmeric has been used for centuries in India for its healing properties. The herb's inflammation-fighting compounds are now recognized and being researched.

For joint pain, the recommended dosage is 400 to 600 milligrams (mg) of turmeric capsules (containing 95% curcumin), taken 3 times a day. Or you can take ½ to 1 teaspoon of turmeric liquid extract, mixed into ½ cup of water, 3 times a day. You should feel better within a week.

If there is no improvement after a week, then it may not help relieve your joint pain. Take comfort in knowing that turmeric has excellent antioxidant, disease-fighting properties and is good for your digestion.

◆ Bruce Fife, ND, director of the Coconut Research Center in Colorado Springs, Colorado (*www.coconutresearchcenter.org*) and author of *Coconut Cures* (Piccadilly Books), uses turmeric in the following ginger-tea recipe to restore health to joints affected by rheumatoid arthritis. Use as much fresh ginger (available in the produce section of most supermarkets and grocery stores) as you like. In fact, the more ginger, the better—it helps to reduce inflammation.

Bring ½ cup of water to a boil. Cut the ginger into thin slices, add them to the hot water and simmer for 5 minutes. Remove the pan from the heat and discard the ginger. Stir ¼ teaspoon of powdered turmeric and 1 tablespoon of unflavored gelatin into the water. Add 1 tablespoon of coconut oil, and continue to stir until the gelatin is dissolved. Then add ½ to 1 cup of calcium-enriched orange juice. Drink this tea once or twice a day.

◆ Mix 1 tablespoon of unfiltered apple cider vinegar (available at health-food stores) in an 8-ounce glass of water, and drink it 2 or 3 times a day. Give it a fair chance to work—at least a week or so.

As a bonus, the apple cider vinegar may also help you lose weight, but be careful because too much vinegar can cause gastritis or heartburn.

According to the Johns Hopkins Arthritis Center in Baltimore, joint pain is strongly associated with body weight. Being just 10 pounds overweight increases the force on the knee by 30 to 60 pounds with each step.

Go to the "Weight Control" section on pages 325–329—you'll find suggestions for taking a load off your feet, your knees, your back…you get the picture.

> ☎ **FYI: Lighten Arthritis Pain**
> The results of a recent study suggest that losing weight, even just 1 pound, can slow the progression of arthritis. When participants in the study lost weight, it made walking a lot less painful. For each pound they lost, they enjoyed a 4-pound reduction in the force on their knees.

Asthma

During an asthma attack, bronchial tubes narrow and secrete an excess of mucus, making it very hard to breathe. Asthma in certain people may be attributed to exercise, allergies or emotional problems—or possibly a combination of all of these factors.

> ⚡ **CAUTION:** Asthma is a serious condition, and it can be fatal if left untreated. If someone is having an asthma attack and cannot breathe, DO NOT try these remedies—call 911 and get him/her to the emergency room.

But there are encouraging words from Isaac Eliaz, MD, director of the Amitabha Medical Clinic in Sebastopol, California (*www.amit abhaclinic.com*). He says that at least 99% of the more than 17 million Americans with asthma can lead symptom-free lives without taking a ton of medication. *To help you do that, here are the doctor's recommendations...*

◆ *Pycnogenol* is a pine-tree extract that contains a potent anti-inflammatory, which can help prevent airway-narrowing inflammation. In a clinical trial, subjects who used pycnogenol showed improvement in how easily they could breathe. The dose used in the study was 250 milligrams (mg), 3 times a day. Pycnogenol is available in health-food stores.

◆ Eat an apple a day—with the skin—and you will get the fruit's rich supply of lung-nourishing *flavonoids*. According to British research, eating an apple daily could reduce the risk of an asthma attack by 20%.

◆ If you drink soy milk, stop for a few weeks and see if your asthma flare-ups subside. The results of an Australian study showed that soy-milk drinkers had more wheezing and full-blown asthma attacks than those who did not drink soy milk.

Genetically modified soy milk that has a high sugar content may increase inflammation in airways, causing spasms when exposed to irritants, such as pollen and mold.

◆ For just 20 minutes a day, meditate, visualize, do yoga or another relaxing activity—anything that will have you breathing slowly and deeply.

According to Dr. Eliaz, breathing this way helps when asthma attacks strike. Deep breathing calms the nervous system, preventing the airway spasms that trigger asthma attacks in the first place.

For a helpful breathing exercise, *see* "Deep-Breathing Exercise for Hypertension" on page 312.

Back Pain

It is estimated that 8 out of 10 people have, at some point in their lives, experienced disabling back pain. Also estimated is the amount spent for the diagnosis and treatment of back pain— more than $5 billion annually.

A simple acupressure massage can relieve stress-induced back pain instantly by triggering the reflexology point that is linked to the spine. Apply firm pressure from the big toe of your left foot, along the inner sole, all the way down to the heel. Then do the same thing on your right foot. There now...feel better?

> **CAUTION:** It's extremely important that any back pain be evaluated by a medical professional to rule out serious illness or injury. If your back pain is chronic, persistent or severe, see a doctor.

Bad Breath, Gum Disease And Toothaches

Natural remedies can help ease the pain of a toothache and, in some cases, alleviate problems caused by nervous tension and low-grade infections. But since it is difficult to know what is causing mouth problems, make an appointment to see your dentist as soon as possible. More important, have the dentist see your teeth and gums.

◆ Coconut oil kills germs that cause bad breath, tooth decay and gum disease, according to Bruce Fife, ND, director of the Coconut Research Center in Colorado Springs, Colorado (*www.coconutresearchcenter.org*) and author of several books, including *The Coconut Oil Miracle* (Avery).

Brush your teeth daily using a mixture of ⅛ teaspoon of baking soda and

½ teaspoon of organic extra virgin coconut oil (available at health-food stores).

◆ If your gums feel sore, massaging them with coconut oil should bring relief.

Bladder Infection

Also *see* "Urinary Problems" on page 324.

The most common *symptoms* of a bladder infection or urinary tract infection (UTI) are...

◆ Frequent urination
◆ Strong, painful urge to urinate
◆ Pain or burning when urinating
◆ Foul-smelling or bloody urine
◆ Fever (with a moderate to severe bladder infection)

The most common *causes* of bladder infections are...

◆ Holding in urine
◆ Constipation
◆ Improper wiping
◆ Exposure to irritating substances, such as soap and bubble baths

> **CAUTION:** If you think you have a bladder infection or UTI, it's very important to check with your health-care professional before trying any of the following remedies.

◆ Put 1 teaspoon of olive oil and 1 teaspoon of finely minced garlic into a glass of warm water and drink it 3 times a day, before meals. These three glasses a day should help destroy the bacteria that's causing the bladder infection.

◆ Chop 1 large onion. Put the onion in a pot with 2 cups of regular milk, and boil it down

to 1 cup. Strain out the onion pieces and drink ½ cup of the onion milk. Four hours later, drink the other ½ cup.

> **NOTE:** When you have a bladder infection, *do not* drink carbonated beverages and stay away from salty and rich foods. Keep it simple—broth, salad, fruit. Also, drinking 100% cranberry juice can help relieve and prevent bladder infections.

★ Blueberries Help Bladders

A study conducted at Rutgers University in New Jersey found that eating a handful of blueberries daily may help prevent bladder infections. This is because blueberries contain a polymeric compound that keeps bacteria from sticking to the bladder wall.

Blisters

A blister is a local swelling of the skin that contains watery fluid. Resist the urge to pop it because you run the risk of infection.

If the blister is open and oozing, that means there is an infection present. Apply antibiotic ointment and—if it gets worse—get professional medical attention as soon as you possibly can.

◆ If the blister is open and *not* infected, cover it with a bandage during the day and take off the bandage when you go to bed. Let the blister dry out.

◆ If the blister is intact, but it's still painful, soak your foot in regular cold milk to reduce the pain and swelling. You can also apply a cold compress (for 10 minutes at a time) to relieve the inflammation.

★ Keep Things Slick

To prevent blisters, apply any type of antiperspirant to the bottom of your feet before you go jogging or hiking. The antiperspirant should prevent the friction that causes blisters.

You can also use other types of lubricants to prevent blisters, such as petroleum jelly (available at drugstores) and BodyGlide (available at sporting goods stores).

Blood Cleanser

Ben Kim, DC, a chiropractor in practice in Barrie, Ontario (*www.drbenkim.com*), promotes the benefits of seaweed as an excellent blood cleanser, believed to support optimal brain function.

■ Recipe ■

Here is Dr. Kim's family recipe for a traditional Korean seaweed soup...

Mi-Yuk Gook

> 1 package of dried seaweed* (1 ounce is enough for 4 servings)
> 6 cups of vegetable broth or organic chicken broth
> 2 teaspoons of sesame oil
> naturally brewed soy sauce or sea salt, to taste
> 1 teaspoon of garlic, minced (optional)

1. Soak the seaweed in water for 2 hours or until soft. Drain and rinse really well, as dried seaweed can come with a lot of dirt, just like spinach.

2. Put all ingredients, including seaweed, into a large pot and bring to a boil, then simmer for 5 minutes to allow all the flavors to come together.

Koreans traditionally enjoy this seaweed soup with a bowl of white or brown rice—sometimes together in the same bowl.

*If you buy the seaweed in a Korean market, ask for 1 package of seaweed for soup. If you shop at a health-food store, buy 1 package of nori seaweed.

Brain Boosters

The adult human brain is about the size of 2 clenched, average-sized adult fists...it weighs approximately 3 pounds...and has about 1 million individual neurons or nerve cells—give or take a few.

The brain is an incredible organ with an almost infinite capacity for storing information. Recalling that information is another story, though. *Here are some suggestions to banish brain-fog moments, sharpen your focus and be on high alert when you need to be...*

◆ Jump-start your day *hydrotherapeutically.* That's a fancy way of saying—take a shower! Begin with warm water, then make it hotter for 10 seconds (not *burning* hot), then cold again for another 10 seconds, then hot again for another 10 seconds. (Do you notice a pattern forming here?) Repeat the hot/cold cycles 5 times.

Hot water dilates blood vessels for a circulation surge...cold water constricts blood vessels for a slowdown in circulation. This switching act revs up the morning's sluggish blood flow, sending oxygen to the brain, which should make you more alert and focused for the rest of the day.

◆ If you are right-handed, brush your teeth with your left hand, and if you're left-handed...well, you know. This challenging little exercise stimulates the nondominant side of your brain and encourages it to develop new nerve-cell connections.

If you really want to pack on those new nerve-cell connections, do a crossword puzzle with your nondominant hand. In no time, you'll be wanting to know when *Jeopardy!* will be holding auditions in your area.

◆ Breakfast is the most important meal of the day when it comes to being your sharpest for work, school, a meeting, an interview—or as a contestant on *Jeopardy!* Researchers find that people score higher on thinking tests when they eat the right breakfast foods.

A study conducted at Tufts University in Boston proved that children who ate instant oatmeal for breakfast the day of testing performed significantly better on tests of short-term memory, spatial memory and listening skills than those who ate either cold cereal or no breakfast.

The Tufts' scientists believe that the high fiber and protein content in oatmeal helps to slow down digestion, which promotes a slower and more sustained release of *glucose* (a simple sugar that is the body's main source of energy) into the bloodstream.

The controlled release of glucose seems to influence the way the brain uses it, especially when it comes to memory performance. So, maximize mental function starting with breakfast—preferably oatmeal.

◆ People who take a daily B-complex supplement tend to be more alert and less affected by stress throughout the day. Be sure to follow the recommended dosage on the label. *Consider the contents and value of the B-complex components...*

  ◆ Vitamin B-1 (thiamine) is used by the brain to help convert glucose (blood sugar) into fuel. Without it, the brain rapidly runs out of energy.

  ◆ Vitamin B-3 (niacin) deficiency can produce agitation as well as anxiety, as well as mental and physical slowness.

  ◆ Vitamin B-5 (pantothenic acid) is needed for hormone formation as well as the uptake of amino acids plus the brain chemical acetylcholine, which combine to prevent certain types of depression.

  ◆ Vitamin B-6 (pyridoxine) is needed for the manufacture of serotonin, melatonin and dopamine—hormones that promote a sense of well-being.

  ◆ Vitamin B-12 is important in the formation of red blood cells. A deficiency may lead to an oxygen-transport problem known as *pernicious anemia*. This disorder can cause

mood swings, paranoia, irritability, confusion, dementia, hallucinations or mania, eventually followed by appetite loss, dizziness, weakness, shortage of breath, heart palpitations, diarrhea and tingling sensations in the extremities.

◆ Folic acid is necessary for the production of SAMe (S-adenosyl methionine), a powerful nutrient that helps prevent depression.

◆ When you learn something new, go to sleep for several hours right afterward, instead of staying awake and practicing or studying whatever you learned. Researchers at the Harvard Medical School in Boston found that you will remember your new facts better after you awaken.

◆ When you need on-the-spot smarts, put your index finger on the *Renzhong* (the acupressure point in the middle of your *philtrum*, which is the spot between your nose and upper lip). Press in and try to stay that way for 30 seconds.

◆ Maybe allergies or smog or too little sleep is making you feel as though you're struggling to think straight. If so, put a golf ball between your palms and roll it around, massaging your *adrenal reflex areas*—they are located halfway down the long first metacarpal bones of the hands below the thumbs.

Reflexologists believe that there are reflexes on the hands (and feet) that correspond to all parts of the body. Stimulation of the appropriate reflexes can activate the body's own natural healing system. This reflexology exercise ought to clear out the cobwebs.

◆ Hold your breath as long as you can without turning blue. Studies show that taking in extra oxygen, like when you're preparing to hold your breath, gives you a burst of energy and will boost your alertness by 60%.

◆ Alan R. Hirsch, MD, director of The Smell and Taste Treatment and Research Foundation in Chicago (*www.smellandtaste.org*), says that the distinctive smell and taste of butterscotch instantly switches the brain back to the moment it first absorbed new information, making it easier to recall facts.

So, eat butterscotch candy when you're learning new information and when you need to get the data from the "tip of your tongue."

◆ Snack on walnuts, a super brain food. They are rich in omega-3 fatty acids…and great for heart health, too.

◆ If you have to think on your feet, grab a handful of raw pumpkin seeds. *Tyrosine*, an amino acid found in pumpkin seeds, helps your mind work like a well-oiled machine.

◆ If accuracy counts, surround yourself with a citrus scent. Suck on a lemon drop, or put a couple of drops of lemon oil on a cotton ball and put it in your work space. Studies have shown that workers exposed to the smell of lemon made 50% fewer errors.

◆ Eat blueberries to keep your memory sharp. Researchers at Tufts University in Boston found that *anthocyanin*, the chemical in blueberries that gives them their beautiful blue color, also encourages the growth of new brain cells.

◆ Color consultant Leatrice Eiseman (*www.colorexpert.com*) suggests keeping purple in your line of sight. If you use a computer, make the color purple part of your desktop, wallpaper or screen saver. Accessorize any work area with shades of purple.

The regal color combines the energy and excitement of red with the confidence and serenity of blue. The result is a calming influence and an alert, active mind.

◆ Eating certain fatty fish—such as salmon, tuna, halibut, mackerel, herring or sardines—is believed to keep your mind agile. It will improve memory, hand–eye coordination and high-level problem solving. Fish is also said to lessen anger, hostility, cynicism and mistrust. Eat fish 2 or more times a week to get those brain-boosting omega-3 fatty acids.

CAUTION: Some types of fish contain dangerous levels of mercury or other contaminants that can be toxic when consumed in high quantities. With this in mind, the Food and Drug Administration (FDA) and the Environmental Protection Agency (EPA) have issued guidelines for consumption—especially for women who are pregnant (or who may become pregnant), nursing mothers and young children.

The FDA suggests that women and young children eat no more than 12 ounces (2 average meals) per week of a variety of fish and shellfish that are lower in mercury.

Certain fish—including shrimp, tilapia, salmon, pollock and catfish—generally contain low levels of mercury. Fish such as shark, swordfish, king mackerel and tilefish tend to have higher levels, and should not be consumed as often.

For more information, visit the FDA food safety Web site at *www.cfsan.fda.gov/~frf/sea-mehg.html* or the EPA Web site at *www.epa.gov/ost/fish/*.

◆ Make exercise more fun by working out to music—you'll also make it easier to organize your thoughts and heighten your alertness.

According to a study conducted by Charles Emery, PhD, professor of psychology at Ohio State University in Columbus, subjects who worked out on a treadmill while listening to music (such as Vivaldi's *The Four Seasons*) scored significantly higher on a test of verbal fluency. It was shown that an exercise/music combination stimulates the brain's *cortical region*, the seat of logic and analytical thinking.

Breast-feeding

Breast-feeding helps to protect your baby from developing gastrointestinal trouble, respiratory problems, ear infections and allergies. Nursing your baby for at least 6 months may also boost your child's intelligence, and protect him/her against obesity later in life.

You may know all of that already, but do you know that breast-feeding also benefits *you* in many ways? It helps the nursing mother lose weight, lower her stress levels and reduce post-partum bleeding, may reduce her risk of developing some types of cancer and may protect her against osteoporosis later in life. *If you are breast-feeding, here is valuable information…*

According to Ben Kim, DC, a chiropractor in practice in Barrie, Ontario (*www.drben kim.com*), "Seaweed is amazingly effective at stimulating healthy breast-milk production in nursing moms." Dr. Kim advises women to eat seaweed soup during pregnancy and the nursing period as a virtual guarantee of healthy breast-milk production.

See "Blood Cleanser" on page 295 of this chapter for Dr. Kim's family recipe for the traditional Korean seaweed soup, *Mi-Yuk Gook.*

Bronchitis

Bronchitis is an inflammation of the bronchial tubes and can be caused by bacteria, viruses, breathing in certain chemicals or smoking.

In fact, 80% to 90% of emphysema and chronic bronchitis cases are caused by smoking. So if you smoke—whether you have chronic bronchitis or want to avoid getting it—STOP SMOKING!

CAUTION: If you have *chronic* bronchitis—or any serious lung condition that is marked by a productive cough (with sputum) and/or shortness of breath (especially with asthma or chronic obstructive pulmonary disease)—you must work with a health care professional to reduce your risk of lung damage.

If you have been diagnosed with *acute* bronchitis—the kind that lasts a week or so and is generally caused by a viral infection (which may begin while you have a cold or sore throat)—consider the following treatment for your inflamed bronchial tubes…

Put 1 quart of filtered or springwater in a pot, then add 3 tablespoons of dried oregano and 3 average-size cloves of garlic that have been chopped *with the skins on.* Let it boil for 10 minutes, then take the pot off the fire and let the mixture steep for 5 minutes. Next, put a towel over your head and neck and bend over the steaming pot. Breathe deeply and exhale. Keep doing that for 5 minutes.

CAUTION: Be extremely careful not to get too close to the hot pot—you could get a steam burn.

Warm up the liquid and repeat the steam treatment every few hours, especially before bedtime. It should help you sleep through the night. (Again, *please* be careful not to get too close to the steam.)

Make another pot of oregano-and-garlic water and drink it throughout the day—½ cup at a time. You may want to add honey and lime juice to make it more palatable.

Bruises

Bruises generally appear when the skin has undergone some form of trauma (minor or not) that caused little blood vessels to break. This can happen from bumping into the edge of a table or from something more serious like a car accident.

Most minor bruises will go away on their own with time (usually after going through a rainbow of colors), but these remedies may speed up the healing process...

◆ A popular Mayan remedy to reduce swelling and promote the healing of a bruise is to cut a lemon in half and rub the pulp over the bruise. Do this every hour until you go to bed, and there should be a big improvement by the time you wake up.

> ⚡ **CAUTION:** If there is broken skin along with the bruise, be warned that applying lemon juice will *sting*!

◆ Before you go to bed, soak a washcloth in a mixture made from equal parts water and apple cider vinegar. Wring out the cloth and wrap it around the bruised and swollen area— be sure it's not too tight, or you can cut off your circulation.

Then put a layer of plastic wrap on the washcloth (to protect your bedsheets) and cover the plastic wrap with a towel. Hold it in place with a large bandage or medical tape, and let it stay that way overnight. In the morning, there should be a tremendous improvement—hopefully, no swelling and just a minimal amount of bruising.

◆ Increase your intake of vitamin C. Taking up to 2,000 milligrams a day can help reduce the pain and inflammation from a bruise.

Carpal Tunnel Syndrome

This condition results from swollen tendons that compress the median nerve within the carpal tunnel canal in the wrist. It's usually accompanied by numbness, swelling, soreness, stiffness, weakness, tingling, discomfort and pain...*a lot* of pain. It tends to be caused by continual, rapid use of your fingers, wrists and/or arms.

At the first sign of carpal tunnel–type pain, warm about ¼ cup of olive oil. Take it off the heat before it starts to boil. When the oil is cool enough to touch, massage it into your skin from your elbow to your wrist.

Even though you may hit some very sore and painful spots, keep massaging and try to dissolve the pain. Every couple of minutes, stop and manipulate the fleshy webbed acupressure area between your thumb and forefinger, then go back to massaging.

Stop after a reasonable amount of time— or when your hand is too tired to continue. Just let your wrist rest until the next day. And, even though it may feel fine the next day, do the wrist-to-elbow olive oil massage once a day for a full week. If there is someone else who can do it for you, that's even better.

The recommended dosage for carpal tunnel inflammation is the same as for arthritis joint pain—400 to 600 milligrams (mg) of turmeric capsules (containing 95% curcumin), taken 3 times a day. Or take ½ to 1 teaspoon of turmeric liquid extract mixed into ½ cup of water, 3 times a day. You will know the turmeric is working if you feel relief within a week.

Cholesterol

In 2004, the US government revised the guidelines for what is considered a dangerous level of cholesterol. Previous levels were a maximum of 100 milligrams per deciliter (mg/dL) of low-density lipoprotein (LDL or "bad") cholesterol, and the new recommendation is to have LDLs no higher than 70 mg/dL.

These guidelines are for very high-risk people with heart disease as well as multiple, poorly controlled risk factors (such as diabetes, high blood pressure and smoking), and who are being treated with medication. But even people with moderately high risk (for example, those who have already had a heart attack) should keep their LDL levels well below 100 mg/dL.

We have always believed (and our research proves) that certain foods—such as apples, avocados, fenugreek, garlic, kiwi, flaxseed, beans and, of course, oatmeal—can help lower cholesterol. While continuing our research, we heard about a woman who was advised by a

Heart-Healthy Treats

How many times have you thought, "If only candy were good for me!" Well, in fact, researchers have found that dark chocolate (when eaten in moderation) can be good for your heart. The *stearic acid* in dark chocolate is converted in the body to *oleic acid*, which is the main fatty acid in olive oil…and we all know how heart-healthy olive oil is.

Also, dark chocolate is chock full of antioxidant-rich compounds known as *flavonoids*. Flavonoids may help to increase HDL ("good") cholesterol levels by as much as 10%, according to Penny Kris-Etherton, PhD, professor of nutrition at Pennsylvania State University in University Park.

The results of a long clinical trial conducted by Mary Engler, PhD, RN, and her colleagues at the University of California in San Francisco, showed improvement in subjects' blood vessel function after they consumed small daily doses (about 1.6 ounces) of flavonoid-rich dark chocolate over an extended period of time.

Dr. Engler concluded that eating a small amount of dark chocolate every day is good for most people. The higher the cocoa content, the better. Some manufacturers, such as Lindt and Chocolove, list the cocoa content on the label of the chocolate bar.

Personal Preference

I've been a milk chocolate person most of my life, and I always found dark chocolate to be bitter. But now I eat Lindt's 85% cocoa, which is very bitter, and I love it. The secret is to break off a small piece and let it dissolve in your mouth (rather than chew it). It tastes great, lasts a long time and I'm satisfied eating less.—*Lydia*

CAUTION: Keep in mind that, while flavonoids are great for your blood vessels, they don't cancel out fat and calories. It's important to stick to the recommended amount (about 1.6 ounces) of dark chocolate daily.

In addition, it's not true that the more chocolate you eat, the healthier you'll be. So if you are on a sugar-free diet, even a small daily dose of chocolate may do you more harm than good. Talk to your doctor.

Also, don't try this remedy if you are allergic to chocolate.

Butter Replacement

Pour extra-virgin olive oil in a wide-mouth jar with a tight-fitting lid, and refrigerate it. It will solidify and then you can use it as a healthy spread on bread or toast, in place of butter.

doctor at the Mayo Clinic in Rochester, Minnesota, to eat a handful of walnuts daily.

The Mayo Clinic reviewed the results of some small studies, which showed that walnuts can significantly reduce blood cholesterol levels. Rich in polyunsaturated fatty acids, walnuts may also help keep blood vessels more healthy and elastic.

All nuts are high in fat calories, and many doctors would advise you to add walnuts to your diet ONLY as a substitute for other foods that contain high levels of saturated fats, such as cheese, butter and fatty meats.

We start the day by eating ½ cup of cooked oatmeal, which is high in fiber and provides 20% of our daily vitamin A. We add cinnamon and some raisins for iron and potassium…or blueberries for antioxidants and vitamin C…as well as walnuts for omega-3 fatty acids. We sweeten it all with a natural sweetener called stevia (available at health-food stores).

Colds and Flu

The common cold can wipe you out, and the influenza virus—which is characterized by inflammation of the respiratory tract and fever, chills and muscular pains—can really knock you down for the count. *If you're feeling run down, have a red, runny nose, chest congestion and that achy-all-over feeling, this remedy may help…*

Pour 1 cup of Epsom salt (available at drugstores) into the bathtub and fill it with hot water. Then add 2 cups of 3% hydrogen peroxide (the inexpensive kind that you get at the drugstore). When the bath is still warm, but cool enough to not burn you, get in and soak for 30 minutes. Then dry off quickly, put on cotton bedclothes and get under the covers.

The bath should help relieve the achiness that comes with a cold and it should also promote a good night's sleep, which will help you get over your cold more quickly.

Cold Sores

About 85% of all Americans are prone to getting cold sores. This unsightly blemish is caused by the *herpes simplex* virus, which bursts into bloom when you least want it—usually, it's when your resistance is low because of a cold, the flu, pregnancy, sunburn, your wedding day or some other stressful factor.

Cold sores generally take about 2 weeks to clear up. *Here are a few suggestions that may speed up the healing process…*

◆ Dab a cold sore with a swab that's been dipped in a little vodka—the alcohol will help dry it out. But be warned that the alcohol will also sting.

★ **The Ears Have It!**

The second you get that tingly feeling on your lip and know that it's the start of a cold sore, rub your finger against the back of your ear.

Then, with that same part of your finger, rub the spot the cold sore is starting to emerge. This should make it disappear. (We can't help but wonder HOW someone discovered this remedy!)

Be sure to wash your hands thoroughly after touching the cold sore—the virus is contagious and can be spread to other people (and body parts) very easily.

◆ Puncture a vitamin E gel capsule—400 international units (IU)—then squeeze out the oil and cover the cold sore with it. Do this 3 times a day. By the third application, the pain should be gone. By the end of the next day (the sixth application), the cold sore should be healed.

★ **Go for the Gold!**

Rubbing a gold ring over a tingly cold sore spot may also put the sore into remission. Hey, it's worth a try.

Colic

Doctors aren't sure what causes a baby to get colic (it could be an allergy or indigestion—or just the child's disposition). But whatever the cause, it's hard to listen to a baby cry from such discomfort. *This remedy may bring relief…*

Put a clean, soft towel on your bed and place the baby on the towel. Then pour a little castor oil on your hand and gently rub the baby's tummy with it. It may take about 10 minutes for the castor oil to kick in and the colicky episode to abate, so be patient.

Constipation

If you are constipated more often than every once in a blue moon, you might want to limit your intake of certain foods that are known to cause constipation. They include milk, cheese, ice cream, unripe bananas, heavily salted and spiced foods, chocolate, alcoholic beverages and products made with white flour.

Foods that help keep you regular are very ripe bananas, figs, dried plums/prunes (of course), flaxseed, avocados, cooked cabbage, apples, oatmeal and salads. Try to vary these foods in your daily diet, and remember—natural inexpensive constipation relievers should not present any side effects if used in moderation.

> **NOTE:** Constipation is a common problem that may be a symptom of disease or lead to more serious ailments. It is important to consult a medical professional before starting any self-help treatment.

This saline laxative for the relief of occasional constipation generally produces results in 1 to 6 hours. For adults (12 years of age or older), dissolve 1 to 2 teaspoons of Epsom salt (available at drugstores) in 4 ounces of water and drink it. Take no more than 2 doses per day.

> **CAUTION:** Epsom salt is made with magnesium and *shouldn't* adversely affect anyone on a salt-restricted diet, but we urge you to check with your health care professional before trying the previous solution.
> In addition, people with kidney disease or renal failure should NOT use this remedy under any circumstances.

Contact Lenses

New technology and materials have made contact lenses more comfortable and more convenient than ever. *If you have lenses—or are thinking about getting them—here's another thing to cross off your concerned list…*

If you're among the people who think it's possible to lose your contact lens in the back of your head, there's no need to worry. The *conjunctiva*, a clear lining that covers the inner lid and connects to the eyeball, makes it impossible for a lens to slip into your head.

If your contact lens gets stuck, retrieve it by flushing your eye with a sterile saline solution (available at drugstores).

Cough

The cough center in your brain is generally motivated by an irritation in the respiratory tract. In other words, a cough is nature's way of helping you loosen and get rid of mucus that's congesting your system.

If you want to get rid of a nagging cough, follow the recommendation of Jane Guiltinan, ND, faculty member at Bastyr University Center for Natural Health in Seattle...in a large glass, combine the juice from ½ lemon (about 4 teaspoons) with ½ cup of warm water. Then stir in 1 tablespoon of table salt and ¼ teaspoon of cayenne pepper.

Gargle with this solution for as long as possible and as deeply as you can tolerate it. Then spit it out. *DO NOT SWALLOW IT.*

Dandruff

As dead cells fall off the scalp, new cells form beneath them. We all lose skin cells this way, but with dandruff this process is faster...a greater number of cells are shed in clumps, often big enough to be seen. If you have dandruff, wear light-colored clothes so that it's not as noticeable. *Then check out the remedies below to help dandruff disappear...*

◆ Are you sure that you have dandruff and not just a buildup of hair spray, styling gel or mousse? Cut back on the products that can cause flakiness, and see what happens. But if you still have dandruff, then it's time to try thyme.

Bring 1 cup of water to a boil, add 2 heaping tablespoons of dried thyme and let it simmer for 7 to 10 minutes. Strain out the thyme and let the water cool. Meanwhile, shampoo your hair as usual. Once the brew is cool, and while your hair is still damp, gently massage the thyme water into your scalp. *Do not rinse it out.*

◆ Get an aloe vera plant. The night before you're going to shampoo your hair, cut off a piece of the lowest leaf of the plant. Peel off the skin of the leaf, and squeeze the gel on your hair and into your scalp. Cover your hair with a bandanna or scarf and sleep that way.

The next morning, when you wash your hair, do not use shampoo. Instead, foam up the aloe gel. This treatment is good for your hair and can, surprisingly, help you get rid of dandruff quickly.

Depression (The Blues)

According to a survey, the average person spends 3 days every month feeling a little sad. There are a variety of things that might make you feel mildly down—from the weather to pressures at the office and/or problems with your partner. *Perk up during those occasional down days with these suggestions...*

> ⚡ **CAUTION:** If you are having trouble coping or feel sad and deeply depressed for more than a few days at a time, seek professional assistance to help pinpoint the cause and recommend treatment. Severe depression can lead to suicide, so seek help immediately.

◆ Don't stop reading just because you see the word *exercise*. Because, according to a study from the University of Texas Southwestern Medical Center and the Cooper Institute (both in Dallas) performing 30 to 40 minutes of moderate aerobic exercise—a brisk walk, a few laps in the pool or pedaling a bike—3 to 5 times a week, could help to alleviate many of the symptoms of mild depression.

You may have to push yourself to do it, but give exercise a try for a few weeks—when you start to feel a whole lot better, it will have been worth it.

> ✎ **NOTE:** Do not start any exercise program without permission from your doctor. Trying to do too much too soon can lead to injury—which can make you more depressed. Consult your health care professional for a physical evaluation and instructions on how to start an exercise routine.

Positive Affirmations

Words have power—great power. Our subconscious acts on our words and thoughts without discrimination. And so we should be careful about what we think and say.

That's why affirmations are wonderful. They are positive programming for the subconscious and, as a bonus, they also make us feel better consciously.

Start by assigning an appropriate affirmation to yourself. Write it down on an index card and read it over and over—at least 7 times in a row, out loud if possible—time and time again throughout the day. Think about the meaning of it, and when you say it—mean it. Even if you memorize it and say it by rote, it will impact your subconscious, and your subconscious will act on it.

Louise L. Hay, Science of Mind minister, metaphysical lecturer and author of *Power Thoughts* (Hay House, *www.hayhouse.com*), says that an affirmation is like planting a seed. *She graciously provided us with a few of those seeds...*

◆ I now choose to release every negative, destructive, fearful idea and thought from my mind and my life.

◆ My body is always working toward optimal health. I am happy and healthy.

◆ I trust life to be wonderful. I see only good ahead of me.

At some point in time, you may want to create your own appropriate, meaningful affirmation by pinpointing whatever is your physical or emotional challenge, its possible underlying cause and the outcome you want. When that time comes, keep it simple, strong and personal.

One of our favorite affirmations is a classic that was created by Émile Coué (and altered by José Silva)...*every day in every way I'm getting better, better and better!*

◆ When you sing out loud, you produce brain vibrations that trigger the release of *endorphins*—chemicals in the brain that can elevate mood and help kill pain. Find a song that you like to sing and then personalize it with happy and positive lyrics that will lift your spirits.

◆ Restore calm and contentment by using the Chinese art of *qigong*. While lying down or standing up, use your palm to rub the area around your belly-button in a clockwise motion. After doing it for 3 minutes, hold your hand over the area (not touching your skin) for 5 seconds.

This process is believed to unclog energy blockages so that your *chi* (life energy) can flow freely, which should put you back into happy balance.

◆ Chase away the blues by petting a friendly dog. Scientists at the University of Missouri in Columbia found that petting a dog increases levels of the get-happy hormone *serotonin*. (Interacting with a *robotic* dog caused a dip in serotonin levels.)

◆ You know how having a *bad-hair day* (BHD) makes you feel totally unattractive? Marianne LaFrance, PhD, professor of psychology at Yale University in New Haven, Connecticut, conducted a study and found that having a BHD can make both men and women feel almost worthless. Restore your happiness-inducing self-confidence by doing whatever it takes to make your hair look its best.

◆ Psychologists and color consultants agree that the color pink conveys calm and helps to soothe. So think pink! It's an attractive and flattering color when worn by men as well as women.

In addition to wearing it, put a vase of pink flowers on your table or desk. Put pink accents around your work space and/or house. Be in the pink. The more, the merrier!

Diarrhea

Diarrhea is a common condition that is often caused by overeating...a bacterial, viral or parasitic infection...mild food poisoning or intolerance...an adverse reaction to medication...or emotional anxiety. It's important to drink clear fluids during and after a bout in order to avoid electrolyte depletion and dehydration.

> ⚡ **CAUTION:** If diarrhea persists, it may be a symptom of a more serious ailment. Get professional medical attention.

Having diarrhea is no fun. Apple cider vinegar (preferably unfiltered, available at health-food stores) will let nature take its course, and will lessen the intensity and get you back in control in a relatively short time.

Take 1 teaspoon of apple cider vinegar mixed in 8 ounces of water, both before meals and in between. That means 6 glasses a day. But it's worth it for all the good it does. Also, the *pectin* (a natural fruit enzyme) in the vinegar will add bulk to the stools and help destroy some types of bacteria that cause diarrhea.

Dry Eye Syndrome

Tear ducts that do not produce enough fluid to keep the eyes moist can result in an uncomfortable dry-eye condition that is characterized by irritation, burning and a gravelly feeling. You may be more at risk for dry eye if you're a long-term contact-lens wearer...or you have had LASIK vision-correction surgery...or you have high blood pressure or rheumatoid arthritis...or if you're getting on in years, especially if you're a woman.

Researchers at Brigham and Women's Hospital and Schepens Eye Research Institute in Boston conducted a Women's Health Study. They found, based on 37,000 women who were enrolled in this landmark study, that women who reported eating at least 5 servings of tuna per week had a 68% reduced risk of dry eye syndrome compared with women who ate only 1 serving per week.

In addition to tuna, it's a good idea to eat foods that are rich in omega-3 fatty acids—such as salmon, halibut, mackerel, herring, sardines, walnuts and pumpkin seeds—ideally, at least 3 times a week.

> ✎ **NOTE:** See the CAUTION on page 297 for more information about mercury and other toxic contaminants that are found in fish, and also the US government's guidelines on limiting fish consumption.

Also, dry eyes may be relieved by eating ground flaxseed and/or flaxseed oil daily (follow the recommended dosage on label), both available at health-food stores. You can also take omega-3 supplements. Follow the dosage on the bottle.

Eczema (*Atopic Dermatitis*)

Eczema is a chronic skin disease that is very uncomfortable, but not contagious. It tends to show up most often on elbows, knees and wrists, and may be triggered by allergies.

> ⚡ **CAUTION:** Persistent or chronic eczema is best treated by a health-care professional.

◆ A Japanese study reported that drinking oolong tea reduced itching and inflammation in people suffering from eczema. Drink 34 ounces (about 1 liter) of oolong tea (available at supermarkets and health-food stores) throughout the day, after meals and between lunch and dinner. Its antioxidant properties relieve itching, redness and swelling.

> ✎ **NOTE:** Oolong tea is NOT caffeine-free, so you should not have it close to bedtime if you're sensitive to caffeine.

◆ To help reduce inflammation from eczema, take 1 tablespoon of flaxseed oil daily.

◆ A popular European treatment is evening primrose oil. The usual dose of this omega-6 fatty acid is 2 to 4 grams a day, taken with food. To soothe cracked skin, you can also use evening primrose oil externally.

◆ We recently heard about an eczema remedy that worked when nothing else did—it is Crisco, the vegetable shortening our grandmother used for cooking and baking (available at supermarkets).

The woman we heard about applied Crisco to her flared-up areas of eczema 2 to 3 times a day until the eczema was gone.

> **NOTE:** Applying Crisco is neither easy nor practical, especially if you go to work. Then again, having eczema is not easy. If you can give this remedy a try, do so for at least 1 or 2 weeks. If the symptoms start to disappear, continue with the Crisco until the eczema is all gone. (Petroleum jelly may also work.)

Edema

Occasional swelling of the legs, ankles or feet may be due to water retention from getting too much salt in your diet. But whatever the cause, it's important to talk to your health care professional to determine *exactly* why it's happening—underlying causes of edema can be heart failure, kidney disease, lymphoma, *deep vein thrombosis* (DVT), bone fracture or some other injury.

And while you're talking to your doctor, be sure to ask him/her about the following herbal remedies to make sure that it's OK for you to take them…

◆ For decades, the herbal preparation horse chestnut (capsules are available at health-food stores) has been used to relieve the swelling and pain of a variety of vein conditions, including varicose veins and chronic venous insufficiency.

Horse chestnut helps reduce inflammation, facilitate blood flow, reinforce the strength of the vein walls and promote their elasticity. Follow the dosage instructions on the bottle.

> **NOTE:** Horse chestnut should be used *only* for chronic venous insufficiency—not for any other type of edema.

◆ Butcher's broom (capsules are available at health-food stores) has been a traditional medicine for treating vein disorders for more than 50 years. In addition to relieving leg pain and swelling, it can help with itching, numbness and cramping. Follow the dosage instructions on the bottle.

Energy Boosters

Dale Carnegie—public speaker and motivational pioneer—believed that "our fatigue is often caused not by work, but by worry, frustration and resentment."

Author Eric Hoffer contends, "Men weary as much of not doing the things they want to do as of doing the things they do not want to do."

Those are important words that may give you food for thought. If you're always tired, take a look at your life and chances are, you'll be able to figure out what's causing your fatigue. Then figure out how to make some positive changes.

While you're figuring that out, here are some picker-uppers for a quick energy boost…

◆ Grab a food that's rich in the essential mineral *selenium*—such as brazil nuts, celery, broccoli, yogurt, cottage cheese, mushrooms, fish and cabbage. Studies show that selenium can help bolster your mood as well as your energy levels.

◆ Singing out loud brings extra oxygen into your body and releases feel-good endorphins, which should give you a right-then-and-there burst of energy.

◆ If you just can't carry a tune, take a deep breath. As you exhale, slowly say the vowels *A-E-I-O-U*.

According to John M. Ortiz, PhD, of the Institute of Applied Musicology in Dillsburg, Pennsylvania (*www.soundpsych.com*) and author of *The Tao of Music* (Weiser), the vibrations produced while making those sounds radiate through your body. They actually function as an internal massage that soothes and revives your entire system.

◆ After standing all day, or sitting for long periods of time, your circulation is diminished and blood pools in your legs and feet. Your energy decreases because blood is not being reoxygenated quickly enough by your heart. Reverse the situation by elevating your feet and letting the pooled blood become recirculated with more oxygen. Your energy level will also be elevated.

✳ Walk Away DVT

To help prevent *deep vein thrombosis* (DVT, the formation of a blood clot that can be extremely dangerous—and even fatal), it's important to exercise the legs on a regular basis. Just take a brisk 30-minute walk every day.

And, do not sit or lie down for extended periods of time without moving your legs—if possible, get up and move around every 30 to 60 minutes to help prevent clots.

◆ If sitting with your feet up isn't practical, slip off your shoes, reach down and rub your feet. Massage the acupressure point in the webbed area between the first and second toes of each foot for 2 minutes. The stimulation will give you an energy surge.

◆ If you're among other people (such as at a long meeting or presentation) and you feel as though you're going to nod off instead of being alert, press your elbows against your sides and press your knees together for a few seconds. Exerting a lot of pressure this way will increase your blood circulation, and you should feel more awake and responsive.

◆ Alan R. Hirsch, MD, director of The Smell and Taste Treatment and Research Foundation in Chicago, has found that scents can influence our energy levels. Dr. Hirsch's studies show that wearing perfume or cologne that you love improves your self-esteem as well as your energy level.

In addition, the scent of cinnamon stimulates the *trigeminal nerve*, the area of the brain that governs wakefulness and raises energy levels. Have cinnamon at breakfast-time—sprinkle it on toast, hot oatmeal, cold cereal or even coffee. Or, during the day, put a drop of cinnamon oil on the inside of your wrist and sniff the invigorating scent.

Erectile Dysfunction

Male impotence or *erectile dysfunction* can be caused by certain psychological problems, such as stress, anxiety, depression, fear or guilt… high blood pressure or cholesterol…hormonal abnormalities, such as low testosterone levels… and prescription and over-the-counter medications. (Incidentally, cigarette smokers are more likely to suffer from erectile dysfunction than nonsmokers—cigarettes decrease the blood flow through veins and arteries.)

If any of these things have been interfering with your ability to perform, you should take appropriate measures to correct the situation.

First and foremost, talk to your doctor—especially if you think your performance problems may be related to medication. Erectile dysfunction can also be a symptom of a more serious condition, such as hypertension, diabetes or vascular disease, so it's best to get checked by your physician.

Meanwhile, to help *boost* your efforts, here's an interesting Native American remedy you may want to try…

Cornsilk tea helps to prevent impotence, and it's also said to enhance a man's sexual performance. Take the silken hairs from 6 ears of corn, and boil them in 3 cups of water for 10 minutes. Strain out the silk, let the tea cool and drink the 3 cups throughout the day. Do the same thing the next day and the day after that—for a total of 3 days in a row. You will then be ready to test this remedy.

Cornsilk tea is a mild diuretic, which is the reason it's believed to make a man ready and "good to go."

Fertility

There are some persistent myths out there that many people believe about fertility. But we feel it's important to dispel these mis-*conceptions*. *Here's the full truth…*

◆ Overall good health doesn't necessarily mean that a person is fertile.

◆ Weight (either overweight or underweight) can affect a person's ability to conceive.

◆ Sexual positions do NOT play a part in the success of conception.

◆ The results of some recent studies concluded that a man's underwear—no matter how brief or tight—does NOT cause a decrease in sperm count.

◆ Ovulation day is the *last* day on which to conceive. Having sex on the 2 days prior

to ovulation offers the greatest chance of conception.

This fact is so important that we repeat it below…along with other suggestions that may help stack the deck in your favor.

◆ Ladies, just say "no" to champagne and wine. One study showed that downing 1 alcoholic beverage a day will cut your odds of conceiving by half. Not so for men. No matter how much alcohol they drink, their fertility remains the same. (That said, smoking can significantly reduce a man's potency.)

◆ Men, take royal jelly—up to 1,000 milligrams (mg) a day—to increase your sperm count and make those little swimmers more aggressive.

For an ovulation calculator, visit *www.baby hopes.com/ovulation-calendar,* or consider a trip to your drugstore to check out the following…

◆ **Fertility monitor and test strips**—Based solely on hormone monitoring, the monitor and test strips display a woman's personal level of fertility (low, high or peak) and her chance of conceiving.

◆ **Digital basal thermometer**—Used to monitor body temperature. A temperature increase near the middle of a woman's menstrual cycle can indicate when ovulation is occurring.

◆ **Ovulation test kit**—This tests for the *luteinizing hormone* (LH) surge, which lets a woman know when she is about to ovulate. Having sex 2 days prior to ovulation generally gives the best chance of conception.

Fever

The average human body temperature is 98.6°F. *Fever* is a term that refers to a temperature that is higher…typically above 100°F in adults. Fever is a *symptom* of illness—not a disease itself. It is the body's response to an outside stimulus, usually an infection.

There are 2 schools of thought with regard to treating adults' fever—either let it run its course, or bring it down. In general, a fever below 104°F can be allowed to run its course...but if it's any higher than that—or if the fever persists for more than a day or so—contact your physician. You may need emergency medical attention.

In the meantime, you can cool a fever by pouring a little bit of rubbing alcohol on a soft cloth and massaging it on the insides of your elbows, in back of your knees and also on your forehead and neck.

⚡ **CAUTION:** DO NOT use rubbing alcohol on a child. Rubbing alcohol applied externally can be toxic to a child.

Food Poisoning

According to Medline Plus (*www.nlm.nih.gov/medlineplus*), a service of the US National Library of Medicine and the National Institutes of Health, food poisoning affects between 60 and 80 million people worldwide each year.

Food poisoning tends to occur at picnics, large social functions and in school cafeterias. These are situations where food may be improperly refrigerated, or food-preparation techniques may not be sanitary.

The most common causes of food poisoning are undercooked meats and eggs, improperly refrigerated dairy products (like mayonnaise mixed in coleslaw or potato salad) and unwashed produce. *The next time you're in charge of the coleslaw and burgers, here's a preventive measure...*

When added to food, spices like garlic, cloves, cinnamon, oregano and sage may help to prevent food-related *pathogens* (the living microorganisms in food, including *E. coli* and *Staph aureus*) from proliferating in improperly prepared foods.

Daniel Y. C. Fung, PhD, professor of food science and an internationally acclaimed microbiologist, and his team of researchers at Kansas State University in Manhattan, discovered that moderate amounts of spices—that is, enough to actually taste the garlic, cloves or cinnamon, etc.—will help prevent raw or undercooked food from making eaters sick.

That said, the best way to prevent food poisoning is to practice meticulous food preparation—wash your hands and all cooking/preparation surfaces thoroughly and cook foods to the recommended safe temperature. (For more information, *see* "Thermometers/Cooking Temperatures" on pages 99–100 of Chapter 4, "The Best-Ever Food Secrets.")

Gout

Gout tends to come on suddenly—but you'll know when you have it. Caused by a buildup of uric acid in the joints, it usually settles in a person's big toe or knee. Gout can be extremely painful, but is also extremely treatable.

Your gout symptoms should subside if you can avoid consuming mushrooms, oatmeal, shellfish, salmon, sardines, anchovies, asparagus, legumes, meat (especially organ meat, such as liver), meat gravies, yeast products (including bread and beer), alcoholic beverages, soda, fried foods, rich desserts, pastries and spices. *In addition, these remedies should help...*

◆ Drink celery-seed, dandelion or yarrow tea after meals. If the tea is loose rather than in tea bags, follow the brewing instructions on the box. (All of these teas are available at health-food stores.)

◆ If it's corn season, simmer 3 fresh corncobs in 1 quart of water for 15 minutes. Discard the cobs, and pour the water in a jar and refrigerate it. After each meal, heat up and drink 1 cup of the corncob tea.

♦ Eating 4 ounces of fresh bing cherries a day is the best way to treat gout. You can also flush the excess uric acid out of your system by drinking 6 ounces of cherry juice 2 or 3 times a day, or taking 1 tablespoon of cherry concentrate 3 times a day.

♦ *Quercetin* (available in health-food stores) is a flavonoid* that inhibits uric acid production —in the same way that prescription drugs do.

The recommended dosage is 1,000 milligrams (mg) of quercetin taken along with 1,000 to 1,500 mg of *bromelain* (an enzyme that enhances the absorption of quercetin), 2 to 3 times daily between meals. Bromelain can also help reduce the inflammation that is caused by gout.

> **⚡ CAUTION:** Do not take aspirin for gout pain. Doing so can raise levels of uric acid in your system.

*Flavonoids are plant substances that act as antioxidants and anti-inflammatories in the body.

> **★ Sensual Gout Prevention**
> To prevent gout, have sex! Yes, sexual activity (specifically ejaculation) helps to reduce uric acid levels in fertile men. So, that should give you something to think about...or something to do in the name of preventive medicine.

Guilt

Is something nagging at you? Something that you regret or feel remorseful about? Follow the findings of Los Angeles–based psychologist Yvonne Thomas, PhD (*www.yvonnethomasphd. com*), and get your mind to release the buildup of this negative, guilty feeling. (And if that's all there is to it, then you may not even need the following exercise.)

Before doing the "good-bye guilt" exercise, ponder this—is it possible that the thing about which you feel guilty has been forgotten by everyone except you? Depending on your answer to that question, all you may need to do is forgive yourself.

Otherwise, just take a pen and paper and write down whatever it is that's bothering you. Then tear the paper into tiny pieces and throw it away, along with the guilt or regret. Gone! We hope you start to feel lighter and better, right then and there.

Gum Disease

See "Bad Breath, Gum Disease and Toothaches" on pages 293–294.

Hair

Spraying, teasing, blow-drying, setting, volumizing, coloring, perming—all are forms of hair torture. No wonder your mane is dry and damaged! *Never fear, my dear—help is here...*

In a small bowl, thoroughly whisk together ⅛ cup of your favorite shampoo along with 1 teaspoon of avocado oil (we use high-quality Maranatha oil, available at health-food stores) and ½ tablespoon of coconut milk (available at supermarkets). Shampoo as usual, then rinse. This doctored-up shampoo should nourish your hair and leave it with a wonderful shine.

> **✎ NOTE:** If you have very long hair, double the amounts in the avocado/coconut/shampoo formula.

Headache

There are about 150 different categories of headache, and nearly everybody suffers from an occasional bout. But 45 million Americans endure regular headaches several times a week—most typically, the so-called *tension headaches*, which can be brought on by fatigue, hunger, stress or overexertion.

Some 28 million people suffer from *migraine headaches*, which scientists now believe result from inherited abnormalities in certain areas of the brain and are triggered by changes in weather or sleep patterns, fatigue, food sensitivity, stress and other factors.

Other types of headaches are generally caused by sinus problems, hormonal changes... even eating ice cream too fast.

> ⚡ **CAUTION:** Regularly recurring headaches might be caused by eyestrain or allergies—or something more serious. Seek professional medical attention immediately if the headache comes on suddenly, is very painful or is accompanied by a fever.

Whatever the reason for your aching head, here are some remedies that should help the pain go away...

◆ Prepare a cup of green tea with sprigs of fresh mint, or combine a green tea bag and a peppermint tea bag to make a big, strong cup of headache-relieving tea. Drink the minty tea and your headache should fade away in about 15 minutes. (Drinking 1 or 2 cups of regular coffee at the onset of a tension headache—NOT a migraine—can help prevent it from getting worse.)

◆ If you feel a headache starting, peel a small piece of fresh ginger (available in the produce section of most supermarkets) and chew it. It's strong and may be hard to get used to, but it beats having the headache.

◆ Migraines—especially morning migraines— can be related to biorhythm disturbances. These problems may be caused by low levels of *melatonin*—a naturally occurring hormone that regulates the body's biological rhythms, such as sleep cycles.

A small but significant study was conducted at the Hospital Israelita Albert Einstein in São Paulo, Brazil—it gave 40 test subjects 3 milligrams of melatonin 30 minutes before bedtime, every night for 3 months.

At the end of the study, more than ⅔ of the patients said that the frequency of their migraines was reduced by 50% or better. Some patients had no subsequent migraines. And, of the subjects who continued to develop migraines, the melatonin helped to decrease their frequency, intensity and duration.

> ✍ **NOTE:** If you would like to take melatonin to help prevent migraines, discuss the appropriate dosage with your health professional. Melatonin may eventually lose its effect if high doses are taken for too long.

◆ To prevent migraines, mix 2 teaspoons of unfiltered apple cider vinegar (available at health-food stores) and 2 teaspoons of honey in an 8-ounce glass of water. Drink it once or twice a day.

This remedy works like magic for some (former) migraine sufferers. So, if you're not allergic to honey, and you're not on a sugar-restricted diet, it's worth a try.

Hiccups

A hiccup is a spastic contraction of the diaphragm—the large circular muscle that separates the chest from the abdomen.

A movement of some kind—or a disruption in your breathing pattern—can put an end to the spastic contractions. There are dozens of ways to do that.

And we thought we had heard them all, but then we came across this great cure for the hiccups—stand up straight with your arms reaching for the sky, and wiggle your fingers. (Try it—what have you got to lose?)

Hypertension (High Blood Pressure)

More than 65 million Americans have been diagnosed with *hypertension* (high blood pressure). If you're among those people, obviously you're not alone. We urge you to discuss your lifestyle with your doctor and, once and for all, do something to change whatever is causing the problem. *These remedies may also help...*

◆ Blood pressure readings can vary by as much as 40%, depending on the time of day you do the testing. At a recent annual meeting of the American Society of Hypertension (*www.ash-us.org*), it was reported that the best time to check your blood pressure is during the morning through midday—blood pressures tend to be higher at the end of the day. Also, blood pressure is generally higher in winter than in summer.

◆ Taking your blood pressure at home is a good way to monitor the success of your efforts between doctor visits. It also gets you used to having your blood pressure taken so that you won't be nervous when you're cuffed in the doctor's office.

◆ Some research studies have shown that eating dark chocolate daily helps decrease blood pressure. Before you make a dash for the candy counter, check out "Heart-Healthy Treats" on page 300. But check with your health care professional before indulging, especially if you are on a special diet.

Deep-Breathing Exercise for Hypertension

If you are among the millions of Americans who have been diagnosed with high blood pressure, consider doing a simple breathing exercise to help get your numbers down.

Once a day, lie on your back and put a book on your stomach, right over your belly-button—sure, go ahead and use this book—and gently inhale to the count of 7 and exhale to the count of 10, moving the book up and down. Do this for 10 minutes.

Deep-breathing exercises like this calm the muscles surrounding the small blood vessels and allow blood to flow more freely. This helps lower blood pressure.

Indigestion

Mild indigestion usually produces 1 or a combination of symptoms—stomachache, heartburn, nausea and vomiting or gas (flatulence). *If you are suffering from a minor tummyache, here are some remedies that might help...*

CAUTION: Severe indigestion or chronic stomach pain may be a symptom of something more serious than you think, such as a heart attack or pulmonary embolism—seek medical attention immediately.

◆ Grate the peel of an organic grapefruit. Spread out the tiny grated bits on paper towels and let them dry overnight. Then store them in a jar with a lid and label it clearly. Keep it in your medicine cabinet...then, whenever you have an upset stomach, take ½ to 1 teaspoon of the grapefruit bits. Chew them thoroughly before swallowing.

◆ If you're traveling, bring along all-natural peppermint toothpaste. As soon as you have that upset stomach feeling, swallow ½ tea-spoon of the toothpaste. (Check the label first to make sure it's safe to swallow.)

◆ If you're in a restaurant, order peppermint tea, or carry strong peppermint candies with you. (There are always a few Ricolas or Al-toids in each of our purses.)

Insect Bites/Stings

For an insect bite or sting, home treatment is often all that is needed. The problem is, you may not be at home when you're bitten or stung. *Here are a few remedies that should be appropriate for the great outdoors…*

CAUTION: If you have a history of being allergic to stinging insects, keep an anti-histamine or a physician-prescribed emergency sting kit with you at all times.

If any insect bite gets very swollen or seems out of the ordinary, get professional medical attention immediately.

◆ As soon as you know you've been bitten by a bug, take 3 leaves from 3 different kinds of trees, and mash them with your fingers (unless you happen have a mortar and pestle outside with you).

When the juice of the leaves comes out, apply it to the bite. In minutes, the pain should be gone as the bite starts to heal.

NOTE: Make sure that you get the leaves from *trees*, and not plants growing on the ground—rubbing poison ivy or poison oak on your skin would be much worse than an insect bite!

◆ If you're at a picnic and you get an insect bite or sting, apply mustard to the area to help relieve the pain, itch and redness. You can also use ice cubes or a paste made from the table salt and water to bring down the swelling.

FYI: The Great Greek Way
In the 6th century, BC, Greek scientist Py-thagoras (he of the famous mathematical the-orem) used mustard to treat scorpion stings. We don't know exactly why it works, but mustard is very healing.

Insomnia

Trouble falling asleep…waking up too early and not being able to fall back asleep…fre-quent awakenings…and waking up feeling unrefreshed—each of these problems is a symptom of insomnia.

In a survey conducted by the National Sleep Foundation (*www.sleepfoundation.org*), 58% —more than half—of American adults reported having insomnia at least a few nights a week. More women than men are insomniacs, in part because of hormonal changes, such as premen-strual syndrome (PMS), menstruation, pregnancy and menopause.

Male or female, if you consistently can't get a good night's sleep, take a look at your life. Once you figure out what may be keeping you awake, talk to your doctor (it's always a good idea to discuss sleep problems with a health care professional). Then you can make the nec-essary changes to get more restful sleep. *Until then, these remedies might help…*

◆ Do you exercise at night and then have trouble falling asleep? *A-ha!* Exercising right before getting into bed will energize you and boost your alertness, making it harder to fall asleep. Instead, exercise at least 3 to 6 hours prior to bedtime—this will help you fall asleep and stay asleep.

◆ When you go to bed, say a prayer and, as studies confirm, you should fall asleep easier and wake up fewer times during the night. The act of praying relaxes the body and mind, and may contribute to your well-being.

◆ In a glass jar with a lid, combine 2 tablespoons of unfiltered apple cider vinegar (available at health-food stores) with 1 cup of honey. Keep the closed jar next to your bed. When you have trouble sleeping, take 2 teaspoons of the mixture, close the jar again, and expect to be asleep within 20 minutes.

◆ In terms of melatonin (a naturally occurring hormone that regulates biological rhythms, such as sleep cycles)…more is definitely *not* better. In fact, Richard Wurtman, MD, director of MIT's Clinical Research Center in Cambridge, Massachusetts, believes that taking too much melatonin will eventually cause it to have no effect at all.

After analyzing several studies, Dr. Wurtman and his research team learned that even just 300 micrograms (mcg) is all that's needed for restful sleep. Most people take 10 times that amount, and then they lie awake, wondering why the melatonin isn't working.

Intestinal Parasites

There are 3 major groups of intestinal parasites that can wreak havoc with a person's gastrointestinal tract—*protozoans* (organisms having only 1 cell), *nematodes* (roundworms) and *cestodes* (tapeworms).

Parasites can make their way into a person's intestine orally via uncooked or unwashed food, contaminated water and/or hands, as well as through skin contact with larva-infected soil or contact with animals. People can also become infected if they kiss or have oral sex with a partner who is infected.

CAUTION: Infection from parasites can be serious and debilitating. It's important to work with a health professional who is experienced in treating parasites—most people will need to take an antibiotic.

While you're waiting for your doctor's appointment, you may want to brace yourself and try the following drink…

◆ Licensed naturopathic physician Nancy Caruso, ND, based in Clarkston, Michigan, suggests adding 1 smashed clove of garlic to ¼ cup of extra-virgin olive oil—drink this concoction 3 times a week for 5 weeks. Your excessive gas and bloating should disappear, along with the parasites.

NOTE: Although extra-virgin olive oil is a healthy monounsaturated fat, keep in mind that ¼ cup (4 tablespoons) contains a whopping 480 calories and about 56 grams of fat (enough fat for an entire day).

We recommend that if you drink Dr. Caruso's tonic, you try to reduce your overall calorie and fat intake for that day.

◆ If you're traveling in countries where papaya is readily available, you should eat this fruit every day. It will help digestion and prevent intestinal parasites, especially if you're eating foods that you're not used to eating.

More important than the papaya meat are the seeds inside the papaya. Eat 1 teaspoon of the raw seeds daily. They have a surprisingly peppery taste. They also contain *papain*, a protein-digesting enzyme that breaks down the cell walls of the parasites.

✳ Don't Drink the Water!

The best way to prevent parasitic infection is to avoid consuming local water (and ice cubes) when you travel—many local water systems are untreated and unsanitary. Be sure to wash all raw fruits and vegetables with clean bottled water, and wash your hands thoroughly after handling them.

Itchy Skin

Dry skin is the most common cause of minor itches…but if you keep scratching it, it could turn into a rash. Other itches are caused by more serious conditions, like eczema or poison ivy. If the itch or rash is persistent, see a doctor.

◆ For generalized itching, take stinging nettle capsules (available at health-food stores…follow the recommended dosage on the label).

◆ Colloidal oatmeal—oatmeal that is finely ground or pulverized—is great for therapeutic baths. Use tepid water in the bath—hot water will further inflame the itchy area, and dehydrate your skin rather than lubricate it. Add several cups of the oatmeal to the bath as it's filling up. Then soak in it for 10 minutes. Pat your skin dry—do not rub it.

CAUTION: If your skin is severely inflamed, do *not* take an oatmeal bath. It can be irritating.

FYI: Slippery When Wet!
When colloidal oatmeal mixes with water, it becomes slightly milky and gives the water a slimy consistency. That's good because it coats the skin…moisturizing, softening and protecting it. The bad part is that the bathtub will become very slippery.

Please be *extremely careful* getting out of the tub or have someone help you out. And be sure to clean the tub thoroughly when you're done, so that whoever uses it next does not slip and fall.

Also *see* "Eczema" on pages 305–306—the oolong tea remedy has been known to suppress the allergic reaction that causes itchiness and skin inflammation.

Jellyfish Sting

With more than an estimated 2,000 species of jellyfish, only about 70 are toxic to humans. But *only* doesn't help when you want to swim, sail or surf in unfamiliar waters. To be safe, ask the lifeguards or other locals what to be aware of with regard to jellyfish and other sea urchins in the water.

And remember—even detached tentacles found on the beach pose a hazard to humans. They can still sting if touched.

Use the following remedies to treat the sting as soon as possible, and it should go away in a day or so. In the meantime, it might be a good idea to see a doctor—just to make sure that the bite isn't serious.

CAUTION: If you're stung by a jellyfish or any kind of sea urchin, and you develop muscle spasms and find it hard to breathe, get medical treatment immediately.

◆ Most jellyfish are not dangerously poisonous, but their sting can be painful. It can burn, and you may break out in a puffy rash that may blister. Do not rub the stung area. It will spread the venom.

If you—or someone helping you—need to touch the stung area, wear gloves, if possible. Jellyfish venom can be easily spread to exposed hands and then to other body parts.

◆ Putting fresh water on the sting will cause the release of more venom. Put saltwater or ice on the area instead—this will neutralize the venom and cool the heat. Applying distilled white vinegar will also help to deactivate the toxins.

◆ If you're stung on a hairy part of your body, shave it. You'll remove the stingers and some of the venom that's embedded in the hair.

◆ If you have access to some adhesive tape, apply it to the stung area. When the sticky tape is pulled off, it should take some of the stingers with it.

♦ For quick relief from a painful jellyfish sting, pour saltwater (saline), beer, vodka or wine on the stung area. These liquids help to dry out the stingers, which will relieve the pain from the venom. (And—although it's a less savory option—urine works, too.)

> ✎ **NOTE:** If you are stung by a stingray, hot water works best to get out the barbs.
> If you are stung by a Portuguese man-of-war, DO NOT apply alcohol or urine—both can cause the release of more venom.

Liver Cleansers

The average adult human liver weighs about 3 pounds and is roughly the size of a football. It's located in the upper-right-hand part of the abdomen, behind the lower ribs.

The liver has more than 200 functions—including converting food into chemicals that the body needs to stay healthy...eliminating toxic substances from the blood...controlling the production and excretion of cholesterol...producing bile (which is essential for digestion)...and at least another 196 other jobs. Gosh—and you thought *you* were busy!

> ⚡ **CAUTION:** If you have hepatitis (inflammation of the liver) or any other problem with your liver, be sure to talk to a health professional before trying any of these remedies.

Needless to say, it's important to take care of your liver. *According to Mayan folk medicine, the best liver cleansers are...*

♦ **Lemon and water**—Add the juice of 1 lemon (about 2½ tablespoons) to an 8-ounce glass of lukewarm water. Have this drink before you even eat breakfast. It's a fantastic way to start your day.

♦ **Parsley**—Eat fresh parsley in salads, or juice ½ cup of the leaves along with ½ beet and 1 carrot for a sweet, healthy drink.

♦ **Radish leaves**—The most nutritious part of the plant are the dark green leaves, which are packed with minerals and vitamins. Wash them thoroughly and add to salads or soups.

♦ **Onions**—Ancient Mayan healers believed that eating cooked and/or raw onions will keep the liver clean, healthy and working well.

Menopause

The North American Menopause Society (*www.menopause.org*) sponsored a Gallup survey that revealed that more than half (51%) of the respondents (American women between the ages of 50 and 65 who had reached menopause) said they were the happiest and the most fulfilled now, compared to how they felt when they were in their 20s, 30s or 40s.

If you are suffering from menopause-related depression, that Gallup survey should help cheer you up and give you hope. *And so should the following remedy...*

Boil 1 tablespoon of dried rosemary in 1 pint of water for 5 minutes. Let it steep for 10 minutes. Then strain out the herb and drink the tea—1 cup between breakfast and lunch... another cup between lunch and dinner.

Rosemary, an herb that was among the Mayans' most important spiritual healing plants, acts as an antidepressant for many menopausal women. It is rich in vitamins A and C as well as the minerals phosphorus, iron, magnesium and zinc. The herb is a wonderful tonic for the nervous system.

Menstrual Cramps (*Dysmenorrhea*)

Most cases of *dysmenorrhea* (severe menstrual cramps) are caused by very strong uterine contractions. More than half the women who menstruate experience these severe cramps.

And, according to the American College of Obstetricians and Gynecologists (*www.acog.org*), approximately 1 out of every 10 women experience menstrual pain that is so severe that she is unable to perform her normal routine for several days each month.

Well, help is finally here for those women who are mildly to intensely affected during that time of month…

◆ Yarrow tea (available at health-food stores) is extremely effective when it comes to easing menstrual cramps (and both of us speak from experience!).

Put 1 teaspoon of yarrow or 1 tea bag in a cup of just-boiled water. Let it steep for about 7 minutes. If it's loose tea, strain and drink. If it's a tea bag, remove it and drink.

Drink 3 cups throughout the day if cramps persist. One cup daily would usually do it for each of us.

◆ If you've run out of yarrow tea, and you're doubled over with cramps, drink a few ounces of pickle juice from the jar in your refrigerator. (For some reason, this saying comes to mind—"What doesn't kill you, makes you stronger.")

NOTE: In some cases, painful cramps may be caused by a deficiency in *acetylcholine*, the neurotransmitter that stimulates your muscles to work. Pickle juice contains acetic acid, which helps the body make the much-needed acetylcholine. So drink a little pickle juice—it's worth a try until you get some yarrow tea.

Muscle and Joint Pain

If you're experiencing muscle and/or joint pain, see your health-care professional for a diagnosis—it's a good idea to get a checkup to find out *exactly* what's causing that pain.

Also, take a look at your daily routine. Do you carry a heavy shoulder bag or briefcase? Are you a mom, dad or child-care worker who's constantly lifting and carrying small children? Does your job require some type of movement that may be causing this discomfort? If you figure out that the pain is due to a repeated physical pattern of activity, break the pattern and the pain will probably go away.

Whether the pain is recurring, or a 1-shot deal, the following remedy should help…

Add 2 cups of Epsom salt (available at drugstores) to a warm bath, and relax in it for 20 minutes or more. The salt's natural mineral—magnesium sulfate—relieves and soothes aches, pains, soreness, stiffness and stress.

CAUTION: Keep Epsom salt away from your mouth, nose and eyes. The delicate tissues can become irritated.

Nail Fungus

Nail fungus is usually caused by a mild trauma that makes the nail—usually the big or little toenail—vulnerable to a fungal infection. And you don't have to walk around barefoot on a shower floor or in a locker room to get an infection. Fungi are everywhere—in the air, in the dust and even in the soil.

To help prevent a fungal infection, wear comfortable shoes and hosiery that allows your feet some breathing space. Wash your feet daily and dry them thoroughly.

Also, keep your toenails trimmed and, before using pedicure tools, be sure to thoroughly disinfect them with rubbing alcohol.

If you already have an infection, use the following remedy every day to help eliminate fungus and make your nails more resistant to developing future infections...

Combine 1 quart of warm water and ½ cup of apple cider vinegar (available at health-food stores) in an appropriate-sized basin or bowl (a sturdy plastic shoebox also works well for soaking either a hand or a foot).

Soak the affected toenails or fingernails in the vinegar solution for 15 minutes, then towel-dry your foot or hand. Follow that with a hair dryer set on *warm* for 1 or 2 minutes.

As the final step of this treatment, prepare a mixture of equal parts tea tree oil (a powerful fungus fighter) and lavender essential oil (a strong antimicrobial agent), and dab the solution on the infected nails.

NOTE: Nails take a long time to grow out completely—about 3 months for fingernails and 6 months for toenails. So be aware that, if you try this remedy, you may have to stick with it for a while.

Nausea

Nausea is an uneasiness in the stomach that may lead to vomiting—which can be a great relief. But it's not always convenient to relieve yourself if you're not at home.

Here are a few suggestions to relieve nausea, whether you're at home, at someone else's home, at a restaurant—or anyplace else, for that matter...

◆ Both of us carry either peppermint Altoids or Ricola cough drops at all times. These strong peppermint candies help make the nausea disappear as they settle the stomach.

◆ When you're feeling nauseous, sniff a piece of lemon or orange peel. To intensify the peel's scent, keep squeezing it as you sniff.

◆ Smelling the printer's ink from a black-and-white newspaper can relieve queasiness.

CAUTION: Severe indigestion or nausea may be a symptom of a more serious ailment, such as a heart attack or pulmonary embolism. If the nausea persists, seek medical attention immediately.

Nosebleed

Nosebleeds tend to be quite minor and can be brought on by several things—allergies, cold weather, sinus infection and other illnesses. When your nasal passages are irritated by rubbing, picking or blowing, the tiny blood vessels break...and the blood flows.

CAUTION: Nasal hemorrhaging—blood flowing copiously from both nostrils—requires immediate medical attention. Call 911 and get to the nearest hospital emergency department.

Also, recurrent nosebleeds may be a symptom of an underlying ailment. Seek appropriate medical attention.

◆ For an *occasional* nosebleed, the first thing to do is to gently blow your nose. Then pinch the fleshy part of your nostrils closed for 10 minutes. (If the nosebleed hasn't stopped after 10 full minutes, you should go to the emergency department.)

◆ You can also stop the nosebleed with lavender oil. Apply the oil with your finger, a cotton swab or a cotton ball. The oil should be soothing to your nasal membranes as it stops the bleeding.

CAUTION: Licensed naturopathic physician Nancy Caruso, ND, based in St. Clarkston, Michigan, recommends using only *therapeutic grade* essential oil (available at health-food stores or through naturopathic doctors) to treat nosebleeds.

If you use an adulterated essential oil (oil that's cut with alcohol or other chemicals), it will burn the inside of your nose.

Poison Ivy/Oak/Sumac

Poison weeds—such as ivy, oak and sumac—grow in just about every part of the United States. And these weeds all produce the same sort of uncomfortable reactions. Chances are, if you're allergic to 1 weed, you're allergic to them all. It's estimated that as many as 10 million Americans are affected by these plants.

> **NOTE:** Poison oak is to the West Coast of the US what poison ivy is to the Eastern part of the country. So the poison ivy remedies here should also be effective for treating poison oak.

◆ If you know that you brushed up against poison ivy, rinse off the area as soon as possible—within 3 to 5 minutes. Any cool liquid will work—water, soda, beer...the trick is to wash it off *quickly*.

The fast washing will help to neutralize or deactivate the poison ivy's *urushiol oil*—the nasty stuff that causes the itchy blisters.

It's important to use cool/cold water only—either warm or hot water will open the skin's pores and let in the urushiol oil.

◆ If you don't have time to wash away the oil —and you already have itchy blisters—then put ½ cup of baking soda in a bowl and add cold, black, brewed coffee...keep adding until it's the consistency of thick paste.

Apply the paste and leave it on until it flakes off by itself. This paste should take away the itch and help dry out the blisters. Keep reapplying it until the itching stops.

◆ If you don't brew your own coffee, then make a baking soda paste—mix 1 tablespoon of baking soda with 1 teaspoon of water. Glop it on the affected areas, let it dry and eventually flake off. This paste should take away the itch and help dry out the blisters.

◆ Truth be told—neither of us has had personal experience with the following whiskey remedy. We heard about it from several reliable sources, but we urge you to proceed with caution. And you should always be aware of your surroundings in areas that have poison ivy.

To help prevent poison ivy infections, moisten a washcloth with whiskey, and rub your exposed body parts with it before going into areas that might have poison ivy.

> **CAUTION:** Do not use whiskey on broken skin—the alcohol can sting! And NEVER apply alcohol to children's skin—it can be toxic.

◆ Another way to prevent poison ivy infections is to spray exposed skin with a deodorant that contains *aluminum chlorohydrate* (such as Right Guard). This active ingredient prevents the urushiol oil from sticking to skin.

◆ You have to *really* want to immunize yourself to try this remedy...first, get a goat and let it graze in a patch of poison ivy (this will not harm the goat).

Once the goat has eaten the poison ivy, put on gloves, cover up the rest of your body, and then milk the goat. Throw away that first milking. The *second* milking is the one to drink. Drink at least 2 cups of goat milk, and it will immunize you for a year. We *kid* you not.

Sinus Problems

Sinus conditions can be caused by changes in the weather, by a room that's overheated, by air-conditioning, by dust, by...gosh, by anything that collects in a person's mustache.

Symptoms of a sinus condition include a runny nose, nasal congestion, headache, neck ache, teary eyes, swollen eyelids—and then some. To discover your sinus trigger, pay attention to when and where symptoms begin.

And to help alleviate the symptoms, try the following elixir...

You can clear up sinus congestion with a "brace-yourself" cocktail. In a pot, combine 1 cup of tomato juice, 1 teaspoon of finely minced fresh garlic, ¼ to ½ teaspoon of cayenne pepper (depending on your hot-spice tolerance) and 1 teaspoon of lemon juice.

Heat the mixture until it's warm, but not too hot to drink. Pour it in a 10-ounce glass and brace yourself—then drink it. Expect good results quickly.

Sore Throat

A sore throat is a mild inflammation and should go away in about 3 days. But if it lasts longer, see your health care professional and get tested for strep throat—this bacterial infection of the throat and tonsils *must* be treated with antibiotics.

But mild sore throat pain can be alleviated with this soothing drink...

In a mug, mix ¼ teaspoon of cayenne pepper, ½ teaspoon of ginger powder and 1 rounded tablespoon of honey. Add 8 ounces of just-boiled water and stir. When the mixture is cool enough to drink, stir it some more and take a big sip. While the mixture is in your mouth, lean your head back, then lean your head to the right and then to the left, and finally, swallow.

Continue doing this with the rest of the drink. When you get down to the bottom of the mug, discard the residue. If your throat is still sore a few hours later, have another mug.

✳ Swab Away Sore Throats

To prevent sore throats, gently and carefully give your ears a once-over with a cotton swab dipped in 3% hydrogen peroxide—every day. Doing this should help prevent a sore throat.

Stress and Anxiety

There are as many symptoms and outward manifestations of anxiety as there are reasons for it. According to the National Health Interview Survey—reported by the Health Resource Network (a national nonprofit health education organization, *www.stresscure.com*)—75% of the general population experiences at least some stress every 2 weeks. Tranquilizers, antidepressants and antianxiety medications account for about 25% of all prescriptions that are written in the US each year.

We're hoping that you'll find positive, natural ways to cope and won't need a prescription. *Here are some ways to help you calm down, chill out, hang loose and feel happy—or at least feel happier...*

◆ Turn up the music—literally. According to a report in *Athletic Insight, The Online Journal of Sport Psychology* (*www.athleticinsight.com*), it's hard to hold on to or focus on negative thoughts while listening to loud music.

⚡ **CAUTION:** Be careful not to listen to music that is so loud that it can cause hearing loss or other damage to your ears.

Extended exposure to any noise above 90 decibels may injure your hearing—as a guideline, normal conversation is about 50 to 60 decibels, and most "loud music" is around 100 decibels.

◆ According to neurologist David Perlmutter, MD, founder of the Perlmutter Health Center in Naples, Florida, people who supplement with 1 or 2 grams of fish oil daily tend to have lower levels of stress hormones during anxiety-producing situations. The fish oil's DHA (a healthful fatty acid) helps regulate *serotonin*, the brain's feel-good chemical.

◆ Soothe your tension by stimulating the acupressure point (*Yingtan*), which is ¼" above the midpoint of your eyebrows. Once you've located it, use your middle finger to tap on it lightly for 10 seconds. Hey, just by stopping you'll feel better.

◆ Add magnesium, the antistress mineral, to your daily supplement regime. Nan Kathryn Fuchs, PhD, a nutritionist practicing in Sebastopol, California, and editor of the Women's Health Letter (*www.womenshealthletter.com*), says that when under stress, the body uses more magnesium than normal, and it takes it from anywhere it can—like your vital organs and bones.

Supply your body with 300 milligrams (mg) of magnesium daily to help cope with stress, and not at the expense of your organs and bones.

◆ Breathing easy is a key to relaxation, especially in stressful situations, such as having a job interview or speaking in public. Wearing too-tight clothes may be keeping you from breathing freely from the abdomen. Men, loosen your belts and ties. Ladies, loosen your belts and wear larger pantyhose that do not constrict your waistlines.

Wearing more comfortable clothes will allow you to expand your stomach as you take a few deep breaths. Those deep breaths will help you feel relaxed and less stressed, plus the inhaled oxygen will give you a boost of energy.

◆ Calm down with a very simple and effective eye exercise from clinical psychologist Fred Friedberg, PhD, author of *Do-It-Yourself Eye Movement Techniques for Emotional Healing* (New Harbinger). *Follow these instructions…*

Select 2 objects in front of you—something in the extreme right of your field of vision, and the other in the extreme left. Then, as you think about how stressed you are, move your eyes from 1 object to the other as fast as you can, 25 times.

Pause for a moment, then repeat the eye movement another 25 times…then pause and repeat for a third time. This repetitive side-to-side action slows your heart rate, blood pressure and breathing, which should make you feel a lot calmer.

◆ Soak a washcloth in ice-cold water and put it on the nape of your neck. Keep it there for about 10 minutes…enough time for the cold to constrict blood vessels and slow circulation to the head. That decreases activity in the brain's stress-storing region (the *hippocampus*), making it easier to shut down your anxiety-causing thoughts.

◆ Aromatherapy may make your drive time a lot more pleasant. Use 1 or 2 drops of essential oil (available at health-food stores) on a cotton ball, and tape it to your dashboard or wherever the scent will waft to your nostrils.

Need a picker-upper? Use peppermint oil for alertness, and cinnamon oil to increase blood flow. Have a problem with road rage? Calm down with some lavender or jasmine oil. Does traffic cause you anxiety? Orange oil will help to quell those nerves.

◆ Summer seems to be the most stressful season for women, according to Amy Niles, former president and CEO of the National Women's Health Resource Center in Red Bank, New Jersey (*www.healthywomen.org*). We wonder—could it simply be the mere thought of putting on a bathing suit?

Whatever the reason, chill out by walking barefoot and activating reflexology points in the soles of your feet. Doing this should have an immediate soothing effect from head to toe. Just be sure that wherever you walk barefoot—in your home, out on the patio, around the pool, on the lawn or at the beach—it's clean and free of stuff you don't want to be stepping on.

Walking barefoot is also a good idea for men who suffer from summer stress.

◆ Mitchell L. Gaynor, MD, senior medical oncology consultant at The Strang Cancer Prevention Center in New York City and author of *Sounds of Healing* (Broadway Books), said, "I've never found anything more powerful than sound and voice and music to begin to heal and transform every aspect of people's lives."

And so, to prevent stress, *sing…sing a song.* The breathing patterns used for singing are said to create chemical changes in the body that lower levels of the stress hormone *cortisol.* This helps to prevent stressful, anxious feelings. We know from experience that singing is an upper—it really does make you feel happier.

✳ **Stress-Busting Advice**

David J. Schwartz, PhD, author of *The Magic of Thinking Big* (Fireside) and an authority on motivation, gave great advice when he said, "To fight fear—act. To increase fear—wait, put off, postpone."

Both work. It's up to you—and only you—to dispel your fear by plunging in and doing whatever needs to be done, or to do nothing except let that fear fester and grow.

Skin Blemishes/Stretch Marks

Skin is among the human body's largest and heaviest organs. The average adult's skin measures 19 square feet and weighs about 9 pounds. The thinnest sections of skin are on your eyelids…the thickest are on your palms and the soles of your feet. Stretch marks occur when the skin gets stretched (obviously) and suffers small micro-traumas under the outer layer.

To help prevent stretch marks—or to speed the healing of them or any scars or blemishes on your 19 square feet of skin—you should know about coconut oil. *And we're here to tell you about it…*

Bruce Fife, ND, director of the Coconut Research Center in Colorado Springs, Colorado (*www.coconutresearchcenter.org*)—and the man we refer to as "The Coconut King"—recommends the daily use of extra-virgin coconut oil (available at health-food stores or on-line at *www.simplycoconut.com*) to help prevent stretch marks. It's especially appropriate for pregnant women and body builders, who are prone to developing stretch marks.

If you already have stretch marks or scars or blemishes of any kind—such as cuts, burns, insect bites, warts, moles—they will heal faster and with less scarring (if any) when treated with coconut oil.

Fife says to put the container of coconut oil in hot water until the oil is very warm—that way, it will be absorbed more efficiently and penetrate deeper into the skin. Massaging the oil into your skin also increases absorption.

The secret to getting the best and fastest results is to keep the coconut oil on the injured skin continually until it's healed. Apply the oil as often as is practical throughout the day.

It also helps to cover the oil with a bandage made from a piece of clean, white cloth or gauze, then put a piece of plastic wrap over the gauze and keep it all in place with medical tape. (Adhesive bandages like Band-Aids don't work well because the oil tends to dissolve the adhesive, causing them to slip off.)

Sties

If you develop a painful red bump on your eyelid, then you probably have a sty. A sty occurs when the oil glands around the eyelid get infected and inflamed. The classic remedy for when you feel a sty coming on (you know, that annoying little twinge each time you blink) is to rub a gold ring across it. *But when it's too late to "go for the gold" because the sty has already blossomed, try this remedy…*

Cut a potato in half and, with the edge of a spoon, scrape out about 3 tablespoons of raw potato. (Be sure to scoop—using a grater will make the potato too watery.)

Then roll up the glob of potato in a clean white handkerchief...or a triple layer of cheesecloth...or unbleached muslin, then lie down and place the poultice over your closed eye. Keep it there for about 40 minutes. When you take off the poultice, gently clean the area around your eye with a damp cloth.

If that annoying twinge doesn't ease off by bedtime, then apply a fresh poultice again before you go to sleep. Expect the sty to keep getting better until it completely disappears within a few days.

CAUTION: If the sty doesn't improve after 2 days, contact your doctor. You may have an eye infection or other serious problem that needs to be treated with a topical or oral antibiotic.

Sun Damage

Studies show that 80% of sun damage is from "incidental exposure"—such as waiting outside for a bus, walking to your car or sitting in a restaurant with the sun shining in. So, even though the average person may not be basking on the beach, he/she is exposed to the sun for about 18 hours a week...enough to cause skin damage if protective measures aren't taken. *So, listen up—for the sake of your skin...*

A moisturizing lotion can put a barrier between damaging sunlight and your skin. Choose a lotion with a *sun protection factor* (SPF) of at least 30—this means that, if you begin to burn after 10 minutes, SPF 30 extends your protection about 30 times longer, depending on your complexion and/or skin type, the strength of the sunlight, and the brand and amount of sunscreen you apply.

Most products are good at screening out the sun's UVB rays—the type of ultraviolet rays that cause sunburn and skin cancers. But you want a product that also offers protection against UVA rays—the kind that put wrinkles in your skin. Any of these ingredients—*oxybenzone* or *titanium dioxide* or *parsol 1789*—will help block out some of the UVA rays. Use the lotion daily—women, before applying makeup...men, after shaving.

Toothaches

See "Bad Breath, Gum Disease and Toothaches" on pages 293–294.

Tongue Burn

Which muscle of the body, proportional to size, is the strongest? Yes, it's the tongue! Well, with all the talking we do, it's no surprise that it gets lots of exercise.

Aside from helping us form words, whistle and blow bubbles with gum, the tongue makes it possible for us to enjoy food. Taste buds are located in different areas of the tongue, mostly around the edges. They are sensitive to 5 specific tastes—bitter, sour, salty, sweet and *umami* (the taste that is associated with monosodium glutamate—MSG).

It was probably 1 of those tasty foods that caused you to burn your tongue. *Here are a couple of soothing suggestions...*

◆ If you've just eaten spicy-hot food and you feel as though your tongue is on fire, swish whole or 2% milk, sour cream or yogurt around in your mouth. (Indian restaurants, which tend to serve very spicy food, always have yogurt in the kitchen.)

◆ When you eat something made with chili peppers or cayenne pepper and you burn your tongue, quickly eat a piece of chocolate. *Casein*, a protein in chocolate, seems to attach to and remove the *capsaicin*—the *hot-hot-hot* chemical compound found in chili peppers—from the tongue's nerve receptors. In any case, it's a good excuse to eat a piece of chocolate!

Urinary Problems

Also *see* "Bladder Infection" on page 294.

The urinary system includes the kidneys, ureters, bladder and urethra—organs and ducts that are involved in the body's release and elimination of urine.

The average adult bladder holds about 24 ounces of urine. When the walls of the bladder are stretched, nerve impulses trigger the urge to urinate. That usually happens when the bladder contains 10 to 16 ounces of urine.

The kidneys, which are located in the back of the abdomen, 1 on each side of the spine, are the principal organs of the urinary system. They filter the blood—all of it—once every hour.

Yes, the urinary system is extremely complex and, when something goes wrong, it needs to be properly diagnosed and cared for.

CAUTION: Any problem with the urinary system is a serious condition that should be evaluated and treated by a health care professional. Talk to your doctor before trying any natural remedy.

◆ A recent study conducted by Robert Levin, PhD, director of research at the Albany College of Pharmacy in Albany, New York, showed that eating ¾ cup of fresh grapes daily can prevent problematic urination urgency and frequency in men who have enlarged prostates.

Why? Because an enlarged prostate can compress the urethra, which reduces blood flow to the bladder and may cause muscle damage. That muscle damage can be responsible for increasing the urgency and frequency of urination. The grapes' antioxidants help protect against possible muscle damage.

CAUTION: An enlarged prostate can be a sign of cancer. If you are having difficulty with urination, it's important to consult your physician.

In addition, some prostate problems can be a symptom of a more serious condition—see your doctor for a thorough checkup.

◆ If you have a urinary tract infection (UTI), consider the following advice from Bruce Fife, ND, director of the Coconut Research Center in Colorado Springs, Colorado (*www.coconut researchcenter.org*) and author of *Coconut Cures* (Picadilly Books).

He says to drink 6 to 8 glasses of water and consume at least 3½ tablespoons of organic extra-virgin coconut oil (available at health-food stores) every day. Divide the oil into equal doses and take them throughout the day.

Start doing this the moment you suspect an infection is coming on. The earlier you start treatment, the quicker the problem will be resolved.

CAUTION: If you think you have a bladder infection or UTI, it's very important to check with your health care professional before trying any natural remedies. You may need to take an antibiotic.

◆ Drink 100% unsweetened cranberry juice (not juice blends) or take cranberry supplements to get the powerful antioxidants called *proanthocyanidins*. Look for grapeseed extract (also called *pycnogenol* or PCO) and follow the dosage instructions on the label.

Warts

The medical term for the common wart is *Verruca vulgaris*. (Don't you think a wart looks like a *Verruca vulgaris*?) Most warts appear on the hands and face—warts that appear on the sole of the foot are known as *plantar warts*. Warts are generally thought to be caused by some type of virus.

No other ailment is as rich in handed-down, ridiculous remedies as warts. For example—rub the wart with a stolen egg, then wrap the egg in brown paper and leave it at a cross-roads. When a stranger picks up the package and breaks the egg, the wart will be transferred from you to that stranger.

The most incredible thing about some of the outrageous remedies we've heard is that they actually work for some people! Here are a couple of *sensible* remedies that should work... and you don't even have to steal an egg.

◆ For plantar warts, mix 1 teaspoon of baking soda with 1 tablespoon of castor oil to create a paste. Put it on the plantar warts and cover with a small, square bandage. Apply a fresh mixture of the paste every morning and evening until the warts are gone. It could take anywhere from 1 week to 1 month.

◆ Dab some tea tree oil (available at health-food stores) on the warts with a cotton swab or cotton ball, and cover them with a bandage. Do this twice a day. Be consistent and patient.

CAUTION: Genital warts are a symptom of a sexually transmitted disease which *must* be treated by a health-care professional.

Weight Control

We won't bore you with talk about eating sensibly and exercising to lose weight—we're sure you've heard it all before.

But what you may not know are some suggestions that can help you stick to that sensible eating plan, speed up your metabolism and expand your healthful menu with interesting foods and beverages, as well as promote behavior modification, which will help you make healthier choices. *Read through the hints below with an open mind, then go to the supermarket with an adventurous spirit...*

◆ Bored with celery and carrot snacks? Enjoy the fresh, licorice-like taste of fennel stems and fronds, either raw or cooked. Fennel (available at most supermarkets and grocery stores) is a good digestive aid and may even help to lower blood pressure. There are only 12 calories in 3½ ounces.

◆ Have a *mochaccino* without the cost and without the calories. Mix 1 packet of sugar-free hot cocoa mix with 1 teaspoon of instant coffee. Add hot water (according to package directions) and stir. As a special treat, add a dollop of Cool Whip Lite (2 tablespoons contain 20 calories and 1 gram of fat).

◆ In a study, people who suppressed their mid-morning hunger pangs by eating 1 tablespoon of peanut butter every day lost nearly twice as much weight as those people who didn't eat the nutty spread.

Additional research reveals that daily peanut-butter eaters (limited to only 1 tablespoon a day) tend to eat 333 fewer calories a day on average.

Go Nuts for This Spread!
Try to eat all-natural peanut butter rather than commercial brands, which may have a lot of added sugar. We eat Maranatha Organic Peanut Butter (available at health-food stores). It has no sugar, no salt, no hydrogenated oils, no trans fats...nothing but dry-roasted peanuts and incredibly good taste.

◆ At your next meal, compare your serving sizes (*see* page 326) to the "correct" serving sizes that we should all be eating. Then gradually work your way down to the proper size portion.

One serving…	Is the size of…
1 cup of cereal flakes	a closed fist
3 ounces of cooked meat	a deck of cards
3–4 ounces of grilled or baked fish	a checkbook
½ cup of pasta	an ice cream scoop
½ cup of fruit	a tennis ball
1 serving of bread	a cassette tape
½ cup of vegetables	a light bulb
1½ ounces of cheese	4 dice
1 teaspoon of butter	a thumb tip
2 tablespoons of peanut butter	a ping pong ball

> ✍ **NOTE:** Keep portions smaller by serving food on small plates.

◆ There is a Zen Buddhist technique called "mindful eating," which is also known as "conscious eating." It means to pay attention to the smell, taste and texture of your food, and try to enjoy every mouthful.

Also be aware of your honest feeling of satisfaction. Keep asking yourself how hungry you are. Then establish a rating system from 1 to 5, with 1 being very hungry and 5 being very full. Learn to stop yourself when you reach 3 or 4.

◆ A study that was reported in the *Journal of Clinical Endocrinology & Metabolism* revealed that drinking 2 liters (½ gallon) of water over the course of the day will burn up to 100 calories total. Based on the findings of that study, bodybuilding.com concluded that by drinking cold water, most people will burn even more calories because the body has to work harder to bring the water up to 98.6°F.

> ✍ **NOTE:** For more information on the *Water-Induced Thermogenesis* study, visit the Web site for the *Journal of Clinical Endocrinology & Metabolism*—*http://jcem.endojournals.org*.

◆ Get on the scale—often. This may sound like simple advice but there's science behind it. It was demonstrated in a study conducted at the University of Minnesota with more than 3,000 overweight or obese adults over a two year period.

The results showed that people who weighed themselves every day lost twice as much weight as people who weighed themselves once a week. And people who reported that they never weighed themselves gained an average of four pounds.

There are many reasons that this tactic works—the researchers suggest that it might be the regular monitoring. We know—because Joan does this herself—that it helps to spot the extra pound or two and take action immediately.

Regardless of the reasons, weighing yourself costs nothing, takes only seconds, and the scale is probably right in the bathroom.

So take our word, and hop on it.

◆ There's a lot of talk about the many benefits of green tea, including its ability to increase the amount of calories the body burns. The credit is not due to the small amount of caffeine it contains, but to a powerful antioxidant called *epigallocatechin gallate* (EGCG).

When you shop for green tea, check the label—it should say that the tea used is standardized for caffeine and EGCG. Also make sure it's unsweetened and/or sugar-free. Drink up to 8 cups of green tea a day, along with eating a healthy, balanced diet. And (sorry to have to remind you) exercise regularly.

> ✍ **NOTE:** As a bonus, drinking green tea may help lower your cholesterol.

◆ If you are a couch potato, then laugh off the pounds by watching humorous television programs. In a study conducted at Vanderbilt

Use Your Nose to Lose Weight

"**T**he stronger the flavor of the food, the stronger its power to satisfy and reduce hunger," says Alan R. Hirsch, MD, neurologist, psychiatrist and director of The Smell and Taste Treatment and Research Foundation in Chicago. *Based on his extensive research, Dr. Hirsch offers the following suggestions...*

◆ Sniff each bite of food quickly 5 times before eating. Fast sniffs signal food messages to the brain—this decreases hunger and works to satisfy the appetite without consuming excess calories.

◆ The odor molecules of fresh-cut strawberries travel directly to the *limbic system* of the brain (which is involved in emotional behavior). From there, the molecules activate the *hypothalamus* (the brain's satiety center) and trick it into believing that you've eaten more than you have.

So, if you want to feel full faster, put some fresh-cut strawberries on your plate and *sniff-sniff-sniff-sniff-sniff*.

◆ Choose to eat hot foods. The heat and steam from the food send flavor molecules up the back of the throat and into the brain's satiety center faster than cold foods.

◆ Keep a bar of chocolate with you (we suggest dark chocolate). When the snack urge takes hold, sniff the candy—but don't eat it.

Just the smell of food can trick your body into thinking you've already eaten it.

University in Nashville, researchers found that subjects who watched TV shows that made them laugh burned up 20% more calories than non-laughers. The researchers calculated that laughing for 10 to 15 minutes a day could burn about 50 extra calories. And that's no joke!

◆ In restaurants, at home or at other people's dinner parties, eat the amount of food that's right for you, then place your eating utensils (probably a knife and fork) crisscrossed to form an X on top of the remaining food. As the plate sits there in front of you, the X will signal *NO MORE*.

And if that's not enough to stop you from mindlessly munching on the rest of the food, you'll think twice about picking up soiled silverware.

◆ A great way to sneak in exercise is by walking a dog. If you don't want to get your own, walk your neighbor's pooch or volunteer at a local animal shelter.

According to researchers at the College of Veterinary Medicine's Research Center for Human–Animal Interaction at the University of Missouri–Columbia, subjects in their study group averaged a weight loss of 14 pounds during a 1-year walking program.

◆ If you walk on a chilly day (with or without a dog), you can boost your metabolic rate by up to 4 times, due to muscle tensing when you shiver. That means you're burning off a lot of extra calories. Just don't stop off at the corner coffee shop for a calorie-laden caramel latte to warm you up.

◆ If you feel a food binge coming on, take a walk...a brisk walk. Your urge to binge will cool down as your body heats up.

◆ Two short exercise sessions a day will stimulate the metabolism more than 1 longer session. Take a brisk 15-minute walk in the

Compounding Pharmacy

A compounding pharmacy customizes medication to meet individual patient needs, based on the specifications set by the prescribing physician. Compounding pharmacists have studied chemical interactions and compatibilities more thoroughly than all other health care professionals, plus they have the ability to prepare various dosage forms.

Scott Berliner, RPh, a natural pharmacist and nutritional educator practicing in Monroe, New York, explained to us that there are situations where compounding use becomes a necessity. *He cites these examples...*

◆ When medications are not available commercially and an alternate chemical or dosage form is required. Another scenario may be that a patient is allergic to a preservative in a prescription medication.

◆ When medications are not stable, small quantities can be prepared more frequently to ensure stability.

◆ When commercial medications need alteration. A patient may need a different dosage form (lozenge instead of capsule...liquid instead of tablet), flavor (especially for children) or strength (seniors often require doses lower or higher than others).

Example: Mr. Berliner makes an anti-inflammatory that is 5 times as strong as ibuprofen, yet it does not upset the stomach and can be applied directly to the inflamed site to bring down swelling. His pain medications are made without Tylenol and can be time-released for extended action.

Mr. Berliner is owner and president of Life Science Pharmacy, Life Science Nutrition and VetRxLife Science Pharmacy. In his practice at Life Science Pharmacy (845-781-7613, *www.life sciencepharmacy.com*), all medications are made in a sterile laboratory from raw material using Food and Drug Administration (FDA)-approved, United States Pharmacopoeia (USP)-approved and National Formulary (NF)-approved products.

To find a compounding pharmacist in your area, contact the International Academy of Compounding Pharmacists' referral service at 800-927-4227 or *www.iacprx.org*.

morning and another in the afternoon. Do this 5 days a week for a full month, and see if it makes a big difference on the scale.

◆ Sit at the edge of a chair with your spine straight and stay that way for 10 minutes. Do this while you're in front of your computer and again when you're in front of the TV.

Sitting erect, unsupported, for 10 minutes twice a day will help tone your core (midsection) muscles. You should see a difference within 2 weeks.

◆ Daily prayer or meditation stimulates the *amygdala* (the part of the brain that controls emotional behavior) and activates the release of *serotonin*, a neurotransmitter that helps curb cravings.

In some studies, subjects prayed daily and lost weight without dieting or exercising. Of course, prayer *plus* a sensible diet and exercise routine is ideal and most advisable for good health as well as weight loss.

NOTE: Do not start any exercise program without permission from your doctor. Trying to do too much too soon can sometimes lead to injury.

Consult your health-care professional for a physical evaluation and instructions on how to start an exercise routine.

◆ Colorado–based nutritional expert Marc David, former workshop leader at Kripalu Center for Yoga and Health in Lenox, Massachusetts, and author of *The Slow Down Diet: Eating for Pleasure, Energy, and Weight Loss* (Healing Arts Press), said that the practice of praying before eating a meal—and by this, he meant heartfelt praying, not just rattling off a few words of thanks for the food—puts the body into a relaxation response. The effect of regular prayer before meals is that you can completely change your digestive metabolism in less than 1 minute.

Changing your metabolism through prayer means you can absorb nutrients better, have greater blood flow and oxygen to the stomach and manufacture more digestive enzymes. We *pray* it works for you. ■

■ Products ■

RESPeRATE

This is a medical device for lowering blood pressure. It is not a drug and has no side effects, and has been cleared by the Food and Drug Administration (FDA).

The relaxing treatment takes only 15 minutes a day (at least 3 days a week…more often is better). With earphones and a portable CD player, the simple and pleasant 15-minute sessions guide your breathing to therapeutic levels.

Source: InterCure, Inc., 877-988-9388, *www.resperate. com.*

CAUTION: If you take blood pressure medication, continue to take it as directed under your doctor's supervision, even while you are using the RESPeRATE system.

Automatic Blood Pressure Monitor with Comfit Cuff

Have you heard about "white coat syndrome"? That happens when your blood pressure rises because you're nervous when seeing your doctor. You can keep track of your blood pressure at home, and here's an easy-to-use home test that remembers and stores your blood pressure history—and may even detect an irregular heartbeat. According to the manufacturer, this technology is particularly important for people with certain forms of arrhythmia or heart disorders.

The Cuff fits arms that are 9" to 17" around.

(Ask a salesperson for another size if this does not fit.) Comes with an illustrated instruction manual, a brochure explaining blood pressure, 4 AA batteries, an AC adapter and a storage case.

This monitor is available all over the country at retail and drugstores.

Source: Omron Healthcare, Inc., 877-216-1333 for customer service, *www.omronhealthcare.com.*

NOTE: Omron also has a Wrist Blood Pressure Monitor that only weighs about 9 ounces and is great for travel.

Purebrush Antibacterial Toothbrush Purifier

We never want to be without this product! We think it's an important way to help maintain good health. Why? This purifier eliminates the dark, moist environment that allows microbes to thrive and multiply in a toothbrush holder.

We don't even like to think about germs or bacteria that can spread from 1 toothbrush to another, making family members sick. You can even reinfect yourself with your own toothbrush.

Purebrush self-starts with each use, holds up to 4 toothbrushes at a time, bathes the toothbrush(es) in warm disinfecting germicidal ultraviolet light for 1 hour, and turns off automatically.

This purifier has been clinically proven to eliminate 99.9% of all yeast, molds, viruses, bacteria and illness-causing microorganisms from your toothbrush.

Source: Murdock Laboratories, Inc., 800-439-2497, *www.purebrush.com.*

InnerScan Body Composition Monitor

This high-tech scale is a sleek addition to the bathroom. And it's a great gift for any health-conscious person.

An easy-to-read LCD screen displays your weight, calculates your body fat percentage, body water percentage and bone mass.

This machine can estimate how many calories you can consume within the next 24 hours to maintain your current weight, which is helpful for dieters.

The monitor can store personal details for up to 4 people between the ages of 7 to 99. There's also a Guest Mode for anyone who wants a reading just once. Four AA batteries are included.

Source: Tanita Corporation of America, Inc. To find a store, call 847-640-9241 or visit *www.tanita.com.*

CAUTION: Do not use the body composition feature if you are pregnant, or have a pacemaker or any other electronic implanted medical device.

CardioChek® Cholesterol Monitor

In the comfort and convenience of your own home, find out between doctor's visits whether your diet, exercise and medication are affecting your cholesterol numbers.

The CardioChek® Cholesterol Monitor gives a reliable total cholesterol reading within 1 minute using just 1 drop of blood. It also includes information on your triglycerides, ketone and glucose levels. The monitor is compact, portable and the batteries are included.

Source: Polymer Technology Systems, 877-870-5610, *www.cardiochek.com.*

NOTE: A test strip is required for each cholesterol test. These strips must be purchased separately because they have an expiration date.

CHAPTER 13

Care for Your Fuzzy Friends

Your dog…he's your best friend, your partner, your defender. You are his life, his love, his leader. He will be yours—faithful and true—to the last beat of his heart, so you owe it to him to be worthy of such devotion.

Thousands of years ago, cats were worshipped as gods. And the cats seem to have never forgotten this. A wise man once said, "In order to keep a true perspective of one's importance, everyone should have a dog that will worship him and a cat that will ignore him." We say, "Whoever said you can't buy happiness never had a pet."

In the United States, humans are outnumbered by their domestic animals. According to the *2005–2006 National Pet Owners Survey,* which was conducted by the American Pet Products Association (APPA), pet ownership is at its highest level, with 63% of all U.S. households owning a pet.

Aside from freshwater fish (139 million), cats are the most popular pets (90.5 million), followed by dogs (73.9 million). Think about it —almost 91 million cats and 74 million dogs… that's a lot of kitty litter and poop scooping!

For more information on pet products or to learn more about the APPA Pet Owners Survey, contact the organization at 800-452-1225 or *www.americanpetproducts.org.*

Naming Pets

The most popular dog name in the United States is "Max." The second most popular name is "Jake," and then "Buddy." The most popular name for cats is "Tigger."

If you're in the market for a pet's name, stay away from those with only 1 syllable, which may sound like a command. For instance, "Sid" can sound like "sit," and "Joe" can sound like "no." Names like these may confuse a pet, especially when you train it to obey commands.

For pet-name suggestions, or if you want to know the meaning of your pet's name, visit Amy Lyden's informative Web site at *www.bowwow.com.au* for answers.

It has been estimated that American pet owners spent $36.3 billion on their companion animals in 2005 (the most recent year for statistics)—this includes veterinary care, food and treats, supplies and grooming services. The hints in this section may help you save some of that money, while still giving your pet the best care possible.

PET SAFETY

Although having a pet is generally a wonderful experience, it comes with many responsibilities, including keeping your pet safe. Much like children, pets sometimes have a way of getting into things that can be dangerous to them. *Here are some tips that should help keep your pet out of harm's way...*

No "Strings" Attached

We've all seen cartoons of cats frolicking with balls of yarn. But that's the only place it should happen. In real life, yarn, twine, ribbon and tinsel can choke a cat—either the cat can swallow it, or get tangled up in it during play.

Keep those stringy things out of kitty's reach, and invest instead in some safe toys for your furry friend.

Electrical Cords

If your pet wants to live dangerously by chewing on electrical cords or household wiring of any kind, rub the cords with a dry bar of soap. If the smell of the soap doesn't deter him/her, then the taste certainly will.

Ensure Your Pet's Safety

In America, a companion animal is lost, stolen or goes missing every 30 seconds. Collars and identification tags may not be enough to keep your pet safe. They can fall off—or be removed—and the animal can slip out of a collar. *But tattoos and microchips are forever...*

Tattoos

There are several companies that work with veterinarians to tattoo ID numbers on all pets. The number is then entered into a national database, along with the owner's name and contact information.

When a tattooed animal is found and brought to a humane society, municipal animal shelter, SPCA, breed club, police station or veterinarian, the person in charge will call the Tattoo-A-Pet's toll-free number.

A live 24/7 operator will put the tattoo number into the database. If the number is in the database, the animal owner's name and contact information will be retrieved, and he/she will be contacted—and soon reunited with his no-longer-lost pet.

If you want this kind of protection for your pet, find out more by visiting *http://tattoo-a-pet.com* or call 800-TATTOOS (828-8667).

Microchips

The microchip is the size and shape of a grain of rice. Your pet's veterinarian injects the chip through a needle between the animal's shoulder blades. (In birds, the chip is injected under the wing.)

This 10-second procedure causes the same amount of "Yelp!" as any other injection—well, maybe a bit more since a bigger needle is used. The numeric ID code stored on the chip corresponds to the owner's contact information in a database.

If you're interested in this kind of protection for your pet, find out more by visiting *www.avidid.com* or call 800-336-AVID (2843).

✎ **NOTE:** Implanted microchips may not be compatible with all scanners. Check with your pet's vet and the local animal shelter and/or animal control officer for the most compatible brand for your area.

Toxic Plants

We hate to tell you this, but there are more than 700 kinds of plants that may be poisonous to your pet. Chances are, you've never even *heard* of most of the plants, let alone have them in your home or on your property.

But there are some common plants that are toxic, which you may have in your garden...or sitting in your living room...or hanging overhead—such as hydrangea, Easter lilies, tiger lilies, daffodils, larkspur, foxglove, lily of the valley, philodendron, dieffenbachia, schefflera, asparagus fern, rhododendron and azaleas, as well as the leaves and stems from tomato plants.

Holiday greenery—such as holly, mistletoe, ivy and poinsettias—can also make your cat or dog sick. If you have any of them decorating your house, be sure they're in a place where your pet won't be able to nibble on them. And, as a rule, it's a good idea to keep pets out of all vegetable and flower gardens.

If you think that your pet has eaten a poisonous plant, look for symptoms—diarrhea, loss of appetite, vomiting, mouth swelling and excessive salivation—then take your pet to the veterinarian. Since treatment is based on the type and amount of the plant that was eaten, if possible, bring along a leaf from that plant.

Before bringing home a new plant, check the list of the most frequently encountered toxic plants. It's available on the ASPCA's Poison Control Center Web site at *www.apcc.aspca.org*, or call customer service at 888-426-4911.

If your pet has been exposed to a poisonous plant, you can call the ASPCA Hot Line at 888-426-4435 (there may be a charge for a consultation).

The Humane Society of the United States (HSUS) also has a list of plants that are toxic to cats and dogs on its Web site, *www.hsus.org*.

Accidental Falls

Accidental falls from high places kill or injure thousands of animals annually. The only time your pet should be allowed on a balcony or terrace unsupervised is if the area is screened in or the pet is on a leash (just make sure it's short enough so that he can't jump over the edge and hang himself).

Install tight-fitting screens on all open windows or make sure that any existing guard rails are secure.

Professional Pet Care

When you must travel and can't take your pet with you, wouldn't it be comforting to have a reliable pet-sitter? The National Association of Professional Pet Sitters (NAPPS) has a database of certified members available throughout the country. For more information, visit the NAPPS Web site at *http://petsitters.org*.

Fire

Stick several brightly colored "Pet Alert" decals (available at pet stores) on the doors or windows of your home.

If there's an emergency when you are away from home, the decals will let the firefighters know how many—and what type of—pets need saving. If possible, include the pets' names and a brief physical description of each.

Pools/Water

♦ It's important to be just as attentive with puppies around a swimming pool as you would be with a young child. Better yet, put up a fence to keep pets away from the pool or any body of water.

If a fence is not possible, and your dog is determined to stay poolside, teach him how to get out of the pool. Do this by getting in the pool with him and guiding him to the steps. Keep doing this until he can swim to the steps and get out of the pool by himself.

◆ Not all dogs are natural swimmers. If you're taking your dog out on the water, you may want to put a life vest (available at most pet stores) on him. Even if your dog can swim, a life vest can save his life in emergency boating mishaps.

The Kitchen

◆ Store or throw away food, including leftovers, as soon as possible—don't leave anything out on a kitchen counter where your pet can get to it. Meat bones can choke or damage a pet's throat or intestinal tract.

◆ You may mean well, but shoveling leftovers into your pet's bowl is not doing him any favors. If there's a little too much fat in the food scraps, it may affect the pet's digestive system in a very negative way.

Also, you may not realize that some food may contain ingredients (such as onions or chocolate) that can be harmful.

◆ Be sure that your garbage can is impenetrable. Just as you don't want your pet getting at food on the counter, you don't want him getting at the discarded food in the garbage.

◆ If your pet pokes his paws into places that may be dangerous for him, install child-safety locks on your kitchen cabinets—for example, the cabinets in which you keep household cleaning products.

The Bathroom

◆ Do not leave plugged-in appliances—such as a blow-dryer, curling iron, electric rollers or face steamer—unattended. A pet may pull it off a counter and burn himself (or accidentally start a fire). If you're lucky, your pet won't get hurt, but you may have to replace the broken appliance.

◆ Do not give your pet access to water unless it's in a bowl for him to drink. Keep toilet-seat covers down…keep sinks and the bathtub empty.

◆ All medications should be stored in a secure or locked cabinet. You don't want your pet showing you how easy it is for him to chew through a child-proof pill bottle.

Every Room in the House

◆ Examine venetian-blinds cords and drapery tiebacks to make sure that they won't accidentally turn into a noose when a playful pet has access to them.

◆ Think twice about having lit candles around if you have a dog or cat who may want to make a game of playing with or putting out the flame—or whose tail may be at the same height as the fire.

◆ Regular exposure to secondhand smoke can lead to allergies and other health challenges for your pet. (We won't even begin to get into the harm it can do to you.)

Birds' delicate respiratory systems are especially affected by smoke. Do not allow any visitors in your home to light up…for the sake of your pets.

The Garage and Driveway

You know the little dark syrupy puddles that pool under or near a car? Chances are, it's *ethylene glycol,* which is antifreeze. Sometimes the liquid is bluish-green or pink. Dogs and cats like to lick it because it tastes sweet.

But antifreeze is extremely toxic to pets—a few licks could be fatal—so be sure to check regularly for spills and thoroughly clean up any leaks. If you have a supply of toxic solutions stored in the garage (or basement), keep them in a secure place where pets cannot get access to them.

> **NOTE:** If you notice any antifreeze leaks, sprinkle some sawdust or kitty litter on the spill to absorb the liquid, then mop up any remains. And have your car checked because it shouldn't be leaking antifreeze!

MEDICINE FOR CATS & DOGS

Several pet owners we know have to sedate themselves before going through the ordeal of giving medicine to their pets. We found some ways to make the job more humane…maybe even easy. *Read through these suggestions, which may help you help your pet…*

Giving Your Cat Medicine

◆ It's not easy to get a cat to swallow a pill. You may need someone to help you keep the cat in place. Start by holding your cat firmly either on your lap or between your knees.

To open his/her mouth, put pressure on each side of his jaw. Place the pill as far back on the tongue as possible and then close his mouth. Hold it closed until he swallows. You may have to gently massage his throat to make that happen.

◆ A gentler way of dealing with medicine in pill form is to mash it and combine it with enough milk or tuna juice to make a paste. Then spread the tasty paste on the cat's paw or nose, and he'll do what comes naturally… lick it up.

◆ It is easier to get a cat to lick liquid medicine than to pop a pill. Drip the liquid on his fur—on any area his tongue can reach.

Giving Your Dog Medicine

◆ If your dog won't take a pill, stick it in a clump of peanut butter, cheese or any yummy food that he would consider a rare treat.

◆ If your dog won't eat food that contains liquid medicine, add some plain yogurt to cover up the strange smell. If he balks at that, then you have no choice but to force the medicine down his throat.

Prevent messy spills by putting your dog in the bathtub (make sure that there is a rubber mat or non-skid pads on the tub floor). It also helps to have an assistant who can hold your dog still.

Pull out the corner of the dog's lower lip, forming a pocket. Dispense the medicine into that pocket a little at a time. Hold the dog's jaws closed until he swallows. You or your assistant should be able to get him to swallow by gently rubbing his throat.

> **NOTE:** When administering any supplement or medication, it's best to check with your pet's veterinarian to determine the appropriate dosage, based on the animal's weight. *The general weight classifications for dogs are…*
>
> ◆ **Miniature:** Less than 10 lbs.
> ◆ **Small:** 11 to 20 lbs.
> ◆ **Medium:** 21 to 50 lbs.
> ◆ **Large:** 51 to 80 lbs.
> ◆ **Extra-large:** More than 80 lbs.

⑤ Pet Prescriptions

When you buy medication directly from your veterinarian, chances are you pay top dollar. However, more than 600 veterinary drugs are approved for human use (such as certain anti-depressants and antibiotics), and are likely to be available at your local pharmacy.

This means that you can save money by buying the *generic* form of your pet's prescribed medicine at your local pharmacy. Ask your pet's veterinarian for a prescription and for appropriate dosage instructions.

WEATHER

Humans are not the only creatures who suffer from extremes of heat or cold. You should be aware that weather conditions affect your pet. It's important to keep your pet comfortable and happy—so here are some safeguards to help protect him/her in all types of weather.

> ⚡ **CAUTION:** Cats should not go outside when the temperature dips below 0°F. Their ears have very little protective fur, and frostbite can set in very easily. Dogs should not go outside when it's –10°F or below. Then again, neither should you.

Cold-Weather Insulation

If your pet goes outside during the cold months, feed him 10% to 20% more food and supplement his diet with healthy *essential fatty acids* (EFAs), such as flaxseed oil, black currant–seed oil, cod-liver oil (available at health-food stores) and olive oil. Dosage for a cat or a small dog is only about ⅛ teaspoon of oil daily. The EFAs along with the extra calories help pets build insulation against the cold.

White Cats and the Sun

White cats do not have protective pigment, so it's important to keep them inside on sunny days when there is snow on the ground. The sun reflects off the snow and increases the cat's risk of developing skin cancer.

Dogs Walking in Snow

Chemicals like rock salt, which is used to melt snow or make it less slippery, can irritate a dog's paws. And what does he do? He licks his sore paws, ingesting those nasty chemicals, and that can make him sick.

You can prevent that from happening by protecting your dog's paws *before* he goes outside. Put small plastic sandwich bags over his paws, keeping them in place with rubber bands. If they're too slippery (or if your dog simply won't wear them), cover his paws with baby socks, also kept in place with rubber bands.

Clean Your Dog's Unprotected Paws

If your dog went out in the snow without protection, as soon as you both get home, wash his paws with a mixture of 1 tablespoon of baking soda and 1 cup of warm water. It will soothe the burning caused by the rock salt.

Prevent Stuck Pads

When your dog is going out in clean, pure, out-in-the-country, unsalted snow, spray the bottom of his paws with nonstick vegetable spray so that the snow won't get packed between his pads.

Soothe Winter Paws

Dry winter air and walking on snow and ice can cause a dog's pads to become cracked and sore. Massage a little petroleum jelly into his pads and between the toes to soothe them.

The Calm During the Storm

If your dog or cat gets frightened during a thunderstorm, you can calm him down by pressing his *Tin Yang* acupressure point.

It's located in the center of the forehead, a little higher than the eyes and a little lower than where the animal's eyebrows would be—if he had eyebrows. Use your thumb to press that point for 2 minutes.

According to an acupressure practitioner, when an animal is frightened, his *chi* (life energy) becomes scattered. The *Tin Yang* point stimulation will distract him from his fear of the thunder by refocusing his life energy and replacing that fear with a wonderful sense of safety. This remedy may be used whenever your pet is in need of calming.

NOTE: You can find a certified veterinarian-acupuncturist by visiting *www.ivas.org*, the Web site of the International Veterinary Acupuncture Society.

To learn more about the benefits of acupressure for your pet, for training programs or to locate an acupressure practitioner, visit *www.animalacupressure.com*.

Dog Days of Summer

During the summer, protect your dog from the sun's strong rays. Keep him indoors or in the shade between 10:00 a.m. and 4:00 p.m.

If you do take him out in the sun for a long stretch of time between those hours, then ask your pet's vet to recommend a nontoxic sunblock (SPF 15 or 30) to put on the tips of his ears, the top of his nose and around his mouth—any of the places where there's hardly any protective fur.

CAUTION: If you have a molded-plastic pet carrier, DO NOT use it in hot weather. If you need to transport your pet in it, be aware that the heat inside can build up and present a real danger to your pet.

FOOD & DRINK

Did you know that when dogs eat, they rely on their sense of smell more than on their taste buds? Did you realize that cats can't taste sweets? And it's just as well since sweets are not good for cats and dogs. Here are some important details about food no-no's for pets and other ideas to make the most of mealtime.

Chocolate? Never!

Chocolate, especially baking chocolate, can be toxic to both cats and dogs. Don't leave a candy dish with Hershey's Kisses or other wrapped chocolates lying around. Your pet may be able to smell the chocolate and eat it with the foil.

In case you're wondering, it's the *theobromine*, an alkaloid in chocolate, that affects the animal's central nervous system and heart muscle. As little as 2 ounces of milk chocolate can be fatal to a puppy.

CAUTION: If you discover that your dog has ingested chocolate, call your veterinarian immediately. You can also contact your local emergency vet clinic (check the *Yellow Pages*), animal hospital or poison control center for instructions.

Grapes, Currants and Raisins? Never!

It's been discovered that grapes, currants and raisins can cause kidney failure in dogs and possibly in cats as well. The toxic amount is 1 ounce for every 2.2 pounds of body weight.

The reason these fruits are poisonous is still unknown. So, if your pet swallows more than a few grapes, currants or raisins, call your vet immediately. Prompt treatment can often result in a full recovery.

Onions? Bad!

Onions are a no-no for dogs and cats because they can cause *anemia* (low blood iron) and possibly death. You may not remember the onions in your leftovers, which is another good reason not to feed your pet leftovers.

Symptoms to watch for include vomiting, diarrhea and poor appetite—contact your pet's vet if you think he consumed onions.

NOTE: Garlic also can be toxic to dogs and to cats.

Yogurt for Gas Prevention

Twice a day, feed your pet some plain yogurt— 1 teaspoon for every 10 pounds of body weight. The yogurt's friendly bacteria, *Lactobacillus acidophilus*, helps break down food quickly in the intestines, improving digestion and preventing gas buildup.

To reduce excess flatulence, add ¼ teaspoon each of dill and fennel to the yogurt.

Dry Food vs. Canned Food

Many vets recommend dry food over canned food. Dry food is just that…dry. Canned food is

Beware of These Foods

Here is a list of foods (provided by the Humane Society of the United States, *www.hsus.org*) that are potentially poisonous to pets…

- Alcoholic beverages
- Apple seeds
- Apricot pits
- Avocados (toxic to birds, mice, rabbits, horses, cattle and dairy goats)
- Cherry pits
- Candy (particularly chocolate, which is toxic to dogs, cats and ferrets…and any candy containing the sweetener Xylitol)
- Coffee (grounds, beans, chocolate-covered espresso beans)
- Hops (used in home beer-brewing)
- Macadamia nuts
- Moldy foods
- Mushroom plants
- Mustard seeds
- Onions and onion powder
- Peach pits
- Potato leaves and stems (green parts)
- Raisins (excessive intake of red grapes should also be avoided)
- Rhubarb leaves
- Salt
- Tea (caffeine)
- Tomato leaves and stems (green parts)
- Walnuts
- Yeast dough

sticky and will stay on your pet's teeth, attracting odor-causing bacteria.

Dry food has an abrasive crunch that can help polish your pet's teeth. The best thing to do is mix a bit of water or oil into the dry food to soften it. Your pet will get all the teeth-cleaning benefits of dry food without the stinky breath that may result from canned food.

An equal mix of dry and canned food might be better for cats, who don't have a thirst mechanism and might not drink enough water.

Canned Food

If you feed your pet an entire can of wet food at a time, it's easier and more efficient to open each end of the can and push out the food with a lid, rather than to scoop out the food with a spoon. Just make sure no metal splinters get into the food.

Dry-Food Storage

If you store big economy-sized bags of dry food in your garage or basement, keep hungry 4-legged critters from getting into them—put the bags of food in big plastic garbage cans with secure lids.

Cat's Bowl

A deep, narrow bowl is a no-no for a cat because it's not roomy enough for his/her whiskers. As you may know, a cat's whiskers have sensitive nerve endings. A shallow bowl or saucer—the wider, the better—will allow him to enjoy his food and water in comfort.

Bowl Placement

Your pet will be more comfortable and secure if he faces the room when he eats and drinks. Place his food and water bowls 2 or 3 feet away from any wall so that there's enough room to position himself behind the bowls, facing out into the room.

When the bowls are placed against the wall, the pet has to eat with his back to the room. That may make him feel vulnerable and nervous, and he will scarf down his food as quickly as he can.

Place Mat

Put a place mat of some kind—an old bathtub mat, a frayed towel or a section of a no-longer-used runner—under your pet's bowls. The idea is to keep the bowls in place, and keep the floor clean and dry.

If the place mat doesn't work for you, glue a rubber jar ring to the bottom of the bowl to keep it in place while your pet eats.

Making Cat's Food Appetizing

If your cat is acting finicky about his food, trickle some oil or water from a can of tuna fish on whatever you're serving. This should whet his appetite.

Garden Water Dish

Create a permanent place for your pet's outdoor water dish. But instead of a dish, use a Bundt pan (most supermarkets sell them), which has a big hole in the middle. Hammer a stake into the ground where you want the dish to be, then place the pan around it.

> **NOTE:** As with any outdoor water dish, make certain that you thoroughly clean it every day. Birds, insects and bacteria can get into it, making it potentially harmful for the pet to drink the water.

Hydrate Outdoors

If you and your dog go outside on a sunny summer day, be sure to bring a bottle of water and a Frisbee. After playing catch, turn over the Frisbee and use it as a saucer for the water.

FLEAS

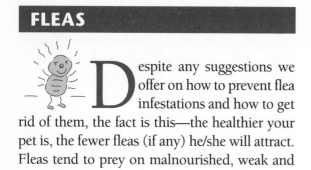

Despite any suggestions we offer on how to prevent flea infestations and how to get rid of them, the fact is this—the healthier your pet is, the fewer fleas (if any) he/she will attract. Fleas tend to prey on malnourished, weak and sick animals.

One of the most effective ways to improve the health of any animal (including us humans) is to improve the quality of its diet. And the best way to improve the diet is by including more wholesome, natural foods and fewer processed, commercial foods.

If you're willing to put in the time preparing food for your pet, rather than just opening a can or a bag, we suggest that you pick up a good book like *Dr. Pitcairn's New Complete Guide to Natural Health for Dogs and Cats* (Rodale Books) by Richard Pitcairn, DVM, PhD, and Susan Hubble Pitcairn, and let it guide you.

Meanwhile, here are some ways in which you can help your pet fight fleas and win....

Check for Fleas

Get your pet to stand on a large piece of white paper, then brush him. If he has fleas, you will see tiny black specks land on the paper. And they will probably be moving.

Lemon Chaser

Thinly slice 2 lemons and place the slices in a pot with a quart of water. Boil for 1 hour, then let it steep overnight.

In the morning, strain out the lemon and keep the liquid in a jar or spray bottle. Once a day, groom your pet with a flea comb, then spray or sponge his coat with the lemon water.

⚡ **CAUTION:** Test a bit of the tonic on a small patch of your pet's skin first to make sure he's not allergic to citrus oil.

The smell of citrus repels fleas. The elixir may also help heal your pet's flea-bitten skin. And if that's not enough, the astringent properties in lemon will help to clean and brighten your pet's coat.

Fleas Hate Vinegar

Add distilled white vinegar to your pet's drinking water—1 teaspoon to each quart of water.

B-1 Without Fleas

Brewer's yeast (available at health-food stores) is rich in vitamin B-1 (thiamin) and—when added to your pet's diet—is said to build your pet's immune system and help repel fleas. The recommended dosage is 1 rounded tablespoon for each 50 pounds of pet.

The good news is that your pet may not be bothered by fleas...the bad news is that brewer's yeast may cause excess gas. To minimize the gas situation, feed the brewer's yeast to your pet in small amounts—in plain yogurt and other moist foods.

⚡ **CAUTION:** According to Alfred Plechner, author of *Pet Allergies* (Very Healthy Enterprises), brewer's yeast is among the most common allergens...along with beef, wheat, eggs and corn. If your pet has a history of food allergies, have his veterinarian test him before using brewer's yeast.

Cat Coat Shiner and Flea Repellent

Rub mayonnaise into your cat's skin and fur, then wipe him clean with a damp washcloth. It should give him a shiny coat while helping to keep fleas away.

Flea Collar

Many pets have had a bad experience with side effects from a commercial flea collar's overly powerful ingredients.

Instead, try this simple and safe herbal flea collar…soak a piece of heavy and smooth twine—long enough so it fits securely around your pet's neck—in pennyroyal oil (available at health-food stores) for 24 hours. Then hang it up in the bathtub until it stops dripping.

When it's dry, tie the twine around your pet's identification collar to repel fleas. Fleas hate pennyroyal!

> ⚡ **CAUTION:** DO NOT use pennyroyal if you, your pet or *anyone* in your household is pregnant, including other pets.

Flea-Repellent Pillow

◆ Drive fleas away by attacking their keen sense of smell. Make a small pillow or sachet bag and fill it with cedar chips or shavings, or chamomile leaves—loose or in tea bags. Attach the sachet securely to your pet's collar, especially since fleas tend to work their way up to their victim's head.

◆ You can also use a small piece of an old pillowcase, and make a little pillow. Fill it with equal parts (about ½ cup each) of rosemary and oregano, and keep it in the doghouse or attach it to the pad on your pet's bed.

Getting Fleas Where They Live

Get rid of fleas on your pet by combing his coat thoroughly, especially around the neck and head. Check your pet-supply store for flea combs. These combs have closely set teeth and will dig out the fleas and flea eggs.

Dip the comb in a clean, empty 32-ounce jar filled with water, and add 1 tablespoon of liquid dish detergent. Then comb and dip, comb and dip until your pet is flea-free.

Old-Fashioned Soap and Water

Bathe your dog once a week with Dr. Bronner's Peppermint Soap (available at health-food stores) or any good, natural dog shampoo (a friend of ours recommends Green Ban). Doing this will go a long way in controlling fleas.

Salt Them Away

Fleas live and breed in carpeting and on furniture. If you have a serious infestation of fleas, you must vacuum (at least every week) all the areas where your pet hangs out.

Then sprinkle common table salt in all of those same places and, after 48 hours, vacuum again. Repeat the procedure—sprinkle salt, and 48 hours later, vacuum.

Hopefully by then, the vacuum will have sucked up all of the original fleas and those that hatched during the 4-day salting.

You may be surprised to know that fleas love salt so much that they will probably gorge themselves to death on it.

> ✎ **NOTE:** It's not necessary to change the vacuum bag in between each cleaning, since the fleas sucked into the vacuum are (or will be) dead.
>
> But if the thought of them being in the vacuum bag bothers you (as it would us!), then by all means replace the bag.

Let Fleas Take a Powder

There are all kinds of flea powders available. Some contain harsh pesticides and potentially harmful chemicals.

If you use a flea product and you suspect that your dog is having an adverse reaction to it—signs to look for include thrashing and/or foaming at the mouth—immediately bathe the animal with mild soap and rinse him off with lots of water. If he does not seem to be getting any better, call your local emergency veterinary clinic and take him for treatment right away.

Once your pet is fine, be sure to report the incident to the manufacturer of the product as well as to the Environmental Protection Agency (*www.epa.gov*).

CLEANING & GROOMING

Acccoording to author James Gorman, "Cats are the ultimate narcissists. You can tell this because of all the time they spend on personal grooming. Dogs aren't like this. A dog's idea of personal grooming is to roll in a dead fish." Of course, they look so adorable doing it, who could be mad? *To groom your pet properly, these hints should help…*

Dog Hair–Catcher

Before each bath, put a hair catcher (available at home-improvement, bed/bath and hardware stores) over the drain to prevent hair clogs. The catchers generally come in 2 sizes. Measure the diameter of your drain before you go to the store.

Eye and Ear Protection

◆ Before giving your pet a bath, pop a drop of castor oil in each of your pet's eyes. This will protect the eyes from soap.

◆ To protect your pet's ears from water during a bath, gently place a cotton ball in each ear. Be sure not to push it in too deep!

✱ **Best Water Temperature**
Cats and dogs prefer lukewarm bath water... not too hot and not too cold.

Soft and Shiny Coat

To make your pet's coat extra-nice, put ¼ cup of baking soda in his bath water.

> ⊘ **CAUTION:** Do not use this remedy if your pet is on a low-sodium diet. He/she might ingest or absorb the baking soda, which is high in sodium. Use cornstarch instead.

Stop the Water Shake

Don't you just hate it when your dog does that post-bath shake and water goes flying everywhere? The shake starts at the dog's nose. The second you see that happening, gently but quickly, grab hold of his nose and you'll quell his urge to shake.

(FYI: Heads or Tails?

Dogs generally shake only if their heads get wet. When bathing your pet, wash his body in the tub first and try to clean his head and neck separately.

Dry Shampoo

Massage baking soda into your pet's fur and then brush it out. The baking soda rubdown and brush-out will clean his coat and get rid of any unpleasant pet odor.

⚡ CAUTION: Do not use this remedy if your pet is on a low-sodium diet. He/she might ingest or absorb the baking soda, which is high in sodium. Use cornstarch instead.

De-Skunking

*Oh, nooooo…*Fido just got sprayed by a skunk and he smells *terrible*. First, check the dog's eyes. If his face was sprayed, his eyes will probably be red and watering. Although the spray isn't blinding, it can be very painful—contact your veterinarian for help.

But if the dog's eyes seem to be OK, then you can proceed with the de-skunking. *Here's what you'll need…*

> 1 pair rubber gloves
>
> 1 bucket of lukewarm water
>
> 1 teaspoon mild liquid soap or dish detergent
>
> 1 quart 3% hydrogen peroxide (it's important that the bottle is fresh, not yet opened)
>
> ¼ cup baking soda

Put on the gloves. Mix the soap in the bucket of water, and wash the dog with it. The soap will break up the oils in the skunk spray. Then combine the hydrogen peroxide and the baking soda in a wide, open container.

While the mixture gurgles, it should be worked into the dog's fur—be sure to focus on the areas where he was sprayed.

⚡ CAUTION: Be sure to keep the skunk-wash solution away from the dog's face and eyes. And if you'll be rinsing his head, put a washcloth over his eyes to protect them.

Wait 5 to 10 minutes, and then rinse off the dog using lukewarm water. The oxygen-producing chemical reaction between the hydrogen peroxide and baking soda should get rid of the skunk smell.

⚡ CAUTION: Do not use this remedy if your pet is on a low-sodium diet. He/she might ingest or absorb the baking soda, which is high in sodium.

✱ Skunk-Solution Alternative

If you don't want to use baking soda to clean the skunk smell, try this—wear rubber gloves and rub your dog's coat with distilled white vinegar, tomato juice or cola. Then bathe and shampoo your dog thoroughly.

Shedding

There are cleansing wipes made especially for dogs and cats—they're available at Petco and other pet stores. Rub them on your pet to pick up loose hair and get rid of any unpleasant pet smell. You can also use a baby wipe to clean your shedding pet.

Suction Up the Hair

With the small upholstery-brush attachment in place, carefully vacuum the just-shed loose hair that's still on your pet and will be all over everything if you don't vacuum it up right away.

Nonstop Shedding

If your pet's shedding seems to be year-round rather than seasonal, work a little lanolin or olive oil into his coat every day. Within a few weeks, there should be a noticeable difference for the better.

Removing Burrs, Tree Sap, Gum

You'll want to wear rubber gloves for this…work vegetable oil or baby oil into the sticky tangled areas of your pet's coat to break up the gunk. This will make it easier to extricate without causing yelps or whimpers.

Cornstarch can also be used to de-gunk your pet. Pour a little on the problem area and patiently work it in, de-gunking the mess.

Nail Care

Here are a few natural and inexpensive answers to the dreaded pet nail-clipping job…

◆ **Dogs**—Walk your dog twice daily on a paved surface. City streets and sidewalks are perfect.

   If you're not in a city, then you might have a paved driveway. Get out the Frisbee or a ball and play fetch on it.

◆ **Cats**—Get a big piece of corrugated cardboard and provide a toy—even if it's just a piece of aluminum foil sculpted into a ball—and let him play on the corrugated cardboard every day.

The idea is that the rough surfaces of the pavement or corrugated cardboard will file down your pet's nails as they romp across them. How's that for a *peticure!*

> **NOTE:** Although these ideas might work for some dogs and cats, many others still require their nails to be trimmed regularly.

CALMING INFLUENCES

Chances are, the calmer you are…the calmer your pet will be. The problem is, the more your pet acts up…the faster you turn into a nervous wreck. So both of you—calm down! *These suggestions should also help…*

Respect Your Pet's Hangouts

Take note of the places your pet likes to hang out. Cats tend to be territorial animals that want their place in the sun, while most dogs enjoy looking out of windows.

Do not place a plant, a lamp or anything similar in your pet's favorite spots that could block the sun or obscure the view.

Nervous Reaction to Strangers

If you're into alternative treatments, then this suggestion is a "gem"—place a jade charm on your pet's collar. It will lie in the vicinity of his/her heart *chakra*, which is the energy center that influences your pet's ability to feel love.

Jumping on Furniture— Foiled!

If your pet insists on getting on furniture that's off limits, put a big piece of aluminum foil on the taboo couch, chair or table. Next time he jumps up—SURPRISE!—the noise and glitter will scare him off. Keep the aluminum foil on the furniture until your pet is no longer interested in it.

It is believed that the vibrations emanating from the jade will make your pet more affectionate and generally calmer. If it works, it should help to take the trauma out of meeting new people.

When Company Comes

If your pet acts up—barks, runs around wildly, jumps up on your guests—when company comes, circumvent that behavior by calming him right before your guests are due to arrive.

Acupressure will get him into a relaxed state—just press the tips of both of his ears between your thumbs and index fingers, then pulse the spots for 45 seconds. There's no guarantee that this remedy will work, but it's certainly worth a try.

If your pet is calm, but your *company* acts up, try the pressing and pulsing on *them*.

Petting the Pet

Animals prefer to be petted the way their fur lies. So always "go with the flow" and don't rub him the wrong way.

FOR DOGS ONLY

American humorist Franklin P. Jones once remarked, "Scratch a dog and you'll find a permanent job." True…but considering the unconditional love you receive in return, we're sure you'll agree that it's worth it. *Here are some ideas that will help you do the permanent job more effectively and with ease…*

Stop the Barking

◆ If your dog barks for no apparent reason, spritz a little lemon juice (or plain water) in his/her mouth and say, "Quiet!" Just be careful not to get any lemon juice in his eyes.

◆ Fill a small jar or tin with pennies or marbles. When your dog barks when he shouldn't, shake the noisy jar in his direction and firmly say, "No!"

Stop Hole Digging

Our friend's dog kept digging holes in their yard. The vet recommended that she fill in the holes with some of the dog's own feces, then cover the poop with dirt. As disgusting as it sounds, it worked. Once she did that, the dog stopped digging holes in the yard.

We've also heard that pinecones can be an effective deterrent.

✳ Mr. Clean Paws

When your dog comes inside after playing in the yard, catch him at the door, before he can track in dirt, and use a baby wipe or doggy wipe to swipe his paws clean.

While you're at it, clean in between his toes to get any caked-on mud.

Stop Furniture and Paw Chewing

◆ Boredom may cause your pet to chew on wooden furniture legs—or on his own paws. To prevent this type of destructive behavior, interact with him more, or get him some good chew toys or a companion.

◆ Dogs don't like the taste or the scent of hot chili sauce or strong-smelling soap, so rub some on the furniture that he likes to munch on so much.

◆ To get him to stop gnawing on his paws, wipe them with a little oil of cloves (available at health-food stores).

Leaving Dogs Home Alone

◆ If you go out during the day and your dog is home alone, put on the radio or television for him. Let an easy-listening station or the newscasters on CNN keep him company—and possibly keep burglars away.

◆ Make your pet feel safe and protected by providing a sheltered space for him—something with walls or sides, like a crate, is ideal. Place it in a spot where you spend lots of time and put something of yours inside. An old, worn T-shirt is perfect.

A pet that feels supported physically will be happier and more emotionally stable.

> **FYI: Crate Training Advice**
>
> A lot of information is available about crate training. We found 2 good Web sites that provide details on the different kinds of crates, how to buy a crate, proper furnishings, good locations, guidelines for introducing the crate to your dog, when *not* to use a crate…and more.
>
> Visit the American Dog Trainers Network at *www.tonypassera.com/thedogsite/www/new/*…and Dumb Friends League at *www.ddfl.org/behavior/crate-train.pdf*.

◆ If your pet goes into a panic when you leave him alone, and he starts chewing and clawing the furniture—Bach Rescue Remedy to the rescue! It's a safe, flower-essence solution, and it's available at health-food stores.

About 30 minutes before you plan to leave your dog alone, add 4 drops of Rescue Remedy to his water dish or a treat that he loves. By the time you leave, he should be calm and no longer hell-bent on chomping on your couch. (We just hope you don't have to leave your pet alone to go to the health-food store to get it.)

> **CAUTION:** If your dog consistently shows anxious, insecure and/or destructive behavior (such as urinating, chewing, excessive barking, etc.) when you leave him alone, this suggests separation anxiety or a more serious problem. Consult your veterinarian or a professional trainer for advice.

Doghouse Wood

The best wood for an outdoor doghouse is cedar. It stands up well to weather, keeps dogs cool in warmer months and repels fleas and ticks.

There are some treated woods that contain arsenic compounds, pesticides and other potentially harmful chemicals. If a dog chews on the treated wood, he can develop skin sores or even be poisoned.

> **✳ In the Doghouse**
>
> Foam rubber is soft as well as comfortable and makes excellent bedding in a doghouse or crate. Be sure to cover the foam with a zippered pillowcase or some other kind of fabric cover (which will make it easier to clean).
>
> The covering should be securely sewn or zipped closed, so that it cannot be chewed open by your pet. If the foam is ingested by the dog, it can be very harmful to his health.

Giving Away Puppies

If your dog has a litter and you plan to give the puppies away, put pieces of cloth in the Mama-dog's bed—1 piece of cloth for each puppy.

Give 1 of those pieces to each adoptive family to use in their new puppy's bed. The cloth should help prevent the puppy from crying for its birth mother.

> **NOTE:** In general, puppies should not be weaned from their mothers any earlier than 6 weeks of age.

Adopting a Puppy

◆ Ask for something that smells of the puppy's birth mother. If it's not possible, you can help your frightened little charge make it through the night by keeping a ticking clock near him to simulate his mother's heartbeat.

◆ Let the puppy cuddle up to a warm hot-water bottle that's wrapped in a soft blanket. Or place something large you've just taken off—an old T-shirt or sweat pants (nothing small that could be chewed and/or ingested)—in his bed. Your scent nearby will help him feel more secure.

> **NOTE:** Don't give puppies anything you don't want destroyed! Puppies love to chew, especially if they're stressed or bored.

FOR CATS ONLY

The author and Shakespeare scholar Mary Bly (who also publishes under the pseudonym Eloisa James) said this about the difference between the most popular household pets—"Dogs come when they're called…cats take a message and get back to you later."

And author Ellen Perry Berkeley summed it up perfectly when she said, "As every cat owner knows, nobody owns a cat." Cats may appear to be very independent, but they do need tending to. *Here are some helpful hints…*

Pick-Me-Up

Would you like to be picked up by the scruff of your neck? Neither would a cat. Do it right with 1 hand on his/her chest, under the ribcage, while the other hand gives him support under the rump and hind feet.

Cat Litter

Cats are like people in that they like their toilet privacy. So put your cat's litter box in an area that doesn't have lots of traffic. *Here are some more suggestions regarding cat litter…*

Clean Kitty's Litter Safely

Toxoplasmosis is a parasitic disease that can be transmitted to humans through contact with a cat's feces.

To protect yourself, always put on disposable rubber gloves to clean the litter box.

> **CAUTION:** People who have compromised immune systems and pregnant women should *never* clean a cat's litter box. Contracting toxoplasmosis is extremely dangerous and can damage a developing fetus.

Kitty Litter—Cheaper Is Better

Expensive cat litter that clumps when it gets wet, making it more scoopable, can actually be harmful to the cat—and to the person who does the scooping.

If a cat licks himself after using the litter box, he can ingest the litter dust, and the person who scoops the litter can inhale the dust. *Sodium bentonite* is the chemical that causes the clumping. A buildup of this chemical can be poisonous and result in respiratory and digestive problems for both humans and cats.

Opt for cat litter that contains no chemicals and no additives. There is a big selection. Visit a pet shop or supermarket, or let your fingers do the walking on the Internet.

Litter Box Deodorant

Layer the bottom of the litter box with baking soda, then add the litter.

Swimming-Pool Style

Cats prefer to have their litter at different levels for the different things they need to do. Arrange the litter like the water in a swimming pool—ranging from deep at 1 end to shallow at the other end.

CAT-ALOG

This section includes unique suggestions that we couldn't *cat*-egorize. But we hope that these ideas make you and your feline friend happier housemates.

Marking *Your* Territory

Whenever your cat goes to an off-limits area of the house, use a plant mister or water gun to spray water on him. After a few gentle sprays, he'll get the hint.

Bringing in a New Cat

To make a new addition welcome by your cat-in-residence, rub the new kitty with a cloth or towel and put it next to your current cat's food bowl (and if you can do this *before* the new cat arrives, so much the better).

Let Cat #1 get used to the scent of Cat #2 while associating it with something good (his meals). It should help the cats to become fast friends.

Fur-Ball Prevention

A hair mass that forms in a cat's stomach is better known as a hair ball or fur ball. Fur balls are the result of the cat swallowing hair as he grooms himself. But if the cat's digestive system is kept lubricated, the swallowed hair will pass through and out before a fur ball is formed.

Here's what to do—feed your cat sardines in oil once a week. If that doesn't totally stop the fur balls, then mix ½ to 1 teaspoon of vegetable oil or olive oil into his food every day.

You can also put ¼ to ½ teaspoon of petroleum jelly on the cat's paws once a day, and let him lick it off.

Repel with Cat's Sense Of Smell

As soon as your cat jumps up on an off-limits piece of furniture, wet a cotton ball with distilled white vinegar and dab it on his mouth. Then put the cotton ball on a piece of plastic wrap or a plastic bag and leave it on the furniture as a reminder.

You can also spritz the cat with a spray bottle filled with equal amounts of distilled white vinegar and water. We just hope *you* don't mind the smell of vinegar.

Stop Furniture Scratching

- Wipe Tabasco or chili sauce on the furniture's woodwork, let it dry, then buff it with a soft cloth. Cats are repelled by the spicy smell.

- If you don't want to put hot sauce on the furniture, sprinkle cayenne pepper on strips of tape and carefully attach the tape to any woodwork the cat likes to scratch.

- Use lemon polish on furniture—cats hate the citrus smell. If the cat scratches the furniture's upholstery, rub it with lemon-scented soap.

- If the soap might harm the fabric, place small plastic bags that contain lemon peel on the upholstery. Anyone who wants to sit on the chair or couch simply has to move the bags…not remove the cat.

- A scratching post will keep your cat's claws in good shape, and may divert his attention away from scratching valuable furniture.

  To keep reviving your pet's interest in the scratching post, sprinkle some (if possible, freshly harvested) catnip on it every other week. Trimming the cat's nails weekly may also help.

PUPPY & KITTEN OVERPOPULATION

And now for a public service announcement…every day, more than 50,000 puppies and kittens are born in the United States. Only 1 out of 5 of these animals is properly cared for in a happy home…the other 4 are homeless, neglected or abused.

These tragic statistics (from veterinarian Holly Frisby at *www.dogsonly.org*) mean that millions of animals wind up in rescue shelters, and 4 million to 6 million of those animals are destroyed each year—simply because nobody wants to adopt them.

Fact: In 6 years, 1 female dog and her offspring can be the source of 67,000 puppies.

The solution to the problem starts with you and your pet. Please read the following information so that you can be a well-informed and responsible pet owner.

Benefits of Spaying Female Pets

- Eliminates "heat" cycles
- Prevents accidental pregnancies
- Prevents unwanted offspring
- Reduces risk of breast tumors or cancer

- Significantly reduces undesirable behavior
- Prevents uterine infections, which are common in older pets

Benefits of Neutering Male Pets

- Significantly reduces prostate and testicular disease or cancer
- Reduces undesirable behavior
- Eliminates urine odor of male cats

When to Spay or Neuter

Check with your veterinarian for his/her specific recommendations. But in general, the best time to spay or neuter your pet is when he/she is about 6 months old—sometimes earlier.

Spaying your female pet *before* her first heat cycle greatly reduces the risk that she will develop breast tumors and cancer. Neutering your male pet *before* he develops undesirable behavior patterns is better than trying to undo those antisocial, embarrassing behaviors after they happen.

Low-Cost Programs

There are many low-cost and free spay-and-neuter programs that can help animal lovers do their part in controlling the pet overpopulation.

Bob Barker, former host of television's long-running game show *The Price Is Right* and an animal-rights advocate, established a foundation that funds qualified clinics and organizations so that they may provide low-cost or free spay-and-neuter services.

For a list of spay-and-neuter services in your state, visit *www.petsandanimals.org*. Or call Friends of Animals in Darien, Connecticut, for a directory of participating veterinarians nationwide—800-321-7387.

SPAY/USA, a program of the North Shore Animal League America, provides the names, numbers and prices for low-cost spay-and-neuter programs in your local area.

For more information, visit *www.spayusa. org* or call 800-248-SPAY (7729). ■

■ Products ■

No-Bark Collar

Do you have a neighbor with a noisy dog? This simple-to-use collar helps the dog break the barking habit, painlessly. Fits any size dog. Requires a 9-volt battery (not included).

Source: Miles Kimball, 800-546-2255, *www.mileskimball.com.*

UPCO has a great catalog with more than 200 detailed, illustrated pages with a huge selection of products for dogs, cats, birds and other pets.

We're listing some of our favorites here, but we encourage pet owners to explore the catalog for themselves.

Freeze-Dried Ice Cream for Dogs

We haven't sampled this ourselves, but our friend's Fido did—and he begged for more. This is a *real* treat made out of *real* ice cream, and it's rich in calcium and vitamin A. It's freeze-dried, so it will keep for years without refrigeration (but we're sure your dog will gobble it up before its expiration date). It comes in 2 canine favorite flavors—vanilla and peanut butter.

Car Harness

If you buckle up for safety, shouldn't your dog be safe, too? The harness (comprised of chest and shoulder straps) is safe and easy to use. The adjustable security strap, which is connected to the harness above your pet's shoulders, fits into any standard seat belt clip. Comes in 5 sizes.

Homeopet—Nature's Natural Medicine

Homeopet medicines are all naturally grown and scientifically formulated in a 100% organic solution, free of all chemicals. They have been clinically used on dogs, cats, fish, birds, rabbits, hamsters, ferrets and pot-bellied pigs. They're deemed safe for puppies, kittens, pregnant and nursing animals—*but be sure to check with your pet's veterinarian before trying them.* There are no known side effects from these fast-acting liquids. There are many formulas for specific ailments, including Anxiety, Joint Relief, and Skin and Itch Relief.

We have heard plenty of recommendations for this brand. Our neighbor's dog takes the Anxiety Formula, and she can attest to its effectiveness during a thunderstorm, at the vet's office or whenever she leaves her pet home alone. The drops give the pet—and the owner—a sense of calm. Also, our cousin volunteers at a dog shelter where they use the Homeopet line successfully.

Pee Post

The Pee Post is a pheromone-treated yard stake that encourages pets to do their "business" in a specific area of the yard. This simple and clever training device will help you maintain your lawn and garden, and makes cleanups easier.

Source: UPCO, 800-254-UPCO (8726), *www.upco.com.*

Gel-Pedic Pet Bed

This bed is available in 5 sizes, ranging from "toy" to "large," and is designed in a natural nesting shape for your pet's security and comfort. The bed is made of soft yet supportive GelFoam, which can be especially beneficial for dogs with arthritis—the GelFoam shapes to the contour of the pet's hips and joints, relieving any pressure that might be causing pain.

The GelFoam also provides insulation to keep your pet cool in the summer and warm in the winter. The embedded aroma of natural eucalyptus helps to repel fleas and mites, and keeps the bed smelling fresh.

Source: Gel-Pedic/Splintek, 888-PET-PADS (738-7237), or 816-531-1900, *www.gelpedic.com.*

Magical Recipes

Our mother and both of our grandmothers were truly kitchen magicians. We always appreciated their to-die-for foods and baked goods, and now we marvel at the strength it took these 3 short, chubby dynamos to conjure up great eats.

They grated and ground and kneaded and rolled and mixed and shook and strained and drained and mashed and sliced and diced and minced and beat and pummeled and stirred and whipped. These were the days before food processors, blenders, electric mixers, graters and peelers. In short, they had no shortcuts.

Inspired by our mother and our grandmothers, but making full use of today's conveniences, we've created this eclectic collection of dessert recipes, ranging from easy (get out the cake mix!) to complex (using more than a half dozen ingredients). We feel that each recipe has a magic of its own.

And by *magic* we mean...

◆ A unique preparation method (let the cookies stay in a turned-off oven overnight)

◆ Something strangely wonderful (a singing cake...cancer-fighting muffins)

◆ An ingredient you may never have used before or even heard of (miso...coconut flour)

◆ Something outrageously decadent (Creamy Coffee Cheesecake)

◆ A surprising ingredient (a cake made with baked beans and tomato sauce, another with eggplant and a believe-it-or-not scrumptious cake made with cherry cola, cocoa powder, mayonnaise and sauerkraut)

With most of these recipes, you may want to play "Guess What's in It?" with your guests... but *after* they've enjoyed eating it.

A few of the recipes that were contributed by family and friends come with their own glaze or frosting. Other recipes refer you to the "Toppings" section so that you may select another that's more to your liking.

Remember, these recipes are for dessert and party treats! They are not recommended for daily consumption...not if you want to eat healthily—and especially not if you want to lose weight. These are for special occasions... for gift-giving...or for that occasional break-the-rules binge. If a child is having a sleepover party, preparing 1 of these recipes would be a fun togetherness project. What kid wouldn't enjoy making Popcorn Cake?

351

But before you begin, you may want to breeze through these...

BASIC BAKING TIPS

Here are some general baking recommendations to keep in mind when preparing these recipes. We hope these hints make your culinary experiences easier and more enjoyable.

◆ Preheat the oven for at least 15 minutes before baking.

◆ When a recipe calls for eggs, unless otherwise specified, use *large eggs*. The general rule (again, unless otherwise specified) is to use them when they're at room temperature for greater cake volume.

◆ When a recipe calls for the juice of 1 lemon, figure on 2 to 3 tablespoons of juice. When a recipe calls for lemon zest, figure on getting 1 tablespoon from an average-sized lemon.

◆ When a recipe calls for melted chocolate, you want to melt it *slowly* to avoid scorching it. Break the chocolate into small pieces, and either put it in a glass cup or ramekin and let it sit in a pan of hot water, or place the chocolate pieces in a double boiler over hot (not boiling) water and stir.

You can also melt chocolate in a microwave. Be cautious and follow the recommended *time* instructions that come with your microwave.

◆ When a cake recipe calls for nuts or dried or candied fruits, and you want to prevent them from sinking to the bottom of the pan while baking, be sure to *dredge* them. That means toss them with flour, sugar or other dry ingredients so that they are coated before putting them in the cake batter.

◆ For beating cake batter—use an electric mixer and keep it going for at least 2 minutes.

◆ Any cake batter that contains butter or other fat should be baked in a greased pan. If it's an extra-rich batter, grease and flour the bottom of the pan, even if it's a nonstick pan and even if you use parchment paper.

Unless otherwise specified, there's no need to grease the sides of a pan. If a cake can cling to ungreased pan sides, it will rise more evenly all around.

◆ Batter should always be put in a cool pan. The batter should not fill the pan to the top. It is ideal for the pan to go in the oven ½ to ⅔ full.

◆ When making a layer cake, use a soup ladle or ice-cream scoop to divide the batter between the 2 cake pans to ensure that the layers end up being the same size.

◆ For best results, bake on the oven's middle rack—not the top or bottom racks.

◆ To test if a cake is done, insert a toothpick (or a piece of uncooked spaghetti) into the center. If it comes out clean, it's done. If you touch the cake and it springs back, that also means it's done.

◆ When baking cookies, keep in mind that a cookie sheet that is not filled to capacity will take less time to bake than a sheet that is full.

◆ When a cookie recipe calls for butter or margarine, the stick form is best. When a label says *spread*, *whipped*, *light* or *diet*, chances are the butter or margarine contains water or air and less fat by volume. Using it will cause cookies to spread excessively during baking, and they will be less tender.

We hope you have as much fun making these recipes as we did, and that you derive as much pleasure from pleasing the people around you by feeding them these extremely yummy treats.

CAKES

O K, get ready to bake some fun (and slightly unusual) cake recipes! You should definitely tell your guests what's in these wonderful confections—however, you may want to wait until *after* they've told you how delicious they are.

Avocado Cake

> 1 cup sugar
> ½ cup butter
> 2 eggs
> 1 cup mashed avocado
> ½ cup buttermilk
> 1 teaspoon baking soda
> 1½ cups all-purpose flour
> ½ teaspoon nutmeg
> ½ teaspoon cinnamon
> ½ allspice
> ½ cup raisins
> ½ cup chopped walnuts

1. Preheat oven to 350°F.

2. Cream sugar and butter, add the 2 eggs and avocado and mix well.

3. Add the baking soda to the buttermilk and add to the batter.

4. Add spices to flour and add to the batter all at once and mix well.

5. Dust the raisins and walnuts lightly with flour and add to the batter.

6. Pour into well-greased Pyrex pan (8" x 10") and bake for 35 to 40 minutes. (This can be stored or frozen. It is also delicious served warm with or without a tart lemon sauce.)

> ✐ **NOTE:** To ice this cake, see the recipe for Avocado & Banana Ice Cream on page 359, or use any of the icings in the "Toppings" section on page 360.

Baked Beans in Tomato Sauce Cake

> 1 8-ounce can vegetarian baked beans in tomato sauce
> 1 cup white sugar
> ½ cup vegetable oil
> 1 large egg and 1 egg white
> ½ teaspoon vanilla extract
> 1 cup all-purpose flour
> ½ teaspoon ground cinnamon
> ¼ teaspoon baking soda
> ¼ teaspoon baking powder
> ½ cup chopped walnuts (optional)
> ½ cup chopped raisins (optional)

1. Preheat oven to 325°F. Lightly grease and flour an 8.5" x 4.5" loaf pan, or spray it with nonstick cooking spray.

2. Empty the can of baked beans (with sauce) in a large bowl, and mash the beans. Then stir in the sugar, oil, eggs and vanilla extract. Mix until smooth.

3. In a separate bowl, combine flour, cinnamon, baking soda and baking powder and mix thoroughly. Then add the mixture to the bean batter, and mix thoroughly until smooth. If you're adding walnuts and/or raisins, do so and mix the batter again.

4. Pour the batter into the prepared loaf pan. Bake for 55 to 60 minutes, until a toothpick inserted in the center of the cake comes out clean.

5. Place the pan on wire rack until the cake cools. When it has cooled, frost it with the Cream Cheese Frosting (recipe below).

Cream Cheese Frosting

> 1 3-ounce package cream cheese
> 1 tablespoon milk
> 2½ cups sifted confectioners' sugar
> ½ teaspoon vanilla extract

Blend cream cheese and milk. Add sugar and blend well, then stir in the vanilla extract. Spread the frosting on cooled cake.

Cherry Cola–Chocolate–Mayonnaise–Sauerkraut Bundt Cake

From the "Foodly Yours" column, *Star-Gazette* (Elmira, NY) by Pat Ernst Dugan, food journalist and recipe creator.

2 cups all-purpose flour

⅓ cup unsweetened Dutch-process cocoa powder

1¼ teaspoons baking soda

¼ teaspoon baking powder

3 eggs

1½ cups sugar

1 teaspoon vanilla extract

1 cup light mayonnaise

1 cup cherry cola

1 cup sauerkraut, washed, drained and chopped

1. Preheat oven to 350°F. Spray a Bundt pan heavily with vegetable cooking spray.

2. Sift flour, cocoa, baking soda and baking powder together on a sheet of waxed paper.

3. In a large bowl with mixer on high speed, beat eggs, sugar and vanilla extract. Reduce speed to low and beat in mayonnaise. Add flour-cocoa mixture alternately with cola. Stir in drained sauerkraut.

4. Bake in prepared Bundt pan for approximately 45 minutes. Cool 10 minutes. Remove from pan onto serving plate.

Chiffon Cake

By Bruce Fife, ND, from *Cooking with Coconut Flour: A Delicious Low-Carb, Gluten-Free Alternative to Wheat*. Piccadilly Books.

This recipe makes either a chiffon or Bundt cake, depending on the type of tube pan used.

12 eggs, separated

½ teaspoon cream of tartar

½ cup butter, melted

½ cup coconut milk

1 cup sugar

1 teaspoon salt

1 teaspoon vanilla extract

1 cup sifted coconut flour

½ teaspoon baking powder

Glaze Frosting (recipe below)

1. Preheat oven to 325°F.

2. Combine egg whites and cream of tartar in a large bowl. Using an electric beater, beat until stiff peaks form. Set aside.

3. In a separate bowl, mix together the butter, coconut milk, egg yolks, sugar, salt and vanilla extract.

4. Combine coconut flour with baking powder and quickly whisk into batter until moistened. Batter will thicken if stirred for too long or allowed to sit for more than a minute or so—before it thickens, pour it gradually over beaten egg whites, folding with rubber spatula until just blended. Do not overmix.

5. Pour batter into a greased tube pan. Bake for 1¼ hours or until knife inserted into cake comes out clean.

6. Turn pan upside down on its center funnel to cool. Let cool for at least 30 minutes, remove cake from pan and cover with the Glaze Frosting.

Glaze Frosting

⅓ cup butter, melted

2 cups powdered sugar

1½ teaspoons vanilla extract

2 to 4 tablespoons hot water

Combine melted butter, sugar and vanilla extract. Stir in hot water, 1 tablespoon at a time until glaze is desired consistency.

Chocolate Potato-Flake Cake

From our uncle, Larry Koster.

2 cups all-purpose flour

2 cups sugar

1 cup instant potato flakes

4 teaspoons baking powder

½ teaspoon salt

1 package instant chocolate pudding

1 cup butter

¾ cup milk

¾ cup water

4 eggs

1. Preheat oven to 350°F. Grease and flour a 10" or 12" Bundt pan.

2. Mix all of the ingredients together, then beat at medium speed for 4 minutes.

3. Pour the batter into the Bundt pan and bake for 55 to 65 minutes, until toothpick comes out clean. Let it stand in the pan, on a cooling rack for 30 minutes. Then spread on the glaze.

Glaze

1½ cups powdered sugar

2 tablespoons cream cheese or butter

½ teaspoon vanilla extract

2 or 3 tablespoons milk or cream

3 to 5 tablespoons chopped nuts

1. Mix all of the ingredients together except the nuts.

2. Beat on low speed until smooth. Then spoon it on top of the cake. Top it off by sprinkling chopped nuts on it.

Creamy Coffee Cheesecake

By Marie Nadine Antol from *Confessions of a Coffee Bean.* Square One Publishers. *www.squareonepublishers.com.*

Yield: 9" cheesecake

Crust

1½ cups graham cracker crumbs

¼ cup powdered sugar

6 tablespoons butter, melted

Coffee Filling

32 ounces cream cheese, softened

¾ cup sugar

2 teaspoons instant coffee granules

1 teaspoon hot water

2 eggs

1 cup sour cream

3 tablespoons Kahlúa or Tia Maria liqueur (optional)

Topping

1½ cups sour cream

2 tablespoons sugar

½ teaspoon vanilla extract

⅛ teaspoon salt

1. To prepare the crust, place all of the crust ingredients in a medium-sized bowl, and toss with a fork or mix with your hands until well-blended.

2. Place the crust mixture in a 9" springform pan or a deep-dish pie pan. Using the back of a spoon or your hands, press the crumbs firmly around the bottom and sides of the pan. Refrigerate the crust for at least 1 hour, or until very cold.

3. To make the filling, place the cream cheese in a large mixing bowl, and beat with an electric mixer until very soft. Add the sugar and beat into the cream cheese.

4. Dissolve the instant coffee in the hot water, and beat into the cream cheese mixture. Then beat in the eggs, 1 at a time, until well-blended.

5. Add the sour cream and the liqueur, if desired, to the filling, and beat slowly until thoroughly combined.

6. Pour the filling into the chilled crust and bake in a preheated 350°F oven for 40 minutes, or until the filling is set and a knife inserted in the center comes out clean.

7. Place the pan on a wire rack, and cool for 40 to 60 minutes, or until the cake reaches room temperature.

8. To make the topping, place the sour cream in a medium-sized mixing bowl and gently stir in the remaining ingredients. When well-blended, spread the topping over the cooled cheesecake.

9. Bake the "topped" cheesecake in a preheated 425°F oven for 5 minutes, or just long enough to set the sour cream. Allow to cool on a wire rack. Refrigerate for at least 4 hours before cutting into wedges and serving.

> **NOTE:** This coffee cake actually has coffee in it and takes some doing, but it will be worth it.

Eggplant Pudding Cake

1 package (2-layer size—18.25 ounce) yellow cake mix (DO NOT use mix that has pudding added for extra moisture)

1 package (4-serving size) vanilla flavor instant pudding and pie filling

2 cups peeled and grated eggplant (about 1 pound)

1 cup sour cream

4 eggs

½ cup vegetable oil

½ teaspoon nutmeg

¼ teaspoon cinnamon

⅛ teaspoon salt

1. Preheat oven to 350°F. Grease and lightly flour a Bundt pan.

2. In a large mixing bowl, combine all of the ingredients. Blend, then beat at medium speed with an electric mixer for 4 minutes. Pour into the prepared Bundt pan.

3. Bake for 1 hour and 10 minutes, or until the cake tests done. *Do not underbake.*

4. Remove from oven and cool in pan for 15 minutes. Remove from pan and let it finish cooling on a rack. Dust with powdered sugar.

This cake freezes great…if there's any left.

> **NOTE:** You don't have to like eggplant to enjoy this cake—you really can't tell there's eggplant in it. It just tastes good.

Popcorn Cake

8 cups dry-popped popcorn

4 ounces chocolate chips

½ cup peanuts, broken in half

¼ cup margarine or butter

¼ cup peanut butter, smooth with no additives (we use Maranatha)

5 ounces miniature marshmallows

1. Line an angel food–cake pan with aluminum foil.

2. In a large bowl, combine popcorn, chocolate chips and peanuts. Set aside.

3. In a saucepan, melt margarine or butter over low heat. Stir in peanut butter and marshmallows. Keep stirring continually until every little marshmallow has melted.

4. Pour marshmallow mixture over popcorn mixture as you gently stir the popcorn, so that it all gets coated.

5. Pack mixture into prepared pan, pressing down firmly. Let it cool completely. Then remove from pan and cut into slices to serve.

Singing Cake

A friend sent us this recipe and said to time it so that you put it in the oven right before your guests are due to arrive. Then, once the cake is baking and your guests are there, invite them into the kitchen to listen to the cake sing.

We were intrigued and—even though we were in the midst of working on this book and weren't about to have company—we wanted to test this recipe and hear the cake sing. We went so far as to set up a tape recorder, thinking we would send the tape to our editor, along with the recipe.

So, we measured out all of the ingredients, then carefully followed the directions and put the cake in the oven. We waited and listened. No singing. No humming. We even would have settled for whining. But nothing. Not a sound.

We left the cake in the oven for close to an hour, hoping at least to hear the refrain from *New York, New York*. But ours was the Marcel Marceau of cakes—absolutely silent. Once it was out of the oven and had finished cooling, we tasted it —and, it was so good, it made *us* sing!

While we can't speak from experience in terms of the cake singing, we've heard that it does work. If you have the time, patience and ingredients, try it and let us know what happens.

> 1 cup butter
>
> 2 cups firmly packed brown sugar
>
> 3 eggs, separated
>
> 2 squares bitter chocolate, melted
>
> 1 cup raisins
>
> 2 teaspoons cinnamon
>
> 1 teaspoon ground cloves
>
> 4 cups flour, sifted
>
> 1 cup strawberry jam
>
> 1 cup chopped walnuts
>
> 2 teaspoons baking powder
>
> 1 cup buttermilk

1. Preheat oven to 350°F.

2. In a large bowl, cream the butter and sugar.

3. Add the egg yolks and stir. Add melted chocolate and stir. Add raisins and stir. Add cinnamon, ground cloves and flour, and stir. Stir in the jam and walnuts. Now, rest your hand from all of that stirring.

4. Beat the egg whites until stiff.

5. Add baking powder to the buttermilk and quickly stir it into the cake mixture.

6. Fold in the stiff egg whites.

7. Quickly pour the mixture into the greased and floured angel food–cake pan. Bake until the cake stops singing—about 45 minutes.

> **NOTE:** We think that this cake is delicious without any topping. But if you want the "icing on the cake," please select 1 from the "Toppings" section on page 360.

COOKIES

Crispy Potato Chip Cookies

From B. L. Ochman.

Yield: About 4 dozen

> 1 cup vegetable shortening or unsalted butter
>
> 1 cup granulated white sugar
>
> 1 cup light brown sugar
>
> 2 eggs, well beaten
>
> 1 teaspoon baking soda
>
> 2 cups all-purpose flour
>
> ½ teaspoon water
>
> 1½ teaspoons vanilla extract
>
> 1½ to 2 cups potato chips (salted or unsalted), coarsely crushed
>
> 1 6-ounce package butterscotch or peanut butter chips

1. Preheat oven to 350°F.

2. In a large bowl, cream the shortening with the sugars until smooth, then add the beaten eggs.

3. In a separate bowl, combine the baking soda with the flour. Mix them together thoroughly. Then slowly pour this dry mixture into the large bowl with the wet mixture. Combine thoroughly.

4. Add the water, vanilla extract, crushed potato chips and butterscotch or peanut butter chips to the large bowl and mix thoroughly.

5. Lightly grease a cookie sheet, or line it with parchment paper. Drop rounded teaspoonfuls onto the cookie sheet 2" apart.

6. Bake for 9 to 12 minutes. Cool cookies on a wire rack.

Bet you can't eat just 1 of these treats!

Overnight-Delight Cookies

Yield: 5 to 6 dozen cookies

> 2 egg whites
> pinch salt
> 1 teaspoon vanilla extract
> ⅔ cup sugar
> 1 cup chopped walnuts
> 1 6-ounce package semisweet chocolate
>   chips

1. Preheat oven to 350°F for at least 20 minutes.

2. Beat egg whites, salt and vanilla extract until soft (not stiff) peaks form.

3. Add sugar—1 tablespoon at a time—and continue beating until very stiff peaks have formed.

4. Add walnuts and chocolate chips.

5. Drop teaspoonfuls of mixture on a large, ungreased cookie sheet. Turn off the oven. Place the cookie sheet in the oven and leave overnight. Do not open the oven until the next morning.

OTHER GOODIES

Almond Crisped Rice Treats

By John and Jan Belleme from *The Miso Book*. Square One Publishers. *www.squareonepublishers.com.*

Yield: 16 treats (2" squares)

> ½ cup unsalted almond butter*
> scant ½ cup rice syrup (available at health-food stores and many supermarkets)
> 2 teaspoons sweet white miso** (available at health-food stores) mixed with 2 teaspoons water
> ½ teaspoon vanilla extract
> ⅛ teaspoon almond extract
> 2½ cups crispy brown rice cereal

1. Preheat oven to 350°F.

2. Combine the almond butter, rice syrup, miso and vanilla and almond extracts in a medium-sized bowl and mix well.

3. Add the cereal and gently toss until evenly coated.

4. Press the mixture into an unoiled 8" square baking pan. Bake for 12 to 15 minutes or until the edges are lightly browned. Allow to cool on a wire rack.

5. Cut into 2" squares and serve.

*Maranatha Almond Butter—100% organic, raw almonds, no salt added and available at health-food stores—is our favorite.

**Miso is a fermented soy food usually made from cooked soybeans and cultured grains, such as rice and barley. Scientific studies have confirmed miso's reputation as a very healing food. *The Miso Book* goes into detail about the many health benefits derived from incorporating miso into your daily diet, along with tasty recipes.

Avocado & Banana Ice Cream

Yield: 2 servings

1 frozen banana, cut in small pieces
1 ripe, average-sized Haas avocado
3 tablespoons lemon juice
½ cup soy milk
sugar or sugar substitute (before you add sweetener of any kind, taste it after it has been blended)

1. Blend all the ingredients in a blender until creamy.

2. Eat it this way, or put it in an ice-cream maker or in the freezer until it has the consistency of ice cream.

Or you can also use it to make an avocado/banana smoothie. Just add more soy milk and ice and blend.

Or you can use it as a topping on the Avocado Cake (*see* page 353).

Orange Bran Flax Muffin Magic (also known as Breast Cancer–Prevention Flax Muffins)

Yield: 18 muffins (a profound number that symbolizes *chai,* meaning life, according to Jewish numerology)

1 cup oat bran
1 cup all-purpose flour
1 cup flaxseed, ground (we use Barlean's Forti-Flax, available at health-food stores)
1 cup natural bran
1 tablespoon baking powder
½ teaspoon salt

2 oranges, whole, washed, quartered and seeded
1 cup brown sugar
1 cup buttermilk
½ cup canola oil
2 eggs
1 teaspoon baking soda
1½ cups raisins

1. Preheat oven to 375°F.

2. In a large bowl, combine the oat bran, flour, flaxseed, bran, baking powder and salt. Set aside.

3. In a blender or food processor, combine oranges, brown sugar, buttermilk, oil, eggs and baking soda. Blend well.

4. Pour orange mixture into dry ingredients and mix until well blended.

5. Stir in raisins. (White chocolate chips can be substituted for the raisins.)

6. Fill paper-lined muffin tins almost to the top and bake for 18 to 20 minutes or until wooden toothpick inserted in the center of the muffin comes out clean.

7. Let the muffins cool for 5 minutes, then transfer them to a cooling rack.

NOTE: According to Christiane Northrup, MD, a leading expert on women's health, flaxseed is the best source of anticancer and phytoestrogenic compounds (lignans), a concentration more than 100 times greater than other lignan-containing foods, including grains, fruits and vegetables.

When you buy flaxseed for these muffins, be sure the label says that the flax is from cold-milled select flaxseed and that it is 100% organic (which means pesticide- and herbicide-free). That milling process gently frees vitamins, minerals, amino acids, lignans and phytonutrients without damaging the delicate omega-3 fatty acids.

TOPPINGS

I f the topping that is included in a recipe doesn't appeal to you—or if you feel like being adventurous—here is a varied selection from which to choose. Any of these toppings can be the perfect cover for your culinary creation.

NOTE: The level of sweetness in these recipes is controllable by the amount of sugar used. Even though we are in the minority, we think the average topping is too sweet, and so we caution you to gradually add the sugar and keep tasting it, so that you stop before you mix in too much.

Chocolate Fudge Frosting

2 cups sugar

¼ cup light corn syrup

½ butter or margarine

½ cup milk

2 1-ounce unsweetened chocolate squares, coarsely grated

1 teaspoon vanilla extract

1. In a heavy saucepan, over low heat, stir all of the ingredients except vanilla extract. When the chocolate melts, bring it to a rolling boil while constantly stirring. Then boil it for 1 minute.

2. Take it off the heat and beat it until it's lukewarm. Then stir in the vanilla extract and continue stirring, and when it reaches a desirable spreading consistency, it's good to go…enough to frost on 2 8" or 9" cake layers.

Lemon Sauce

1 cup water

⅓ cup sugar

1 tablespoon cornstarch

2 tablespoons butter

1 tablespoon lemon juice

½ teaspoon vanilla extract

Boil until clear and serve warm over cake.

Peanut Butter Frosting (Broiled)

2 tablespoons butter, softened

1 cup packed dark brown sugar

⅔ cup peanut butter

¼ cup milk

⅔ cup chopped peanuts

1. Combine and cream butter, sugar and peanut butter.

2. Add milk and stir well. Keep stirring as you mix in nuts.

3. Spread over warm cake.

4. Place frosted cake under broiler, about 4" to 5" from the heat source. Leave it there until topping bubbles and browns lightly. It will happen quickly, so stay with it every second to prevent it from scorching.

5. Let the cake cool at least 30 minutes before serving it.

Quick-and-Easy Tropical Frosting

1 9-ounce container of Cool Whip

1 small can crushed pineapple

1 package vanilla instant pudding

1. Combine and beat ingredients thoroughly.

2. Frost and refrigerate. ■

Index

PRODUCTS INDEX

RECIPES INDEX